Building English Skills

Blue Level

Building English Skills

Purple Level

Yellow Level

BLUE LEVEL

Orange Level

Green Level

Red Level

Gold Level

Silver Level

Aqua Level

Brown Level

Plum Level

Pink Level

Cherry Level (K)

Chapter 8 Writing Different Types of Paragraphs   155

Contents

Prepared by the Staff of
THE WRITING IMPROVEMENT PROJECT

Joy Littell, Editorial Director, McDougal, Littell & Company

J. A. Christensen, East High School, Salt Lake City, Utah

Stephen G. Ham, New Trier Township High School East, Winnetka, Illinois

William H. Horst, Henrico County Schools, Virginia

Alice E. Johnson, Librarian, Evanston Township High School, Evanston, Illinois

Patricia Phelan, Chairman of the English Department, Hale Jr. High School, San Diego, California

Debbie Rosenberger, teacher and writer; formerly, Henrico County Schools, Virginia

Marcia Baldwin Whipps, East High School, Salt Lake City, Utah

The Staff wishes to thank the more than 1500 students who contributed samples of their writing for analysis.

Consultants

Dr. Patsy M. Davis, Assistant Professor, College of Education, Department of Curriculum and Instruction, University of Tennessee, Knoxville, Tennessee

Beth Johnson, English Department Chair, Polk County School District, Lakeland, Florida

Karen Kutiper, Language Arts Coordinator, Alief Independent School District, Houston, Texas

Adrian W. McClaren, English Consultant, Memphis City Schools, Memphis, Tennessee

Julia S. Nichols, English Department Chair, North Area II, Memphis, Tennessee

Harry H. Raney, Teacher, Memphis School District, Memphis, Tennessee

Carolyn C. Walter, Educational Consultant and Writer, Chicago, Illinois

ISBN: 0-86609-308-7   TE ISBN: 0-86609-309-5

Acknowledgments: Simon & Schuster: For entries from *Webster's New World Dictionary, Student Edition;* copyright © 1981 by Simon & Schuster, Inc. Macmillan Publishing Company: Chapters 1, 2, 5, and the Handbook contain, in revised form, some materials that appeared originally in *English Arts and Skills, Grade 10,* by Ronald J. Wilkins et al, copyright © 1965, 1961 by The Macmillan Company. Used by arrangement. (Acknowledgments are continued on page 760)

85 86 87 88 / 12 11 10 9 8 7 6 5 4 3

THE McDOUGAL, LITTELL ENGLISH PROGRAM

Building English Skills

Blue Level

Joy Littell, EDITORIAL DIRECTOR

McDougal, Littell & Company
Evanston, Illinois
New York   Dallas   Sacramento

Handbook

6.0 Agreement of Subject and Verb 559

7.0 Pronoun Usage 580

8.0 Adjective and Adverb Usage 608

9.0 The Right Word 627

10.0 Capitalization 643

11.0 End Marks and Commas 659

12.0 The Semicolon, the Colon, the Dash and Parentheses 680

13.0 The Apostrophe 693

14.0 Quotations 702

Chapter 1

Building Your Vocabulary

Most children entering grammar school know between three and four thousand words. Most adults, on the other hand, use up to ten thousand words on a regular basis and recognize another thirty to forty thousand words in print.

Such a large vocabulary is an essential tool in the modern world. It can determine how well you understand the thousands of new ideas and concepts that will be developed during your lifetime. It can also, to a great extent, determine how successful you will be in school and on the job.

In this chapter, you will learn several important techniques for improving your vocabulary. By applying these techniques, you will increase the number of words available for use in your own speaking and writing. You will also improve your ability to interpret and understand written material.

Part 1   Learning Word Meanings from Context

When you read, you will sometimes come upon words that are unfamiliar to you. Whenever this happens, you should attempt to discover the meaning of the unfamiliar word. This process will enable you to interpret the passage that you are reading and to add the word to your own written and spoken vocabulary.

Often you can find clues to the meanings of unfamiliar words within the material you are reading. In other words, clues to the meaning of a word can come from the **context** in which the word is used. The context of a word is the sentence or group of sentences in which the word appears.

Several types of context clues can help you discover the meaning of an unfamiliar word. The following are among the most common:

1. Definition or Restatement
2. Example
3. Comparison
4. Contrast

When you have learned to use these clues, you will be able to determine the meanings of many unfamiliar words quite easily.

Definition or Restatement

Of all context clues, the easiest to detect and understand are **definition** and **restatement**. Sometimes a writer will actually define a word, especially if the word is a technical term that many readers are likely not to know. Consider the following example:

> Metal can be made more flexible by *annealing*, which is a process of heating followed by slow cooling.

The definition of *annealing* is given directly, following the words *which is*. *Annealing* is a "process of heating followed by slow cooling."

More often, a writer will restate the meaning of a word in a less precise form than a dictionary definition.

> Throughout the trial the jury was *sequestered*—they were not allowed to contact anyone outside the courtroom.

Even if you do not know the word *sequestered,* the context of the passage points to the words "not allowed to contact anyone." One dictionary definition for *sequestered* is "hidden or kept away from others." Thus the context provides a restatement of the meaning of the word *sequestered.*

Writers will often signal a definition or restatement by using a form of the verb *to be (is, are, was, were)* or one of the following key words and phrases:

Words Signaling Definition or Restatement		
which is	or	also known as
that is	in other words	also called

Whenever you read one of these key terms, be alert to a possible definition or restatement. You can also use these key words when you need to explain a difficult or unusual word in your own writing.

One form of definition or restatement is not signaled by a key word at all. This is the **appositive**, a restatement of the same idea in other words. An appositive is set off from the rest of the sentence in which it appears by a comma, a pair of commas, a dash, or a pair of dashes. Consider the following example:

The top of the table was finished with a *veneer*. If you do not know the meaning of *veneer,* you cannot tell from this sentence whether it is a tool, a kind of paint, or a kind of wood. In the following sentence, however, an appositive phrase explains the meaning of the word:

> The top of the table was finished with a *veneer*, a thin sheet of wood.

A definition or restatement in context will enable you to determine the meanings of many unfamiliar words quickly and easily. You can also use definition or restatement to explain uncommon or unusual words in your own writing and speaking.

Example

Definition and restatement explain the meanings of unfamiliar words in a fairly direct manner. Most context clues are less straightforward. For example, instead of simply stating the meaning of a word, a writer may give examples that illustrate the word. By examining these examples, you can often get a reasonable idea of the word's meaning.

> The university had several excellent *entymologists* on its staff. These included Dr. Tower, a specialist on flying insects, and Dr. Mistri, an expert on the effects of pesticides on insects.

The second sentence does not define the meaning of *entymologist* directly. However, it does give two examples. Since Dr. Tower and Dr. Mistri both study insects, an *entymologist* must be someone involved in this field of study.

Examples and key terms can also work in the opposite way. A familiar term may help you to understand the meaning of an unfamiliar example. Consider the following sentence:

> Many American Indian languages, such as *Chippewa* and *Tillamook*, are extremely complex.

Even if you do not know what *Chippewa* and *Tillamook* are, you can still understand these examples because they are introduced by the familiar term *American Indian language*.

The following words often signal examples as context clues:

Words Signaling Examples				
like	such as	for instance	other	these
including	for example	especially	this	these include

Whenever you read one of these key words, look for any examples that follow. Whenever you must explain an unfamiliar term in your writing, consider providing examples of your own.

Comparison

A writer may provide clues to the meaning of an unfamiliar word by drawing a comparison using other, more familiar terms, objects, or ideas. By observing the similarities between the things described, the reader can then form a good idea of the meaning of the unfamiliar word. Consider this example:

> The *dirigible,* like a huge silver balloon, floated above the stadium with an advertising banner streaming out behind it.

The context does not fully reveal what a *dirigible* is. However, the comparison does allow you to form a mental image of what it might look like. The comparison allows you to conclude that a dirigible is some sort of balloon-like aircraft.

Comparisons are often signaled by certain key words:

Words Signaling Comparisons				
like	in the same way	resembling	similarly	identical
as	similar to	likewise	also	related

Be alert to a possible comparison whenever you come across these key terms. Remember also that comparison is an excellent method for explaining unfamiliar terms in your own writing.

Contrast

Sometimes a writer will provide a clue to the meaning of an unfamiliar word by contrasting it with something familiar. By deciding what the unfamiliar word does *not* mean, you can get some idea of what it does mean. Consider the following example:

Zinc is a naturally-occurring element. *Einsteinium,* on the other hand, is not.

In the above example, the key words *on the other hand* offer an important context clue. Based upon the contrast indicated by these words, you can conclude that Einsteinium is an element that does *not* occur naturally. In other words, it is a manufactured element. The following chart lists some other key words and phrases that signal contrasts:

Words Signaling Contrasts			
but	however	on the other hand	dissimilar
although	on the contrary	unlike	different

Be alert to a possible contrast whenever you read the key words listed above. You may also want to use this technique to explain an unfamiliar term to readers of your own writing.

Exercises Learning Word Meanings from Context

A. Using the context clues that you have studied, determine the meaning of the italicized word in each passage. Write your own definition for each word. Then tell what context clue you used to determine the meaning, definition or restatement, example, comparison, or contrast. Look the word up in a dictionary to check your definition.

1. Before shipping *frangible* objects, such as delicate glassware or electronic equipment, pack them carefully with foam padding.

2. An *opaque* fog fell upon the coast; we couldn't even see the lighthouse two hundred feet away.

3. Most *Felidae,* including the tiger and the familiar housecat, have long tails that are useful in maintaining balance.

4. The President and the Prime Minister expressed *consonant* ideas; in other words, they were in agreement on most issues.

5. After the fire, most people responded to the call for help compassionately. A few, however, *callously* refused.

6. Julie was extremely *loquacious*, but her friend rarely said a word.

7. Many European *Märchen*—including "Cinderella" and "Jack and the Beanstalk"—have existed for hundreds of years and are known throughout the world.

8. Jean, although she had been the most *voluble* of us all before the concert began, fell silent as soon as the first mournful note of the oboe sounded.

9. The many kinds of *phobia* from which people suffer include hydrophobia (fear of water), agoraphobia (fear of open spaces), claustrophobia (fear of closed places), and ailurphobia (fear of cats).

10. Gold is a *ductile* metal. It can be bent or hammered without breaking.

B. Write a passage using each of the following words. Explain the meaning of each word by providing the type of context clue indicated in parentheses. Refer to the lists of key words provided in this chapter.

1. **sentinel**	a person or animal set to guard a group	(definition or restatement)
2. **deciduous tree**	a tree that sheds its leaves every year	(example)
3. **abacus**	a frame with beads or balls that slide back and forth; used for doing arithmetic	(comparison)
4. **steppe**	a large area of flat land in which there are few trees	(contrast)
5. **predator**	an animal that hunts other animals	(example)

6. **balalaika**	an instrument with a triangular body and three strings	(comparison)
7. **pedagogue**	a teacher, especially of small children	(definition or restatement)
8. **vertebrate**	any animal that has a spinal column	(contrast)

Part 2   Inferring Word Meanings

Clues to the meaning of a word are not always as clear and straightforward as the ones that you studied in Part 1. Sometimes you may have to "read between the lines" to find the context clues. This process of reading between the lines to reach a conclusion is called **inference**. Among the types of inference you may use when determining the meaning of an unknown word are:

1. Inference from main idea and supporting details
2. Inference from cause and effect
3. Inference from implied comparison or contrast

Inference from Main Idea and Supporting Details

The main idea of the following paragraph concerns the meaning of *eclectic*. As you read the paragraph, pay close attention to how it is developed, and decide what the main idea is.

> You have only to turn on your radio to see how *eclectic* America's musical tastes are. At any time of day you are sure to find jazz, rock, show tunes, and country-and-western songs. A twist of the dial may bring you "easy listening" music, a string quartet, a symphony, or an opera. Turn the dial again, and you may find electronic music.

Notice that the paragraph is developed by details. These details show the wide variety of music that a person can find on the radio at any time. The main idea of the paragraph is that America's musical tastes are *eclectic*. Since this main idea is supported by details showing a wide variety of types of music, *eclectic* must have a meaning that is close to "widely varied."

Inference Based on Cause and Effect

If an unfamiliar word is used in the context of a cause–effect relationship, you will have a strong clue to the meaning of the word. As you read the following paragraphs, decide what would cause Mrs. Anderson to behave as she does.

> Murray's *mendacity* quickly became famous around the little town. In fact, it was the only thing he was known for. The story is told that one day he ran into Mrs. Anderson's drugstore in a raincoat, carrying an umbrella. Water was dripping off his clothes onto the floor.
> "It sure is raining out there!" declared Murray. Mrs. Anderson looked at him skeptically. Then she walked to the door of the shop and stepped outside. She came back soaking wet.
> "Why did you do that?" asked Murray.
> "Just checking," said Mrs. Anderson.

What kind of reputation would Murray have to have to cause Mrs. Anderson to check his statement about the rain? He would have to have a reputation for *lying*. Therefore, *mendacity* must mean "lying."

Inference Based on Comparison or Contrast

Often writers will provide you with details that enable you to make a comparison or contrast between a specific word and other material in the paragraph. Such implied comparisons or contrasts can be useful when you are trying to determine the meaning of an unfamiliar word. In the following passage, for example, you are given details that enable you to contrast two attitudes that a person takes. This contrast should allow you to infer the meaning of the word *dour*.

Throughout the first hour that I spent sitting on the dock, the man fishing beside me sat wearing a *dour* expression. The only sound that I heard from this fellow was a sigh now and then. Then he caught a flounder. At once he began to smile. He introduced himself, and for the next hour kept up a constant stream of anecdotes, reminiscences, and jokes.

By contrasting the details presented in this paragraph, you can determine that a *dour* person is someone who does not smile, whistle, or chatter. Therefore, dour must mean something like "gloomy."

Exercise Inferring Word Meanings

Read each of the following passages completely. Then reread each passage, paying particular attention to the italicized word or words. Based on your understanding of the passage, try to infer the meaning of each italicized word. Write your own definition of the word. Then, check your definition in a dictionary.

1   As a young man, Dennis decided that he was going to get ahead at all costs. He never accepted an invitation unless he thought that he could benefit by it. He never did anyone a favor unless he felt certain that it would be returned twofold. He remembered a person's name only if the person could be useful to him. Largely because of this *calculating* attitude, Dennis found that he had few friends.

2   Sometimes, the loss of one sense leads to *augmentation* of the others. People who lose their sight, for example, often experience an increased ability to hear, smell, taste, and receive *tactile* sensations. Thus, a blind person can easily read the raised dots of the Braille alphabet, while the same task is nearly impossible for a sighted person.

3   I sat staring out the window at the willow trees. Their branches waved slowly in the breeze. It was a warm, lazy day, and my thoughts drifted backward to other such days in Louisville years before. I was shocked out of this *reverie* by the bell attached to the door. Someone had come into the shop.

4   The defendant took the stand. He was dressed in a neat gray suit, with a white shirt and a dark blue tie. He walked with a sure and easy stride, and took the oath with a calm and steady voice. He looked at each member of the jury in turn. When he turned his eyes to me, I saw that they had an open, honest look. I was surprised. He did not resemble the *malefactor* I had pictured in my mind.

5   Roman *hegemony* reached its height under the emperor Augustus. All Europe, with the exception of Germany, was under Roman rule. To the north, Roman power extended to nearly all of Great Britain. North Africa, Turkey, and much of the Middle East were also under the control of Rome.

Part 3   Recognizing Prefixes

All English words are made up of one or more of these parts:

Prefix   a word part that is added to the beginning of another word or word part

Suffix   a word part that is added to the end of another word or word part

Base Word   a complete word to which a prefix and/or a suffix may be added

Root   a word part to which a prefix and/or a suffix may be added. A root cannot stand alone.

The word *unquestionable*, for example, is made of the prefix *un-*, the base word *question*, and the suffix *-able*. *Incredible* is made of the prefix *in-*, the root *cred*, and the suffix *-ible*.

One way to increase your vocabulary is to learn to analyze the word parts of unfamiliar words. We will begin by looking at prefixes. Read the following examples:

PREFIX		BASE WORD		NEW WORD
dis	+	appear	=	disappear
re	+	appear	=	reappear
pre	+	arrange	=	prearrange

Each of these words is formed by adding a prefix to a previously existing word. If you know the meaning of the prefix and the meaning of the base word, the meaning of the new word is easy to figure out.

The following chart contains several prefixes that are useful to know because each has a single, unchanging meaning:

Prefixes Having a Single Meaning

Prefix	Prefix Meaning	Examples	Word Meaning
bene-	good	benefit	anything for the good of a person or thing
circum-	around	circumscribe	to draw a line around
com- con- col- cor-	with, together	constructed	put together
equi-	equal	equidistant	equally distant
extra-	outside	extra-curricular	outside the curriculum
inter-	between, among	international	between or among nations
intra-	within	intrastate	within a state's boundaries
intro-	into	introvert	one who only looks within at his or her own thoughts
mal-	bad	maltreat	to treat badly
mis-	wrong	misspell	to spell wrong
non-	not	nonworking	not working
pre-	before	predawn	before dawn
sub-	under or below	subzero	below zero

Many prefixes, however, have more than one meaning. The following chart lists some common prefixes of this kind.

Prefixes Having More Than One Meaning

Prefix	Prefix Meaning	Examples	Word Meaning
ab-, a-	not away up, out	abnormal absent arise	not normal to be away rise up
dis-	opposite of depriving of away	distrust dispirit dispatch	the opposite of trust to deprive of cheerful spirits to send off or away
in- ir- il- im-	not in, into very	incomplete impossible irregular investigate illustrious	not complete not possible not regular to look into shining brightly, famous
pro-	in favor of forward, ahead	procapitalism propel	in favor of capitalism to push forward
re-	again back	replant repay	to plant again to pay back
super-	over and above very large	superhuman supertanker	more than human very large tanker
trans-	across beyond	transatlantic transnational	across the Atlantic beyond national boundaries
un-	not the opposite of	unafraid untie	not afraid the opposite of tie

Exercises Prefixes

A. Replace each italicized phrase with a single word. Each word should contain one of the prefixes you have learned. You may want to check the spelling in a dictionary.

1. Stealing is not *legal*. Stealing is _____ .
2. It is *not probable* that a lion will make a good pet. Lions are _____ pets.

3. My respect for her *is not measurable*. My respect for her is _____ .

4. Jesse James was a *very famous* outlaw. James was _____ .

5. Please *tell* that story *again*. Please _____ that story.

6. That ship sails *across the Pacific*. It is a _____ ship.

7. The explorers went on a search *outside the territorial boundaries*. It was an _____ search.

8. The delicate instrument was *wrongly used*. The instrument was _____ .

9. This area is *not residential*. It is a _____ area.

10. The check was *dated beforehand*. The check was _____ .

B. Determine the meaning of the prefix and the base word in each word below. Try to determine the meaning of each word by adding the meaning of the prefix to the meaning of the base word.

1. *pre*plan
2. *extra*ordinary
3. *pre*judge
4. *mis*judge
5. *a*political
6. *sub*marine
7. *non*poisonous
8. *extra*sensory
9. *intra*city
10. *mal*function
11. *equi*lateral
12. *con*current
13. *non*violent
14. *pre*test
15. *circum*navigate

C. The prefix *in-* has three distinct meanings.

in- = not	EXAMPLE:	incorrect
in- = in or into	EXAMPLE:	input
in- = very	EXAMPLE:	invaluable

The prefix *in-* often becomes:

ir- before a word beginning with *r*	EXAMPLE:	irregular
il- before *l*	EXAMPLE:	illegible
im- before *b, p,* or *m*	EXAMPLE:	imbalance

Decide which meaning of *in-* applies in the following words:

1. insert
2. incapable
3. indebted
4. insensitive
5. infamous
6. illogical
7. immigrate
8. irresponsible
9. irrelevant
10. imperfect
11. illiterate
12. inactive

14

Part 4   Recognizing Suffixes

Another way to determine word meaning is to look for suffixes. Like prefixes, each suffix has its own meaning or meanings. Once you know suffixes and their meanings, you can attach them to base words or roots to form new words. Look at the following examples:

BASE WORD		SUFFIX		NEW WORD
appear	+	-ance	=	appearance
adjust	+	-ment	=	adjustment
arrange	+	-ment	=	arrangement
care	+	-less	=	careless
friend	+	-ship	=	friendship

Study the following groups of suffixes. Once you learn their meanings, you will further increase your ability to recognize the meanings of unfamiliar words.

Noun Suffixes

Some suffixes, when added to a base word or root, form nouns. These are called **noun suffixes**.

Noun Suffixes That Mean "One Who Does Something"

Suffix	Example	Word Meaning
-ant	commandant	one who commands
-eer	auctioneer	one who auctions
-er, -or	photographer	one who takes photographs
-ist	geologist	one who studies or is experienced in geology
-ician	magician	one who performs magic

Notice that all the words listed above refer to people who do something. The suffixes *-ant, -eer, -er, -ist,* and *-ician* tell you that the word describes a person who does something.

Noun Suffixes That Make Abstract Words

Suffix	Examples
-ance, -ence	vigilance, independence
-ation, -ition	imagination, condition
-dom	freedom
-hood	womanhood
-ice	cowardice
-ism	realism
-ment	encouragement
-ness	kindness
-ship	friendship
-tude	gratitude
-ty, -ity	frailty

All of the words listed are abstract words. They describe a state of being. For example, *heroism* is the state of being heroic. *Frailty* is the state of being frail. What abstract word would describe the state of being romantic?

Exercises Suffixes

A. From each of the words listed below, form another word by adding a noun suffix that means "one who does something."

1. electric
2. biology
3. novel
4. politics
5. racket
6. engine
7. machine
8. beauty
9. manage
10. mathematics
11. profit
12. ideal

B. The following words can be changed so that they function as abstract nouns. Add a suffix that will change each word so that it can function as a noun. (Be careful of spelling changes as you form the nouns. Remember to check a dictionary if you are not sure of the spelling of a word.)

1. nonviolent	4. friendly	7. real	10. limit
2. wise	5. equal	8. assign	11. child
3. note	6. judge	9. add	12. resign

Adjective Suffixes

Some suffixes, when added to a base word, create adjectives—words that are used to modify nouns and pronouns. Such suffixes are called **adjective suffixes**.

Adjective Suffixes That Mean "Full of"

Suffix	Example	Word Meaning
-ous	furious	full of fury
-ose	verbose	wordy (full of words)
-acious	vivacious	full of vivacity
-ful	harmful	full of harm

The suffixes listed below mean "relating to," "pertaining to," or "like." These suffixes also create adjectives when added to base words or roots. For example, the word *music* is a noun. When the suffix -al is added to it, it becomes the adjective *musical*.

Adjective Suffixes That Mean "Relating to," "Pertaining to," or "Like"

Suffix	Example	Word Meaning
-al	musical	relating to music
-ant	triumphant	relating to triumph
-ic	heroic	pertaining to a hero; like a hero
-ical	economical	pertaining to economy
-ative	talkative	relating to talk
-ish	childish	relating to a child; like a child
-ive	active	pertaining to action

The following adjective suffixes mean exactly what they say. If you understand the meaning of the base word or root, you will understand the meaning of the combination.

Adjective Suffixes That Mean What They Say

Suffix	Example	Word Meaning
-able, -ible	readable convertible	able to read able to be converted
-most	topmost	being at the very top
-less	senseless	without sense (less sense)
-like	lifelike	like life

Exercises Adjective Suffixes

A. What clues do the suffixes give you to the meaning of the following words? Try to determine the meaning of each word. Then check the word in a dictionary.

1. bookish	6. additive	11. historical
2. cautious	7. peerless	12. reducible
3. grandiose	8. laughable	13. uppermost
4. wakeful	9. foremost	14. communicative
5. angelic	10. biological	15. exultant

B. Look up the meaning of *inflammable*. Why could this word be misinterpreted?

C. Many of the words in the following list may be unfamiliar to you. However, you should be able to determine their meanings from what you have learned about prefixes and suffixes. Use each word in a sentence that shows your understanding of its meaning.

1. impractical	6. misinformation
2. uninformative	7. inexactitude
3. imprecision	8. unservicable
4. maladjusted	9. disillusionment
5. immobility	10. melodious

Part 5 Roots and Word Families

Another way to develop your vocabulary is to become familiar with **roots**. A root is the part of a word that contains its basic meaning. A root cannot stand alone. A great many roots used in our language originally came from Latin or Greek. Each of the following Latin and Greek roots is responsible for a whole family of English words. If you know the meanings of these roots, you will be able to unlock the meanings of many unfamiliar words.

Greek Roots

The following chart lists some commonly used Greek roots. Notice that some of these roots have more than one meaning.

Useful Greek Roots

Root	Meaning	Examples of English Words
anthrop	human	anthropology
aster, astr	star	asterisk
auto	self, alone	automobile
bibl	book	Bible
bi, bio	life	biology
crac, crat	govern	democracy
dem	people	epidemic
geo	earth	geoscience
graph	write	paragraph
gram	write	grammar
log	word, reason	catalog
logy	study of	geology
metr, meter	measure	meter
nom, nym	name, word, law	economic
phil	love	philharmonic
soph	wise, wisdom	sophisticated
theo	god	theology
therm	heat	thermometer

Exercises Using Greek Roots

A. Each of the following words contains two or more Greek roots. Give the meanings of these roots. Then, define the word based upon your study of its parts. Check your definition in a dictionary. Note any differences between the root meaning and the dictionary definition.

1. bibliophile
2. demography
3. autobiography
4. astrology
5. astronomy
6. philosophy
7. metronome
8. geothermal
9. autocratic
10. bibliography

B. Each of the following words contains one Greek root plus a prefix, a suffix, or both. Give the meanings of these word parts. Then, define each word based upon your study of its parts. Check your definition in a dictionary. Note any differences between the root meaning and the dictionary definition.

1. *therm*al
2. mis*anthrop*ic
3. *graph*ic
4. *metr*ic
5. an*onym*ous
6. *program*
7. il*log*ical
8. *log*ician

C. Complete the following sentences based upon your knowledge of Greek roots. Then check your answer by using a dictionary.

1. The Greek word *adelphos* means "brother." Therefore, the name *Philadelphia* means _____ .

2. The Greek word *morph* means "shape" or "form." Therefore, the word *anthropomorphic* means _____ .

3. The Greek word *pseudes* means "false." Therefore, the word *pseudonym* means _____ .

4. The Greek word *psyche* means "mind" or "soul." Therefore, the word *psychology* means _____ .

5. An *antonym* is a word that is opposite in meaning. Therefore, the Greek prefix *anti-, anto-* must mean _____ .

6. The Greek word *nautes* means "sailor." Therefore, the word *astronaut* means _____ .

7. The Greek prefix *ana-* means, among other things, "backward." Therefore, the word *anagram* means _____ .

8. The Greek word *kryptos* means "hidden." Therefore, the word *cryptogram* means _____ .

9. The Greek prefix *syn-, sym-* means "together." Therefore, the word *symbiosis* means _____ .

10. The word *synonym* means _____ .

Latin Roots

The following chart lists some of the most commonly used Latin roots. Notice that some of these roots have more than one meaning.

Useful Latin Roots

Root	Meaning	Examples of English Words
capt	take, hold, seize	capture
cede, ceed, cess	go, yield, give away	recession, proceed
cred	believe	credit, creed
dic, dict	speak, say, tell, utter	dictate, dictionary, dictator
duc, duct	lead	induce, conductor
fac, fec	do, make	factory, defector, fact
mit, miss	send	missile, dismiss
pon, pos, posit	place, put	component, deposit, position
port	carry	porter, portable
scrib, script	write	description, scripture
spec	look, see	spectacle, spectator
stat	stand, put in a place	statue, stature
tract	pull, move	tractor, retract
vers, vert	turn	versatile, invert, vertical
vid, vis	see	video, vista
voc, vok	call	invoke, vocation
vol	wish	volunteer, malevolent

Exercises Using Latin Roots

A. Each of the following words contains one Latin root plus a prefix, a suffix, or both. Tell what each word part means. Then, write a definition for each word. Finally, check your definition in a dictionary.

1. *cap*tive
2. ex*port*
3. in*cred*ulous
4. in*cess*ant
5. trans*pose*

6. trans*mit*
7. bene*fac*tor
8. in*scribe*
9. re*voke*
10. *vis*ible

11. con*vert*
12. con*duc*tive
13. in*spec*tor
14. *stat*ic
15. *tract*ion

B. Using your knowledge of Latin roots, choose words from the list provided to complete the following sentences.

benediction	evoked	receded
benevolent	imports	remit
captivated	induction	reverted
credible	intractable	stationary
envision	mission	vocation

1. The performer *took hold* of the audience. The performer _____ the audience.

2. Please *send back* your payment. Please _____ your payment.

3. The place where soldiers are *led into* the army is called the _____ center.

4. She told a very *believable* story. She told a very _____ story.

5. At low tide, the level of the ocean water *went back down.* The water _____ .

6. We were *sent* to find water. Finding water was our _____ .

7. A person who *wishes good* for others is _____ .

8. Teaching is my *calling* in life. Teaching is my _____ .

9. Dr. Jekyll *turned back* into Mr. Hyde. He _____ to his other personality.

10. Coffee is *carried into* our country from Brazil. Our country _____ from Brazil.

11. The quarterback *stood in one place*. He remained _____.

12. I can *see* many changes coming in the next few years. I _____ many changes over the next few years.

13. Alex has made his decision and *cannot be moved*. He is _____.

14. The song *called forth* memories of her past. The song _____ memories of her past.

15. The chaplain *uttered a blessing*. The troops listened to this _____.

Word Families

A **word family** is a group of words that have a common root. You can develop your vocabulary by recognizing these roots and looking for them in difficult or unfamiliar words.

As you have learned, the Latin root *scrib, script* means "write." Many English words contain this root:

*scrib*e   *script*
*scrib*ble   *script*ure

Many additional words that contain this root have prefixes added in front of the root.

sub*scrib*e   post*script*
pre*scrib*e   tran*script*

Other words that contain this root have prefixes and suffixes.

pre*script*ion   in*script*ion
de*script*ion   de*scrip*tive

All of the words listed above belong to the same word family. All of them are derived from the Latin root *scrib, script* which means "write."

Being able to identify the root in a longer word will help you unlock its meaning. Also, seeing how words are grouped into word families will give you a method of sorting out the new words you read or hear.

Exercises Word Families

A. Listed below are several different word families. For each word family, identify the Latin root. Then add two other words to each family. Tell why each new word belongs to the family.

1. capture recapture caption	5. spectacle introspection specimen	9. repose postpone position
2. incredible credence creditor	6. vision television visual	10. recess procession secede
3. remit commit mission	7. import export portable	11. duct conduct reduce
4. diction predict dictation	8. vocalist provoke vocabulary	12. station status static

B. For each of the following words, identify the word family. Make a chart and fill it in. Use your knowledge of prefixes, suffixes, base words, roots, and word families. The first line has been completed for you.

WORD	FAMILY	ROOT MEANING	WORD MEANING
1. transmit	mit, miss	send	send across
2. dictator			
3. reverse			
4. circumspect			
5. vocal			
6. benefactor			
7. malevolent			
8. substation			

Part 6 Applying Your Vocabulary Skills

You have now learned several useful methods for determining the meanings of unfamiliar words. The following exercises are much like the vocabulary questions on standardized tests—they will provide practice in using the methods that you have learned.

Section 1: *Learning Word Meanings from Context.* Use context clues to select the best definition for the italicized word in each passage. Write the letter that represents the best definition.

1. Ms. Bell prefers to spend her vacation in a *bucolic* place—a farm or a cabin in the woods.

   (A) relating to a vacation, carefree
   (B) friendly
   (C) relating to the countryside, rustic
   (D) far away

2. She did have one *idiosyncrasy*, a very odd habit that startled new acquaintances.

   (A) a foolish act
   (B) peculiar behavior
   (C) hobby
   (D) strange acquaintance

3. Marietta likes the quiet of the library, as opposed to the *cacophony* of the cafeteria.

   (A) clutter
   (B) crowd
   (C) food
   (D) noise

4. The whale came into existence fairly recently, but the shark, a truly *primordial* beast, has been around for millions of years.

   (A) ancient
   (B) frightening
   (C) wild
   (D) unknown

5. The minister's living quarters, or *manse*, were connected to the church.

   (A) church
   (B) congregation
   (C) pulpit
   (D) home

6. The speaker tried to *repress*, or hold back, her anger at the heckler's remarks.

  (A) excuse (C) ignore
  (B) control (D) explain

7. The local college is offering several classes in *horticulture*, including one on growing flowers, one on caring for fruit trees, and one on tending a vegetable garden.

  (A) home improvement (C) growing plants
  (B) interior decorating (D) outdoor recreation

8. *Terrestrial* animals, unlike their counterparts in the water, have to support their own weight.

  (A) large (C) heavy
  (B) land (D) warm-blooded

9. The school's halls were *labyrinthine*, so Mr. Bolenger drew up a map to help the new students find their way through the many corridors.

  (A) long (C) narrow
  (B) like a maze (D) brightly decorated

10. Leroy loved the *lugubrious* melodies of funeral marches and sad, old folk songs.

  (A) low (C) ancient
  (B) frightening (D) mournful

Section 2: *Inferring Word Meanings.* Read each passage carefully. Determine the meaning of each italicized word. Write the letter that represents the best definition of the word.

1. Most of the debris from the wrecked ship had sunk to the bottom. Amid the remaining *flotsam*, rescue workers found only a life preserver, some timber, and a single sailor's cap.

  (A) floating debris (C) nets
  (B) water (D) sailors

2. Rock music is *ubiquitous* nowadays. Not only do we hear it on television and on the radio, we also hear it in cars, elevators, grocery stores, and even in dental chairs.

(A) everywhere (C) modern
(B) loud (D) soothing

3. Many creatures undergo a complete *metamorphosis*. The butterfly, for example, begins life as a caterpillar and then changes into its adult form. The frog begins life as a tadpole and only later develops the shape and habits of the adult animal.

(A) awakening (C) life
(B) examination (D) transformation

4. Ancient Sumeria was a *hagiocracy*. All important decisions were made by priests. They passed the laws, settled disputes, and collected taxes in the form of grain.

(A) country ruled by force (C) city
(B) country ruled by (D) nation
religious leaders

5. The sloth may be the most *dilatory* animal in existence. Scientists have to combat boredom when studying these creatures because it takes them so long to do anything.

(A) slow-moving (C) gentle
(B) little-known (D) interesting

6. Carlotta and I both read the passage several times very carefully, examining each word. Nonetheless, her *exigesis* differed from mine. This was because the author did not make clear what he meant by "courage."

(A) book (C) author
(B) interpretation (D) assignment

7. *Arachnids* are sometimes good to have around. They help farmers by eating insects, and their webs can be beautiful.

(A) insects (C) spiders
(B) garden (D) flowering plants

8. Though Dr. Grumwald had great faith in the *salubrious* effects of the new medicine, his patient continued to get worse.

(A) dangerous   (C) medicinal
(B) harmful   (D) healthful

9. Many people of the time considered Bach's music *ephemeral*. However, millions of people still listen to this music today, over two hundred years later.

(A) beautiful   (C) short-lived
(B) complicated   (D) long-lived

10. Hyenas are cautious, cowardly creatures. Jackals, on the other hand, are known for their *temerity*.

(A) recklessness   (C) friendliness
(B) cowardliness   (D) behavior

Section 3: *Analyzing Word Parts.* Use your knowledge of prefixes, suffixes, base words, and roots to tell the meaning of each italicized word. Circle the letter that represents the best definition.

1. *disclaim*

(A) deny any claim to, disown
(B) to treat well
(C) to be under a claim or obligation
(D) to claim again, repeat a claim

2. *irrefutable*

(A) not in favor of
(B) very large
(C) leading into
(D) not capable of being refuted or disproved

3. *malformation*

(A) something overhead or above
(B) something straightened or lined up
(C) something that is badly formed
(D) something that is well formed

4. *transcontinental*
   - (A) spanning or crossing a continent
   - (B) within a continent
   - (C) not a continent
   - (D) outside of a continent

5. *extragalactic*
   - (A) located within the galaxy
   - (B) deprived of a galaxy
   - (C) located outside the galaxy
   - (D) equal to the galaxy in size

6. *superstructure*
   - (A) a structure built below something else
   - (B) a structure built on top of something else
   - (C) outside the structure
   - (D) inside the structure

7. *presuppose*
   - (A) falsely believe
   - (B) support beforehand
   - (C) believe beforehand
   - (D) apply pressure to

8. *intra-atomic*
   - (A) outside an atom
   - (B) within an atom
   - (C) not atomic
   - (D) around the atom

9. *equipotential*
   - (A) having no potential
   - (B) having great potential
   - (C) having equal potential
   - (D) having potential for evil

10. *atypical*
    - (A) like everything else
    - (B) normal
    - (C) a kind or type
    - (D) not like everything else

SUMMARY AND APPLICATIONS

1. Developing your vocabulary will increase your understanding of the speech and writing of other people. It will also help you to express your own ideas clearly and precisely.

2. One way to increase your vocabulary is to use context clues to figure out the meaning of unfamiliar words. Context clues are definition or restatement, example, comparison, and contrast.

3. A second method for improving your vocabulary is to infer word meanings from main ideas and supporting details, from descriptions of cause and effect relationships, or from implied comparisons or contrasts

4. A third method for improving your vocabulary is to understand the meanings of prefixes, suffixes, base words, and roots.

Applications in Other Subject Areas

Science / Math. Many terms that you use in science and math contain Latin and Greek roots. Find ten such words in your textbooks. Write them down and circle the root or roots.

All Subjects. Use the techniques studied in this chapter to determine the meanings of unfamiliar words used in your classes and textbooks. Record these new words and their meanings in a vocabulary notebook. The notebook should contain separate pages for each class.

	History
○ *empire*	*a number of lands under one ruler*
confederation	*an alliance or league of individual people or estates*

Chapter 2

Using the Dictionary To Build Word Power

One of the first reference works you learned to use was probably a dictionary. How many times, as a child, were you told to "look it up" when you had a question about the spelling or meaning of a word? Most adults still use dictionaries primarily for this purpose: to find the proper spelling or definition of a word that they do not know. However, modern dictionaries have many important uses beyond these traditional ones.

In this chapter you will learn how to use the dictionary to increase the precision and power of your vocabulary. You will also learn a great deal about how dictionaries are organized and what kinds of information can be found in them. By learning to use the many kinds of information contained in modern dictionaries, you can improve your writing, reading, and speaking in many ways.

Part 1 Finding Information in the Dictionary

Abridged and Unabridged Dictionaries

In the reference section of your school or public library, you have probably seen a huge dictionary placed on a special stand. This is an **unabridged dictionary**. This massive volume contains several hundred thousand detailed entries. Occasionally you will need to use an unabridged dictionary. For most of your work, however, you will find it much more convenient to use an **abridged dictionary**. The smaller size of the abridged dictionary makes it easier to use.

In addition to standard abridged and unabridged dictionaries, there are many specialized dictionaries of technical terms in fields as diverse as theater and computer science. See the list of specialized dictionaries given on page 329 of Chapter 14.

Since dictionaries differ in their organization, symbols, and abbreviations, you will probably find it most helpful to use one dictionary consistently. Even if you don't have a dictionary of your own, you should become familiar with a dictionary in your classroom or library. A thorough understanding of one particular dictionary will prove more beneficial than an incomplete understanding of the organization of several dictionaries.

What's on a Dictionary Page?

As you study the information given below, refer to the dictionary page reproduced on pages 36 and 37.

1. Guide Words. The two large words printed at the top of the page are **guide words**. These indicate the first and last words entered alphabetically on that page. You should check the introduction to the dictionary to see how words are alphabetized in that dictionary. (For example, is *St. Louis* entered under *st-* or *sa-*?) The guide words should help speed up your process of locating a word.

2. Entry. All of the information about a word in the dictionary is called an **entry**. In the example on pages 36 and 37, each entry follows this general pattern:

    a. entry word
    b. pronunciation (or pronunciations)
    c. part of speech
    d. etymology
    e. definition (or definitions)
    f. synonymy
    g. words derived from the entry word
    h. cross-reference

Not every item is included for every entry.

3. Key. In most dictionaries, the bottom right-hand page contains a **key** to the pronunciation symbols and other symbols used in the dictionary. There is usually a fuller set of symbols and abbreviations in the front or back of the book.

What's in a Dictionary Entry?

A closer look at the entry for the word *enmity* on page 36 will help illustrate the entry items listed above.

Entry Words. Printed in dark type, the **entry word** is divided into syllables. Occasionally, when you are writing, you may need to divide a long word, putting it on two lines. Custom dictates that such division occur only between syllables. Check the syllabication in order to divide the word correctly.

Sometimes you may see what appears to be two entries for the same word. Such entries are **homographs**—words that are spelled alike but have different meanings. A *story*, for example, may be a "tale or narrative" or a "floor of a building." Because of these distinct meanings, most dictionaries give at least two entries for the spelling *s-t-o-r-y*.

In addition to listing complete words, many dictionaries also list word parts such as the prefix *trans-* and the suffix *-ist*. Such entries are useful in determining the meanings of combined forms such as *trans-oceanic* or *romanticist*.

Pronunciation. Following the entry words, the pronunciation is given in parentheses. Since different dictionaries use different pronunciation and accent symbols, it is important for you to understand the system your dictionary uses. By using the pronunciation key at the bottom of the page, you can determine the pronunciation of *enmity*. If a word has more than one acceptable pronunciation, or if the word is pronounced in different ways at different times, those differences will be explained.

Part of Speech. The letter *n*, following the pronunciation indicates that *enmity* is a noun. If the plural of a noun is not formed by simply adding -*s* or -*es* to the singular form, most dictionaries give the correct spelling of the plural form at this point. The designation *pl.* **-ties** tells that the plural form is *enmities*.

Etymology. The material within the dark brackets gives the etymology of the word *enmity*. **Etymology** is the tracing of a word back to its origins. The symbols < OFr < L. tell that the word comes from an Old French word which was derived from the Latin word *inimicus*. The word ENEMY in small capital letters is a cross-reference. By turning to the entry for *enemy*, you can learn that the Latin word *inimicus* is a compound of the prefix *in-*, meaning "not," and the word *amicus*, meaning "friend."

Definition. Following the etymology, you find the definition of the word *enmity*. Frequently, this may be your only reason for looking up a word, but as you can see, each dictionary entry gives much more than just the definition.

Synonymy. The abbreviation *SYN.* after the definition indicates the **synonymy**. Here you find words that are similar in meaning to *enmity*. This synonymy points out the slight differences in the meanings of *enmity, hostility, animosity,* and *antagonism.*

Derived Words. Following some of the entries on this page (for example, *enlist* and *ensign*), you will notice additional words, printed in bold type and divided into syllables. These are words that are derived from the entry word. These words are so closely related to the entry word that the editors of the dictionary did not feel it necessary to list them as separate entries.

Cross-Reference. In the discussion of the etymology of *enmity,* you saw an example of **cross-reference**. The word ENEMY printed in small capital letters tells you to turn to another entry for additional information about the etymology of this word. Note also the cross-reference at the end of the entry for *ensue.*

Other Information. Abbreviations and symbols are used in many dictionaries to provide additional information about particular entries. In some dictionaries, for example, the symbol ‡ is used to describe foreign words or phrases, while the symbol ☆ is used to indicate a word or phrase that originated in America. Whatever dictionary you use, make sure that you are familiar with the abbreviations and symbols listed in the front or the back of the book.

Exercise Learning How To Use the Dictionary

Answer the questions below by referring to the sample dictionary page on pages 36 and 37.

1. What is an etymology? a synonomy?
2. Where could you learn more about the origin of *entail?*
3. Where would you find a synonymy of words similar in meaning to *ensue?*
4. The abbreviations *vt.* and *vi.*, as in the entry for *enlist,* often give students problems. The abbreviation *vt.* indicates that in this sense the verb is *transitive,* one that takes a direct object. *vi.* means that the verb is *intransitive,* one that does not take a direct object. Study the entry for *enlist* and write one sentence using *enlist* as a transitive verb and one using it as an intransitive verb.
5. What does the double dagger symbol (‡) before the entry *en rapport* indicate? Why is there no such symbol before *en masse, ennui,* and *entente?*
6. What does the symbol ☆ indicate before the second definition of *enlistment?*
7. What does the symbol < mean?
8. What does the hyphen indicate before the entry *-ent?*
9. Study the synonymy following the entry for *enmity.* Use each of the synonyms in a sentence. Write your sentences so that the differences in the meanings become clearer.

en·list (in list′) vt. 1. to enroll in some branch of the armed forces 2. to win the support of; get the help or services of [to enlist men in a cause] 3. to get (another's help, support, etc.) —vi. 1. to join some branch of the armed forces 2. to join or support a cause or movement (with in) —en·list′ee′ n.

enlisted man any man in the armed forces who is not a commissioned officer or warrant officer

en·list·ment (-mənt) n. 1. an enlisting or being enlisted ☆2. the period for which one enlists

en·liv·en (in liv′n) vt. to make active, lively, interesting, or cheerful; liven up or brighten [to enliven a party by playing games] —en·liv′en·er n. —en·liv′en·ment n.

en masse (en mas′; Fr. än mäs′) [Fr., lit., in mass] in a group; as a whole; all together

en·mesh (en mesh′) vt. to catch in or as in the meshes of a net; entangle

en·mi·ty (en′mə tē) n., pl. -ties [< OFr. < L. inimicus, ENEMY] the bitter attitude or feelings of an enemy or mutual enemies; hostility

SYN.—enmity denotes a strong, fixed feeling of hatred, whether hidden or openly shown; hostility suggests open enmity shown in active opposition, attacks, etc.; animosity suggests bitterness of feeling, usually in personal relationships, that tends to break out into open hostility; antagonism stresses the opposition of persons, forces, etc. that compete or work against each other

en·no·ble (i nō′b'l) vt. -bled, -bling 1. to raise to the rank of nobleman 2. to give a noble quality to; dignify —en·no′ble·ment n. —en·no′bler n.

en·nui (än′wē; Fr. än nwē′) n. [Fr.: see ANNOY] a feeling of being very bored and tired of everything; boredom

e·nor·mi·ty (i nôr′mə tē) n., pl. -ties [< Fr. < L. < enormis, irregular, immense < e-, out + norma, rule: for IE. base see KNOW] 1. great wickedness [the enormity of a crime] 2. a very wicked crime 3. enormous size or extent: generally considered a loose usage

e·nor·mous (i nôr′məs) adj. [see prec.] 1. very large or very great; huge 2. [Archaic] very wicked; outrageous —e·nor′-mous·ly adv. —e·nor′mous·ness n.

en route (än rōōt′, en) [Fr.] on or along the way

Ens. Ensign

En·sche·de (en′skhə dā′) city in E Netherlands, near the German border: pop. 136,000

en·sconce (in skäns′) vt. -sconced′, -sconc′ing [EN- + sconce, a small fort] 1. [Now Rare] to hide; conceal; shelter 2. to place or settle snugly [to ensconce oneself in an armchair]

en·sem·ble (än säm′b'l) n. [Fr. < OFr. < L. < in-, in + simul, at the same time] 1. all the parts considered as a whole; total effect 2. a whole costume, esp. of matching or complementary articles of dress 3. a company of actors, dancers, etc. 4. Music a) a small group of musicians performing together b) their instruments or voices c) the performance together of such a group, or of an orchestra, chorus, etc.

en·shrine (in shrīn′) vt. -shrined′, -shrin′ing 1. to enclose in or as in a shrine 2. to hold as sacred; cherish [enshrined in memory] —en·shrine′ment n.

en·shroud (-shroud′) vt. to cover as if with a shroud; hide; veil; obscure [towers enshrouded in mist]

en·sign (en′sin; also, and for 4 always, -s'n) n. [< OFr. < L. < insignia: see INSIGNIA] 1. a badge, symbol, or token of office or authority 2. a flag or banner; specif., a national flag, as one displayed on a ship 3. Brit. Army formerly, a commissioned officer who served as standard-bearer ☆4. U.S. Navy a commissioned officer of the lowest rank, ranking below a lieutenant junior grade —en′sign·ship′, en′sign·cy n.

en·si·lage (en′s'l ij) n. [Fr.] 1. the preserving of green fodder by storage in a silo 2. green fodder so preserved; silage

en·sile (en sil′) vt. -siled′, -sil′ing [Fr. ensiler] to store (green fodder) in a silo

en·slave (in slāv′) vt. -slaved′, -slav′ing 1. to put into slavery; make a slave of 2. to keep complete control over; dominate; subjugate [she was enslaved by her work] —en·slave′ment n. —en·slav′er n.

en·snare (-sner′) vt. -snared′, -snar′ing to catch in or as in a snare; trap —en·snare′ment n.

en·snarl (-snärl′) vt. to draw into a snarl or tangle

SYN.—**enormous** implies a going far beyond what is normal in size, amount, or degree [an enormous room; enormous expenses]; **immense** implies size beyond the usual measurements but suggests that great size is normal for the thing described [redwoods are immense trees]; **huge** usually suggests a great mass or bulk [a huge building; huge profits]; **gigantic**, **colossal**, and **mammoth** originally implied a likeness to a *giant*, the Colossus of Rhodes, and an extinct elephant (the mammoth), and therefore these words emphasize the idea of great size, force, importance, etc., now often in an exaggerated way; **tremendous** literally suggests that which causes awe or amazement because of its great size

e·nough (i nuf′) *adj.* [OE. *genoh*] as much or as many as needed or wanted; sufficient [*enough* money to pay the bills] —*n.* the amount or number needed or wanted —*adv.* **1.** as much or as often as necessary; sufficiently [the stew is not adequately *enough*] **2.** fully; quite [oddly *enough*] **3.** just adequately; tolerably; fairly [he played well *enough*]

e·now (i nou′) *adj., n., adv.* [Archaic] enough

en·plane (en plān′) *vi.* **-planed′, -plan′ing** to board an airplane

en·quire (in kwīr′) *vt., vi.* **-quired′, -quir′ing, -quir′ies** *same as* INQUIRE —**en·quir′y** *n., pl.* **-quir′ies**

en·rage (in rāj′) *vt.* **-raged′, -rag′ing** to put into a rage; make very angry; infuriate —**en·rage′ment** *n.*

‡**en rap·port** (än′ rä pôr′) [Fr.] in harmony; in sympathy; in accord

en·rapt (in rapt′) *adj.* enraptured; rapt

en·rap·ture (-rap′chər) *vt.* **-tured, -tur·ing** to fill with great pleasure or delight; also **en·rav′ish**

en·rich (in rich′) *vt.* to make rich or richer; specif., *a)* to give more wealth to *b)* to give greater value or effectiveness to [to *enrich* a curriculum] *c)* to decorate; adorn *d)* to fertilize (soil) *e)* to add vitamins, minerals, etc. to (bread, etc.) for more food value —**en·rich′ment** *n.*

en·roll, en·rol (in rōl′) *vt.* **-rolled′, -roll′ing** **1.** to record in a list **2.** to enlist **3.** to accept as a member —*vi.* to enroll oneself or become enrolled; register; become a member —**en·roll′ee′** *n.*

en·roll·ment, en·rol·ment (-mant) *n.* **1.** an enrolling or being enrolled **2.** a list of those enrolled **3.** the number of those enrolled

en·sue (in sōō′, -syōō′) *vi.* **-sued′, -su′ing** [< OFr., ult. < L. *insequi* < *in-*, in + *sequi*, to follow] **1.** to come afterward; follow immediately [we met and a long friendship *ensued*] **2.** to happen as a consequence; result [the damage that *ensued* from the flood] —see SYN. at FOLLOW

en·sure (in shoor′) *vt.* **-sured′, -sur′ing** [< Anglo-Fr. *enseurer*: see EN- & SURE] **1.** to make sure; guarantee [measures to *ensure* accuracy] **2.** to make safe; protect [safety devices to *ensure* workers against accidents]

-ent (ənt, 'nt) [< OFr. *-ent*, L. *-ens* (gen. *-entis*), stem ending of certain present participles] **1.** *a suffix meaning* that has, shows, or does [*insistent*] **2.** *a suffix meaning* a person or thing that [*superintendent, solvent*]

en·tab·la·ture (en tab′lə chər) *n.* [MFr. < It. *intavolatura* < *in-*, in + *tavola* < L. *tabula*, TABLE] *Archit.* **1.** a horizontal structure supported by columns and composed of architrave, frieze, and cornice **2.** any structure like this

en·tail (in tāl′) *vt.* [< ME. < *en-*, in + *taile*, an agreement < OFr. < *tailler*, to cut: see TAILOR] **1.** *Law* to limit the inheritance of (real property) to a specific line or class of heirs **2.** to have as a necessary part or result; involve; require [the plan *entails* work] —*n.* **1.** an entailing or being entailed **2.** an entailed inheritance **3.** the order of descent for an entailed inheritance —**en·tail′ment** *n.*

en·ta·moe·ba (en′ta mē′ba) *n. same as* ENDAMOEBA

en·tan·gle (in taŋ′g'l) *vt.* **-gled, -gling** **1.** to make tangled, or catch in a tangle; ensnare or ensnarl [the fishing lines became *entangled*] **2.** to involve in difficulty [they *entangled* him in a bad business deal] **3.** to confuse; perplex —**en·tan′gle·ment** *n.*

en·tente (än tänt′) *n.* [Fr. < OFr. < *entendre*, to understand] **1.** an understanding or agreement, as between nations **2.** the nations, etc. having such an understanding

en·ter (en′tər) *vt.* [< OFr. *entrer* < L. *intrare* < *intra*, within < IE. base *en-*, in] **1.** to come or go in or into **2.** to force a way

fat, āpe, cär; ten, ēven; is, bite; gō, hôrn, tōōl, look, oil, out; up, fᵘr; get; joy; yet; chin; she; thin, then; zh, leisure; ŋ, ring; ə for a in ago, e in agent, i in sanity, o in comply, u in focus; ' as in able (ā′b'l); Fr. bàl; ë, Fr. coeur; ö, Fr. coq; ü, Fr. duc; r, Fr. cri; H, G. ich; kh, G. doch; ‡foreign; ☆ Americanism; < derived from. See inside front cover.

Part 2 The Multiple Meanings of Words

Many of the words listed in the dictionary have more than one meaning. A good way to develop your vocabulary is to learn additional meanings for words that are already part of your vocabulary.

Of course, you know the word *front*. But you may not know that *Webster's New World Dictionary of the American Language* (Students Edition) gives 15 noun definitions for *front*, 2 adjective definitions, 5 definitions as a transitive verb, and 2 definitions as an intransitive verb—24 definitions in all. Examine the entry below. How many meanings of *front* do you know?

Dictionary Entry for *front*

front (frunt) **n.** [< OFr. < L. *frontis*, genitive of *frons*, forehead]
1. outward behavior or appearance, esp. when merely pretended [to put on· a bold *front*] **2.** the part of something that faces forward; most important side **3.** the first part; beginning [toward the *front* of the book] **4.** the place or position directly before a person or thing **5.** a forward or leading position or situation ☆**6.** the first available bellhop, as in a hotel **7.** the land bordering a lake, ocean, street, etc. **8.** the most forward area, where actual fighting is going on in a war **9.** a specified area of activity [the home *front*] **10.** a broad movement in which different groups are united in order to achieve certain political or social aims ☆**11.** a person who serves as a public representative of a business, group, etc., as because of his prestige ☆**12.** a person, group, etc. used to cover up some activity, esp. an illegal one [the barber shop was a *front* for the numbers racket] **13.** a stiff shirt bosom, worn with formal clothes **14.** a face of a building; esp., the face with the principal entrance **15.** *Meteorol.* the boundary between two masses of air that are different, as in density —**adj. 1.** at, to, in, on, or of the front **2.** *Phonet.* sounded toward the front of the mouth [*i* in *bid* and *e* in *met* are *front* vowels] —**vt. 1.** to face; be opposite to [our cottage *fronts* the ocean] **2.** to be before in place **3.** to meet; confront **4.** to defy; oppose **5.** to supply or be a front to [white stone *fronts* the building] —**vi. 1.** to face in a certain direction ☆**2.** to be a front (senses 11 & 12) (with *for*) — **in front of** before; ahead of

---

Exercises The Multiple Meanings of Words

A. Study the dictionary entry for *front,* shown on page 38. Write a sentence for each specific meaning of *front.*

B. Study the following dictionary entry for the word *cell.* Write a sentence illustrating each meaning of *cell.*

Dictionary Entry for *cell*

cell (sel) **n.** [< OFr. *celle* < L. *cella* < IE. base *kel-*, to conceal, from which also come HALL, HELL & HULL¹] **1.** a small room or cubicle, as in a convent or prison **2.** a very small hollow, cavity, or enclosed space, as in a honeycomb, or in a plant ovary **3.** any of the smallest organizational units of a group or movement, as of a Communist party **4.** *Biol.* a small unit of protoplasm, usually with a nucleus, cytoplasm, and an enclosing membrane: all plants and animals are made up of one or more cells **5.** *Elec.* a container holding electrodes and an electrolyte, used either for generating electricity by chemical reactions or for decomposing compounds by electrolysis —**celled adj.**

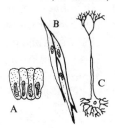

CELLS
(A, epithelial;
B, smooth muscle;
C, nerve)

C. The word *slip* is used in twelve different ways in the following sentences. Explain the meaning of the word as it is used in each of the sentences.

1. Ruth *slipped* softly from the room.
2. The ship *slipped* its moorings.
3. It must have *slipped* my mind.
4. We all wrote our names on a *slip* of paper.
5. Mother bought *slips* for the pillows in the guest room.
6. Ed *slipped* on a piece of ice yesterday.
7. The *Queen Elizabeth* occupies a special *slip* in the harbor.

8. She is a *slip* of a girl.
9. Marie asked for a *slip* of Aunt Susan's ivy.
10. Why don't you *slip* off your coat?
11. The hunter *slipped* his dog.
12. Bill made a bad *slip* while talking with the principal.

D. In the following sentences, the italicized word is used in a different sense from the usual one. Determine its meaning if you can. If not, consult a dictionary.

1. The men *scoured* the countryside for the lost boy.
2. An American *school* of painting began with Benjamin West.
3. I could not find the book I wanted in the *stacks*.
4. He converted his assets into *liquid* form.
5. Because of the dangerous *list*, the captain called all hands.
6. His profit *margin* on the T-shirts was too low.
7. If the *pilot* is successful, the show will become a series.
8. Mom *pinked* the edges of the seam to prevent raveling.
9. *Base* metals, such as iron, are not used for jewelry.
10. The highway's *cloverleaf* was jammed with cars.

E. Each of the following words has several different meanings. Consult the dictionary entry for each word. Use each word in three sentences to illustrate three meanings.

1. rail   3. pledge   5. bark
2. tip   4. keep   6. square

Part 3 Refining Your Vocabulary

By now you should have some understanding of the importance of developing a large vocabulary. However, just knowing the meanings of a large number of words is not enough. You must use the words in your writing and speaking, and use them correctly. Developing your vocabulary also requires refining. As you add words to your vocabulary, you must constantly work to use the words correctly. You can help to refine or sharpen your vocabulary through the correct use of synonyms and antonyms.

Synonyms

Think for a moment of the color blue. What do you picture in your mind?

Now picture as many other shades of blue as you can.

Just as there are various shades of the color blue, there are various shades of meaning to the words we often call synonyms. Examine the synonymy given below for the word *quick*.

Dictionary Entry for *quick*

quick (kwik) **adj.** [OE. *cwicu*, living < IE. base *gwei-*, to live]
1. [Archaic] living **2.** *a*) rapid in action; swift [a *quick* walk, a *quick* worker] *b*) prompt [a *quick* reply] **3.** lasting a short time [a *quick* look] **4.** able to understand or learn rapidly **5.** sensitive [a *quick* sense of smell] **6.** easily stirred; fiery [a *quick* temper] —**adv.** quickly; rapidly [come *quick*!] —**n. 1.** the living, esp. in **the quick and the dead 2.** the sensitive flesh under a fingernail or toenail **3.** the deepest feelings [cut to the *quick* by the insult] —**quick'ly adv. —quick'ness n.**
SYN.—**quick** implies a natural ability or tendency to respond rapidly in action, thought, or feeling [a *quick* mind]; **prompt** suggests a being willing or a being disciplined to respond immediately to a demand, request, etc. [*prompt* to obey; a *prompt* acceptance]; **ready** implies a being prepared, inclined, or willing to act at once in a specified way [her *ready* wit]—see also **SYN.** at AGILE and FAST[1]—**ANT. slow**

Note that this synonymy gives cross-references to another synonymy under the entry for *agile*. The synonymy for *agile* is shown below.

Dictionary Entry for *agile*

ag•ile (aj''l; *chiefly Brit.* -īl) **adj.** [Fr. < L. < *agere*, ACT] **1.** quick and easy of movement; nimble **2.** keen and lively [an *agile* wit] —**ag'ile•ly adv. —a•gil•i•ty** (ə jil'ə tē) **n.**
SYN.—**agile** and **nimble** both imply quickness and lightness of movement, but **agile** stresses general skill and ease in the use of the limbs, while **nimble** suggests quick sureness in carrying out a particular act [*nimble* fingers at the keyboard]; **quick** implies speed or promptness with no indication of the degree of skill; **spry** suggests nimbleness, esp. as displayed by a vigorous, elderly person; **sprightly** suggests liveliness, gaiety, etc.—**ANT. torpid, sluggish, lethargic**

The Thesaurus. One book that is of great use to writers is the dictionary of synonyms or *thesaurus.* Here is a sample entry.

---

81. SPECIALTY

(object of special attention or preference)

.1 NOUNS **specialty,** speciality, **line, pursuit, pet subject, field,** area, main interest; **vocation** 656.6; **forte, métier, strong point,** long suit; specialism, specialization; technicality; **way,** manner, **style,** type; cup of tea [informal], bag *or* thing [both slang], weakness [informal].

.2 **special, feature,** main feature; **leader,** lead item, leading card.

.3 **specialist,** specializer, **expert, authority,** savant, scholar, connoisseur; technical expert, technician; pundit, critic; amateur, dilettante; fan, buff, freak *or* nut [both slang], aficionado.

.4 VERBS **specialize, feature; narrow, restrict,** limit, confine; specialize in, **go in for,** be into [slang], have a weakness or taste for, be strong in, follow, pursue, **make one's business;** major in, minor in; do one's thing [slang].

.5 ADJS **specialized,** specialist, specialistic; technical; **restricted, limited,** confined; **featured,** feature; **expert, authoritative,** knowledgeable.

A thesaurus can help you to find a synonym with the precise shade of meaning that you are seeking. However, when you use a word from a thesaurus, check the meaning in a dictionary. A thesaurus lists words that are similar but not identical in meaning.

Exercises Using Synonymies

A. List at least four synonyms for each of the following words. Use each synonym in a sentence that illustrates its specific meaning.

1. error   2. crowd   3. pleasure

B. Use each word in the following three groups of synonyms in a sentence. Make sure that each sentence highlights the particular shade of meaning possessed by that word.

1. prompt	2. nimble	3. hasty
quick	spry	fast
ready	agile	swift

C. Each of the following groups of words may be considered synonyms. Consult the dictionary entries of synonymies for these words. Use each word in a sentence that illustrates the specific meaning of that word.

GROUP A

1. wind
2. breeze
3. gale
4. blast
5. gust
6. zephyr

GROUP B

1. secret
2. stealthy
3. covert
4. furtive
5. clandestine
6. surreptitious
7. underhanded

GROUP C

1. rescue
2. deliver
3. redeem
4. ransom
5. save

GROUP D

1. go
2. depart
3. leave
4. withdraw
5. retire
6. quit

Antonyms

Some words in English have exact opposites; day—night, short—long, hot—cold. Many other words do not have exact opposites, but they do have words whose meanings are different enough to be called antonyms. Antonyms are useful when you want to make a contrast in order to focus attention on a particular idea. Skillful use of antonyms will help you convey your meaning effectively and emphatically.

A. Following each of the synonymies on page 41, you will see an antonym or antonyms for the entry word. Use each of these antonyms in a sentence. If possible, use the contrasting entry word in the same sentence.

B. Give an antonym or antonyms for each of the following words:

1. careful	5. cheap	8. prelude
2. transitory	6. continue	9. combustible
3. famous	7. cosmopolitan	10. despondent
4. humane		

C. Select five of the sets of antonyms you have given in Exercise B. Use each of these sets of antonyms in a sentence.

Part 4 Interesting Word Origins

Many English words have interesting origins. The word *senator* comes from the Latin word meaning "old." The Roman Senate was a council of elders.

A person who is fond of luxury, comfort, and costly pleasures may be called a *sybarite.* This word comes from Sybaris, an ancient Greek city in southern Italy famous for its luxury.

Exercises **Interesting Word Origins**

A. Check the etymology of each word below in a good dictionary. Write a brief description of the background of each word.

1. agriculture	8. intoxicate	15. emancipate
2. belligerent	9. landau	16. guerrilla
3. carnival	10. league	17. gymnasium
4. corduroy	11. lieutenant	18. pedigree
5. curfew	12. mob	19. sinecure
6. czar	13. nausea	20. tenor (voice)
7. delta	14. ogle	

B. Look up the etymologies of these four words:

1. dexterous   3. gauche
2. adroit   4. sinister

Why do the first two words have favorable meanings, and the last two words uncomplimentary meanings?

Words Derived from People's Names

Many of the words we use are derived from the names of people or literary characters. The term *malapropism,* meaning "the act or habit of misusing words ridiculously," comes from Mrs. Malaprop, a character in Richard Brinsley Sheridan's eighteenth-century play *The Rivals.* Mrs. Malaprop was noted for her misuse of words. For example:

He is the very pineapple of politeness.

Exercise Words Derived from People's Names

Each of the following words is related to a person or a literary character. The etymology for each word in a good dictionary should tell you the person to whom the word is related. Check each word in a dictionary and write down the name of the person or character from whom it is derived. Then use each word in a sentence.

1. cereal   13. mesmerize
2. chauvinist   14. pantaloon
3. galvanize   15. pasteurize
4. gerrymander   16. quixotic
5. guillotine   17. sandwich
6. leotard   18. saxophone
7. lynch   19. sequoia
8. macadam   20. shrapnel
9. martial   21. sideburns
10. maudlin   22. teddy bear
11. maverick   23. vulcanize
12. mercurial   24. watt

SUMMARY AND APPLICATIONS

1. Dictionaries are useful tools for increasing the size and precision of your vocabulary. They are essential also for reference in many different subject areas.

2. Dictionaries are available in both abridged and unabridged forms. There are also many specialized dictionaries of terms from particular technical or professional fields.

3. Most dictionaries contain the following:

Guide words	Entry words	Etymologies
Pronunciation keys and respellings	Part of speech abbreviations	Synonymies
	Definitions	Entries
		Derived Words

Check the material at the front and back of your dictionary for additional elements, including special symbols and abbreviations.

Applications in Other Subject Areas

Geography / History / Social Science. Many dictionaries include among their entries the names of important people and places. Some dictionaries list these names in the body of the dictionary alongside other entries. Other dictionaries list names of places in a special section called a *gazetteer*. Find the names of at least five famous people, five places, and five important events in your classroom dictionary. Write these names, along with the information provided about them.

Foreign Language. Look in your dictionary for the list of abbreviations. This list will contain abbreviations for the names of many languages that have contributed to the growth of English. Then, look through the text of your dictionary for words that have interesting etymologies. Find at least ten of these words and describe, in writing, what languages they are derived from.

Chapter 3

Selecting Language for Your Purpose

You live in an age of specialization. Years ago, for example, a student could decide to become a doctor. Today, that same student could decide to become a podiatrist, psychiatrist, cardiologist, neurologist, pediatrician, endocrinologist, or opthalmologist. Similar changes have taken place in law, government, business, science, and many other areas.

Every technical or professional field creates its own specialized vocabulary. By using this vocabulary, or **jargon**, people in the same field can communicate efficiently with one another. Most of these terms are used only by specialists. Some, however, have spilled over into common usage.

In order to understand and communicate in today's complex society, you must have a familiarity with many specialized vocabularies. You must also understand when these terms are appropriate to use in your own writing and speaking.

Part 1 Terms from Specialized Areas

The Vocabulary of Sports

Sports is one area where the presence of a specialized vocabulary is immediately obvious. How many words from the following chart do you recognize? How many do you use?

The Vocabulary of Sports

BASEBALL

batting average	diamond	bunt	strike zone
squeeze play	sacrifice	dugout	line drive
double play	bull pen	pop fly	earned-run
ground out	slider	pennant	average

BASKETBALL

field goal	foul	dribble	free throw
zone defense	forward	rebound	jump ball
technical foul	assist	traveling	

FOOTBALL

field position	blitz	fumble	touchdown
I-formation	draw	rollout	end zone
interference	lineman	gridiron	clipping
interception	kickoff	sideline	receiver
four-three defense	down	holding	line of
huddle	safety	offside	scrimmage

HOCKEY

defensemen	offside	rebound	boarding
power play	puck	hat trick	hooking
neutral zone	goalie	flip pass	slap shot
icing the puck	forward	charging	face-off

A. Choose any twenty words listed in the chart on page 48. Look up the words in a dictionary and copy their definitions. Do any of the terms have definitions not related to the sport?

B. Choose any two sports not listed in the chart on page 48. Then, using an encyclopedia and a dictionary, put together a list of ten specialized terms used in each sport. Define these terms.

C. Pretend that you are a sports announcer. Describe in a paragraph a moment of play-by-play action from a sport that you enjoy. Use at least five terms from the vocabulary of sports.

The Vocabulary of the Arts

We enjoy sports either as participants or as spectators. We enjoy the arts in the same way. The arts include such diverse creative activities as music, dance, literature, painting, sculpture, photography, and the theater. Learning specialized terms used to describe the arts will help you to understand and appreciate the arts more fully.

The Vocabulary of the Arts

MUSIC			
counterpoint	vivace	major	scale
diminuendo	tempo	minor	atonal
crescendo	largo	rhythm	forte
allegro	sharp	timbre	adagio
harmony	flat	pitch	andante

DANCE			
tour en l'air	barre	turnout	arabesque
choreography	jeté	entrechat	pirouette
pas de deux	kick	en pointe	corps de ballet
chorus line	attitude	soft shoe	

LITERATURE

alliteration	plot	setting	parable
criticism	theme	climax	folk tale
protagonist	tone	ballad	allegory
antagonist	mood	fable	fiction
point of view	epic	legend	parody
character	myth	essay	poetry
motivation	irony	prose	satire
biography	genre	simile	metaphor

VISUAL ARTS

texture	color	form	medium
composition	hue	shape	palette
abstract	value	sketch	design

THEATER

proscenium	scrim	makeup	director
stage manager	set	comedy	scenery
melodrama	cast	tragedy	costume
projection	farce	drama	property
blocking	pace	lighting	production

Exercises **The Vocabulary of the Arts**

A. Choose twenty words from the chart on pages 49 and 50. Look up these words in a dictionary and copy their definitions.

B. The terms of specialized vocabularies come from a variety of sources and may go through many changes. Answer the following questions by choosing words from the list provided below.

adagio	jeté	pace	pitch	turnout
folk tale	mood	palette	sketch	value

1. Name three terms that were originally from other languages.
2. *Compound words* are made from two smaller words. Name two terms that are compound.

3. Name three terms that can be used in more than one art.
4. Name four terms that describe things outside the arts.

C. Write a description or review of a favorite work of art. Use at least five of the terms in the chart on pages 49 and 50.

The Vocabulary of the Mass Media

Closely connected with the world of the arts is the field of the mass media. The **mass media** are means of communication that reach a large audience. These include *broadcast media* such as radio, television, and the movies, and *print media* such as newspapers and magazines. The broadcast media are all products of the twentieth century. Therefore, many of the words used to describe these media are relatively recent. Because much of our understanding of the modern world comes from the media, everyone needs to be familiar with its basic vocabulary.

The Vocabulary of the Mass Media

BROADCAST MEDIA

station break	network	simulcast	location
anchorperson	spinoff	videotape	dead air
variety show	sponsor	air time	prime time
cinematography	credits	exterior	docu-drama
instant replay	sitcom	interior	back lot
film editing	set	producer	sound track
documentary	dub	director	close-up
camera angle	pan	montage	laugh track

PRINT MEDIA

major news story	ears	masthead	dateline
wire service	deck	edition	syndicated
feature article	byline	analysis	watch dog
news briefs	column	caption	classified ads
free lance	lead	reporter	human
headlines	filler	stringer	interest story
circulation	cut	editorial	

Exercises The Vocabulary of the Mass Media

A. Choose twenty terms listed in the chart on page 51. Look up these words in a dictionary and copy the definitions.

B. Answer the following questions by referring to the list of words provided and to a dictionary.

anchorperson	docu-drama	simulcast
cinematography	dub	sitcom
dateline	ears	stringer
deck	network	

1. Name three terms used to describe the mass media that are compound words.

2. *Blends* are words made by combining parts of two other words: motor + hotel = motel. Name four terms used to describe the mass media that are blends.

3. Name four terms used to describe the mass media that have different meanings outside this field.

C. Choose one of the following topics. Write a composition using at least four of the terms listed in the chart on page 51.

a. The quality of television news
b. The variety of programming on television
c. The variety of stories in newspapers
d. Careers in journalism

The Vocabulary of Business

Business includes all activities that provide goods or services for profit—finance, banking, commerce, or manufacturing. Most workers in this country are employed by businesses. Today there are over four million businesses in the United States, and the number continues to grow. Even if you never work in a business yourself, you will still be directly affected by the actions that businesses take. Therefore, it is a good idea to familiarize yourself with the specialized vocabularies that businesses use.

The Vocabulary of Business

board of directors	labor	capital	competition
installment plan	land	inputs	marketing
profit motive	goods	outputs	recession
executive officers	trade	services	depression
free enterprise	union	finance	liabilities
cost of living	assets	regulation	accounting
proprietorship	debit	market	prime rate
partnership	credit	interest	production
corporation	stocks	supply	wholesale
stockholder	bonds	demand	personnel
production	trust	inflation	consumer
commodities	retail	monopoly	price index

Exercises The Vocabulary of Business

A. Choose fifteen terms from the chart on this page. Look these up in a dictionary and copy their definitions.

B. Read the following article from a city newspaper. Write down any terms or labels that could be considered jargon. Using a dictionary or some other reference source, translate the article.

Dow edges up 3.35 points, but market showing mixed

Stocks were mixed throughout the day Thursday as the market modestly extended its slight advance in the previous session.

Steel, oil-service and forest-products issues rose, but several defense, mining, oil and drug stocks fell back.

The Dow Jones average of 30 industrials edged up 3.35 to 1,254.67. The measure climbed 3.25 on Wednesday to give it a gain of 36.48 over the past seven sessions.

Gainers held a 9-7 edge over losers on the New York Stock Exchange, but the NYSE's composite index was up .04 to 95.93.

The American Stock Exchange market value index was up 0.36 to 219.94.

Big Board volume totaled 80.74 million shares, against 83.38 million Wednesday.

The Vocabulary of Science

Most astronomers today believe that a quasar is a composite structure of engine and fuel—a massive black hole (the super-compacted remnant of what was once a very large star or group of stars), surrounded and fueled by a ring of inflowing gas and dust, called an accretion disk. Both are located at the center of a galaxy, but the brilliant splash of light and radiation that shows up as a quasar on Earth-based telescopes comes from matter in the disk, enormously accelerated and heated by the black hole's powerful gravitational fields.

What would you guess is the source of this paragraph? A text-book? An encyclopedia? It is actually a paragraph from an article in the *Los Angeles Times*. It was written for the general public, yet it is packed with specialized scientific vocabulary.

The sciences today are exploding with new concepts such as *quasar*. Each new discovery calls for a precise scientific term. Scientists often rely on combining Greek and Latin roots to make words that will be understood outside the English-speaking community. For this reason, the language of science is becoming an international language.

The Vocabulary of Science

BIOLOGY			
microorganism	cell	enzyme	catalyst
amino acid	organ	protein	organism

ASTRONOMY			
constellation	planet	nebula	big bang
black hole	phase	quasar	cosmology
light-year	nova	red shift	

CHEMISTRY			
molecule	gas	liquid	solution
formula	base	titrate	element

EARTH SCIENCE			
hydrosphere	fault	atmosphere	lithosphere
paleontology	volcano	biosphere	geology

PHYSICS			
electromagnetic	fission	fusion	mechanics
relativity	entropy	quantum	

ANTHROPOLOGY			
Homo sapiens	taboo	ritual	culture
ethnography	custom	primate	archaeology

PSYCHOLOGY			
psychosis	cortex	synapse	anxiety
psychometry	neuron	neurosis	cerebrum

SOCIOLOGY			
assimilation	caste	alienation	demography

Exercises The Vocabulary of Science

A. Choose any ten words from the chart on pages 54 and 55. Look these words up in a dictionary and define them.

B. Using a dictionary for reference, define each of these terms as it applies to the field of science. Then use the word in a sentence that demonstrates your understanding of the term.

1. cell	8. astronomy	15. volcano
2. microorganism	9. cosmology	16. atmosphere
3. chromosome	10. quasar	17. Homo sapiens
4. vitamin	11. constellation	18. primate
5. lunar	12. nebula	19. biosphere
6. pulmonary	13. nova	20. cortex
7. pathology	14. planet	

The Vocabulary of Computer Science

Familiarity with computers has become an essential part of a modern education. Computers are no longer used only by professionals in the field. Many non-specialists also use computers. When you do banking, use a credit card, make an airline or theater reservation, or place a long-distance call, you are using the services of a computer. In the future, computers will play an even larger role in our lives. For this reason, it is important to learn the basic vocabulary of computer science.

The Vocabulary of Computer Science

microprocessor	bit	program	simulation
computer-enhanced	byte	COBAL	software
key punch	disk	BASIC	printout
time-sharing	tape	FORTRAN	terminal
processing	drum	memory	central
debugging	file	hardware	processing unit
punch card	input	interface	
programmer	output	binary	programming language
flowchart	bug	data base	

Exercises The Vocabulary of Computer Science

A. Look up and define fifteen words from the chart on this page.

B. Answer the following questions by referring to a dictionary and to the chart on this page.

1. *Acronyms* are words that are made from the first letters of other words: FBI = Federal Bureau of Investigation. Name two computer terms that are acronyms.
2. What does the prefix *micro-* mean in *microprocessor*? What does the prefix *inter-* mean in the word *interface*?
3. What are the origins of the terms *data, binary,* and *memory*?
4. A *bug* is an insect. Why would computer specialists use this term to describe an error?
5. What are the various meanings of the word *terminal*?

Part 2 The Levels of Language

How are your writing and speech affected by the increasing growth of these specialized vocabularies? Should you try to use them in writing but not in speaking? Should you avoid them completely and leave them to the experts in each field?

A general guideline is to use technical terms when they are appropriate to your purpose and audience, or when they are necessary to the precise communication of ideas. Words that are less exact would be the wrong words to use. However, there are more specific guidelines for language choice. These may be applied to all aspects of language and communication.

To choose appropriate vocabulary for any occasion, you must first identify both the situation and the audience. Once you pinpoint this information, you should select the appropriate level of English. The following diagram shows the different levels of your language.

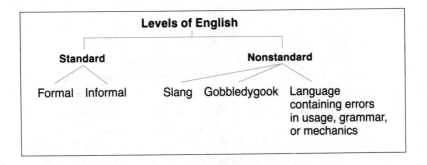

Standard English

Language that is suitable at all times and in all places is known as **standard English**. There are two levels of standard English: formal and informal.

Formal English is language appropriate to circumstances that are serious, dignified, or ceremonial. You sometimes hear formal English in sermons, public speeches by government officials, graduation addresses, and lectures. However, formal English is used more often in writing than in speaking. You will find it in scholarly journals, legal papers, business reports, and many textbooks. The following is an example of formal English:

> One of the oldest surviving religions in the world, with an unbroken succession of seers and teachers, is practiced by millions of people living in the vast subcontinent of India; it is known as Hinduism. The term "Hinduism" was coined in relatively recent times. Modern Hindus use this Western term simply as a convenience when speaking or writing English. Among themselves they prefer to call their religion *sanatana dharma* ("eternal religion"), since it was not founded by any historical person but is based upon eternal principles that were "heard" by the *rishis* (sages or seers) who lived during a very remote period in history.—S. A. NIGOSIAN, *World Religions*

Informal English is the comfortable, correct language used in everyday situations. Also known as **colloquial English**, it is the language of conversation and informal talks. It is also the written language of most newspapers and magazine articles. Consider the following example of informal English:

> The citizens of Farmington, Utah, will never forget the sound. "The trees were popping and the boulders rolling," recalls Steve Moon of the fire department. "Anybody who wouldn't be nervous listening to *that* coming down the hill would have to have something wrong with them." What came down that hill was mud: tons of soggy, slippery, onrushing mud. The same thing was happening in the neighboring town of Bountiful, where 1,000 people had to be evacuated. Mud slides and floods all last week caused millions of dollars of damage and the loss of 16 homes in Utah and in western Nevada, where a mucky avalanche descended from aptly-named *Slide Mountain.*
>
> —*Time*

The chart on the following page describes the differences between formal and informal English.

It is important to realize that there are similarities as well as differences between formal and informal English. Both levels use correct grammar, spelling, and punctuation at all times.

Characteristics of Formal and Informal English

	FORMAL	INFORMAL
Tone	Serious, reserved, academic, ceremonial	Personal, friendly, casual
Vocabulary and Mechanics	Sometimes uses longer or more complicated words Avoids contractions, clipped words, and slang Uses correct grammar, spelling, and punctuation	Uses simpler words Often uses contractions and clipped words Avoids slang Uses correct grammar, spelling, and punctuation
Organization	Longer, carefully constructed sentences	Sentences of a great variety of lengths Similar to conversational English
Appropriate Uses	Reports or serious essays Legal, academic, religious, or other professional documents Formal speeches, debates, or interviews	Writing intended for a general audience Conversations, letters Informal talks
Audience	Readers of scholarly material Readers of professional documents Persons in positions of authority	Friends, co-workers Most general audiences

Nonstandard English

Language that does not conform to the accepted standards of grammar, usage, and mechanics is called **nonstandard English**. Nonstandard English is chiefly a form of spoken English. If it appears in print, it is usually in the dialogue of a character in a story or a play. In the following work of fiction, the author, Ring Lardner, deliberately uses nonstandard English. Look for the mistakes in grammar and spelling in this portion of a letter a rookie baseball pitcher is writing to his friend.

> Next morning half the bunch mostly vetrans went to the ball park which isn't no better than the one we got at home. Most of them was vetrans as I say but I was in the bunch. That makes things look pretty good for me don't it Al? We tossed the ball round and hit fungos and run round and then Callahan asks Scott and Russell and I to warm up easy and pitch a few to the batters. It was warm and I felt pretty good so I warmed up pretty good . . . So I went in and after I lobbed a few over I cut loose my fast one. Lord was to bat and he ducked out of the way and then throwed his bat to the bench. Callahan says What's the matter Harry? Lord says I forgot to pay up my life insurance. He says I ain't ready for Walter Johnson's July stuff.
>
> —RING LARDNER

Notice the misspelling of *veteran*, the incorrect verb forms *throwed, don't it,* and *ain't,* and the double negative *isn't no better.* These are typical examples of nonstandard English.

Slang. Another characteristic of nonstandard English is the overuse of **slang**. This term refers to all words and phrases that are not accepted as standard English. Slang often seems colorful and interesting when it is first used, and sometimes it even becomes accepted as standard English. (The words *carpetbagger, hobo, highbrow,* and *killjoy,* for example, began as slang.) However, if you read a novel from the 1920's and run into such terms as *lounge lizard, sockdolager,* and *the cat's pajamas,* they will probably be meaningless to you. In the same way, recent slang terms will probably fade away within a few months. Due to the temporary nature of slang, it is best to avoid it in most situations.

If you use slang, use it with caution. Slang is never appropriate in formal writing or speech. It may be used occasionally in informal conversations. Use it sparingly in informal writing if it is appropriate. For instance, you may use slang in dialogue.

Exercises Using the Levels of Language

A. Choose a topic from the arts or sciences. Write a paragraph on this topic using the formal language of a report. You may find it helpful to use some of the terms defined in this chapter. Then, using informal English, rewrite your paragraph as though you were going to include it in a letter to a friend.

B. The following report contains several different levels of language. Rewrite the report. Eliminate all nonstandard English and replace inappropriate phrases and slang.

> When you shine a beam of light through a prism, the light is broken up into the colors of the rainbow: violet, blue, green, yellow, orange, and red. These colors are called *spectra*. The spectra are really neat to look at because they're pretty and everything, but they are also useful to scientists. Astronomers, in particular, really get into using spectra for research.
>
> By shining the light of distant stars through a spectrograph, astronomers can produce rainbow-like spectra for objects that are way, way out there in space somewhere. By studying these spectra, scientists can figure out lots and lots of interesting things, like what stars are made out of and how far away they are and how fast they're traveling through space. Given the value of such information, one can conclude that sometimes things that look really great are also extremely useful.

Gobbledygook

The Dictionary of Occupational Titles lists over forty thousand types of jobs in existence today. The specialized vocabularies, or jargons, of these occupations have helped to create a common abuse of language.

Gobbledygook is writing that is hard to understand because it uses too many uncommon words or too much technical jargon. Writing of this sort is often found in government and business publications. The following is an example of gobbledygook:

> Extra supplies may be requisitioned in accordance with procedures outlined in the revised operational manual by entering on the appropriate form the source of the extraordinary requisition request, the amount in which said extraordinary request exceeds the annual budgetary allotment designated for that supply category, and written permission for said request from the highest-ranking authority available.

To avoid writing gobbledygook yourself, you should aim for simple, direct language. Avoid words and constructions that are unnecessary, too fancy for the subject, too formal for the situation, or too unfamiliar for you to handle. To decide if your language is appropriate, keep these guidelines in mind:

1. Ask yourself what you are trying to say. Your point must be clear to you before you can make it clear to anyone else.
2. Make sure your ideas are controlling your choice of words, and not the other way around.
3. Choose words that are precise and concrete.
4. Use technical jargon only when a simpler term will not convey your meaning.
5. Don't pile up unnecessary words and phrases to try to dignify your subject.
6. When revising your writing, cut out unnecessary repetition.

Exercises Recognizing Gobbledygook

A. Match each passage of gobbledygook on the left with the corresponding famous quotation on the right.

1. Humankind, taken *in toto*, is such that the individuals comprising this group are coequal in their inceptive or primal state.

a. "I know why the caged bird sings."
— PAUL LAURENCE DUNBAR

2. Past experience seems to indicate that the events concomitant to love are unlikely to proceed in an orderly or expected manner.

3. Pulchritude lies not in the object of perception but in the subjective impressions of the perceiver.

4. Indulgence in censurable behavior is an attendant human frailty in sharp contrast to the exoneration of others who indulge in censurable behavior, which is a quality one might well associate with deity.

5. The causal or determining factors that underlie the euphonious vocalizations of immured avifauna lie within the scope of my personal ratiocination.

b. "To err is human, to forgive divine."
—ALEXANDER POPE

c. "All men are created equal."
—THOMAS JEFFERSON

d. "Beauty is in the eye of the beholder."
—MARGARET WOLFE HUNDERFORD

e. "The course of true love never did run smooth."
—WILLIAM SHAKESPEARE

B. Now reverse the procedure by translating five of the following well-known proverbs into gobbledygook. You may want to consult a thesaurus for synonyms.

1. All's well that ends well.
2. A bird in the hand is worth two in the bush.
3. A penny saved is a penny earned.
4. A watched pot never boils.
5. Flattery will get you nowhere.
6. Too many cooks spoil the broth.
7. Don't put off till tomorrow what you can do today.
8. A rolling stone gathers no moss.

SUMMARY AND APPLICATIONS

1. Specialized vocabularies have contributed enormously to the growth of the English language. These terms allow efficient communication within and about an area of specialization.

2. Learning the words and phrases of specialized fields will help you to understand more of what you hear and read in school, on the job, and in everyday life. These terms are also useful in your own writing and conversation.

3. Informal English is appropriate for everyday use. Formal English is appropriate for use on serious, dignified, or ceremonial occasions.

4. Avoid nonstandard English, including all language containing improper grammar, usage, and mechanics. Use slang only for added color in a dialogue or story.

5. Avoid gobbledygook in all circumstances. Good writing is clear and direct.

Applications in Other Subject Areas

History / Social Studies. The field of politics and government, like the other fields that you have studied in this chapter, makes use of many specialized words and phrases. Look into a history or social studies text. Put together your own list of words from the jargon of politics and government and define these terms by referring to textbooks or to a dictionary.

Computer Science. One problem that the manufacturers of computers face is how to make explanations and instructions understandable to the average user. Find information on how to do some simple task on a basic home computer. Write up a set of directions that would enable someone unfamiliar with the computer to complete the task. Avoid using jargon unless you explain the term.

Chapter 4

Combining Ideas in Sentences

Most writers know that they must carefully consider *what* they say whenever they write. Many, however, don't realize that they must be equally concerned with *how* these ideas are expressed. Consider the following group of sentences:

> We were all hungry. It was after the game. We stopped at an all-night diner. We had hamburgers. We had clam chowder.

This paragraph is choppy and monotonous. Each sentence is short and contains only one simple idea. We can improve the style of the paragraph by combining its ideas into one sentence.

> We were all hungry after the game, so we stopped at an all-night diner where we had hamburgers and clam chowder.

The new sentence flows smoothly and shows how the ideas are related. Consequently, it is more interesting to read.

Good writers vary the length and complexity of their sentences. This chapter will teach you how to use this skill in your own writing. It will help you to develop a clear and interesting writing style of your own.

Part 1 Joining Sentences

Often two sentences express similar ideas that are of equal importance. Such sentences can usually be joined by a comma and the word *and*.

> Diane began work at noon. Sue joined her at one o'clock.
> Diane began work at noon, *and* Sue joined her at one o'clock.

If two sentences express contrasting ideas of equal importance, they can often be joined by a comma and the word *but*.

> I went to bed early. I could not get to sleep.
> I went to bed early, *but* I could not get to sleep.

When two sentences express a choice between ideas of equal importance, they can often be joined by a comma and *or*.

> Is Greg going to the game? Is he taking you to the movies?
> Is Greg going to the game, *or* is he taking you to the movies?

Exercises Joining Sentences

A. Join each pair of sentences by following the directions in parentheses.

1. Will Tom be able to rejoin the team? Will he have to sit out the whole season? (Join with **, or**.)
2. I remembered the eggs. I forgot the butter. (Join with **, but**.)
3. Jane sanded the tabletop. Phil assembled the base. (Join with **, and**.)
4. Would help arrive in time? Would we be stranded on the mountaintop all night? (Join with **, or**.)
5. Rain began to fall in torrents. The players sprinted for the shelter of the dugout. (Join with **, and**.)
6. Lucille is not as fast as Joan. She has more endurance. (Join with **, but**.)
7. Pine is much less expensive than oak. It is not as sturdy. (Join with **, but**.)
8. My parents are on a business trip. I'm staying with Jeff's family. (Join with **, and**.)

9. Would you like to go to a movie? Should we go to a concert instead? (Join with **, or**.)

10. The tax bill passed easily. The leash law was defeated by a wide margin. (Join with **, but**.)

B. Join each pair of sentences by using **, and** or **, or** or **, but**. Be prepared to explain your choices.

1. Jenny thought that she had finished the test. She had overlooked the last problem.

2. Chris ran after the bus. She was not able to catch it.

3. Add the cubed potatoes. Then simmer the soup for an hour.

4. You can walk from Knox Street to Third Avenue. You can take the crosstown bus.

5. Motorcycles are economical. A car offers better protection from the weather.

Part 2   Joining Sentence Parts

Sometimes the ideas expressed by two sentences are so closely related that some words are repeated. The repetition is unnecessary and awkward. The ideas would be much better expressed if they were joined in one sentence and the repeated words were eliminated. When the sentence parts express similar ideas of equal importance, they can usually be joined by *and*.

Carl runs the hurdles. *He runs* the hundred-meter dash.
Carl runs the hurdles *and* the hundred-meter dash.

When the sentence parts express contrasting ideas, they can usually be joined by *but*.

We found the door. *We* could not open it.
We found the door *but* could not open it.

When the sentence parts express a choice between ideas, they can usually be joined by *or*.

Do you want tacos for dinner? *Do you want* gyros *for dinner?*
Do you want tacos *or* gyros for dinner?

Exercises Joining Sentence Parts

A. Join the related parts in each pair of sentences by following the directions in parentheses. Eliminate the italicized words.

1. We will take the train to El Paso. *We will take* the bus *to El Paso*. (Join related parts with **or**.)

2. We led for most of the game. *We* lost in the final seconds. (Join related parts with **but**.)

3. Phil did not want to go at first. *Phil* changed his mind at the last minute. (Join related parts with **but**.)

4. Success may come overnight. *Success may come* after years of struggling. (Join related parts with **or**.)

5. I'd like to go to Denver. *I'd like to go to* San Francisco. (Join related parts with **and**.)

6. We have plenty of asparagus. *We have* no broccoli. (Join related parts with **but**.)

7. I stopped at Dan's house. *I* asked him to come to dinner. (Join related parts with **and**.)

8. Parker would have to inch his way along the narrow ledge. *Parker would have to* risk everything in a leap across the chasm. (Join related parts with **or**.)

9. The brown bear rolled over in the sun. *It* yawned. (Join related parts with **and**.)

10. Wash the cut with disinfectant to prevent infection. Bandage it carefully *to prevent infection*. (Join related parts with **and**.)

B. Join the related parts in each pair of sentences by using *and, but,* or *or.* Eliminate repeated words.

1. I want to become a biologist. I want to become a Grand National Stock Car driver.

2. I bought my mother some flowers for her birthday. I took her out to dinner for her birthday.

3. My cousin Benjamin was here this morning. My cousin Benjamin left before noon.

4. The shopping cart rolled down the hill. It rolled into the oncoming traffic.

5. I ran well at the start. I dropped out after the first hill.

Part 3 Adding Single Words

Sometimes only one word in the second sentence of a pair is really important to the meaning. The one important word can be added to the first sentence, resulting in one sentence that is a much tighter and more effective way of expressing the idea.

> Betty was able to fix our radiator. *It was* leaking.
> Betty was able to fix our leaking radiator.
>
> Chris stared at the fender. *It was* dented.
> Chris stared at the dented fender.

Sometimes the form of the important word must be changed by adding *-ing* or *-ed.*

> Betty was able to fix our radiator. *It had a* leak.
> Betty was able to fix our leaking radiator.
>
> Chris stared at the fender. *It had a* dent.
> Chris stared at the dented fender.

At other times, you may have to add *-ly* to the word.

> My uncle visited us in Richmond. *It was a* brief *visit.*
> My uncle visited us *briefly* in Richmond.

Often, the word ending in *-ly* can be placed in any of several positions in the sentence.

> My uncle arrived at the party. *His arrival was* unexpected.
> *Unexpectedly,* my uncle arrived at the party.
> My uncle arrived *unexpectedly* at the party.

Exercises Adding Single Words

A. Combine each pair of sentences by adding single words. Eliminate the italicized words. Follow any special directions.

1. Susan had a cold. *The cold was* severe.
2. John returned all the books. *They were* overdue.
3. Sgt. Bass studied the window. *The window was* broken.

4. A boy stood in the aisle. *He was* whimpering.

5. The reports are in that pile. *They are* complete. (End the important word with **-ed**.)

6. Diana talked about her mountain-climbing adventures. *The talk was* endless. (End the important word with **-ly**).

7. The silence was shattered by a wolf. *It* howled. (End the important word with **-ing**.)

8. A buzzard glided toward the ground. *It made* circles *as it flew.* (End the important word with **-ing**.)

9. The truck driver had parked on the bridge. *Such parking is* illegal. (End the important word with **-ly**.)

10. Mrs. Walker spoke of her childhood memories. *She* treasures *them.* (End the important word with **-ed**.)

B. Combine each of the following pairs of sentences by adding the important word from the second sentence. Decide on your own whether to change the form of the important word.

1. We had some of Jon's lasagna for dinner. It was delicious.
2. Officer Page caught the car at the light. It was speeding.
3. Jane walked along the deserted street. Jane was nervous.
4. This glass should be thrown out. It has a crack.
5. A cat was curled up in a spot of sun. It was asleep.

Part 4 Adding Several Single Words

You may be able to add several single words to a sentence. Adding several words will allow you to combine more than two sentences if one states the main idea and each of the others adds only one important detail to the main idea.

> Cathy told a story to a group of kindergarten children. *The story was* thrilling. *It was an* adventure *story. The children were* delighted.

> Cathy told a thrilling adventure story to a group of delighted kindergarten children.

Sometimes you will have to use a comma or commas when you add more than one word to a sentence. Sections 11.14 and 11.15 in the Handbook will provide you with information on the use of commas.

> Jackson hit a home run into the upper deck at Yankee Stadium. *It was* long *and* towering.
>
> Jackson hit a long, towering home run into the upper deck at Yankee Stadium.

Sometimes you can join the words with *and*.

> My attention wandered during the second act. *The second act was* long. *It was also* tedious.
>
> My attention wandered during the long and tedious second act.

Remember that changes in the endings of the important words may be necessary.

> A building dominates the downtown area. *It is made of* glass. *It* glitters.
>
> A glittering glass building dominates the downtown area.

Exercises Adding Several Single Words

A. Combine each group of sentences by adding the important words. Eliminate the italicized words and follow any special directions given in parentheses.

1. At the end of the film, a snake crushed several buildings. *The snake was* huge. *The buildings were* tall.

2. Frank threw a pitch to Becky. *It was* low *and* outside. (Use a comma.)

3. Becky hit a line drive right at Jeff on third. *It* sizzled. (End the important word with **-ing**.)

4. The fox circled the chicken coop. *He was* crafty *and* old. (Do not use a comma or *and*.)

5. A slice of sun peeked over the horizon. *The slice was* thin. *The sun was* fiery *and* red. (Do not use a comma or *and*.)

6. In the light I could just make out a face. *The light was* dim. *The face was* weathered.

7. We reached the summit after a climb. *The climb was* long. *It was also* exhausting. (Join the important words with **and**.)

8. Strips of orange peel add flavor to a stew. *The strips should be* thin. *The orange peel is* tangy. *The flavor is* unusual.

9. John gave a sigh of relief. *It was* long. *It was* low. *It was* heartfelt. (Use commas.)

10. The next meet will be held in Westlake's pool. *This is the next meet on the* schedule. *Westlake's pool has* heat. (End the important words with **-ed**.)

B. Combine each group of sentences by adding the important words from the second sentence to the first sentence. Changes in the endings of the important words may be necessary.

1. Dan found a letter in a book on the shelf. The letter was crumpled. It was old. The shelf was dusty.

2. The stranger stood alone in the night. It was still and damp.

3. The commuters enjoyed their ride on the cars. The ride was swift. It was also comfortable. The cars were new and lightweight.

4. The loon's cry is odd. It is a cry made of laughs and whoops.

5. I'll have eggs and juice. Fry the eggs and chill the juice.

Part 5　Adding Groups of Words

You may find that one sentence contains an important group of words that can be added to another sentence. When the group of words gives more information about someone or something, it should be added near the words that name the person or thing.

The man had a suspicious look. *He was* beside my father.
The man beside my father had a suspicious look.

A box stood in the corner. *It was* filled with old clothes.
A box filled with old clothes stood in the corner.

I was startled by a dark figure. *It was* standing in the doorway.
I was startled by a dark figure standing in the doorway.

I was startled by a dark figure. *I was* standing in the doorway.
Standing in the doorway, I was startled by a dark figure.

When the group of words describes an action, it should be added near the words that name the action.

> Our cat was hiding. *She was* under the sofa.
> Our cat was hiding under the sofa.

In some cases, the group of words restates the meaning of another word in the sentence. In such cases you will have to separate the group of words with a comma or a pair of commas.

> My secret dream was to climb Mount Everest. *Mount Everest is* the world's highest peak.
> My secret dream was to climb Mount Everest, the world's highest peak.

> My friend is a football fanatic. *My friend is* Al Peters.
> My friend, Al Peters, is a football fanatic.

> Alaska is twice the size of Texas. *Alaska is* our largest state.
> Alaska, our largest state, is twice the size of Texas.

When the group of words adds more information to the entire main idea of the other sentence, it may be added at the beginning or at the end.

> I drove to the abandoned factory. *I drove there* in the late afternoon.
> In the late afternoon, I drove to the abandoned factory.
> I drove to the abandoned factory in the late afternoon.

> I decided to change my plans. *I did it* for Joan's sake.
> For Joan's sake, I decided to change my plans.
> I decided to change my plans, for Joan's sake.

Usually, you can add a group of words to a sentence without making any change in form. Sometimes, however, you will have to change one of the words. The new form of the word will often end in *-ing*.

> Huge tankers moved slowly into the harbor of the city. *They* carried shipments of oil.
> Huge tankers carrying shipments of oil moved slowly into the harbor of the city.

Remember that more than one group of words can be added to a sentence. You may have to use a variety of techniques to combine them.

> A cloud of fog crept into the area. *It* arrived at dusk. *The fog* blanketed the city.
> A cloud of fog crept into the area at dusk, blanketing the city.

Exercises Adding Groups of Words

A. Combine each group of sentences by adding a group of words or groups of words to one of them. Eliminate the italicized words.

1. Mr. Perkins was waiting. *He was* in the lobby.

2. A tall woman stood on the corner. *She* carried a briefcase. (Add **-ing** to one of the words in the group.)

3. *I was* opening the envelope. I found three pages. *They were* from my laboratory report.

4. We watched without moving. *We were* dazzled by the beauty of the falls.

5. A rainbow arched across the sky. *This happened* after a storm.

6. Katy spent every summer in the country. *She stayed there* with her grandmother.

7. John Layne praised the opposition. *This happened* after the game. *He is* our starting quarterback.

8. The construction crew worked busily. *They worked* through the day. *They* stopped only for a quick lunch break. (Add **-ing** to one word in the last sentence.)

9. Diana was chosen for the all-star team. *She was* a short girl. *She was* playing in her first full season.

10. The downtown area was entirely reconstructed by 1884. *It had been* destroyed by fire in 1882.

B. Combine each group of sentences by adding a group of words or groups of words to one of them.

1. Cliff had no idea that he was being watched. He was standing alone. He was beneath a streetlamp.

2. We had been reading *I Am Third*. *I Am Third* is the autobiography of Gale Sayers.

3. Archaeologists flocked to the site of the ancient city. It had been discovered by Professor Greene and her students.

4. Dr. Watson settled back in an overstuffed chair. He began another fascinating story. The story was about one of Holmes's famous cases.

5. Rosa was concentrating fiercely. She was concentrating on her term paper. Rosa did not hear the telephone ringing. It was in the next room.

Part 6 Combining with *Who, Which,* and *That*

You have just seen that a group of words in one sentence often describes a person or thing in another sentence. Sometimes, the introductory word *who, which,* or *that* is needed to combine the two sentences.

Who is used to add a group of words that describes a person. If the added group of words is essential to the meaning of the sentence to which it is added, it should *not* be set off by commas. If the added group of words is not essential to the meaning of the sentence, then it should be set off by commas.

> To be successful, a candidate needs supporters. The supporters must be willing to work long and hard for victory.

> To be successful, a candidate needs supporters who are willing to work long and hard for victory. (The added information is essential to the sentence. It tells *what kind of supporters.*)

> William Golding was awarded the Nobel Prize for literature in 1983. He is best known for the novel *Lord of the Flies.*

> William Golding, who is best known for the novel *Lord of the Flies,* was awarded the Nobel Prize for literature in 1983. (The added information is not essential to the sentence.)

Which and *that* are also used to add groups of words. They are used to add words that refer to things. When the added information is essential to the meaning of the sentence, use *that.*

When the added information is not essential to the sentence, use *which* and set off the group of words with a comma.

> A pulsar is an object in space. It emits radio waves.
> A pulsar is an object in space *that* emits radio waves.
> Instead of the usual house plants, try growing herbs. They are both attractive and useful.
> Instead of the usual house plants, try growing herbs, *which* are both attractive and useful.

Exercises Combining with *Who, Which,* and *That*

A. Combine each of the following pairs of sentences by following the directions in parentheses. Eliminate the italicized words.

1. Chip hasn't come to practice all week. *Chip* didn't miss a single workout last year. (Combine with **, who.**)

2. Most rocks from the "seas" of the moon are basalts. *Basalts* are formed from volcanic lava. (Combine with **, which.**)

3. The movie has been nominated for an Academy Award. I saw *the movie* last night. (Combine with **that.**)

4. Our voices were drowned out by the roar of the waterfalls. *The falls* cascaded from two hundred feet above us. (Combine with **, which.**)

5. The man had found the stolen briefcase under a table in a coffee shop. *The man* returned the missing documents. (Combine with **who.**)

6. The guest speaker was Dr. Esther Blair. *Dr. Blair* described what a large ocean farm of the future might be like. (Combine with **who.**)

7. Did you see the note? I left *the note* on the refrigerator. (Combine with **that.**)

8. Carlos discovered the solution to the math problem. *The math problem* had stumped the rest of the class completely. (Combine with **that.**)

9. Charles Schultz created the *Peanuts* comic strip. *He* is probably the most famous cartoonist in the country. (Combine with **, who.**)

10. The tomatoes and herbs came from our backyard garden. He used *the tomatoes and herbs* to make this spaghetti sauce. (Combine with **that.**)

B. Combine each of the following pairs of sentences. Decide on your own whether to use **, who** or **, which** or **, that.**

1. Larry suddenly returned to town. Larry hadn't written to me or called since he moved away last year.
2. The engine in the two-door coupe has a turbocharger. The turbocharger boosts the engine's power.
3. Carl has been taking lessons in Portuguese. He hopes to go to Brazil as an exchange student next year.
4. Esther's bicycle trip will take her through twelve states. She has been planning the trip since last winter.
5. The composition is entitled "Lagrima." Maria played the composition at her guitar recital.

Part 7 Combining Sentences Using Substitution

Read the following pair of sentences.

> She *jogged* to school and back every day. *This* helped to increase Corey's stamina.

Notice that *This* in the second sentence refers to the entire idea in the first sentence. This pair of sentences and others like it, can be combined in one smooth statement.

> Jogging to school and back every day helped to increase Corey's stamina.

The word *jogged* was changed to *jogging*, and the italicized words were eliminated.

Here is another example of sentences combined by using *-ing*.

> *He had always* watched the sun rise over the ocean. When he moved to Utah, Brad missed *that experience.*

> When he moved to Utah, Brad missed *watching* the sun rise over the ocean.

Notice that the word *watched* was changed to *watching*, and that the italicized words were eliminated.

Exercises Using Substitution

A. Combine each group of sentences by using **-ing**. Eliminate the italicized words.

1. *Janet* worked at an after-school job. *This responsibility* kept Janet from joining the track team.
2. *Phillip* refused to pay his debts. *That* led Phillip into serious trouble.
3. *Martha* visited the statewide science fair. *This* was the beginning of Martha's interest in science.
4. *Some people* get a good night's sleep before a test. *Others* cram until late at night. *The first* is a much better strategy than *the second.*
5. *Many people* recycle paper. *This* saves forests, energy, and money.
6. *We* booed when the other team took the court. *That* was a mistake that we later regretted.
7. *Mrs. Benson* competed in the city marathon. *That* was the high point of Mrs. Benson's fitness program.
8. Our guests discussed politics and world affairs at dinner. *They* enjoyed *that.*
9. *We will* hold our meetings in the evening. We hope that *that* will increase attendance.
10. *Music lovers can* listen to a record. *They can* see a live performance. *The first* can never take the place of *the second.*

B. Combine each pair of sentences by using **-ing**. Decide on your own what words should be eliminated.

1. Maria missed the last bus home. That meant that Maria would be at least an hour late.
2. He climbed the Matterhorn at sixty years of age. That brought Mr. Daniels his greatest thrill.
3. People have to rest in bed after an illness. That can be depressing for an active person.
4. I discovered Parkinson's true identity. That enabled me to solve the mystery.
5. Cliff slipped as he rounded the final turn. That cost Cliff a first place medal.

Part 8 Combining To Show Causes and Effects

Explanations are certain to play an important role in your writing. Most explanations take the form of a statement of cause and effect. In other words, you state that something happened because of something else. The following example uses the word *because* to make the cause-and-effect relationship clear.

> Many household cleaning products are toxic. They should be kept out of the reach of children.
>
> *Because* many household cleaning products are toxic, they should be kept out of the reach of children.

Notice that a comma separates the two sentences. The words *since* and *for* are also useful for indicating causes in combined sentences.

> The young actor was very nervous. He had never been on stage before.
>
> *Since* he had never been on stage before, the young actor was very nervous.
>
> The parade was postponed. It began to rain.
>
> The parade was postponed, *for* it began to rain.

The words above are added before the cause in the combined sentence. You can also add words before the effect. The following words are the ones most commonly used to indicate effects:

so	as a result	thus
therefore	consequently	

If you use the word *so* to indicate an effect, you can still join the sentences with a comma. If you use one of the other words or phrases from this list, you will have to use a semicolon (;) before the word and a comma after it.

> Many household cleaning products are toxic. They should be kept out of the reach of children.
>
> Many household cleaning products are toxic; therefore, they should be kept out of the reach of children.

Exercises Combining To Show Causes and Effects

A. Combine each of the following pairs of sentences by using the key words given in parentheses.

1. People should eat some foods that are high in fiber every day. Fiber is important to digestion. (**since**)
2. We forgot to patch the tent. We all got wet. (**; consequently,**)
3. Crosstown traffic has been rerouted to the south. The 16th Street bridge is being repaired. (**because**)
4. The 16th Street bridge is being repaired. Crosstown traffic has been rerouted to the south. (**; therefore,**)
5. Nelson didn't attend last week's meeting. He didn't realize that he was on the nominating committee. (**because**)
6. The crowd cheered throughout the candidate's speech. It was impossible to hear what she said. (**; as a result,**)
7. Janet loved the movie *Excalibur*. I loaned her a book of Arthurian legends. (**, so**)
8. The opposing team fumbled the ball several times. We were ahead by two touchdowns by the end of the first quarter. (**; thus,**)
9. It is difficult to write about the history of chess. The origin of the game is a mystery. (**, for**)
10. The school had to close early. The heat failed. (**because**)

B. Combine each of the following pairs of sentences in two ways. First, combine to show that one of the sentences is a cause. Then combine to show that one of the sentences is an effect.

1. The message had been transmitted in code. We couldn't tell what it meant.
2. Andy had practiced his solo for weeks. He felt calm when the night of the concert arrived.
3. The northern hemisphere is tilted towards the sun in the summer. It receives more direct rays of the sun at that time.
4. I had an hour to wait between buses. I decided to walk along the river for a while.
5. Lee had never seen a condor before. She was astounded by the bird's ten-foot wingspan.

Review Exercises Combining Ideas in Sentences

A. Join each pair of sentences by using , **and** or , **or** or , **but**.

1. Would you like to borrow my pen? Do you prefer to use a pencil?

2. The birds haven't discovered the feeder. The squirrels have.

3. I made that feeder myself. Then I mounted it on a tall pole.

4. Would a taller pole discourage the squirrels? Will I just have to put up with them?

5. The class was almost over. I still had three essay questions to answer.

B. Join the related parts in each pair of sentences by using **and**, **or**, or **but**. Eliminate the italicized words.

1. You might make the table with ash. *You might make the table with* birch.

2. They peered through the dusty window. *They* couldn't see anyone inside.

3. Glen asked several questions. *Glen* still wasn't certain that he understood the problem.

4. We can meet in the park today at noon. *We can meet* in the park tomorrow at three.

5. I have many relatives living in St. Louis. *I have many relatives living in* Oakland.

C. Combine each of the following pairs of sentences by adding the important word. Eliminate the italicized words and follow any special directions in parentheses.

1. A wind blew from the mountains. *The wind was* cold.

2. I had just begun my job. *It was my* first.

3. Detective Bass questioned the witness. *His questioning was* merciless. (End the important word with **-ly**.)

4. This project could not have been completed without the help of many people. *They were* tireless.

5. Sunlight glittered on the windowpanes. *They had* frost *on them*. (End the important word with **-ed**.)

D. Combine each group of sentences by adding the important words. Eliminate the italicized words and follow any special directions in parentheses.

1. Early that morning, a message arrived from the crew members. *The message was* mysterious. *The crew members were* missing.
2. Parker gave a speech. *It was* calm *and* thoughtful. (Use a comma.)
3. Could my voice be heard over the crowd? *My voice* trembled. *The crowd* screamed. (End the important words with **-ing**.)
4. I started the day with a plate of eggs. *They were* fluffy. *They were* scrambled. (Do not use a comma.)
5. A dog loped along beside me as I ran. *It was* large. *It was* shaggy. *It was* gray. (Use two commas.)

E. Combine each group of sentences by adding a group of words or groups of words to one of them. Eliminate the italicized words.

1. Mrs. Daniels was standing. *She was* at the side of the stage.
2. A trio of music students wandered through the park. *They were* playing violins.
3. *I was* turning the corner. I ran into two people. *They were* from my old neighborhood.
4. We sat motionless in our seats. *We were* stunned by the ending of the film.
5. Confetti littered Main Street. *This was* after the parade.

F. Combine each of the following pairs of sentences by following the directions in parentheses. Eliminate the italicized words.

1. King Oliver was a strong influence on Louis Armstrong. *King Oliver* played cornet during the 1920s. (Combine with **, who**.)
2. The boy has started his own landscaping business. *The boy* lives next door to me. (Combine with **who**.)
3. Pedestrians are a major cause of automobile accidents. *These pedestrians* do not use crosswalks. (Combine with **who**.)
4. Jeannie has been learning to operate a video camera. *Jeannie* hopes to become a television director. (Combine with **, who**.)
5. The person will be notified by telephone. *The person* has won the raffle. (Combine with **who**.)

G. Combine each of the following pairs of sentences by following the directions in parentheses. Eliminate the italicized words.

1. You may see as many as a hundred meteors per hour during the Perseid meteor shower. *The Perseid meteor shower* occurs in August. (Combine with **, which**.)
2. All fish have gills, but a few kinds also have lungs. *The gills* remove oxygen from the water. (Combine with **that**.)
3. I had missed the bus. *The bus* would have taken me directly to Des Moines. (Combine with **that**.)
4. The package is on the table in the hall. *The package* arrived for you. (Combine with **that**.)
5. The new interstate highway follows the route of an old wagon trail. *The new interstate highway* will be open to traffic tomorrow. (Combine with **, which**.)

H. Combine each group of sentences by using **-ing**. Eliminate the italicized words.

1. *I* finished my history paper. *That* gave me a real sense of accomplishment.
2. *The Andersons* refinish old furniture. *That* has brought the Andersons a second income.
3. *Lucille* explained her position in a calm and logical way. *That* won Lucille the respect of everyone in the audience.
4. *Bill* brags. *That* has cost Bill many friends.
5. *People* plan ahead. *This* can prevent wasted time and effort.

I. Combine each of the following pairs of sentences by using the key words given in parentheses.

1. The picnic site was changed at the last minute. Many people were confused, and a few were very annoyed. (**; as a result,**)
2. The growing season in this area is long, and the soil is fertile. Agriculture has always been an important industry. (**because**)
3. The bookstore was not open. I came back later. (**, so**)
4. The football team had spent six hours riding on a bus. Most of the players were tired when the game started. (**since**)
5. The football team had spent six hours riding on a bus. Most of the players were tired when the game started. (**; consequently,**)

1. Learning to combine ideas in sentences will help you make your writing clearer and more interesting.

2. Sentences and sentence parts expressing ideas of equal importance can often be joined by using a comma plus *and, or,* or *but.*

3. Single words can sometimes be taken from one sentence and added to another. Sometimes single words from several sentences can be added to another sentence. Occasionally, one must add *-ed, -ing,* or *-ly* to single words when moving them to another sentence.

4. Sometimes one or more groups of words can be taken from a sentence and added to another sentence.

5. Sometimes a group of words can be added to a sentence by using *who, which,* or *that* or by adding *-ing* to a key word.

6. Cause and effect relationships can be shown by adding groups of words beginning with *because, since, for, so, therefore, as a result, consequently,* or *thus.*

Applications in Other Subject Areas

Current Events / Social Studies / Mass Media. Written sentences can be reread if their meaning is unclear. Spoken sentences cannot be reviewed in this way. For this reason, authors of public speeches and news broadcasts try to keep their sentences short and simple. Authors of magazine articles and books, on the other hand, can use longer sentences that combine several ideas.

Choose a topic or controversy that is in the news. Write a brief report or editorial on this subject for broadcast on the air. Use short, simple sentences. Then, rewrite your report or editorial for publication in a magazine. This time, combine your sentences to produce good written copy.

Chapter 5

Improving Your Sentences

The problems of writing are largely problems with individual sentences. By improving your sentences, you automatically improve your paragraphs, compositions, reports, and letters.

The following are some of the most common weaknesses found in sentences:

Some sentences have a shortage of ideas or do not provide enough information.

Some sentences contain too many ideas and should be broken up into smaller units.

Some sentences do not make sense.

In this chapter you will learn how to solve these problems by revising sentences written by other young people like you. You will be using a method of writing improvement that has been tested with thousands of students. This method does not rely on the principles of grammar. Instead, it focuses on improving writing by eliminating problems of meaning and sense.

Part 1   Avoiding Empty Sentences

> The reason I like the Pittsburgh Steelers is that they are my favorite team.

Sentences that say too little are **empty sentences.** Grammatically they may be complete, yet they are lacking in ideas, in substance. One reason is that they may contain words or groups of words that repeat the idea contained earlier in the sentence. Here is an example of this kind of writing:

> The reason I like the Pittsburgh Steelers is that they are my favorite team.

This is writing in a circle. The idea of *liking* is repeated. The writer begins by saying that he *likes* the team. He ends with the same idea expressed in the word *favorite.* The sentence is empty because no reasons for liking the team are given. The writer could have said this:

> The Pittsburgh Steelers are my favorite team because they have a strong passing game, an aggressive defense, and a winning spirit. I particularly admire Terry Bradshaw's passing.

Sentences are empty because the writer does not take the trouble to think about what he or she wants to say. The reader gets the impression that the writer is just trying to fill space.

Exercises   Revising Empty Sentences

A. Revise the following sentences.

Suggestions

1. Read each sentence. Ask yourself, "What idea is repeated?"
2. Supply the necessary facts or ideas.
3. Write more than one sentence if you need to.

1. I am interested in ceramics because it is an interesting hobby.
2. It is impossible to learn a new language so quickly because people are not able to do it.

3. I wanted to play on the team because I always wanted to be a basketball player.

4. During those few days I began to admire her qualities because her character was so fine.

5. Mike had three reasons for choosing the book he was reading, and his reasons were all good ones.

6. If you're just starting, the $75 model is a good guitar for a beginner.

7. The fight, of course, was silly, and we were both foolish for fighting.

8. The hero was the typical kind of man that you have seen many times in everyday life.

9. I liked the Robert Redford movie because it was an excellent movie.

10. My sister Fran is always joking, and she never does anything but joke around.

B. Revise these sentences.

1. I'd like to be a lifeguard because I'd love to do that and get paid for it, too.

2. I flunked the test because I didn't deserve to pass.

3. You should always put stereo speakers at least ten feet apart from each other because ten feet apart is the best distance for them to be.

4. Scott Joplin is popular because a lot of people like his songs.

5. More women are going into politics than ever before, and there should be more people like Chief Justice O'Conner in public office.

6. Inflation has become a huge problem, and everyone has to pay higher and higher prices for food, clothing, TV repairs, and other things, and these prices keep going up.

7. I think I should tell you everything in the story up to the ending, but I don't think I should tell you the ending.

8. I prefer to be with some people because they are my friends.

9. My freshman year was a good one because it was my first year.

10. I liked that waltzing bear best because it was a bear that could dance.

Part 2 Avoiding Padded Sentences

> In my opinion, I think soccer is the best team sport ever invented.

Padded sentences are ineffective sentences that contain unnecessary words. Padding can result from the following:

repetition of the same word or idea
repetition of *that*
use of such fillers as

> *on account of the fact that* . . .   *what I believe is* . . .
> *the reason is that* . . .   *the thing* . . .

Repetition of the Same Word or Idea

PADDED: *In my opinion, I think* soccer is the best team sport ever invented.

        (An opinion is a thought. Eliminate one or the other.)

BETTER: In my opinion, soccer is the best team sport ever invented.

BETTER: I think soccer is the best team sport ever invented.

PADDED: This book is a *biography of the life of* Jimmy Carter.
        (Since *biography* means *the life of*, one of these is unnecessary.)

BETTER: This book is a biography of Jimmy Carter.

BETTER: This book is about the life of Jimmy Carter.

Repetition of *That*

PADDED: It is obvious *that* since I like music so much *that* I should study it.

BETTER: It is obvious *that* since I like music so much, I should study it.

PADDED: The captain thought *that* if she turned south *that* she would run out of the storm.

BETTER: The captain thought *that* if she turned south, she would run out of the storm.

The Use of Fillers

PADDED: When the boys ran away, *the reason was that* they were frightened.

BETTER: The boys ran away because they were frightened.

PADDED: *On account of the fact that* we still depend on foreign oil, we may have more energy problems.

BETTER: Because we still depend on foreign oil, we may have more energy problems.

PADDED: *What I believe is* that love solves many problems.

BETTER: I believe that love solves many problems.

PADDED: *The thing* I am looking forward to being is a social worker.

BETTER: I am looking forward to being a social worker.

Long sentences can sometimes be simplified without losing any of their thought by reducing clauses to phrases or to appositives:

PADDED: We have a garage *that has an automatic door opener.* (adjective clause)

BETTER: We have a garage *with an automatic door opener.* (prepositional phrase)

PADDED: We attended the demonstration *that was given in the laboratory.* (adjective clause)

BETTER: We attended the demonstration *given in the laboratory.* (participial phrase)

BETTER: We attended the demonstration *in the laboratory.* (prepositional phrase)

PADDED: Jo Anne Smith, *who is our top-ranking student,* won a scholarship to Yale. (adjective clause)

BETTER: Jo Anne Smith, *our top-ranking student,* won a scholarship to Yale. (appositive)

Exercises Revising Padded Sentences

A. Revise the following sentences. Omit the padding.

1. The beginning of the unpleasantness started when Sue refused the invitation.
2. The reason why Agnes decided on a green dress was on account of the fact that she has red hair.
3. In his opinion, he thought I owed the teacher an apology.
4. The unbelievable number of accidents that are caused by sheer carelessness on our highways is staggering.
5. I did not like to retrace my footsteps back down the deserted street.
6. Jo thought that if she applied that she could get the job.
7. Since I have finally reached the ripe old age of sixteen years of age, I hope to get a job this summer.
8. What the salesman wanted us to know was the fact that we did not have to pay the total cost in order to have the bicycle delivered.
9. The reason that Mike wanted to lose a few pounds was that his favorite slacks did not fit him.
10. The class prepared a program that was dedicated to Mozart, who was a great musician.

B. Revise these sentences.

1. The beginning of it all started with the invention of the computer.
2. During the 1960's there was a great change in people's attitudes at the time.
3. I believe it is time for a great leader to come along who will really lead our country, like Abraham Lincoln.
4. Deaf people are usually safe drivers because they are aware of their handicap of not being able to hear.

5. On account of the fact that our house has been sold, we will be moving away soon.

6. The thing I am bothered about most is about the weight that I have gained.

7. Dan did not have any gray paint to paint the steps with, so he used brown paint to paint the steps.

8. What I don't like about shirts is a shirt that has no pockets.

9. The reason that we were late was the fact that we missed the plane.

10. Babe Didrikson was a woman who was a great athlete.

Part 3 Avoiding Overloaded Sentences

> I want to be a doctor because I want to help people who suffer, but I will have to study many long years in medical school before I will be qualified as a doctor.

Overloaded sentences are sentences that say too much. They carry too many ideas. They mix up important ideas with unimportant ones, and the reader is unable to sort them out. In some cases, ideas are even repeated.

What can you do to avoid overloaded sentences?

1. First, decide on the main ideas.
2. Decide which ideas can be combined into one sentence.
3. Write the main ideas as one sentence, following the usual sentence pattern of subject—verb—object.
4. Write separate sentences for the other ideas.
5. Write simply and clearly.

The following sentence tried to say too much.

> I want to be a doctor because I want to help people who suffer, but I will have to study many long years in medical school before I will be qualified as a doctor.

Let's look at the steps necessary to revise that sentence. These are the main ideas.

I want to be a doctor.
I want to help people who suffer.
I will have to study for many years to be qualified.

Two of these ideas can be combined smoothly into one sentence: the desire to be a doctor and the reason for the desire.

I want to be a doctor because I want to help people who suffer.

The remaining ideas, which are also related, should be expressed in another sentence.

To be qualified as a doctor, I will have to study for many years.

This is how the original overloaded sentence now reads.

I want to be a doctor because I want to help people who suffer. To be qualified, I will have to study for many years.

The following are additional examples of overloaded sentences. In the revisions, unimportant words and ideas have been omitted. Study these sentences carefully. Think about how you can use the same revision techniques in your own writing.

OVERLOADED: I drove out of town on a dark, lonely road, and I happened to see a car pulled up at the side of the road, which made me feel sorry for the poor people standing beside it, and, like the Good Samaritan I am, I stopped to see if I could help.

REVISED: As I drove out of town on a dark, lonely road, I happened to see people standing near a car pulled up at the side of the road. Like a Good Samaritan, I stopped to see if I could help.

OVERLOADED: I like all kinds of books, and it makes no difference to me whether other people think a book I am reading is dull, as long as I like it.

REVISED: I like all kinds of books. It makes no difference to me whether other people think the book I am reading is dull, as long as I like it.

Exercises Revising Overloaded Sentences

A. Revise each of the following sentences.

Suggestions

1. Look for the main idea and concentrate on putting it into a sentence.
2. Leave out words or ideas that are unnecessary or that get in the way.
3. Write more than one sentence if necessary.

1. There was a science fair at the museum, and Jack Gorman's robot caused a great deal of excitement, and people came from miles around to watch him give a demonstration of it.

2. Scientists say that foods eaten as soon as possible after picking contain more vitamins and that prolonged cooking results in a lack of these very essential substances.

3. The Japanese hold two festivals every year devoted to dolls, the Girls' Festival which is on March 3, and the Boys' Festival which is on March 5, and during these festivals they display dolls that have been passed down in their families for generations.

4. Mathematics is a subject that trains your mind and helps you to solve problems, which helps in future life because so many people can't think straight or solve their problems.

5. He liked playing baseball and played it well, which is unusual because in 1900 there weren't many good players and baseball wasn't a popular game.

B. Revise these sentences.

1. The American Kennel Club, an organization of dog breeders in the United States, recognizes over 125 breeds of dogs, which shows that there are many different breeds of dogs.

2. I like the movie more than the book because in the movie the characters seem real, and they don't seem real in the book.

3. While I am covering various stories, I will be able to learn many new things and understand things I know even better and also help the paper's readers to be able to learn and understand different things that happen in the world.

4. No one even asked me to go home with her, but as I was walking home by myself thinking of my first unhappy day at school and of the dreary days ahead, a friendly voice called out behind me, "Hi! I'm Patsy Walker."

5. To me, sleeping is fascinating because I consider it a time of dreams that allow me to visit strange places where anything might occur as though I were Alice in Wonderland and had fallen through a rabbit hole into a land of fantasy and make-believe.

C. The following sentences contain the kinds of problems you have been working with. Revise the sentences. Some of them are empty, padded, *and* overloaded.

1. I want to be a deep-sea diver, and my reason for choosing this profession is that this is the thing that interests me most in life.

2. Whales and dolphins are marine creatures that live in water, but they are not fish, which are also marine creatures that live in water, because they are mammals, which means they are warm-blooded.

3. What I believe about criticism is that some kinds of criticism are good, but other kinds of criticism are harmful, and harmful criticism is criticism that tears a person down instead of helping the person to grow and develop.

4. We have two English setters, Melissa and Storm, and English setters are such a rare breed that whenever we take them walking people stop and ask what kind of dogs they are.

5. Billy the Kid was America's best-known outlaw, and not many people know that he had a baby-faced look and did not look like an outlaw at all and that he never used his real name.

Part 4 Keeping to the Point

Omit details that interrupt the meaning of a sentence and have no connection with the main idea.

What is wrong with the following sentence?

> The editor of the school paper, who has six Siamese cats, called a meeting of the staff and gave out the assignments for the final issue.

The editor's interest in cats has nothing to do with the staff meeting. The clause *who has six Siamese cats* is, therefore, a detail that interrupts the sentence and has no connection with the main idea. It should be omitted.

Do not allow irrelevant details to slip into your writing. Keep your ideas clear and to the point.

Exercises **Keeping to the Point**

A. Revise the following sentences. Omit details that do not belong.

1. Harold's older brother, who has three children, is completely different from Harold in appearance and interests.

2. The school band, which had brand new uniforms, was invited to play at a band competition in Washington, D.C.

3. Supersonic passenger planes, which make a terrible noise when they take off, have made it possible for people to travel around the world in a single day.

4. The all-girl rock group, in which there are several redheads, toured the state all summer.

5. The book I am reading, which has a blue cover and many illustrations, contains information about the most recent developments in the field of electronics.

6. Many of my friends, who are tall and very pretty, are fond of bowling.

7. Last Saturday I saw a basketball game, which I prefer to football, that went into double overtime.

8. At Grandmother's house, a table was prepared on which there was an abundance of bread, butter, cake (which my father is not allowed to eat because of his diet), colored eggs, ham, chicken, and other food.

9. The play was about a nineteenth-century doctor named Treves who lives in London, which was founded as a Roman trading post around A.D. 43, and his famous patient, John Merrick.

10. I want to work in television or radio because the audience will be doubled in ten years, when I'll be ten years older and will have my driver's license and my own car, and more technicians will be in demand.

B. Revise these sentences. Each sentence may have more than one problem.

1. While I am on this earth, I want to do something that the people I leave behind me after I am gone will remember me for.
2. I used to live with my parents in Woodland Hills, which is a suburb of Los Angeles, but now I live with my mother in an apartment in the city, which is called "the city of angels" in spite of my presence.
3. It wasn't until last year, after Uncle Dan died in St. Francis Hospital, that I realized what a wonderful friend I had lost.
4. In 1947, the year in which Tennessee Williams won the Pulitzer Prize, Thor Heyerdahl sailed on a raft from Peru to Polynesia in one hundred and one days to prove that prehistoric people could have made long ocean voyages across the sea in rafts.
5. Robert Frost was born in San Francisco — a city in which cable cars still operate — but his poetry deals primarily with New England, in the eastern part of the United States.

Part 5 Keeping Related Sentence Parts Together

Do not separate sentence parts that belong together with constructions that should be written elsewhere. Doing so causes your readers to lose the train of thought and makes the sentences sound choppy.

AWKWARD: *I am,* as soon as I have saved enough money, *going to buy* a portable radio. (Parts of the verb phrase are separated.)

BETTER: As soon as I have saved enough money, *I am going to buy* a portable radio.

AWKWARD: *Julie,* after falling from her bike, *assured* us she was not hurt. (Subject and verb are separated.)

BETTER: After falling from her bike, *Julie assured* us she was not hurt.

AWKWARD: I *found,* inside the envelope that Mother handed me, *an invitation* to a surprise birthday party. (Verb and object are separated.)

BETTER: I *found an invitation* to a surprise party inside the envelope that Mother handed me.

Exercises Keeping Related Parts Together

A. Revise each of the following sentences. Bring the separated parts closer together.

Suggestions

1. Read each sentence to yourself. Read it in more than one way, moving the parts around. Listen to the sound and sense of the sentence as you say it with the parts in different places.
2. Revise the sentence to bring the separated parts closer.

1. The coach wouldn't, no matter how much we reasoned with him, put Jack back in the game.

2. The crippled plane, because the pilot wanted to use up most of the fuel before landing, circled the field for three hours.

3. We could have, if we had worked together, won the state championship last year.

4. I feel that I could, if I had an interest in chemistry, learn the subject more thoroughly.

5. Many college graduates receive, on account of their additional training and knowledge, higher salaries.

6. I, because I was in town, decided to buy my parents their anniversary present.

7. Are there people in other galaxies who are discovering, by scientific methods that we do not know, important facts about our own solar system?

8. My parents are, for the whole month of August, doing volunteer work at a center for disadvantaged children.

9. I have, although my friends would not believe it, two medals and a trophy for diving.

10. The gleeman, since there was neither television nor radio at the time, reported news of current happenings to the people.

B. Revise these sentences.

1. This 1924 airmail stamp is, I am told, worth $400.
2. There have been, throughout history, only seven basic jokes.
3. Wolves, in spite of what many think, never attack people.
4. The Hawaiian Islands were, in 1778, discovered by Captain James Cook.
5. The coach announced that she had resigned after the game.
6. Most of Sam's snapshots had, until he got his new camera, a washed-out look.
7. My bicycle and I are frankly no longer friends.
8. It had, even though it was a late-model car, a suspiciously low price.
9. Offices of all sizes have electronic computers, keeping up with progress.
10. According to a psychologist, people are not very trustworthy who often insist that they are telling the truth.

Part 6   Combining Ideas Effectively

Avoiding Overuse of *and*

Although *and* is a useful conjunction for joining ideas that have a relationship indicating *addition,* its overuse creates a decidedly uninteresting style. Careful writers avoid using *and's* to join a string of ideas like the following:

> I went to the library, and when I got there it was closed, and I was worried because I had to get a book for English, and I knew I would get into trouble if I didn't have it, and I read the sign and noticed that the hours were listed, and . . .

A reader quickly loses interest in a string of ideas like this. The writer's responsibility to a reader is to present ideas in a logical, coherent way. The secret of good writing is to take the time to *reread, revise,* and *rewrite.*

Using Compound Sentences Correctly

To the reader, the value of a compound sentence is that it joins related ideas.

Some people act before they think, and they live to regret it.

Sometimes a writer joins unrelated ideas because he or she does not take time to plan beforehand. Sometimes a writer leaves out an in-between thought through carelessness or haste. The reader is confused and has to stop and ask, "What is the connection between the first and the second idea?" There is no clear connection; the ideas are not related.

You can handle this problem by expressing the thought omitted. It may be necessary to write two sentences to do so.

CONFUSING: The time hand on the electric scoreboard stopped, and the visiting team won the game.

IMPROVED: The time hand on the electric scoreboard stopped. *As a result, extra seconds were allowed for play*, and the visiting team won the game.

CONFUSING: The rain came down in torrents, and the janitor's wife had to entertain unexpected visitors alone.

IMPROVED: The rain came down in torrents. *Because the janitor was working late to take care of the flooded cellar*, his wife had to entertain unexpected visitors alone.

Using Linking Words Correctly

Conjunctive adverbs and other linking words are also used to combine related ideas:

RESULT	ADDITION	
consequently	also	in fact
hence	besides	likewise
therefore	furthermore	moreover
thus	indeed	

EXCEPTION OR CONTRAST		ALTERNATIVE
however	still	at the same time
nevertheless	yet	on the other hand
nonetheless		otherwise

Notice how the use of linking words makes specific relationships clear in these sentences.

> Joe made the varsity; *consequently*, he will have to spend many hours in after-school practice. (result)
>
> Studying languages disciplines your mind; *furthermore*, it makes communication with people from other nations possible. (addition)
>
> The play had been widely promoted; *nevertheless*, the audience was small. (contrast)
>
> It may snow tonight; *on the other hand*, there may be just a light frost. (alternative)

The choice of different connecting words can change the meaning of a sentence.

> Auto racing is a dangerous sport; *nevertheless*, he wants to try it. (exception or contrast)
>
> Auto racing is a dangerous sport; *therefore*, he decided not to try it. (result)

Exercises Combining Ideas Effectively

A. Revise the sentences on the following page. Some of them contain too many *and*'s. Others are compound sentences joining unrelated ideas.

Suggestions:

1. Check the sentence for too many *and*'s.
2. Pick out the main ideas.
3. Combine related ideas.
4. Locate the compound sentences that join unrelated ideas.
5. Supply the details needed to make good sense.
6. Write more than one sentence if necessary.

1. The plane zoomed overhead, and it made a great deal of noise, and it was a 747 and was flying nonstop from Rhode Island to California.

2. The game went into overtime, and the coach did not appear for his broadcast at the local studio.

3. I love to watch the snow start its long journey from the sky and fall to the ground, and the snowflakes lie there in all shapes, big ones, little ones, round ones, and people finally step on them or shovel them away.

4. He was watching a television play, and he decided it was the worst he had ever seen, and he was disappointed that this channel would offer such a program, and he turned it off.

5. The bugle corps lined up for the precision drill and maneuvers, and they carried the trophy home in triumph.

6. The train pulled out of the station, gradually picking up speed, and Jim went home disappointed.

7. The girl who had the leading role in the school play got the measles, and I hoped they would let me try out for the part, and they did, and I had only three days to rehearse.

8. The audience filed into their places for the first American performance of the Brazilian rock group, and the total box-office receipts were very high.

9. I thought my mother and father didn't love me any more on account of my new baby sister, and my mother sensed my feelings, and she told me she loved all of us and not one more than the other.

10. The traffic was very light, and we all got bad sunburns at the beach.

B. In each of the following sentences, supply a linking word that makes clear the relationship between the parts. If an additional linking word can be used to indicate a different relationship, be prepared to explain what the relationship is.

1. He did not want to go; _____, I insisted upon his making an appearance.

2. Perhaps it would take me years to learn the procedure; _____, I might master it in six or seven months.

3. There is very little scenery in this play; _____, you must use your imagination.

4. I'm not a poor driver; _____, the traffic officer always stops me and threatens to give me a ticket.

5. Mr. Black acknowledged that it was Art's fault; _____, he pointed out that Bob was responsible to a certain extent, too.

6. Amy felt like going to bed early; _____, she had promised to write to Trisha that night.

7. Many of the girls I know ski very well; _____, they are willing to take me along with them.

8. I have always wanted to be a physical education teacher; _____, I am interested in observing the methods used by my own teachers.

9. Farming had been a tradition in my family; _____, my interest in it was not surprising.

10. He had eaten more than anyone else; _____, he did it in half the time.

11. Everyone says that the show was the best we've ever had; _____, we sold very few tickets.

12. You will have to sign the documents; _____, you will have to be accompanied by your parents.

13. By reading a book you can find yourself floating down the Mississippi on a riverboat; _____, you can experience the thrill of climbing the Swiss Alps.

14. You must follow the directions that came with the kit; _____, you will not be able to assemble the model.

15. The cast of the annual school play was posted; _____, Jane's name appeared at the top of the list.

Part 7 Subordinating Ideas Correctly

Another way to join ideas effectively is to use the complex sentence. The main idea is then expressed in the main clause and the less important idea in the subordinate clause.

SUBORDINATE IDEA   MAIN IDEA

After I had located the article, I read it rapidly.

It must be emphasized that only the writer of the sentence can determine whether ideas are of equal value or whether one is subordinate to the other. To one writer, the ideas in the following sentence may be equally important.

I located the article, and I read it rapidly.

(Turn to Section 3.5 in your Handbook for a list of subordinating conjunctions and the precise relationships they show between main and subordinate ideas.)

Problems in Joining Ideas

Two additional problems in joining ideas are *faulty coordination* and *faulty subordination*.

Faulty Coordination. Although it is true that the writer alone knows what the main idea in a sentence is, there are times when he or she may mistakenly coordinate two ideas that obviously are not of equal value and cannot be joined by *and*. The reader is uncomfortably aware that one idea is dependent upon the other in some way.

FAULTY: The rainfall was not sufficient, and the roses drooped on their stems.

Here, logic determines that the roses drooped *because the rainfall was not sufficient*. Therefore, the sentence is an example of faulty coordination.

REVISED: *Because the rainfall was not sufficient,* the roses drooped on their stems.

FAULTY: The carpet was white, and my parents were afraid that it might get soiled easily.

REVISED: *Because the carpet was white,* my parents were afraid that it might get soiled easily.

Faulty coordination can be corrected by changing one of the clauses into a subordinate clause, a phrase, or an appositive.

103

FAULTY:	Some students do not concentrate on their work, and they have difficulty in learning.
REVISED:	Some students have difficulty in learning *because they do not concentrate on their work.* (subordinate clause)

FAULTY:	She listened to John's excuse, and she broke out laughing.
REVISED:	*After listening to John's excuse,* she broke out laughing. (phrase)

FAULTY:	Joy won first prize in the state instrumental competition, and she is a soloist in our orchestra.
REVISED:	*Joy, a soloist in our orchestra,* won first prize in the state instrumental competition. (appositive)

Faulty Subordination. Faulty subordination occurs when the writer states the main idea in the subordinate clause. Confusion results from a sentence structure in which an idea that should precede another is placed after it instead.

FAULTY:	Because the coat was too expensive for me, it was an imported cashmere.
REVISED:	Because the coat was an imported cashmere, it was too expensive for me.

FAULTY:	Everyone else was in swimming while Buzz and Joe tied all the clothes in knots.
REVISED:	While everyone else was in swimming, Buzz and Joe tied all the clothes in knots.

Exercises Coordinating and Subordinating Ideas

A. Revise the sentences to correct faulty coordination.

1. I listened to my father's advice, and I decided to take math.
2. Edna won the fifty-yard dash, and she is our best runner.
3. The pictures did not turn out well, and I had taken every precaution.

4. Mark Twain became a very popular writer, and he had great obstacles to overcome.

5. My older sister bought a used car, and it is a 1980 Firebird.

6. We won the league games for three successive years, and we have permanent possession of the trophy.

7. I had prepared my lesson thoroughly the night before, and I wasn't worried about the test.

8. Dolores has decided on her career, and it is marine biology.

9. All preparations had been carefully made, and the rocket exploded.

10. Bacteria have built up an immunity to certain antibiotics, and new medicines have to be produced.

11. Our school has many brilliant students, and we did not get a National Merit Scholarship.

12. Don was listening to his new stereo recordings, and he did not notice how late it was.

13. Fred kept looking and he still couldn't find the ball.

14. I sometimes think about death, and it is something that happens to everyone.

15. Mr. Armanda told me to interview Miss Carnahan, and she is the candidate's chief speech writer.

B. Revise the sentences to correct faulty subordination.

1. Not being able to knit, she could not read the directions.

2. Joan is the top-ranking student in her class, although she is not going to college.

3. Yesterday I was walking down the street when I met a friend I hadn't seen in years.

4. Hurrying to help him, Ted saw his little brother in tears.

5. There was to be an important meeting of the student officers after school, although the president left at the regular time.

6. Wolves are rare because they are an endangered species.

7. I stepped off the plane at Kennedy Airport, when I noticed a crowd waiting behind the fence.

8. Dad was busy with his monthly report because he hardly heard a word I said.

9. Dashing out of the house, she grabbed a sandwich.

10. People who don't like this neighborhood value privacy.

Part 8 Making Sentence Parts Parallel

The coordinating conjunction *and* joins sentence parts of equal value: noun and noun, verb and verb, phrase and phrase, clause and clause. The constructions are then **parallel.** If *and* is used to join constructions of different kinds, there is a **lack of parallelism.** Study the following sentences and determine what constructions are joined by *and.* Note the revisions made to achieve parallelism.

FAULTY: Pat wanted a *view* of the West and *to ride* horseback. (noun and infinitive)

REVISED: Pat wanted *to see* the West and *to ride* horseback. (infinitive and infinitive)

FAULTY: Everyone needs *sympathy* and *to be noticed.* (noun and infinitive)

REVISED: Everyone needs *sympathy* and *attention.* (noun and noun)

FAULTY: The principal asked us *to stand* and *that we remain silent for one minute.* (infinitive and clause)

REVISED: The principal asked *that we stand* and *that we remain silent for one minute.* (clause and clause)

FAULTY: She requested *help* with her exercise and *that I explain the procedure again.* (noun and clause)

REVISED: She requested *help* with her exercise and another *explanation* of the procedure. (noun and noun)

REVISED: She requested *that I help her with her exercise* and *that I explain the procedure again.* (clause and clause)

Lack of parallelism often occurs when the pronouns *which* and *who* are used in a sentence. Avoid using *and who* or *and which* unless there is a preceding *who* or *which* to balance it.

FAULTY:	This is a popular *book* and *which you can get in the school library*. (*and* joins a noun and a clause.)
REVISED:	This is a popular book, which you can get in the school library.
SIMPLER:	You can get this popular book in the school library.

FAULTY:	Carlotta is a brilliant *woman* and *who has a great future*.
REVISED:	Carlotta is a brilliant *woman*, and *she has a great future*.
REVISED:	Carlotta is a brilliant woman who has a great future.
SIMPLER:	Carlotta is a brilliant woman with a great future.

The fault can be corrected by making sure that the *and* joins two similar constructions. In the revision, *and* may be omitted altogether.

Exercises Parallelism

A. Revise these sentences to make the constructions parallel.

1. Dad visited his birthplace and where he grew up.

2. At last I came to a road I knew and which would take me home.

3. When you get to know him, you will consider him to be friendly and that he is also helpful.

4. We are going on a trip to Atlantic City and which is a popular resort.

5. In high school chemistry, you will learn about distilling water and to analyze compounds.

6. In this course you will learn accuracy and to work fast.

7. Everyone wants to avoid accidents and being sick.

8. Our neighbors are the Deckers and who won a trip to Mexico last month.

9. Jo had to choose between taking singing lessons and to learn ballet.

10. My brother wanted a trip around the world and to fly in a supersonic plane.

B. Revise these sentences.

1. She has many accomplishments: horseback riding, dancing, skin-diving, and a champion swimmer.
2. We decided to investigate further and that we might find clues in the locked room.
3. The coach was a man of experience and who never got impatient.
4. My brother has a job gassing up cars, picking up trash, and he runs errands.
5. We ate in a Chinese restaurant and there was a traditional Chinese opera that we also saw.
6. Gloria did not want a job taking dictation or be a filing clerk.
7. Following the trail is easier than to cut through the woods.
8. The salad dressing splattered on the table, on the rug, and got spots on Mr. Grimly's suit.
9. The typical American changes jobs seven times, and a change of career three times.
10. Laura is a good babysitter and reliable.

Review Exercises   Revising Sentences with Various Problems

A. Revise the following sentences. They contain various problems you have dealt with in this chapter.

1. In my opinion, I think the spring jackets in the basement are better buys than the ones on the main floor.
2. Although we enjoyed the trip through the mountains, the roads were terrible.
3. I like to watch professional tennis because it is an exciting sport to watch.
4. How to program a computer is something I haven't learned how to do yet.
5. I think that it was really fortunate that we had a spare tire.
6. The mayor personally cut the cake herself.
7. I'm afraid that I have to admit that I bungled the job.
8. Mom and Dad were in a state of shock because they were shocked by the size of the dinner check.

9. The last person on the show, who was a stand-up comedian, was a very funny fellow.

10. The electrician touched a live wire when she was mildly jolted.

B. Revise these sentences:

1. Hank Aaron hit more home runs in his career than any other baseball player, and he hit 733 home runs.

2. I was startled by Selma's remark because I just sat there and said nothing.

3. Our trip to Disney World was, in spite of the long waits in line, fun for every member of the family.

4. When my brother Jack came home from college, he said his grades were so low he needed a snorkel, but I knew he was only joking because he always gets good grades.

5. My grandmother is a successful accountant, a professional clarinetist, and raises German shepherds.

6. Dad found two matching wedding bands in the rented boat, so what he did was put a notice in the paper.

7. When I was only three years old, my family moved from Boston to Louisville, and we have lived in Louisville ever since.

8. The Queen of England can fix your car because she is a trained mechanic, and she learned how to fix cars during World War II.

9. Our fuel pump broke and our car had to be towed to the garage and so we missed the first act of the play.

10. Scientists have landed some equipment on Mars, including a seismometer, and they have studied the earthquakes that take place on Mars, but they call the earthquakes on Mars "Marsquakes."

1. Good writers review their work carefully and revise awkward or repetitious sentences.

2. Empty sentences repeat what the reader already knows.

3. Padded sentences contain unnecessary words or phrases.

4. Overloaded sentences contain too many ideas and must be divided into more than one sentence.

5. Some sentences contain unrelated ideas or fail to demonstrate how the ideas contained in them are related.

6. Some sentences contain faulty subordination or parallelism.

7. Always revise your sentences to avoid these problems. This process will bring clarity and precision to all of your writing and speaking.

Applications in Other Subject Areas

Business. In Chapter 3, you learned about an incorrect use of language called "gobbledygook." This type of language occurs when a speaker or writer obscures ideas with unnecessary terms and long, rambling sentences. It is common in business documents. Find an example of "gobbledygook" in a set of directions, a legal document, or a piece of technical writing. Discuss with your class how these pieces of writing could be improved through the use of the sentence revising techniques suggested in this chapter.

Speech. Choose one of the topics listed below. Without thinking about the topic beforehand, talk into a tape recorder for one minute. Say anything that comes into your mind about the topic. Analyze your "speech," looking for empty, padded, overloaded, or poorly-constructed sentences. Consider how you might correct any errors that you have found.

        television commercials   pep rallies
        lasting friendships   homework

Chapter 6

The Process
of Writing

Everyone is familiar with the mazes found in puzzle books and magazines. To begin a maze, you place a pencil at a given starting point. Then you start to search for the best route through the twisting paths before you. As you continue, you make a dozen wrong turns and hit several dead ends. With patience, though, you eventually reach your goal.

Writing is very similar to exploring a maze. As you begin to write, you have many paths and goals to choose from. At first you may make false starts and experiment with several different approaches. Finally, you discover the right path.

This exploration of ideas is all part of the **process of writing.** The process consists of three main stages: pre-writing, writing the first draft, and revising. Each stage plays an important role as you search for the best way to express your thoughts.

Part 1 Pre-Writing

You would not go on a trip without planning where you were going. Similarly, you should not begin a piece of writing without considering what you will be writing about and how you can effectively present your ideas. This planning process is called **pre-writing.**

Careful attention to the pre-writing stage simplifies the actual writing that follows. Complete each of the following steps as part of the planning process.

1. Select and limit your topic.

Choosing a topic. Unless you are writing on an assigned topic, you will have the opportunity to select one of your own. You will probably have the greatest success with a topic that interests you or with which you are most familiar. Therefore, begin by asking yourself these questions:

What do I know about?

What would I like to learn more about?

What interesting experiences have I had or observed?

What interesting subjects have I read about?

What is happening to me or around me that I could record?

This is just one way you can begin your search for topics. You might also try several of the techniques listed on page 113.

As you begin to gather ideas, save them in a writing file. Clip interesting newspaper or magazine articles. Write down thought-provoking facts, quotations, and opinions on note cards. Store all of these items in a file box or writing folder. Refer to your file when you need inspiration for writing.

Limiting a topic. Topics must be limited so that they can be thoroughly explored within the limits of your paper. You cannot, for example, write a two-hundred word essay about "Maps." However, you could write one about "How to use a world atlas." Similarly, do not choose a topic that is too narrow or you will end up "padding" your writing with unnecessary words.

Pre-Writing Techniques

Journal Writing. Keep a spiral notebook in which you record interesting ideas, thoughts, feelings, impressions, and experiences. Write in your journal on a regular basis. Like your writing file, a journal can provide you with hundreds of ideas for writing. It also allows you to practice your writing skills in a totally unstructured way.

Reading. Skim magazines, books, and newspapers for intriguing topics, or for stories that trigger your imagination. Keep a list of possible subjects. You might also record specific facts or quotations that strike you as particularly interesting.

Discussions and Interviews. Listen carefully for the opinions and stories that emerge in everyday conversation. Remember that every individual has a unique background and special experiences to share. You may also want to question certain people directly about their interests, opinions, or background. Such interviews often provide fascinating results.

Brainstorming. This technique may be done by yourself or with others. It simply means starting with one idea and then building on it or branching out from it. The general topic "buildings," for example, could lead to topics as varied as "stained glass windows," "European castles," and "Frank Lloyd Wright."

Clustering. Clustering is actually a type of brainstorming. Begin by writing a word or phrase on a piece of paper. Circle it. Now, outside this circle, write down any word or phrase that you associate with that "nucleus" word. Put each new idea in its own circle and connect it with the nucleus. Branch out from the new circles in a similar manner. When a brand-new train of thought begins, start again at the nucleus. (See page 185 for an illustration of clustering.)

2. Determine your purpose.

Once you have limited your topic, you can focus your writing even more by deciding exactly what you want to say about your subject. Start by determining what you want to accomplish — your *purpose*. Here are some helpful questions you can ask yourself.

Do I want to analyze my subject? describe it? explain it?

Do I want my writing to entertain my readers? inform them? persuade them?

What main ideas do I want my readers to grasp?

Is there a certain *mood*, or atmosphere, I want to create?

What *tone*, or attitude toward my subject, do I want?

After you have determined your purpose, you can begin to make several important decisions about how you will present your ideas. Will you write a fictional piece, a personal essay, or a report? Will you write formally or informally? What details will you select? For longer pieces of writing, you may wish to include a statement of your topic and controlling purpose. This is sometimes called a **thesis statement**.

3. Identify your audience.

Writing is a form of communication involving at least two parties—the writer and the reader. Therefore, any written piece is directed at a particular audience. That audience may be a teacher, a friend, or even an entire group or community.

Identifying your audience allows you to continue the decision-making process. It will determine the level of language you use. (See Chapter 3, "Selecting Language for Your Purpose.") It can also help you choose an appropriate vocabulary and pertinent supporting information. Finally, knowing your audience will help you select effective methods of development and presentation. Ask yourself these questions:

How old are my readers?

How familiar are my readers with my subject?

What are my readers' attitudes or opinions towards my subject?

The answers to these questions are very important. With them, you can make sure that the language and information in your paper suit your particular readers.

4. Gather your supporting information.

The details you will use to develop your ideas are based on your topic, the purpose of your paper, and your audience.

The topic, of course, is the major determining factor. Every piece of information must relate to the topic directly. However, the purpose of the paper may help you to sort out information, too. For example, you would probably not include statistics in a paragraph that is intended solely to entertain. Finally, your audience will determine how much background information you need, as well as how specific you can get.

You can find supporting information by using many of the same pre-writing techniques discussed earlier—brainstorming, reading, discussion, interviewing, and observation. Use your own knowledge, as well as information from outside sources. As you gather information, take careful notes.

5. Evaluate and organize your information.

After you have gathered your information, evaluate your notes.

Are all necessary details included?

Are there any unrelated ideas that should be deleted?

Should other details be added for accuracy or clarity?

Now organize your notes. Group details that seem to be related. These "groups" can help you to see gaps in your information. They may also signal possible paragraph divisions.

Next find an effective order. For example, the details in a paragraph that explains a process would be organized in the order in which they occur. A composition that describes a new invention might be presented so that familiar ideas precede difficult ones.

Keep in mind that all pre-writing activities are designed to help you begin writing in a thoughtful, organized manner. Many of the decisions you make at this point can be changed or adjusted.

Study this example of pre-writing notes for a paragraph:

1. Possible topics
   the drama workshop
   the championship baseball game
   hot summer day *
   my first biology experiment
2. Narrowed topic
   hot summer day - my impressions
3. Purpose
   to re-create my feelings on a hot
     summer day   mood - irritation, discomfort
                  tone - serious
4. Audience
   my classmates and teacher
5. Specific details
   ② heavy, hot air of August -date?
   afternoon sune
   ④ animals in sprinkler dog, birds
   ⑤ me sitting on porch -me or use
   ① no rain - 19 days   another person's
                        point of view?
   ⑦ Ann and Mark arguing
   ⑧ argument concerned a TV show
   ⑥ no breeze, no energy
   ③ burned lawn
   baby brother in baby poole
6. Order of details
   Spatial - as the person on the porch
     looks around

A. Copy this section of one writer's pre-writing notes for a paragraph. Delete any unrelated details and add details that you think would make the notes more complete. Group details that are related. Finally, number the details or groups in the order you would present them in a paper.

Narrowed topic: How people waste energy

Specific details:

electricity is expensive
unnecessary appliances that use energy—can-openers, etc.
leaving lights on when not necessary
uses of solar energy
gas prices have risen_____% in the past 10 years
leaving the TV on while no one is there
cars that burn energy/fuel
leaving heat/air conditioning on unnecessarily
letting water leaks remain unfixed
gas heating versus electric heating

Order of details?

B. Make a pre-writing plan like the one on page 116. Save the notes for use later in this chapter.

Part 2 Writing a First Draft

If you have paid careful attention to the pre-writing activities, writing the rough draft is a relatively easy task. Simply write in sentence and paragraph form those ideas that you have gathered and organized. Do not worry about details such as spelling and punctuation. You will have the opportunity to correct such errors later, during revision. Leave space between lines to make corrections.

Many people make the mistake of trying to write a perfect paper on the first attempt. In reality, a first draft is simply a chance to experiment with the ideas from your pre-writing notes. A draft is also an opportunity to explore entirely new possibilities. In fact, you will find that many of your best ideas don't come to you until *after* you begin to write.

As you work on your draft, begin to rework your material. Add new details. Delete others that you no longer think are interesting or relevant. Modify your purpose or organization if necessary. You may even want to start over as a new approach or more exciting idea occurs to you. As you continue to revise, keep your main idea, purpose, and audience in mind in order to keep your material unified.

Remember, a first draft is only an experiment. It is *not* the final product. Treat it this way, and you will be much more relaxed as you begin to write.

FIRST DRAFT

It hadn't rained in nineteen days. The thick, hot air hung over the city like a blanket. A sprinkler sprayed the patch of lawn. The water had attracted sparrows and a large dog. Kathy Newman sat on the front steps faning herself with a newspaper. She barely had the energy to move her arm. Inside, her sister and brother argued noisily. Kathy sighed and looked at the sky for the much needed rain.

Compare this draft to the pre-writing notes on page 116. What details has the writer added? Have any been eliminated? Notice that she has also changed the *point-of-view* of the paragraph so that it concerns another person, not the writer herself. Despite all these changes and improvements, the paragraph needs a great deal more work. These changes will be handled in the next stage: revising.

Exercise Writing a Rough Draft

Using your pre-writing notes from Exercise B in Part 1, write a rough draft of your paragraph. Remember that changes and revisions in your plan are often desirable at this point.

Part 3 Revising

Revision is often considered the key to the writing process. Although it is usually presented as the last stage of the process, it actually plays an important role from the moment you begin your pre-writing activities. You are revising, for example, when you narrow a topic. You are revising as you evaluate pre-writing notes or work on a rough draft.

At this point in the process, you must revise your rough draft. With a critical eye, read what you have written. You may even want to read it out loud. Often you will hear problems that you might otherwise miss.

First, read the draft for content. Concentrate on the ideas and information presented. Ask yourself the following questions.

Is my topic clear?
Are all details related to the topic?
Are there details that do not belong in a particular section or in the writing as a whole?
Should any details be added to help clarify the topic?
Is the purpose clear and has it been accomplished?
Will my audience understand the information presented?

Next, read to check your method of presentation.

> Will your reader be able to follow your ideas?
> Is your organization clear?
> Do sentences flow logically from one to the next?
> Does your organization suit your topic and purpose?

Finally, read aloud for style. Check for precise language and solid sentence structure. Make sure that the level of language, tone, and mood suit the writing and do not change.

As you revise in each of these areas, remember that you may complete a second or third draft. Write a final draft only when you are completely satisfied with your revisions.

REVISION

There had been no rain for ~~It hadn't rained in~~ nineteen days. The motionless thick, hot air hung over the ~~city~~ town like a sweltering blanket. On Lincoln street, the Newman's sprinkler hissed as it ~~A sprinkler sprayed the~~ small, scorched patch of lawn. ~~The water had attracted sparrows and a large dog.~~ Nearly, Kathy Newman sat on the front steps fanning herself with a newspaper. She watched listlessly ~~She barely had the energy to move her arm.~~ as several bedraggled sparrows and a large, panting dog moved onto the damp ground. Inside the house, her sister and brother argued shrilly ~~noisily.~~ Kathy sighed and searched ~~looked at~~ the sky for signs of the much needed rain.

Proofreading

Proofreading means checking for errors in grammar, usage, mechanics, and spelling. You should save this step until you have completed your content revision, since you often catch errors in mechanics as you revise.

To help identify and correct any remaining errors, refer to reference books as well as the Sections on grammar, usage, and mechanics in this textbook. You may also wish to use the proofreading symbols on page 125.

Exercises Revising Your Writing

A. Look at the revised paragraph on page 120. Compare it with the first draft and answer these questions.

What content changes have been made?
Where was the organization modified?
There are also several changes in wording. What effect do they have?
Were any errors in grammar or mechanics spotted? Do any remain?
Read both drafts aloud. Which draft accomplished the purpose best? Why?

B. Revise the rough draft of the paragraph you wrote for the Exercise in Part 2. Proofread your paper for errors in spelling and mechanics.

Part 4 Preparing the Final Copy

When you are satisfied with your revision, prepare your final copy. Carefully transfer all changes from your rough draft. Make your copy as neat as possible. If you make too many errors in copying, begin again. Follow the manuscript form your teacher requires, including proper headings and margins.

When you have finished your final copy, proofread it one last time. Make corrections neatly.

There had been no rain for nineteen days. The motionless air hung over the town like a sweltering blanket. On Lincoln Street, the Newman's sprinkler hissed as it sprayed the small, scorched patch of lawn. Nearby, Kathy Newman sat on the front steps, fanning herself with a newspaper. She watched listlessly as several bedraggled sparrows and a large, panting dog moved onto the damp ground. Inside the house, her sister and brother argued shrilly. Kathy sighed and searched the sky for signs of the much-needed rain.

Exercise Making a Final Copy

Prepare the final copy of your paragraph. Be sure to follow all the guidelines required by your teacher.

Guidelines for the Process of Writing

Pre-Writing

1. Select a topic that interests you.
2. Narrow the topic until it can be thoroughly developed in a specified length.
3. Decide on your purpose.
4. Use your understanding of purpose and audience to determine your type of language and choice of details.
5. Gather and list details that you could use to develop your topic.
6. Evaluate and organize your list of details. Delete unrelated ideas. Add new ones. Put your details into a logical order.

Writing the First Draft

1. Keeping your audience and purpose in mind, begin to write.
2. Let your thoughts flow freely. Modify your initial plans for content and organization, if necessary. Do not be too concerned with grammar and mechanics at this point.

Revising

Read what you have written. Answer the following questions:

1. Did you stick to your topic?
2. Did you include everything you wanted to?
3. Are there any unnecessary or unrelated details?
4. Is each main idea clearly expressed and thoroughly developed?
5. Do tone, mood, and level of language remain consistent?
6. Do your ideas flow smoothly?
7. Is your writing organized logically, with a beginning, a middle, and an end? Are the ideas presented in an order that makes sense?
8. Is your writing interesting and lively? Is there variety in the type and structure of your sentences?
9. Is your word choice vivid and precise?
10. Do the language and the content suit your audience?
11. Have you accomplished your purpose?

Revise as necessary. Then proofread your work, using the checklist on page 124.

Proofreading Checklist

Proofread your paper by answering the questions below. Additional instruction on each concept may be found in the indicated Sections.

Grammar and Usage

Are compound and complex sentences written and punctuated correctly? (Sect. 3)
Are there any sentence fragments or run-ons? (Sect. 4)
Have you used verb tenses correctly? (Sect. 5)
Do all verbs agree with their subjects? (Sect. 6)
Have you used the correct form of each pronoun? (Sect. 7)
Have you used adjectives and adverbs correctly? (Sect. 8)

Capitalization

Did you capitalize first words and all proper nouns and adjectives? (Sect. 10)
Are titles capitalized correctly? (Sect. 10)

Punctuation

Does each sentence have the proper end mark? (Sect. 11)
Are marks such as colons, semicolons, apostrophes, hyphens, and quotation marks used correctly? (Sect. 12, 13, 14)

Spelling

Are plurals and possessive forms spelled correctly? (Sect. 13, 16)
Did you check all unfamiliar words in the dictionary? (Sect. 15)

Form

Were corrections made neatly? (Sect. 17)
In your final copy, is the writing legible?
Have you used the proper heading and margins?
Did you follow all points of the manuscript form required by your teacher?

Proofreading Symbols

SYMBOL	MEANING	EXAMPLE
$\wedge$	insert	would *have* gone
$\equiv$	capitalize	United states
/	make lower case	our club President
$\sim$	transpose	th i e r
delete	delete	finished the (the) race
¶	make new paragraph	....be complete. ¶ Another reason
$\smile$	close up space	head line
$\odot$	period	....and stop⊙Before going...
$\wedge$	add comma	However few people

SUMMARY AND APPLICATIONS

1. The process of writing is a process of thinking and rethinking, writing and revising. It is essential to good composition. It is also a means of training yourself to think through problems thoroughly and logically.

2. Careful attention to pre-writing steps makes actual writing much easier. Pre-writing includes choosing a topic, deciding on the audience and purpose for the writing, and gathering and organizing ideas.

3. The first draft is the writer's opportunity to experiment with the ideas developed during pre-writing. Attention to mechanical details is not important at this time.

4. Revising and proofreading are the final stages of the process of writing. The writer checks for complete coverage; a consistent tone, mood, and level of language; sound organization; and a precise vocabulary. Finally, the writer proofreads for errors in grammar, capitalization, punctuation, and spelling.

Applications in Other Subject Areas

Science. When you conduct a scientific experiment, you must follow a strict process. Like the process of writing, this process involves careful planning and organization, a well thought out procedure, and a clearly presented final paper, or lab report. Write a set of guidelines for conducting and writing up an experiment. Divide your guidelines into stages, and clearly list all steps.

Math. To find the solution to a problem in math, you often depend on a process, or formula, for problem solving. Find such a procedure in your algebra or geometry book (how to find the area of a triangle, how to solve a certain type of algebraic equation). Write the procedure in paragraph form, using a specific problem as an example.

Chapter 7

Writing Effective Paragraphs

The process of writing is more than just a series of steps that you go through to complete a writing assignment. It is also a path to clear thinking. As your writing skills develop, you will find that your abilities to focus on ideas and organize them effectively have also increased. Such skills are invaluable in every area of oral and written communication.

One of the first skills required for effective writing is the ability to organize your ideas into paragraphs. In this chapter, you will examine the basic elements of good paragraphs. You will also learn a variety of techniques for writing paragraphs that communicate your ideas clearly.

Part 1 Elements of a Good Paragraph

A paragraph is a group of sentences that deal with a single topic or idea. Usually, one sentence, the **topic sentence**, states the main idea of the paragraph. The single idea of the topic sentence is then supported with other related sentences. These supporting sentences satisfy the reader's curiosity by giving details that further explain or support the main idea. They also build onto and support each other. Often, a concluding statement sums up the idea stated in the topic sentence.

Well written paragraphs are characterized by unity and coherence. **Unity** is the relationship of the sentences in a paragraph to the topic sentence. **Coherence** is the relationship of sentences to each other.

Unity. When all of the sentences in a paragraph are related directly to the topic sentence, the paragraph has unity. Unity can be destroyed by the inclusion of one or two sentences that do not relate to the topic sentence. Sometimes the lack of unity is so pronounced that you have only a series of disconnected sentences, not a paragraph.

Coherence. When the sentences in a paragraph are arranged in logical order, the paragraph has coherence and its ideas flow together smoothly. Logical orders vary, depending on the subject of the paragraph. The three most common orders are chronological, spatial, and order of importance. Each of these orders is discussed in detail later in this chapter.

Let's examine the following paragraphs to see how well they meet the requirements of a good paragraph.

EXAMPLE 1

After six weeks of feeding the lemon shark from the target, we gave him the big test. We put the target into the water at the appointed time but with no food on it. The shark rushed at the target with his mouth open, then swerved aside when he found no food. The second time, and for eight more times, he came in slowly, looking over the target without touching it. Finally, he nuzzled the empty target and set off the automatic bell. We quickly tossed out a reward piece of food wrapped in string that hit the water with a splash just to the left of the target. The shark quickly grabbed the food, cutting the string with his teeth. After that he repeatedly pushed the empty target and then took the food tossed to him, proving that he had associated pressing the target with getting food.—DR. EUGENIE CLARK

This is a well written, well organized paragraph. When you read the topic sentence, "After six weeks of feeding the lemon shark from the target, we gave him the big test," you are interested in knowing what the "big test" is. The next seven sentences then describe what happened during the test. Every sentence is related to the topic sentence. Thus, the paragraph has unity. The sentences also relate well to each other. The ideas flow comfortably from sentence to sentence. Therefore, the paragraph has coherence.

EXAMPLE 2

Study the following example.

Life at 1308 Carlisle Street was like a circus, with something always going on in at least three places at once. You never had time to think about yourself; you just tried to deal with each emergency as it came up—a fight between the twins, a bone stuck in little Randolph's throat, the baby crying—and go on to the next one. It was fun, like any circus, but going to the circus once a year was one thing, Louretta thought; living with it all the time was something else.—KRISTIN HUNTER

Example 2 is also characterized by unity and coherence. In the topic sentence, the writer describes life at 1308 Carlisle Street as a three-ring circus. In the rest of the paragraph she develops this comparison by noting similarities between three emergency situations at home and a circus. She also points out the difference between time spent at a circus and time spent at home. The ideas flow logically from one to the other. The paragraph begins with a description of 1308 Carlisle and ends with Louretta's personal reaction to this circus-like atmosphere.

EXAMPLE 3

Now study this example. As you read, list the topic sentence and the ideas covered by the paragraph. Then examine your list carefully and answer the questions that follow.

Preschool children are the single largest television audience in America, spending a greater number of total hours and a greater proportion of their waking day watching television than any other age group. According to a recent survey, children in the two-to-five age group spend an average of 30.4 hours each week watching television, while children in the six-to-eleven group spend 25.5 hours. Action for Children's Television is a parent-founded organization dedicated to improving the quality of programming for children. Watching television is essentially a passive experience for both children and adults. Another survey documented a weekly viewing time of 34.56 hours for preschool boys and 32.44 hours for preschool girls. Still other surveys suggest figures up to fifty-four hours a week for preschool viewers. Even the most conservative estimates indicate that preschool children in America are spending more than a third of their waking hours watching television.

Check to see whether or not this paragraph is unified. Do all the sentences in the paragraph relate to the topic sentence and to each other? The topic sentence states the main idea of the paragraph: preschool children are the single largest television audience in America. The second sentence supports this idea with several statistics. The third and fourth sentences, however, introduce ideas (Action for Children's Television, television a passive experience) that do not relate to the number of hours children spend watching television. These sentences weaken the unity of the paragraph and make coherence impossible. They should be removed.

EXAMPLE 4

Check the following paragraph for unity and coherence.

The problems of urban growth are painfully apparent. One of the worst is "urban sprawl." Many cities also face tax starvation. Homes, schools, stores, factories, and highways spread across open land in an unplanned crazy-quilt pattern, smothering the countryside with confusion. They continue to depend on many of the services—hospital care, sewer lines, water supplies, and amusements—which are highly developed in the central cities. Another problem is the clash between the spreading city and the older political units—towns, villages, and counties—that lie in its path. Some authorities cite Los Angeles as a prime example of both problems and wryly call it "a hundred suburbs in search of a city."

After reading the topic sentence, you assume that all the ideas in the paragraph are going to relate to the problems of urban growth. All the ideas do, in fact, relate to these problems. However, the ideas are so disorganized that you probably had trouble understanding the relationship.

To begin an analysis of the paragraph, look at Sentence 1. It is a clear, well written statement of the main idea of the paragraph. Sentence 2 begins to explain the idea by identifying one of the problems of urban growth: urban sprawl. Sentence 3, however, does not continue with the discussion of this problem. It introduces the new idea "tax starvation" without relating it to urban growth. The coherence, or flow, of the paragraph is disrupted. This sentence should, therefore, be deleted.

Sentence 4 returns to the original idea of the paragraph. It defines "urban sprawl," the problem identified in Sentence 2. Sentences 2 and 4 can be combined to make a new sentence that reads, "One of the worst is 'urban sprawl,' in which homes, schools, factories, and highways spread across open land in an unplanned crazy-quilt pattern, smothering the countryside with confusion."

Sentence 5 has more than one problem. First, it begins with the pronoun "they," which refers to the homes, schools, stores, factories, and highways named in the previous sentence. The pronoun is used in an attempt to make these sentences flow together. However, the connection that the pronoun establishes between the two sentences is faulty. Homes, schools, stores, factories, and highways do not depend on hospital care, sewer lines, water supplies, and amusements; people do.

Another problem with Sentence 5 is that, even if the pronoun were removed and corrected, the idea expressed in the sentence would still be unclear. Does the writer mean that the expanding areas do not have sufficient services, or that they overburden the existing ones? The idea should be clarified or removed.

Sentences 6 and 7 return once again to the original idea, the problems of urban growth. They should be retained because they explain the main idea of the paragraph.

After the specified changes are made, the paragraph reads as follows:

> The problems of urban growth are painfully apparent. One of the worst is "urban sprawl," in which homes, schools, stores, factories, and highways spread across open land in an unplanned crazy-quilt pattern, smothering the countryside with confusion. Part of this confusion stems from the failure of the city planners to provide enough services—hospital care, sewer lines, water supplies, and amusements—to adequately meet the needs of the new areas. Confusion also results from the clash between the spreading city and the older political units—towns, villages, and counties—that lie in its path. Some authorities cite Los Angeles as a prime example of both problems and wryly call it "a hundred suburbs in search of a city."

The unrelated idea of tax starvation was deleted, and the problem of lack of services was tied in better to the rest of the paragraph. The paragraph is now well written and well organized. All the ideas stick to the point and work together, resulting in a feeling of unity and coherence.

Teach yourself to be aware of the topic sentence and important ideas in the paragraphs you read and write. In the process, you will be learning to organize your thoughts and think logically. This will ensure unity and coherence in your own writing.

Exercise Identifying Well Written Paragraphs

Study the following groups of sentences. Identify those that are well written paragraphs and those that are not. Revise the latter by rearranging sentences, by dropping sentences, by adding information, or by making other changes that transform the groups of sentences into coherent, unified paragraphs.

1   No one could escape from the city. The mainland was two miles away, across an expanse of wild water that no boat could survive. All four bridges were down. Men, women, and children crouched in their houses, staying close to the walls because that was the safest place if the roof came down. Houses were collapsing; people were dying. No one knew how many, no one knew when his or her turn would come. The wind blew on—and on—and on.

2   McIver knew that the first few moments of a jump were always crucial. The opening shock of the orange chute jerked him straight up. He threw his head back to check the rigging. It was perfect. He pulled on the toggle held in his left hand, allowing a jet of air to escape from an opening in the back of the chute. This maneuver compensated for the strong wind, and he drifted steadily toward the landing site.

3   Native Americans have contributed a great deal to American farming methods. The white settlers in Colonial America might have starved if they had not copied Indian farming methods. Many places in the United States have names of Indian origin. Approximately half of the states have Indian names. At least one group, the Pima, had a well developed irrigation system.

4   As the first mist of morning rose over the hills, Vyry poked among the rubble and the warm ashes of her gutted home, trying to salvage any possible possession. At first, she was just another part of the gray mist that enfolded her. Occasionally she found an iron pot or a fork and a spoon in the charred remains piled near the blackened chimney that had once been part of her kitchen. A little wind blew among the ashes, and sometimes the dust blew into her face. Then she would slowly straighten up and, carefully blinking her eyes, let the tears wash her eyes clean before bending down to continue her dismal search.

5   About five in the afternoon we submerged and set our course for the North Pole. The geographic North Pole does not coincide with the magnetic North Pole. All through the night, as

we sped northward, the ice detector and television scanned the surface in vain for patches of thin ice. The nuclear submarines Nautilus and Skate reached the North Pole in 1958 and 1959, respectively. Our belief that we would find thin ice frequently enough to surface at will seemed overly optimistic. Our plan to surface precisely at the North Pole looked hopeless.

6   It was a warm, sunny day without a cloud in the sky. The day before had also been bright. I was standing by a weathered old tenement house. The paint had peeled from the walls; and what had been a front porch was now a mass of splintered, rotted wood. The house had once been the elegant home of a meat-packing tycoon. Servants had scrubbed the steps and polished the brass and answered the door in starched uniforms. Down the dirty street, I could see a little girl standing in the shadows. She held a doll with a broken head in her arms. She had long, blonde hair, and she was crying.

7   Who are the Mexican people? That may be an impossible question to answer because we are so highly diverse and even unpredictable. We are peace-loving and friendly, yet we started the first bloody revolution in the twentieth century. We are vindictive and unforgiving, yet for three centuries we patiently worked on our own land as peons for those who had taken it from us in conquest. We are fiercely emotional and hot-blooded, yet in ancient times we were intellectual enough to chart the heavens and build magnificent pyramids with geometrical precision. We are a cosmic people whose racial identity spanned an ocean and enshrined the best of two worlds.

8   As you move toward the baggage-claim area, you may see a family group which you can identify by the striking similarity in the way they walk. Walking away from the departure area, you see three travelers making hurried arrangements in telephone booths. Others on their way to the baggage-claim counter who have been met by family or friends usually appear the happiest and walk with a great deal of enthusiasm. An airport is an excellent spot for viewing all types of people and emotions. Those who are waiting to be met keep rising on their toes and looking around.

Part 2   Pre-Writing: Choosing a Topic

In Chapter 6 you learned some basic guidelines for selecting a topic for writing. Important considerations are these:

1. **Subject.** Choose a subject in which you are interested and which you think will interest your readers. Use the pre-writing techniques discussed in Chapter 6.
2. **Size of Topic.** Limit your subject so that it can be developed clearly in the length you have chosen for the paragraph.
3. **Purpose.** Decide what you want to accomplish with your writing.
4. **Audience.** Identify the people who will read your writing. How can you focus your topic to appeal to those readers?

After you have made these initial decisions, you will write a topic sentence. This sentence will help you further refine your topic and purpose.

The Topic Sentence

As you learned in Part 1, the topic sentence states the main idea of the paragraph. The rest of the sentences in the paragraph must develop this main idea. Therefore, a good topic sentence is extremely important for the development of a paragraph.

A good topic sentence meets the following requirements:

A. A topic sentence presents a general statement.

A topic sentence must be broad enough so that it can be supported or explained by specific detail. It must be wider in scope, or more general, than the rest of the sentences in the paragraph. Here are three good topic sentences that are general statements.

1. Anpao stopped and stared at the ground.
2. Los Angeles has a vaguely Mexican atmosphere, which cannot be captured in words or concepts.
3. The fall was a beautiful scarf of warm, hazy days that trailed leisurely over the Panhandle.

These sentences contain very little specific information. Each states what the paragraph is about. Each is general enough to be developed with specific details.

Let's see how the writer of one of these topic sentences explained the general statement.

> *Anpao stopped and stared at the ground.* On the trail lay the most beautiful objects he had ever seen. There was a war shirt, a shield, and a bow and arrows. Anpao had never seen such handsome weapons. He had never seen such a noble war shirt. His own clothes had become shabby from the long journey in the desert. His last pair of moccasins was torn, and his hair was knotted and filthy. He crouched so he could gaze at the beautiful things on the ground. It seemed as if someone had surely left them there so any passerby could take them. But Anpao would not touch them. He got up and walked carefully around the objects and continued on his way.—JAMAKE HIGHWATER

The writer first makes the general statement, "Anpao stopped and stared at the ground." Then he gives specific information about what Anpao sees on the ground; about what Anpao looks like, which affects his response to what is on the ground; and about Anpao's reaction to what he sees.

B. A topic sentence limits the scope of a paragraph.

A topic sentence makes a general statement—a statement that is broader in scope than the rest of the paragraph. However, if a topic sentence is *too* general, the remainder of the paragraph will have to be either extremely long in order to explain the idea, or it will have to contain nothing but general statements. A topic sentence, therefore, must limit an idea so that it can be developed completely in one paragraph.

Here are examples of topic sentences that are too broad.

1. He liked all kinds of fresh fruit.
2. I like comedies, especially film comedies.
3. Mathematics is useful in many areas of everyday life.

Each of these topic sentences would require several paragraphs for adequate development. If an attempt were made to develop any one of them in one paragraph, the paragraph would contain nothing but several broad generalizations, as in the following example.

> He liked all kinds of fresh fruit. He liked the way they felt in his hand, and he liked the way they smelled. Best of all, he liked the way they tasted.

To communicate the basic idea of liking fruit more clearly, the topic sentence must be limited to a specific kind of fruit and to a specific situation, as in the following sentence.

> The cherry was a smooth, shiny marble in the child's possessing hand.

The idea in this sentence can be developed into a paragraph with the addition of specific details.

> The cherry was a smooth, shiny marble in the child's possessing hand. He stared at its roundness in fascination and thought he had never seen anything so beautifully red. It was flowers and summer days, and the brightest stones under the warmest streams. He held all these starry things burning together in his palm and smiled a secret smile that he felt to the tips of his toes. He pressed the fire-jewel, the robin feather, the drop of blood hard between thumb and finger and felt it squish into water. A warm, sweet smell rose up; and, with the tip of a small tongue, he licked the tart juice from his fingers. "The sun would taste like this if you could bite it," he sighed.

C. The topic sentence establishes a contract between reader and writer.

The writer is saying, in effect, "Look, I have an idea that I want to explain to you." The reader is responding, "All right, explain it to me." If the writer holds to the contract, the rest of the paragraph will explain the idea introduced in the topic sentence.

Here is an example of a topic sentence.

> Computers can make millions of calculations a second using facts stored in their electronic memories, yet these remarkable machines have a basic limitation.

In this sentence, the writer makes a contract in which she says, "I want to tell you about a limitation of computers." She then proceeds to fulfill her contract by explaining the limitation.

Computers can make millions of calculations a second using facts stored in their electronic memories, yet these remarkable machines have a basic limitation. They can do only what they are instructed, or "programmed," to do. They are no more skillful or accurate than the people who work on them, for if the programming is wrong, the answers will be wrong.

All the ideas in the paragraph are related to the topic sentence. This sentence controls the content of the entire paragraph.

Key Words. Notice that in the above example, the idea that controls the content of the paragraph is contained in the key word *limitation*. This is true of most topic sentences; the main idea is presented in one or several key words within the sentence.

1. Pierrot was a gentle dog.
2. The calmness of the night was almost oppressive.
3. Breakfast on Saturday mornings was lazy and unhurried.

In topic sentence 1 the key word is *gentle*; in sentence 2 it is *calmness*. In sentence 3 the key phrase is *lazy and unhurried*. Each word or phrase sets the direction of the entire paragraph. Paragraph 1 will focus on Pierrot's gentleness. Paragraph 2 will give details that reinforce the idea of calmness. Paragraph 3 will explain what made the breakfasts so lazy and unhurried.

D. The topic sentence catches the reader's attention.

Even if a topic sentence meets the first three requirements, it will do little good if it does not encourage the reader to continue reading. Look at the following topic sentences.

1. I am going to tell you about a person I knew named Simon.
2. My trip to Salt Lake City last summer was interesting.
3. I have a friendly dog.

Each sentence could be developed into a paragraph, yet many readers might not be interested in reading the paragraph because of the dull opening sentence.

In contrast, the following topic sentences would be much more likely to intrigue the reader enough to read beyond the opening sentence.

1. Simon was tough, intelligent, and determined to live.
2. Salt Lake City, Utah, has a law against carrying an unwrapped ukelele on the street.
3. Having an overly friendly dog cost me a job.

After reading each of these sentences, you probably found yourself asking questions such as these: What was wrong with Simon? Why was he so determined to live? How did such a silly law get passed? Does Salt Lake City have any other silly laws? What did the dog do? How could a dog's behavior cause a person to lose a job? Each sentence has caught your attention and has made you want to read further.

Exercises Working with Topic Sentences

A. Read the following paragraphs carefully. Identify those in which the writers have kept their contracts with their readers by developing the idea in the topic sentence and by giving enough information about it. Suggest possible revisions for those paragraphs in which the writers have not kept their contracts.

1 Kitty O'Neil has earned the title "fastest woman alive." She has driven superpowered vehicles on land and water. Handicapped children are her special interest. Herself deaf since infancy, she encourages deaf children to set high goals for success. Ms. O'Neil eats mostly spinach and other vegetables to keep in shape for her demanding job as a television and movie stuntwoman. She is the only woman member of Stunts Unlimited, a group of highly trained performers whose services are always in great demand.

2 Numerous reports of the yeti, or Abominable Snowman, have come from the Himalayas for some two hundred years. Villagers relate stories about it that date back many generations, and some claim to have recently seen the yeti. The first Westerner to have published an account of the yeti was B.H. Hodg-

son in 1832. Since then, more than forty Westerners have described sighting the yeti or its footprints.

3   I always thought I'd like to sky dive. When I was little, I used to like to go swimming. Near the lake was a huge tree with a branch that reached out over the water. The other kids would climb up there—ten, maybe fifteen feet—hold their noses, and jump off; but I was always afraid of heights.

4   I knew with a terrifying certainty that I was no longer alone in the house. The hall clock chimed with comforting regularity. Rex yelped softly in his sleep. Outside a loose shutter banged familiarly against the shingles.

5   One day we heard Mrs. Cook's dog barking down beside the swamp at the base of the cornfield. We ran out to see what had happened. When we got there, the dog was standing still, with his tail straight up in the air, barking hysterically. There, lying beside a log, was a big, old snake with fishy scales all over his body. Aldine, Junior, and I stood there in a trance looking at it, too scared to move. We had never seen one like this. It was so big it didn't even look like a snake. It looked big enough to swallow us whole. Finally the snake slowly made its way back into the swamp, leaving a trail of mashed-down grass behind it.

B. In the following paragraphs, the topic sentences have been removed, leaving only the supporting details. For each paragraph, write a topic sentence that is more general in scope than the details, but is limited enough to be adequately developed by the details.

1   In height, a bamboo plant can range anywhere from a dwarf twig, barely three inches tall, to a climber thrusting 200 feet skyward. In width, it can be a slender tendril of *sasa* one-tenth of an inch across or a hulking, seven-inch-wide pillar of *madake*.

2   The eyes, a camel's only truly beautiful feature, are double-lashed in a heavy fringe that screens out blowing sand. The ears and nostrils can be closed up tightly for the same purpose. The

feet, disproportionately large at the bottom of skinny shins, are splayed and padded, the better to move over sand without sinking.

3   A calculator was propelled through a snowblower last winter; another was run over by a trailer truck. Both proved still usable after minor repairs. A calculator lost by a California survey crew on a 5000-foot mountain, where summer temperatures soar above 100 degrees and winter brings ten feet of snow, blinked instantly to life when found by a hunter a year and a half later.

4   The dunes were covered with mats of sand flowers, which are red and have tiny eyes that are sometimes pink and sometimes white. Yuccas grew tall among the rocks of the ravine. Their heads were clustered with curly globes no larger than pebbles and the color of the sun when it rises. Lupines grew where the springs ran. From the sunny cliffs, in crevices where no one would think anything could grow, sprang the little red and yellow fountains of the comul bush.—SCOTT O'DELL

5   When I can leave my office in time so that I can spend thirty or forty minutes in spading the ground, in planting seeds, in digging about the plants, I feel that I am coming into contact with something that is giving me strength for the many duties and hard places that await me out in the big world. I pity the man or woman who has never learned to enjoy nature and to get strength and inspiration out of it.—BOOKER T. WASHINGTON

C. Following is a list of subjects. For each subject, write topic sentences that could be developed into effective paragraphs. Then select two topic sentences from this list, or write two on other subjects that interest you. Save these for use later in the chapter.

1. Frisbee throwing	7. Communities
2. First-aid	8. Animal behavior
3. Nutrition	9. Nonverbal communication
4. Careers	10. A neighbor
5. Advertising slogans	11. Saving money
6. Television drama	12. Comic books

Part 3   Pre-Writing: Gathering Ideas

After you have selected a topic and written the topic sentence, the next step is to gather information to develop your main idea. The pre-writing techniques discussed in Chapter 6—brainstorming, clustering, discussion, and reading—are all excellent means of generating ideas. You will find that the types of details you gather can be classified in four ways:

1. Sensory details
2. Facts or statistics
3. Specific examples
4. Incidents and anecdotes

Each type serves a special purpose and can make unique contributions to a piece of writing.

Using Sensory Details

You already know that the use of vivid, precise words helps a writer to communicate experiences and feelings. The most effective way to re-create an experience for the reader is through the use of details of sights, sounds, and smells. Such details, if they are presented using carefully chosen adjectives and specific verbs, allow a reader to visualize and hear a scene almost as well as if he or she were actually a part of it. Look at the following example.

> The twilight was white, and it lasted for a long while. The sky became a curious blue-green that soon faded to white. The air was soft gray, and the arbor and trees were slowly darkening. It was the hour when sparrows gathered and whirled above the rooftops of the town, and when in the darkened elms along the street there was the August sound of the cicadas. Noises at twilight had a blurred sound, and they lingered—the slam of a screen door down the street, voices of children, the whir of a lawnmower from a yard somewhere.—CARSON McCULLERS

The writer of this paragraph uses sensory details to create a soothing impression of deepening twilight. She begins her development of the paragraph by using phrases that appeal to the reader's sense of sight—the twilight was white; the sky became a curious blue-green; the air was soft gray; the arbor and trees were slowly darkening; the darkened elms.

She also uses phrases that appeal to the sense of hearing—the sound of the cicadas; noises...had a blurred sound; the slam of a screen door; voices of children; the whir of a lawnmower.

Also notice the writer's choice of verbs. Instead of stating that the sparrows flew, she says they "gathered and whirled." This gives the reader a mental image of the movement of the birds.

Exercise Developing a Paragraph by Using Sensory Details

Close your eyes and imagine yourself in one of your favorite places. It might be a still lake, a bustling street, a ski slope, or even a place in your home where you go to be alone. Jot down notes about what you would see, hear, smell, taste, feel, and experience in this place. You may want to concentrate on the details that make the strongest impression. Write a topic sentence for a paragraph that would describe this place. Then list your sensory details below the sentence. Be sure to use vivid, specific words that describe these sensory details. Save your work for use later in this chapter.

Using Facts or Statistics

Sometimes a topic sentence can best be supported with details that provide concrete data about an idea. The following example shows how the topic sentence can be supported with facts or statistics.

> The so-called typical American family—made up of a breadwinning father, a homemaking mother, and two dependent children—is no longer typical. According to recent government statistics, 7.3 percent of American households are made up of single parents with one or more children at home.

Of the total number of households, 28 percent consists of both a father and a mother who are wage earners. A surprising 32.4 percent consists of married couples with no children or none living at home. In all, only 17 percent of American households fit the traditional pattern.

The writer begins with a general topic sentence. She then supports her main idea with four statistics. In the closing sentence, the writer reinforces the topic sentence by stating that only 17 percent of American families could fit the old definition of "typical."

Exercise Developing a Paragraph by Using Facts or Statistics

Each of the following topics can be developed into a paragraph that uses facts or statistics. Choose two of the topics or make up two of your own. Research the topics, and then write a limited topic sentence that can be developed into a paragraph. List the facts and/or statistics you would use to develop your topic sentence. Save your work for use later in the chapter.

1. Our vanishing wildlife
2. New American immigrants
3. The Olympic Games
4. The care and feeding of pets
5. Major highway accidents
6. Coal as a form of energy
7. Fish hatcheries

Using Specific Examples

Some paragraphs may be developed best through the use of examples. Following is a paragraph developed with one specific example.

Datsolalee, the greatest designer and weaver of baskets among the Washo people, created works of art that are treasured by collectors of American handicrafts. One of her most famous baskets, "Myriads of Stars Shine over the Graves of Our Ancestors," contains 56,590 single stitches, over thirty-six stitches to the inch. Requiring more than a year to create, its design reflects her view of tribal history and life.

The writer begins the paragraph with a general statement about the artist and her importance. She then describes one basket that is representative of the artist's finest work.

In the following paragraph the writer uses several specific examples to support the general idea in the topic sentence.

In the untamed man's world that was the Old West, women went through unimaginable ordeals to stay alive, to reach their goals, to contribute in some way to the development of the frontier. Sarah Royce, traveling with a pitifully small and ill-equipped party, faced death from starvation in the desert before she reached California, there to bear a son who would become a prominent educator and philosopher. Bethenia Owens endured the dismay of other women and the derision of men to become a licensed, practicing physician. Clara Shortridge Foltz fought social pressure to study and practice law. Abigail Scott Duniway raised a family, supported an invalid husband, and was pelted with rotten eggs when she barnstormed for women's right to vote.

The writer begins with a general statement that concerns the ordeals endured by women in the Old West. He supports the statement with four examples of women who survived and achieved despite trials and hardships.

Exercise Developing a Paragraph by Using Specific Examples

Choose two of the following subjects or make up your own. Write two topic sentences. Then write down one or two examples that could be used to develop each sentence. Save your work.

1. The influence of "big money" on sports
2. Styles of sneezing
3. Television coverage of major events

4. Supermarkets: non-food items
5. Great cities
6. Noncompetitive sports
7. Challenging games
8. Desert plants and animals
9. Conflicts
10. Teens in the news
11. Acts of heroism
12. Memorable books

Using an Incident or an Anecdote

Developing a topic sentence through the use of an incident or anecdote can give a more personal or informal touch to a paragraph. With this type of development, the topic sentence presents a general idea; the body of the paragraph illustrates the idea through an incident or anecdote taken from the writer's own experiences.

The following is an example of a paragraph developed by using an incident.

Adults often have vivid memories of childhood experiences that at the time seemed insignificant. I have never forgotten something that happened to me when delivering the laundry that my mother washed and ironed. We were in need of money, and Mother had hurried through this batch of laundry so that it could be delivered and we could be paid for the weekend. I took the bundle of clothes to a small apartment in a private house, entered, and called out. No one answered. I called out again and again; then I went into the next room, part of which was cut off by a screen. I peeped around the screen and caught a glimpse of the young woman whose laundry I was delivering. She was sitting as quietly as a mouse, a book in her hands. I suspect she knew who was calling, and I can only guess that she did not answer because she did not have the money to pay. I could not bring myself to let her know that I knew she was there. I left the laundry and went home without the money. Mother did not scold me; somehow she managed that weekend.

—MARIAN ANDERSON

The writer could have developed the topic sentence with several impersonal statements about childhood experiences that are long remembered. Instead, she relates an incident that illustrates her point. The paragraph "comes alive" with the description of that one incident.

Exercise Developing a Paragraph by Using an Incident or Anecdote

Choose two of the topic sentences listed below, or write two sentences of your own. For each make a list of details related to a specific incident or anecdote that develops the topic. Save your work for use later in the chapter.

1. Jealousy can destroy friendships.
2. Complaints sometimes result in actions.
3. Relatives can also be friends.
4. Some things you just have to learn for yourself.
5. Loneliness can be an excellent teacher.
6. My father/mother is an understanding person.
7. I met an important challenge—and won.
8. Learning to cook isn't as easy as it looks.
9. Daydreams can come true.
10. People can be unexpectedly generous.

Part 4 Pre-Writing: Organizing Ideas

After making an informal list of all the information and ideas you think you might use to develop your paragraph, the next step is to determine the best order in which to present them. Your paragraph should be organized in a way that will enable the reader to understand how your ideas are related to each other.

In deciding on the organization of your paragraph, you should consider your audience, your purpose, and the type of information you have gathered. Ask yourself the following questions about each piece of information:

Does this idea support the topic sentence?
How does this idea relate to my other details?
Does this piece of information logically follow another in time
or in degree of importance?
Is this idea more familiar to my readers than another?

If you begin to organize your ideas with these questions in mind,
you are helping to make sure that your paragraph will have unity
and coherence.

There are five basic methods of organization.

1. Chronological order, or time sequence
2. Spatial order
3. Order from least important to most important idea
4. Order from most familiar to least familiar idea
5. Order by comparison or contrast

Chronological Order

When you use chronological order, you arrange your details in
the order in which they happened. This type of organization is
generally used in paragraphs developed by an incident or anecdote, as in the following paragraph.

I felt sick as I saw the cobra's head hit Grace's hand, but the
snake did not bite. He struck with his mouth closed. As rapidly
as an expert boxer drumming on a punching bag, the snake
struck three times against Grace's palm, always for some incredible reason with his mouth shut. Then Grace slid her hand
over his head and stroked his hood. The snake hissed again and
struggled violently under her touch. Grace continued to caress
him. Suddenly the snake went limp and his hood began to close.
Grace slipped her other hand under the snake's body and lifted
him out of the cage. She held the reptile in her arms as though
he were a baby. The cobra raised his head to look Grace in the
face; his dancing tongue was less than a foot from her mouth.
Grace braced her hand against the curve of his body and talked
calmly to him until he folded his hood. He curled up in her
arms quietly.—DANIEL P. MANNIX

The writer is describing one minute of a tense confrontation between a woman and a cobra. By putting the details in chronological order, he allows his readers to experience the event moment by moment, just as they would if they were present in the room.

Spatial Order

The type of organization that presents details in the order in which a viewer might notice them is called **spatial order.** This type of organization might proceed from side to side, from top to bottom (or the reverse), or from near to far (or the reverse). Spatial order is especially useful in presenting visual details. It allows the reader to "see" a scene as though his or her eyes were actually scanning it. In the following example the writer begins by describing objects that are near and then carries the reader away from the foreground of the garden to more distant scenes.

> I opened the gate and stepped into a beautiful garden. Huge poppies in vivid rows of orange and yellow nodded sleepily in the hot August sunlight. Back of these, tall spires of larkspur in a gamut of brilliant blues waved their lovely arms and trembled at each butterfly's shy kiss. The riotous marigold flaunted her golden gown against the lush cool green of an untrimmed privet hedge. In the center of a grassy circle, a flock of sparrows quarreled with two bluejays over the right to bathe in a white marble bird bath. But in a nearby syringa bush, a cheery robin, oblivious to the confusion, sang lustily. Three weeping willow trees at the rear of the garden sheltered a rustic bench. In the midst of all this loveliness I sat and dreamed.
>
> —RAY BRADBURY

Least to Most Important Idea

This type of organization is useful for developing paragraphs when the purpose is to make some kind of point. These types of paragraphs often use facts and statistics or specific examples. Select the specific statements you want to use according to the impact you think they will have on the reader. By beginning with the least important idea and ending with the strongest statement, you can build your ideas to a climax or emphasize a particular point. The paragraph below was developed in this way.

Is traditional handwriting in the schools obsolete? Supporters of the new italic method of writing insist that it is, at least for young children. First of all, say the critics, the letter forms now taught call for motor coordination that many youngsters simply do not have. Secondly, these letters are confusing to youngsters because they bear little resemblance to the typefaces that students are simultaneously learning to read. Finally, the traditional letter forms were not designed to accomplish the combination of legibility, speed, and ease necessary to good writing.

The writer of the paragraph has carefully arranged the material within it so that the simplest reason, which involves children's motor coordination, comes first. The final sentence in the paragraph presents the strongest reason. By organizing the paragraph in this manner, the writer ensures that the best reason is the one most likely to be remembered.

Most to Least Familiar Idea

When you use this method of organization, you start with ideas that are familiar to your reader. Then you move from this comfortable base to new concepts. In the paragraph below the writer begins with a well-known fact, and then lists more technical and scientific statements supporting the topic sentence.

All of us must be conscientious about brushing our teeth regularly after eating. Food residue clings to the surfaces of the teeth and, if not removed by thorough brushing, will form acids. These acids destroy the tooth enamel, and then decay sets in. Bad breath is one result. More seriously, teeth may be lost, abscesses may form, and infection may spread to other parts of the body. The ultimate result will be lengthy, perhaps painful, and certainly expensive trips to the dentist.

Comparison or Contrast

This method of organization can be used with almost any type of development. By using comparison or contrast the writer points out the similarities or the differences between two or more things. By using comparisons, this writer shows how two cities are alike.

Writing in the Boston *Globe* in 1970, Ian Menzies suggested that Boston and San Francisco are "the two most exciting cities in the nation." There are certainly strong similarities. Both have water on three sides, strikingly similar skylines, and almost equal land areas. Both have a similar mix of scholarship, of history, and of the arts. While one has a Puritan heritage, the other Spanish, both are controlled by an Irish-Italian political structure which is slowly yielding its control to emerging minority populations.

The writer introduces the idea of comparison in the second sentence. He then proceeds to point out several similarities between Boston and San Francisco, similarities in physical, cultural, and political characteristics. By repeating the word *both*, he reinforces the idea of comparison throughout the paragraph.

In using contrasts, you are showing how the facts, examples, or incidents are different. In the following paragraph, the writer presents a "before" and "after" description of a young man. This creates a sharp contrast that points out that something wonderful or exciting has happened to the young man.

I could scarcely believe the man coming out of the house to be the same one who had so recently entered it. Surely, this alert young fellow with flushed, eager face and shining eyes had nothing in common with the pale, dejected-looking creature who a few minutes before had passed me. I had carefully observed him then and had noted the beaten, hopeless look in his eyes. How his shoulders had sagged, and his footsteps had lagged as though bound on a fruitless errand! Now his upright figure, with its squared shoulders, was vibrant with life. His lips were parted in a half smile; and as he passed me, he was humming a lilting tune.

Exercise Choosing a Method of Organization

Look at the topics listed below. For each topic, state the method of organization that would result in the best possible presentation of ideas. Then choose two of the topics, or two of your own, and make up pre-writing notes. Show the details you would use to develop the topic, as well as the order in which you would present them. You may want to use two of the lists you developed for earlier parts of this chapter.

1. Understanding laser discs
2. The great race
3. Why _____ is a terrific place
4. A plane's-eye view
5. Old movies versus new

6. Peering into a hallway
7. Reasons to travel by car
8. How _____ have changed
9. How to make a sculpture
10. How a video-disk works

Part 5 First Draft and Revision

In Chapter 6, you learned that the first draft is the writer's attempt to find out more about what he or she wants to say. The primary purpose of the rough draft is to get some of the ideas from the pre-writing stage down on paper.

As you work on this draft, you may think of new ideas or ways to modify and refine the ideas you already have. It may be necessary to return to the pre-writing stage to re-evaluate your organization, choice of supporting details, or even the topic itself.

In writing the first draft, you should not be concerned about grammar or punctuation. Worrying about the mechanics of writing at this point will only distract you. It is more important to let your ideas flow freely.

Exercise Writing a First Draft

Look through the pre-writing notes you developed for Part 4 of this chapter. Choose a set that interests you, and write a rough draft of a paragraph.

Revising the Rough Draft

Every writer should be prepared to work through several drafts before reaching a final product. Review the discussion of revision in Chapter 6, "The Process of Writing." Now examine your rough draft. Give thoughtful consideration to your choice of details and method of organization. Also check for unity and coherence, and for precise word usage. Consult your dictionary and thesaurus for words that might result in more vivid descriptions.

The example below is a revised rough draft of the paragraph on pages 144-145, which is developed using specific examples.

Datsolalee,   weaver

~~The~~ greatest designer and ~~weever~~ of baskets ~~was an Indian woman named Datsolalee.~~ She was one among of the Washo people, ~~Datsolalee~~ created works of art that are ~~valued~~ treasured by ~~many who collect~~ collectors of American handicrafts. ~~I know a woman who has one of her baskets.~~ One of her ~~greatest~~ most famous baskets is "Myriads of Stars Shine over the Graves of Our Ancestors." Requiring more than a year to create, its design reflects her view of tribal history and life. ~~It~~ contains 56,590 single stitches, ~~which is~~ over thirty-six stitches to the inch.

Look at the different types of revisions the writer made. Some sentences were combined to create a closer relation between ideas. The idea about a woman owning a basket was deleted because it interrupted the unity of the paragraph. The next to last sentence was moved to the end of the paragraph to improve the organization. By improving some word choices, the writer presents clearer images for the reader. Finally, the writer proofread her paper for errors in grammar, usage, and mechanics.

Exercise Revising the Rough Draft

Revise the rough draft you wrote for the exercise on page 152.

SUMMARY AND APPLICATIONS

1. A paragraph is a group of sentences dealing with a single topic.

2. The topic sentence of a paragraph is a general statement of what the paragraph will be about.

3. When all of the sentences in a paragraph develop the topic sentence and relate logically to each other, the paragraph has unity and coherence. Remember that unity and coherence are important to any clear expression of ideas.

4. Paragraphs can be developed with sensory details, facts, statistics, examples, incidents, or anecdotes.

5. Ways of organizing paragraphs include the following five methods: chronological order, spatial order, order of importance, order of familiarity, and comparison-contrast. Whenever you are given a writing assignment in one of your classes, choose the most appropriate organizational method for your presentation.

Applications in Other Subject Areas

Social Studies / Fine Arts. Choose a topic from each of the areas below. Develop a set of pre-writing notes for each topic that you choose. How does your choice of details and method of organization differ for each category or topic?

SOCIAL STUDIES	FINE ARTS
ghost towns	a famous painting
the Alamo	the sound of a particular instrument
missionaries in Hawaii	a type of dance

Science. The skills of paragraph writing are also the skills of logical thinking. They teach you to analyze and organize data. Find some old lab reports you have written up for a biology or chemistry class. How is organizing a lab report similar to organizing a paragraph? How is it different? How does the structure of a lab report help lead you toward a conclusion? Does a paragraph do the same thing? Write your answers in paragraph form.

Chapter 8

Writing Different Types of Paragraphs

In the preceding chapters, you studied the steps in the process of writing and different ways of developing and organizing a paragraph. Now you are ready to take this knowledge one step further.

As you read a story or an article, you are probably aware of the many different types of paragraphs that make up the larger composition. Some paragraphs relate events, others provide descriptions, and still others explain ideas. Together, these paragraphs allow both writer and reader to explore many different aspects of a topic and to gain a complete understanding of it.

As a writer, you too must learn to compose these various types of paragraphs. This chapter takes a close look at four basic kinds: narrative paragraphs, descriptive paragraphs, expository paragraphs, and persuasive paragraphs.

Each of these types of paragraphs has a unique purpose. In this chapter we will explore ways of developing each type into a unified, coherent piece of writing.

Part 1   The Narrative Paragraph

The narrative paragraph tells, or narrates, a story. It can be based on fact, on imagination, or on a combination of both. The narrative is a simple, natural form of writing in which the author relates an incident.

Since the narrative paragraph tells a story rather than develops a single idea, it does not always have a topic sentence. Instead, a writer may begin a narrative paragraph with a description of the first incident or action in the story. The writer may also begin with a general statement that sets the stage for the narration that follows.

Point of View

The narrative may be presented from two points of view. The paragraph written in the **first person** is told from the point of view of the writer, or of the writer's main character. A first person narrative uses pronouns such as *I, my, me, we,* and *our.* The following is an example of this type of narration.

> I turn from the window and flop down on the bed, shoes and all. Perhaps because of what happened this afternoon or maybe just because I see my brother Charley so seldom, my thoughts hover over him like hummingbirds. The cheerful, impersonal tidiness of this room is a world away from Charley's walk-up flat and a hundred worlds from the bare, noisy shanty where he and the rest of us spent what there was of childhood. I close my eyes, and side by side I see Charley of my boyhood and the Charley of this afternoon, as clearly as if I were looking at a split TV screen. Another surge of love, seasoned with gratitude, wells up in me.—EUGENIA COLLIER

When using the **third-person** point of view, the writer tells a story from the point of view of someone outside the action of the story. When this point of view is taken, pronouns such as *he, she,* and *they* are used. Compare the example on the following page with the one above.

In the summer of 1887 Nellie Bly was in New York, and the first three months were the worst of her life. It was hot, the hottest summer the city had known. Every day brought new accounts of people sickening and dying of the terrible, stifling heat. Work must go on; somehow people dragged themselves out of their homes in the mornings, hurried into the slight protection of the buildings where they worked, sat sweltering until it was time to go home, drooping, panting, perspiring in the horse trolleys, or slowly walking the streets. They crowded the brownstone stoops or the fire escapes in the evenings and hoped in vain for a cool breeze that would let them sleep at night.

—IRIS NOBLE

Pre-Writing

Selecting Details for a Narrative Paragraph. Although the narrative paragraph is a natural form of writing, care must be taken with its development. To gather details for a narrative paragraph you must recall, or create, all of the details needed to tell the story to the reader. Make sure that you don't leave out anything that is important to the development of the story. You must also be certain to confine the details to the main topic. Avoid straying from the subject. Finally, use vivid, descriptive words.

Organizing a Narrative Paragraph. The narrative paragraph is usually written in chronological order; that is, the events are related in the order in which they happened. The chronological order in some paragraphs is clear and direct from beginning to end.

It was George Crum, an American Indian, who chipped the first potato. In 1853 Crum was employed as a chef at a posh resort in Saratoga Springs, New York. One evening a particularly fussy guest kept returning his French fries because they were "too thick." Crum grabbed a potato, sliced it into paper-thin pieces, and plunged them into boiling fat. The resulting golden, curling chips were proclaimed delicious by the stubborn diner. They were known as Saratoga chips until the turn of the century. Thereafter, they were called potato chips.

—BRUCE FELTON AND MARK FOWLER

In the preceding paragraph, the incident took place in a short, precise period of time. However, when a paragraph relates an event taking place over a longer period of time, the writer needs a means of indicating the order and the passing of time. To do this, the writer uses transitional devices. **Transitional devices** are words and phrases that suggest the relation of the ideas in the paragraph. In narrative paragraphs, time words and phrases, such as the ones below, are the kinds most commonly used.

Time Words and Phrases

A POINT IN TIME		
one month	next year	at midnight
two days	yesterday	tonight
tomorrow	last week	at this moment

ORDER OF TIME		
next	soon	immediately
then	instantly	the next day
later	finally	the following Friday

PERIODS OF TIME		
for a moment	during the day	for a long time
for an hour	after a week	during the winter

ACTIONS REPEATED IN TIME		
seldom	occasionally	once
sometimes	frequently	twice

A BREAK IN TIME		
meanwhile	before this happened	at the same time

When the chronological order is clear, as in the paragraph about George Crum, time words and phrases merely reinforce the coherence of the paragraph. However, in paragraphs where the passage of time is less clear, transitional words and phrases are essential. For instance, the flow of the following paragraph would be very uneven without the use of transitional devices.

My dad's a tinkerer with a creative bent, and he leaps at a chance to solve difficult problems. *When* a friend complained of being unable to rid his attic of a colony of squirrels, Dad *immediately* volunteered his services, suggesting the use of a flashing yellow light to scare them out. The two men installed it *one Saturday afternoon* and *after an hour* slowly opened the attic door. The light was working, but not in the way my father had expected. Around it, in a perfect semi-circle, sat the squirrels, staring in fascination at the yellow light.—DAVID TOBIT

Notice how this writer goes from one period of time to another, making smooth transitions with the italicized words. These devices are subtle reminders to the reader that time has lapsed and another event is introduced.

Exercise Writing Narrative Paragraphs

Select one of the topics from the box, or another of your choice. The topic may be real or imaginary. Develop the topic into a narrative paragraph. Complete each of the steps on the following page.

Possible Topics
1. A Bad Day at School
2. I Learned Something About Myself
3. A Family Celebration
4. A Night To Remember
5. A New Kid Comes to School
6. It Pays To Be on Time
7. We Thought We'd Won the Game
8. A Practical Joke
9. A Natural Disaster
10. The Worst/Best Moment of My Life

Pre-Writing: After you have selected the topic for your narrative paragraph, list at random all the thoughts, feelings, sights, sounds, and smells associated with this incident. Next, limit your ideas by identifying the peak point or points of the experience. Focus on the effect the experience had on you or your main character. Also decide on the impression you want your readers to have when they have finished reading your paragraph.

Write a topic sentence that identifies your narrowed topic and the impression you want to give your readers. Organize your details, using chronological order.

First Draft: Using the list of ideas from your pre-writing notes, write the rest of your narrative paragraph. Be sure to include transitional time words and phrases that will indicate time periods and create a smooth flow of events.

Revision: Read over your rough draft carefully several times. Have all important events and ideas been included? Does your paragraph flow smoothly from idea to idea?

When you are satisfied with the content of your writing, check the spelling, grammar, and punctuation in your paragraph. Then write the final copy.

Part 2   The Descriptive Paragraph

A descriptive paragraph paints a word picture that appeals to the reader's senses: sight, hearing, taste, touch, and smell. Through careful selection of words, a writer can also create a certain **mood:** a feeling of tranquility, excitement, happiness, sorrow, or fear.

Pre-Writing

Selecting Details for a Descriptive Paragraph. The purpose of your paragraph will determine your selection of details. Which sensory details will best convey the impression you want to give the reader? Some descriptive paragraphs appeal to one sense only.

Others appeal to a combination of senses. All descriptive paragraphs, however, strive to create a feeling within the reader about the scene that is being described.

Read the following paragraph written by Mark Twain. Pay particular attention to the choice of details, emphasized by careful word choice. Notice how the use of these details results in a vivid image and a distinct mood.

> I still keep in mind a certain wonderful sunset that I witnessed when steamboating was new to me. A broad expanse of the river was turned to blood; in the middle distance the red hue brightened into gold, through which a solitary log came floating, black and conspicuous. In one place a long, slanting mark lay sparkling upon the water; in another the surface was broken by boiling, tumbling rings that were as many-tinted as an opal. Where the ruddy flush was faintest, was a smooth spot that was covered with graceful circles and radiating lines, ever so delicately traced. The shore on our left was densely wooded, and the somber shadow that fell from this forest was broken in one place by a long ruffled trail that shone like silver; and high above the forest wall a clean-stemmed dead tree waved a single leafy bough that glowed like a flame in the unobstructed splendor that was flowing from the sun. There were graceful curves, reflected images, woody heights, soft distances; and over the whole scene, far and near, the dissolving lights drifted steadily, enriching it, every passing moment, with new marvels of coloring.—MARK TWAIN

What sense or senses are appealed to in this paragraph? What mood is created?

Organizing a Descriptive Paragraph. Many descriptions of places and objects are primarily visual in appeal. These descriptions contain details that are organized in **spatial order.** Sometimes the order of ideas is direct and easy for the reader to follow. At other times, the order may be a little less straightforward. Spatial order is often clarified through transitional devices such as the ones shown in the chart that follows.

Words and Phrases Showing Spatial Order

DIRECTIONS

left	through	around
right	into	between
above	ahead	among
below	behind	in front of
center	across	in back of
up	toward	forward
down	away from	backward
past	against	parallel

DISTANCE

foreground	on the edge of	close to
background	in the center of	next to
first	approximately	leading to
last	twenty feet	far
halfway	about ten miles	near
beyond	twenty kilometers	long
distant	remote	short

AREA OR SPACE

outside	field	hall
inside	plain	stairway
interior	hillside	stage
exterior	acre	alley
lawn	hut	street
garden	villa	road
courtyard	mansion	narrow
park	closet	wide

In the writing of experienced authors, less structured patterns of spatial organization are common. In such writing, good transitional devices are essential, for without them a reader could not follow the descriptions. Read the following examples and identify the transitional devices used by these writers. Notice how space words lead you from one place to another.

1. From Near to Far (Or the Reverse)

The front garden was a small square with a privet hedge. There she stood, trying to soothe herself with the scent of flowers and the fading, beautiful evening. Opposite her small gate was the stile that led uphill, under the tall hedge between the burning glow of the cut pastures. The sky overhead throbbed and pulsed with light. The glow sank quickly off the field; the earth and the hedges smoked dust. As it grew dark, a ruddy glare came out on the hilltop, and out of the glare the diminished commotion of the fair.—D.H. LAWRENCE

Notice how the writer begins with concrete details of a figure in the garden nearest him. Then he leads the reader visually out of the garden to the distant pastures and up to the darkening sky. He uses transitional words such as "front," "opposite," and "overhead" to make this order clear.

2. From Top to Bottom (Or the Reverse)

In the following description the writer gives details of a man's face from the eyes down.

Outside, a man walking along the edge of the highway crossed over and approached the truck. He was not over thirty. His eyes were very dark brown and there was a hint of brown pigment in his eyeballs. His cheek bones were high and wide, and strong deep lines cut down his cheeks, in curves beside his mouth. His upper lip was long, and since his teeth protruded, the lips stretched to cover them, for this man kept his lips closed.

—JOHN STEINBECK

3. Circular

In describing a bedroom in a Spanish hacienda, the writer of the following paragraph begins with the "great high beds" and moves around the room. She leads the reader completely around the room, ending with the table beside the bed.

The bedrooms in the house were completely carpeted; there were great high beds with feather mattresses. A gilt-framed mirror hung over the washstand, which had a white marble top;

there were a couch and large chairs. On the papered wall hung portraits of members of the family, the frame in gold with a strip of red velvet next to the glass; a table was at the bedside with a candle-holder and a basket which was filled with fruit or cakes when the room was occupied. —NINA OTERO-WARREN

Describing a Person

Describing a person is different from, and in many ways more difficult than, describing a place or object. That is because the writer must try to capture intangible qualities such as personality and character. The skillful writer can do this by describing the person's outward characteristics in such a way as to indicate inner qualities. The writer may also choose to describe the person's inner self directly, or to do a little of both.

The writer of the following paragraph concentrates on observable qualities. He gives details about the fisherman's appearance, disposition, and approach to work.

Jukichi Oyama, master fisherman, owner of the "Taihei-maru," had a face like leather, well tanned by sea winds. The grimy wrinkles on his hands were mixed indistinguishably with old fishing scars, all burned by the sun down into their deepest creases. He was a man who seldom laughed but was always in calm good spirits, and even the loud voice he used when giving commands on the boat was never raised in anger. While fishing, he seldom left his place on the sculling platform at the stern, only occasionally taking one hand off the oar to regulate the engine.—YUKIO MISHIMA

From the description of external characteristics, a reader can infer many things about the fisherman's inner qualities.

1. He is a hard worker.
2. He respects those who work for him.
3. He is at peace with himself.
4. He is a disciplined person.
5. He is dedicated to his work.

The writer of the next paragraph takes an entirely different approach. He includes no details about physical appearance, but focuses directly on the character of his father.

> My father was a quiet, unpretentious man. He was naturally conservative and cautious, and generally displayed common sense in what he said and did. He never went to school; such education as he had was self-acquired. Later in life I appreciated the fact that his self-development was little less than remarkable. He had a knowledge of general affairs and was familiar with many of the chief events and characters in the history of the world. The quality in my father that impressed me the most was his high and rigid sense of honesty. I could not conceive of him as a party to any transaction that was questionable in the least. I think he got his greatest satisfaction in life out of the reputation he had built up as a man of integrity.
>
> —JAMES WELDON JOHNSON

Exercises Writing Descriptive Paragraphs

A. Choose a topic from the box, or make up your own. Following the steps in the writing process listed on the next page, develop a paragraph that appeals to as many senses as possible.

Possible Topics

1. A summer morning
2. Riding a Go Kart
3. A drugstore
4. An amusement park
5. Walking outside after or during a rainstorm
6. A school gymnasium during a basketball game
7. Dawn
8. Midnight
9. A classroom during a test
10. A school dance

Pre-Writing: Narrow your topic by selecting a specific part of the experience that you want to describe. What impression do you want to convey to your reader? Which details will help create this impression? What would be the best organization for these details?

First Draft: After organizing the ideas in your pre-writing notes, write a topic sentence that will give the reader a preview of your paragraph. Complete the paragraph using vivid and precise words that will bring the scene alive for your reader. Use appropriate transitional devices to add coherence.

Revision: Review your first draft carefully. Does it leave the desired impression? Can you condense ideas into more concise sentences? Can you combine several sensory details into one coherent sentence?

Check to see that the organization of your paragraph follows a logical spatial order with smooth transitional phrases. Then improve your material by looking up more interesting synonyms to substitute for unexciting language. When you are satisfied with the content, check punctuation, sentence structure, spelling, and grammar. You are now ready to write the final copy.

B. Following is a list of topics that may be developed into paragraphs describing people. Choose one, or make up a topic of your own. Then, following the steps on the next page, write a paragraph that reveals some of the inner qualities of the person.

Possible Topics
 1. A gymnast at an important meet
 2. An instructor at a dog obedience school
 3. A waiter or waitress
 4. A little boy trying to tie his shoes
 5. An artist at work
 6. A patient in the waiting room of a clinic
 7. A roller skater
 8. A customer or sales clerk at a store
 9. A bus driver
 10. An unforgettable character you've known

Pre-Writing: Write your impressions of the person, including such things as physical appearance, character, disposition, admirable qualities, contradictions of character, and distasteful habits. Determine the strongest point of your description, the aspect of the person that you want to highlight. Which details will give emphasis and support to your subject? How will you present them?

First Draft: After you have decided on the dominant impression of your paragraph, organize your pre-writing notes accordingly. Write your topic sentence and complete your draft with details that would create a real, three-dimensional character.

Revision: Go over your draft several times. Does every detail reinforce what you wanted to tell about the character? Can you add other details about the character's physical appearance or personality? Proofread for minor errors, and then write your final copy.

Part 3 The Expository Paragraph

A friend asks you how to repair a bicycle. Your history teacher asks you to name the events leading to the Vietnam war. A stranger wants to know the location of the nearest bus stop. In each of these situations, you are being asked to explain something.

A paragraph that is written to explain something or convey information is called an **expository**, or **explanatory**, paragraph. It can be developed in a variety of ways, depending on the subject of the paragraph and the writer's purpose for writing.

There are three main types of expository paragraphs:

1. Paragraphs that explain a process
2. Paragraphs that define
3. Paragraphs that give reasons

The Paragraph That Explains a Process

The simplest form of the expository paragraph is the paragraph that explains a process. Such a paragraph may simply explain how to do something, as in the following example:

The forward roll will give you your first sensation of being upside down in tumbling. You have probably done this stunt many times, but let us analyze the correct movement. To get into the starting position, put your hands flat on the mat, shoulder width apart, your fingers pointing forward, knees between your arms. From here, push off with your feet and rock forward on your arms. Just as you feel yourself falling off balance, tuck your head down between your arms. Keep your chin on your chest and put the back of your head on the mat. Keep rolling, and as the weight comes off your hands and you roll onto your back, grasp your shins and pull yourself up onto your feet. That's all there is to the forward roll.   —NEWTON C. LOEN

This paragraph gives very exact, precise instructions for completing the process. Whenever you are composing a paragraph that explains a process, make sure that your pre-writing notes list all of the details, facts, or steps necessary for the successful completion or understanding of the process. Avoid using technical terms that your reader might not understand, or make sure that you define such terms in context. Most paragraphs that explain a process can best be organized in chronological order. As you write the first draft, include transitional words and phrases to make the order of the ideas even more definite.

All of these guidelines must also be followed in the second type of "process" paragraph—the paragraph that explains how something works. Read this paragraph about how bats navigate. Do you have a good understanding when you are finished reading?

The bat is the only mammal that can fly. Because bats are nocturnal creatures, they need a good navigational system to enable them to fly and find food in the dark. Some bats use their vision and sense of smell to find their way. Others navigate by means of echoes. To use this method, the bat emits a series of short, high-frequency sounds while flying. The sounds strike any nearby objects and the echoes bounce back to the bat. The bat's sensitive hearing picks up these echoes. Depending on the strength of the echoes and the amount of time it took them to return, the bat can then judge the distance to and movement of the object.

Exercise Writing To Explain a Process

Choose one of the topics from the box, or make up one of your own. Then write a paragraph explaining the process. Follow the writing steps shown below.

Possible Topics
1. Explain how a microscope works.
2. Give directions for how to complete some art, industrial education, or home economics project.
3. Describe how a telephone or some other communications device works.
4. Tell how to approach a strange animal.
5. Explain how to make a good first impression.

Pre-Writing: Narrow your subject and write a topic sentence that indicates your specific topic, purpose, and audience. What are the steps of the process? What details are needed to present the process clearly? In what order should they be presented?

First Draft: Get the steps of the process down on paper. Include all the details your reader would need to understand the process completely. Use transitional devices to make the order of the process clear.

Revision: Go over your rough draft several times. Are your instructions or descriptions complete? Has anything been left out? Have you used only terms your reader would understand? Are there any errors in spelling, usage, or mechanics?

The Paragraph That Defines

Since an expository paragraph is one that explains, it is often used to define an unfamiliar term, object, or idea. To do so, a paragraph of definition first places the term to be defined in a general category, and then identifies several distinguishing characteristics of the term. These characteristics help to separate the term being defined from others closely related to it. To make the description precise, sensory details, facts, and statistics are often used.

Generally, the details in a paragraph of definition are organized from most general to most specific. This is the method used in the following example.

> Iceboats are small, speedy boats that resemble sailboats. They are used for winter sport in northern climates. An iceboat has a long body and is supported by three runners. One runner is attached to the body of the boat, and the other two are at the ends of an *out-rigger*, or crosspiece, that runs across the boat. The sail of an iceboat resembles that of a sailboat, and is attached with steel wires to hollow masts and spars. Iceboats can be as short as ten feet, but most are somewhat longer. They can reach speeds of up to one hundred miles an hour.

The writer begins this paragraph by placing iceboats in a general category, small boats, and by comparing them to the more familiar sailboats. The sentences that follow give specific characteristics that distinguish iceboats from other craft. Notice how the writer has used both descriptive details and statistics to accomplish this purpose. The types of details are quite common in paragraphs of definition. So are explanations of the object's function, purpose, or use.

Exercise Writing a Paragraph of Definition

Choose one of the topics from the box, or make up one of your own. Write a paragraph of definition. Complete each of the writing steps on the following page.

Possible Topics

1. A recent invention
2. Radar
3. Braille
4. A type of car, boat, or plane

5. An odd insect
6. A type of game
7. The African veldt
8. A Moog synthesizer

Pre-Writing: Decide whether the term to be defined needs to be narrowed further. Then analyze it carefully. To what general class does your subject belong? What are its identifying characteristics? Could sensory details, facts, or statistics best be used to describe it? What would be the most effective method of organization?

First Draft: Use your pre-writing notes to get your ideas down on paper. Try to choose precise words that will present the characteristics of your subject clearly.

Revision: Examine your rough draft from the point of view of your reader. Is the term placed in a general or familiar category that helps to identify it? Do the characteristics help distinguish the term from closely related ones? Do the details that are presented illustrate these characteristics? When your definition is complete, carefully check your paper for mechanical correctness.

The Paragraph That Gives Reasons

An explanatory paragraph attempts to explain why something is true or why something should be. The writer states that something is true *because* something else is true or occurred first, or that an action or idea is right *because* certain facts support it.

For this type of writing, a good topic sentence is especially important. Sometimes the topic sentence is a statement of opinion. It presents a particular view on a subject. This view may be a simple belief or idea or a controversial statement requiring a great deal of proof. In either case, the topic needs strong reasons to support it.

The reasons in an expository paragraph can be facts, statistics, examples, or anecdotes. They should provide logical support for your topic sentence. Look at the following paragraph.

> I was born in the wrong century. The signs of my out-of-placeness are everywhere. My shelves are filled with Victorian novels. I don't have a food processor. I eat fatback. I spank my children. I think everyone should take Latin. I believe in duty, work, fidelity, and suffering. I think too much fun is not a good thing.—SUZANNE BRITT JORDAN

Notice that the writer organized her examples, or supporting ideas, from least important to most important. This is a common organizational method for this type of paragraph.

Exercise **Writing To Provide Reasons**

Choose a topic from the box or make up your own. Write a paragraph giving reasons. Complete each of the steps below.

Possible Topics

1. Explain why you love a particular type of music, or the music of a specific group.

2. Find an editorial in a local newspaper. Write a paragraph telling why you agree or disagree with it.

3. Do you hope there is life on other planets? Tell why or why not.

4. Do you like yourself tremendously or think that you could use some improvement? Explain your feelings.

5. Should a person ever try to achieve the impossible, or does this simply lead to frustration? Explain.

Pre-Writing: Write a topic sentence that states an idea or belief. Make sure that this sentence also reflects your narrowed topic, your purpose, and your audience. What facts, statistics, examples, or incidents could be used to support your topic? What method of organization would be most effective?

First Draft: Using your pre-writing notes, get your ideas down on paper. You may think of better supporting reasons as you write. As long as each one could be logically linked to your topic sentence by the word "because," include them.

Revision: Go over your rough draft several times. Do all of your reasons relate logically to your topic sentence? Are your reasons organized to have the best effect on the reader? Remember to do a final check for errors in grammar, usage, and mechanics.

Part 4 The Persuasive Paragraph

A persuasive paragraph is actually a more specific type of explanatory paragraph. It is set apart from other kinds by its purpose and by the nature of its topic sentence.

The purpose of a persuasive paragraph is to persuade readers to accept the logic behind an opinion or to adopt the opinion as their own. The choice of subject matter is limited to ideas about which there are at least two ways of thinking.

The topic sentence of a persuasive paragraph states the writer's way of thinking about a subject. It establishes the writer's point of view, which is justified by supporting statements.

Giving Opinions and Reasons

Persuasive paragraphs are of two basic types. In the first, the element of persuasion is weak. The purpose of the paragraph is simply to explain to the reader why the writer feels a certain way or holds a particular belief. To accomplish this goal, the writer states an opinion in the topic sentence, then follows with reasons to support that opinion. You read an example of this type of paragraph under "The Paragraph That Gives Reasons" in Part 3.

Stating Propositions and Supporting Arguments

In the second type of persuasive paragraph, the element of persuasion is much stronger. Its purpose is to convert the readers to the opinion held by the writer.

The topic sentence in this type of paragraph is a definite proposition of belief. In other words, it is a clear statement of a conclusion that the writer has reached and that the writer wishes the readers to reach after reading the arguments presented in the paragraph. At first reading, a proposition of belief might appear to be a statement of fact. Closer examination, however, will reveal that it deals with a question that is open to debate.

The following are three examples of propositions of belief.

1. The passion of Americans should not be politics, baseball, or money, but education.
2. Our football team is the best in the state.
3. The threat of famine facing the hungry nations is the responsibility of the entire world.

Every persuasive paragraph contains two parts: a *what* and a *why*. The proposition of belief stated in the topic sentence is the *what*. The arguments given to support the *what* are the *why*.

Pre-Writing

Gathering Convincing Information. When you wish to write a strong persuasive paragraph, keep these three things in mind.

1. To present an effective argument for one side of a question, you must study and understand the arguments that support the opposite point of view.
2. Your audience consists of readers whose beliefs about the question at hand may be different from yours. You are not writing for readers who already think the way you do. Thus, your arguments must be as strong as possible.
3. Your supporting arguments can take the form of facts, statistics, examples, anecdotes, comparisons, or contrasts. In other words, you have available all the methods you used for developing other kinds of explanatory paragraphs.

Organizing The Persuasive Paragraph. After you have gathered the supporting arguments for your persuasive paragraph, you want to present them in the most forceful, effective manner. There are five main ways of organizing this type of paragraph.

1. Present the weakest argument first, building up to the strongest argument as a forceful conclusion.
2. Use the strongest argument first to gain attention and support. Then present other arguments.
3. Begin with an argument your readers are most likely to agree with, and gradually lead them to those ideas that they may take exception to.

4. Show weaknesses in the argument(s) against your position, then follow with arguments in favor of your position. This is a form of comparison and contrast.
5. Start with arguments in favor of your position and follow with a discussion of the weaknesses in arguments against your position. This is also comparison and contrast.

For each paragraph you will need to decide the best order of presentation based on the strength or weakness of each of your arguments. Another point to remember as you write is that an opinion, by its nature, cannot be "right" or "wrong." Therefore, the opinions held by your opponents are also valid. *Never* attack an opposing view by using harsh, unreasonable, or biased language. Let your reasons argue for you. See Chapter 12, "Critical Thinking," for a more in-depth discussion of persuasion.

Now read the following paragraph. Look for the elements of good persuasive writing.

In the 1960's, the National Park Service instituted a "forever wild" doctrine designed to keep the parks of North America as natural as possible. This policy has proven harmful to two common species inside the parks—humans and grizzly bears— and should be dropped or modified. In an attempt to preserve the wilderness and the natural instincts of the animals, the Park Service had closed down dumping sights and forbidden hotel-keepers to leave out food for the bears. Unfortunately, the grizzly bears, which had grown used to human attention, began to prowl closer to camps and vacation homes. The results have been predictable, but tragic. Bears have been shot or have fallen victim to poachers. People have been mauled and even killed. In other words, the "forever wild" idea simply won't work when people already have invaded the environment. As Montana Wildlife biologist John Craighead says, "Man is now a definite part of the ecology and must be accommodated."

In this paragraph, the writer clearly states an opinion in the second sentence. He then supports this opinion with many different types of reasons. The reasons are organized so that the opinion of an authority, possibly the writer's strongest support, is presented last, where it will have an impact on the reader.

Notice, too, that the writer did not neglect the ideas of the opposition. Reasons supporting the "forever wild" are mentioned, and not criticized unduly. The writer presents both sides using reasonable language and lets his information do its own persuading.

Exercise **Writing To Persuade**

Choose one of the topics from the box or make up one of your own. Write a persuasive paragraph on some aspect of the topic about which you feel strongly. Complete the steps below.

Possible Topics
1. The use of grades in school
2. Freedom of the press
3. The results of "progress"
4. Small high schools *versus* large high schools
5. The role of the family in today's society
6. Compulsory education
7. Meeting the future
8. Censorship
9. The legal driving/voting age
10. Equal opportunity

Pre-Writing: Narrow your topic to a specific issue. Then write a topic sentence that identifies your opinion on that issue. Find facts, statistics, or incidents that support your opinion. Which of these reasons are most effective? How should you present them?

First Draft: Use your pre-writing notes to get your ideas down on paper. Remember to use well-thought-out reasons and reasonable language.

Revision: Go over your rough draft. Is your opinion clearly stated? Do all your reasons logically support your opinion? Have you included specific details to support your claims? Have you arranged your reasons in the most effective order?

Guidelines for Writing and Revising Paragraphs

These Guidelines will help to remind you of the qualities necessary for good paragraphs. However, your writing procedure should also follow the steps in Guidelines for the Process of Writing on page 123.

1. Does the paragraph deal with only one main idea?

2. Does the topic sentence state the main idea?

3. Does the topic sentence control and limit the ideas that are discussed in the rest of the paragraph?

4. Does the paragraph have unity and coherence?

5. Are there enough details—facts, statistics, examples, incidents, or anecdotes—to develop the paragraph fully?

6. If it is a narrative paragraph, is it developed in chronological order? Does it use time words and phrases?

7. If it is a descriptive paragraph, does it use vivid sensory details? Does it present these details in a logical order? Does it use space words and phrases? If the paragraph describes a person, does it try to capture the essence of the person? Does it appeal to the senses?

8. If it is an expository or a persuasive paragraph, does it clearly explain a process? give reasons? define? Is the supporting material presented in an effective order? Is the purpose of the paragraph clear to the reader?

SUMMARY AND APPLICATIONS

1. There are three main types of paragraphs: narrative, descriptive, and expository.

2. Narrative paragraphs relate events. They can be written in the first or third person, and are generally organized in chronological order.

3. Descriptive paragraphs create word pictures through the use of sensory details. These details are usually organized in spatial order.

4. Expository, or explanatory, paragraphs can explain a process, give definitions, or offer reasons to support an idea. The most common methods of organization for this type of writing are *most familiar to least familiar idea,* and *least important to most important idea.*

5. Different topics require different types of paragraphs. Whenever you are writing for any of your classes, choose types of paragraphs that are appropriate to your material.

Applications in Other Subject Areas

Social Studies. Historical subjects can be approached in many different ways. For example, an event can be related as a story, told about factually, or analyzed. Choose a famous event, such as a battle or the appearance of the first car or plane. Write up this event in any three of the following ways:

1. As a description
2. As a story, or narrative
3. As a factual account
4. As a paragraph that provides reasons for success or failure
5. As an explanation of a process

Math. You often use special tools in math class: a compass, a protractor, a calculator, or a slide rule, for example. Choose one of these tools and write a paragraph explaining how to use it.

Fine Arts. Write a brief review of a performance you have just witnessed. Describe the performance vividly, choosing precise verbs and adjectives.

Chapter 9

Writing a Composition

When you studied the different types of paragraphs, you learned that ideas may be expressed in many different ways. Sometimes you put together details to create a description. At other times, you tell stories or explain a concept or process. All of these possibilities are open to you because you understand the many different ways in which the elements of a paragraph can be arranged.

Sometimes, however, the options afforded by a paragraph are not enough. You need more time to develop your ideas, more room in which to discuss them. When this is the case, you can develop several paragraphs and make them work together. The result of this is another type of writing—the composition. By learning how to write a composition you provide yourself with a whole new range of possibilities for self-expression.

In this chapter, you will learn all of the elements of a good composition. You will also learn how to apply the process of writing to create a composition of your own.

Part 1   What Is a Composition?

At the beginning of Chapter 7, the paragraph was defined as follows:

> A paragraph is a group of sentences that deal with a single topic or idea. Usually, one sentence, the topic sentence, states the main idea of the paragraph. The single idea of the topic sentence is then supported with other related sentences.

The definition of the composition is only slightly different:

> A composition is a group of paragraphs dealing with a single topic or idea. Usually, one paragraph, called the **introductory paragraph**, states the main idea of the composition. The **body**, or middle paragraphs, are related to the introductory paragraph. They further explain or support the main idea. The **conclusion**, or final paragraph, pulls all of the information together.

The following examples illustrate the similarities between the organization of the paragraph and the organization of the composition.

A PARAGRAPH

The destruction caused by the tidal wave was total. On the beach where the village had stood not a house remained, no wreckage of wood or fallen stone wall, no little street or shops, no docks, not a single boat. The beach was as clean of houses as if no human beings had ever lived there. All that had been was now no more.—PEARL S. BUCK

A COMPOSITION

THE BIG WAVE

The purple rim of the ocean seemed to lift and rise against the clouds. A silver-green band of bright sky appeared like a low dawn above the sea. The castle bell began to toll a warning, deep and pleading. Would the people hear it in the roaring wind? Their houses had no windows toward the sea. Did they know what was about to happen?

Under the deep waters of the ocean, miles down under the cold, the earth had yielded at last to the fire. It groaned and split open and the cold water fell into the middle of the boiling rocks. Steam burst out and lifted the ocean high into the sky in a big wave. It rushed toward the shore, green and solid, frothing into white at its edges. It rose, higher and higher, lifting hands and claws.

The wave came nearer and nearer, filling the air with its roar and shout. It rushed over the flat, still waters of the ocean. It reached the village and covered it fathoms deep in swirling water, green laced with fierce white foam. The wave ran up the mountainside, until the knoll where the castle stood was an island. All who were still climbing the path were swept away—black, tossing scraps in the wicked waters.

Then with a great sucking sigh, the wave swept back again, ebbing into the ocean, dragging everything with it, trees and stones and houses. It swept back over the village and returned slowly again to the ocean, subsiding, sinking into a great stillness.

Upon the beach where the village had stood not a house remained, no wreckage of wood or fallen stone wall, no little street of shops, no docks, not a single boat. The beach was as clean of houses as if no human beings had ever lived there. All that had been was now no more.—PEARL S. BUCK

The paragraph deals with a single idea—the destruction caused by a tidal wave. The topic sentence states this idea. The other sentences support the main idea by describing the destruction.

The composition also deals with a single idea. However, the idea is broader than that of the paragraph because the composition describes the entire process of destruction. The introductory paragraph implies that something dangerous is about to happen. The rest of the paragraphs further explain this idea by developing one particular aspect of the disaster:

1. The cause of the wave
2. The approach and arrival of the wave
3. The retreat of the wave
4. The results of the wave

Notice that the composition has five paragraphs. For purposes of explanation, all compositions selected as examples for this chapter will be made up of five paragraphs. However, there is no limit to the length a composition can be. It can contain as many paragraphs as there are ideas.

Part 2 Pre-Writing: Deciding on a Subject

When you begin the process of writing a composition, your first step is to choose a subject. The following guidelines are important to keep in mind:

1. **Choose a subject that interests you.** Without interest on your part you will have a difficult time creating interest on the part of your readers.
2. **Choose a subject that is familiar to you.** The better you know a subject, the more information you are likely to have about it. You will then be able to write with confidence.
3. **Choose a subject that has value for you.** If you feel strongly about a subject, you will work harder to convey those feelings to your audience. You will therefore communicate something of value to your readers.

Observation, brainstorming, clustering, and journal-writing are all techniques that will help you discover what you know or would like to know. These techniques can also uncover hidden thoughts and tell you more about yourself. Knowing who you are is important to your writing. Remember, you are unique. There is no other person in the world just like you. No one acts the same or thinks the same. No one else has lived a life exactly like yours. Your experiences, your thoughts, your feelings, and your imagination provide an almost endless source of subjects for interesting compositions. You need only identify them.

The writer of the following composition drew from his own uniqueness, from his own experiences, to explain what "growing up" meant to him.

UNDERSTANDING OF A SORT

On a hill I stood and whispered to the far sea. I was ten, not really much younger than I am now. And yet, almost a decade separates that little boy I was from the bigger boy I am. Understanding of a sort has come between us—or perhaps it is a loss of understanding.

The sea was bluer then, I think. Ten years ago the little boy thought that seas are blue because the water is blue—all the way to the bottom. Now the bigger boy knows that seas are blue because they reflect the sky. The bigger boy wishes that the little boy had never found out.

The tide is coming in. Tides, the bigger boy has been told, come in because of the magnetism of the moon. The little boy thought the tide comes in because on the shore a good water mother calls it to her arms. Lying on the hill, the little boy used to wait and try to hear her call, but she always called so softly that he never could hear her. If ever he had heard her, he planned to run down the hill to the beach and hunt until he found her in one of the coves. She would have room in her arms, he was sure, for him as well as for the sea.

When the little boy, ten years ago, stood on the hill and watched the sea, he stood in another land, apart from the country of drab people and dingy towns. They did not exist for him. But the years have brought a growing in the towns and people about him. The vines of reality climbed over him and after a while he became part of them. Now they are forever with him.

The bigger boy I am cries again to be the little boy I was; but the voice comes back to me as a hollow echo. A wall of understanding has been built between us. But there—the water mother is calling in the sea. I think I almost hear her.

This very personal experience resulted in a beautiful, somewhat sad story. You probably have had similar experiences of your own. Draw on those memories. Also remember that you can use your imagination. Expand on dreams, create new people and places, and think about the future. Develop ideas that no one has ever thought of before.

A. Study the following suggestions for composition topics. On a sheet of paper, list those that interest you. Then think about your own experiences. Add at least ten topics to your list. Some may be on imaginary subjects and situations. Keep your list for future reference.

1. My Fondest Dream	9. Things I Don't Need
2. At the Dinner Table	10. My Nicest Compliment
3. My Own Prejudices	11. A Terrible Party
4. Growing Older	12. My Best Friend
5. Souvenirs	13. My Dog and Me
6. My Kid Sister/Brother	14. My Worst Fear
7. The Day I Met Fear	15. A Kind Gesture
8. The Quiet Times	16. Losing

B. Choose four subjects from the list you developed in Exercise A. Begin jotting down more specific topics based on these subjects. Save this list.

Part 3 Pre-Writing: Narrowing the Subject

In writing a paragraph, you must choose an idea that can be treated adequately and satisfactorily within the limits of the paragraph. The same holds true in writing the composition. You must choose a subject that is narrow enough to be developed completely in the space allowed.

Subjects taken from personal experience may not have to be narrowed if you select a subject because you have one specific experience in mind. On the other hand, a general subject such as "A Perfect Day" may catch your interest but still be too unfocused for development in a composition. If this is the case, some creative thinking may help you focus on a topic. Often it is helpful to work on this narrowing process in stages so that you don't overlook any possibilities.

For instance, a writer exploring the subject of "A Perfect Day" decided that clustering might help her identify different possibilities. Her first thoughts concerned different categories into which all days could be divided. She came up with the following ideas: school days, vacation days; fall, spring, summer, and winter days. She quickly decided that the school/vacation division interested her more, so she began to concentrate on that.

After listing some ideas for a perfect school day, the writer chose to pursue the idea of a perfect vacation day. While not as broad as her original subject, "vacation days" was still a large category that required further refining. More brainstorming helped her narrow her subject further. Look at this writer's notes. The starred items show which details the writer decided to focus on.

PRE-WRITING IDEAS

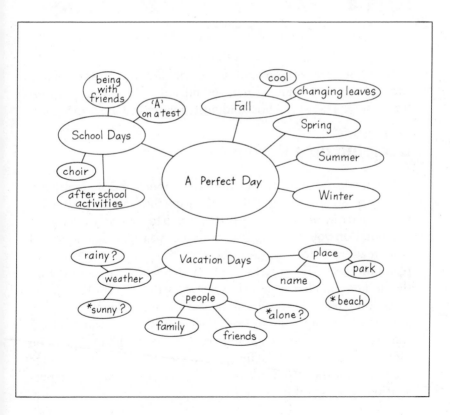

From this narrowing process, the writer's topic emerged. She decided to write about "Time Spent on the Beach." Of course, this topic can still lead the writer to many different types of writing. She needs to focus her narrowed subject even more. The next step in the process of writing allows a writer to do just that. It involves identifying your purpose and audience.

Exercise Narrowing Your Subject

In your last assignment you selected four possible composition subjects. Select one of these subjects and narrow it for development in a short composition. Use clustering, brainstorming, or other pre-writing techniques to help you focus on a topic.

Part 4   Pre-Writing: Determining Purpose and Audience

To refine your composition topic completely, you must make two additional decisions. First, you must decide on your purpose for writing. Then you should identify whom you are writing for.

Deciding on a Purpose

In Chapters 6 and 7 you learned the importance of identifying your purpose for writing. Briefly, determining your purpose helps you to narrow your subject further and to choose the type of presentation you will use. For example, you may decide to tell your readers a story, to describe something for them, or to explain an idea to them. Later, this choice will have an effect on the details you choose and the way you will organize them.

As you select a purpose, you may also want to decide on a *tone* and *mood* for your composition. Do you want it to be humorous? sad? serious? Do you want your readers to laugh? to cry? to be moved by the beauty or ugliness of the scene you are describing? Do you want them to think seriously about the idea you are presenting, or to see it in an amusing way?

The writer of "Time Spent on the Beach" decided to write a descriptive composition. She planned to show how a walk on the beach can affect her feelings. She also decided that the mood of her composition would be one of increasing calm. These decisions led the writer to consider other pre-writing elements. She decided that sensory details might best develop her idea. She also wondered if chronological order might be a likely method of organization.

Identifying Your Audience

It is important, first of all, to know the age group for whom you are writing. The reason for this is simple. Your pre-writing and writing decisions will change depending on whether you are writing for young children, your classmates, or adults. The words you choose, the amount of information you include, and the explanations you give may all change a great deal.

Besides the age of your audience, you should know whether you are writing for readers who have some knowledge of the subject or for readers who are unfamiliar with it. This, too, will influence the amount and difficulty of information you will select and present.

To clarify this point, read the following two introductory paragraphs, both written on the subject of water safety but for two entirely different audiences. As you read, decide what age groups the paragraphs are intended for.

EXAMPLE 1

Summer is about half over. What do you plan to do before school starts again? In one neighborhood nine-year-old Bryan hopes to go camping with his dad and catch lots of fish. Erin, who is one year older, wants to practice her roller skating and win the softball tournament. Eleven-year-old Danny plans to read some good books and get lots of sleep. All three of them want to swim as much as they can in the nearby lake. Before they take another plunge, however, they need to review some swimming safety rules.

EXAMPLE 2

I want to remind you, at the start of a new fishing season, that although rivers are often breathtakingly beautiful in the eyes of an angler, they can take your breath away permanently. It is essential to realize the power of water to kill, and treat it accordingly—not with fear but with respect, and with an awareness that you're not immortal. If you fish sizable rivers, there are things you can do to avoid injury or drowning.

The first paragraph is written for young readers; the second is written for older readers with special expertise in fishing. The writers chose their words and details for their specific audiences.

Once these decisions are made, you are ready to begin gathering information for your composition.

Exercises Determining Your Purpose and Audience

A. Decide on a purpose for your composition. Include this information in your pre-writing notes.

B. Identify the audience for your composition. Consider how this audience will affect your choice of details and type of vocabulary. Include this information in your pre-writing notes.

Part 5 Pre-Writing: Planning the Composition

Planning is a necessary part of writing a composition. It allows the actual writing to go much more smoothly. The planning process involves three separate, equally important steps.

1. Gathering ideas
2. Identifying main ideas
3. Organizing ideas

By following these steps, you can be confident that your composition says something worthwhile. You can also be sure that your ideas are presented in a way that can be easily understood.

Gathering Ideas

If you write about a subject that is not completely familiar to you, you may have to do some outside reading to gather details. When you write from personal experience or knowledge, however, you are already familiar with your subject. You have all the information you need, stored in your memory. To retrieve this information, you must first spend some time thinking about your subject. Brainstorming and clustering are often helpful techniques to use at this stage. You can then write down the ideas you want to include in your composition. Record them on notebook paper or on note cards, using one card for each idea. Putting your ideas on note cards has an advantage in terms of organization since you can easily group and regroup your ideas.

When the writer of "Time Spent on the Beach" was limiting her topic, she realized that sensory details might be a good means of development. Therefore, she made the following list:

"Time Spent on the Beach"

sun setting
fresh air revives me
beach—where I go to be alone
~~walk in woods to be alone, too~~
lighthouse lights
trees in distance
dinner—picnic with cousins
~~family outings common with us~~
gulls crying overhead
can hear boats unloading
wet sand on toes
day of fishing and swimming
~~fished for the first time when I was four~~
dog—soft, damp fur
sunburn
cousins visiting

Remember that your pre-writing notes are not final. Ideas may be added or deleted at any time. In the list above, the writer has already reconsidered some ideas. She deleted those that she felt were unrelated to her topic. She will keep refining her list in the next pre-writing step—identifying main ideas.

Exercise Writing Down Ideas

Make a list of information related to your composition topic. This information may include sensory details, facts and statistics, and incidents or anecdotes. Record your ideas in your pre-writing notes.

Identifying Main Ideas

Your next step in planning is to try to determine how your ideas are related to each other. In other words, you want to group similar ideas together for possible development as paragraphs.

The writer of the sample composition studied her pre-writing notes for possible idea clusters. She found three groups:

1. Sound details
2. Sight details
3. Touch details

After careful consideration, her headings, with the related ideas underneath, looked like this:

Sound Details
   gulls crying overhead
   boats unloading
   waves roaring and beating

Sight Details
   sun setting
   trees in distance
   lighthouse lights

Touch Details
   dog—wet, damp fur
   fresh air fills lungs
   wet sand on toes
   sunburn stings

After grouping your ideas, you may find that you have several "extra" pieces of information that do not fit under your main idea headings. These may be deleted from your notes. However, if the details are appropriate, you may want to include them in your introduction or conclusion.

As your ideas take shape, you will also be adding information to expand on your thoughts. For instance, the writer of the sample composition added "waves roaring and beating" to her notes.

Occasionally, you may know what main ideas you want to develop *before* you have brainstormed minor details. When this occurs, simply "fill in" your pre-writing notes by adding supporting details to the main ones.

Exercises **Identifying Main Ideas**

A. Following is a list of ideas. Decide which two could be used as general headings. Identify them. Then list the remaining ideas under the appropriate headings.

1. walking into a room full of strangers
2. meeting new people
3. encourage people to talk about themselves
4. uncomfortable situations
5. some parties and dances
6. ways to relieve the tension and start conversation
7. listen to what others say and comment on it
8. starting a new job
9. joining a club or team
10. ask questions about another's interests

B. From the following list of ideas, choose the three general headings. Then group the remaining ideas under those headings.

1. service to society
2. description of career
3. attitudes that are looked for
4. income
5. qualifications
6. personal satisfaction

7. physical and personal qualities
8. rewards of this career
9. opportunities
10. kinds of work involved
11. education/skills that are needed
12. places where such work is done

C. Organize the ideas for your composition. Identify your main ideas. Then group specific, related details underneath them.

Organizing Ideas

Your writing plan is now nearly complete. You have gathered your ideas, identified main ideas, and placed your details in related groups. All that remains is to delete those ideas that are of little importance, add new ideas that would improve your composition, and organize your material into a logical order.

"Logical order" is simply an order that is easy for your readers to follow. As with paragraphs, however, there is no single order that is correct for a composition. Each composition presents an organizational problem of its own. The solution can be reached if you follow a two-step process:

1. Arrange groups of related ideas into logical order
2. Organize the ideas within each group

Now review the different types of organization you might use.

Chronological Order. The simplest and most natural order is *chronological.* This means placing ideas in the order they occurred. This order is often used for narrative compositions or for those explaining a process.

Spatial Order. This type of order is usually used for description. Details are presented in the order a writer wishes the reader to picture a person, place, or object.

Order of Importance. Ideas can also be organized in *order of importance*; that is, from the least important to the most important idea. This order is often used for explanatory compositions that give reasons or persuade. Look at the following example.

The threats

    Loss of wildlife
    Loss of water supplies

The causes

    Accidental seepage of industrial waste
    Accidental collisions of oil tankers
    Deliberate piping of industrial wastes directly into the water

The remedies

    Informal individual and collective action
    Formal national and international legislation

In this example, the writer is concerned about the death of wildlife and the loss of water supplies. The most important ideas that she will present are the remedies for these losses. These ideas come at the end of the writing plan.

Comparison and Contrast. Depending upon the material, audience, and purpose, a writer could also organize ideas using *comparison and contrast*. The writer of the composition on waterfowls, for example, could have described present threatening conditions and contrasted those with more ideal conditions resulting from environmental remedies.

You will recall that the writer of "Time Spent on the Beach" thought that chronological order might be a good order for her composition. She would present the sensory details of the beach in the same order that she became aware of them.

1. Sight Details

    sun setting
    lighthouse lights
    trees in distance

2. Sound Details

    boats unloading
    gulls crying overhead
    waves roaring and beating

3. Touch Details

> wet sand on toes
> fresh air fills lungs
> pet dog and the feel of wet, damp fur

Notice that the writer dropped "sunburn stings" under "Touch Details." Even though it fit logically under this category, the writer decided that including this detail interrupted the mood that she was trying to create. Notice, too, the order of the details *within* the first and second groupings. The writer has chosen to organize these details in spatial order (far to near). She hopes that by doing so she will cause the reader to picture the details in a natural way.

Exercises Organizing Ideas

A. The following exercise gives three lists of ideas that might be used for compositions. Rearrange each of the lists into an order that seems best for each subject. Remember that there is no one correct order for any particular group of ideas.

1. MARKET GARDENING

   selling the products
   selecting seed
   planting
   preparing the soil
   deciding what to plant
   gathering the products
   cultivating
   preparing the products for market

2. TENNIS: A GOOD GAME FOR STUDENTS

   increase in mental alertness
   relaxation from study
   joy of competition
   health
   pleasure
   interaction with others
   improvement in circulatory system

3. AUTOMOBILES SHOULD BE BANNED FROM CITIES

Public transportation is more efficient than the automobile.

The automobile is the major source of air pollution.

Accidents involving pedestrians and automobiles are common.

Automobiles contribute to noise pollution.

Dependence on automobiles hurts everyone.

Automobiles are inefficient for moving large numbers of people.

New freeways remove land from residential, business, and recreational use.

Money spent on new roads and road repairs could be put to better use elsewhere.

The automobile is a nuisance and a health hazard.

Many automobiles carry only one driver.

B. Organize your own groups of ideas. If necessary, rearrange the ideas within each group so that they are presented more effectively.

Part 6 Writing the Rough Draft

As you begin writing the first draft of your composition, a major part of your work is already finished. Your topic has been selected and narrowed, your audience and purpose have been determined, and your ideas have been gathered and organized into a logical pattern.

Now it is time to write your rough draft. Remember that at this point you are simply exploring ideas and approaches. Do not worry about fine-tuning your ideas until you begin to revise.

The Introductory Paragraph

When you made your writing plan, you were working primarily on the middle, or body, of your composition. Because a good composition always contains a beginning, a middle, and an end, you now need to consider the introductory paragraph.

The introductory paragraph of a composition serves two important functions and must, therefore, be written with great care. First, a good introductory paragraph catches the reader's attention. Second, it gives the reader an indication of what the composition is about.

Catching the Reader's Attention. A good writer avoids dull and uninteresting opening statements, such as these:

1. In this paper, I am going to tell you about where I go to find peace.
2. Hang-gliding is an exciting sport.
3. There are three important reasons why automobiles should be banned from our cities.

There is nothing in these sentences to make the reader want to read further. How lacking in interest they are compared with the following paragraphs which are based on the same subjects as the topic sentences above. The first paragraph is the final version of the introduction to "Time Spent on the Beach."

1   As I walk down the beach, I escape from a day filled with interruptions, little cousins, and chaos. Venturing further, I walk on seeking peace.

2   "What am I doing here?" A surge of panic raced through my body as I felt the wind begin to tug at the contraption strapped to my arms. "I could break a leg, an arm. I could be killed!" At that moment, the full pressure of the wind caught at the hang-glider's sail, and I was lifted upward, upward, held aloft only by the rising currents of air.

3   The automobile has got to go! We have reached a point in the growth of our cities where we can no longer allow this primitive mode of transportation to eat up our land, waste natural resources, pollute our atmosphere, and cause so many needless deaths and injuries.

In these introductory paragraphs, not only have the writers given an indication of what their compositions will be about, but they have done so in a way that catches their readers' attention and stimulates curiosity.

Types of Introductory Paragraphs. There are many types of introductory paragraphs. Each provides a different approach to the material that will be presented in the composition. When choosing the approach that will be the most effective, the writer must consider both the subject and the purpose of the composition.

Four types of introductory paragraphs are illustrated by the following examples:

1. THE PARAGRAPH THAT MAKES A DIRECT APPEAL

Have you ever felt embarrassed because you didn't know what to say? If the answer is yes, you're not alone. If you've ever felt tense, timid, or tongue-tied in social situations—or if you've been so frightened that you've gone out of your way to avoid them—you need some advice on how to deal with them.

—ALICE FLEMING

In this type of introductory paragraph, the writer speaks directly to the reader. The subject of the composition is introduced. This approach is particularly effective for involving the reader in your topic.

2. THE PARAGRAPH THAT USES A PERSONAL APPROACH

Halloweens I have always considered wilder and richer and more important than even Christmas morn. The dark and lovely memories leap back at me as I see once again my ghostly relatives, and the lurks and things that creaked stairs or sang softly in the hinges when you opened a door.—RAY BRADBURY

In this type of introductory paragraph, the attitude of the writer toward the subject is immediately apparent. A composition that begins with this approach will probably go on to describe a personal experience and the writer's feelings about the experience.

3. THE PARAGRAPH THAT DESCRIBES AN OVERALL EFFECT

November chills. Raw rain flays the sullen fields and black roofs. Sunlight touches the earth, but shyly. Most mornings are dusted with frost. Storm sashes rattle in the wind. Snow flurries swirl from a lonely sky and whip the flinty earth. It is the time for man-made warmth.—HERB DANIELS

This type of paragraph is effective in "setting the scene" for a composition. It often is used as the opener for a description or for a narrative based on a real or imaginary experience. A writer who uses this approach must be careful to evoke a mood that will be consistent with the content of the composition.

4. THE PARAGRAPH THAT AROUSES CURIOSITY

Suppose there were no critics to tell us how to react to a picture, a play, or a new composition of music. Suppose we wandered innocent as the dawn into an art exhibition of unsigned paintings. By what standards, by what values would we decide whether they were good or bad, talented or untalented, successes or failures?—MARYA MANNES

This type of paragraph invites the reader to find the answer to a question by reading the rest of the composition. It is especially effective for compositions whose purpose is to explain an idea.

Exercises Writing Introductions

A. Read the following opening statements and decide which ones have definite reader appeal. Rewrite those that are lacking in appeal. You may use more than one sentence in your revision.

1. Habits are first cobwebs, then cables.
2. This composition is about learning to ski.
3. My kid sister is a difficult person to live with.
4. Nobody goes to the hardware store for a loaf of bread.
5. I would like to tell you about an interesting trip I took.
6. The first time I met Joe Benton, I thought he was a great guy; now I think he's crazy.
7. When I think of New Orleans, I think of food.
8. My hobby is interesting.
9. Our camping trip turned out to be an exciting experience.
10. My teacher has asked me to write a paper about censorship.

B. Write the introductory paragraph for your own composition. Review it until you are satisfied that it will catch your readers' attention and that it accurately states the subject of the composition.

The Body

The major part of a composition is **the body.** It is in these paragraphs that the ideas indicated in the introductory paragraph are developed or explained.

Remember that the writer of "Time Spent on the Beach" began her composition like this:

> As I walk down the beach, I escape from a day filled with interruptions, little cousins, and chaos. Venturing further, I walk on seeking peace.

The introduction indicates that the writer will describe how her walk on the beach brought her peace.

Working from her writing plan, the writer then composed the following first draft of the body paragraphs. Notice how she more fully developed her original notes. Of course, other changes will still be made later on, as the writing process continues.

SAMPLE FIRST DRAFT

> It is now seven oclock and the sun begins to hide behind the hills. It's rays reflect the heat that beat upon the day. But it is cooler now, and both the sun and I begin "to rest." As it darkens, something that catches my eye is the blinking light of the lighthouse. Up ahead the trees clumped together down the side of the hill stand still like soldiers at ease.
>
> In the distance, sounds of the oar boats loading and unloading their wears in the nearby harbor. Above the squaking of gulls and the flapping of their wings is present. The rush of waves at my feet keeps a constant roar, like a drummer beating out the same notes over and over. These sounds blend into one beautiful, mystical melody.
>
> As I walk on, my toes grip the damp, hard-packed sand. I continue ahead as the fresh air surges into me, giving me a burst of new life. Feeling that I am no longer alone, I turn around to see my dog creeping behind me like a detective searching for clues.

In this rough draft, the writer of "Time Spent on the Beach" expanded and modified some of her original details. This act of "reshaping" is a continuous part of the process as your writing takes a more definite—but still not final—form in your rough draft.

Notice that the body of the composition is divided into three paragraphs, each one developing a different main idea from the writing plan. The first line of each paragraph is also indented. A paragraph indentation signals the reader that a new idea is about to be introduced. Indentations make a composition appealing to the eye of the reader by breaking up the typing or writing on the page.

Achieving Unity and Coherence

In addition to paragraphing, you should also use **transitional devices** to provide signals for your reader. Transitional devices give a composition a feeling of unity and coherence. As your ideas develop in your rough draft, these transitional words and phrases tie them together. There are six basic transitional devices.

1. Using a Word or Phrase That Indicates Time. Such words include the following:

first	before	meanwhile	until
next	after	in the meantime	finally
then	afterwards	eventually	today

The chief servant clapped his hands and a door opened through which there came servants, all with wings on their backs, bearing golden trays laden with meat, fish, pomegranates, and persimmons, pineapples, and peaches. A tall servant with a long white beard carried a golden goblet full of wine. Atzel was so starved that he ate ravenously. The angels hovered around him, filling his plate and goblet even before he had time to ask for more.

When he had finished eating, Atzel declared he wanted to rest. Two angels undressed and bathed him. Then they brought him a nightdress of fine embroidered linen, placed a nightcap with a tassel on his head, and carried him to bed with silken sheets and a purple velvet canopy. Atzel immediately fell into a deep and happy sleep.—ISAAC BASHEVIS SINGER

2. Using a Word That Shows the Relationship Between Ideas. Such words include the following:

also	because	therefore	moreover
too	and	besides	similarly

In the dining room, my father still sat on the floor. His shoulders sagged and he looked up at me with dull, unseeing eyes. Within a single morning, on a perfect June day, my young father had become an old man. Looking down at my father, I deliberately ignored the soldiers and their authority to tell me what I might and might not do—and asked for my father's permission to go to my mother. He nodded and patted my head.

My mother too had changed. Usually she was composed and fastidiously groomed, but now her face was flushed and her beautiful crown of braids was tumbling down . . . .

—ESTHER HAUTZIG

3. Using a Word That Shows an Opposite Point of View. Such words include the following:

but	while	on the other hand	nevertheless
however	although	in contrast	yet

I ordered stock and played records on request, emptied ashtrays and dusted the windows' cardboard displays. Louise and her partner, David Rosenbaum, showed their pleasure by giving me a raise; and although I was grateful to them, I could exhibit my feelings only by being punctual in coming to the shop and being efficient at work and coolly, grayly respectful.

At home, however, life shimmered with beautiful colors. I picked up my son from the baby-sitter's every evening. He was five years old and so beautiful his smile could break the back of a brute.—MAYA ANGELOU

4. Using a Word That Repeats a Word Used Earlier.

Barclay's attitude to the railroad was about the same as toward the modern world in general. He had entered lightheartedly into the whirl and crash and crush, the grand babel of building, the suction and spouting, groaning, and whining and breaking of steel—all the riotous, contagious movement around him.

He had entered into the rough camaraderie of the railroad with all the hot energy of youth. It was a rugged, new experience that kindled his vagabonding mind and body. There was a rude poetry in the roar and rush and rattle of trains, the sharp whistle of engines and racing landscapes, the charm of a desolate mining town and glimpses of faces lost as soon as seen. He had even tried to capture some of those fleeting, piled-up images in writing.—CLAUDE McKAY

5. Using a Synonym for a Word Used Earlier.

Standing in front of the lioness, he shouted something unintelligible in a raucous voice. The fur all over her body seemed to stand up, and she backed away from him apprehensively. Then he began talking to her in a soft, cooing voice. She relaxed at once and came closer to him. As he backed away from her she followed him. Then he barked a command in a sharp voice and although he continued to back away, Mumma stood still, watching him.

Without taking his eyes off the animal, he said to me, "The most important part of controlling an animal is the tone of your voice. Once you can get an animal to react to your tone, you can control it completely."—DAMOO DHOTRE

6. Using a Pronoun That Refers to a Word Used Earlier.

"Let me see now," said Great-grandma. "Let me see..." With no fuss or further ado, she traveled the house in an ever-circling inventory, reached the stairs at last, and took herself up three flights to her room where, silently, she laid herself out under the snowing-cool sheets of her bed and began to die.

—RAY BRADBURY

Exercises Studying and Writing Body Paragraphs

A. Study the following pairs of paragraphs carefully. Identify the transitional device, or devices, that each writer has used to tie together the paragraphs and the ideas within them.

1   After I had returned from India, I entered into a correspondence with Ved, whose letters were surprisingly mature for a boy in his teens. They were clearly the work of a resourceful mind. What impressed me particularly was his supple use of the English language.

I met Ved for the first time in the spring of 1952. He came to our home with his father, then in the United States as a visiting Fulbright professor. There was nothing about Ved that suggested a handicapped person. He used no cane. He had no Seeing Eye dog. He didn't wait for people to lead him from one place to another. Not once did his father take him by the hand. Yet he moved about easily.—NORMAN COUSINS

2   Even though my father was desperately hard pressed during the Great Depression, today I feel less pity for him. I know it was the hard work that kept him going vigorously and happily right up almost to his 85th birthday.

It was hard work, in fact, that hacked a civilization out of a formidable wilderness. A willingness to work, more than any other characteristic, has distinguished every immigrant group— from the Pilgrims and Puritans to the Haitian, Cuban, and Asian refugees. We owe our national success, I say, far more to plain hard work than to good government.—HENRY LEE

3   For seven years there had been too little rain. The prairies were dust. Day after day, summer after summer, the scorching winds blew the dust, and the sun was brassy in a yellow sky. Crop after crop failed. Again and again the barren land must be mortgaged, for taxes and food and next year's seed. The agony of hope ended when there was no harvest and no more credit, no money to pay interest and taxes. The banker took the land. Then the bank failed.

In the seventh year a mysterious catastrophe was worldwide. All banks failed. From coast to coast the factories shut down, and business ceased. This was a Panic.

—LAURA INGALLS WILDER

4   Marget was my first love. I met her when she joined our sixth-grade class.

She stood before the class, her blue, frightened eyes sweeping back and forth across the room until they came to rest on my face. From that very first day we became friends—Marget, just fresh from Sweden, and I, a sixth generation American.

—CARRIE A. YOUNG

5   The heat pressed down on me, as if suddenly in league with gravity. My pack sagged. And then all at once, a thread of clear water was sparkling on bare rock. I walked up beside it with light and springing step. The thread broadened. Half a mile, and I camped in the shade of some green creekside bushes. Soon I was stretched out cool and naked on my sleeping bag.

The little creek, still less than a foot wide, bubbled and babbled past so close that I could reach out whenever I wanted to and scoop up a cupful of cool drinking water. All I could see was green foliage and a hint of glaring rock beyond. That, and the sparkling creek and the oddly humped, blue-gray rock over which it flowed.—COLIN FLETCHER

6   I was about ten feet in front of Kitty as we got near the corner. The thing about Kitty is that you have to beat her to the corners if you're going to win a bicycle race that she's in. She always slowed down more than most people when she got to the corners, but she made up for it when she got on the straight runs. The only people on the block that she couldn't beat were Kwami and me, but she was getting pretty close to me, too. Anyway, I was just about ten feet in front of her when we hit the corner. I reached down and switched into fifth gear and leaned into that corner perfectly and was just about ready to straighten out and really do it to the finish line when I saw this lady named Drusilla.

Well, I saw her and then again I didn't see her. That is, I didn't see her in time. All of a sudden she popped up from between two parked cars, and I jerked my handlebars so I wouldn't hit her. I think I shouted "Watch out!" or something like that, too. When I jerked the handlebars, the bike started skidding and went right at her. I went over the handlebars and smack into the middle of the street. I hit so hard I thought I was going to pass out. I actually bounced on the pavement!

—WALTER DEAN MYERS

7   Ollie spent the early afternoon sitting on the rail in front of The Chicken Shack Restaurant, watching the cooks sling the wire baskets of chicken in and out of the frying fat. They were too sweaty and tired to tell her to move from in front. "Ruining the business," the owner used to fuss.

Later she stood between the laundry and shoe store, watching some men pitch pennies against the building. She waited for a while, squeezing a rubber ball in her hand. If I can just get the wall for a minute, she thought, maybe somebody'll come along and we'll have us a good game of handball. But the men went right on pitching while other ones were waiting their turn. They'd be there for hours, so Ollie left.—TONI CADE BAMBARA

B. Write the first draft for the body of your composition. Use your writing plan to guide you. Keep in mind appropriate transitional devices that will help tie your ideas together. Also remember that additions and changes are still likely at this time, and usually desirable.

The Conclusion

After you have finished the draft of the body of your composition, you are ready to write the **conclusion**. The concluding paragraph ties all the ideas together and indicates to the reader that the composition is finished.

The writer of "Time Spent on the Beach" wrote this concluding paragraph:

> Calm now, I turn back, for the sun is hidden from sight. My walk has not only allowed me to escape for a short time but it has also renewed me for my return to reality.

You will notice that the conclusion *repeats* some of the ideas from the introductory paragraph. This is one method that can be used to create a strong conclusion.

Another effective way to end a composition is to *summarize* or *comment upon* your story or opinion in a short, concluding statement. This was the approach used by the writer who ended her composition in this manner:

Whether accidental or deliberate, environmental pollution is a dangerous threat to both our wildlife and our water supplies. Individuals and governments cannot stand idly by; they must present a unified front in order to remedy this problem.

The following is another effective ending. This writer ended with some appropriate lines of poetry that indicate "the end."

Had it been worth struggling out of bed at 4:30 a.m. to go hiking after a view? I had to think it was. I could always take a nap later in the afternoon, but there would have been no way to make up the fresh, golden beauty I had seen. Robert Frost's words kept running through my mind as I headed for home.

"So dawn goes down to day.
Nothing gold can stay."

Exercises   Finishing Your Composition

A. Write the concluding paragraph for your composition.

B. Decide on a title for your composition. You can take the title from your pre-writing notes, or write a new one.

Part 7   Revising the Composition

You now have a complete draft of your composition, but you are not finished. Revision is the "fine tuning" stage. You have actually been revising throughout the writing process. You reworked your pre-writing notes, rethought approaches, and considered and rejected different methods of organization. As you wrote your rough draft, you probably found yourself scratching out words and ideas and inserting others. Now, nothing must escape your attention. Your concern with ideas, word choice, unity, coherence, and style must be precise.

To avoid becoming careless or overwhelmed, go through your rough draft several times. Focus your attention on just one or two areas at a time. You may need to make several drafts. Correcting problems in this manner should aid your concentration.

My Escape from Reality

~~Time Spent on the Beach~~

As I walk down the beach, I ~~leave behind~~ escape from a day filled with

interruptions, little cousins, and chaos. ~~As I~~ venture_ing fur-

ther, I ~~am looking for~~ walk on, seeking peace.

It is now seven o'clock and the sun, like a shy child, begins to hide behind

the hills. It's rays reflect the ^or bold yellow, red, and orange heat that beat upon the day.

But it is cooler now, and ~~both the sun and~~ I begin "to rest." like the sun,

As ~~it~~ the sky darkens, something ~~that~~ catches my eye, a man-made star, ~~is the~~ blinking twinkling,

light of the lighthouse. Up ahead, the trees, clumped to-

gether down the side of the hill, stand, as still, as ~~like~~ soldiers at

~~ease.~~ attention

In the distance, ^the muffled sounds of the oar boats loading and un-

loading their ~~wears~~ wares in the nearby harbor. Above, me, I hear the gulls the ~~squak-~~

~~ing of gulls~~ squawking and ~~the flapping of their wings is present.~~ The

rush of waves at my feet ~~keeps a constant roar, like a drum-~~

mer beating, out the same notes over and over. All These sounds

blend into one beautiful, soothing mystical melody.

As I walk on, my toes grip the damp, hard-packed sand.

I continue ahead, and ~~as~~ the fresh air surges into me, giving me

a burst of new life. ~~Feeling~~ Sensing that I am no longer alone, I turn

around to see my dog creeping behind me like a detective

searching for clues. It almost seems as if he's been sent from the "real world" to find me and bring me back.

My walk has not only allowed me to escape ~~from reality~~ for a short

time. Calm now, I ~~must~~ turn back, for the sun is hidden from

sight. My "escape" has also renewed me for my return to reality. but it

Analysis of the Revision

1. Vivid, specific modifiers, such as "bold yellow, red, and orange" have been added. Adjectives such as these enliven descriptions by giving the reader a sense of immediacy and sharing in the experience. One strength of this composition is its many fresh, well-chosen comparisons.

2. Coherence has been strengthened. For example, the revised composition includes an additional sentence at the end of the fourth paragraph. This new sentence creates a link between the fourth paragraph and the conclusion.

3. Unity is strengthened by changing the title of the composition and revising the introduction. The word "escape" is now used in the title, introduction, and conclusion.

4. Sentence variety has been improved. In her first draft, the writer began both sentences in the introduction with "As." The beginning of the second sentence was changed in revision. Because she used several comparisons, the writer also overused the word "like."

5. Many errors in grammar and mechanics were spotted.

Proofreading

In the distance, there are the muffled sounds of the ore boats loading and unloading their wares in the nearby harbor. Above me, I hear the gulls squawking and flapping their wings. At my feet, the rush of waves beats out the same notes over and over. All these sounds blend into one beautiful, soothing, mystical melody.

You will catch many errors in grammar, capitalization, punctuation, and spelling during revision. However, you still need to proofread your paper a final time. The preceding paragraph shows errors found during this final check. When you are satisfied with your composition, make a final neat copy.

Now read the final version of "My Escape from Reality."

MY ESCAPE FROM REALITY

As I walk down the beach, I escape from a day filled with interruptions, little cousins, and chaos. Venturing further, I walk on seeking peace.

It is now seven o'clock, and the sun, like a shy child, begins to hide behind the hills. Its bold yellow, red, and orange rays reflect the heat that beat upon the day. But it is cooler now, and, like the sun, I begin to "rest." As the sky darkens, a man-made star, the twinkling, blinking light from the lighthouse, catches my eye. Up ahead, the trees, clumped together down the side of the hill, stand as still as soldiers at attention.

In the distance, there are the muffled sounds of the ore boats loading and unloading their wares in a nearby harbor. Above me, I hear the gulls squawking and flapping their wings. At my feet, the rush of waves beats out the same notes over and over. All these sounds blend into one beautiful, soothing, mystical melody.

As I walk, my toes grip the damp, hard-packed sand. I continue ahead, and the fresh air surges into me, giving me a burst of new life. Sensing that I am no longer alone, I turn around to see my dog creeping up behind me like a detective searching for clues. It almost seems as if he's been sent from the "real world" to find me and bring me back.

Calm now, I turn back, for the sun is hidden from sight. My walk has not only allowed me to escape for a short time, but it has also renewed me for my return to reality.

Exercise Completing Your Composition

Revise your rough draft. When you are satisfied with the content, proofread your material. Then make a clean, final copy.

Guidelines for Writing and Revising Compositions

As you write a composition, follow the steps in Guidelines for the Process of Writing on page 123. Use the following Guidelines after you have written your first draft.

1. Has the subject been narrowed to a topic that can be covered in a few paragraphs?

2. Does the composition deal with a single topic or idea?

3. Does it have an introduction, a body, and a conclusion?

4. Does the introduction present the main idea? Does it catch the reader's interest?

5. Does the body explain or support the main idea?

6. Does the conclusion restate the main idea, summarize the information, or comment upon it?

7. Do the paragraphs work together to develop a single topic or idea that is the subject of the composition?

8. Is the composition appropriate for the audience for which it is intended? Is the purpose clear?

9. Are the ideas presented in a clear, logical order?

10. Does the composition have unity? Are the supporting ideas in each paragraph related to the topic sentence? Is each paragraph directly related to the main idea in the introductory paragraph?

11. Does the composition have coherence? Are there transitional devices that tie the paragraphs together?

12. Is the title meaningful and interesting?

Additional Guidelines

If it is a narrative composition, are the events told in the order in which they happened?

If it is a descriptive composition, does it use specific sensory details to paint a word-picture? Are the sight details presented in spatial order?

If it is an explanatory composition, does it explain how something is done or why something is believed to be so? If the composition gives instructions, are the steps organized in chronological order? In a composition that supports an idea with reasons, are the reasons organized logically? Are the reasons convincing?

SUMMARY AND APPLICATIONS

1. A composition is a group of paragraphs that develops a single idea.

2. A composition has three main parts. The introductory paragraph of a composition tells what the composition will be about. The body paragraphs develop this idea. The final paragraph, or conclusion, summarizes the information or comments on it. It also signals that the composition is finished.

3. Narrow the subject of the composition to an idea that can be covered within the specified limits of the paper.

4. Organize information for a composition by taking notes, identifying main ideas, grouping details under these main ideas, and putting the material in logical order.

5. As you write rough drafts, remember that change and new ideas are expected, even desirable, at this point.

6. Revise for content, unity, and coherence. Proofread your material when the content changes are complete.

7. Follow these steps when you write compositions for all subjects and purposes.

Applications in Other Subject Areas

Mass Media. Articles in magazines can be viewed as expanded compositions. Look at an article from a publication such as *Time* or *Newsweek*. Identify the introductory paragraph, or paragraphs. Look for topic sentences and supporting ideas. Notice how the articles were concluded. Bring your article to class for discussion.

Speech. A speech could be considered an "oral composition." For example, it contains all of the same main parts: an introduction, a body, and a conclusion. In what other ways are the two types of communication similar? How are they different? What problems are encountered in one and not the other?

Chapter 10

Types of Compositions

If you were asked to put some music on a stereo, your reply would probably be "What kind?" The term *music* is much too general to be used without further clarification. Similarly, if you were about to read or write a composition, your first thought would be "What kind of composition?" You would want to know what purpose the composition had or what kind of subject matter it involved.

In Chapter 8, you became familiar with the four main types of paragraphs—narrative, descriptive, expository, and persuasive. Each had its own particular purpose and characteristics. In this chapter, you will apply your knowledge of these paragraphs to writing different types of compositions. You will also gain further practice in the development of effective compositions.

Part 1 The Narrative Composition

The narrative paragraph relates something that happened; in other words, it tells a story. The narrative composition does the same thing. A narrative can be a work of fiction, such as a short story or novel, or it can be a work of nonfiction, such as a newspaper article, a biography, or a journal.

There are two main types of narrative compositions: the **simple narrative** and the **complex narrative.** As its name implies, the complex narrative is longer and more complicated than the simple narrative. Both, however, contain the same basic elements of character, setting, conflict, and theme.

The Elements of a Narrative

The **characters** are the people (or animals) in the story. Those who are active in the narrative, and upon whose actions or experiences the story depends, are the *major characters.* Those whose actions are less significant are the *minor characters.* Because of its short length and simple structure, a simple narrative will often have only one or two characters. On the other hand, a complex narrative will often have several characters, both major and minor.

There are a number of ways of describing characters in a narrative. The writer can simply present detailed descriptions of the characters, telling the reader outright what is important to know about the character. The writer can also choose more subtle methods, such as showing actions that are characteristic of the person or telling what the person is thinking. Finally, the writer can reveal the character through dialogue.

The **setting** is the place where the events in a narrative happen. Setting includes the time frame of the story and the conditions under which the events occur. In some narratives, the setting is a key element, having an impact on both the characters and the events. In other narratives the setting plays a minor role and is only a background for the action of the narrative.

Conflict is the struggle or problem that is central to the narrative. Conflict usually is brought about because of something the character, or characters, want. There are four basic types of conflict.

Types of Conflict

THE INDIVIDUAL AGAINST A SUPERNATURAL FORCE: the struggle against God or the gods (as in ancient myths and legends). Also the struggle against the devil or evil forces.

THE INDIVIDUAL AGAINST NATURE: the struggle to survive natural catastrophes, such as floods, earthquakes, and hurricanes. This type of conflict would also include the struggle between human beings and any members of the animal or plant world.

THE INDIVIDUAL AGAINST SOCIETY: the struggle against social forces, such as injustice, prejudice, and loss of individual freedom. It also includes the struggle of one individual against another.

THE INDIVIDUAL AGAINST HIMSELF: the struggle within the mind or conscience of an individual as he or she attempts to make a personal decision.

The **theme** is the central idea of the narrative. It is the dominant impression or idea that the writer wants to convey to the readers. Through the theme, a writer can share ideas, moods, morals, or philosophy.

The Simple Narrative: Pre-Writing

A simple narrative takes a reader through an event from its beginning to its conclusion. It is, in a way, similar to the type of story you would tell a friend in conversation, the type of story that begins "Let me tell you about something that happened the other day."

A simple narrative requires the same pre-writing steps as any composition. For example, you must select a topic, determine your purpose, and identify your audience. However, some of the pre-writing considerations are unique to this type of composition.

Selecting a Subject. The topic for a simple narrative need not be a spectacular event such as a narrow escape or a last-minute rescue. Ordinary events can make good topics, too. Your experiences at a football rally, at a county fair, or on a surfboard are all topics that can be turned into enjoyable stories. Just be sure that the story has a high interest level or some special significance that you can communicate to a reader.

Choosing a Point of View. Every narrative composition, whether it is a simple narrative or a complex narrative, has a narrator through whose eyes the story is told. The writer of the composition can choose to have the narrative relate events either in the first person or in the third person.

In the **first person** type of narrative, the narrator can be either an observer of the action or a participant in it. In either case, the description of events is limited to what the narrator can know and see at any one time. The description of thoughts and feelings is limited to those of the narrator only. He or she does not have access to, and therefore cannot relate, the thoughts and feelings of the other characters.

Following are two sentences written in the first person. In the first, the narrator is an observer of the action. In the second, she is a participant.

1. Looking through the bars of the fire escape, I saw a German shepherd pawing through the garbage piled next to the building.
2. With great effort, I summoned the last of my depleted strength and jumped the final hurdle.

In the **third person** type of narration, the narrator functions in one of three ways. He or she may "see" and describe all the externally observable events, even those that take place at the same time. The narrator may not, however, describe what is going on in the minds of the characters.

A second kind of third-person narrator relates events through the eyes of one character. He or she has access only to the thoughts and feelings of that character and to the events observed by the character.

A third kind of narrator is omniscient. He or she knows everything, including what goes on in the minds of all the characters.

Following are three sentences written in the third person. In the first, the narrator describes external events only. In the second, the narrator describes the thoughts of one character. In the third, the narrator reveals the thoughts of two characters.

1. Raul pushed aside the heavy blue drape and entered the dimly lit room.
2. Henry hesitated for a moment, reluctant to commit himself to such drastic action.
3. Robin and Eric examined the arrowhead carefully, each anticipating the fine addition it would make to his collection.

Determining Characters, Setting, and Conflict. If a narrative is to have impact on the reader, the characters and setting must seem very real to the reader. If there is a conflict, it must be clearly defined. Before you begin to write, therefore, ask yourself questions such as the following:

FOR CHARACTER: Who are my characters?
What do they look like?
What do they do? What do they want?
How do they feel about themselves and their situation?

FOR SETTING: Where does the story take place?
What does the area look like?
What is the time frame of the story?

FOR CONFLICT: What problem or situation must the characters work through?
Which of the four types of conflict am I dealing with?
Is the conflict serious or humorous?

Once these aspects of the story are clear to you, begin selecting details that will enable you to make each element just as clear to your reader.

Selecting a Tone and Mood. You remember that the **tone** of a piece of writing is the attitude that the writer (or narrator) takes toward the subject. The tone may be serious, critical, amused, sentimental, or angry, for example. The mood is the atmosphere or feeling that the reader experiences as he or she reads. A writer may create a mood of terror, tranquility, celebration, or confusion.

Unless both tone and mood are clear in the mind of the writer, the resulting story may be a confusing blend of attitudes and emotions. As you work on your pre-writing notes, make some definite decisions concerning each of these elements. Then keep in mind the tone and mood you have selected as you choose the details and descriptive words for your story.

The Simple Narrative: First Draft

As you compose the first draft of a narrative, refer to your pre-writing notes in order to remember the decisions you made. Also keep the following characteristics of a well-written narrative in mind:

Unity in the narrative means sticking to the story. Each event should in some way contribute to the unfolding of the story.

Unity is enhanced by transitional devices that tie together the paragraphs and the ideas within the paragraphs. In the simple narrative, unity is also enhanced by structure. The main idea is given in the introductory paragraph and each paragraph that follows explains or supports that idea.

Coherence in the narrative is the relation of one event to another and the order in which these events are described. In most narrative compositions, events are related in chronological order.

Emphasis is the means by which your central idea is communicated to your reader. In the pre-writing stage, you made a decision about the ideas, moods, messages, or events you want to communicate to your reader. As you write your first draft, you stress those details that are important to the main idea, and focus less strongly on the others.

Remember that a first draft is simply your first attempt at getting your story down on paper. You can strengthen any element of the story as you revise.

The Simple Narrative: Revising

As was pointed out earlier, a narrative cannot be effective unless the story seems real to the reader. This means that word choice must be carefully thought out so that the reader has a strong impression of the setting, each character, and every action in the story. As you revise, make sure each sentence presents its idea as vividly as possible. Use concrete nouns, precise modifiers, and lively verbs.

The other characteristics of a good narrative must also be considered as you revise. Strengthen unity, coherence, and emphasis. Make sure, too, that the elements of tone, mood, and point of view are consistent.

Now read the following example of a simple narrative:

SILENT SONG

I'll tell you a story about birds. This happened near the sea, in Puerto Saavedra, Imperial del Sur. On Lake Budi some years ago, they were hunting down the swans without mercy. The procedure was to approach them stealthily in little boats and then rapidly—very rapidly— row into their midst. Swans, like albatrosses, have difficulty in flying; they must skim the surface of the water at a run. In the first phase of their flight they raise their big wings with great effort. It is then that they can be seized; a few blows with a bludgeon finish them off.

Someone made me a present of a swan: more dead than alive. It was of a marvelous species I have never seen anywhere else in the world: a black-throated swan—a snow boat with a neck packed, as it were, into a tight stocking of black silk. Orange-beaked, red-eyed.

They brought it to me half-dead. I bathed its wounds and pressed little pellets of bread and fish into its throat; but nothing stayed down. Nevertheless, the wounds slowly healed, and the swan came to regard me as a friend. At the same time, it was apparent to me that the bird was wasting away with nostalgia. So, cradling the heavy burden in my arms through the streets, I carried it down to the river. It paddled a few strokes, very close to me. I had hoped it might learn how to fish for itself, and pointed to some pebbles far below, where they flashed in the sand like the silvery fish of the South. The swan looked at them remotely, sad-eyed.

For the next twenty days or more, day after day, I carried the bird to the river and toiled back with it to my house. It was almost as large as I was. One afternoon it seemed more abstracted than usual, swimming very close and ignoring the lure of the insects with which I tried vainly to tempt it to fish again. It became very quiet; so I lifted it into my arms to carry it home again. It was breast high, when I suddenly felt a great ribbon unfurl, like a black arm encircling my face: it was the big coil of the neck, dropping down.

It was then that I learned swans do not sing at their death, if they die of grief.—PABLO NERUDA

Analysis. In this composition, the writer tells the story of his experience with an injured swan. He and the swan are the only characters in the story. The setting is a lake by the sea "some years ago." The story is told from the first-person point of view.

The conflict in the story is that of the individual against nature. In this case, however, it is nature that suffers from the contact. The theme centers on the tragedy of the death of a spirit—the swan's, and perhaps a person's.

Both the tone and the mood the author brings to these ideas are those of sadness and grief. These feelings are reflected in the sorrowful atmosphere of the story. All of these emotions are emphasized by phrases such as "without mercy," "more dead than alive," "wasting away," "heavy burden," and "remotely, sad-eyed."

The writer achieves unity by describing only the events that relate to the main idea of the composition. He does not stray from the main idea by describing the lake, his home, or any actions unrelated to the experience with the swan.

The writer achieves coherence by organizing the narrative in chronological order. He describes what happened in the order that it happened.

The writer achieves emphasis by the skillful selection and arrangement of details. The emphasis throughout is on the writer's thoughts, feelings, and actions during his futile attempts to save the swan. All the other details are included because they have some direct or indirect relationship to these thoughts and feelings. The writer has grouped all the details around the central idea of the composition—the tragedy of the swan's death. In the first paragraph, he describes the swan hunting that resulted in his caring for the injured swan. In the second paragraph, he provides a vivid description of the bird. In the third and fourth paragraphs, he tells of his actions to save the swan and of the uselessness of physical help in the presence of the death of the swan's spirit. This is the theme, or central idea of the composition. In the final paragraph, the writer tells what he brought with him from the experience.

Exercise Writing a Simple Narrative

Check your writing journal for possible subjects for a narrative composition. They can be based on events in which you participated, on events that you observed, or on events that someone described to you. They can be based on fact, on imagination, or on a combination of both.

After you have listed several possible subjects, complete the following steps:

Pre-Writing: Select and narrow your topic. Then answer the following questions: Who are the characters in your narrative? What is the setting? What is the central idea or theme that you want to convey? What tone and mood will you want your story to demonstrate? What point of view will you use?

First Draft: Write your story as though you were telling it to a friend. Keep unity, coherence, and emphasis in mind.

Revision: Look at your work critically. Does your opening paragraph catch the reader's attention? Does your setting help create the desired mood? Did you give the appropriate details to develop life-like characters and a vivid setting? Is the story told consistently from the same point of view? Is the order logical and easy to follow? Should you add more details or delete some events to create a stronger impression or clearer conflicts? Does your writing have unity and coherence?

The Complex Narrative or Short Story

The **complex narrative,** or short story, contains the same basic elements of character, setting, and conflict as the simple narrative. In the complex narrative, however, these elements are developed with much greater detail.

A more significant difference between the simple and the complex narrative lies in their structures. In the simple narrative, the writer describes events that lead to a conclusion, achieved in the final paragraphs. In the complex narrative, the writer builds to a climax, the turning point or high point of the story. Usually, the climax takes place close to the end of the story. The events that follow the climax resolve the conflict.

In addition to a unique structure, most short stories have the following five identifiable characteristics:

1. An immediate introduction to the setting, the major characters, and the beginnings of the conflict.
2. A tight structure in which every detail is significant.
3. A structure in which the end is enfolded in the beginning.
4. A title whose meaning often does not become clear until the end of the story.
5. Dialogue, or conversation, that gives a feeling of believability to a story and that brings the characters to life. Effective dialogue uses language that suits the person represented; in other words, the character must speak as his or her real-life counterpart would.

Now read this example of a complex narrative.

LATHER AND NOTHING ELSE

He came in without a word. I was stropping my best razor. And when I recognized him, I started to shake. But he did not notice. To cover my nervousness, I went on honing the razor. I tried the edge with the tip of my thumb and took another look at it against the light.

Meanwhile, he was taking off his cartridge-studded belt with the pistol holster suspended from it. He put it on a hook in the wardrobe and hung his cap above it. Then he turned full around toward me and, loosening his tie, remarked, "It's hot as the devil. I want a shave." With that he took his seat.

I estimated he had a four-days' growth of beard, the four days he had been gone on the last foray after our men. His face looked burnt, tanned by the sun.

I started to work carefully on the shaving soap. I scraped some slices from the cake, dropped them into the mug, then added a little lukewarm water, and stirred with the brush. The lather soon began to rise.

"The fellows in the troop must have just about as much beard as I." I went on stirring up lather.

"But we did very well, you know. We caught the leaders. Some of them we brought back dead; others are still alive. But they'll all be dead soon."

"How many did you take?" I asked.

"Fourteen. We had to go pretty far in to find them. But now they're paying for it. And not one will escape; not a single one."

He leaned back in the chair when he saw the brush in my hand, full of lather. I had not yet put the sheet on him. I was certainly flustered. Taking a sheet from the drawer. I tied it around my customer's neck.

He went on talking. He evidently took it for granted that I was on the side of the existing regime.

"The people must have gotten a scare with what happened the other day," he said.

"Yes," I replied, as I finished tying the knot against his nape, which smelled of sweat.

"Good show, wasn't it?"

"Very good," I answered, turning my attention now to the brush. The man closed his eyes wearily and awaited the cool caress of the lather.

I had never had him so close before. The day he ordered the people to file through the schoolyard to look upon the four rebels hanging there, my path had crossed his briefly. But the sight of those mutilated bodies kept me from paying attention to the face of the man who had been directing it all and whom I now had in my hands.

It was not a disagreeable face, certainly. And the beard, which aged him a bit, was not unbecoming. His name was Torres. Captain Torres.

I started to lay on the first coat of lather. He kept his eyes closed.

"I would love to catch a nap," he said, "but there's a lot to be done this evening."

I lifted the brush and asked, with pretended indifference: "A firing party?"

"Something of the sort," he replied, "But slower."

"All of them?"

"No, just a few."

I went on lathering his face. My hands began to tremble again. The man could not be aware of this, which was lucky for me. But I wished he had not come in. Probably many of our men had seen him enter the shop. And with the enemy in my house I felt a certain responsibility.

I would have to shave his beard just like any other, carefully, neatly, just as though he were a good customer, taking heed that not a single pore should emit a drop of blood. Seeing to it that the blade did not slip in the small whorls. Taking care that the skin was left clean, soft, shining, so that when I passed the back of my hand over it not a single hair should be felt. Yes. I was secretly a revolutionary, but at the same time I was a conscientious barber, proud of the way I did my job. And that four-day beard presented a challenge...

The man, who had kept his eyes closed, now opened them, put a hand out from under the sheet, felt of the part of his face that was emerging from the lather, and said to me, "Come at six o'clock this evening to the school."

"Will it be like the other day?" I asked, stiff with horror.

"It may be even better," he replied.

Once more he leaned back and shut his eyes. I came closer, the razor on high.

"Are you going to punish all of them?" I timidly ventured.

"Yes, all of them."

The lather was drying on his face. I must hurry. Through the mirror, I took a look at the street. It appeared about as usual; there was the grocery shop with two or three customers. Then I glanced at the clock, two-thirty.

The razor kept descending. Now from the other sideburn downward. It was a blue beard, a thick one. He should let it grow like some poets, or some priests. It would suit him well. Many people would not recognize him. And that would be a good thing for him, I thought, as I went gently over all the throat line. At this point you really had to handle your blade skillfully, because the hair while scantier, tended to fall into small whorls. It was a curly beard. The pores might open, minutely, in this area and let out a tiny drop of blood. A good barber like myself stakes his reputation on not permitting that to happen to any of his customers.

And this was indeed a special customer. How many of ours had he sent to their death? How many had he mutilated? It was best not to think about. Torres did not know I was his enemy. Neither he nor the others knew it. It was a secret shared by very few, just because that made it possible for me to inform the revolutionaries about Torres's activities in the town and what he planned to do every time he went on one of his raids to hunt down rebels.

His beard had now almost entirely disappeared. He looked younger, several years younger than when he had come in. I suppose that always happens to men who enter and leave barbershops. Under the strokes of my razor, Torres was rejuvenated; yes, because I am a good barber, the best in this town, and I say this in all modesty.

A little more lather here under the chin, on the Adam's apple, right near the great vein. How hot it is! Torres must be sweating just as I am. But he is not afraid. He is a tranquil man, who is not even giving thought to what he will do to his prisoners this evening. I, on the other hand, polishing his skin with this razor but avoiding the drawing of blood, careful with every stroke—I cannot keep my thoughts in order.

Confound the hour he entered my shop! I am a revolutionary but not a murderer. And it would be so easy to kill him. He deserves it. Or does he? No! No one deserves the sacrifice others make in becoming assassins. What is to be gained by it? Nothing. Others and still others keep coming, and the first kill the second, and then these kill the next, and so on until everything becomes a sea of blood. I could cut his throat, so, swish,

swish! He would not even have time to moan.

But I'm shaking like a regular murderer. From his throat a stream of blood would flow on the sheet, over the chair, down on my hands, onto the floor. I would have to close the door. But the blood would go flowing, along the floor, warm, indelible, until it reached the street like a small scarlet river.

I'm sure that with a good strong blow, a deep cut, he would feel no pain. He would not suffer at all. And what would I do then with the body? Where would I hide it? I would have to flee, leave all this behind, take shelter far away, very far away. But they would follow until they caught up with me. "The murderer of Captain Torres. He slit his throat while he was shaving him. What a cowardly thing to do."

And others would say, "The avenger of our people. A name to remember"—my name here. "He was the town barber. No one knew he was fighting for our cause."

And so, which will it be? Murderer or hero? My fate hangs on the edge of this razor blade. I can turn my wrist slightly, put a bit more pressure on the blade, let it sink in. The skin will yield like silk, like rubber, like the strop. There is nothing more tender than a man's skin, and the blood is always there, ready to burst forth. A razor like this cannot fail.

But I don't want to be a murderer. No, sir. You came in to be shaved. And I do my work honorably. I don't want to stain my hands with blood. Just with lather, and nothing else. You are an executioner; I am only a barber. Each one to his job. That's it. Each one to his job.

The chin was now clean, polished, soft. The man got up and looked at himself in the glass. He ran his hand over the skin and felt its freshness, its newness.

"Thanks," he said. He walked to the wardrobe for his belt, his pistol, and his cap. I must have been very pale, and I felt my shirt soaked with sweat. From his trousers pocket Torres took some coins to pay for the shave. And he started toward the door. On the threshold he stopped for a moment, and turning toward me he said,

"They told me you would kill me. I came to find out if it was true. But it's not easy to kill. I know what I'm talking about."

—HERNANDO TELLEZ

Exercises | Understanding the Complex Narrative

A. Answer the following questions about "Lather and Nothing Else." Save your answers for use in Part 5 of this chapter.

1. Who are the main characters of this story? What are they like? What details support your opinion?
2. What is the setting of the story? the point of view?
3. What is the main conflict in the story? How is it resolved?
4. How is unity achieved in this story? What lends coherence to the flow of events? How is the main idea emphasized?
5. What would you say the theme, or message, of the story is? Find evidence in the story to support your answer.

B. Following the steps described in the exercise for writing a simple narrative, compose a short story. Remember, however, to develop your characters, plot, setting, and conflict more thoroughly and to include the characteristics shown on page 221.

Part 2 The Descriptive Composition

Description is generally used in conjunction with other types of writing. There are instances, though, when writers have been so strongly moved by a place, a scene, or a person that they communicate their feelings in a descriptive composition.

As you saw when you studied the narrative composition, the process of writing must be adapted to suit different types of writing. Now you will use the process in a descriptive composition.

Pre-Writing

When you write a descriptive composition, follow all of the usual pre-writing steps of selecting a topic, identifying your purpose and audience, and gathering and organizing details. Refer to Part 2 on the descriptive paragraph in Chapter 8 to remind you of some of the pre-writing options you have for this type of composition. Then study the material that follows, which mentions some special pre-writing considerations.

Point of View and Organization. In the narrative composition, point of view refers to the way that the narrator tells the story. In the descriptive composition, point of view refers to the physical place from which the writer views the object of description.

The details in a descriptive composition, as in a descriptive paragraph, must be grouped in some way and then arranged in a logical order. Possible orders include spatial order, chronological order, and any number of original orders conceived and carried out by the writer.

No matter what organizational pattern you choose to follow, however, you must make sure it reflects a specific physical point of view. You must choose a position from which to view the object or scene that is the subject of your composition, and keep this point of view consistent.

By selecting a specific point of view, you narrow your subsequent choice of details to those that can be sensed from that given point. For example, if you decide to describe a traffic jam from the top of a tall building, you will include only those things that can be heard, seen, touched, tasted, and smelled from that vantage point. If you decide to place yourself in the midst of the traffic jam, your choice of details will be entirely different.

Mood. The mood of a descriptive composition often depends on the mood a writer was in as he or she viewed a scene. Suppose you are looking down at a city street. The sky is dark. Heavy, black clouds are moving in from the west. The wind is blustery, and thunder rumbles in the distance. You may feel depressed, melancholy. This is the mood that will be reflected in your description of the scene. To achieve this mood, you would use words such as *dismal, oppressive, dreary,* or *cold.*

On the other hand, suppose the sight of an oncoming thunderstorm fills you with excitement. The details of the scene would remain the same, but your description of them would change. Now you would use words such as *powerful, brisk*, and *electric* to create an entirely different mood.

First Draft

As you write your first draft, experiment with word choice and the presentation of ideas, and details. During this process, however, use the following information to guide the types of decisions you make.

Unity. The purpose of the descriptive composition is to create a single, unified impression in the mind of the reader. You achieve this by maintaining a definite point of view. You include only those details that contribute to the desired impression. You make sure that each sentence relates to the topic sentence of the paragraph and that each paragraph relates to the introductory paragraph.

Because it strengthens the impression in the mind of the reader, precise language reinforces the unity of a descriptive composition. The writer creates precise language in three main ways.

1. By using strong verbs; for example, *grabbed* instead of *took* and *marched* instead of *walked*.
2. By using specific nouns; for example, *collie* instead of *dog* and *daisy* instead of *flower*.
3. By using adjectives, adverbs, and prepositional phrases; for example, *the sprightly old woman* instead of *the woman*, tumbled *head-over-heels* instead of *tumbled*, and *slept quietly under the cherry tree* instead of *slept*.

Coherence. Coherence, or clarity, in description is achieved through the logical arrangement of ideas. The logical orders specific to description were discussed previously in the section on point of view, and in Chapter 8.

The Artistic Description, or Personal Essay

There are two types of descriptive compositions: practical and artistic. The practical description appeals to the intellect. It is an objective description that holds strictly to external details and facts. You might see this type of description in an encyclopedia article, a travel brochure, or an academic report. The artistic description, on the other hand, uses description to appeal to the emotion, and to the imagination. It is a type of **essay**—a short composition in which the writer expresses some sort of opinion or personal view. In contrast to the description, the artistic description is primarily subjective. Therefore, the mood the writer creates is very important.

Read the following artistic description.

WINTER HAPPENING

Once in the year there comes *the snow*. There are all manners of snow, both cruel and kind, but there is one snow that people think of as *the snow*. It is the symbol of all snows, the childhood miracle that remains forever an image larger than all the bitter snows that come before and after.

The snow falls slowly in soft clusters like fairy snowballs. The clusters are so slow, so far apart that children can stand and catch them on their tongues. The snow clings where it falls, pure as wool blankets. The thistles become flowers. The wild carrot blooms again. Everything is unbelievably still.

The snow falls to the proper depth, to the exact moment when all ugliness is covered, to the weight that the twig and branch can bear without breaking. It knows precisely when to stop. All night *the snow* remains motionless unless a twig is shaken by an owl or a weasel. It hardens a little with a light crust, to bear the weight of the wild things walking in the night.

The morning comes slowly and begins with a gray whiteness. The ground is stitched with tiny tracks that end suddenly in round, damp holes, or vanish where a small thing flew upward. Rabbit tracks wander along the raspberry thickets, and the sycamore balls have little caps of fur. It is best in this white grayness before the sun has come through the ascending clouds. The brooding, silent, closed-in world of *snow* and whiteness, motionless except for the birds, a timeless moment like an enormous pearl, a moment of stillness before the sun, and the thousand-diamond glitter and the rainbowed sound of light.

Even children, whose first thought is to tramp it and scrape it into balls, stand for a moment in awe. They drink in the miracle that is to become forever *snow*, *the snow* that is almost too beautiful to be borne.—JOSEPHINE W. JOHNSON

The writer's physical point of view is in the midst of the snow. Her mood is one of serenity, of peace.

The single, unified impression communicated to the reader is also one of serenity. The writer creates this impression by maintaining a consistent point of view and mood, and by carefully choosing details that elicit feelings of serenity in the reader.

The writer also achieves unity by repeating the phrase "the snow" and by constructing the composition so that each paragraph develops the main idea presented in the introductory paragraph.

The writer achieves coherence through the logical arrangement of ideas into chronological order. She describes the snow falling at night, then its appearance in the morning.

The writer achieves emphasis by including numerous details in the body paragraphs to describe "the snow," the central idea of the composition. The falling of the snow and its appearance in the morning are the two most important ideas in relation to the central idea. The writer, therefore, gives these two ideas the largest amount of space.

Exercise Writing a Description

Following the techniques described in Chapter 9, "Writing a Composition," write a descriptive composition of five paragraphs. The composition may be either practical or artistic. Begin by choosing and limiting a subject. Once you have a topic, complete the following steps:

Pre-Writing: Narrow your subject to fit a five-paragraph composition. Decide on your audience and your purpose. Decide on your physical point of view and mood. Finally, gather, group, and organize your ideas and notes into a writing plan.

First Draft: Write a rough draft, using your writing plan as a guide. Try to use vivid, precise words in your descriptions.

Revision: Check to make sure that all ideas are related to each other and to the introductory paragraph. Does your composition have unity, coherence, and emphasis? Did you use strong verbs, precise nouns, and vivid descriptive words and phrases?

Part 3 The Expository Composition

Expository writing is the type of writing you will do most often in school, and probably later on in your chosen career. The purpose of expository writing, also called explanatory writing, is to pass on information or to explain something such as a process, a term, a thought, or an idea. It is the type of writing you use to write reports, give directions, or argue a point.

The Composition That Explains a Process

This type of composition tells how to do something, or how something works. The writer's goal, or purpose, is to explain the process so that it may be easily done or understood by the reader. Therefore the composition is usually written in a very direct, straightforward style. The composition that explains a process usually has the characteristics listed below. These are useful to keep in mind during the pre-writing and drafting stages.

The Composition That Explains a Process

Purpose:	to explain a process
Audience:	readers unfamiliar with the process
Types of Development:	facts, details, steps of the process, examples
Type of Organization:	usually chronological, with the paragraphs in the composition organized so that each paragraph refers to a different step of the process, or to one phase of execution such as the gathering of materials

Read the composition on the following page. Look for the characteristics listed in the chart.

MAKING A HOLOGRAM

Imagine going to a movie where the characters appear in three dimensions around you. Or picture yourself slipping a cassette into a special machine and having a band spring from the projector to perform a concert in your living room. Such scenes may be possible in the near future because of the development of an exciting technique called holography. Holography is the process by which a three-dimensional image of an object is created. Similar to photography, holography records the image of an object on a light-sensitive plate or film. The resulting hologram, however, has the depth and appearance of a real object and appears to take up the same amount of space. The process by which this is accomplished is as fascinating as the image itself.

In order to understand how a hologram is created, it is helpful to know a few things about the human eye and how it "sees" things. When you look at an object, your eye receives patterns of light reflected from the object's surface. Your eye then sends these patterns to the brain, and the brain interprets them, creating an image of whatever it is that you are looking at. A hologram can make your brain "see" an object by reproducing precisely—light wave for light wave—the pattern that would be produced by the object itself.

The simplest holograms, called transmission holograms, create this light pattern through the use of a special light called a *laser*. The waves in a beam of laser light are all the same length. Therefore they are predictable and controllable. To make a transmission hologram, holographers split the beam of laser light into two parts. One part of the beam is used to illuminate an object placed in its path. The other part is sent on a separate path and then reunited with the other portion. When the two parts of the beam are brought together again, they create an interference pattern that matches exactly the light waves reflected from the surface of the object. This pattern is recorded on a special light-sensitive plate and then developed like an ordinary photograph.

There is one more step to the process, however. In ordinary photography, you can see the image simply by looking at the photograph under any light source. However, if you were to look at a developed holographic plate, all you would see is a pattern of light and dark lines. In order to create the image, a beam of laser light must be passed through the plate to reproduce the original light patterns. These patterns are picked up by the viewer's eye, which then "tricks" the brain into seeing the object as though it were actually present.

The image created by a transmission hologram appears to the viewer as an object behind a window because of the intervening holographic plate. However, more recent advances in the field have produced "reflection" holograms in which the image appears in front of the plate, as well as "integral" holograms that the viewer can walk around and see from all sides. As technology in this field advances, holograms will seem so real that the viewer will constantly have to be reminded that they are, in truth, only images. These images, however, may be the best imitations of reality that it is possible to make.

In general, this composition explains the technique of holography by outlining the steps of the process in chronological order. However, the writer realized that the concept of holography would more than likely be unfamiliar to the readers. Therefore, the writer incorporated one other element that makes the explanation easier to understand. Rather than begin immediately with a step in the holographic process, the writer introduces the explanation by relating holography to two more familiar processes—photography and human sight. Readers are thus provided with familiar material to which they can add additional information. This slight departure from straight chronological order is a logical solution to the problem of explaining a complex idea to an audience with little background in the area.

The Composition That Defines

Like the paragraph of this type, the composition that defines is used to introduce the reader to an unfamiliar term, object, or idea. It begins by placing the term to be defined in a general category, and then goes on to identify several distinguishing characteristics of the term. This type of writing is commonly seen in encyclopedias and reports. The following characteristics should be considered during the pre-writing and drafting stages:

The Composition That Defines

Purpose:	to define an unfamiliar term
Audience:	readers unfamiliar with the term
Types of Development:	sensory details (description), facts, statistics, examples
Types of Organization:	usually general to specific, or most familiar to least familiar. The first paragraph presents general, or familiar, information, and each succeeding paragraph dwells on more specific characteristics. These latter details may be grouped by type (appearance, function, applications) or in any of several ways that may be determined by the types of details used.

Read the following composition that explains what a coat of arms is.

THE COAT OF ARMS

Anyone who has ever read a book about knighthood or been fascinated by the nobility of Europe has heard of the term "coat of arms." Yet few people understand exactly what a coat of arms is. Basically, the term refers to a design used to distinguish an individual family or to authenticate official documents. The phrase itself comes from a practice knights once had of sewing these designs on the surcoats that they wore over their armor.

Originally, the coat of arms was simply a means by which one knight could identify another on the field of battle. It was developed during the Middle Ages, when the use of armor made it nearly impossible for knights to tell friends from enemies. Since symbolism was very important in medieval times, the symbol chosen by each knight often commemorated an important event in his life, or some outstanding quality. Some of these identifying symbols developed during the Crusades. Others evolved during tournaments or pageants.

As the number of coats of arms increased, so did the amount of confusion. Therefore, *heralds* began to supervise the selection of colors and symbols and developed a standard for the coat of arms. In general, the coat of arms consists of three parts: the shield, the crest, and a motto. The shield is the main element of the coat of arms. It contains the surface, or *field*, on which is placed the design. The crest is more of an ornamental device that is used above the field. The motto is a word, phrase, or sentence chosen as an expression of the goals or ideals of an individual or family.

The shield may involve quite an elaborate design. It begins with carefully selected colors, or *tinctures*, that represent two metals, seven colors, and various furs. Lines of various types and meanings divide the shield into more than one tincture. On this background of color are placed the figures, or *charges*, of the design. Charges are anything that can be symbolized in form and color. They include divine beings, animals, people, and objects that have some special meaning.

Today, countries such as Great Britain still use heraldic symbols, but more to show the ancestry of a family than to record its accomplishments. These devices are also used on official documents, and to represent entire states or provinces. No matter what they are used for, however, the rich history and colorful meanings of the coats of arms make them fascinating reminders of an exciting and romantic past.

This composition defines a device that would be unfamiliar to most Americans: the coat of arms. In general, the composition is developed with details and facts, and is organized from most general to most specific. It begins with a general statement that a coat of arms is a design used to distinguish families and authenticate documents. It then goes on to provide more specific information about the historic background and the individual elements that resulted in this design.

Notice, however, that the composition also utilizes chronological order as it explains how the modern coat of arms evolved. It also mixes different types of development where appropriate.

The Composition That Gives Reasons

This type of composition makes a statement of an idea or opinion in the first paragraph and then presents reasons why it is true or should be true. The statement of the idea or opinion, sometimes called the **thesis statement**, controls the content of the entire composition.

The Composition That Gives Reasons

Purpose:	to defend or to give reasons supporting an idea
Audience:	those who do not understand the idea or the writer's attitude toward it, or those who disagree with the idea
Types of Development:	facts, statistics, examples, incidents, and anecdotes. Your choice of supporting details will often depend on the *tone* of your composition. Facts, statistics, and examples would work best in a more serious composition, while an incident or anecdote would be more suitable for a humorous, informal, or artistic piece.
Types of Organization:	least to most important, most to least familiar, comparison and contrast. The kind of organization you use will depend entirely on the types of reasons you gather and the strength of those reasons. Even chronological order may be used if you are supporting an idea with a long anecdote. The way ideas are grouped into paragraphs also varies. Usually, however, each paragraph in this type of composition develops a specific reason using any of the ways mentioned under "Types of Development." These paragraphs are then arranged so that the most powerful reason is presented last, as a climax.

The following composition is an example of this last type of expository writing.

HIDDEN MESSAGES

Since the 1950's, a curious method of sending information has been available to those who wish to use it. This method is called *subliminal communication*. It involves sending messages that can be recorded by the human brain, but which are below the level of consciousness. With subliminal messages, ideas can be planted within a person's mind without that person necessarily being aware of them. In recent years, subliminal communication has become the focus of a great deal of renewed interest—and the subject of heated debate as well.

Both the fascination with and the fear of subliminal communication spring from the ways in which the messages are sent. A message can be as simple as an image "hidden" in a photograph. It can take the form of an inaudible message underneath the background music in stores and businesses and on audio cassettes. It can appear as a brief visual image, with a duration of no more than 1/30 of a second, between the frames of a movie or television show. A message can even flash from a program onto the screen of a home computer.

Those who support the use of subliminal messages say that this system is a harmless and efficient method of accomplishing many goals. First of all, the messages can be used to aid in law enforcement. In one supermarket, for example, broadcasting the subliminal message "Be honest" underneath the store's background music was said to have cut shoplifting by nearly 70%. Subliminal messages can also be used for a number of painless self-improvement projects. Special cassettes and computer programs are now on the market that use subliminal messages to help people lose weight, increase self-confidence, improve eating habits, and increase their reading speed.

Despite these attractive aspects of subliminal messages, critics of the method have equally strong reasons for opposing its use. One argument states that such messages take away from the freedom of choice. Subliminal commercials, for example, can plant a desire for a product in a person's mind for which he or she has no real need. More important, however, is the fact that subliminal messages cannot be easily detected. Therefore, harmful or dangerous messages could be transmitted to the public without anyone being aware of them.

Are subliminal messages, then, a marvelous development in communication, or a threat to our welfare? Until the effects of such methods are better understood, perhaps no one can say for certain. What is obvious, though, is that this method of communicating ideas is one that must be closely watched and carefully evaluated.

In this composition, the writer has divided supporting information into three groups. The first group, which was developed in the first body paragraph, included examples of subliminal messages and some facts about them. The second and third groups included reasons why people support the use of these messages, and reasons why some people oppose it. Other types of support, such as the statistic about shoplifting, were also used. Again, by incorporating types of development other than the main one of reasons, the writer produces a more in-depth composition. An organization that utilizes both order of familiarity and comparison and contrast further aids the presentation.

No matter what type of expository composition you write, always follow the basic steps of gathering, grouping, and organizing ideas that are discussed in Chapter 9, "Writing a Composition." Use the guidelines discussed above during this process. Remember, however, that more than one type of development or organization may be used within a single composition. You need only make sure that each element achieves a specific purpose and does not disrupt the unity of the composition. Also keep in mind that the entire composition must demonstrate unity, coherence, and emphasis.

Exercise Writing an Expository Composition

Choose a subject suitable for development into an expository composition. Then, develop your subject into a five-paragraph explanation that exhibits the characteristics of unity, coherence, and emphasis. Use the writing steps on the following page.

Pre-Writing: After you have selected a subject, narrow your topic to suit the purpose and audience of your composition. Focus on a specific purpose: Will you explain a process, define a term, or give reasons to support an idea? What details, facts, or examples are needed for a clear explanation? What are the main steps or points? What is the most effective way to organize the material so that your subject will be clear to your readers?

First Draft: Using your pre-writing notes, get your ideas down on paper. As you write, concentrate on thorough explanations and clear transitions.

Revision: As you read over your composition, try to pretend that you do not understand the process or theory that you explained. Mentally "walk" through each step. Did you leave anything out? Is the explanation given objectively and in a logical order? Did you stick to the main idea in the introduction?

Part 4   The Persuasive Composition

The persuasive composition is an emotional appeal aimed at persuading the readers to accept the writer's opinion as their own. It is closely related to the explanatory composition in that it seeks to explain an idea through the use of facts or statistics, one or more examples, an incident or an anecdote, or comparisons or contrasts.

Essentially, the persuasive composition is an expansion of the persuasive paragraph. Both have the same characteristics and techniques of development. The writer states an opinion or belief and then gives reasons and factual arguments to support the topic statement. In addition, both are aimed toward readers who will most likely *oppose* the idea being presented, whereas in other types of writing the reader is more passive, reading merely for information or entertainment.

In Chapter 8, the following sentences were used to describe the persuasive paragraph.

The choice of subject matter is limited to ideas about which there are at least two ways of thinking.

The topic sentence of a persuasive paragraph states the writer's way of thinking about a subject. It establishes the writer's point of view, which is justified by supporting statements in the rest of the paragraph.

Chapter 8 also included these points to keep in mind when writing a persuasive paragraph.

To present an effective argument for one side of a question, you must study and understand the arguments that support the opposite point of view.

Your audience consists of readers whose beliefs about the question at hand are different from yours. You are not writing for readers who already think the way you do.

The same four ideas are also true for the persuasive composition. Possible methods of organization are also the same for both. They are listed on the following chart.

Methods of Organizing the Persuasive Composition

1. Present the weakest argument first, building up to the strongest argument as a forceful conclusion.
2. Use the strongest argument to gain the reader's attention and support at the beginning, then present other supporting arguments.
3. Begin with an argument your readers are most likely to agree with, and gradually lead them to those that they may take exception to.
4. Show weaknesses in the argument(s) against your position, then follow with arguments in favor of your position. This is a form of comparison and contrast.
5. Start with arguments in favor of your position and follow with a discussion of the weaknesses in arguments against your position. Again, this is another order of comparison and contrast.

Finally, the guidelines for using reasonable language and good persuasive techniques also apply to all persuasive writing. In addition, remember to make a strong ending. You can save a strong point for last, you can make an emphatic restatement of your opinion or show what the consequences of your view are, or you can ask your readers to take action on your idea.

Pre-Writing: Planning the Persuasive Composition

In order to be convincing, you should think through the details both for and against your position. This type of writing involves the presentation of reasons that compel the reader not only to acknowledge your view as valid, but also to accept it as his or her own. Each detail of your composition should be arranged in a logical order that will be the most effective and to the point.

As you write, however, you have to be aware of the doubts and objections in the mind of the reader. Your plan of writing should include efforts to satisfy those doubts and objections.

Study the following outline for a persuasive composition.

PROPOSITION OF BELIEF: The jury system should be abolished.

  I. It makes just verdicts hard to secure.
    A. Juries are often uninformed.
    B. Juries are often prejudiced.
      1. Many are influenced by church or society affiliations.
      2. Many are prejudiced against large corporations.
  II. The trial of all cases by judges would be better.
    A. Judges are experienced in working with complicated legal cases.
    B. Most judges try to rise above their prejudices.
    C. Judges are less likely to be moved by the eloquent arguments of lawyers.
    D. Judges are not easily deceived by witnesses.
  III. The substitution of judges for juries would not be a dangerous innovation.
    A. Appellate and Supreme Courts function without juries.
    B. Many lawyers have long favored the substitution.

As with the persuasive paragraph, the writer begins with a proposition of belief. She then gives three reasons or arguments, to support her proposition.

I. It makes just verdicts hard to secure.
II. The trial of all cases by judges would be better.
III. The substitution of judges for juries would not be a dangerous innovation.

In anticipation of the arguments that the opponents of this proposition might raise, the writer has listed, under the main headings, supporting statements that are constructive to her own arguments and destructive to those of her opponents.

Exercise Writing a Persuasive Composition

Think of several subjects that are being discussed at school, in your community, or in the media. Choose one about which you have a strong opinion and write a five-paragraph persuasive composition.

Pre-Writing: After careful analysis of your selected topic, write your statement of belief. List all the arguments both for and against your position. Consider the best means of presenting a convincing argument. Should you use facts or statistics, examples, or comparisons or contrasts? What is the most logical organization for your composition? Make an outline for your composition. Be sure to anticipate opposing views.

First Draft: Using the notes and outline from your pre-writing, write an introductory paragraph that presents your statement of belief in a way that will capture the reader's attention. Then build the body of the composition around convincing reasons for the reader to adopt your views. Remember to use reasonable language. End with a strong conclusion that will reinforce your position and unify the composition.

Revision: Did you state your position clearly? Have you followed through with relevant facts or examples to support your opinion? Does your composition consider and answer opposing views? Does your paper have unity and coherence?

Part 5 The Composition About Literature

Writing about various types of literature is an important step in the development of your writing skills. It utilizes the writing process you have already learned and at the same time adds some interesting new dimensions.

Most significantly, writing about literature differs from other types of composition in the respect that it requires you to use your skills of interpretation and analysis. In an analysis, you look at the elements of a work and reach some conclusions about them. You develop your own ideas about the piece. Your purpose, then, in writing about literature is to explain your ideas or conclusions to your readers.

Most often, you will have to write this type of composition about a story or poem you have just read. Although some of the specific elements of the pre-writing differ, the same basic techniques can be applied as you prepare to write about either of these types of literature.

Pre-Writing: Analysis and Interpretation

Analyzing a piece of literature is similar to putting together a jigsaw puzzle. A good puzzle builder begins by placing all the puzzle pieces face up on a table and studying them in order to find identifiable patterns, relationships among the pieces, and the overall shape and form of the picture. You will find it helpful to follow much the same process in analyzing literature. You must break a story or poem down into its elements in order to examine how these parts are related.

In analyzing literature, you should follow these steps.

Step 1   Read the story or poem.

Step 2   Take notes on the elements of the story or poem.   These elements might include some or all of the ones presented in the chart on the following page.

Elements of Fiction	Elements of Poetry
Setting	Purpose
Mood	Theme
Point of View	Form (free verse, couplet, stanzas, etc.)
Theme	
Characters (description, importance, motivations)	Sound devices (rhyme, alliteration, assonance, consonance, etc.)
Conflict	Imagery (metaphor, simile, personification, etc.)
Turning Point/Climax	

Step 3 **Choose a topic and determine a purpose.** Once you have taken notes, decide which aspect of the piece interests you most. Sometimes you will decide to deal with just one of the elements. For instance, you might write about the growth of one character, how the writer creates the mood, or the theme. At other times, you might want to discuss the effect of one or more elements on another. For instance, you might write about how setting affects a character, what the relationship is between the point of view and the plot, or how the major conflict contributes to understanding the theme.

Step 4 **List the points you wish to cover.** Also gather support for each idea by carefully selecting details, lines, or passages from the piece you are analyzing.

Step 5 **Organize your ideas.** Group your ideas and put them in logical order. As with other types of writing, your topic will often help to determine the most logical method for organizing your material. For example, if your topic is a discussion of the growth of one character, a logical order would be chronological. Or, you could present the elements that caused the change according to the amount of impact they had on the character.

Writing and Revising the Analysis

Take time with the pre-writing steps of analyzing and interpreting fiction. This gives you the material you need to begin writing a first draft. Write your first draft to get your ideas down on paper. As always in the process of writing, you will develop and refine your ideas as you write. You will be adding, deleting, and rearranging ideas to fit your topic and purpose in your first draft as well as in subsequent revisions.

In later revisions, check your writing for unity, coherence, and full development as well as for correct grammar, usage, and mechanics.

Below is a sample analysis of "Lather and Nothing Else," which you read in Part 1 of this chapter. It is the final product of many drafts and revisions. The writer has chosen to discuss the conflict that the main character faces and to explain how it is resolved. As you read, look at the ways the ideas are grouped and the order in which they are presented. Also, notice how well each point is supported with actual lines from the story.

HONOR AND NOTHING ELSE

A character gets a shave in a barbershop. On the surface, there is not much suspense in a summary of Hernando Tellez's short story "Lather and Nothing Else." But there is literally a life-and-death struggle going on. Although the story has two characters who are on opposite political sides, this conflict is not between them. The main conflict in the story is an internal one, a life-and-death struggle that takes place in the main character's mind.

When Captain Torres, a leader of the existing regime, comes into his shop for a shave, the barber/narrator of the story immediately becomes uneasy and senses a conflict within himself. At first, he defines his conflict in political versus professional terms, "Yes. I was secretly a revolutionary, but at the same time I was a conscientious barber, proud of the way I did my job. And that four-day beard presented a challenge." In other words, the barber is faced with a dilemma. As a revolutionary, should he take this opportunity to slit Torres's throat? Or, as a "conscientious barber," should he carefully shave Torres and take "heed that not a single pore should emit a drop of blood"?

Rather than resolving his conflict, the barber heightens his internal struggle by identifying what others would think and do. He realizes that other revolutionaries have probably seen Torres enter his shop and he feels a "certain responsibility" to take this opportunity to kill Torres. After all, as he says, "…so it was going to be difficult to explain how it was that I had him in my hands and then let him go in peace, alive, clean-shaven." He also considers how Torres's murder will make him a hero among the revolutionaries. On the other hand, the barber realizes that Torres's murder would end his life in the village and that he would have to flee. Those supporting the existing regime would pursue him and call him "the murderer of Captain Torres." They would consider his actions "a cowardly thing to do."

The barber also tries to resolve the question of whether he should kill his enemy by justifying Torres's death and rationalizing that it would not hurt. The barber thinks that Torres's death would be quick and painless, "I'm sure that with a good strong blow, a deep cut, he would feel no pain. He would not suffer at all." The narrator also thinks that Torres deserves to die because of the pain and death that he has inflicted upon the revolutionaries. However, even as he considers killing the Captain, the barber knows that Torres's death would not end the struggle between the existing regime and the revolutionaries. The barber acknowledges this when he says, "What is to be gained by it? Nothing. Others and still others keep coming, and the first kills the second…"

Considering others' opinions and trying to justify the murder do not settle the barber's conflict. It is only resolved by coming to terms with himself, by realizing what he is and what he is not. At the moment of resolution, the barber declares, "But I don't want to be a murderer." The barber cannot bring himself to be treacherous, to betray his customer's trust, to kill Torres in cold blood. He puts his decision in terms of his profession, that he stains his hands with lather—not with blood. However, there is more to it than this. The barber's hands are clean—with lather, soap; but his work and his actions are also clean and honorable. He cannot be any other way.

With this realization, the internal life-and-death struggle is resolved: Torres will live, and the barber's honor will also survive.

Exercises Writing About Literature

A. Reread "Lather and Nothing Else." Choose a different element to analyze. Following the steps presented in Part 5, write your own analysis. You may want to use your answers to the exercise in Part 1 that follows the story.

B. Read another story assigned by your teacher or one of your own choosing. After you have read the story, complete the following three steps.

Pre-Writing: Identify the various elements of the story. What is the major conflict? Who are the characters? How would you describe them? What is the mood of the story? the point of view? Identify the elements that interest you and determine your topic and purpose. What method of organization best suits your topic?

First Draft: Use your pre-writing notes to get your ideas down on paper. Use details from the story to support your ideas. Look for new insights.

Revision: Go over your rough draft several times. Is your main idea clearly stated? Are your reasons convincing? What story details can you add to support your ideas?

SUMMARY AND APPLICATIONS

1. Narrative, descriptive, and explanatory compositions each have specific purposes and characteristics. All well-written compositions, however, exhibit the characteristics of coherence, unity, and emphasis.

2. Both simple and complex narrative compositions are used to relate events or incidents. They include the elements of character, setting, conflict, and theme.

3. Descriptive compositions use sensory details to "paint a word picture" of places, scenes, or people. Such descriptions may be practical or artistic.

4. Expository, or explanatory, compositions can be used to explain a process, define a term or idea, or provide reasons for a statement or opinion. A special type of composition that gives reasons is the composition that persuades.

5. The composition about literature is an analysis of a story or poem. It requires the writer to identify the elements of the piece and look for relationships among them.

Applications in Other Subject Areas

Speech. Each type of composition presented in this chapter can be converted to an equally distinctive type of oral presentation. The steps for preparing the material remain the same—only the final product differs. Choose one of the ideas below and prepare an oral presentation to deliver in front of your class.

    a. A story, to be performed as dramatically as possible.
    b. A descriptive piece, perhaps with slides or music.
    c. A demonstration, complete with props.
    d. A persuasive speech, possibly in the form of a lawyer addressing a jury.

All Subjects. Look for examples of each of the main types of composition in your textbooks for science, social studies, math, industrial arts, and home economics. In class, discuss which types of writing are most common in each area, and why you think this is so.

Chapter 11

Writing a Report

Your knowledge of the world increases every day. Usually you acquire information quite informally. You pick up facts and ideas through observation, conversation, and the media. Sometimes, however, your information-gathering is more direct, systematic, and purposeful. At this point in your life, this type of information-gathering is usually related to school projects. Later it may be a part of your job. Often you will have to present the information you collect in the form of a report.

A **report** is a piece of writing based on material from sources outside your personal knowledge and experience. First, you seek and gather specific information on a subject. Then you examine and organize all the separate bits of information. Finally, you transform them into a unified, coherent piece of writing.

In its purpose and source of information, then, a report differs from the compositions that you have studied so far. However, a report does involve the same stages of pre-writing, drafting, and revision.

Part 1 Pre-Writing: Choosing and Limiting a Subject

If you are not assigned a specific topic, your first step in writing a report is choosing a subject. To find possible subjects, you will want to consult the sources available to you. Other people, such as your teachers, friends, or neighbors, might be able to suggest subjects. In addition, school and public libraries have thousands of books on an almost unlimited variety of subjects. Your textbooks also mention people, places, and events that are potential subjects.

As you consider possible subjects, keep in mind that you will have to spend some time doing research. Therefore, it is important that you choose a subject that interests you. Also try to choose one that you feel you can make interesting to a reader.

Limiting a Subject

Subjects that require research may need to be narrowed. To narrow your subject effectively, you need to consider two things:

1. the amount of information available on a subject
2. the length of your report

For example, suppose you had been asked to write an eight- to ten-paragraph report. You are interested in writing about whales. This is far too broad a subject for thorough treatment in such a short report. However, this subject does contain a number of more specific topics. Among these are the following:

Types of whales
The life of whales
Whaling (early or modern)
The "Save the Whales" movement
The International Whaling Commission

Any of these topics are more suitable for a short report in terms of length and amount of available information.

When you are narrowing a topic, you may find it helpful to read a short encyclopedia article on your general subject. You may also want to check the index or table of contents of a book dealing with the particular subject you have in mind. For instance, a writer interested in writing a report about American music checked the table of contents for *A Short History of Music in America* and found sixteen general headings covering the development of American music. Each of these subjects was still too broad for a short report. The writer noted, however, that the table of contents was broken down into subheadings. Under "The Second Decade and World War I" he discovered the following:

EARLY JAZZ

Origins
Dixieland Jazz
Musicians

After skimming the sections on the three specific topics suggested by this part of the table of contents, the writer chose to research and write about the origins of jazz.

Exercises Pre-Writing: Choosing a Report Topic

A. The following subjects are too general for a short report. Narrow each one so that it is suitable for a five-to-ten-paragraph paper. You may need to do some reading on a few of the subjects.

1. Sky Diving
2. Women in the Work Force
3. Hispanic-Americans
4. Dancing
5. Animal Migration
6. Native American Culture
7. Photography
8. Immigration
9. Life in Old England
10. Endangered Species
11. Superstitions
12. Advertising
13. Energy Sources
14. Weather
15. The Olympic Games
16. America's Relationship with Great Britain

B. Look at the list of topics that you developed in Exercise A. Choose five that interest you. Then add five more topics of your own. Be sure to narrow each one so that it is appropriate for an eight-to-ten-paragraph report. Keep this list.

Part 2   Pre-Writing: Preparing To Do Research

Once you have identified an interesting or exciting topic, you may be eager to head toward a library and lose yourself in the books. However, a little more planning at this point will make your later research work more efficient and effective.

Identifying Your Purpose

The subject of a report, like that of any composition, may be approached in several different ways. Identifying your purpose will help you to clarify your approach and focus your research.

You may decide that the purpose of your report is merely to **inform** your readers about your topic. In this case, you select facts and details that help your readers understand the topic. For instance, if the writer researching jazz decides to tell about "The Origins of Jazz," he would limit himself to looking for details that would identify the various roots of jazz.

A slightly more complex purpose would be **to analyze** a topic. In this case, you rework your topic so that it focuses on the "why" or "how" of a subject. Then you select and organize your information in a way that helps your readers draw their own conclusions about your topic. The writer of the sample report, for example, could choose to write about "The Impact of New Orleans on the Origins of Jazz." He would then collect information that showed how jazz was affected by the people and atmosphere of New Orleans.

A third type of purpose is **to compare and contrast** two elements within a topic. You begin this sort of paper by researching each element separately. Then you analyze your data for common or contrasting points. The writer developing the jazz topic could use a comparison and contrast approach if he decided to compare the origins of jazz with the origins of folk music. At this point, you may wish to refine your topic with a **statement of purpose.** This statement, sometimes called a **thesis statement,** may be used in the introduction of your report.

Identifying Your Audience

Identifying your audience will help you to decide what background information to include in your report. It will also tell you how technical you can be in your explanations and terminology, or word choice. This step is very important. You may gather excellent information on your topic. Without an adequate idea of your audience's background and knowledge, however, your presentation of this information may cancel out the excellent research.

The writer of "The Origins of Jazz," for example, identified his audience as the classmates in his English class. He could not assume that all of them would be familiar with the technical terms of music, or even that all of them would know what jazz is. On the other hand, if this report had been for classmates in an advanced music class, the writer could have assumed that his audience had a similar and more technical background.

Making a List of Questions

In addition to identifying your purpose and audience, you can prepare to do research by making a list of questions concerning your topic. This list should identify areas that you are curious about or that you think your readers might be interested in. The questions will help you clarify what you are looking for as you get involved in your research and keep you from wasting time gathering irrelevant information.

After a little preliminary reading, the writer interested in jazz came up with the following list of questions.

–What is jazz?
–How, where, and when did jazz originate?
–What is ragtime?
–What is ragtime's relationship to jazz?
–What is jazz's relationship to the blues?
–What are the characteristics of jazz?

As you begin your own research, questions such as these will help you decide which information to record. Of course, as your research progresses you may want to revise your questions or add others. You may also want to record some information that does not strictly "fit" into the categories that the questions suggest. As long as this information *does* fit your topic, purpose, and audience, do not hesitate to record it. Remember that, like all the tools of pre-writing, the technique of forming questions is simply a guide.

Exercise Pre-Writing: Preparing To Do Research

Choose a topic from the list you made in Part 1. This will be the topic of your report. Determine the purpose and audience for your report and record these in your pre-writing notes. Then make a list of eight to ten questions that you would like to answer as you research your report.

Part 3 Pre-Writing: Gathering Information

With your preliminary work complete, you are now ready to go to the library. If you have not already done so, read some general encyclopedia articles on your subject. Then, use the *Readers' Guide to Periodical Literature,* a newspaper index, and the card catalog to find newspaper articles, magazine articles, and books concerning your topic. You may also want to consult other specialized reference books in your research. For further instruction on using the library effectively, see Chapter 14, "Using the Library and Reference Works."

Making a Working Bibliography

When you identify a book or article that you think may be helpful in your research, record the information concerning that source on a 3″ × 5″ card. Follow the guidelines shown in the chart on the following page. Use a separate card for each source and assign each card a number. This list is your **working bibliography.**

1. **Books with a single author.** Give the author, last name first; the title of the book; the place of publication; the publisher's name; and the year of publication. Put the library call number in the upper left-hand corner of your card.

2. **Books with two or more authors.** List all the authors, but reverse the name order of only the first author listed. Record all other information as in Guideline 1.

3. **Articles in encyclopedias.** Give the title of the article, the name of the book or set, and the year of the edition.

4. **An essay in a collection of pieces by different authors.** Give the author, last name first; the title of the essay; the title of the collection; the name(s) of the editor(s); the place of publication; the publisher's name; the year of publication; and the page numbers of the essay.

5. **An article from a magazine.** Give the author, last name first (unless unsigned); the title of the article; the name of the magazine; the date of the magazine; and the page numbers of the article.

6. **An article from a daily newspaper.** Give the author, last name first; the title of the article; the name of the newspaper; the edition of the newspaper; the date of the newspaper; and the section, page number(s), and columns of the article.

The writer of the report on jazz had these bibliography cards:

Book

ML
3561
.J3
E765
1975

Erlich, Lillian. ③
What Jazz Is
All About.
New York: Julian
Messner Co., 1979

ML
3561
.J3
H44

Borneman, Ernest. ①
"The Roots of Jazz."
In Jazz.
Ed. Nat Hentoff and
    Albert J. McCarthy.
New York: DaCapo Press,
1974, pp. 3-14.

Lees, G. ⑥
"Emergence of Jazz."
High Fidelity,
Aug. 1978,
pp. 16-17.

"Jazz." ⑤
The World Book
    Encyclopedia.
1984 ed.

Exercises Pre-Writing: Making a Working Bibliography

A. Make up bibliography cards for the following sources. Use 3″x5″ cards or draw rectangles on a sheet of paper. Organize and number them as you would for a report.

1. *Visitors from Beyond: the Comets* by Willy Lay and Brice Adams, call number 5523.6, published in 1969 by McGraw-Hill in New York
2. *Comets, Vagabonds of Space* by David Sargent, call number QB 721.4, published in 1982 by Doubleday in Garden City, New York
3. *World Book Encyclopedia's* article on "Halley's Comet" by Joseph Ashbrook, volume 6, 1981, p. 24
4. "Search for Halley's Comet Stepped Up at Kitt Peak" in *Astronomy*, p. 69, March 1982 issue
5. "Halley's Comet Returns to Earth" by T. Dickinson in *MacCleans*, p. 60, November 8, 1982
6. "Comet Trekking" in the *Chicago Tribune*, Chicago final edition, November 1, 1982, section 1, page 7, column 2

B. Make a working bibliography for your report. Use 3″x5″ cards to record your information. Follow the guidelines and examples given in this lesson for recording and arranging sources. Save your cards.

Taking Notes

As you read your sources, take notes on the information that you feel is significant to your topic, audience, and purpose. Write this information on 3″x 5″cards also, putting only one idea on each card. Record the page number of the source of information on each card. Finally, number the note card to correspond with the number of the bibliography card that identifies the source of your information.

Rewording Information. An important point to keep in mind when taking notes is this: *Never take credit for someone else's work.* When using information from another source, do not copy the material word for word in your notes and then later write it into your report as if it were your own. To do so is to be guilty of **plagiarism**—the uncredited use of another person's material.

The easiest way to avoid plagiarism is to paraphrase, or re-word, material as you put it into your notes. Begin by reading the passage carefully. Then put the meaning of the passage into your own words. As you paraphrase, make sure that you maintain the original sense or meaning of the source.

Notice how the writer researching jazz transferred information from his source to his notes.

ORIGINAL SOURCE

> Of these, the most prevalent was the work song. Character-istically, the work song was cast in call-and-answer form; the song leader would throw out a vocal line, which the workers would answer with a short phrase, perhaps no more than a single syllable timed to the pull of the oars or the fall of the hammer.

Note Made from the Source

> Workers used a ②
> leader-and-response
> pattern in their
> songs.
>
> ─p.35

Quoting a Source Directly. Occasionally an author will explain something so well or describe something so vividly that you will want to quote his or her exact words. When this is the case, copy the material accurately on your note card. Put quotation marks around the quoted material, both in your notes and later in your report. In addition to using quotation marks, you should give credit within the body of your report by mentioning the author's name and the title of the source. The page number where the quote may be found is shown in parentheses following the closing quotation marks.

The writer of "The Origins of Jazz" researched his topic in several sources and recorded dozens of ideas on 3"x5" cards. Four of his cards are shown here.

Each Sunday, slaves ⑤
in Congo Square,
New Orleans, danced,
clapped, and beat
drums.
           page 54

                ⑥
slave spirituals:
one source of
the blues
          page 16

"The African concept of ③
music as a communal,
creative activity was
always there. It is
at the heart of Afro-
American folk music—
and of jazz." page 45

⑥

New Orleans: Congo Square celebrations called "bamboulas" page 17

Separating Fact from Opinion

A report should consist only of facts. Therefore, you need to be able to distinguish fact from opinion as you take notes. A **fact** is a verifiable piece of information. It can be proven true by checking an encyclopedia, an authority, or other reliable sources.

An **opinion**, on the other hand, cannot be proven. It is simply a statement of someone's personal feelings on a subject. An opinion is often signaled by judgment words, such as *best* and *worst,* or by phrases containing the words *should* or *ought to.* See Chapter 12 for more information on fact and opinion.

Exercises Pre-Writing: Taking Notes

A. Assume that you are writing a report on Halley's Comet. Use this article from page 24 of the *World Book Encyclopedia* to write five note cards. Be sure to paraphrase the material.

> **HALLEY'S COMET** is a brilliant comet named for the English astronomer Edmund Halley. It appears every 76 to 79 years. Before Halley made his investigations, most people believed that comets appeared by chance. But Halley believed that comets belonged to the solar system and took definite paths around the sun at regular intervals. He found that the paths taken by certain comets in 1456, 1531, and 1607 were identical with the path of a comet observed in 1682. He decided that the same comet made all these paths. He correctly predicted that it would appear in 1759, and at regular intervals thereafter.

B. Take notes on 3"x5" cards for your own report. Follow the guidelines outlined in this section for documenting sources and recording information. Save your notes.

Using Graphic Aids

As you do your research don't overlook the graphic aids that accompany a source you are using. Often picture captions, illustrations, sketches, diagrams, maps, tables, and charts contain facts that could develop your report.

Common Graphic Aids

TYPE	PURPOSE	STUDY TIPS
Pictures Sketches Diagrams	To illustrate text To show the parts or functions of the subject (diagrams and some sketches only)	Read caption or title Relate picture, sketch, or diagram to text Pay particular attention to labels of parts
Maps	To display geographical areas or geographical distribution	Read caption or title to determine the purpose of the map Look for the *legend* or *key* (list of symbols and abbreviations; indication of scale or size)
Tables Charts	To list information To compare information	Read caption or title Check key, if there is one, to determine how information is organized
Graphs	To show relationships between groups or sets To show changes over time	Read caption or title Read all labels of parts of the graph Determine what relationship is being shown between groups or sets

Interviewing

As part of your preliminary research, you may have talked with an expert on your subject. Now is the time to return to that expert to gather further information.

Begin by making specific arrangements with the interviewee concerning the time and place of the interview. Then arrive promptly with your "homework" done. This means that you have done enough background reading on the topic to feel comfortable with the concepts and terms that the expert is likely to use. You should also have prepared a list of specific questions that you wish to ask your authority. Make sure these questions are worded to avoid "yes" and "no" answers. Using phrases such as "Could you explain..." will accomplish this purpose.

Although an interview is a "non-print" source, the information that you gain from it should be recorded and documented. During the interview, you may take notes on paper or make a tape and later identify and transfer individual facts to 3"x5" cards. Another method is to write single questions from your interview list at the top of 3"x5" cards. As you ask the questions, record the expert's answer beneath the question on the card.

Make a bibliography card for your interview source which includes the name and title of the expert; the nature of the communication (letter, telephone, or personal); and the interview date.

The writer of "The Origins of Jazz" spoke with his high school band director. The bibliography card looked like this:

Imes, Gary, music instructor. Personal interview on the origins of jazz. October 7, 1983.

④

A. Study the following map from page 36 of the *World Book Encyclopedia*, volume 9. The map shows the distribution of population among Japan's four major islands. Make a note card based on the map.

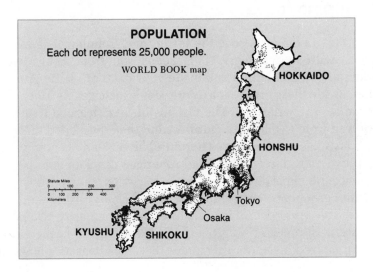

B. Consider your report topic. Could an authority be a source? Prepare ten interview questions that you could ask such an expert.

Part 4   Pre-Writing: Organizing a Report

At this point in the process of writing a report, you have dozens of note cards. These cards, however, are in no logical order. Before you can begin writing a rough draft, you need to take some time to make sense out of all the data you have collected. You also need to decide how this material could be presented in a unified and coherent way.

The only way to accomplish these tasks is to organize your ideas in relation to each other. You can begin this process by sorting your information—grouping similar ideas together. The value of putting a single fact on each note card now becomes clear. You can arrange, rearrange, add, and delete information as the pattern of your material takes shape.

Grouping Ideas

Often in a longer report, the sorting and grouping of ideas will be a multi-step process. This keeps you from being overwhelmed by facts. First subdivide your data into large groups, then divide these groups into increasingly manageable units. For instance, the writer of "The Origins of Jazz" learned that jazz evolved from two foreign cultures, and then developed through various stages in America. Therefore, he divided his note cards into two piles: foreign roots and American development.

Once this initial division was made, the writer was ready to make further groupings. He began by subdividing his cards on foreign roots. The writer determined that he could again make two piles: Western European background and West African background. He organized his note cards under these headings as follows:

Western European Background of Jazz

- Blacks working as American house servants heard the Western European songs of the whites
- Field workers heard snatches of Irish or Scottish airs whistled by their overseers
- Blacks adapted the ballads and hymns played by fiddlers at parties and balls

West African Background of Jazz

- "The African concept of music as a communal, creative activity was always there"
- West Africans used percussion instruments as a principle means of expression
- West African music used two to six drums
- West African music emphasized rhythm—similar to jazz
- Rhythm passed down in speech, song, and body movement

- West Africans followed no 4 beat measure of time or absolute accent rules
- West African music created a single mood—similar to jazz
- West African culture developed highly complicated rhythms
- West African music used repetition to create a hypnotic effect
- West African music had no regular pitch, time, or timbre

The writer went through a similar process with his note cards on "American Development." He identified three subgroups:

Growth and Development of Jazz in America

New Orleans Music
Early Music of American Blacks
Blues

Next the writer grouped his note cards under these headings.

New Orleans Music

- Each Sunday, slaves in Congo Square, New Orleans, danced, clapped, beat drums
- Celebration in Congo Square called *bamboula*
- Drummers beat out old West African rhythms
- Ragtime developed in New Orleans
- Origin of ragtime—music of military brass bands
- Blacks combined music of bands and Congo Square rhythms

Early Music of American Blacks

- Blacks brought rhythms and music to America from Africa
- Combined African music with European music of the whites
- Black folk music emerged—work songs, plantation cries, field "hollers," spirituals
- Leader-response pattern quite common

Blues

- Developed along with ragtime
- First blues by band leader W.C. Handy, who wrote down the African sounds of black music
- Key characteristics of blues—the "blues" note and the leader-response pattern of early black and West African music

Once these initial groupings had been made, the writer studied them carefully, looking for further refinements in his organization. He had these thoughts as he examined his notes.

1. Almost every group of ideas mentions something about the West African origins of the different types of music. This seems to indicate that this is a key group of notes.
2. Since the characteristics of West African music are repeated in other groups, perhaps some of the details can be deleted from the West African grouping.
3. The Western European group of notes is very small and the information on it is mentioned again in the idea group "Early Music of American Blacks." Perhaps the Western European notes could be incorporated into this other group.
4. The information under "New Orleans Music" involves *two* main idea groups: The rhythm of the Congo Square celebrations and the development of ragtime. These should probably become separate groups.

With these ideas in mind, the writer formed new groupings. Notice how the titles of the groups have also been modified.

West African Ties to Jazz

The Growth and Development of Jazz in America
> New Orleans (Congo Square rhythms)
> New Orleans (ragtime)
> The Folk Music of the Blacks
> The Blues

When you organize your own notes, make sure that you go through a similar process of thought, organization, more thought, and re-organization. The time you spend now will be time saved later.

Exercise Pre-Writing: Organizing Your Information

Divide your note cards from Part 3 into related groups. You may need to break this process into several steps. Begin by identifying large categories. Then break these categories down further.

Determining the Order of Information

Once you have grouped your information, you must determine a logical order in which to present it. As you have done with other types of writing, consider your topic, your purpose, and your audience. Then decide which of the organizational methods you learned in Chapter 8 would be most appropriate.

Reports are often organized from least important idea to most important idea, or from most familiar concept to least familiar concept. However, a topic such as "The Social Impact of 'Brown vs. the Board of Education'" might be developed through comparison/contrast of social conditions before and after the famous court case. It could also be developed in a chronological order that presents social changes since the court case.

Sometimes the facts themselves will determine the order. The writer of "The Origins of Jazz" found this to be true. He had these thoughts in determining the order of his information.

1. I've already noticed that the West African origins of jazz are important to every other concept in the paper. Therefore, this key paragraph should probably be presented first.
2. The American blacks brought the West African music and rhythms to America. The paragraph on the early music of the American blacks, then, would make a good transition from West African origins of jazz to the development of jazz in America.
3. The three remaining forerunners of jazz—the Congo Square music, ragtime, and the blues—each contributed an important element to jazz. They also follow a roughly chronological order in their development. If I follow this same order in my report, my reader will be able to see clearly how and when each element of jazz was added. This order will also make transitions between groups easy to handle as I write my rough draft.

With these considerations in mind, the writer reorganized his groups of note cards yet another time. He also organized the ideas *within* each group so that they flowed logically.

You should follow a process similar to this in thinking through your organization. Of course, your topic will require different considerations. The overall method, however, will be the same.

Making an Outline

Some writers feel comfortable composing their rough draft from their note cards. Most writers, however, feel more secure putting their information and organization into a formal outline before they begin to write. An outline provides you with a concise summary of your ideas. Constructing an outline also gives you another opportunity to check your logic and organization.

Each group of note cards becomes a major division in an outline. The key idea of the group becomes the division's main heading. The individual note card facts become major points underneath the heading. See Section 18 for more information on outlining.

The final outline for "The Origins of Jazz" is shown below:

I. West African influence
   A. Origins of jazz
   B. Similarities between jazz and West African music
      1. Single mood
      2. Hypnotic effect
      3. Use of percussion
      4. Irregular pitch, time, rhythm, vibrato
      5. Communal, creative activity

II. The folk music of the blacks
   A. Was a combination of West African music and Western European ballads and hymns
   B. Included several types of folk music
      1. Work songs
      2. Plantation cries
      3. Field "hollers"
      4. Spirituals
   C. Contained emotional power later a part of jazz

III. The music of Congo Square
   A. Was part of celebration held by blacks—"bamboula"
   B. Used rhythms of West Africa
      1. Highly complex
      2. No four-beat measures or absolute rules of accent
      3. Played on drums while others danced and clapped
      4. Later an important jazz element

IV. The development of ragtime
   A. Originated in military bands of the French
      1. Horn and woodwind sound
      2. French quadrilles
   B. Combined brass band music and the rhythm of Congo Square drums
   C. Developed from ragtime bands
V. The blues
   A. Appearance
   B. Introduction by W. C. Handy
   C. Key characteristics
      1. The "blue note"
      2. The leader-response pattern
      3. Repetition of phrases

Notice how this outline reflects all of the writer's earlier decisions concerning the grouping of ideas in logical order.

Exercise Pre-Writing: Organizing Your Report

Examine the groups that you formed earlier with your note cards. Put the groups and the ideas within them into a logical order. Then, using your note cards, prepare an outline for your report.

Part 5 Writing the First Draft

Like the various types of compositions, a report has three main divisions: the introduction, the body, and the conclusion. Each of these serves a specific purpose for the report's audience.

The Introduction

Before reading a report, your audience has three questions:

 – What is the topic of the report?
 – What is the purpose of the report?
 – Why should I read this report?

A good introduction answers all three of these questions for your readers. For instance, consider the two paragraphs below as possible introductions for the report on the origins of jazz.

1   In this paper, I am going to tell you about the origins of jazz. Jazz has many different roots.

2   What's as American as apple pie? One possible answer is— Jazz! This lively music, with its strong rhythms and unusual tonal effects, is uniquely American. Like America, however, it is the product of many different cultures and styles. Indeed, the origins and growth of jazz are as rich and varied as the music itself.

Although the first paragraph does introduce the topic and purpose of the report, it does nothing to capture the readers' interest and attention. Unless readers have their own reasons for continuing to read the report, there is nothing in the first paragraph to motivate them.

The second paragraph also presents the topic and purpose of the report, but it does so in a much livelier way. By beginning with a question, the writer of the second paragraph immediately engages his readers and makes them feel as though they are a part of the discovery process. The writer then uses the paragraph to provide a simple definition of jazz, and a clear idea of what the rest of the paper will cover. This not only gives his readers a valuable frame of reference for absorbing new information, but also leaves them with several questions in their minds for which they will seek answers:

– What foreign cultures contributed to jazz?
– How did they contribute?
– What are the "styles" that are a part of jazz?

Exercise First Draft: Writing an Introduction

Write an introduction for your report. In introducing your topic and purpose, try to engage your readers' attention. If necessary, use your introduction to provide your readers with background concerning the subject.

The Body

In writing your body paragraphs, you will reap the rewards of all your previous preparation. If you have done a careful job of gathering and organizing your information, a great deal of your work for this section is done. Writing your body paragraphs will primarily involve putting your notes in sentence form and filling in the details. Your outline and note cards should provide you with all of the information you need.

Each body paragraph will cover the information listed under one of your outline headings. The key idea of each heading will be used to write the topic sentence for each paragraph. The sentences that follow will develop the key idea.

As you write, make sure you use transitional devices to tie together the paragraphs and the ideas within them. Also remember that, in working on the drafts of your report, it is likely that you will still be adding, deleting, and rearranging ideas. This is to be expected as your ideas take firmer form as sentences and paragraphs on a page.

The writer of "The Origins of Jazz" developed his main outline divisions into five body paragraphs. In working on his rough drafts, he followed the natural writing process of reorganizing details and adding and deleting information. (See pages 273-274 for the final version of the body paragraphs.)

Exercise First Draft: Writing the Body Paragraphs

Use your outline from Part 4 to write the body paragraphs of your report. Strengthen the unity of your report by adding, deleting, or reorganizing your material as necessary.

The Conclusion

The writer of "The Origins of Jazz" wrote this conclusion:

> By the early part of this century, these various forms of music had achieved enormous popularity. Their mournful strains and infectious rhythms were heard throughout the country.

Soon the blues joined with the rhythms of the brass bands. From this music, a new and completely American form of music was born—jazz!

You will notice that the conclusion *repeats* one of the ideas from the introductory paragraph. This, of course, is one means of signaling "the end" to readers. The conclusion of a report can also indicate an ending to your readers by restating your main point, briefly summarizing your facts, or showing a final step in a progression. The above conclusion does all of these things.

Exercise Writing the Conclusion

Write the conclusion to your report. Make sure that it ties the report together and provides it with a definite finish.

Part 6 Revising Your Report

The complete report on "The Origins of Jazz" appears on pages 273-274. This is the final version, the result of several previous drafts. Although revision is an ongoing part of the writing process, it is most important as you work on your rough drafts. A multistep revision process often works best. Use the Guidelines on pages 123 and 177 to help you with your work.

After you have revised the content of your drafts, remember that the revision of a report involves one additional step. *Check your facts for accuracy.* Check the spelling of names and terms, the accuracy of dates, and the correct relationship of ideas.

When all your revisions are complete, proofread your material for errors in grammar, usage, and mechanics. Make a clean, final copy. Then proofread once more for careless errors in copying. Use the Checklist on page 124 to guide your corrections.

Exercise Revising Your Report

Read, revise, and proofread your report. Make a final copy.

THE ORIGINS OF JAZZ

What's as American as apple pie? One possible answer is —
Jazz! This lively music, with its strong rhythms and unusual tonal
effects, is uniquely American. Like America, however, it is
the product of many different cultures and styles. Indeed,
the origins and growth of jazz are as rich and varied as the
music itself.

No one really knows just how and where jazz was born. It is
safe to assume, however, that jazz had its origins in Africa. There
are several clearly identifiable links between West African music
and jazz. For instance, West Africans used music to develop a
single mood and to create an almost hypnotic effect by using
repetition. They also used percussion instruments as a principle means of expression. In addition, West African music ignored regularities of pitch, of time, of timbre, and of vibrato.
Each of these characteristics is also true of jazz. In *What Jazz
Is All About,* Lillian Erlich mentions one other common
element of the two types of music. She writes, "The African
concept of music as a communal, creative activity was always
there. It is at the heart of Afro-American folk music — and
of jazz." (p. 45)

How, then, were these West African roots transferred to
America? It was the Afro-American slaves, pulled from their
homeland and thrust into a vastly different culture, who brought
the characteristics of African music to this country. Once here,
blacks learned the ballads and hymns of Western Europe from
the whites around them. Incorporating elements of their West
African musical heritage, they transformed these ballads and
hymns into their own folk music. These were the work songs,
the plantation cries, the field "hollers," and the spirituals heard
and sung by the early slaves as they gave vent to their loneliness, frustration, and sorrow. From this music came the emotional power that is the first root of jazz.

In New Orleans, this unique music of the black slaves was
taken a step further. Each Sunday, blacks would gather on
Congo Square for a celebration, a *bamboula*. There they re-
called the rhythms of their West African homeland, rhythms

passed down from parent to child in speech, song, and body movement. These highly complicated rhythms were orderly, but the order was unique to that West African culture. There were no four-beat measures of time or absolute rules of where the accent had to fall. In Congo Square, musicians would beat these rhythms on drums of many sizes, and the others would dance and clap. Thus, the beat of jazz was born.

Another element of jazz also developed in New Orleans. Through its years as a French colony, the people who lived in this city on the Delta had heard the strident music of the military brass band and had danced to the rhythms of French quadrilles played by some of these same bands. By the late 1800's, these sounds and rhythms were combined with the beat of the Congo Square drums. This syncopated form of melody became known as "rag" or "ragtime." The music was played by small brass bands made up of the descendents of the earlier slaves who had established the "beat" in Congo Square. The distinctive jazz sound of horns and woodwinds began to emerge. Later, pianos and string instruments were also added.

Along with ragtime came "blues." In the early 1900's, a band leader named W.C. Handy began to write down some of the sounds of black music that he heard while traveling around the South. He adapted music so that it could be played by the "rag" bands. A key characteristic of this sound was the "blue note," a remnant of West African music. Blue notes were certain tones in the scale that were sung just a bit flat and which then slid into the next note. The leader-response pattern and repeated phrases of early black music also made their way into the blues. In this pattern, one singer made a statement and a chorus repeated it, created a variation in it, or made an exclamation about it. The wail and pattern of the blues was complete.

By the early part of this century, these various forms of music had achieved enormous popularity. Their mournful strains and infectious rhythms were heard throughout the country. Soon the blues joined with the rhythms of the brass bands. From this music, a new and completely American form of music was born—jazz!

Part 7 Preparing a Bibliography

When the facts and details of your writing come from sources outside yourself, you must include a list of those sources with your report. This is a bibliography. It comes at the end of the paper.

To prepare your bibliography, look over your bibliography cards. Discard any sources that you did not use. Alphabetize your list by the author's last name or by the title of the source if no author is given. Copy all the information from your bibliography cards.

The writer of the sample report had the following bibliography, which included an essay, two books, a personal interview, an encyclopedia article, and a magazine article.

Bibliography

Borneman, Ernest. "The Roots of Jazz." In *Jazz*. Ed. Nat Hentoff and Albert J. McCarthy. New York: DaCapo Press, 1974, pp. 3-14.

Collier, James L. *The Making of Jazz: A Comprehensive History.* New York: Dell Publishing Co., 1978.

Erlich, Lillian. *What Jazz Is All About.* New York: Julian Mesner Co., 1979.

Imes, Gary, music instructor. Personal interview on the origins of jazz. October 7, 1983.

"Jazz." *World Book Encyclopedia*. 1984 ed.

Lees, G. "Emergence of Jazz." *High Fidelity,* August 1978, pp. 16-17.

Notice that periods follow the author's name and the end of the entry. A period is also placed after a book title. Notice, too, that all lines after the first line are indented.

Exercise Preparing a Bibliography

Use your bibliography cards to make a bibliography for your report. Follow the form given in the lesson. Position the bibliography at the end of your report, either directly after your conclusion or on a separate sheet of paper. Proofread your final copy.

SUMMARY AND APPLICATIONS

1. A report is a piece of writing in which the writer gathers information from outside sources and presents it clearly and accurately. The skills of report-writing can be used for school projects, to write newspaper articles, and in business.

2. Reports can inform the reader, analyze a topic, or compare or contrast subjects. The topic and purpose of the report, as well as the audience, determine the kind of research needed.

3. Prepare a working bibliography on 3″ x 5″ note cards. Also record research information on 3″ x 5″ cards. This includes any material gathered in interviews or from graphic aids. Be sure to record facts, not opinions. Also record information in your own words.

4. A bibliography is the list of outside sources used in the report.

5. For longer reports, a multi-step process of organization and revision is often necessary.

Applications in Other Subject Areas

Business. One common type of business report requires the writer to analyze and draw conclusions from data, organize the material, and present it in a form that can be read and understood by those outside the business. Look at the following chart. Write a short report that presents *and* analyzes the information.

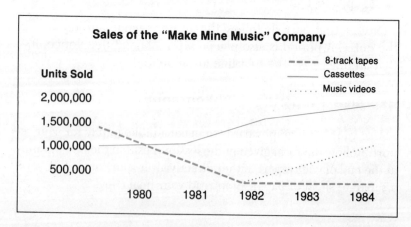

Sales of the "Make Mine Music" Company

- - - - 8-track tapes
——— Cassettes
. . . . . . Music videos

Units Sold

2,000,000
1,500,000
1,000,000
500,000

1980   1981   1982   1983   1984

Chapter 12

Critical
Thinking

Most decisions are fairly easy to make. You probably have little difficulty deciding what clothes you will wear or what music you will listen to. However, many of the most important decisions that you will make in your lifetime will not be so easy. Buying a car, choosing a career, selecting a candidate for political office—these decisions are all much more difficult.

To make these important decisions, you must understand the principles of sound critical thinking. You must know how to gather reliable, factual information, how to evaluate the options of others, and how to form sound opinions of your own. You must also be able to recognize illogical statements and improper appeals to emotion. By studing the principles in this chapter, you will find that decisions in your life will be easier to make. You will also come to think and write more clearly and precisely as you present your own ideas.

Part 1 Establishing Facts

Webster's New World Dictionary defines a **fact** as a "thing that has actually happened or that is really true." A fact, then, is entirely different from something you imagine, guess, or feel.

Statements of fact can be proved true or false. If you state that your team lost last week, for example, you have made a statement of fact, one that can be checked by someone else.

There are two methods for checking statements of fact:

Observe the claim for yourself.
Consult a reliable source.

The ability to prove the truth of statements of fact is important when you do research, when you are reading or listening to the ideas of others, and when you are attempting to express your own ideas and opinions. The following guidelines will help you when attempting to verify statements of fact:

How To Check Factual Statements

1. **If possible, check facts through personal observation.** Trust your senses. If a classmate says, "It's raining outside" or "There are new bleachers in the gymnasium," check these statements by looking outside or by going to the gymnasium. If a salesperson tells you that a particular sweater is hand-woven, look at the label and the material to confirm this.

2. **If personal observation is impossible, consult a reliable source.** Such sources can be reference works or other people. If you are wondering whether you answered a test question correctly, you can consult your textbook, handouts, or classroom notes. If someone tells you that ninety percent of the universe is made of hydrogen, you can ask a chemistry teacher or look in an encyclopedia.

3. **If you use an outside source, make sure that it is up-to-date.** An encyclopedia published in the 1960's will describe smallpox as a commonly-occurring communicable disease. Today, thanks

to a world-wide vaccination program, the disease has been completely conquered. Because facts change, you must always make sure that your sources reflect current knowledge.

4. Make sure that the statement is consistent with other known facts.
When two statements of fact contradict one another, one of them must be wrong. Further research is often required to determine which statement is true. For example, a recent book claimed that the Mayans, an ancient people of South America, had the ability to launch manned flights into space. However, archaeologists point out that the methods of transportation pictured in Mayan art are fairly primitive. The claim for ancient space travel contradicts known facts and, more than likely, the theory is false.

5. Make sure that the source of the statement is reliable and unbiased. A statement is *reliable* if it is based upon expertise or personal experience. For example, encyclopedias are generally reliable sources because the articles in them are usually written by experts.

A statement is *unbiased* if it does not reflect the prejudices of the person making the statement. For example, a report in a medical journal on the effects of smoking is likely to be unbiased. A statement on the same subject made by the owner of a tobacco shop might not be.

Exercises Checking Facts

A. Check the truth of each statement below by consulting the reference work listed in parentheses. Correct false statements.

1. The Los Angeles Rams have won seven division championships, but no Super Bowls. (almanac)
2. Sudan is a tiny African nation bordering on both Ethiopia and Chad. (atlas)
3. Enrico Fermi, the renowned chemist, discovered uranium. (encyclopedia)
4. The name *Joseph* is Hebrew in origin and originally meant "He shall add." (dictionary)
5. Abraham Lincoln had two daughters, but no sons. (textbook, encyclopedia)

6. Mesopotamia was one of the "cradles of civilization." (encyclopedia)

7. A popular food in Great Britain is skittles. (dictionary)

8. The average rainfall in Death Valley is half an inch per year. (almanac)

9. The people of Finland speak Danish. (encyclopedia)

10. Mackinac Island gets its name from an American Indian word meaning "large turtle." (dictionary)

B. None of the following statements are true. Identify each statement as out-of-date, inconsistent with other known facts, or both. Be prepared to defend your answers in class.

1. The most popular form of music in America is the *swing*, which is played by the "big bands."

2. Plants cannot survive in areas where there is little rainfall.

3. People who live outside major urban areas like New York or Boston have no access to the arts.

4. Few women receive college educations.

5. A reusable space vehicle will be a reality in only five years.

Part 2 Distinguishing Between Fact and Opinion

You do not always use factual statements; many of the statements that you make are opinions. An opinion is a statement that cannot be proved with absolute certainty. One way to tell facts from opinions is to ask the following question: Can this statement be proved? If the statement can be proved, it is a fact. If the statement cannot be proved, it is an opinion. Consider the following statements:

STATEMENT OF FACT: Between 1954 and 1974, Hank Aaron hit 733 home runs.

STATEMENT OF OPINION: Hank Aaron is the greatest baseball player who ever lived.

The first statement can be proved by referring to an almanac containing sports records. Since the statement can be proved, it is a fact. The second statement cannot be proved with certainty. People can disagree about it. Therefore, it is an opinion.

Types of Opinions

You can express an opinion in any of three ways: You can make a judgment; you can make a prediction; you can make a statement of obligation. Each of these ways is described below.

Judgments. A judgment is an opinion about something's value. To say that the sun is shining and the temperature is in the 80's is to state a fact. However, if someone says, "It's a beautiful day," this is an opinion. The difference lies in the word "beautiful." This is a judgment word. The word tells you that the speaker values the day highly. Because judgment words express personal opinions, it is possible for people to disagree about statements containing them. Here are some other judgment words:

pretty	valuable	dishonest	mean
attractive	worthless	good	moral
unattractive	cheap	bad	immoral
ugly	honest	kind	wonderful

Predictions. A prediction is a statement made about the future. "The sun will rise tomorrow" seems like a valid statement, yet there is always the chance that it will not. "We're going skiing" is a prediction. So is "I will get my cast off next week." Until these things have actually happened or failed to happen, you cannot prove these statements true or false.

Statements of Obligation. A statement of obligation tells not how things are but how someone feels things should be. The key words in statements of obligation are *should, ought to, must,* and similar terms. "You *should* study accounting," and "People *ought to* grow their own vegetables," both contain words of obligation. Like statements of judgment and predictions, statements of obligation cannot be proved true or false. Therefore, they are opinions.

Exercise   Fact or Opinion?

Below are twenty statements. Decide whether each is a statement of fact or an opinion. If it is an opinion, tell whether it is a judgment, a prediction, or a statement of obligation.

1. Cable television has taken many viewers away from the commercial television networks.

2. President Johnson supported the 1964 Civil Rights Act.

3. Halloween used to be known as *All Hallow's Eve*.

4. Some hospitals offer training programs in Nuclear Medicine Technology.

5. Cable television companies offer wonderful sports programming.

6. President Johnson's birthday should be made a national holiday.

7. By the end of the decade, most Halloween celebrations will be held indoors.

8. Nuclear Medicine Technology provides several wonderful career opportunities.

9. Carrots contain Vitamin A, which is essential to developing night vision.

10. You ought to eat at least one carrot per week.

11. The surface temperature of Venus is 850 degrees Fahrenheit.

12. Most members of the Actor's Equity union are unemployed.

13. America should have been named after Christopher Columbus.

14. The state of Pennsylvania does not have a state song.

15. The Florida Everglades are mysterious and interesting.

16. Someone ought to write a theme song for the state of Pennsylvania.

17. Due to the high surface temperature of Venus, no person will set foot on the planet in our lifetime.

18. Acting is a poor career choice.

19. The Florida Everglades contain many plants and animals that are not found elsewhere in the United States.

20. America was named by a German mapmaker who incorrectly believed that Amerigo Vespucci was the first European explorer of the New World.

Part 3   Supporting and Evaluating Opinions

When you express an opinion, you want it to be one that others will respect and possibly agree with. Similarly, when someone else offers an opinion, you want to examine it closely to see whether or not you agree with it.

One simple test can be used to evaluate both your own opinions and the opinions of others: check to see whether the opinion is supported by facts.

Suppose, for example, that someone says, "You should earn mostly A's if you want a college scholarship." This is a statement of obligation. After some thought, you realize that it is a sound opinion because it can be supported by the following facts:

> Colleges consider grade averages and test scores when awarding scholarships.
>
> Most graduating seniors who are awarded scholarships to college have grade averages better than B+.
>
> National Merit Scholars have B+ to A grade averages.

Now assume that you make the prediction, "I could get a scholarship without earning A's." If you want this opinion to be accepted, you must support it with facts such as the following:

> Several scholarships are available that are based solely on economic background.
>
> Some athletic scholarships are not based upon grades.
>
> Many businesses offer scholarships to children of employees that are not based upon academic achievement.

When you evaluate a statement of opinion, make sure that you also evaluate the facts on which the opinion is based. In other words, make sure that the facts come from a reliable, unbiased source and that they are not out-of-date or inconsistent with other known facts. You should also make sure that the opinion itself does not contain *overgeneralizations, errors in reasoning,* or *improper appeals to emotion.* Parts 4, 5, and 6 of this chapter will describe these characteristics of weak opinions.

Supporting and Evaluating Opinions

A. The following statements are all opinions. Tell whether each opinion is a judgment, a prediction, or a statement of obligation. Write one statement of fact that supports or contradicts each opinion.

1. Someday there will be a colony of people on the moon.
2. Every student ought to learn at least one foreign language.
3. Solar energy is the best energy source available.
4. The world's population must not be allowed to outstrip available food and shelter.
5. Computers will be in every American home by the end of the century.

B. Choose three of the following topics and write statements of opinion concerning them. One opinion should be a judgment. One should be a prediction. One should be a statement of obligation. Then, write two statements of fact to support each of your opinions.

Television	School	Marriage
Sports	Movies	Rearing Children
Books	Music	Careers

Part 4 Dealing with Generalizations

Generalizations are broad statements based upon particular facts. Suppose, for example, that you observe that your cat sheds a great deal of fur in the spring. Suppose that you then observe that several other cats also shed fur at this time of year. You might make the following generalization: "Cats shed fur in spring."

Your process of reasoning could be diagramed as follows:

Cat$_1$ sheds fur in spring. $\Big\}$

Cat$_2$ sheds fur in spring. $\Big\}$ Specific, related facts

Cat$_n$ sheds fur in spring. $\Big\}$

Therefore, cats shed fur in spring. ······· generalization

Of course, after you have made this generalization, you might discover a cat that does not shed its fur in spring. This one fact would make the generalization false. To be absolutely certain that the generalization is true, you would have to observe all of the cats that are alive today. Because it is impossible to gather all of the necessary facts to prove the generalization, you can never be absolutely certain that it is true. Generalizations, like opinions, are only as good as the facts that support them.

Overgeneralizations

Making generalizations based upon insufficient facts is called **overgeneralizing**. Overgeneralizations are usually harmless exaggerations used to express personal feelings. Examples of this kind of overgeneralization include the following:

Every time we plan a picnic, it rains.
There's always a long line at the cafeteria.

No one expects such overgeneralizations to be taken literally.

On the other hand, some overgeneralizations are actually harmful. If you decide not to eat in a certain restaurant or not to buy a certain product because of a single unfortunate experience, that is your decision. But if you attempt to influence others by stating that the restaurant serves spoiled food or that the product falls apart, you are being unfair.

The examples in the paragraph above are quite trivial and harmless. However, overgeneralizations can sometimes be influential and even dangerous. Consider the statement "Labor unions are responsible for the high cost of living." This type of statement could be used in a political campaign or to influence support for a piece of legislation. It is not only an overgeneralization, but it is also harmful in its effect.

Another harmful type of overgeneralization is the **stereotype**. In this sort of statement, an entire group—often separated out by religion, ethnic background, economic level, or nationality—is wrongly identified as sharing certain characteristics or being responsible for some particular event. Such statements are inaccurate, harmful, and irresponsible.

One way to keep from making overgeneralizations is to be careful about using words that name entire groups of things. The word "teenagers," for example, refers to every individual teenager, and should not be used by itself except in statements that are indeed true of teenagers. The statement "Teenagers love rock music" is an overgeneralization because it is not true of *all* teenagers.

Another way to avoid making overgeneralizations is to avoid "absolute words"—words that are used to refer to every event or thing of a kind. Common absolute words used in overgeneralizations are listed on the chart below. Use these words with care when you speak and write. Also, watch for them in your reading and in test questions.

Absolute Words			
all	everyone	none	nobody
every	everybody	no	nowhere
each	everywhere	no one	never

Instead of "absolute words," use words that limit the range of the statement that you are making. Such words are called **qualifiers**. The following are some of the most commonly used qualifiers:

Qualifying Words			
most	usually	seldom	occasionally
many	generally	rarely	at times
much	frequently	hardly ever	tends to be
few	often	a small number	infrequently
some	sometimes	almost	not often

Be sure to choose the most precise qualifier. Notice how the overgeneralizations on the next page—statements that are obviously untrue and harmful—are made more accurate by the use of qualifying words.

Qualifying Generalizations

Teenagers are irresponsible. (overgeneralization)

Some teenagers are irresponsible.

A few teenagers are irresponsible.

All politicians are dishonest. (overgeneralization)

Some politicians are dishonest.

A few politicians are dishonest.

Exercises Dealing with Generalizations

A. For each of the following topics, write one overgeneralization. Then, rewrite your overgeneralization, adding qualifiers to make the generalization accurate.

Extra-curricular Activities   Smoking
Homework   Exercise
Music   Soap Operas

B. Identify the overgeneralizations in the following paragraph and correct them by rewriting as necessary. Underline any qualifiers that you use in your revision.

Everyone loves to go camping. There is nothing quite as nice as pitching a tent under the stars and "roughing it" for a while. It is therefore fortunate that every major city in the U.S. has excellent camping facilities nearby. However, no one can ever really enjoy these facilities because campers don't respect one another's rights. When people are in a campground, they play loud music and leave litter lying about. This is odd because people go camping to escape the noise and clutter of everyday life. The only possible solution to this problem is to close down state parks until people learn how to behave themselves in public places.

Part 5 Detecting Fallacies in Reasoning

Overgeneralizing is just one of the mistakes, or **fallacies**, that occur in reasoning. Fallacies result in weak opinions and lost arguments. You must be aware of common fallacies so that you can avoid them in your own speaking and writing and recognize them in the speaking and writing of others.

Fallacies of Cause and Effect

To find the causes of an event, we usually look at the events that occurred just before the event that we are trying to explain. However, there can be errors associated with this method. One of these errors is the **single cause fallacy**. This occurs whenever an event that has several causes is mistakenly described as having only one cause. For example, to say that the American Civil War was caused by tensions over the issue of slavery is an example of the single cause fallacy. Many differences between the North and South led to the war.

Another common error in reasoning about cause and effect is known by the Latin name **post hoc, ergo propter hoc**. The phrase means "after this, therefore because of this." The fallacy occurs when someone assumes that one event was caused by another simply because two events were close to one another in time. For example, early explorers noticed that after breathing the air near swamps, people developed a disease characterized by chills and fever. Therefore, they named the disease *malaria*, which means "bad air." It was later discovered that the actual cause of the disease was a parasite spread by mosquitos found in swampy areas.

Exercise Avoiding Fallacies of Cause and Effect

Identify the logical fallacy in each of the following passages.

1. Susan does not eat properly and never exercises. She also worries a great deal and stays up late at night. Last week she went

to a doctor, saying only that she always feels tired. The doctor told her to go to bed every evening by 9:30.

2. Tim never believed in superstitions until something happened to prove one of them to him. One day Tim attended a speech meet at a school that was undergoing some new construction. On the way into the school, Tim walked under a ladder. As a result, he lost every round in which he competed.

3. Those students who do poorly on examinations simply don't study enough.

4. Just before the crime rate started to increase, television networks started to air lots of detective shows. Therefore, these shows must have caused the increase in the crime rate.

5. America is a wealthy nation today because Americans are willing to work hard for what they want.

Vague or Undefined Terms

Some weak or meaningless statements can result from using words that are vague or difficult to define. This is especially true with regard to many words that are used to describe people. The word *old*, for example, must be used very carefully. Who is to say when being young ends and being old begins? The word *intelligent* is another example. There is no real agreement as to what constitutes an intelligent person. Anyone who uses this term must therefore define the term when it is used. Consider the following opinions. Which terms contained in these opinions are too vague?

> *The Old Man and the Sea* is an appropriate book for high school students.
> Colleges and universities should only accept the right kind of people.
> The statement made by the speaker was improper and in poor taste.

Whenever you evaluate an argument or an opinion, and whenever you put together an argument or an opinion of your own, make sure that the words used are clearly defined. Otherwise, the argument or opinion will be weak or unclear.

A. Often people have great difficulty agreeing upon a definition for a given word. To demonstrate this, try conducting this poll:

1. Choose five people whom you know. These can be friends, relatives, or teachers.
2. Ask each of these people the following questions:
   a. What is a radical?
   b. What is a liberal?
   c. What is a conservative?
3. Record the answers to your questions carefully. Then, gather your answers together and bring them to class for discussion.

B. Write your own paragraph, identifying yourself as a *radical*, a *liberal*, or a *conservative*. In the body of the paragraph, explain what you mean by the term.

The Either/Or Fallacy

Whenever you are listening to an argument or opinion, be alert to the use of the word *or*. This word is often used to present alternatives or to classify things by placing them in groups.

> ALTERNATIVE: The speech team must *charge additional dues* **or** *cancel the banquet.*

> GROUPS: The residents of the neighborhood were all either *wealthy businessmen* **or** *entertainers.*

There is nothing wrong with presenting two alternatives or placing things in two groups. Just be sure that you do not give the impression that there are only two alternatives or groups when there are actually more. If you were to do so, you would be committing the **either/or fallacy**. If, for example, you were to classify all people as either friends or enemies, you would be ignoring or misjudging those people who do not fit into either category. If you were to say that "By 1990 everyone in the U.S. will either live in the country or in large cities," you would be leaving out the many alternate possibilities between these two extremes.

False Analogy

An **analogy** is a comparison of two things. Analogies are useful for explaining unfamiliar things in familiar terms. For example, you might describe the force of gravity as being like elastic bands connecting all of the objects in the universe to one another. This would be fine as long as you were aware that there are important differences between gravity and elastic bands. Gravity, for example, does not break at great distances.

Assuming that two things are similar when they are not is a common fallacy known as **false analogy**. For example, someone might say: The United States and the Soviet Union are like two fighters in a boxing ring. This is a poor analogy because the things being compared are not really similar. Boxing gloves are not quite as lethal as nuclear weapons, and powerful countries do not have to go along with the judgments of outside referees. Before using an analogy, test it by asking these questions:

1. Are the two things I am comparing really similar?
2. Does the analogy suggest similarities that do not exist?

Exercises Avoiding the Either/Or Fallacy and False Analogies

A. The following statements all contain the words *either*, or *or*. Tell why each statement is an example of the either/or fallacy.

1. Either you like rock and roll music or you are a snob.
2. All people are either leaders or followers.
3. Take vitamins regularly or you will become malnourished.
4. A high school graduate must either go to college or get a job.
5. There's no in-between when it comes to mathematics. You either love it or you hate it.

B. What similarities exist between the two items in each analogy below? What differences exist? How good is each analogy?

1. Taking a test is like participating in a beauty contest.
2. The brain is a kind of computer.
3. Life is like a baseball game.

Circular Reasoning

Sometimes people try to prove a statement simply by repeating it in other words. Suppose, for example, that you want to prove the statement "Mr. Donegal is an excellent gardener." You cannot offer the statement "He is really good at caring for plants" as proof of the first statement because the two statements mean roughly the same thing. Offering a restatement as proof is a common fallacy known as **circular reasoning** or **begging the question**.

Stacking

The fallacy of **stacking** occurs when someone ignores facts that contradict the position that he or she wants to prove. Suppose, for example, that you favor purchasing new band uniforms and that you have the following facts:

1. Over half of the band uniforms now owned by your school are threadbare.
2. The judges of the state band competition that you are entering will consider the quality of your uniforms when judging your band's performance.
3. Ninety percent of the student population is opposed to buying new band uniforms.

If you were to present the first two facts but ignore the third, you would be committing the error of stacking.

Equivocation

Equivocation is the error of taking unfair advantage of the multiple meanings of words. Suppose, for example, that you read an advertisement for "genuine Indian rugs." You purchase one of these rugs, take it home, and discover that the label says "Made in America" instead of "Made in India." You then take the rug back to the store and are told, "Well, the design is Indian, isn't it?" The salesperson has taken unfair advantage of the fact that the phrase "Indian rug" has more than one meaning.

Exercises Avoiding Circular Reasoning, Stacking, and Equivocation

A. Identify the fallacies in each of the following:

1. You read the following headline in a disreputable newspaper:

SCIENTISTS RAISE THE DEAD

You then read the article and find out that it is about excavating the tomb of an Egyptian king.

2. Biology is much more interesting than geology because life science holds more fascination than earth science.

3. In Shakespeare's play *Macbeth*, three witches tell the hero that he will not be harmed until the forest of Birnam moves to Dunsinane hill. Since Macbeth knows that trees cannot walk, he feels secure. However, near the end of the play, a rebel army cuts branches from Birnam Wood to carry in front of them for protection as they march on Dunsinane Castle.

4. Jules Breton's painting, "Song of the Lark" is one of the most beautiful works of art ever produced because it is so pretty and is such a pleasure to look at.

5. The film *E.T.* was popular because so many of the people who saw it, liked it.

B. Below you are given a question and a series of facts. Using these facts, write one paragraph that commits the fallacy of stacking. Then write another paragraph that presents the facts in a well-balanced manner.

Should schools be in session year-round?

FACTS	
Pro	More time would be available for learning. More class time could be devoted to each subject.
Con	Most students and teachers oppose year-round school. Year-round school would cost taxpayers more money.

Part 6　Recognizing Improper Appeals to Emotion

Often other people will try to persuade you by appealing to your emotions. A charity, for example, might use this technique to gain sympathy and donations for disaster victims. A political advertisement might use an emotional appeal to create respect and admiration for a particular candidate. There is nothing wrong with such appeals to emotion as long as they are not misleading. However, many of the commonly used emotional appeals are, in fact, misleading. It is therefore important that you learn to recognize them.

Snarl Words and Purr Words

Sometimes words are used not to communicate ideas or information, but simply to create an emotion in the reader or listener. **Purr words** such as *fresh, exciting, new,* and *marvelous* are used to create positive emotions. **Snarl words** such as *disgusting, ridiculous, lazy,* or *unimaginative* are used to create negative emotions. For example, one very successful jingle from a car commercial was "Baseball, hot dogs, apple pie, and Chevrolet." The commercial gave some specific information about the cars. It then used purr words to strengthen the listener's positive feelings about the product.

Irrelevant Personal Attacks

People who disagree about an issue should be careful to limit their discussion to the issue itself. They should not bring statements about each other's character into their discussion. To do so would be to commit the error of making an **irrelevant personal attack**, a technique also known by the Latin term *ad hominem* (to the man). Consider the following excerpt from a political debate:

CANDIDATE A: If I am elected, I will make money for education, my number one priority...

CANDIDATE B: If you vote for me, you will keep that lazy
spendthrift, Candidate A, out of office.

The first candidate is addressing a genuine issue. The second
candidate is ignoring the real issue and leading the discussion off
track by making an irrelevant personal attack.

Bandwagon/Snob Appeal

Sometimes people are pressured by others to adopt some belief or to take some action simply in order to conform. This is
called the **bandwagon** appeal. For example, if everyone you know
suddenly started wearing scarves in the summertime, there would
probably be a great deal of pressure on you to "jump on the
bandwagon" and wear them also.

A variation of the bandwagon technique is called **snob appeal**.
This is a kind of reverse bandwagon in which people are encouraged to do, not what everyone does, but what is done only
by a select group of people. For example, if someone were to tell
you that you should wear scarves in the summertime because all
of the really stylish people are wearing them, this person would
be attempting to influence you through snob appeal.

Transfer

Sometimes people will attempt to associate your feelings about
one thing with another, unrelated thing. This is called **transfer**.
Advertisers make use of transfer when they associate their clients'
products with famous people, popular events, or interesting places.
For example, many Americans have strong, positive feelings about
the Olympic Games. Therefore, an advertiser might show a group
of people watching an Olympic competition while drinking a
particular soft drink. Some politicians make use of this technique when they have themselves photographed holding babies
or standing under the statues of national heroes.

Testimonial

A **testimonial** is a personal endorsement of an idea or a product. Testimonial can be a powerful persuasive technique, especially if the person making the testimonial is famous and popular. For example, a well-known model might be hired to make a testimonial on the quality of a cosmetic. A famous sports hero might volunteer to make a testimonial for a political candidate.

Unfortunately, the people who make testimonials are often unqualified. A baseball player is not necessarily an expert on politics. When you hear a testimonial, ask two questions:

1. Does this person speak from personal experience?
2. Does this person speak from expertise?

Exercise Improper Appeals to Emotion

Identify the improper emotional appeals in the passages below by choosing the correct types from those provided in parentheses.

1. Join the select few who will not settle for anything less than the latest in video technology. Buy new "SensoriVision." (irrelevant personal attack, snob appeal, testimonial)

2. You all know me. As a student council delegate for the past two years, I have helped to bring many exciting activities to our school, including the popular Student/Teacher Variety Show. If you like what I have done in the past, I would urge you to support my choice for student body president, Carlotta Rodriquez. (snarl words, bandwagon, irrelevant personal attack, testimonial)

3. I don't think he should be allowed to represent our school in the state mathematics contest. After all, he doesn't dress properly. (transfer, irrelevant personal attack, bandwagon)

4. Remember October nights, football games, autumn leaves, bonfires, campouts, hayrides, and jack-o'-lanterns? Recapture these moments with a tall, refreshing glass of Opal Orchard's Apple Juice. Opal Orchard's—It's a little taste of October. (snob appeal, testimonial, irrelevant personal attack, transfer)

5. Twenty major cities already have this law on the books. Our town should,too. (transfer, testimonial, bandwagon)

SUMMARY AND APPLICATIONS

1. The principles of critical thinking can help you avoid weaknesses in your own speech and writing and to recognize them in the speech and writing of others.

2. Facts can be proved by observation or by reference to authority. Opinions cannot be proved, but can be supported by facts.

3. Three common types of opinion are judgments, predictions, and statements of obligation.

4. Avoid overgeneralization and stereotyping.

5. Learn to recognize and avoid the major logical fallacies (single cause; *post hoc, ergo propter hoc;* vague or undefined terms; either/or; false analogy; circular reasoning; stacking; and equivocation).

6. Learn to recognize and avoid improper appeals to emotion (snarl words, purr words, bandwagon, snob appeal, transfer, irrelevant personal attacks, and testimonial).

Applications in Other Subject Areas

Mass Media. Put together a scrapbook of improper emotional appeals by finding examples of each of the following in magazine advertisements:

snarl words	transfer
purr words	testimonial
bandwagon	snob appeal

Fine Arts. Find a review of a movie, play, or television show in a newspaper or news magazine. Determine the author's overall opinion of the work being reviewed. Then, list the facts provided to support this opinion. Did the author support the opinion well? Why or why not? Then, write your own review of a movie, play, or television show. In the pre-writing stage of your work, be sure to gather sufficient facts and details to support your opinion.

Chapter 13

Study Skills and Test-Taking

Being a high school student is no easy task. Enormous pressures are placed on you every day. You must study for exams and quizzes. You must complete compositions, reports, and other projects. You must devote hours to practicing your skills in mathematics, English, and other subject areas. In addition to these academic demands, you must fulfill many social obligations and other outside responsibilities. In short, you are required to do a great deal in very little time.

In order to succeed in meeting your responsibilities, you must be extremely well organized. Learning the study and test-taking skills discussed in this chapter will help you use your time wisely and effectively. Learning these skills will also help you in later life by improving your organization abilities and by improving your scores on college and job-related examinations.

Part 1 Establishing Study Habits

You know that careful planning can make writing easier. In a similar way, a well thought out study plan can make completing assignments and taking tests much simpler. Learn to approach your study sessions logically, using the following guidelines:

1. Study in a suitable environment. Your study area should be quiet, free of distractions, and well lighted. It should also be well supplied with study tools, including pens, pencils, paper, and a dictionary.

2. Understand your directions before beginning an assignment. If your instructions are written, read them through carefully and completely before starting to work on the assignment. If your directions are oral, be sure to list all of the required steps in their proper order. Associate each step in every assignment with a key word that describes what you must do. Such words include *answer, explain, research, memorize, write, read, draw, solve,* or *review.* Know precisely what you must do, and when the assignment must be turned in.

3. Schedule your study time carefully. Record all assignments in an assignment notebook. This notebook should contain columns for each of the following:

   a. Name of class
   b. Assignment
   c. Materials needed to complete assignment
   d. Date assignment is given
   e. Date assignment is due

Refer to this notebook daily. Break long-term assignments— ones that cover several days or weeks—into separate steps. Then assign times for the completion of each of these steps.

Make up a weekly study schedule showing all of your personal commitments and the times available to complete particular assignments. Schedule at least two twenty- to forty-minute study sessions per day (You may need more). Allow yourself ten-minute breaks between study sessions. Always tackle your hardest assignments first, while your mind is fresh.

4. Use the SQ3R method for reading textbooks. This is one of the most effective approaches to studying written material. It consists of five steps: Survey, Question, Read, Recite, and Review.

Using SQ3R

Survey the material. Look over the entire article or selection to get a general idea of what you will be reading. Read the introduction and also the summary, if there is one. Check the titles and headings and look at any illustrations.

Question. Prepare a set of questions. Decide what questions you should be able to answer at the end of your reading. Use any study questions presented in the book or provided by your teacher. You can also make up your own questions by turning each title and heading into a question. Pictures, maps, or charts can also be used to make up questions.

Read the selection. Look for the answers to the questions as you read. Also identify the central thoughts in each section.

Recite the answers. After you finish your reading, recite in your own words the answers to your prepared questions. Make notes on the answers. Also make sure you have grasped any other important points of the selection and record those, too.

Review the selection. Quickly read over your notes and look over the main points in the book to impress them on your memory. Look up the answers to any questions you are still not sure of.

---

5. Take notes as you read and listen. Write legibly in a notebook, using phrases and abbreviations. You may want to use a modified outline form, putting main points at the margin and indenting details under these points.

6. Adjust your reading speed. Slow down for difficult, detailed, or new material; speed up for material that you are surveying and for easy or familiar material. There are two kinds of fast reading, each with its own method and purpose.

Skimming involves moving your eyes quickly over a page or selection, noting titles, topic sentences, and highlighted words or phrases to get a general idea of the content of a selection.

Scanning involves moving your eye quickly across a line or down a page to locate particular information. When scanning, look for key words and phrases that indicate that you are close to the information that you need. Then, stop scanning and read slowly.

Exercises Establishing Good Study Habits

A. Start a daily assignment notebook. Include columns on each page for the name of the course, the assignment, the date the material was assigned, the due date, and materials you will need.

B. Set up a study schedule for this week. Include on this schedule all of your personal commitments. Then, mark study times.

C. Apply the **SQ3R** study method to the rest of this chapter.

Part 2 Studying for a Test

The announcement of an upcoming test may cause you some nervousness and concern. However, if you use the study techniques described in Part 1, you will find that you are already quite well prepared for most examinations. By learning a few additional techniques, you can approach any test confidently.

There are many different kinds of tests. Every type of test has its own special characteristics and strategies. However, learning an effective method of review will help you in tests of all kinds.

Effective review consists of several steps. The first and perhaps most crucial step is to allow yourself sufficient time. As soon as you learn that you are going to have a test, enter on your study calendar the test date *and* dates for reviewing test material.

1. Take down all information given by your teacher concerning the test. Make sure that you know the date of the test, what material the test will cover, and the form that the test will take (essay, short answer, or objective—see pages 304-308).

2. Study from as many different sources of information as possible. Refer to your textbooks, notes, quizzes, papers, and any other materials that contain information that will be covered by the test. Using the SQ3R study method, reread as much of the material as time allows. Look at chapter summaries and introductions. Skim chapters, reading all headings and subheadings and all boldface, colored, or italicized material. Skim your notes.

3. Put together a list of study questions on the material to be covered by the test. Make up questions corresponding to the important information in these materials. Combine your list of study questions with any study guides supplied by your teacher. Keep a separate list of key terms, including definitions, names, dates, important events, formulae, theories, and concepts. Make sure that you study the proper spellings of key terms.

4. Quiz yourself using the questions and the list of key terms from step three. There are several methods for doing this. One method is to write out all of the questions and key terms in test form and to give yourself this test. Another method is to make flashcards, putting your questions and key terms on one side of the cards and answers or explanations on the other side.

5. Find and review answers to any questions that you could not answer in step four.

6. If time permits, repeat steps four and five on several occasions before the exam.

Some students find it beneficial to recopy or outline their notes, highlighting all significant information. This can be a very effective study method because the physical act of writing forces you to concentrate on the material. No matter what type of review you use, however, be sure to get enough sleep before the test.

Exercise Preparing for Tests

Assume that you are being tested on Parts 1 and 2 of this chapter. Make a list of key words and phrases covered in these parts. Also write a list of study questions that cover this material.

Part 3 Taking the Test

Preparation, by itself, is not enough to ensure that you will do well on a test. You must also use your time wisely *during* tests. The following guidelines will help you to get the best results from the preparation that you have done.

Guidelines for Test-Taking

1. **Survey the test and budget your time.**

   a. Glance over the entire test before starting it. Determine how long the test is so that you can pace yourself.

   b. Determine the order in which you plan to answer the questions. Note which questions are worth the most points and which are easiest. Answer these first.

2. **Read or listen to all directions carefully.**

   a. Determine whether or not you are allowed to use materials such as outlines, books, notes, etc.

   b. Make sure that you understand all oral or written directions before you begin work.

   c. Be aware of special requirements given in the directions. For example, if the test is machine scored, you will have to make dark, heavy pencil marks on the answer sheet.

   d. Before answering a specific question, note the type of answer called for. Look for words such as *find, write,* or *explain.* On true/false or multiple choice tests, read all answers before making your choice.

3. **Save difficult questions for last.**

   Return to these after you have completed the rest of the test. You will often find that some questions on a test suggest answers to other questions.

4. **Save time for review, proofreading, and revision.**

   Look over the test after you finish it. Return to any questions that you have not answered. Check your answers to difficult questions a second time.

Part 4   Types of Test Questions

Once you understand the general strategies for test-taking, you can concentrate on some more specific ones. These strategies are determined by the types of tests and test questions you are dealing with. If you familiarize yourself with these questions and techniques, you will be able to complete tests more confidently.

The most common sort of examination is the **objective test**. Objective tests may consist of *multiple choice, true/false, matching, completion,* or *short answer questions*. Also common are **essay** questions on examinations. Each type of test question requires particular strategies.

Multiple Choice Questions

On **multiple choice** tests, the student is asked to choose the *best* answer from among a group of answers that are provided on the test. The strategies listed below are useful for completing multiple choice tests:

1. Read through all of the choices before deciding on your answer.
2. Always eliminate incorrect answers first.
3. Choose the most complete and accurate answer.
4. Be wary of choices that contain words such as *totally, always, never, only,* or *forever.*
5. Pay particular attention to choices such as *none of the above* or *all of the above.*

EXAMPLE

Which of the following literary forms did *not* begin as part of the oral tradition?

    a. the epic   c. the ballad
    b. the novel   d. the folktale

True/False Questions

On **true/false** tests, the student tells whether statements are true or false. The following strategies are useful:

1. If part of a statement is false, the whole statement is false.
2. Statements with absolute words like *all, always, only,* and *everyone* are frequently false.
3. Statements with qualifying words like *generally, probably, sometimes, usually, often,* and *most* are frequently true.

EXAMPLE

All primates are monkeys. *false*

Matching Questions

On **matching** tests, the student matches items in one column with items in a second column. The following strategies are useful:

1. Check the directions to see how many times each item can or must be used.
2. Read all of the items in both columns before pairing them.
3. Match items that you are certain about first.
4. Cross out items as you use them.
5. Be careful. If you have to change one answer, you may be forced to change several other answers as well.

EXAMPLE

1. Antoine Becquerel → **A.** discoverer of radium
2. Michael Faraday → **B.** discoverer of radioactivity
3. Marie Curie → **C.** inventor of electric motor
4. Guglielmo Marconi → **D.** inventor of the radio

Completion (Fill-in-the-Blank) Questions

On **completion** tests, the student is asked to fill in gaps in statements provided on the exam. The following strategies are useful:

1. Make sure your answer fits grammatically into the slot.
2. If several words are needed to answer the question, write in all of them.
3. Write legibly, and be sure that your spelling, grammar, punctuation, and capitalization are correct.

EXAMPLE

A shape that has four sides, with opposite sides parallel, is called a _parallelogram_.

Short Answer Questions

On **short answer** tests, the student is asked to answer questions briefly in complete sentences. The following strategies are useful for short answer tests:

1. Answer in complete sentences.
2. Be sure that you answer all parts of the question.
3. Check your grammar, spelling, punctuation, and capitalization.
4. Write legibly.

EXAMPLE

When and by whom was the Buddhist religion founded?

The Buddhist religion was founded by Gautama Buddha in the sixth century B.C.

Essay Tests

An essay test measures both knowledge of content and your writing skills. The following strategies are useful:

Pre-Writing

1. Read the question carefully, looking for words that tell you what you must do. Such words include *compare, describe, explain, interpret,* or *summarize.*
2. Determine precisely what information the essay should contain. In other words, make sure that your essay contains the ideas or information requested in the essay question.
3. If the essay question is divided into parts, organize your essay into corresponding sections, each covering a part of the essay question.
4. Quickly make a modified outline of the major points and supporting details that you want to cover.
5. Write a controlling idea that includes a brief restatement of the question and a general statement of your answer. These will appear in the introduction to your essay.

Writing

1. Unless otherwise instructed, double space your essay so that you can easily make corrections later.
2. If you are asked to write a long essay, divide the essay into several paragraphs. Make sure that every paragraph has a topic sentence, good supporting ideas, and transitions that tie ideas in the paragraph together.
3. Make sure that the essay itself has an introduction, a body, and a conclusion.
4. Write legibly, and be careful about matters of spelling, punctuation, and capitalization.

Revision

1. Check your answer to make sure you have included all important ideas.
2. Save time to proofread your essay.
3. Correct all errors in grammar, usage, and mechanics.

Exercises **Taking Tests**

A. Answer the following questions:

1. When taking a test, save time at the end to _____ .

2. If a test is machine-scored, you should make dark, heavy, marks on the answer sheet with a _____ .

3. Which of the following is a type of objective examination?
   a. multiple choice   d. true/false
   b. matching   e. all of the above
   c. completion   f. none of the above

4. Match the types of tests with their strategies:

   a. true/false

   1. If any part of a statement is false, the whole statement is false.

   b. multiple choice

   2. Make sure your answer fits grammatically into the given space.

   c. completion

   3. Read all of the items in both columns before pairing them.

   d. matching

   4. Pay attention to answers such as *none of the above* or *all of the above*.

B. Write a one-paragraph essay explaining three important effects that television has on the lives of Americans. Give reasons or examples to support your topic sentence, and follow the strategies outlined in Part 4. Allow yourself exactly twenty minutes.

Part 5   Standardized Tests

You are probably familiar with standardized tests. These are tests that allow one person's performance to be compared with those of thousands of others who have taken the test. Standardized tests are often administered in the form of a test booklet, which is accompanied by a special answer sheet that can be graded by computer. You may have already taken standardized tests in any of the following areas: (1) learning ability, (2) learning achievement, (3) aptitude and interest, or (4) personality.

During the next two or three years, you may be taking several standardized tests especially designed for those who wish to attend college. These include tests of academic ability, or aptitude, such as the Preliminary Scholastic Aptitude Test (PSAT), the Scholastic Aptitude Test (SAT), and the American College Testing Program Assessment Test (ACT). Unlike most of the tests that you take in high school, aptitude tests are not meant to measure what you have learned in specific courses. Instead, tests of this kind usually measure basic skills in language and mathematics. They are used to predict how well you will do in the future, in college, or on the job.

In addition, some college programs require applicants to take tests of achievement such as the Advanced Placement Test (APT). Achievement tests measure what you have learned in high school.

Because college entrance examinations cover skills or learning gained over a long period of time, cramming is ineffective as a method of preparation. The best preparation for college entrance examinations is to concentrate on improving your language and mathematics skills by working hard in your high school classes. Another effective method of preparation is to study different types of test questions you are likely to encounter in standardized tests: *antonyms, analogies, reading comprehension, sentence correction, sentence completion,* and *usage questions.*

Antonyms

An **antonym** is a word of opposite meaning. Questions covering antonyms are answered by selecting the choice most opposite in meaning to the given word. These questions test the range of your vocabulary. A typical antonym question looks like this:

EXAMPLE: **Antonyms**

EULOGIZE   A) praise   B) malign   C) support
                D) usurp   E) undermine

To answer an antonym question, use the following strategies:

1. Remember that you must find a word that is *opposite* in meaning. Do not be thrown off by *synonyms*—words that are similar in meaning—that are included among the possible answers.
2. Decide whether the given word is positive or negative, and then eliminate all of the choices that are in the same category as the given words.
3. Remember that many words have more than one meaning. If no word seems to fit your sense of the opposite meaning, think about other meanings for the given word.
4. If you don't know the meaning of a given word, try to analyze the word's prefix or base word in order to define it. See Chapter 1 for more information on word parts.

Analogies

Analogies are pairs of words that are related in some way to each other. In an analogy question, you are given two words that are related to one another in some way. Your job is to find two other words that are related to one another in the same way. A typical analogy question looks like this:

EXAMPLE: **Analogies**

STANZA: POEM::   A) movie: script   B) novel: chapter
                              C) act: play   D) song: melody

To answer analogy questions, use the following strategies:

1. First, determine the relationship between the first pair of words. Then, create a sentence that contains both words and that shows the relationship between them. The first pair of words in the above example can be used as follows:

A *stanza* is a section of a *poem*.

2. Second, find the pair of words from among the answers that can replace the first pair in your sentence:

An *act* is a section of a *play*.

3. Third, recognize the many types of relationships expressed in analogies. The following chart lists many of the most common of these relationships.

Type of Analogy	Example
cause to effect	virus: cold
part to whole	finger: hand
object to purpose	car: transportation
action to object	dribble: basketball
item to category	salamander: amphibian
type to characteristic	owl: nocturnal
word to synonym	antipathy: aversion
word to antonym	antipathy: attraction
object to its material	shoe: leather
worker and creation	composer: symphony
worker and tool	carpenter: hammer
time sequence	sunrise: sunset

Reading Comprehension

Reading comprehension questions test your ability to analyze and interpret written material. In the reading comprehension sections of standardized tests, you must first read a passage and then answer questions about it. The following are some common subjects covered by reading comprehension questions:

1. The central thought of a passage
2. Specific details found in a passage
3. Conclusions based upon statements made in a passage
4. The meanings of specific words in a passage
5. The mood or attitude of the writer of a passage
6. Specific techniques of the writer of the passage

A typical reading comprehension question looks like this:

To answer reading comprehension questions, use the following strategies:

1. Read the question below the passage first. This will help you to focus on the main idea of the passage as you read it.
2. Read all of the choices before you select an answer.
3. Answer questions based upon material in the passage, not upon your own opinions or knowledge.

4. Do not choose an answer simply because the answer is a true statement. Make sure that your choice answers the specific question that is asked.
5. Do not be misled by choices that are partially correct.
6. Refer back to the passage if you need to check an answer.
7. Set a time limit for completing questions on each passage.

Sentence Correction

Sentence correction items examine your ability to eliminate an error in a sentence. You are asked to evaluate the underlined part of a sentence. If it is correct, then choose answer *A*, which repeats the original word or words. If you think the underlined section is incorrect, then select the group of words that is correct. A typical sentence correction question looks like this:

EXAMPLE: **Sentence Correction**

One of the giant meteors <u>are veering from their path.</u>
   A. are veering from their path
   B. are veering from its path
   C. is veering from their path
   D. is veering from its path
   E. veering from its path

To answer sentence correction questions, use the following strategies:

1. Identify the error before you look at the choices.
2. Pay careful attention to grammar, word choice, sentence construction, and punctuation. In the above question, for example, the verb *are veering* and the pronoun *their* do not agree with the subject of the sentence, *one*. Answers *B* and *C* each retain one of these agreement errors. Answer *E* results in a sentence fragment. Answer *D* should be chosen because it corrects both of these errors.

Sentence Completion

Sentence completion questions test your ability to use vocabulary words and to recognize relationships among parts of a sentence. You are given a sentence in which one or two words are missing. You must then choose the word or words that best complete the sentence. A typical sentence completion question looks like this:

EXAMPLE: Sentence Completion

Age did not _____ but actually _____ this artist's output.

A) renew...furthered
B) slow...slacked
C) decrease...increased
D) lengthen...narrowed
E) publicize...secluded

To answer sentence completion questions, use the following strategies:

1. Read the entire sentence carefully, underlining or circling key words. Pay particular attention to words that indicate contrast *(but, however)* or similarity *(and, another)*. For example, the word *but* in the sample question above gives you a clue that the correct word pair will contain words that are opposite in meaning. The correct answer is, therefore, *C)* decrease . . . increased.

2. Try each of the choices in the sentence. Eliminate those choices that make no sense, those that are grammatically incorrect, or those that contradict some other part of the statement.

3. Look for grammatical clues within the sentence. Does the space call for a verb, an adjective, a noun? If the answer is a verb, what tense must the verb be written in to correspond with the rest of the sentence? Asking such questions may help you to eliminate some incorrect answers.

Usage Questions

Usage questions require you to recognize writing that does not follow the conventions of standard written English. Common errors in such sentences include incorrect verb tenses, improper agreement of pronoun and antecedent, lack of parallel structure, incorrect use of idioms, and improper word choices.

In usage questions, four words or phrases are underlined and lettered. You must choose the one underlined part that needs to be corrected. If the sentence is correct as written, mark the *no error* slot on your answer sheet. A typical usage question looks like this:

EXAMPLE: Usage Questions

Her remarks <u>were</u> startling; <u>their</u> <u>affect</u> on the
       A   B   C
audience <u>was</u> immediately apparent. <u>No error.</u>
        D   E

To answer usage questions, use the following strategies:

1. Read the sentence through completely.
2. Check to see that the sentence is not a fragment.
3. Check to see that the subject of the sentence agrees in number with the verb.
4. Check to see whether the pronouns agree with their antecedents.
5. Make sure that verbs are in the correct tense.
6. Check the grammatical construction of the sentence. In particular, check for improper parallelism (See Chapter 5).
7. Check the word choice.
8. Look for misuse of adjectives, adverbs, and other words. In the question above, for example, *affect* is incorrectly used. The word should be *effect*.
9. Look for dangling participles.
10. Remember that the error—if there is one—occurs in an *underlined* portion of the sentence.

General Strategies

No matter what type of question you are answering, certain strategies can be applied to any part of a standardized test. Keep the following guidelines in mind.

Basic Strategies: Standardized Tests

1. Budget your time carefully.

2. Leave the most difficult questions for last.

3. Most standardized tests make use of computerized answer sheets. Students are required to fill in circles corresponding to the correct answer in the test booklet, as follows:

   23. (a)   (b)   (c)   (d)   (e)

   When using such computerized answer sheets, follow these guidelines:

   a. Always fill in the circle for the correct answer completely.

   b. Check your numbering on the answer sheet periodically.

   c. Never make notes or stray marks on the answer sheet. These could be misread as wrong answers by the scoring machine. Instead, write on the test booklet itself or on scratch paper, as indicated in the directions for the test.

4. In the test booklet, cross out the obviously wrong answers, circle key words, and put a check mark next to questions that you will be coming back to.

5. Random guessing is unlikely to improve your score. In fact, on some standardized tests, points are deducted for incorrect answers. Therefore, guessing is not a good idea. However, if you can eliminate one or more of the choices, then your chances of guessing the correct answer are increased.

All of these strategies can help you to increase your chances of success on standardized tests. Remember, too, that a good mental attitude, sensible physical preparation, and the ability to relax can be equally important factors.

Exercises Understanding Standardized Tests

A. Read the following descriptions. Write the type of test question each refers to: antonyms, analogies, reading comprehension, sentence correction, sentence completion, or usage.

1. Includes these types: "item to category" and "causes to effect."

2. Often tests your ability to draw conclusions.

3. Tests your ability to evaluate and correct sentences.

4. Requires an ability to identify words with opposite meanings.

5. Asks you to use vocabulary words and to recognize relations among parts of a sentence.

6. Requires a knowledge of standard and nonstandard English.

7. Requires you to see relationships between pairs of words.

8. Contains four underlined words or phrases.

9. Asks you to interpret written material.

10. Is best answered if one first identifies the error and then chooses the best replacement.

B. Write one example of each type of standardized test question (excluding reading comprehension). Check your questions and answer choices carefully. Use a dictionary and the Handbook Sections of this text to make your questions as challenging and accurate as possible.

SUMMARY AND APPLICATIONS CHAPTER 13

1. Good study skills will teach you to organize your responsibilities and to approach problems logically.

2. Make sure that you understand all directions before beginning any assignment. Record your assignments in an assignment notebook. Schedule your study time carefully and choose a suitable study area. Use the SQ3R study method. Take notes using your own shorthand or a modified outline. Adjust your reading speed to suit the material.

3. When reviewing for a test, use any materials that contain information to be covered by the test. Skim this material. Put together a list of study questions and a list of key terms. Quiz yourself on the material combined in these lists.

4. Know the type of test you will be taking and follow the specific test-taking strategies outlined in this chapter.

Applications in Other Subject Areas

Business / Health. To enter many occupations in the business and health fields, you must first pass examinations that demonstrate your occupational training or skills. The following is a partial list of such occupations:

Real Estate Brokerage Medical Technology
Civil Service Pharmacy
Accounting Nursing
Insurance Nutrition

Choose three of the above fields and do some research to determine what examinations are required for entry into these fields.

All Subjects. Choose a test from one of your classes on which you scored lower than you would like to have scored. Make two columns on a sheet of paper. In one column, list everything you did right when preparing for and taking this test. In the other column, list everything that you could have done to improve your score. Refer to specific guidelines given in this chapter.

Chapter 14

Using the Library and Reference Works

During your high school years, you will often be required to do library research for classes in literature, history, science, and other subjects. Sometimes the purpose of this research will be to find information for use in compositions, reports, and speeches. At other times, you may be asked to use library materials to supplement the textbooks, lectures, and discussions in your classes.

To use the library effectively, you must know what materials libraries contain, how these materials are classified and arranged, and how to locate specific information in books and reference materials. This chapter will give you the basic information that you need to make efficient use of the library.

Part 1 How Books Are Classified and Arranged

It is important for you to understand the classification and arrangement of books in a library. Knowing how and where books are placed will enable you to find any book you need.

The Classification of Books

Fiction. Novels and short-story collections are usually arranged in alphabetical order by author. For example, if you wanted to read the novel *A Separate Peace* by John Knowles, you would first look for the section in the library marked FICTION. Then you would look for books that have authors whose last names begin with *K* and find the book in its alphabetical position. If the book is not there, someone else has borrowed it, or a browser has carelessly returned it to the wrong position. Check to see if the book is out of alphabetical order.

Nonfiction. Most libraries classify nonfiction books according to the Dewey Decimal System. This system, which is named for its originator, the American librarian Melvil Dewey, classifies all books by number in ten major categories.

000–099 **General Works** (encyclopedias, handbooks, almanacs, etc.)

100–199 **Philosophy** (includes psychology, ethics, etc.)

200–299 **Religion** (the Bible, theology, mythology)

300–399 **Social Science** (sociology, economics, government, education, law, folklore)

400–499 **Language** (languages, grammars, dictionaries)

500–599 **Science** (mathematics, chemistry, physics, biology, etc.)

600–699 **Useful Arts** (farming, cooking, sewing, nursing, engineering, radio, television, gardening, industries, inventions)

700–799	**Fine Arts** (music, painting, drawing, acting, photography, games, sports, amusements)
800–899	**Literature** (poetry, plays, essays)
900–999	**History** (biography, travel, geography)

As you can see from the major categories of the Dewey Decimal System, each discipline has a classification number. For example, all science books have a number between 500 and 599, and all history books have a number between 900 and 999. The system becomes more detailed as each of these major groups is subdivided. The table below shows how the subdividing works in the literature category (800–899).

800–899 **Literature**	810–819 **Literature Subdivided**
810 American literature	810 American literature
820 English literature	811 Poetry
830 German literature	812 Drama
840 French literature	813 Fiction
850 Italian literature	814 Essays
860 Spanish literature	815 Speeches
870 Latin literature (classic)	816 Letters
880 Greek literature (classic)	817 Satire and Humor
890 Other literatures	818 Miscellany
	819 Canadian-English literature

Arrangement of Books on the Shelves

You will see at a glance that books are arranged on the shelves numerically in order of classification. Most libraries prominently mark their shelves with the numbers indicating the books to be found in each particular section. Within each classification, books are arranged alphabetically by authors' last names. An exception is individual biographies and autobiographies. These books are arranged alphabetically by the last name of the *person written about*.

Biography. The Dewey Decimal System division for Biography is 920. However, large libraries will often place biographies in a separate section because of the large number of these books. In this case they will have a "B" on the spine of the book and on the catalog card. If you are looking for a particular biography and are unable to locate the 920 division, ask the librarian for assistance.

Reference Books. Reference books of particular types or specific subjects are also shelved together, often with the letter *R* above the classification number.

Exercises How Books Are Classified and Arranged

A. In which Dewey Decimal category would the following information be found?

1. Flying saucers
2. Cost of a college education
3. Rules for soccer
4. History of Buddhism
5. Plays with two characters
6. Tasaday Indians
7. Recipes for pizza
8. Picture of a medieval castle
9. African art
10. Population explosion

B. Using the Dewey Decimal system listed on pages 320 and 321, assign the correct general classification number to these books.

1. *Mythology,* by Edith Hamilton.
2. *How Does a Poem Mean?* by John Ciardi.
3. *Your Legal Rights As a Minor,* by Robert H. Loeb, Jr.
4. *The Aztec Indians of Mexico,* by Sonia Bleeker.
5. *Developing Your Personality,* by Martin Panzor.
6. *I Like Jazz,* by Donald Myrus.
7. *Modern English and Its Heritage,* by Margaret Bryant.
8. *Everyday Life in Classical Athens,* by T. B. Webster.
9. *Math Menagerie,* by Robert Kadesch.
10. *Modern Sociology,* by Marvin Koller.

Part 2 Using the Card Catalog

To determine whether the library has a book you want and where to find it, use the **card catalog**. The card catalog is a cabinet of small drawers or file trays containing alphabetically arranged cards. Each card bears the title of a book that the library has on its shelves. The card also carries the classification number, or as librarians say, **call number** in the upper left-hand corner. (See the illustration below.)

To find your book, write down the call number. If it is a work about literature—for example, *The Pleasures of Poetry* by Donald Hall—the call number will be in the 800 range. (Specifically, works about poetry will be found in 811.)

Go to the section of shelves marked 811, and you will find your book alphabetically placed among those authors' last names that begin with *H*. The same call number you found on the catalog card will be imprinted on the spine of the book near the bottom.

There are usually three cards for the same book in the card catalog: the *author card*, the *title card*, and the *subject card*.

The Author Card. Perhaps you are researching a topic concerning space vehicles and know that there is a book on this topic by Robert M. Powers. You will find the author card in the card catalog, and it will look like this:

629.45   **Powers, Robert M.**

        Shuttle: the world's first spaceship/by
        Robert M. Powers. Stackpole, c 1979
        255 p., ill.

Author cards for all books by an author will be filed together alphabetically according to title. Notice also that books *about* the author are filed *behind* the author cards.

The Title Card. Suppose you do not know the author's name, but do know the title of the book. Look in the card catalog for a card bearing the title at the top as follows:

629.45   **Shuttle**

Shuttle: the world's first spaceship/by Robert M. Powers. Stackpole, c 1979 255 p., ill.

The place of the title card in the catalog is determined by the first letter of the first word in the title. (*A, An,* and *The* do not count as first words.)

The Subject Card. You may not know whether a book has been written about space vehicles. However, because it is of current interest, you suspect that there may be a book about them. If you look through the cards cataloged under the subject *space vehicles,* you will find the following:

629.45   **SPACE VEHICLES**

Shuttle: the world's first spaceship/by Robert M. Powers. Stackpole, c 1979 255 p., ill.

Subject cards are most useful when you want information on a specific topic from a variety of sources. Cards for all books on a particular subject are cataloged together. The subject card may also indicate whether a book has chapters on a single aspect of the topic you are interested in. The publication date on the card will help you find the most up-to-date book on your subject.

Card Information

Notice that all three types of catalog cards (author, title, subject) give the same information.

1. The call number
2. The title, author, publisher, and date of publication
3. The number of pages, and a notation on whether the book has illustrations, maps, tables, or other features

The catalog card will often provide additional information.

4. A brief description of the nature and scope of the book (This will help you decide whether the book will be useful to you.)
5. A listing of other catalog cards for the book

Cross-Reference Cards

Occasionally, in looking up a subject, you will find a card that reads *See* or *See also*. The "See" card refers you to another subject heading in the catalog that may give you the information you want. Let's say you want a book on movies, and you find this card.

```
Movies

        see

Moving pictures
```

It means that the library catalogs all books on movies under the heading *moving pictures.*

The "See also" card refers you to other subjects closely related to the one you are interested in. A "See also" card looks like this:

```
Moving pictures

     see also

Comedy films
Experimental films
Horror films
Indians in motion pictures
Social problems in motion pictures
War films
Women in moving pictures
```

Guide Cards

Besides the catalog cards, you will find guide cards in the cabinet trays. These are blank except for the guide word (general subject heading) on a tab that projects above the other cards. Guide cards aid you in finding other catalog cards quickly. For example, if you want books on the metric system, you will find them easily by means of alphabetically arranged guide cards.

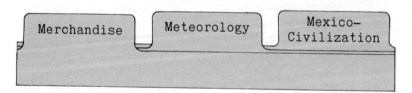

| Merchandise | Meteorology | Mexico–Civilization |

Exercises Using the Card Catalog

A. The figure on the next page represents six trays of a card catalog. The items at the right name authors, titles, and subjects that would be filed in these trays. Copy the list at the right on a separate sheet of paper and write the numbers in the blanks to show in which trays you would find the items listed.

1—	**A—Be**	_____ *Don Quixote*
2—	**Bi—Ca**	_____ Badminton
3—	**Ce—Cr**	_____ *A Bell for Adano*
4—	**Cu—Do**	_____ City Planning
5—	**Du—Er**	_____ *An American Dilemma*
6—	**Es—Fu**	_____ Charlotte Bronte
		_____ *The Environmental Handbook*
		_____ Acting
		_____ Charles Beard
		_____ *A Friend of Caesar*

B. Use the card catalog to find the title, author, call number, and publication date of the following books.

1. A collection of American poetry
2. A book by Anne McCaffrey
3. A book on World War I
4. A collection of fine art reproductions
5. A book by Lewis Carroll

C. What subject cards would give you information about the following topics? Discuss your answers in class.

1. Bali dances
2. The powers of the president
3. Jewelry designs
4. Automobile insurance
5. Writing a research paper
6. Dieting
7. Salem witchcraft trials
8. Civil War Ballads
9. Life on Mars
10. Atomic submarines

D. Using the card catalog, list the author, title, call number, and publication date of all books about two of the following people:

1. Abigail Adams
2. Duke Ellington
3. Golda Meir
4. Adlai Stevenson
5. Rachel Carson
6. Richard Wright

Part 3 Using Reference Works

One of the best ways to get information is to consult a reference work. Suppose your teacher were to ask you to write a brief biographical sketch of the American writer Carl Sandburg. One good source would be *Twentieth Century Authors,* by Kunitz and Haycraft. It may be found in the reference room of most libraries. Knowing the various types of reference works and where they are kept in the library can save you valuable time.

Reference works are tools, and like tools, should be used in definite ways. Most reference works have prefaces that describe how information is arranged, show sample entries, and explain the symbols and abbreviations used in the book. Before using any reference work for the first time, skim the preface.

Nine basic types of reference works are described in this part.

1. Dictionaries. The most widely used reference books in the library are the general dictionaries. There are three major types. The first is the unabridged (complete) dictionary containing more than 500,000 words. Second, there are abridged (shorter) editions, commonly called "desk" or "collegiate" dictionaries. The third group are pocket-sized; they are convenient for checking the spelling of ordinary words, but too limited for high school and college use. Here is a list of reliable dictionaries.

GENERAL DICTIONARIES

The American Heritage Dictionary of the English Language
The Macmillan Dictionary
The Random House Dictionary of the English Language
Thorndike-Barnhart Dictionary
Webster's New World Dictionary of the American Language
Webster's Third New International Dictionary of the English Language

Another group of dictionaries are those dealing with certain aspects of the English language: synonyms and antonyms, rhymes, slang, Americanisms, etymology, and so forth. Finally, there are special-purpose dictionaries that deal exclusively with music, medicine, biography, and many other subjects. The list below is by no means complete, but it provides good source material for you. You may check your school and community library as to the availability of specific-subject dictionaries.

2. Encyclopedias. These are collections of articles, alphabetically arranged on nearly every subject. Guide letters on the spine of each volume and guide words at the top of the pages aid you in finding information. It is best, however, to first check the general index when looking for information. It may list several relevant articles. For up-to-date information on a topic, check the yearbook that many encyclopedias issue. (A word of caution: When you write essays and reports, you must enclose in quotation marks all material taken verbatim from any source.) The following are some of the most reliable encyclopedias:

Collier's Encyclopedia (24 volumes)
Compton's Encyclopedia (26 volumes)
Encyclopaedia Britannica (30 volumes)
Encyclopedia Americana (30 volumes)
World Book Encyclopedia (22 volumes)

The library has many special-purpose encyclopedias dealing with a wide variety of subjects. These encyclopedias are located in the library reference room or area.

ENCYCLOPEDIAS ON SPECIFIC SUBJECTS

The Baseball Encyclopedia
The Concise Encyclopedia of Archeology
The Concise Encyclopedia of English and American Poets and Poetry
The Concise Encyclopedia of Modern Drama
Encyclopaedia of Occultism
Encyclopaedia of Religion
The Encyclopedia of American Facts and Dates
Encyclopedia of Animal Care
Encyclopedia of Auto Racing Greats
Encyclopedia of Careers and Vocational Guidance
The Encyclopedia of Chemistry
Encyclopedia of Gardening
Encyclopedia of World Art (15 volumes)
Grzimek's Animal Life Encyclopedia (13 volumes)
The Illustrated Encyclopedia of Aviation and Space
The Illustrated Encyclopedia of World Coins
The International Encyclopedia of Cooking
International Encyclopedia of Social Sciences (17 volumes)
LaRousse Encyclopedia of Mythology
McGraw-Hill Encyclopedia of World Biography (12 volumes)
McGraw-Hill Encyclopedia of World Drama (4 volumes)
The Mammals of America
The New Columbia Encyclopedia
The Pictorial Encyclopedia of Birds
Universal Encyclopedia of Mathematics

3. Almanacs and Yearbooks. Published annually, almanacs and yearbooks are useful sources of facts and statistics on current events, as well as matters of historical record in government, economics, population, sports, and other fields.

Guinness Book of World Records
Information Please Almanac, Atlas and Yearbook
Statesman's Yearbook
Statistical Abstract of the United States
Women's Rights Almanac
World Almanac and Book of Facts

4. Biographical References. There are brief biographical notations in dictionaries and longer biographical articles in encyclopedias. Often, however, a better source is a specialized work.

American Men and Women of Science
The Book of Presidents
Current Biography
Dictionary of American Biography
Dictionary of National Biography
The International Who's Who
Twentieth Century Authors
Who's Who
Who's Who in the East (and Eastern Canada)
Who's Who in the Midwest
Who's Who in the South and Southwest
Who's Who in the West
Who's Who in American Women

5. Books About Authors. These are excellent reference books.

American Authors: 1600–1900
British Authors Before 1800
British Authors of the Nineteenth Century
Contemporary Authors
Twentieth Century Authors
Twentieth Century Authors: First Supplement
European Authors: 1000–1900
World Authors 1950–1970

6. Literary Reference Books. The following are reference books on the history of literature, on quotations and proverbs, for locating poems and stories, and for information about writers.

> *Bartlett's Familiar Quotations*
> *Cyclopedia of Literary Characters*
> *A Dictionary of Literature in the English Language*
> *Encyclopedia of World Drama*
> *Granger's Index to Poetry*
> *A Literary History of England*
> *A Literary History of the United States*
> Mencken's *A New Dictionary of Quotations*
> *The Oxford Companion to American Literature*
> *The Oxford Companion to English Literature*
> *The Oxford Companion to the Theatre*
> *Poetry Handbook*

7. Pamphlets, Handbooks, and Catalogs. Many libraries have pamphlets, handbooks, booklets, and clippings on a variety of subjects including vocations, travel, census data, and program schedules. They also have a collection of college catalogs. All of these are kept in a set of file cabinets called the **vertical file**. This file can be an invaluable source to you when writing a report or looking for information on careers.

8. Atlases. We usually think of an atlas mainly as a book of maps, but it contains interesting data on a number of subjects. The excellent *National Geographic Atlas of the World,* for example, lists some of the following topics in its table of contents: "Great Moments in Geography," "Global Statistics," and sections on population, temperatures, oceans, and place names. Below is a list of other widely used atlases.

> *Atlas of World History*
> *Atlas of World Wildlife*
> *The Britannica Atlas*
> *Collier's World Atlas and Gazetteer*
> *Goode's World Atlas*
> *Grosset World Atlas*
> *The International Atlas from Rand McNally*
> *Rand McNally Commercial Atlas and Marketing Guide*
> *The Times Atlas of the World*
> *Webster's Atlas with Zip Code Directory*

9. Magazines. The *Readers' Guide to Periodical Literature* lists the titles of articles, stories, and poems published during the preceding month in more than 100 magazines. It is issued twice a month from September through June and once a month in July and August. An entire year's issues are bound in one hardcover volume at the end of the year. Articles are listed alphabetically under *subject* and *author* (and *titles* when necessary).

Excerpt from the *Readers' Guide*

ARMSTRONG, Dave
Falling in love with four-wheel drive. J. A. La-   *title of article*
   tham. il pors Esquire 91:23-30 Je 5 '79 *
ARMSTRONG, Joe
Between the lines. pors N Y 12:5 My 14 '79
ARMSTRONG, Louis
   Louis Armstrong: release of Giants of jazz al-
   bum. J. Vance. por Stereo R 42:142-3 My '79 *   *name of magazine*
ARMSTRONG, Neil A.
   Footprints of Apollo II. E. Keerdoja. il pors
   Newsweek 94:14+ Jl 2 '79 *   *volume number*
ARMSTRONG, Sonia
   Between two worlds. N. M. Nichols. Seventeen
   38:140-1 My '79 *   *page reference*
ARNESON, Howard D.
   (ed) Economic diary (cont) Bus W p 18+ Mr
   19: 16+ Je 4 '79   *date of magazine*
ARNETT Cobb Quartet. See Jazz groups
ARNIE'S (restaurant) See Chicago—Hotels, res-
   taurants, etc.
ARNOLD, Walter   *author entry*
   Trade winds (cont) Sat R 6:58 F 17; 50 Ap 14;
   48 My 12; 47 Jl 7 '79
ARNOLD Bernhard & Company. See Bern-
   hard, Arnold & Company
ARNOLDO Mondadori Editore. See Publishers
   and publishing—Italy
ARNSON, Cynthia
   Charge up Capitol Hill. Nation 228:755-6 Je 23 '79
ARON, Raymond
   Democracy, yes. por Time 114:41 Jl 9 '79 *
ARONS, Stephen
   Book burning in the heartland. il Sat R 6:24-6+   *illustrated article*
   Jl 21 '79
ARREST   *subject entry*
   Bum rap for former mental patients: study by
   Henry Steadman. L. Asher. Psychol Today
   12:102+ Ap '79
     See also   *"see also" cross reference*
     Bail
ARRHYTHMIA. See Heart beat   *"see" cross reference*

Exercises Using Reference Works

A. Find information on one of the following subjects by using the general index of three different encyclopedias. Write a brief report on the topic and tell which encyclopedia was most useful and why.

The Kabuki Theater
Television Advertising
Tools of the Stone Age
American Sculpture
Extrasensory Perception
  (ESP)

Sickle Cell Anemia
Space Travel
Urban Renewal
The Human Circulatory
  System
Bioengineering

B. Using the dictionaries available in your library, write answers to the following questions. Write the title of the dictionary used after each answer. Use as many different dictionaries as possible.

1. What is the origin of the word *Motown?*
2. Give two definitions of the word *masthead.*
3. List three antonyms for the word *flimsy.*
4. Where was the word *chortle* first used?
5. What is meant by the expression "take up the cudgels"?
6. Give three synonyms for the word *patience.*
7. What is an *ombudsman?*
8. Define the word *allegory* and give an example.

C. Use the current issue of *World Almanac* or a similar source to answer the following questions:

1. How can you apply for a patent?
2. What is the address of the National Foundation of the March of Dimes?
3. When should the U.S. flag be displayed?
4. How many Americans have been awarded the Nobel Prize for Literature?
5. What does the 26th amendment to the Constitution provide for?
6. What historic event took place on January 25, 1915?
7. Who was the first woman in space?
8. When will Halley's comet next be visible from the earth?

D. Use the *Readers' Guide* to answer the following:

1. Turn to the "Key to Abbreviations" and write the meaning of the following symbols used in the *Readers' Guide:*

Ap	por	Ja	Jl
il	S	supp	abr
+	Ag	tr	jt auth

2. Using the list of "Abbreviations of Periodicals Indexed," give the complete titles of the following magazines:

Motor T	Sci Am
Eng J	Sr Schol
Sports Illus	Phys Today
Good H	US News
Sat R	Bus W

3. Find three articles on one subject that interests you. Give the title, the author (if given), the name of the magazine, the volume number, the date, and the page numbers for each article.

E. Using the special-purpose dictionaries, encyclopedias, and biographical and literary reference works noted in this chapter, find answers to the following questions. Write the name of the reference work you used after each answer.

1. Define and give examples of a limerick.
2. What was Thomas Jefferson's role in the American Revolution?
3. What is the title of the poem that begins—"Some say the world will end in fire"? Who wrote the poem?
4. Find a picture of Queen Elizabeth II of England.
5. How did Sir Isaac Newton discover the law of gravitation?
6. How did the expression "the real McCoy" originate?
7. Does the country of India get any of its energy from nuclear reactors?
8. What is the "Theater of the Absurd"?
9. What literary reference work includes a discussion of *The Bridge of San Luis Rey?*
10. Who wrote *Leaves of Grass?* Where was this writer born?

SUMMARY AND APPLICATIONS

1. Libraries contain resources in every conceivable subject area. Learning to use the library well will enable you to do research efficiently. It will also provide you with many opportunities for enjoyable reading.

2. Works of fiction are arranged on library shelves in alphabetical order, according to the author's last name.

3. Works of nonfiction are arranged according to the Dewey Decimal classification system.

4. The card catalog holds alphabetically-organized cards for all books in the library. Books may be listed by author, title, and subject.

5. Reference works are generally marked with an "R" and kept in a separate section of the library. They include dictionaries, encyclopedias, almanacs, yearbooks, biographical and literary reference works, pamphlets, atlases, and magazines.

Applications in Other Subject Areas

History. Choose one of the following historical figures. Find information concerning this figure in as many different kinds of resource materials as possible. Record your sources.

Thomas Jefferson   Marie Antoinette
Mohandas Gandhi   Simón Bolívar

Science. Science is the most rapidly changing of fields. Current information on scientific discoveries and research can be found in many available science-related magazines. Go to your library and find at least three different science magazines. Report on three recent discoveries made by scientists.

Chapter 15

Letters, Forms, and Résumés

As you get older, you suddenly begin to face a number of decisions about your future. Some of these decisions concern what you will do next summer, and others concern the rest of your life. How do you go about investigating the many opportunities and courses open to you?

There is only one way to receive specific, accurate information, and that is to deal directly with the source. The most efficient way to accomplish this purpose is to write a business letter. You will receive the information you have requested and have it available to study. You will also establish a contact for any additional facts you need.

Schools and colleges have specific offices for requests from future students. Employment agencies and corporations will inform you as to the availability of jobs—permanent, part-time or temporary. Travel agencies are loaded with information they are eager to mail. Park and resort areas hire seasonal help yearly and they are waiting for requests from potential employees.

In this chapter, you will learn how to write business letters: what to write, where to write, and what to do with the replies you receive. You will also learn the skills of filling out forms, writing résumés, interviewing, and applying for jobs. Each of these skills will help you as you explore the many possibilities the future holds.

Part 1 The Forms of Letters

Just as the business letter has a specific purpose, it also has a specific form. This form is as important as the layout of a baseball diamond. You would not switch first base with the pitcher's mound, or move the catcher in front of the batter. If you did, the game would be confusing to the regular fan. The same kinds of rules apply to a business letter. The reader is accustomed to looking at a certain part of the page for specific information. If you change the form, you will confuse the reader.

While there are different business letter forms, the information is always in the same order and consists of six parts. Compare the examples that follow, noting the parts and their names.

Choose the form that appeals to you and master it. You will be using it frequently in the years ahead.

The **heading** of the letter consists of your address and the date. You always use three lines. The first line contains your street address. The second line is the city, state, and ZIP code. Note that there is always a comma between the city and the state, but none between the state and ZIP code. The third line is the date the letter is written. If you live in a small town that has no street addresses for mailing purposes, or if your mail is delivered to a post office box, you would use a slightly different heading, as shown in the examples on the next page.

P.O. Box 169
Rochester, New York 14617
July 16, 1985

Edmore
North Dakota 58330
July 16, 1985

BLOCK FORM (used only when the letter is typewritten)

1563 New Salem Drive
St. Louis, Missouri 63141   Heading
July 14, 1985

Manager
Specific Personnel Agency, Inc.   Inside Address
620 Broadway
New York, New York 10006

Dear Sir or Madam: Salutation

                                                      Body

....
....
....

....
....

Yours truly,   Closing

John H. Levine   Signature

John H. Levine

1563 New Salem Drive
St. Louis, Missouri 63141
July 14, 1985

Office of Admissions
University of Hawaii
2444 Dole Street
Honolulu, Hawaii 96822

Inside Address

Dear Sir or Madam: Salutation

Body

Closing   Sincerely,

Signature   *John H. Levine*

John H. Levine

The **inside address** includes the department or person to whom you're writing on the first line; the name of the company on the second line; the street address or post office box number on the third line; and the city, state, and ZIP code on the fourth line. If you are not writing to a specific person or department, you would have a three-line address and simply eliminate the first line.

One space is left blank between the inside address and the next part, the **salutation**. This can be one of many, depending upon the inside address.

FOR A DEPARTMENT OR A COMPANY

```
Gentlemen:
Ladies and Gentlemen:
Dear Sir or Madam:
```

FOR A SPECIFIC PERSON, NAME UNKNOWN

```
Dear Sir:
Dear Madam:
Dear Sir or Madam:
```

FOR A SPECIFIC PERSON, NAME KNOWN

```
Dear Mr. Jones:
Dear Mrs. Sorenson:
Dear Miss Sorenson:
Dear Ms. Sorenson:
```

A blank space is left between the salutation and the **body** of the letter, which is the most important part of your letter. You should state your purpose clearly, briefly, and politely. It is always helpful to make a rough draft of this portion of the letter to be certain you have given the necessary information, and that you have no errors in punctuation, spelling, or grammar. This is the only impression the receiver will have of you; make it a good one.

A blank space is left between the body of the letter and the **closing**. This is kept as simple as possible, with only the first word capitalized.

```
Sincerely,     Yours truly,   Respectfully yours,
Truly yours,   Cordially,     Very truly yours,
```

Type or print your name four spaces below the closing, and write your **signature** in the space between.

Whenever you write a business letter, you should have a copy for yourself. This does not mean you write the letter twice, only that you make a photocopy or a carbon copy. Carbon paper is readily available and easy to use, particularly if you type. If you are writing your letter in longhand, you must buy carbon paper made for this purpose.

Typists may sometimes find that their letters do not look as attractive as they should because the letters are short. In this case, double-space the entire letter, leaving extra spaces between the six parts.

Exercises The Forms of Letters

A. Put the following addresses in proper inside-address form, punctuating and capitalizing correctly. Below each address use the correct salutation for the particular address.

1. western airlines vacation department p o box 92931 world way postal center los angeles california 90009
2. personnel manager general telephone co of florida 610 morgan street tampa florida 33602
3. quantas 360 post street san francisco california 94108
4. employment office yellowstone company yellowstone park wyoming 82190
5. admissions office colorado women's college montview boulevard and quebec denver colorado 80220

B. Using one of the letter forms shown, write a letter on a plain piece of paper to one of the addresses in Exercise A. Label all six parts of the letter in the right margin.

Part 2 The Envelopes

A standard 9½″ x 4″ envelope is preferred for a business letter. This size allows sufficient room for the receiver's address and your return address. Also, the insertion of the letter is much easier than with a smaller envelope. You need to learn only one form.

In the upper left-hand corner, write your name on the first line; the street address or post office box on the second line; and city, state, and ZIP code on the third line. Then, in a position in the middle of the envelope, copy the inside address from your letter, line for line. Write from the middle of the envelope to the right, so the address ends up in the bottom corner of the envelope.

In order to ensure that your letter reaches the correct party, check the address, street, and ZIP code. The ZIP code is of primary importance today, as it enables the postal department to sort your letter for delivery as rapidly as possible. If you do not know the ZIP code, call your local post office.

If you use an abbreviation for the name of a state, you *must* use the ZIP code with it. When using these abbreviations, it is not necessary to separate the city and state in the address with a comma; if you do not use the abbreviations, you must use the comma.

After the letter has been written and the envelope addressed, you must fold the letter to fit the envelope. This can be done by folding the letter into thirds so that you will have only two creases. Start at the bottom of the letter and fold up. When folded, your letter should fit easily into the envelope.

Exercises **Addressing Envelopes**

A. Using a plain sheet of paper, turn it sideways and draw two 9½″ x 4″ envelopes on each side, a total of four envelopes. Address the envelopes using the information below. Use your telephone directory, magazines, or your local library to complete the last two envelopes.

1. Advertising Department, Revlon, Inc., 767 5th Avenue, New York, New York 10022
2. *Sports Illustrated,* Time Incorporated, 3435 Wilshire Boulevard, Los Angeles, CA 90010
3. The personnel office of a local company
4. A college in which you are interested

B. Using the letter form you've chosen, write a letter to an imaginary person at an imaginary company. Use the correct form, including salutation and closing. On the back of the paper draw an envelope and address it.

Part 3   Kinds of Business Letters

Business letters are written for many reasons. There are letters requesting information, letters inquiring about employment, letters to colleges and other schools, and many more. They all require that you use the following guidelines.

1. Use plain white 8½″ x 11″ paper. Pastels and decorated stationeries are not appropriate.
2. Use a standard form.
3. Keep a copy for your reference.
4. Use a standard envelope. A letter folded nine times to fit a small envelope looks messy.
5. Check the address and include the ZIP code.
6. Keep the body of the letter brief and specific.
7. Stay within your vocabulary range. Do not use technical terms if you are not certain of their correct usage.
8. Make a rough draft of your letter and check carefully for errors before writing the final copy.
9. Make your handwriting as legible as possible.
10. Approach letters with a positive attitude.

Letters Requesting Information

The one type of business letter you will use more than any other is the request for information. It is used to inquire about employment, college requirements, vacation ideas, or anything else in which you have an interest.

The body of the letter should be brief, with the main emphasis on what information you need and why you need it. If you are writing regarding employment or college, the dates you plan to work or attend are necessary. The order of these three W's—What, Why, and When—will change, but it is much easier on the reader if you write what you want first. The Why should be as concise as possible. A detailed explanation is not only unnecessary, but unwanted. Remember, you are asking for information; make it easy for the reader to reply. Being polite, of course, is a necessity.

General Requests for Information

There are times when you will need more information for a major assignment than is available in the school library. Perhaps you are curious about some particular place, person, or hobby. If you take the time to write a letter requesting this particular information and find an address where it is available, you will undoubtedly receive a reply.

Here is an example of a letter requesting information.

413 Acacia Avenue
Palo Alto, California 94306
August 2, 1985

Energy Research and Development Administration
U.S. Government
20 Massachusetts Avenue, N.W.
Washington, D.C. 20019

Dear Sir or Madam:

At the present time I am preparing a report on energy alternatives for my high school science class. Could you please supply me with some current information regarding the development of solar energy or any other substitutes for current energy sources?

Also, if you have any publications available on this matter, I would appreciate being informed of their titles and cost.

Yours truly,

Rosa M. Ortega
Rosa M. Ortega

Exercise Requesting Information

Choose one of the subjects below and write a rough draft of a letter requesting information.

1. Child Abuse
2. Population Control
3. The Women's Movement
4. Environment Conservation
5. Alcoholism

6. TV Violence
7. Drug Abuse
8. Earthquakes
9. Pollution
10. Civil Rights

Letters About Employment

The letter concerning employment is a formal business letter written to an employer and requesting a job application and interview. If you are writing to a small company and you know the name of the owner or manager, address the letter directly to him or her. If you are writing to a large concern, the Personnel Department handles all the hiring, regardless of the department.

The best business letters follow a four-part format:

1. Purpose. Begin by directly stating the purpose of your letter, that you are applying for a specific job. Refer to a person that told you about the job or to an advertisement. State whether you are looking for full-time, part-time, or temporary work.

2. Qualifications and References. State your age or grade in school and the date when you will be available to work. Identify your experience and any skills that relate to the job you are seeking. List achievements that portray you as an effective worker.

Finally, include references. Make sure that you have gotten their permission first. List their names, positions, addresses, and telephone numbers.

3. Request for Application and/or Interview. Ask for an application and an interview. Tell the employer when and where you can be contacted and include your telephone number.

4. Thank You. Always thank a prospective employer for his or her time.

555 Dover Street
Albuquerque NM 87101
April 23, 1985

Dr. Carla Manos
3333 First Street
Albuquerque NM 87101

Dear Dr. Manos:

I would like to apply for a job as an assistant at your veterinary clinic. Ms. Siebers, my guidance counselor at Albuquerque High, told me that you may have an opening this spring.

I am very interested in someday practicing veterinary medicine, and would welcome this opportunity to learn more about the field. At school, I have maintained a B+ average and am the treasurer of my freshman class. This year, I was in charge of organizing the first school dance. I work hard and am reliable. Both Ms. Siebers and Mr. Walters, our principal, have offered to act as references for me. They can be contacted at 555–1232.

I am available for work after school each day. Also, I will be willing to work full–time during the summer.

I would greatly appreciate your sending me an application form. I would also like to arrange an interview. I can be reached at 555–4321 after 3:00 P.M. on school days.

Thank you for considering me for the position.

Sincerely,

Alex Canteras
Alex Canteras

Write a letter to a real or imaginary company, expressing interest in a part-time or summer job. Address an envelope for your letter.

Letters to Colleges and Other Schools

Letters to all schools follow the same basic pattern.

1421 Kenneth St.
Shreveport, Louisiana 71103
February 21, 1985

Admissions Office
University of Oklahoma
660 Parrington Oval
Norman, Oklahoma 73069

Dear Sir or Madam:

Would you please send me information about the entrance requirements for the University of Oklahoma. I will be graduating from high school in the spring of 1987, and plan to enter the university the following fall.

I am interested primarily in information about your tuition, board and room, and any other major expenses involved in obtaining a degree in Pharmacology.

I would appreciate a copy of your catalog.

Respectfully,

Anthony Lebeaux

Anthony Lebeaux

Be specific about the information you would like. If you are interested in costs, ask about them. If you are "shopping around" and comparing a number of schools, request a catalog. There might be a charge for the catalog, but they will inform you. If you have already decided on a specific major field, state what it is. There may be different requirements for that field, such as specific preparation, a longer course, more expenses. Direct your letter to the Admissions Office. *Barron's Profiles of American Colleges* or a similar reference book in your local library will supply you with the required information for the address.

Part 4   Filling Out Forms

We live in a time when forms have become increasingly important as a means of recording information about different tasks, people, services, and material. You probably have already filled out many types of forms, ranging from hall passes to job applications. In the future, you will encounter many more. Some of these forms will be used by others to make important decisions regarding your schooling, employment, and finances. Learning how to fill out forms correctly is, therefore, extremely important.

The following guidelines may be helpful to you as you complete various types of forms:

1. Read all directions carefully. Skim the form all the way through before making any marks on it. Notice any special requirements indicated in the directions, such as "Print" or "Please type." Then, gather all the information that you will need to fill out the form, such as dates, social security number, and your parents' birthdates.

2. Assemble your tools. Use a good pen, or a typewriter and an eraser. Do not use pencil unless requested to do so.

3. Begin filling out the form line-by-line, rereading all directions. Directions for procedures as simple as filling in your name may vary from form to form.

4. Application forms for a job or for admission to a school have a number of questions in common. Your address, date of birth,

sex, height, weight, color of hair, and color of eyes are normal application entries. Do not make the common mistake of putting the current year for the date-of-birth entry. You will find that there is never enough space for the information requested. When you can, abbreviate. This means that you would put 10-30-85 rather than October 30, 1985.

There may be some questions on the application form that you cannot answer. These include such items as "Military Service," "Name of husband/wife." There is one standard guideline for filling out applications—answer everything! An empty line looks as if you forgot to answer, did not know the answer, or did not want to answer. If the information does not apply to you, insert the initials N.A. This means "not applicable;" it does not apply to you.

5. Application forms consistently ask for references. They sometimes specify personal references; at other times they ask for the names of former employers. A personal reference does not mean your best friend. An employer would like the name of a responsible adult, who has known you for a long period of time, who has some idea of your capabilities, and who knows whether or not you are honest and trustworthy. Family physicians, former employers, teachers, and family friends are ideal. Contact them first and ask if you may use them as references. Have their full names, home addresses, and telephone numbers ready for the application form.

6. When the form is finished, check it for accuracy, spelling, and completeness. Proofread carefully.

7. Return the form to the person, department, or organization specified on the form. In some cases you may wish to make a copy of the form for your own records.

Exercises Filling Out Forms

A. Design a form for students applying for the position of class secretary. Be sure the form provides you with any information you might need, such as the student's year in school, previous experience, skills, and grade point average. Also make sure the form will tell you how the student can be contacted.

B. Examine the application for a social security card that appears below. On your own paper, write out the information needed to answer sections 1, 2, 5, 6, 7, 8, and 10. Use the writing utensil and style indicated in the directions on the form.

A SAMPLE SOCIAL SECURITY FORM

DEPARTMENT OF HEALTH AND HUMAN SERVICES SOCIAL SECURITY ADMINISTRATION				Form Approved OMB No. 0960-0066
FORM SS-5 – APPLICATION FOR A SOCIAL SECURITY NUMBER CARD (Original, Replacement or Correction)	MICROFILM REF. NO. (SSA USE ONLY)			

Unless the requested information is provided, we may not be able to issue a Social Security Number (20 CFR 422. 103(b))

INSTRUCTIONS TO APPLICANT ▶ Before completing this form, please read the instructions on the opposite page. You can type or print, using pen with dark blue or black ink. Do not use pencil.

NAA NAB **1**	NAME TO BE SHOWN ON CARD — First	Middle	Last
	FULL NAME AT BIRTH (IF OTHER THAN ABOVE) — First	Middle	Last
ONA	OTHER NAME(S) USED		

STT
2 MAILING ADDRESS (Street/Apt. No., P.O. Box, Rural Route No.)

CTY STE ZIP	CITY	STATE	ZIP CODE

CSP
3 CITIZENSHIP (Check one only)
☐ a. U.S. citizen   ☐ c. Legal alien not allowed to work
☐ b. Legal alien allowed to work   ☐ d. Other (See instructions on Page 2)

4 SEX
☐ Male
☐ Female

DOS
5 DATE OF BIRTH — MONTH DAY YEAR
6 AGE — PRESENT AGE
7 PLB — PLACE OF BIRTH — CITY — STATE OR FOREIGN COUNTRY

MNA **8** FNA	MOTHER'S NAME AT HER BIRTH — First	Middle	Last (her maiden name)
	FATHER'S NAME — First	Middle	Last

PNO
9 a. Have you or someone on your behalf applied for a social security number before?   ☐ No ☐ Don't Know ☐ Yes
If you checked "yes", complete items "b" through "e" below; otherwise go to item 11.

SSN
PNS
PNY b. Enter social security number   c. In what State did you apply?   What year?

NLC d. Enter the name shown on your most recent social security card   e. If the birth date you used was different from the date shown in item 5, enter it here. — MONTH DAY YEAR

DON
10 TODAY'S DATE — MONTH DAY YEAR
11 Telephone number where we can reach you during the day — HOME OTHER

ASD WARNING: Deliberately providing false information on this application is punishable by a fine of $1,000 or one year in jail, or both.

12 YOUR SIGNATURE
13 YOUR RELATIONSHIP TO PERSON IN ITEM 1
☐ Self   ☐ Other _____ (Specify)

WITNESS (Needed only if signed by mark "X")   WITNESS (Needed only if signed by mark "X")

DO NOT WRITE BELOW THIS LINE (FOR SSA USE ONLY)			DTC	SSA RECEIPT DATE _____
☐ SUPPORTING DOCUMENT- SSN ASSIGNED OR VERIFIED ☐ EXPEDITE CASE ☐ DUP ISSUED SSN			NPN	
DOC NTC CAN		BIC	SIGNATURE AND TITLE OF EMPLOYEE(S) REVIEWING EVIDENCE AND/OR CONDUCTING INTERVIEW.	
TYPE(S) OF EVIDENCE SUBMITTED		☐ MANDATORY IN PERSON INTERVIEW CONDUCTED		DATE
	IDN ITV	DCL		DATE

Form **SS-5** (2-81)

Part 5 Résumés and Interviews

Writing letters and filling out forms are not the only business skills that you will need to develop. You must also learn to present yourself favorably through written résumés and personal interviews.

Writing a Résumé

A **résumé** is a list of your experience, education, and skills. Many schools and employers require résumés instead of, or in addition to, applications. Résumés serve as tools for narrowing a field of applicants. It is therefore essential for you to learn how to write a résumé that conveys a good impression of you.

As with any piece of writing, you may want to work through several drafts of your résumé. All résumés, however, should include the following information:

Personal Data. This section simply includes your name, address, and phone number, including the area code.

Objective. This is a short statement of your purpose. Are you seeking admission to a college or applying for a job? Your objective can be as broad or as narrow as you like.

OBJECTIVE: Position as a sales trainee in a retail organization that gives opportunities for advancement to a position in management.

OBJECTIVE: Salesperson in Sporting Goods Department of Johnson Brothers Company.

Experience. This section should include all paid employment. Also, you may wish to include volunteer jobs that you have held. Names of employers, addresses of the businesses, dates of employment, and job descriptions should be included. Always list your most recent job first, and work back to your first job. Do not be concerned if your experience seems a little sparse right now; you will be surprised how quickly it will increase in the next few years. Put this information in the following order:

Period employed
Name and address of firm
Position held
Duties

Education. Under *education*, list all schools attended, dates, and any special courses of study. Include any honors or awards earned in school. You need identify only high schools and vocational or special training programs. List your most recent school first.

Personal Qualifications and Skills. In this section, you can list all additional items you think might interest the reader. These are the items you might include:

Place and date of birth
Health
Professional memberships
Community groups
Other curricular or extra-curricular activities (academic, athletic, student government, etc.)
Hobbies or special interests
Special skills

References. Give the names, addresses, and telephone numbers of three people who will give you a good reference. It is helpful if one is a previous employer, one a former teacher or school administrator, and one a family friend.

An additional section entitled *Skills* can also be added. This section can be used to highlight your special talents. (See sample résumé, page 355.) Such a section is extremely helpful if you have limited work experience. List your skills under specific categories, as follows:

SECRETARIAL: type 70 wpm, maintained files for Business Education Department; achieved score in the 90th percentile on national accounting test.

MANAGEMENT: scheduled newspaper meetings and deadlines; supervised news staff; arranged fund-raising activities.

353

Completing the Résumé

Now that your rough worksheet is complete, you are ready to revise it into a final copy. The wording in a résumé is quite different from the kind of writing you are used to in school.

First, do not use complete sentences or personal pronouns. This is a compilation of facts, not a paragraph assignment.

WRONG: I attended East High School in Salt Lake City, Utah, where I took many special courses. Some of those of particular interest were retailing and accounting.

RIGHT: East High School
Salt Lake City, Utah
Took special courses in retailing and accounting

Also, choose words that reflect positive attitudes. Use action words when describing your responsibilities and skills. Be specific. Consider the following examples:

DULL, NEGATIVE LANGUAGE

I've only been a shift supervisor for less than one year. My duties were to take care of the restaurant at night.

ACTIVE, POSITIVE LANGUAGE

Promoted to shift supervisor June, 1985. Responsibilities included scheduling, coordinating food preparation, training new employees.

Before you write the final copy, here are some other important guidelines:

1. Use 8½″ x 11″ white paper.
2. Type your résumé or have it typed.
3. Proofread carefully for misspelled words.

Remember, just as certain colors flatter one person but not another, a résumé should be written and set up to flatter you. Look at the sample résumé that follows. It was written by a teenager who has had only one paid part-time job. She decided to develop a skills section and to place it first so her abilities and potential were highlighted. She also has written a career objective statement because she has had little work experience.

ELIZABETH WATTS

222 Hyacinth Drive   Telephone: 555—5555
Tucson, Arizona 85703

OBJECTIVE

Salesperson in clothing department of major
department store or specialty shop

SKILLS

<u>Public Relations/Communications</u>: routed telephone
calls in school's main office; welcomed visitors to
school; interviewed local business merchants and
school staff as newspaper reporter

<u>Clerical</u>: type 65 wpm; take shorthand; maintained
files for Business Ed. Department

<u>Artistic</u>: designed award—winning tailored suit for
school fashion show; coordinated color scheme and
decorated gym for fall orchestra concert

EXPERIENCE

Counselor, Hiawatha Youth Camp, Tucson, Arizona
    June, 1983—August, 1983
    Responsibilities: scheduling activities;
       supervising athletic events; teaching
       handicrafts

EDUCATION

Central High School, Tucson, Arizona
    August, 1982—present
    Course of Study: College Prep with courses in
       fashion merchandising, sewing, art
    Activities: school newspaper, fashion show
       coordinator, orchestra
    Grade Point Average: 3.5

REFERENCES

Mrs. Donna Douglas   Jim Sanchez, Director
Home Economics Instructor   Hiawatha Youth Camp
Central High School   1510 Cattle Road
Tucson, Arizona 85710   Tucson, Arizona 85719

Exercise Preparing a Résumé

Prepare a résumé, using a *Skills* category as instructed in this chapter. Identify the type of job you would be applying for so that the résumé can be tailored to suit this particular job. Include a statement of job objective as well as categories for experience, education, and references.

Interviewing

The interview is often the last step in a job hunt or any other application process. The initial phone call or letter, the application form, and the résumé are simply tools used to determine which applicants will be invited for an interview. If you reach the interview stage, you will know that you have already made a good impression.

The interview is your chance to sell yourself, to present your personality and skills as positively as possible. You need to answer questions honestly and confidently. As with the résumé, focusing on your strongest skills and using positive language will improve your presentation.

As you prepare for the interview, keep the following points in mind.

Appearance is a key to a successful interview. General good grooming and neatness always make a good impression. Neatness demonstrates attention to detail—one of the primary assets of good workers.

Promptness, another strong asset, can be demonstrated by arriving on time or a few minutes early.

Courtesy is a must during the interview. The opening and closing statements will help the interviewer form an impression of you. A polite, friendly introduction and handshake is appreciated by an interviewer. "Hello, my name is _____ . I'm happy to meet with you," is an effective opening statement. When the interviewer has indicated that the interview is over, thank the interviewer for his or her time.

Communications skills involve speaking, listening, and body language. The interviewer will ask several questions relating to your past experiences, skills, ambitions, and availability. He or she will be listening closely to your answers. Speak clearly, using correct grammar. Answer the interviewer's questions completely, honestly, and positively. Listen carefully and maintain eye contact with the interviewer. Sit up straight and avoid nervous hand gestures.

The following questions are similar to those often asked during interviews. How would you answer each one?

Questions Frequently Asked by Interviewers

1. Why are you interested in this job?

2. Why do you feel you could handle the job? What experience do you have?

3. Tell me a little about yourself—your hobbies and interests, for example.

4. What do you like most about yourself? What do you like least?

5. Why do you think you would be the best person for the job?

After an interview, a thank-you call or letter is appropriate. This will indicate to the interviewer both that you are considerate and that you are interested in the job. When writing a thank-you letter, follow the guidelines for effective letter writing covered in Part 3 of this chapter.

Exercises Interviewing

A. Look at the list of commonly asked questions on the chart above. Decide what type of job you might be interested in. Then write out the sort of answers you might give an employer who was interviewing you. Answer honestly, confidently, and positively.

B. Pretend that you are the managing editor of your school newspaper. Prepare a set of questions that you might ask an applicant.

Part 6   Using Skills To Find a Part-Time Job

Teen-age employment has grown dramatically over the past few years. Today, there are over nine million working teen-agers in the United States. Some of these teens work to help meet family expenses or to save money for college or vocational training. Others work simply to gain valuable job experience. If you are not already working, you may decide to begin working sometime soon. If so, there are several steps that you will need to take. The first is determining what sort of job is right for you.

Identifying Your Skills and Responsibilities

Before you begin to look for a job, you must first make sure that you have time for one. School is your full-time job, and nothing should be allowed to interfere with it. In addition to school, you probably also have many family and social obligations. Therefore, a full-time job is probably out of the question.° Even a part-time job may require more time than you can allow. To test whether or not you have enough time to take on a part-time job, make a schedule of your activities for one week. Include all time spent studying and all of your personal obligations or commitments. Examine this schedule and decide upon the number of hours that you can realistically devote to a part-time job. Discuss this schedule with a parent or with a guidance counselor.

If you decide that you have enough time to take on a part-time job, the next step is to assess your skills.

Take a look at the things you like to do and do well. What are your strongest assets? Are you good at mathematics? at com-

---

°Federal and state laws protect teens from overwork and dangerous working conditions. Under Federal law, if you are fourteen or fifteen years old, you may work only up to three hours on a school day and up to eighteen hours per week. (Hours are extended during the summer.) State laws vary and supersede Federal laws. Check with your guidance counselor about your state's child labor laws.

munication? Are you dependable? punctual? What type of work environment do you most enjoy? Do you enjoy working indoors, or would you prefer to work outside? Do you have any marketable skills such as typing, carpentry, or repairing bicycles or small engines? Answering such questions will help you to decide what sort of job is best suited to you. It may also suggest particular job ideas to pursue.

Examining the Job Market

The next step in finding a part-time job is to examine the job market to determine what jobs are available. Local newspapers contain employment ads for both full and part-time jobs. They are usually listed alphabetically by type of job (assistant, manager, auto mechanic, . . .). Most ads identify the job type and provide a telephone number or an address so that you can contact the employer. Some ads list the qualifications and preferred skills of the candidate most likely to be hired.

Other possible sources of information about jobs include guidance counselors, friends, and relatives. Sometimes these people can recommend job possibilities. Letting people know you are looking for a part-time job creates a networking system which sometimes leads to a job tip or referral.

A final strategy is to contact businesses personally to see if jobs are available. Make sure to specify the type of job you are looking for and the hours that you are available.

Exercises   Assessing Your Skills and Examining the Job Market

A. Choose at least five words from the list on the following page that describe activities you have completed. Then, add details telling what you have done, when, and where. Save this list for use in writing letters of application and résumés.

> EXAMPLE: *Built* part of the set for my high school drama club's production of *Oklahoma.*

Advised	Earned	Performed	Supervised
Assisted	Handcrafted	Prepared	Taught
Built	Operated	Repaired	Typed
Cared for	Organized	Served	Won
Designed	Participated in	Sold	Wrote

B. Read each of the following employment ads. Evaluate your suitability for each job. For each job, write a short paragraph explaining why you would or would not apply. Include experience, skills, interests, availability, and personal qualities.

INTERVIEWERS	STOCK
Now hiring Telephone interviewers for Market Research. Will train for evening and weekend hours.	Perm. part-time positions during school year for packing and restocking school supplies.

ANIMAL CARE	SECRETARY
Small animal care work and maintenance for animal hospital. Morning and weekends. Reliable and mature. Exp. preferred.	Perm, part-time, 15 hours per week. Schedule flexible. Typing, bookkeeping, pleasant phone manner. Good opportunity for responsible individual.

Contacting Employers

When you have determined your availability and job skills, you will begin contacting employers either by phone or by letter.

Phone Calls. When you call a prospective employer, give your name and ask if he or she has any openings. Be sure to identify the type of job you are looking for and the qualifications you have. Speak briefly, clearly, and politely, keeping in mind that you may be disrupting a busy work day.

During the call, write down any essential information that you learn, such as the employer's address or the time for an interview. Save salary questions for the interview. Avoid dropping in on employers without first scheduling an appointment. Calling first to ask if you may visit them will show your consideration for others, a key employee asset.

Letters of Application. Instead of making a phone call, you may decide to write a formal letter of application. Follow all the guidelines covered in Part 3 of this chapter. Also, remember that some employers may require a résumé along with your letter of application. If a résumé is requested, complete it according to the guidelines in Part 5.

Completing Employment Forms

If you have contacted an employer by phone, the job application form will be the first sample of your work that the employer sees. In any case, you should always complete the form accurately, neatly, and completely to insure a positive impression. Follow the general guidelines for filling out forms listed on pages 349-350 of this chapter. Also look at the sample application form on page 362.

In addition, some employment applications leave space for you to add any other information that you feel may add to your chances of being hired. Take the opportunity to list special achievements in school, volunteer activities, awards, and honors. You may also list any outstanding personal attributes such as those you listed in the exercises on pages 359 and 360. This is especially important if you have had little actual job experience.

In addition to the job application form, you may also need to fill out other employment forms such as an application for a social security card (see page 351), work permit, or health permit. Such forms are often required by state or federal law. Check with your guidance counselor or employer for information on these forms.

If you complete all these steps well, you may be rewarded with an interview. Review the guidelines for interviewing covered in Part 5. Be prepared, be confident—and good luck!

Exercise Completing Job Application Forms

Look at the application form on page 362. On your own paper, write out the requested information. Use the writing utensil and form you would use on the actual application.

A SAMPLE JOB APPLICATION FORM

Marriott's
GREAT AMERICA ®

P.O. Box 1776, Gurnee, Illinois 60031

APPLICATION FOR
SEASONAL EMPLOYMENT

AN EQUAL OPPORTUNITY EMPLOYER M/F/H

PLEASE PRINT

NAME

LAST   FIRST   MIDDLE

SOCIAL SECURITY NO:

LOCAL ADDRESS
NO   STREET   CITY   STATE   ZIP

LOCAL PHONE: ( )

PERMANENT ADDRESS
NO   STREET   CITY   STATE   ZIP

BIRTHDATE AND
AGE (IF UNDER 21):   DAY / MO / YR

HIGH SCHOOL
NAME   CITY/STATE   GRADE COMPLETED

COLLEGE/OTHER
NAME   CITY/STATE   GRADE COMPLETED: MAJOR

SPECIAL SKILLS (typing, keypunch, languages, crafts, mechanics)

EMPLOYER	DATES EMPLOYED	SALARY	REASON FOR LEAVING	JOB DUTIES
NAME	FROM	START		
CITY	TO	FINISH		
SUPERVISOR				
TELEPHONE				
NAME	FROM	START		
CITY	TO	FINISH		
SUPERVISOR				
TELEPHONE				

IMPORTANT NOTE: All positions are temporary. That is they are seasonal - not year-round positions. The availability date you indicate will have a strong bearing on your application. Failure to comply with the availability you indicate below will affect your future employment status.

I CAN WORK WEEKENDS IN MAY.   YES ____ NO ____

I CAN WORK ANY DAY & ANY SHIFT-BEGINNING ___ MO / ___ DAY / 83

I CAN WORK ANY DAY & ANY SHIFT UNTIL ___ MO / ___ DAY / 83

I CAN WORK WEEKENDS IN SEPTEMBER/OCTOBER. YES ____ NO ____

☐ I WANT PART TIME ONLY.

☐ I WANT TO WORK THE TWO-WEEK PROGRAM.

PLEASE NUMBER FIRST 3 POSITIONS DESIRED
(Number following position is minimum hiring age)
(* Means only a limited number of positions to be filled)

☐ Games/Arcade Host/Hostess 16
☐ Area Host/Hostess (Sweeper) 15
☐ Beer/Wine Attendant 21
☐ Cash Control 19
☐ Character/Escort 16*
☐ Computer Operator 16*
☐ Crafts 16*
☐ Food Host/Hostess 15
☐ Janitorial/Grounds 18

☐ Keypunch Operator 16*
☐ Landscaper 18
☐ Laundry Attendant 16
☐ Mechanic 18*
☐ Merchandise Host/Hostess 15
☐ Nurse (RN, LPN) 18
☐ Nursing Assistant 18
☐ Office Clerical 16
☐ Parking Lot Host/Hostess 16

☐ Ride Host/Hostess 17
☐ Security Host/Hostess 18
☐ Theatre/Sound Technician 16*
☐ Theatre Attendant 15*
☐ Ticket Seller 16
☐ Ticket Taker 15
☐ Wardrobe Attendant 16
☐ Warehouse Attendant 18

☐ Other: _____   Would you accept any position?   YES ____ NO ____

1. Effective business communication skills can help you obtain information, apply to schools, and seek and gain employment.

2. All business letters include the inside address, heading, date, salutation, body, closing, and signature.

3. Business letters should be specific and concise. Types of business letters include requests for information, letters about employment, and letters to colleges and other schools.

4. When completing forms and applications, read all directions before beginning. Complete any form slowly and carefully.

5. A résumé is a list of your experiences, education, and skills. Prepare one that presents your background and qualifications attractively.

6. Prepare for an interview by doing research and developing questions you want answered. Dress well for your interview. Act and speak confidently.

7. Use all of the above skills when you look for a job.

Applications in Other Subject Areas

All Subjects. For your next long report or formal speech, gather some of your information from an organization, such as a museum or research foundation, or from an expert or authority. Use your letter-writing skills to acquire this information.

Mass Media. Examine the classified section of a city newspaper. Read the want ads and other notices under such categories as artists, audio-visual editors, journalists, public relations, and writers. Select one job that appeals to you. Write down a list of questions that you might have about this job.

Chapter 16

Group Discussion

Rehearsing a play, preparing for a football game, planning a dance—these are but a few of the many activities that require working with other people. Whenever people are brought together by a common interest, problem, or goal, they may be considered a group. Groups may be as informal as a gathering of friends after school or as formal as a committee meeting of the Congress of the United States. Groups may exist by themselves, or as part of larger groups such as businesses or schools.

In your lifetime you will probably participate in many such groups. Sometimes you will be expected to join in group discussions. In this chapter you will learn how groups function in discussions, what roles you can play as a group member, and how to deliver a talk to a group. You will also learn how to make group discussions effective and rewarding.

Part 1   Group Organization and Purpose

Group discussions are most effective when they are well organized and have a specific purpose. Whenever a group meets for discussion, it is best to choose a **chairperson** to lead the discussion and to maintain order. Sometimes a group may also wish to elect a **secretary** who can take notes during the discussion. The rest of the group will then act as **participants**, addressing themselves to the discussion topic under the guidance of the chairperson. Effective discussions usually develop in four stages:

1. Statement of subject and purpose. In this stage a group member, usually the chairperson, explains what the discussion is to be about and why the discussion is being held. Common purposes for holding discussions include sharing information, solving problems, and planning courses of action.

2. Definition of key terms and narrowing of topic. At this point, group members agree upon definitions for the words that will be central to their discussion. In a discussion on "Energy Sources," for example, a group might agree to define an energy source as "that which can be used to produce mechanical or electrical power." Defining such key terms helps to clarify the topic for discussion. It also helps group members to avoid needless arguments and misunderstandings.

At this point, the group might also decide to limit the range of their discussion by narrowing their topic. For example, instead of dealing with all energy sources, a group might decide to deal only with such natural sources of energy as wind and the sun.

3. Analysis. In this stage, the group discusses the topic in detail. The goal is to arrive at a plan of action or to reach an agreement, or *consensus*. What happens in the analysis stage will vary according to the nature of the topic and the purpose of the group.

4. Summary. In this stage, a group member, either the chairperson or the group secretary, summarizes the major points made during the discussion by the various members of the group.

Part 2 The Duties of Group Members

The Duties of the Chairperson

At times you may be called upon to act as a group chairperson. Your success depends upon your familiarity with the subject under discussion and the way you carry out your duties as a leader. Study the following guidelines:

1. Prepare for the discussion. Do some preliminary reading and thinking about the subject. Take notes on important points that should be considered.

2. To begin the discussion, introduce the topic or problem. Then state the aim of the discussion. You may also mention important points you think the group will want to consider.

3. Allow time for the introduction, the discussion, and a short summary of the conclusions reached.

4. Keep the discussion orderly. Allow only one person to speak at a time. Ask members of the group to raise their hands if they wish to speak. If several people begin to speak at once, interrupt politely but firmly. Make a statement such as "I'm sure everyone has something important to share. Let's hear from Alana first, then Hal, and then Louis."

5. Give everyone a chance to contribute. If two or more persons wish to speak, call on the person who has so far had only a small share in the discussion.

6. Keep the group's interest at a high pitch. Ask stimulating questions from time to time—especially if the discussion lags.

7. Keep the discussion moving forward. If your group's purpose is to reach a conclusion or consensus on a topic, keep this fact constantly in mind. If your group's purpose is to adopt a plan of action, guide the discussion toward that end. Do not allow the group to get sidetracked by unimportant or unrelated matters.

8. Take notes on key points made during the discussion. These will come in handy when you make your summary.

9. At the end of the discussion, briefly summarize the key points and decisions.

The Duties of a Participant

The success of any discussion will depend in great measure on how well you, as a participant, know your duties and carry them out. If you follow the guidelines given below, you will be able to make useful contributions to the discussion.

1. Take part in the discussion. The purpose of discussion is to bring out different points of view. Even though you may not be as forceful a speaker as someone else, speak up anyway. Your ideas may be just as good as another person's.

2. Speak only when the chairperson recognizes you. In a very large group, you can get the chairperson's attention by standing. In a small group, you can simply raise your hand.

3. Speak correctly and distinctly. Be sure to use acceptable grammar so that your listeners can concentrate on *what you are saying* and not *how you are saying it.* Be sure also that you enunciate clearly and that you speak loudly enough to be heard.

4. Support your statements with facts, examples, or the opinions of experts. If you introduce facts or statistics, be sure they are accurate. If you cite examples, be sure they are relevant to the topic. If you give the opinions of experts, be sure that these opinions were intended to apply to the topic under discussion.

5. Take notes and refer to these notes when speaking. Using a well-organized format, such as a modified outline, record important points as they are discussed. Write down the positions taken by other group members, and note key words or terms that they use. Jot down any questions that you have about what other speakers say. Then, when you are ready to join in the discussion, refer to these notes.

6. Listen attentively. Show your interest in what each speaker has to say by maintaining good posture and good eye contact. Use motions of the head and other gestures to signal to the speaker that you hear, understand, or agree with what is being said. Listen carefully to all speakers. Do not spend most of your time thinking about what you intend to say next.

7. Be courteous and tactful. If you disagree with someone, do not be rude and do not make irrelevant personal attacks. Refer politely to positions taken by other speakers. Ask questions for clarification of other speakers' opinions. Instead of flatly contradicting what another speaker says, indicate your disagreement by asking questions that begin with phrases such as "Isn't it possible that…?" or "Your idea is good, but don't you think that…?" Note areas of agreement when possible.

8. Try to understand the other person's point of view. Do not close your mind to an idea simply because it is not yours. Try to see things as others see them. Consider everyone present as your equal and accept even the least appealing remarks as worthy of your complete attention. Ask an occasional question that will draw out the wisdom hidden in some passing remark. Finally, be ready to recognize and accept an opinion or a solution that is better than one that you yourself may have proposed.

Exercises Group Discussion

A. The following is part of a class discussion. Read it and answer the questions that follow it.

Should Every High School Graduate Go to College?

CHAIRWOMAN: We hear a lot today about the importance of going to college. But is a college education really necessary for success? Many of our parents didn't go to college, but we think of them as successful. The question, then, is this: should we all aim at getting a college education?

JEFF: Madame Chairwoman.

CHAIRWOMAN: Jeff.

JEFF: It seems to me that things being what they are today, each of us—

TOM: (interrupting) You mean that everyone in our class should go to college? Don't be silly.

JEFF: No, not necessarily. I mean that if we think we are college material, we should do everything we can to assure ourselves of getting a college education. My reason for thinking so is that competition is much keener today, and the person who has a college education stands a better chance of meeting that competition.

KATHY: Madame Chairwoman.

CHAIRWOMAN: Kathy. (As the discussion continues, the chairperson recognizes each speaker in turn and by so doing gives him or her the right to speak.)

KATHY: While Jeff has raised a good point, I believe there may be other points that we should discuss in regard to this matter. Let's hear from those who have other arguments, pro or con.

ANNE: Well, why don't you give your own point of view, instead of holding out to get the opinion of others? Don't you *have* a point of view? Well, I have. I know plenty of people who have made a lot of money in business or in industry, and they never had a college education. So I think Jeff is all wrong.

NED: I think that Jeff has a very good argument, and I'd like to go even further with it. Educators and others who know about these things are constantly telling us that the college graduate gets the preference today in all fields leading to executive or administrative positions. We also know that it's impossible to get into the professions today without a college background.

LEO: I agree. However, I want to say a word for the student who has ability and is enterprising but doesn't want to spend the time or the money it takes to get a college education. I don't think this student should feel discouraged about the future. He or she can go to a vocational school and prepare for a trade or service job. Later, the student can take courses in evening schools that will help him or her to advance. Eventually, this person may even own a business. To many people, this kind of career and the independence it offers is the most satisfying of all.

KATHY: So far we've talked about a college education only as an advantage in getting a good job with a good salary. I think there are some other things to consider. What about the social and cultural advantages of a college education?

JEFF: Kathy has a good point. I think the social and cultural benefits of a college education are just as important as the economic values. Social activities can teach you things you don't learn in a classroom. You meet and learn how to get along with all kinds of different people. This can give you more self-confidence in the future.

NED: Kathy mentioned the cultural advantages. Let's not forget them. College gives you the opportunity to learn about a lot of different subjects. It makes you a more well rounded person—someone who has a lot of interests and who can talk about lots of different things. This is useful socially and economically and is also helpful for people who are still trying to decide on their major field of study.

CHAIRWOMAN: It seems to me that we have thrashed out this question pretty well. Before we try to come to a conclusion, maybe we should invite some adults—business or professional people—to talk to us about this. What do you think?

1. How well did the chairperson introduce the subject? Were the topic and purpose of the discussion made clear?

2. How would you rate each student's contribution? Give specific reasons for your answers.

3. Did the group reach a consensus? Why or why not?

B. Form a discussion group with several of your classmates. Elect a chairperson for your group and choose one of the following discussion topics, or another topic of your own. Before you begin your discussion, review your duties as a participant on pages 367 and 368. See how well you can put into practice what you have learned.

1. Should the United States continue to build nuclear power plants and use nuclear power as a basic energy source?

2. Does violence on TV affect people's lives?

3. What type of television programs are most rewarding?

4. Should private citizens be allowed to own handguns?

5. Should school be held year round?

Part 3   Speaking Before a Group

There are many instances when you will be required to speak to groups. Most frequently, you will be asked to deliver an informal talk, which is a brief speech requiring a small amount of background work and practice. Some common informal talks are **introductions, announcements,** and **simple demonstrations**. On occasion, you may be asked to deliver formal talks. These are longer than informal talks and require more thought, time, and preparation. However, the skills required for proper preparation and delivery of these two kinds of talks are quite similar.

Preparing a Talk

The preparation of a talk requires six separate steps. These steps are identical to those of the pre-writing stage of the process of writing. They are listed in the chart on the following page.

1. **Choose a topic and narrow it.** Your topic should be of interest to you and to your audience. Limit the scope of the topic so that you can cover it in the alotted time.

2. **Define your purpose.** Decide whether you wish to inform, persuade, or entertain.

3. **Determine your main idea.** State in a single sentence the main idea that you wish to get across. This main idea may be a general observation or an opinion.

4. **Identify your audience.** Know to whom you will be speaking. Suit your remarks to their backgrounds, ages, interests, and experience.

5. **Gather your information.** Take notes on information that is directly related to your main idea and purpose. Sources of information include your own experience, interviews, and reference material.

6. **Organize your material.** Your talk should have an introduction that interests your audience, explains the title of your talk, and states your main idea. The body of your talk should accomplish your purpose by informing, persuading, or entertaining your audience. Common methods for organizing ideas in the body of a speech include *least important to most important idea* and *most important to least important idea*. Your conclusion should re-emphasize your main idea, summarize your important points, and if appropriate, appeal to your audience to take some action.

Exercise Preparing a Talk

Choose one of the topics below. Then carry out the directions that are listed on the following page.

a. Jobs   e. Television
b. Athletic events   f. College
c. Music   g. Vacations
d. Holidays   h. School

1. Narrow your topic for use in a ten-minute talk.
2. Identify the audience for your talk.
3. Define your purpose.
4. Write a statement of your main idea.
5. Gather information on your topic.
6. Organize your material and write your talk.
7. Revise your talk.

Delivering a Talk

The effective presentation of a formal talk is not easy, but there are things you can remember to ensure your success.

1. Rehearse your talk out loud. You may practice with a tape recorder or by reciting your talk for a friend or a relative. Choose a method of delivery that is comfortable for you. If you prefer to memorize the talk, do so. You may also use notes, but do not read your talk word by word from these notes.

2. Use appropriate non-verbal communication. Maintain good eye contact and posture. Be positive and at ease. Wear clothing that does not draw excessive attention to itself. Use facial signals and gestures to underscore points made in your speech.

3. Speak clearly and pleasantly. Make sure that your audience can hear what you are saying. Do not speak too slowly or too quickly. Vary your pace. Avoid speaking in a monotone. Enunciate your words carefully, and pronounce them correctly.

Exercises Delivering a Talk

A. Read your prepared speech into a tape recorder. Listen to this recording, noticing any problems in volume, speed, pitch, enunciation, and pronunciation. Note areas for improvement. Practice correcting these errors by reading parts of your speech aloud. Then, repeat the process and compare the results.

B. Practice your speech in front of a mirror. Pay particular attention to appropriate facial expressions and gestures.

C. Deliver to your class the talk that you wrote in the previous set of exercises. Follow the guidelines for delivering a talk listed on page 373.

Listening to and Evaluating Speeches

As an audience member, you have several responsibilities. You must be receptive and attentive. You must also be critical without being rude. The following basic courtesies and listening guidelines will help you to fulfill these responsibilities.

1. Listen attentively. Sit up in your seat. Maintain eye contact with the speaker. Do not make noise or talk during the speech. Do not indulge in distracting behavior.

2. Listen for the speaker's main idea and supporting statements. Determine the subject and the main idea of the speech. Listen for other ideas that support or develop this main idea.

3. Offer suggestions to improve the speaker's content and delivery. If you are asked to evaluate a speaker's performance, make positive comments as well as negative ones. Make your comments specific. Avoid attacking the speaker. The chart on the following page will help you to make specific evaluations.

Exercise Evaluating Speeches

Use the checklist on the following page to critique a round of speeches in your class. Be sure your comments are specific and constructive.

Checklist for Evaluating Speeches

CONTENT:

Introduction

_____ gets audience's attention

_____ is brief and to the point

_____ is appropriate to the topic

Body

_____ supports main idea

_____ contains no irrelevant material

_____ states important ideas clearly

_____ develops all ideas thoroughly

Conclusion

_____ is brief

_____ provides a summary of major points
or draws attention back to thesis

PRESENTATION:

Non-verbal

_____ speaker has good posture

_____ speaker is relaxed and confident

_____ speaker has good eye contact

_____ gestures and facial expressions are
natural and appropriate

Verbal

_____ speaker is not too quiet or too loud

_____ speaker's articulation is clear

_____ speaker's pace is not too slow or rapid

_____ speaker's pitch is not too high or low

_____ speaker varies volume, pace, pitch

_____ speaker uses pauses effectively

SUMMARY AND APPLICATIONS

1. Good discussion skills can help you in any situation where you must work with others to make plans, accomplish a task, or solve a problem.

2. The chairperson and participants in a group discussion should prepare beforehand, take notes on key points, and listen courteously to others.

3. The chairperson should introduce the topic, define the purpose of the discussion, and keep the discussion on target. He or she should also give all group members a chance to participate, and briefly summarize the discussion at its close.

4. Participants should speak only when recognized. They should support their statements with evidence, try to understand other viewpoints, be courteous toward other group members, and be tactful when disagreeing.

5. When you are preparing a talk, follow the pre-writing steps of the process of writing.

6. When you are delivering a talk, be aware of your dress, facial expressions, posture, gestures, volume, speed, pitch, and enunciation.

7. When you are listening to and evaluating speeches, be attentive, receptive, and pleasant. To evaluate a speech, refer to specific aspects of the speaker's content and delivery.

Applications in Other Subject Areas

All Subjects. One effective method of preparing for tests or other classwork is to form a *study group*. This is a group that meets outside of class to discuss what has been learned in a particular class. If you are interested in forming a study group for one of your classes, talk to the teacher of the class about the idea.

Current Events. Cut out several interesting articles from a newspaper or news magazine. Develop a statement on the subject that could be questioned or challenged by another person. Form a discussion group to discuss your idea.

Handbook

A detailed Table of Contents appears in the front of this book.

How To Use the Handbook

This Handbook is your reference book. In it the concepts of grammar, usage, and mechanics are organized so that you can study them efficiently and refer to them quickly.

To use the Handbook well, you should first leaf through it to become familiar with its organization and contents. Note especially the following:

Organization of the Handbook

Grammar Sections 1-4 contain grammar rules and explanations. You can refer to these when you have questions about grammar in your own speaking and writing.

Usage Sections 5-9 are a guide to English usage. When you are puzzled about which form of a word to use in your writing, turn to the appropriate part of these sections.

Forms and constructions marked STANDARD are accepted as standard usage—the kind of usage that is appropriate at all times and in all places. Forms and constructions marked NON-STANDARD are not always appropriate.

Mechanics Sections 10-16 offer rules for capitalization, punctuation, spelling, and the formation of plurals. Use this section of the Handbook when proofreading or whenever questions about mechanics arise.

Good Form Sections 17-18 contain information that is useful when you have questions about proper manuscript or outline form.

1.0 The Classification of Words

Words, like people, can be classified according to the jobs they perform. There are eight major groups of words, each with different functions in sentences. These eight groups are called the **parts of speech**.

nouns	adjectives	conjunctions
pronouns	adverbs	interjections
verbs	prepositions	

In addition to these eight categories, there are three other groups of words that perform many of the same jobs performed by the parts of speech. These words are called **verbals** because they are made from verbs.

infinitives   participles   gerunds

These eleven groups of words, the parts of speech and the verbals, make up the language that we speak and write. This Section will describe each of these groups, providing you with terms that you can use to analyze your own speech and writing.

1.1   The Noun

Certain words in the language are used as labels. We use them to identify people, places, things, and ideas.

A noun is the name of a person, place, thing, or idea.

Things include such visible items as *clothes, trees,* and *chairs.* Things may also be items that we perceive with our other senses: *smells, sounds, tastes.* Ideas include all things, such as *beliefs, theories,* and *emotions,* that exist inside the minds of people.

PERSONS	PLACES	THINGS	IDEAS
Matt Dillon	Boston	baseball	love
friend	country	amplifier	charity
priest	arcade	prayer	democracy

A **common noun** is the name of a whole group of persons, places, things, or ideas. It is a name that is common to an entire group: *animal, dish, apple, tent.*

A **proper noun** is the name of an individual person, place, thing, or idea.

A proper noun always begins with a capital letter.

COMMON NOUNS	PROPER NOUNS
dancer	Maria Tallchief
bridge	Golden Gate Bridge
continent	Africa
business	Columbia Pictures
language	Spanish

As the above list shows, some nouns, especially proper nouns, may consist of more than one word. Each word in a proper noun is capitalized.

Any word that can be immediately preceded by *the* is a noun: *the* bridge, *the* dog, *the* language. Most proper nouns, but not all of them, can also be preceded by *the: the* Astrodome, *the* Buick, but not *the* O. J. Simpson or *the* Detroit.

Exercise A: Find all the nouns in the following sentences.

1. The announcer said that the plane for Minneapolis would leave in thirty minutes.
2. Maria Mayer, an American physicist, won the Nobel Prize.
3. John wanted to change the ribbon on his typewriter, but the ribbon would not cooperate.
4. There was a scream of skidding tires and then a metallic thud, followed by the sound of splintered glass.
5. The tourists gathered together at the foot of the Eiffel Tower for a snapshot.
6. The boys and their mother drove through the desert at night.
7. Helen is president of the class, and her brother Philip is the recording secretary.
8. Al wrote a paper about Babe Didrikson and her life in sports.
9. Half of the people in the world can neither read nor write.
10. Andrew Wyeth is well known for his paintings of rural scenes.

Exercise B: Decide which are common nouns and which are proper nouns. Write the proper nouns, beginning each with a capital letter.

1. german, science, language, english
2. lake, lake erie, mountain, mount everest
3. park, joshua national monument, gulf, cape cod
4. village, fairfield township, country
5. labor, labor day, good friday, birthday
6. senator nancy kassebaum, mayor tom bradley, state representative
7. judge, justice thurgood marshall, judge shirley m. hufstedler
8. uncle harry, bridge, rittenhouse square, gettysburg battlefield
9. cathedral, rabbi, saint patrick's cathedral, church
10. college, purdue university, sawyer business college, vocational school

1.2 The Pronoun

It would be awkward to repeat the name of a person or thing every time we wish to refer to it. Instead, we sometimes use other words in place of names. These words are pronouns. They may be used in a sentence in any way that a noun is used.

A pronoun is a word used in place of a noun.

The noun for which the pronoun stands and to which it refers is its **antecedent.**

Sue had changed *her* dress. (*Sue* is the antecedent of *her.*)

The *boys* changed *their* jerseys. (*boys* is the antecedent of *their.*)

Sometimes the antecedent appears in a preceding sentence.

Inspector Hughes was baffled by the appearance of Dr. Dixon on T.V. *He* thought that the doctor had disappeared years before. (*He* refers to the antecedent *Inspector Hughes.*)

There are six kinds of pronouns:

personal pronouns	demonstrative pronouns
compound personal pronouns	interrogative pronouns
indefinite pronouns	relative pronouns

Personal Pronouns

Pronouns used in place of persons' names are called **personal pronouns.**

Bill baked a cake. *He* bakes well.

Personal pronouns are also used to refer to things.

Consuelo bought a *painting. It* was beautiful.

Personal pronouns can be categorized in several different ways.

Person. Pronouns that identify the person speaking are in the **first person.** Pronouns that identify the person being spoken to are in the **second person.** Pronouns that identify the person or thing spoken about are in the **third person.**

First Person (the person speaking)
I, me, my, mine
we, us, our, ours

Second Person (the person spoken to)
you, you, yours

Third Person (the person or thing spoken about)
he, him, his, she, her, hers, it, its
they, them, their, theirs

Number. Pronouns that refer to *one* person, place, thing, or idea are **singular.** Pronouns that refer to *more than one* are **plural.**

SINGULAR: Joni didn't care for the band, but I liked *it* a lot.
PLURAL: Chimpanzees can't talk, but *they* can use tools.

Gender. Pronouns that refer to males are in the **masculine gender.** Pronouns that refer to females are in the **feminine gender.** Pronouns that refer to things are in the **neuter gender.**

The pronoun *it* is neuter because it refers to things. Countries, ships, and airplanes are sometimes referred to by the feminine pronouns *she, her,* and *hers.* Animals may be referred to by *it* and *its* or by *he, his, him, she, her,* or *hers.*

Case. Personal pronouns change their form, or spelling, for different uses in sentences. Consider the following examples:

He made a movie.   *His* movie was a hit.
The Academy gave *him* an Oscar.

This change in form is called a change in the **case** of the pronoun. There are three cases in English: the **nominative case,** the **possessive case,** and the **objective case.** See Section 6 for information concerning the uses of these cases.

The following table shows person and number of all three cases of personal pronouns.

Personal Pronouns

SINGULAR		
Nominative	Possessive	Objective
FIRST PERSON: I	my, mine	me
SECOND PERSON: you	your, yours	you
THIRD PERSON: he, she, it	his, her, hers, its	him, her, it

PLURAL		
Nominative	Possessive	Objective
FIRST PERSON: we	our, ours	us
SECOND PERSON: you	your, yours	you
THIRD PERSON: they	their, theirs	them

Possessive Pronouns. All personal pronouns have one or two special forms that are used to show ownership or belonging. A pronoun that shows ownership or belonging is a **possessive pronoun.**

> The squirrels ate all of *my* peanuts. (ownership)
> Chief Joseph led *his* people wisely. (belonging)

Some personal pronouns have two possessive forms. One of these forms is used in place of a noun, just like other pronouns: *mine, yours, hers, ours, theirs.* The other is used as a modifier before nouns: *my, your, her, our, their.* See the examples on the following page.

This horse is *mine*. (used like other pronouns)
This is *my* horse. (modifies the noun *horse*)
The awards are *ours*. (used like other pronouns)
We claimed *our* awards. (modifies the noun *awards*)

The possessive pronoun *his* functions in both ways.

Exercise: Find the personal pronouns in the following sentences. Find the antecedent of each pronoun.

1. The doctor told the boys that they could use his boat.
2. Bob, your father wants you to call for him.
3. Helen and Karen finished the geometry test first. They found it easier than the history exam.
4. Pygmy marmosets must be small indeed, for they can perch on a single blade of grass.
5. Shirley Temple, the child actress, made her first million before she was ten years old.
6. The Pioneer spacecraft made its way past Pluto.
7. The boys cooked their meals in the open and made their beds of pine boughs.
8. When Jim's power mower broke, the neighbors let him use theirs.
9. Betty has a driver's permit, but she doesn't have it with her.
10. The police found the car, but they couldn't move it.

Compound Personal Pronouns

A **compound personal pronoun** is formed by adding *-self* or *-selves* to a personal pronoun, as follows:

FIRST PERSON:	myself, ourselves
SECOND PERSON:	yourself, yourselves
THIRD PERSON:	himself, herself, itself, oneself, themselves

There are no other acceptable compound personal pronouns. Never say *hisself* or *theirselves*.

Compound personal pronouns are used *intensively* for emphasis or *reflexively* to refer to a preceding noun or pronoun.

The President *himself* welcomed the ambassador. (intensive)
Dawn treated *herself* to a soda. (reflexive)

A compound personal pronoun must have an antecedent.

NONSTANDARD: Ted and *myself* will head the committees.

STANDARD: I will head the committee *myself*.

Exercise: Writing Supply an acceptable compound personal pronoun in each of these sentences. Find the antecedent for each pronoun. Then, tell whether the pronoun is used intensively or reflexively.

1. The doctor (_____) helped Ms. Brown into the car.
2. Our Olympic competitors can be proud of (_____).
3. Eve talked (_____) into asking for a raise.
4. The pigs opened the farmer's gate by (_____).
5. You girls can see the results for (_____).
6. Jack blames (_____) for the accident.
7. Jane, you will have to solve this problem (_____).
8. Einstein (_____) said that thinking is a kind of play.
9. Before renting the mopeds, we tested them (_____).
10. The company president (_____) replied to our criticism.

Indefinite Pronouns

Some pronouns, such as *anyone* and *anything*, do not refer to a definite person or thing. They are called **indefinite pronouns**. Indefinite pronouns often do not have antecedents.

SINGULAR INDEFINITE PRONOUNS

another	anything	either	everything	no one
anybody	one	everyone	neither	someone
anyone	each	everybody	nobody	somebody

both   many   few   several

The pronouns *all, some, none, most,* and *any* may be singular or plural, depending upon their meaning in the sentence.

All of the candy *has* been sold. (singular)
All of the skiers *have* returned. (plural)

Some of the money *is* counterfeit. (singular)
Some of the voters *were* angry. (plural)

None of the cider *is* sour. (singular)
None of the doors *were* locked. (plural)

Demonstrative Pronouns

The words *this, that, these,* and *those* are used to point out, or demonstrate, which one or which ones are meant. For this reason, they are called **demonstrative pronouns.** They always refer to a definite person or thing. The words they refer to may come later in the sentence or in another sentence altogether.

This is the *camera* I won. (*camera* is referred to by *this*.)

On his wall were several Picasso *prints. These* had been given to him by his uncle. (*prints* is referred to by *These.*)

Note: The demonstrative pronouns *this, that, these,* and *those* may also be used to modify nouns: *this hat, those curtains.*

Interrogative Pronouns

When the pronouns *who, whose, whom, which,* and *what* are used to ask questions, they are **interrogative pronouns.**

Who took the pretzels?   *What* is the time?
Whom did you want?   *Which* do you like?
Whose shoes are these?

Relative Pronouns

The words *who, whose, whom, which,* and *that* are sometimes used to combine two ideas, as in the following example:

IDEA 1: Barbara Tuchman is the Pulitzer Prize winning historian

IDEA 2: Barbara Tuchman wrote *A Distant Mirror.*

COMBINED IDEA: Barbara Tuchman is the Pulitzer Prize winning historian *who* wrote *A Distant Mirror.*

Because such words *relate* one idea to another, they are called **relative pronouns**. See Section 3.6 for more information on the use of relative pronouns.

Exercise A: List the pronouns below. Tell what kind each is.

1. Nobody knows how language began.
2. The teacher could not find her grade book.
3. Some of the neighbors formed a car pool.
4. All of the clowns carried water pistols.
5. Who played the part on Broadway?
6. Someone had dropped her sandwich into the pool.
7. What have you done to make Mike so upset?
8. These come from China.
9. Is this the watch you lost?
10. Did anyone but you see the extraterrestrial?

Exercise B: List all of the pronouns in the following paragraph. Tell what type each one is.

Who would have thought one could take a college course on ice cream? I wouldn't have, at least not until my sister told me about the class Professor Philip Keeney teaches at Penn State. Every time he offers this ice cream course, it fills up rapidly. This is not surprising. In fact, the crowds fighting to get into the class bring to mind a famous saying known by everyone: "I scream, you scream, we all scream for ice cream."

1.3 The Verb

A **verb** is a word or group of words that expresses an action, a condition, or a state of being. The word that the verb expresses an idea about is called the **subject** of the sentence.

A verb is a word that expresses an action, condition, or state of being.

Grammatically, the verb is the most important part of the sentence. If you can find verbs and manage them properly, many of your grammar and usage problems will be solved.

Most verbs change their form (their sound or spelling) to show past or present time. They are the only words that do so. This fact can help you decide which word in a sentence is the verb.

The trains *were* on time. (past)
The trains *are* on time. (present)

The Smiths *loved* Arizona. (past)
The Smiths *love* Arizona. (present)

Most verbs also change their form to show the difference between singular and plural in the third person.

Joe *likes* country music. (third person singular)
Sue and Marcella *like* woodworking class. (third person plural)

There are two main categories of verbs: **action verbs** and **linking verbs**.

Action Verbs

An action verb may tell of an action that can be seen.

Loretta *knocked* on the door.
The car *skidded*.

An action verb may also tell of an action that cannot be seen.

Jane *wanted* a new cat.
The ambassador *hoped* for success.

Linking Verbs

Linking verbs do not express actions. Instead, they link subjects to adjectives or to other nouns or pronouns in the sentence.

> Sue *is* captain. (links the subject *Sue* to the noun *captain*)
> Sherman *seems* unhappy. (links the subject *Sherman* to the adjective *unhappy*)

There are three major groups of linking verbs:

> forms of the verb *to be*
> verbs that have to do with the senses
> verbs that express the condition or placement of the subject.

Linking Verbs

Forms of *To Be*	Sensory Verbs
Jim *was* excited. The decorations *were* nice. I *am* tired. You *are* our leader. He *is* a magician. Others: *be, been, being*	Her hair *felt* soft. Garfield *looked* annoyed. My salad *tastes* delicious. The room *smells* musty. His children *appeared* sad. This song *sounds* silly.

Verbs of Condition, or Placement	
The coach *became* elated Our team *remained* ahead. The redwoods *grew* tall.	She *seems* intelligent. The diver *stayed* down.

Sometimes the same verb can be used as both a linking verb and as an action verb.

LINKING	ACTION
Abdul *grew* strong. Paul *sounded* happy.	Pat *grew* radishes. LeRoi *sounded* the alarm.

Main Verbs and Auxiliaries

Many verbs consist of more than one word. They consist of a **main verb** and one or more helping verbs, or **auxiliaries**. Together, a main verb and its auxiliaries are called a **verb phrase**. When a verb consists of more than one word, the last word in the phrase is the main verb.

There are three verbs that can be used either as main verbs or as auxiliaries. Here are their forms:

DO	HAVE	BE		
do	has	is	was	be
does	have	am	were	been
did	had	are		being

AS MAIN VERB	AS AUXILIARY
They *do* all the work.	We *do* enjoy school shows.
Have you the strength?	They *have* lost it.
The marks *were* good.	The fans *were* watching.

The auxiliaries used most often are the forms of *be* and *have*. Other common auxiliaries are the following:

must	may	shall	could	would
might	can	will	should	

AUXILIARY	MAIN VERB	VERB
had	been	had been
was	doing	was doing
had	done	had done
could have	gone	could have gone
might have been	seen	might have been seen
is being	improved	is being improved

Often the parts of a verb are separated by a word or words that are not part of the verb.

She *was* certainly *being* helpful.
It *had* just *stopped* snowing.

Exercise A: Find the verb in each of these sentences. Include all the words that make up the verb. Do not include any word that separates an auxiliary from a main verb.

1. The lighthouse keeper had seen such a storm only once before.
2. The African gray parrot is the most talkative bird in the world.
3. The truck driver was completely blinded by the flash.
4. How did you recognize her?
5. The new school will almost surely be ready by fall.
6. The new law has been poorly enforced.
7. Do you and your brother have enough blankets?
8. The freighter had apparently run aground in the fog.
9. The park benches had been freshly painted.
10. The swimmers were obviously exhausted.
11. The fog was now rapidly lifting from the field.
12. No one has ever returned from that desert.
13. The flaws can easily be seen under a magnifying glass.
14. Have you really been to Saudi Arabia?
15. The oxygen supply in the submarine will last for several weeks.

Exercise B: Writing Find the verb in each of the following sentences. Tell whether it is a linking verb or an action verb. If it is a linking verb, write a new sentence using the same verb as an action verb. If it is an action verb, write a new sentence using the same verb as a linking verb.

1. The baby orangutan looked asleep.
2. Robert Wadlow of Illinois grew to a height of 8 feet, 11 inches.
3. The tornado appeared without warning.
4. These footprints look fresh.
5. A mysterious echo sounded from the mountaintop.
6. The tuba player appeared breathless.
7. Have you ever tasted papayas?
8. The pitcher's arm felt tired.

9. On the deck, we could smell the salty sea air.
10. The sure-footed high wire artists remained calm.
11. The detectives seemed confident about the outcome of their investigation.
12. My Bruce Springsteen albums sounded terrific.
13. The cat looked at the goldfish.
14. Carmine felt tired but happy after the elections.
15. The Jedi warrior grew quiet and thoughtful.

Transitive and Intransitive Verbs

A **transitive verb** carries the action from the subject to the object of the verb. The object is the word that comes after the verb and tells *who* or *what* receives the action.

SUBJECT	TRANSITIVE VERB	OBJECT
Cara	completed	the application.
My neighbor	grows	avocados.
José	entered	the subway.

An intransitive verb expresses an action that is complete in itself; it does not carry action to an object.

SUBJECT	INTRANSITIVE VERB	OPTIONAL MODIFIER
Bret	sang.	
A child	wept.	
The morning	passed	quickly.

Notice that sometimes intransitive verbs are followed by adverbs or other modifiers.

Many verbs may be transitive in one sentence and intransitive in another.

INTRANSITIVE	TRANSITIVE
Everyone *applauded.*	Everyone *applauded* Styx.
Are you *selling?*	*Are* you *selling* your home?
Mr. Berra *called.*	Mr. Berra *called* the lawyer.

Exercise A: Find each verb. Tell whether it is a transitive or an intransitive verb.

1. The band uniforms finally arrived just before Christmas.
2. The trainer stepped into the wounded leopard's cage.
3. The sophomore class has a good attendance record.
4. Greg walked unsteadily to the front of the stage.
5. The author tells a story of her childhood in Wyoming.
6. Our team played well during the first quarter.
7. Once a circus horse stuck his foot into his mouth.
8. Helen enjoys responsibility.
9. The murderer does not appear in this act.
10. All cars have safety belts as standard equipment.

Exercise B: Writing Tell whether the verb in each of the following sentences is transitive or intransitive. Then write sentences using the transitive verbs as intransitive verbs and vice versa.

1. Your work load *will lighten* after this semester.
2. The caboose *hooks* onto the last car.
3. Molly *could kick* a field goal better than any other player on the football team.
4. Randi *played* a beautiful melody from Borodin's Polovtsian Dances on the French horn.
5. *Have* the Morrison's *moved* their furniture into their new house yet?
6. The tall ships *sailed* into the harbor for the last time.
7. She *slipped* on the ice during the final spin of her routine.
8. The explorers *crossed* the Andes by burro.
9. Don't *rush* your meals.
10. Wind *rustled* in the trees above us.

Exercise C: Writing Write ten of your own sentences using each of the following verbs twice. Make the verb transitive in one sentence and intransitive in the other.

dance	change	ring	place
offer	sew	run	swing

1.4   The Adjective

Words that describe or limit the meanings of other words are called **modifiers.** One kind of modifier is the **adjective.** Adjectives are used to describe nouns or pronouns. Carefully chosen adjectives can make your speech and writing precise, vivid, and interesting.

An adjective is a word that modifies a noun or pronoun.

Adjectives are used before nouns and pronouns to answer one of the following questions: *Which one? What kind? How many? How much?*

WHICH ONE:	this, that, these, those
WHAT KIND:	tiny, old, yellow, shy
HOW MANY:	few, three, both, twenty, most
HOW MUCH:	more, less, enough, abundant

Notice that demonstrative pronouns can also function as modifiers:

this book	*that* dog
these apples	*those* people

The Articles

The word *the* is called a **definite article** because it usually refers to a definite or specific thing or person.

The words *a* and *an* are called **indefinite articles** because they refer to no particular thing or person. *A* is used before words beginning with consonant sounds. *An* is used before words beginning with vowel sounds. The sound, not the spelling, determines which word is used.

> They went to *an* auction every Saturday.
> I found *a* history book.
> The bus was *an* hour late.
> It was *a* heated argument.

Proper Adjectives

A modifier formed from a proper noun is a **proper adjective.** A proper adjective is always capitalized.

NOUN	ADJECTIVE	NOUN	ADJECTIVE
Ireland	Irish	East	Eastern
France	French	Shakespeare	Shakespearean
Canada	Canadian	Bible	Biblical

Predicate Adjectives

An adjective that is separated from the noun or pronoun that it modifies by a linking verb is called a **predicate adjective.**

Karen seems *sleepy*. (*seems* links the subject and the predicate adjective.)

We were *exhausted*. (*were* links the subject and the predicate adjective.)

An adjective that follows a linking verb and that modifies the subject is a predicate adjective.

Exercise A: Find each adjective and tell which word it modifies. Ignore the articles.

1. The old house had been empty for several years.
2. The second team played during the last quarter.
3. The new teacher was patient and helpful.
4. One poor elephant was suffering from a bad toothache.
5. The enormous jet cannot land at a small airport.
6. A magnetic field surrounds the entire earth.
7. The new atomic submarines are spacious and comfortable.
8. The water in this lake tastes salty.
9. Many young Americans are making scientific discoveries.
10. The two people in the other car seemed angry.

Exercise B: Follow the same directions as for Exercise A.

1. This little book contains some big ideas.
2. A cold wind drove the deep snow into huge drifts.
3. Steve Cauthen is the young jockey who has won many races.
4. Yesterday Carlita collected sixteen different coins.
5. This new tent easily sleeps several people.
6. Most European students can speak the English language.
7. The library charges fines for overdue books.
8. The hamburger tasted dry and gritty.
9. Some small economy cars are neither small nor economical.
10. Janet Guthrie became famous as the first woman racer in the Indianapolis 500.

Exercise C: Writing Add colorful adjectives to the following sentences to make them more vivid and more precise.

1. The _____ rabbit in the cartoon ate a _____ carrot.
2. A _____, _____ wind was blowing, and the _____ trees were shaking.
3. I love the _____, and _____ days of summer.
4. A _____ fire hydrant had burst, spilling water over the _____, _____ street.
5. The _____ government supports the study of _____ languages by giving _____ sums of money to schools that offer them.
6. Rudi, my _____ friend, just sat there looking _____ and _____.
7. Up the _____ mountain and down _____ slope on the other side, we carried our _____ canoe.
8. There are _____ beasts in these _____ and _____ woods.
9. He may have been a _____ musician, but he wrote one _____ song.
10. Despite all of his _____ efforts, the _____ archaeologist could not decipher the _____ code.

1.5 The Adverb

Nouns and pronouns are modified by adjectives. Verbs and other parts of speech are modified by adverbs. Like adjectives, adverbs help to make writing and speech more interesting and precise.

An adverb modifies a verb, an adjective, or another adverb.

MODIFYING A VERB: Barnes answered *angrily.*

MODIFYING AN ADJECTIVE: It was a *most* enjoyable trip.

MODIFYING AN ADVERB: They moved *rather* cautiously.

Adverbs tell *where, when, how,* or *to what extent:*

WHERE: The family is *inside.*
WHEN: I'll bring you the present *soon.*
HOW: The storm struck *swiftly.*
TO WHAT EXTENT: We did not *fully* understand the question.

Many adverbs are formed by adding *-ly* to an adjective: *perfect-perfectly, quiet-quietly, beautiful-beautifully, happy-happily.* However, not all modifiers ending in *-ly* are adverbs. The following *-ly* words, for example, are adjectives: *friendly, lively, lonely, ugly.*

Many adverbs do not end in *-ly.* The negatives *no, not,* and *never* are almost always adverbs. Many time words, such as *later, often, always,* and *soon,* are always adverbs.

Directive Adverbs

Adverbs that tell *where* (place or direction) about the verb are called **directive adverbs.** They normally follow the verb they modify.

We searched *near* and *far.*   The sign had fallen *down.*
They are waiting *outside.*   The conductor walked *in.*

Many of these directive adverbs are combined with verbs to make idioms; *put off, put through, put up.* An **idiom** is a group of words with a meaning different from the literal meanings of the words taken individually.

Position of Adverbs

A directive adverb normally follows the verb it modifies. An adverb modifying an adjective or another adverb usually comes immediately before the word it modifies. Other adverbs may be shifted from one place in the sentence to another.

DIRECTIVE: The elevator had gone *up.*
(modifies *had gone*)

ADVERB MODIFYING MODIFIER: It was a *very* common name.
(modifies *common*)

OTHER ADVERBS: *Suddenly,* he turned and ran.
(modifies *turned* and *ran*)
He turned *suddenly* and ran.
(modifies *turned*)

Exercise A: Find each adverb and tell which word or words it modifies.

1. The bus almost always arrives late.
2. The entire class worked hard and successfully on the project.
3. Does your car usually start easily on cold mornings?
4. The streets have become rather crowded recently.
5. The auditorium was soon completely filled with impatient, enthusiastic fans.
6. Nearly every city in the United States has a zoo.
7. The doctor gave orders quietly and confidently.
8. Polio is sometimes rather difficult to diagnose.
9. Lately, the summers have been extremely hot.
10. There goes Dr. Harrison now.

Exercise B: Writing Rewrite the following sentences, making them more precise by adding adverbs that answer the questions in parentheses.

1. The doctor approached the sick tiger. (how?)
2. Did Carlotta send for the tickets? (when?)
3. The class had finished the signs. (when?)
4. The plane's fuel supply was exhausted. (to what extent?)
5. David raised his hand. (how?)
6. We had often explored the valley. (where?)
7. The quarterback limped from the field. (how?)
8. The parade grounds flooded. (to what extent?)
9. It was raining cats and dogs. (when?)
10. Do your ballet exercises. (when?)

1.6 The Preposition

The words in English sentences are connected to one another in a variety of ways. One common method of connecting words is by using **prepositions.**

There are seventeen one-syllable prepositions in English.° They are used to show the following relationships.

LOCATION:	at, by, in, on, near
DIRECTION:	to, from, down, off, through, out, past, up
ASSOCIATION:	of, for, with, like

Here are some two-syllable prepositions.

about	against	before	beside	except
above	along	behind	between	inside
across	among	below	beyond	outside
after	around	beneath	during	over
				under

°The word *but* may be used as a preposition with the meaning of *except*. The word *as* may be used as a preposition with the meaning of *except*. The word *as* may be used as a preposition with the meaning "in the capacity of": *As* a firefighter, he has to be able to remain calm under pressure.

A number of prepositions are formed by combining some of the one-syllable prepositions.

into   upon   without   onto   within   throughout

Compound prepositions are formed by combining a modifier with a preposition or by grouping prepositions.

according to	out of	on account of	aside from
prior to	owing to	instead of	by means of
in front of	subsequent to	because of	as to

Objects of Prepositions. A preposition never appears alone. It is always used with a word or group of words that is called its **object.** The object of a preposition usually follows the preposition.

The President walked briskly *into* the *hall.*
Wait *on* the *corner.*

A preposition and its object, along with the words that fall between them, make up a **prepositional phrase.**

into the hall	on the corner
among the ruins	beyond the horizon

Occasionally, a preposition may follow its object. This usually occurs in sentences that contain interrogative or relative pronouns.

Whom did you write the letter *to*? (*whom* is the object of the preposition *to*.)
Is this the town that you came *from*? (*that* is the object of the preposition *from*.)

The object of a preposition may be a single word or a group of words.

WORD: The box fell behind the *refrigerator.*
WORD: After *Tuesday*, we will have a long vacation.

WORD GROUP: Before *baking a cake*, you should read the recipe.
WORD GROUP: Give the package to *whoever answers the door*.

Exercise A: Find each preposition and its object.

1. The truck was stopped at the border and searched for arms.
2. During the centuries, the continents have been drifting apart.
3. Booth jumped to the stage and screamed at the audience.
4. To whom is the announcement addressed?
5. After the game, the crowd rushed for the exits.
6. I read in the paper that there will be no school on Friday.
7. The people of Quebec speak French instead of English.
8. Beyond the city limits there is no rule against fireworks.
9. At half time a band marched onto the field.
10. For many years, the old courthouse had been left in disrepair.

Exercise B: Follow the same directions as for Exercise A.

1. On the weekends Don babysits for his neighbors.
2. The pandas at the Washington Zoo have been put on diets.
3. The dog sniffed around the kitchen for its dinner.
4. Raccoons scurried over immense piles of garbage.
5. Everyone but Marietta had seen the car approaching.
6. California's redwoods tower above the other trees.
7. Karen felt better after her talk with the coach.
8. All but one of the trees died during the winter.
9. Amy rode her bike to school instead of the bus.
10. Aside from the cost, there is no objection to the proposal.

1.7 The Conjunction

Another kind of word used to tie the parts of a sentence together is a **conjunction**. A conjunction may connect single words, or it may connect groups of words called phrases and clauses.

A conjunction is a word that connects words, phrases, or clauses.

There are three kinds of conjunctions: coordinating conjunctions, correlative conjunctions, and subordinating conjunctions.

Coordinating Conjunctions

Some conjunctions are used to connect similar sentence parts. They are called **coordinating conjunctions** because they tie together things of the same kind or order. These coordinating conjunctions are *and, but, or,* and *yet*.

> *Snow* and *sleet* covered the roads.
> The train was *fast* and *comfortable*.
> The traffic moved *slowly* but *steadily*.
> He was *strict* yet *fair*.
> The rocket shot *off the pad* and *into the air*.
> We could *take a walk* or *go for a swim*.
> *They acted human*, yet *I kept noticing their webbed feet*.

For and *so* are also used as coordinating conjunctions to connect groups of words that would otherwise stand alone as separate sentences.

> They called him "Mr. X," *for* no one knew his real name.
> Our television broke, *so* we told stories instead.

Nor is used as a coordinating conjunction only when it is preceded by another negative word.

> The workers had *no* organization, *nor* did they have leaders.
> Betty did *not* have her skis, *nor* did she have her skates.

Correlative Conjunctions

A few conjunctions are used in pairs: *not only . . . but (also)*; *either . . . or*; *neither . . . nor*; *both . . . and*; *whether . . . or*. Such conjunctions are called **correlative conjunctions**.

> Some cats are *not only* independent *but also* aloof.
> *Both* Laurel *and* her brother made the team.
> *Neither* the mayor *nor* his aide would comment on the report.
> We must decide *whether* to stand firm *or* to compromise.

Conjunctive Adverbs

Certain adverbs are used to join main clauses. Main clauses are groups of words that would otherwise stand alone as separate sentences. When used in this way, the adverbs are called **conjunctive adverbs**. A conjunctive adverb is preceded by a semicolon and followed by a comma. The most common conjunctive adverbs are these:

accordingly	consequently	however	therefore
also	furthermore	moreover	thus
besides	hence	nevertheless	still

Note: There is one other type of conjunction known as a *subordinating conjunction*. Refer to Section 3.5 for discussion of conjunctions of this type.

Exercise A: Find and identify each coordinating conjunction, correlative conjunction, and conjunctive adverb.

1. Neither the speeches nor the music was very exciting.
2. Both the Japanese and the Italian delegates opposed the investigation.
3. The search party worked quickly and carefully to find the missing children.
4. We must either sell more subscriptions or give up the paper.
5. The police officer beckoned us forward, but we could not move.
6. The odds were against him, yet Washington drove forward.
7. We were not at home; nevertheless, the package arrived safely.
8. The evidence sounded convincing; still, we believed Northrop innocent.
9. The dictionary is a valuable tool; however, not all dictionaries agree.
10. The sub was lying silently three hundred feet down, so the planes could not detect it.

11. Play the record and think of us.
12. We must leave at once; otherwise, we will be late.
13. Do you know whether Paul or Jane is coming?
14. The outfielders wear glasses; consequently, the sun won't blind them.
15. Wave after wave engulfed the tower, but the light still shone.

Exercise B: Writing Make each pair of sentences into one sentence by joining the italicized words with an appropriate conjunction. Use the type of conjunction shown in parentheses.

1. The test was *fair*. The test was *difficult*. (coordinating)
2. *The players* agreed with the plan. *The owners* agreed with the plan. (correlative)
3. *We wanted to watch the game. Our television was broken.* (coordinating)
4. Germanium is a *rare* metal. Germanium is a *useful* metal. (coordinating)
5. *We arrived late. The movie had barely begun.* (conjunctive adverb)
6. The burglars crept *down the alley*. They went *into the doorway*. (coordinating)
7. *Small children* were placed in the lifeboats. *Their parents* were placed in the lifeboats. (coordinating)
8. You may take *biology*. You may take *art appreciation*. (correlative)
9. These sweaters are *warm*. They are also *attractive*. (coordinating)
10. *You will enjoy the movie. You will enjoy the book even more.* (conjunctive adverb)

1.8   The Interjection

An **interjection** is a word or group of words interjected into the sentence. It is usually followed by an exclamation point.

An interjection is a word or word group used to express surprise or other emotion. It has no grammatical relation to other words in the sentence.

Help!   Oh!   Terrific!   Hold it!   Yeah!   Oops!

1.9   Words Used as Different Parts of Speech

Some words, such as *have, is, do,* are always verbs. The personal pronouns *I, me,* etc., are always pronouns. Many words, however, may be used in sentences in different ways.

The *fire* destroyed sixty acres of trees. (noun)
Among the chief duties of a ranger is *fire* patrol. (adjective)
The manager will *fire* that clerk. (verb)

To identify the part of speech of a word, you must determine how the word is functioning in the sentence.

Verb or Noun?

Some words may be used either as verbs or as nouns. To distinguish between nouns and verbs, determine whether the word names something *or* expresses an action or state of being.

Where can we *store* the boxes? (verb)
The *store* closes early today. (noun)
Dip the meat in the sauce. (verb)
Let's take a *dip* in the pool. (noun)

Noun or Adjective?

A word used to name a person, place, thing, or idea is a noun. The same word may be used before another noun to tell "what kind." When so used, it is an adjective.

Jazz has come of age in America's concert halls. (noun)
Would you call Billie Holiday a *jazz* singer? (adjective)
Plastic is now used in making most toys. (noun)
They bought their child a *plastic* baseball bat. (adjective)

Adjective or Pronoun?

A demonstrative pronoun—*this, that, these,* or *those*—may also be used as an adjective. If the word is used alone in place of a noun, it is a pronoun. If used before a noun to tell "which one," it is an adjective.

This is my Aunt Margaret. (pronoun)
These are Ted's gloves. (pronoun)
That composition is excellent. (adjective modifying *composition*)
Those hamburgers are really good. (adjective modifying *hamburgers*)

In a similar way the words *what, which,* and *whose* may be used alone as pronouns or before nouns as adjectives.

What should I say? (pronoun)
What street is this? (adjective modifying *street*)

Which is your painting? (pronoun)
Which train do I take? (adjective modifying *train*)

Whose can it be? (pronoun)
Whose plan was accepted? (adjective modifying *plan*)

The words *your, my, our, his, her, their* are forms of the personal pronouns used to show possession. Used in this way, they perform the job of adjectives. The words *mine, yours, hers, ours,* and *theirs* are always pronouns. The word *his* may be used either as a pronoun or an adjective. See Section 1.2.

Her yellow Honda is over there. (adjective)
The tiger kitten is *hers*. (pronoun)
The new Volkswagen is *his*. (pronoun)
That is *his* Uncle Charlie. (adjective)

Adjective or Adverb?

Several words have the same form whether used as adjectives or adverbs. To tell whether a word is used as an adjective or as an adverb, decide what other words in the sentence it goes with, or modifies. If the word modifies a noun or pronoun and tells *which one, what kind, how many,* or *how much,* it is an adjective. If the word modifies any other kind of word and tells *where, when, how,* or *to what extent,* it is an adverb.

> The plane flew *low*. (adverb telling *where* about *flew*)
> Sara played a *low* note. (adjective telling *what kind* of *note*)

Adverb or Preposition?

A number of words may be used either as prepositions or as adverbs. One simple test may help you to tell the difference. A preposition is never used alone. It is always followed by a noun or a pronoun as part of a phrase. If the word is in a phrase, it is probably a preposition. If the word has no object, it is probably an adverb.

> Sue put on her coat and went *out*. (*Out* is an adverb. It has no object.)
> Sue put on her coat and went *out* the door. (*Out* is a preposition. It has an object, *door*.)
> The sundial had been knocked *down*. (adverb)
> Will you all please stand *up*? (adverb)
> The cart rolled *down* the hill. (preposition)
> The mountaineers struggled *up* Pike's Peak. (preposition)

Exercise A: Determine the part of speech of each italicized word in the following sentences.

1. A special plane stood waiting *for* the President.
2. It was a hard decision, *for* there were too few facts.
3. We started out with our packs full of food, cooking utensils, clothes, chocolate bars—everything *but* soap.

4. We telephoned on Saturday morning, *but* the office was closed.
5. *After* the accident Carmen drove with great caution.
6. *Above*, we could see the Northern Lights.
7. Are *these* your books?
8. *These* lucky discoveries have greatly benefited mankind.
9. *What* college does your sister attend?
10. *What* are you going to read for your report?
11. The clock is *slow*; it always runs *slow*.
12. *Outside* the window stood a tall, eerie figure.
13. Please take the dog *outside*.
14. *Inside* the house everything was in disorder.
15. We stood on the balcony of the old hotel watching the sun go *down*.

Exercise B: Writing Identify the part of speech of each italicized word. Then, write a new sentence using the word as indicated in parentheses.

1. The *pull* of the sun and moon on the earth creates tides. (verb)
2. *Which* is the problem that bothered you? (adjective)
3. The wind blew *hard* all night long. (adjective)
4. At the North Pole, the sea is very *deep*. (adverb)
5. Our tour guide was left *behind*. (preposition)
6. There will be no *afternoon* games next year. (noun)
7. His last movie did not *further* his career. (adverb)
8. My grandparents have a very *fast* boat. (adverb)
9. By early afternoon, the 1955 Chevrolet had taken the *lead*. (verb)
10. A great crowd gathered *around* the movie star. (adverb)
11. At *what* time will liftoff occur? (pronoun)
12. The *brick* wall was crumbling. (noun)
13. *Promise* me that you will come to auditions. (noun)
14. We visited a wildlife preserve *in* Kenya. (adverb)
15. Many American companies *branch* out into other parts of the world. (noun)

1.10 Verbals

Some words in English are formed from verbs but are not verbs themselves. Such words are **verbals**. These include **infinitives**, **participles**, and **gerunds**. Verbals may be used as many different parts of speech. (See Section 2 for a discussion of verbal phrases.)

1.11 The Infinitive

The **infinitive** is a verb that is preceded by *to*, which is called the "sign of the infinitive." The forms of infinitives are as follows:

ACTIVE PRESENT: to honor
PASSIVE PRESENT: to be honored
ACTIVE PERFECT: to have honored
PASSIVE PERFECT: to have been honored

The infinitive may be used as a noun.

To win was not our only goal. (subject of *was*)
My little brother always wants *to argue*. (object of *wants*)

The infinitive may also be used as a modifier. Used as an adjective it may modify nouns.

Cape Cod is the place *to see*.

The Dodgers are the team *to beat*.

As an adverb, the infinitive may modify adverbs, adjectives, or verbs.

Bob arrived too late *to help*. (modifying the adverb *late*)

The suit was easy *to clean*. (modifying the adjective *easy*)

They started *to laugh*. (modifying the verb *started*)

See Section 2.14 and 3.6 for additional details on infinitives.

1.12   The Participle

A **participle** is a verbal that is used as an adjective. There are several forms of the participle, all widely used.

PRESENT PARTICIPLE:	following
PAST PARTICIPLE:	followed
PERFECT PARTICIPLE:	having followed
PASSIVE PERFECT PARTICIPLE:	having been followed

The present participle always ends in *-ing*. The past participle has several different forms, but usually ends with *-ed, -d, -t,* or *-n.* See Section 5 for more information about participles and their uses.

The participle is always used as an adjective to modify a noun or a pronoun. In the following examples, the arrow indicates the word modified by the participle.

Smiling, Laura accepted the award.

Elated, the class arrived in Washington.

Having been hired, Lana looked forward to her new job.

The paramedics, *working* quickly, hooked up the oxygen tanks.

Note that a participle may follow the word it modifies.

1.13   The Gerund

The **gerund** is a verbal noun that always ends in *-ing.* It is used in the sentence as a noun and in almost every way that a noun can be used.

Debating is Fred's favorite school activity. (subject of the verb)
Tanya likes *skating* and *skiing.* (object of the verb)
Before *writing* a report, be sure of your facts. (object of the preposition)

1.14 Gerund, Participle, or Verb?

You may have noticed that all present participles, all gerunds, and some verbs end in -*ing*. To distinguish among them, remember the following rules:

1. If the word ending in -*ing* is used as an adjective, it is a present participle.
2. If the word ending in -*ing* is used as a noun, it is a gerund.
3. If the word ending in -*ing* is preceded by an auxiliary verb, it is a verb.

PRESENT PARTICIPLE: Rudi loves the musical about the *singing* pirates. (*Singing* is used as an adjective to modify *pirates*.)

GERUND: *Singing* is not the primary activity of real pirates. (*Singing* is used as a noun, the subject of the verb *is*.)

VERB: Do you know what the pirates *were singing* about? (*Singing* is used as a verb, preceded by the auxiliary verb *were*.)

Exercise A: Find the verbals in these sentences. Label them as infinitives, gerunds, or participles.

1. Mark's favorite activity, from childhood on, was swimming in the ocean.
2. I have learned to take notes in class.
3. Long-distance running makes many people feel healthy.
4. That free ice cream cone was an unexpected treat.
5. Denise likes to dance on roller skates.
6. There are courses to improve memory.
7. Playing fairly demands self-discipline.
8. Disappointed, the team left the field silently.
9. Studying is important to most teen-agers.
10. The game warden subdued the bellowing beast.
11. Charlie Chaplin made clowning an art.

12. Coreen wants to study auto mechanics.
13. Laughing, the child grasped the brass ring on the carousel.
14. Most people want to succeed the easy way.
15. Boris wore a frightening mask to the theatre club picnic.

Exercise B: Find the infinitive in each sentence. Tell whether it is being used as a noun or as a modifier.

1. The chess club will be happy to help.
2. The plan is to survey the bottom of the oceans.
3. Althea decided to accept the challenge.
4. I want to work on the problem slowly and carefully.
5. The giant radio antenna is designed to record distant sounds.
6. It was an honor to be nominated.
7. Everyone thinks he or she wants to be told the truth.
8. The last question was supposed to have had two parts.
9. We were glad to have been invited.
10. The lock appears to have been broken.
11. To gain admission to the Air Force Academy, one must be recommended.
12. The tourists asked to be given directions in their own language.
13. The class voted to end the party at midnight.
14. We stayed up late to hear the election returns.
15. It takes patience, practice, and stamina to be a writer.

Exercise C: Tell whether the italicized word in each sentence is a verb, a present participle, or a gerund. If the word is a verb, list its helping verbs. If the word is a participle, tell what word it modifies. If the word is a gerund, tell whether it is acting as a subject of a verb, an object of a verb, or an object of a preposition.

1. *Speaking* publicly was difficult for Thomas Jefferson.
2. *Smelling* smoke, Coretta called the fire department.
3. The lions had been *eating* their noonday meal.
4. The toddler, *racing* down the aisle, knocked over a stack of cans.

5. *Walking* carefully on the rocks, the hikers crossed the stream.
6. Many teenagers earn money by *mowing* lawns.
7. Before *raking* leaves, decide what you will do with them.
8. Do you know when the Chinese ballet troupe is *leaving?*
9. Some people enjoy *standing* in line.
10. Among his teammates he was known for his "*fumbling* fingers."
11. Quick *thinking* saved the ship.
12. Horseback *riding* is Lisa's favorite sport.
13. *Running* at great speed, Pat broke the school's one-mile record.
14. *Singing* in the shower is my only musical outlet.
15. By noon we will have been *traveling* for four hours.

Exercise D: Writing Write three of your own sentences for each of the following words. First, use the word as a gerund. Next, use the word as a participle. Finally, add a helping verb to the word and use it as a verb in a sentence.

driving   building   understanding
writing   pouring

REINFORCEMENT EXERCISES

The Classification of Words

A. Use common and proper nouns. Rewrite each sentence. Substitute a proper noun for each italicized common noun and a common noun for each proper noun. You may have to add or delete the words *the* and *a*.

1. The family had their *car* ferried across the *river*.
2. *Michael* leads his *team* in runs batted in.
3. Did you see *Billy Joel* on the *show*?
4. Drive down the *street* and past the *stadium*.
5. I read a review of the *movie* in *Newsweek*.
6. The *senator* spoke *Spanish* fluently.
7. The *author* read a passage from the *book* to us.
8. The *painting* is one of *Van Gogh's* most famous works.
9. The *president* of the *country* held a press conference.
10. He hopes to be employed by the *company* by next *February*.

B. Identify pronouns. List the pronouns in these sentences. Next to each one, write which kind it is—personal, compound personal, indefinite, demonstrative, or interrogative.

1. This was the costume I wore to the Halloween party.
2. If Steve Carlton himself were the pitcher, the Phillies still could not have beaten them.
3. Although we thought ourselves brave, none of us would pet the tame tiger.
4. Which is most affectionate, Terry's Angora, my alley cat, or your Siamese?
5. No one could figure out how the actors could change their costumes so quickly.
6. The two officers couldn't handle the disturbance themselves, so one radioed for assistance.

7. Does anyone know whom these belong to?
8. Everyone was impressed by the museum's fine collection of Japanese art.
9. Which of the two composers wrote this?
10. Tell me, whose projects were entered in the science fair?

C. Identify verbs. Copy the verbs in these sentences. Put one line under auxiliary verbs and two lines under main verbs. Identify the verbs as action verbs or linking verbs.

1. Have you ever seen the classic movie *It's a Wonderful Life* starring James Stewart?
2. A journey in a space shuttle will soon seem as commonplace as a flight in an airplane.
3. By noon Kathy will have collected dozens of shells for her art project.
4. Ahmad's sister was working patiently on her painting.
5. Alexander the Great had become a famous conqueror by the age of seventeen.
6. The elderly senator had often dreamed about the office of the Presidency.
7. What will you be doing in the year 2000?
8. The wreckage of the plane was spotted at the bottom of the canyon.
9. The exchange students were singing a lively French song.
10. The mountains of the West must have looked unconquerable to the original pioneers.

D. Identify adjectives. Copy the adjectives in the following sentences and the nouns or pronouns that they modify. Underline any predicate adjectives. Ignore articles.

EXAMPLE: Bill felt ill.

<u>ill</u> (Bill)

1. Life was carefree on the islands.
2. Which of the runners had the fastest time?

3. A tiny tugboat towed the enormous supertanker out of the narrow harbor.
4. We discovered an ancient fossil near the base of the mountain.
5. France is smaller than Texas.
6. The fishermen hauled the empty nets onto the deck of the boat and headed for home.
7. After the storm, the crickets remained quiet for a while.
8. Maria operates the finest gallery in town.
9. The inexperienced actor seemed nervous but happy with the script for the new movie.
10. By the end of the game, the players were muddier than the field.

E. Identify adverbs. Copy each adverb in the following sentences. Tell whether it modifies an adjective, a verb, or another adverb. Some sentences may contain more than one adverb.

> EXAMPLE: Which of the computers works most efficiently?
> *Most* modifies the adverb *efficiently*
> *efficiently,* modifies the verb *works*

1. A large calico cat crept silently across the lawn.
2. The game lasted much longer than most because of an extremely long half-time program.
3. Some rock stars are incredibly wealthy.
4. The audience laughed loudest at the routine of the sad clown.
5. The trunk in the attic appeared rather old.
6. A very peculiar odor gradually filled the laboratory and the hallway.
7. Usually, elephants move rather slowly.
8. Can you come to football practice earlier than you did last week?
9. Mysterious voices were heard within.
10. The research assistants handled the dangerous materials very carefully.

F. Identify prepositions. Find each preposition and its object. Underline any compound prepositions.

1. The lights of the airplane were hidden among the stars.
2. In his famous "Gettysburg Address," Lincoln mentioned the need to preserve "government of the people, by the people, for the people."
3. The largest issue of a newspaper in history was a Sunday edition of the *New York Times.*
4. Cousteau listens to marine creatures by means of a special sonar device.
5. The nation's first kindergarten was begun by Margaretha M. Schurz in 1856.
6. The Yukon River flows through Alaska and empties into the Bering Sea, which separates the United States from the Soviet Union.
7. Many of the children of Zaire, a country in the heart of Africa, must row to school across dangerous swamps.
8. Subsequent to the Norman Invasion in 1066, French became the official language of England.
9. Hank remembered his homework as he was going out of the house.
10. Inside its den, the pack rat rested upon its bed of treasures.

G. Identify conjunctions. Find the conjunctions. Identify each as a coordinating or correlative conjunction or conjunctive adverb.

1. Shakespeare did not attend college, but he did master several foreign languages and much of ancient and modern history.
2. A chemical waste dump was found near the reservoir; consequently, many of the city's residents were upset.
3. Elise wants to be either a concert violinist or a veterinarian.
4. Firecrackers and other such explosives are illegal in this state; however, they are not illegal in the adjoining one.
5. The wrestler was too heavy; therefore, he had to enter a higher weight class or postpone his comeback.

6. According to Greek mythology, Zeus was the foremost of the gods, yet even he was subject to fate.
7. The immigration officer asked the refugees whether they were driven from their country or had come of their own free will.
8. The rocking of the boat made me seasick; nevertheless, I enjoyed my tour of the Gulf.
9. Neither rain nor sleet nor my neighbor's Doberman keeps the postal workers from their appointed rounds.
10. It was once believed that there was not only water on Mars but also canals.

H. Use words as different parts of speech. Identify the part of speech of the italicized word in each of the following sentences. Then, write a new sentence using the italicized word as indicated in parentheses.

1. The quarterback almost fumbled the ball, but he made a *fast* recovery. (adverb)
2. Sandi will practice her speech this evening, and Maria will *time* it. (noun)
3. The President's plane flew *straight* from Washington to the disaster site. (adjective)
4. We saw an excellent *show* based upon the life and work of Stevie Smith. (verb)
5. Due to a flat tire, our dinner guests arrived *late in the evening*. (adjective)
6. After her development of the new software, Ms. Martin's company gave her a *raise*. (verb)
7. Will the television network *search* for a new star or cancel the series? (noun)
8. According to British folklore, gnomes are *little* people who live inside the earth. (adverb)
9. After it started raining, I realized that my bicycle had been left *outside*. (preposition)
10. Have you already mailed *those* postcards about the meeting? (pronoun)

I. Identify verbals. In the following sentences, underline the verbals. Indicate whether each is an infinitive, a gerund, or a participle. Some sentences will contain more than one verbal.

1. What famous speech begins with the words "To be or not to be"?
2. Before arguing your point of view, be sure that you know all of the facts.
3. Leaping high into the air, Hernandez caught the ball.
4. The amplifiers made a deafening noise.
5. Barry hopes to attend culinary school and to become a chef.
6. Coach Finney believes that swimming is the best exercise.
7. William Golding did not expect to win the Nobel Prize.
8. The conductor signals the orchestra to begin by tapping his baton on the podium.
9. The toys collected by the fire department are to be distributed by the Salvation Army.
10. The company operates a day-care center for the children of working parents.

The Classification of Words

A. Determine how the italicized words are used in each sentence. Tell whether each is a noun, pronoun, verb, adjective, adverb, preposition, conjunction, interjection, gerund, participle, or infinitive.

1. *Several* of the people *on* the beach played volleyball.
2. Cal *soon* learned that the *plant* with *three* leaves was poison ivy.
3. Although she *seemed* calm, Char was *nervous and* tense about the play.
4. *Wow! That* really sailed out of the stadium!
5. The lighthouse *keeper sounded* the foghorn.
6. Scientists *are finding* many *uses* for the *laser* beam.
7. Belinda *guided* the chestnut-brown horse *along* a wooded trail.
8. Carlos celebrated *his* birthday by *going* to the carnival.
9. For supper we *ate some* of the vegetables that grew in our garden.
10. *Who* actually discovered *America*?
11. *Ashley* used both *palms* and ferns *in* her terrarium.
12. The cafeteria serves hamburgers *or* hot dogs *nearly* every day.
13. *Frequently*, Lisa *uses* a jump rope *to exercise*.
14. The game stopped while Derek hunted *for* his contact *lens*.
15. *Aha!* You're the one *making* that noise!

B. Determine the part of speech of each italicized word in the following paragraph.

A *monsoon* is a seasonal wind often accompanied *by heavy* rainfall. In Japan, monsoons are extremely important because they bring the moisture *that* nourishes *the* country's rice fields. Since the Japanese depend *heavily* on this crop for food—the word "gohan" is used in Japan for both "food" and "rice"—failure of the monsoon *to appear* has *often* resulted in famine. In other words, the monsoon is both a giver *and* taker of life. In early fall, *it* often brings *typhoons,* Pacific Ocean counterparts to Atlantic hurricanes. These *roaring* winds *sometimes* churn up *monstrous* tidal waves that wreak havoc *along* the shorelines of the island kingdom.

C. Identify the part of speech of the italicized word in each of the following sentences. Then, write a new sentence using the same word as indicated in parentheses.

1. When will the band *record* its next album? (noun)
2. The operator of the Ferris wheel assured me that no one had ever fallen *out.* (preposition)
3. We saw several sharks *swimming* in the bay. (gerund)
4. *"Wonderful!"* he said. "I thought you would win first place at the science fair." (adjective)
5. *Help* arrived in the form of a country doctor driving a battered 1963 Chevy. (verb)
6. When the tomato was first introduced to Europe, many people thought that the *plant* was poisonous. (verb)
7. *What* station do you listen to most often? (pronoun)
8. The pitch was *high* and outside. (adverb)
9. The swallows would *dart* back and forth between the feeder and the birdbath. (noun)
10. Spider monkeys hold onto tree branches with their tails to keep from *falling.* (participle)

USING GRAMMAR IN WRITING
The Classification of Words

A. Good writers vary the beginnings of their sentences to avoid the monotony of lines like these:

> *He* was tired. *He* had been hiking too long. *He* dropped his backpack from his shoulders. *He* rested for a moment on a log and took a sip of water from his canteen. *He* noticed that the forest around him was beginning to darken. *He* wasn't likely to find his way back to camp once the sun had set. *He* decided to head back before it was too dark. *He* rose. *He* heard a noise.

Try rewriting the above paragraph. You may add, combine, or delete material. Also try beginning some of the revised sentences with different parts of speech, such as prepositions or verbals. Then, write a second paragraph telling what happens to this lone hiker.

B. Imagine that you are an extraterrestrial stranded on the planet Earth and that you look just like some common animal (a cat or a mouse, for example). Write a radio message to your home planet describing an encounter with an Earthling. In your message, use vivid, precise verbs to make your descriptions come alive. You may find a thesaurus useful as a source of unusual or interesting verbs (See Chapter 2, page 42 for information on using a thesaurus.)

C. Pretend that you are witnessing the final moments of an important sporting event. The score is tied and there is great excitement in the air. Write two paragraphs. In the first paragraph, describe the crowd, the setting, and the general atmosphere. In the second paragraph, describe the action in the concluding moments of the game. Try to make your writing as lively as possible by using vivid adjectives, adverbs, and participles. Label these as follows: *ADJ*—adjective, *ADV*—adverb, and *PART*—participle.

CUMULATIVE REVIEW
The Parts of Speech

Recognizing the Parts of Speech and Verbals. Number your paper from 1 to 20. Decide whether each italicized word or phrase in the paragraphs below is being used as a *Noun, Pronoun, Verb, Adverb, Adjective, Conjunction, Preposition, Interjection, Gerund, Infinitive,* or *Participle.* Write your answer next to the corresponding number. Remember that the part of speech is often determined by how a word is used in the sentence.

About two thousand years ago, the Native Americans *now*
                                                     1
called the Anasazi began *cultivating* crops in the dry, *un-*
                          2   *touched* land that is now Arizona, New Mexico, Utah, *and* Col-
3   4
orado. In their earliest settlements there, the Anasazi built pit
houses, *rounded* structures of logs and mud with woven grass
         5
roofs. *However*, about A.D. 900 the Anasazi began *to make* a
        6   7
new kind of building, the *stone* and adobe pueblo. *These* were
                           8   9
like huge apartment houses. One of the *largest* buildings was
                                        10
Pueblo Bonito, *which* can still be seen in New Mexico. Pueblo
                11
Bonito had several hundred rooms. *Enormous!*
                                   12

Many pueblos were built high on the ledges of canyons. En-
trances into one of these, the Cliff Palace at Mesa Verde in
Colorado, were *through* holes in the roof. Ladders also led up
                 13
to the fields at the top of the cliff. The Anasazi *probably*
                                                   14
removed these ladders when enemies appeared.
15

Around 1300, *these* sites throughout the Southwest were
               16
abandoned. Agriculture *had been* difficult in the best of times.
                        17
Droughts made food even *more* scarce. Many of the Anasazi
                         18
moved east to the Rio Grande *valley*, where their culture sur-
                              19
vived until they were conquered by the Spanish. Today, only
remnants of their culture still exist *among* the Pueblo people
                                      20
of New Mexico.

2.0   The Parts of a Sentence

In English, single words are widely used to convey meaning. The following words, for example, all express complete ideas.

Stop!   Danger.   Poison!

In general, however, meaning is expressed in English by groups of words acting together: *in the morning, playing tight end, Laura laughed*. These groups of words are neither spoken nor written in haphazard order. This is because English sentences have fixed patterns into which words are placed to express meaning.

Even if you think that you know very little about English grammar, you nevertheless have a working knowledge of these basic patterns. A better understanding of how and why such patterns work will help you use language effectively.

2.1 The Sentence

Sentences are used to make statements and to ask questions. To be understood, they must express a complete thought, a complete idea, or a complete question.

If a group of words does not express a complete thought, it is not a sentence. We begin the study of the sentence with a partial definition:

A sentence is a group of words that expresses a complete thought.

INCOMPLETE:	The man in the white suit (What about him?)
COMPLETE:	The man in the white suit sells ice cream.
INCOMPLETE:	Patty Kalember, the actress (Did what?)
COMPLETE:	Patty Kalember, the actress, was a champion swimmer in high school.
INCOMPLETE:	Crossing the road (Who did what?)
COMPLETE:	Crossing the road, we saw glass on the pavement.

Exercise A: Which of the following groups of words are sentences?

1. Immediately recognizing the danger
2. Nobody panicked
3. Like most small children on a roller coaster
4. Waited for the rain to stop
5. Forward, into the heart of the storm
6. Quito, Ecuador, practically on the equator
7. This is an entirely new approach
8. Some highlights of his career
9. Her remarks influenced the campaign
10. An ice-skating rink in the park

Exercise B: Writing Some of the following groups of words are not complete sentences. Find them and make them into complete sentences. Write *Sentence* for those groups that are sentences.

1. Actually, we were not at all surprised
2. No clear-cut plan or ready-made formula for creating school spirit
3. Never spoke to us or even noticed us, even though we were dressed in bright orange
4. They scraped and painted the walls
5. Disappearing in the fog and howling horribly
6. Always asking questions, but never getting an answer
7. Still trying to discourage the plan of the Indian Council
8. Was too much emphasis placed on the commercial
9. The change in population throughout the country

10. Coming to a sudden stop in the middle of the intersection
11. The traffic officer waved furiously
12. Coming into the brightly lighted hall like a duchess
13. Renowned for its excellent service and cuisine
14. There at the pier was a glamorous cruise ship
15. Instead, he dictated a sharp reprimand

2.2   Kinds of Sentences

Sentences may be classified according to structure° or according to the purpose of the speaker or writer. There are four principal purposes served by sentences, as described below.

1. The **declarative sentence** is used to make a statement of fact, wish, intent, or feeling. It is followed by a period.

> Naomi Jones sailed solo around the world in 1978.
> I would like to be a nuclear physicist.

2. The **imperative sentence** is used to state a command, request, or direction. The subject is always *You*. When the subject is not expressed, as is usually the case, *you* is "understood" to be the subject. An imperative sentence is usually followed by a period.

> (You) Please turn off the light.
> (You) Speak to the landlord tomorrow.

3. The **interrogative sentence** is used to ask a question. It is always followed by a question mark.

> How much does it cost?
> Who wrote *To Kill a Mockingbird?*

4. An **exclamatory sentence** is used to express strong feeling. It is always followed by an exclamation point.

> What a surprise that was!   How lucky we were!

° For classification of sentences by form or structure, see Section 3.0.

Exercise A: What kind of sentence is each of the following?

1. Can anyone explain this problem?
2. Brasilia is the capital of Brazil.
3. Throw away those dirty old sneakers.
4. Where does the Queen of England live?
5. Please don't eat the daisies.
6. What a weird riddle that was!
7. Can't we watch something a little more interesting?
8. Her remark was quite uncalled for.
9. Raisins are made by drying grapes.
10. What a day it was for a hike!

Exercise B: Follow the directions for Exercise A.

1. When is the next solar eclipse?
2. Keep your seat belt fastened.
3. Airport controllers must be alert.
4. How crazy this plan seems!
5. Which state has the most national parks?
6. I am taking a vacation from alarm clocks.
7. Oh, look at that magnificent rainbow.
8. Don't expect to learn a foreign language overnight.
9. For many years, Silas lived at the edge of town.
10. Turn left at the next corner.

2.3 Subject and Predicate

There are two parts in every complete sentence. (1) The **subject** is the person, thing, or idea about which something is said. (2) The **predicate** is the idea expressed about the subject.

Every sentence contains a subject and a predicate.

The subject of the sentence is the person, thing, or idea about which something is said.

The predicate tells something or asks something about the subject.

The verb *to predicate* means "to proclaim, declare, preach, or affirm." The predicate of a sentence, therefore, "proclaims, declares, preaches, or affirms" something about the subject.

We may say that a sentence is a group of words that tells something (*predicate*) about a person, place, thing, or idea (*subject*).

A sentence is a group of words expressing a complete thought by means of a subject and a predicate.

SUBJECT	PREDICATE
Dogs	bark.
The dogs in the street	bark at passing fire engines.
Light	shines.
The light at Kennedy's grave	shines as a beacon of courage.

2.4 The Simple Predicate

In every predicate, however long, the key word is the **verb.**°

The simple predicate of the sentence is the verb.

The verb may be a phrase consisting of more than one word: *had seen, should have seen, was singing, had been singing*. The words making up the verb may be interrupted by a modifier. Such a modifier is not part of the verb.

> *were* soon *found*   *had* just *left*
> *was* never *finished*   *had* almost *toppled*

The simple predicate, which we shall hereafter call the *verb*, may be compound. The word *compound* means "having more than one part of the same kind." The parts of a compound verb are joined by a conjunction (*and, or, neither-nor,* etc.).

> She **sang** well *and* **danced** beautifully.
> The motor **sputtered, coughed,** *and* **stopped**.
> You **can** *either* **go** *or* **stay**.

° The **complete predicate** consists of the verb, its modifiers, and complements.

2.5   The Simple Subject

Every verb has a subject. The subject is the word that the verb expresses an idea about. To find the subject, form a question by placing *who* or *what* before the verb.

Holly called yesterday.   Two ships in the fleet sank.

VERB:	called	VERB:	sank
WHO CALLED?:	Holly	WHAT SANK?:	ships
SUBJECT:	Holly	SUBJECT:	ships

Just as there is a key word in the predicate, there is also a key word in the subject of a sentence. This key word is the **simple subject**.

Most domestic chickens rarely fly.

VERB:	fly
COMPLETE SUBJECT:	Most domestic chickens
SIMPLE SUBJECT:	chickens

The simple subject plus its modifiers make up the complete subject.

The subject of the verb may be compound. The parts of a compound subject are normally joined by a conjunction.

> The **brain** *and* **spinal cord** are parts of the central nervous system.
> A **quartet** by Haydn *and* a **quintet** by Mozart were played at the concert.
> *Either* **Sadowsky** *or* **Fisher** will start at quarterback.

Whenever you look for the subject, do not be misled by phrases that appear between the subject and the verb.

> The crops in the field withered during the drought.
> (The subject is *crops*, not *field.*)
>
> All of the contestants felt that the judges were fair.
> (The Subject is *All*, not *contestants.*)

Diagraming. The simple subject and simple verb of a sentence are diagramed as follows:

We sang.

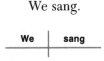

Single word modifiers are placed on slanted lines below the words that they modify.

My aunt sings beautifully.

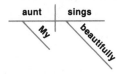

Exercise A: Find the verb and its simple subject. Some parts may be compound.

1. Robert Frost won four Pulitzer Prizes.
2. Once again, the Cardinals have won the World Series.
3. Streams and rivers flowed gently down to the sea.
4. The rocket reentered the atmosphere too quickly.
5. Dudley Moore and Susan Anton have made a television special together.
6. The birch trees swayed and danced in the breeze.
7. Proxima Centauri and our own sun are the nearest stars.
8. The old dog rose slowly, stretched, and then shook himself.
9. All the club members helped with the decorations.
10. Oranges, grapes, and candy filled the basket.

Exercise B: Find the verb and its simple subject.

1. Soup, fruit, and whole-wheat bread are nutritious.
2. Tracy's most cherished possessions are her Pink Floyd and Rolling Stones albums.

3. Many high schools have recently organized coed sports programs.
4. Are Natalia Makarova and Cynthia Gregory famous ballerinas?
5. Neither she nor her friend had come to our party.
6. At the noise, the pigeons took off and flew into the trees.
7. He changed his seat twice, fidgeted, and then left the hall in a hurry.
8. The chill and the dampness of the old abandoned house depressed us.
9. Either the soprano or the alto will sing a solo.
10. Unjust punishment and excessive flogging had turned the officers and crew against Captain Bligh.

2.6 Subjects in Unusual Positions

In most sentences the subject appears before the verb. This subject-verb order is the normal pattern of English sentences. In many sentences, however, this order is reversed.

Questions. In most questions the subject appears between the words making up the verb phrase.

VERB	SUBJECT	VERB
Did	you	ask?
Have	you	eaten?
Can	you	go?
Could	you	have gone?

In most questions beginning with the interrogative words *where, when, why, how,* or *how much,* the subject falls between the parts of the verb: Where **do** *we* **go** from here? In questions beginning with *who* or *what,* the verb may follow the subject in normal order:

Who shouted?   What fell?

Notice that *who* and *what* sometimes function as subjects.

Sentences Beginning with *There* and *Here*. Many sentences begin with *There* or *Here* immediately followed by some form of *be*: *There is, There was, There will be, Here is, Here were,* and so on. Often, *Here* and *There* are introductory words used to get the sentence started. They are never the subject of the verb. In this kind of sentence, the subject follows the verb.

> Here is a new idea. (*idea* is the subject.)
> There were eight puppies in the litter. (*puppies* is the subject.)
> There will be a rehearsal on Saturday. (*rehearsal* is the subject.)

Note: Not all sentences beginning with *Here* and *There* follow the above pattern: *Here we can plant a garden. Here she comes. There he is.* In these sentences, *Here* and *There* are adverbs modifying the verb.

Sentences in Inverted Order. For emphasis or for variety of style in speaking and writing, the subject is sometimes placed after the verb.

> In the audience sat director *Gerald Friedman.*
> On the top of the mountain was a lookout *post.*
> Onto the runway roared the sleek *jet.*

Finding the Subject of the Verb. To find the subject of the verb in any sentence, find the verb first. Then form a question by placing *who* or *what* before the verb. If the sentence is not in normal word order, this technique will still work. However, re-phrasing the sentence in its normal order may help to make the subject clearer.

> INVERTED: From the cellar came a low whine.
> NORMAL: A low whine came from the cellar.

Exercise A: Find the verb and its simple subject.

1. There on the wet grass lay my lost scarf.
2. How much money did you lose?
3. Could you have seen the show from the back row?

4. Here are the missing keys.
5. Over the treetops rose the full moon.
6. Along the hedge crept the cat.
7. There was not a house in sight.
8. Should I have telephoned so early?
9. There might have been a serious accident.
10. Through the tall grasses leaped the kangaroo.

Exercise B: There are eleven sentences in the following paragraph. Number your paper and write the verb and the simple subject of every sentence.

> In the future, robots will be a part of everyone's life. Where will they be found? There will be robots in homes, schools, and businesses. They will perform many of our more tedious tasks. However, there is little resemblance between these robots and humans. Here are the only requirements for a robot "body." First of all, a robot needs a brain, the computer. Also necessary is an arm with claws. Along the arm run cables. These cables transmit instructions from the brain to the claw. A few years ago, would anyone have believed these mechanical wonders?

2.7 Complements

Some sentences, such as *Joan sings*, contain only a subject and a verb. Most sentences, however, require additional words placed after the verb to complete the meaning of the sentence.

These additional words are called **complements.**

SUBJECT	VERB	COMPLEMENT(S)
The shortstop	caught	the baseball.
The class	taught	me a lesson.
Fay	was	a cheerleader.

There are several types of complements, including **direct objects, indirect objects,** and **predicate words**.

2.8 The Direct Object

In many sentences the action verb carries action from the subject to some other word. The verb ties these words together. The word to which the action is carried from the subject is the **direct object.**

Sometimes the direct object tells what receives the action of the verb. Sometimes it tells the result of the action.

RECEIVER OF ACTION:	Sondra baited the *hook*. (baited what?)
RESULT OF ACTION:	Sondra caught a *fish*. (caught what?)
RECEIVER OF ACTION:	The lawyer took the *case*. (took what?)
RESULT OF ACTION:	The lawyer won the *case*. (won what?)

The direct object is a word or group of words to which the verb carries the action from the subject.

Action verbs that carry the action from subject to object are called **transitive verbs**. Action verbs that are not followed by direct objects are called **intransitive verbs**. It is possible for verbs to be transitive in one sentence and intransitive in another.

The fans *were cheering* Chris Evert Lloyd. (transitive)
The fans *were cheering*. (intransitive)

Everyone *knows* the secret. (transitive)
Everyone *knows*. (intransitive)

In some so-called action verbs, the action is not visible. However, the verb still carries the thought from subject to object, tying them together.

Beth *has* high ideas. (has what?)
George *understands* Italian. (understands what?)
Adam *wants* a snowmobile. (wants what?)

The direct object may be compound.

I lost my *hat* and *coat*. (lost what?)
They wanted *fame* and *fortune*. (wanted what?)

Diagraming. In a sentence diagram, the direct object is placed on the main horizontal line after the verb. It is separated from the verb by a vertical line that does *not* cross the main line.

We sang songs.

| We | sang | songs |

Direct Object or Adverb? A direct object tells *whom* or *what* after the verb. To find the direct object, form a question by placing *what* or *whom* after the verb. An adverb following an action verb tells *where, when, how,* or *to what extent* about the verb.

The dog follows the *mail carrier*. (what—direct object)
The dog is *outside*. (where—adverb)
The guests arrived *late*. (when—adverb)

2.9   The Indirect Object

Another kind of complement is the **indirect object**. The indirect object is a noun or pronoun that comes before the direct object in the predicate of a sentence.

The indirect object of the verb tells *to* or *for whom*, or *to* or *for what*, something is done.

We gave *Karen* the award. (*to* Karen)
Joe made his *brother* a sandwich. (*for* his brother)

A verb has an indirect object only if it also has a direct object.

SUBJECT	VERB		INDIRECT OBJECT		DIRECT OBJECT
Ms. Preston	showed		*us*	the	map.
Art	offered	the	*guests*	some	coffee.
I	sent		*Angela*	a	card.

The indirect object may be compound: I asked *Bert* and *Amy* the question.

The words *to* and *for* are never placed before the indirect object. When followed by a noun or pronoun, *to* and *for* are prepositions. The noun or pronoun following the preposition is the object of the preposition.

> Alec gave *Lisa* a sweater. (*Lisa* is the indirect object.)
> Alec gave a sweater to *Lisa*. (*Lisa* is the object of the preposition.)
>
> My grandmother made *me* a pie. (*me* is the indirect object.)
> My grandmother made a pie for *me*. (*me* is the object of the preposition.)

Diagraming. An indirect object is placed on a horizontal line below the verb. It is connected to the verb by a slanted line.

Myron gave me his jacket.

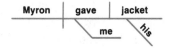

Exercise A: Find both the direct and indirect objects.

1. Jack sent Doreen a card from Hawaii.
2. The principal gave the students her advice.
3. Dad wrote the mayor a letter of apology.
4. The zookeeper gave the elephants a bath.
5. Alicia lent Ernie her ocarina.
6. Phoebe told the teacher her excuse.
7. The box office guaranteed us good seats.
8. David passed Suzanne his eraser.
9. An usher handed me a program.
10. The forlorn Santa offered Sonia his job.

Exercise B: Find the direct and indirect objects.

1. The brief rain brought the farmers no relief.
2. The library issued me a new card.

3. At graduation the superintendent awarded five students scholarships.
4. For Christmas, the vain actor sent everyone his photograph.
5. The guide showed the visitors our sculptures.
6. Danny sends you his best wishes.
7. Navy planes brought the party badly needed supplies.
8. The speaker showed us some slides of New Zealand.
9. The quarterback passed him the ball.
10. The explorers bid the islanders a happy farewell.

2.10 Predicate Words

A linking verb connects its subject to a word in the predicate. The word that is connected to the subject by a linking verb is called a **predicate word**. There are three types of predicate words: the **predicate noun**, the **predicate pronoun**, and the **predicate adjective**.

My favorite holiday is *Thanksgiving*. (predicate noun)

The motor scooter is *hers*. (predicate pronoun)

The quarterback felt *confident*. (predicate adjective)

A predicate word is another type of complement. Since it refers to the subject, it is called a **subject complement**.

Diagraming. When diagraming a simple sentence with a linking verb, slant the line following the verb in the direction of the subject. This slanted line indicates that the predicate word refers back to the subject of the sentence.

George seems well.   Mary is president.

| George | seems \ well | Mary | is \ president |

Exercise A: Find the predicate words in the following sentences. Tell whether each is a predicate noun, a predicate pronoun, or a predicate adjective.

1. This may be our last chance.
2. The new high school looks very modern.
3. Ann seems quite happy at college.
4. The stadium was nearly full of spectators.
5. Harry will probably be our next class president.
6. This is an unusual opportunity.
7. The demolished car was a depressing sight.
8. It should have been she in the winner's circle.
9. The captain of the ship is an old friend.
10. Juanita is clearly the best player on the team.

Exercise B: Make five columns on your paper. Head them *Subject, Verb, Direct Object, Indirect Object*, and *Predicate Word*. Find those parts in the following sentences and put them in the proper columns.

1. The commander gave the troops a stern warning.
2. We have a permanent settlement at the South Pole.
3. After the concert, Billy Joel gave us his autograph.
4. At the icy turn, four cars crashed.
5. Has Jim read the directions carefully?
6. The new jets are sensitive to weather conditions.
7. Deserted towns appear throughout the West.
8. In 1907 two men rowed a boat across the Atlantic.
9. In the first airplane race, one plane was chased by an eagle.
10. For the variety show audition, Benita sang a beautiful song from *Cats*.
11. The rebels appear confident of success.
12. The shop has made us a new table.
13. In the last quarter, Deerfield scored two touchdowns.
14. New sources of energy will greatly change our lives in the next twenty years.
15. The leaders of the expedition were scientists from England.

2.11 Compound Parts of Sentences

Subjects, verbs, objects, predicate words, and predicates may all be compound. That is, they may consist of more than one part *of the same kind*. The parts are joined by a conjunction.

COMPOUND SUBJECT: *Time* and *Stereo Review* are Jerry's favorite magazines.

COMPOUND VERB: The plane *climbed* and *dived*.

COMPOUND DIRECT OBJECT: We want *air* and *sunlight*.

COMPOUND INDIRECT OBJECT: Pam gave *Joe* and *Felicia* lunch.

COMPOUND OBJECT OF PREPOSITION: We drove steadily through the heavy *rain* and *sleet*.

COMPOUND PREDICATE WORD: We felt *warm* and *cozy*.

COMPOUND PREDICATE: The police *halted the bus* and *questioned all of the riders*.

Diagraming. Compound parts are diagramed as follows:

Al and Sue (*compound subject*) sat and listened (*compound verb*).

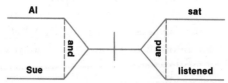

Miller wrote and directed (*compound verb*) this production (*complement shared by the two verbs*).

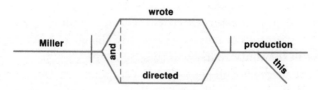

The teacher gave Louis and Josie (*compound indirect object*) the books and records (*compound direct object*).

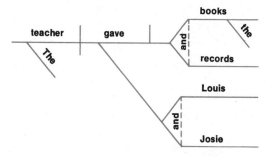

The speeches of the governor and the mayor (*compound object of the preposition*) were brief but informative (*compound predicate adjective*).

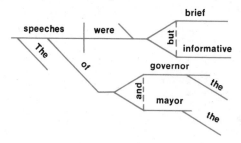

The critics praised the acting but disliked the play (*compound predicate*).

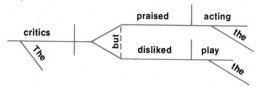

Exercise: Find the compound sentence parts in the following sentences. Label them *Subject, Verb, Direct Object, Indirect Object,* and *Predicate Word.*

1. Robin washed and waxed the new Chrysler.
2. The audience loved the silent Harpo and adored Groucho.

3. Judy sounds tired and unhappy.
4. Waylon and Willie played and sang a slow, quiet ballad.
5. My aunt gave Paul and Jane a comforter.
6. The uniforms were bright and colorful.
7. The zookeeper and the police sought the missing elephant.
8. The three longest rivers are the Nile, the Amazon, and the Mississippi.
9. The passengers and the crew cheered the courageous captain.
10. The ranger found and destroyed the traps.
11. Above the dark storm clouds, the sky was a brilliant blue and gold.
12. Fame and fortune are fleeting.
13. The police arrived and questioned their suspect.
14. Maria sent my family and me a postcard and a souvenir.
15. The President, two generals, and thirty reporters greeted the ambassador.

2.12   The Phrase

A phrase is a group of words without a subject and a verb, used as one part of speech.

A phrase is used as one part of speech. A **verb phrase** is two or more words used as a verb: *would be, could have been.* A **noun phrase** is two or more words used as a noun: *Pan American Highway, Jane Addams High School.* Phrases may also be used as adjectives or adverbs.

2.13   The Prepositional Phrase

The prepositional phrase consists of the preposition, its object, and modifiers of the object.

> *Behind the ramshackle red barn* was an old workhorse.
> The children walked *through the maze.*

The object of a preposition is always a noun, a pronoun, or a group of words used as a noun.

Esther went *to* the opera. (*opera* is the object of *to*.)

The dog went everywhere *with* him. (*him* is the object of *with*.)

After calling the Coast Guard, we resumed the search. (*calling the Coast Guard* is a group of words used as a noun. It is the object of *After*.)

Give the letter *to* whoever answers the door. (*whoever answers the door* is a group of words used as a noun. It is the object of *to*.)

The prepositional phrase is a modifier. It is used either as an adjective or as an adverb. A prepositional phrase that modifies a noun or pronoun is an **adjective phrase.** That is, it is a phrase used as an adjective.

Kirstin is the student *with the long, auburn hair*. (*with the long, auburn hair* modifies the noun *student*.)

The energy *in a single atom* is tremendous. (*in a single atom* modifies *energy*.)

An adjective phrase always comes immediately after the noun or pronoun it modifies.

Note: Adjective phrases can modify subjects, direct objects, indirect objects, and predicate words. Do not confuse a noun or a pronoun in an adjective phrase with the subject, object, or predicate word that it modifies.

Plenty *of tickets* are still available. (*of tickets* modifies the subject, *Plenty*.)

Try some *of these desserts*. (*of these desserts* modifies the direct object, *some*.)

Writing poetry is a lot *of fun*. (*of fun* modifies the predicate word, *lot*.)

A prepositional phrase that modifies a verb, an adjective, or an adverb, is an **adverb phrase.** That is, it is a phrase used as an adverb to tell *where, when, how,* or *to what extent* about the word it modifies.

> Megan put the stereo speakers *on the bookcase.* (*on the bookcase* tells *where* about the verb *put.*)

> The movie was successful *beyond all expectations.* (*beyond all expectations* tells *to what extent* about the adjective *successful.*)

> The hunters rose early *in the morning.* (*in the morning* tells *when* about the adverb *early.*)

When two or more prepositional phrases follow each other, they may modify the same word, or one phrase may modify the object in the preceding phrase.

> They arrived *at the airport on time.* (Both phrases modify *arrived; at the airport* tells *where* and *on time* tells *when* about the verb.)

> Cape Horn is *at the southernmost tip of South America.* (*at the southernmost tip* modifies *is; of South America* modifies *tip.* It tells *which* tip.)

Diagraming. In a sentence diagram, a prepositional phrase extends from the word that it modifies, as follows:

> Eric painted a portrait *of the President.*
> (adjective phrase)

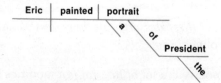

The key was stuck *in the door.* (adverb phrase modifying a verb)

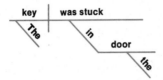

The guests left early *in the morning.* (adverb phrase modifying another adverb)

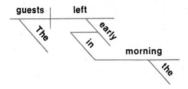

The novel *about life on Mars* has disappeared. (adjective phrases)

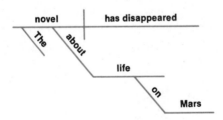

Exercise A: Write each prepositional phrase and the word or words it modifies. Tell whether each phrase is an adjective or an adverb phrase.

1. In the late afternoon we had our first customer.
2. There was a spontaneous burst of applause.
3. John had once been lost on the Yukon River for three days.
4. The jewels had been hidden in a box of rubbish.
5. Can you work at the museum after school?

6. The sudden illness of the leading lady forced a change in our plans.
7. For twenty years the man in the iron mask captured everyone's imagination.
8. Before a holiday, a feeling of excitement pervades the school.
9. A cloud of smoke appeared on the horizon.
10. For two hours Dale clung to the rock with her fingertips.

Exercise B: Writing Add prepositional phrases that modify the italicized words and that answer the questions in parentheses. Tell whether your phrases act as adjectives or as adverbs.

1. We *arrived* (where?) early.
2. A strange cry *was heard* (when?).
3. The radio towers *were visible* (to what extent?).
4. The coral *reefs* (where?) hold many wonders.
5. Coach Samuels benched the *player* (which player?).
6. The waves *hurled* heavy rocks (where?).
7. Jessie *went cycling* (when?).
8. Alicia bought a new *album* (whose album?).
9. The *sound* (what sound?) *drifted* (where?).
10. (When?) America *was* still a *land* (what kind of land?).

2.14   The Infinitive Phrase

You have learned that an infinitive is a verb form, usually beginning with *to: to dance, to dream.* Like other verb forms, the infinitive can have modifiers and complements. An infinitive, its modifiers, and its complements make up an **infinitive phrase.**

to speak confidently	to begin on time
to start a motor	to lend us a hand
to look your best	to be happy

The infinitive may be modified by adverbs or by adverb phrases. These modifiers are part of the infinitive phrase.

Our team has **to practice** *daily.*

Firefighters must be ready **to respond** *at a moment's notice.*

An infinitive made from an action verb may have both direct and indirect objects as complements. These objects are considered part of the infinitive phrase.

Our school offered **to assist** *the fund drive.*
Mary offered **to teach** *Peter the guitar.*

When the infinitive is made from a linking verb, its complement is a predicate word. This complement is also considered part of the infinitive phrase.

She will grow up **to be** *President.*
Be careful not **to appear** *overly anxious.*

Infinitive phrases can be used in many ways. They may function as nouns, adjectives, or adverbs. When they are used as nouns, infinitive phrases can function as subjects, objects, or predicate words.

SUBJECT: *To learn a foreign language* is no simple task.
OBJECT: Rudi wanted *to run in the Boston Marathon.*
PREDICATE WORD: Ava's goal is *to act in a soap opera.*

An infinitive phrase can also be used as an adjective.

We made some sandwiches *to eat on the ferry.* (The infinitive phrase modifies *sandwiches.*)

When used as an adverb, an infinitive phrase may modify a verb, an adjective, or another adverb.

Several friends called *to offer congratulations.*
(The infinitive phrase modifies the verb *called.*)
Their latest song is certain *to be a hit.*
(The infinitive phrase modifies the adjective *certain.*)
We arrived early enough *to see the sun rise over the harbor.*
(The infinitive phrase modifies the adverb *enough.*)

449

Many of the best speakers and writers feel that modifiers in infinitive phrases must be placed before or after the infinitive. Placing an adverb between *to* and the rest of the infinitive is usually considered an error. Such errors are called **split infinitives.**

NONSTANDARD: He hopes *to* substantially *increase* his pay.
STANDARD: He hopes *to increase* his pay substantially.

NONSTANDARD: The spaceship's mission was *to* boldly *go* where no ship had gone before.
STANDARD:: The spaceship's mission was *to go* boldly where no ship had gone before.

Diagraming. The infinitive phrase is diagramed as follows:

We want to have a beach party soon.

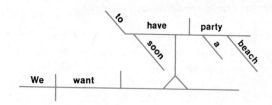

To get a summer job was not easy.

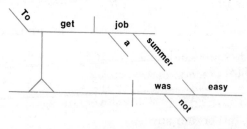

Exercise A: Find the infinitive phrases in the sentences below.

1. As soon as she arrived, Deena made plans to leave town.
2. Unfortunately, Don is sure to win this election.
3. Marla decided to read *I Know Why the Caged Bird Sings* for her report.

4. Congresspersons like to get letters from the voters.
5. I would be happy to give you a recommendation.
6. The Todds are trying to rent their house for the summer.
7. To be sure, we weren't the only amateurs in the group.
8. All of the clerks try to be cooperative.
9. To paint beautifully was his sole pleasure.
10. She wanted to be captain of the volleyball team.

Exercise B: Find each infinitive phrase in the sentences below.

1. Emily's ambition is to write for a newspaper.
2. To study for the test, Molly outlined the chapters.
3. The candidate promised to halt inflation.
4. Record crowds went to see the King Tut exhibit.
5. To open the garage door, you push this button.
6. John Adams was the first President to live in the White House.
7. To stay healthy, you should exercise regularly.
8. *Jaws III* was meant to be frightening.
9. To clean the attic would take hours.
10. It was difficult not to sing along with the performers.

Exercise C: Writing Find and correct the split infinitive in each sentence.

1. We ought to quickly leave.
2. It would be a good idea to regularly telephone home.
3. Your parents should be told that you are going to probably be late.
4. Did the propeller seem to already be broken?
5. The cables appear to deliberately have been cut.
6. A raccoon always tries to thoroughly wash its food.
7. Before we take any action, we want to completely understand the facts.
8. Sheila wanted to eventually become an astronaut.
9. Were you able to finally finish your carpentry course?
10. Ask your friend to occasionally come to our house for supper.

2.15 The Participial Phrase

A participle is a word that is formed from a verb and used as an adjective. It usually ends with -*ing*, -*ed*, -*d*, -*t*, or -*en*: the *singing* sailors, the *worried* executive, the *written* word.

A **participial phrase** consists of the participle, its modifiers, and its complements. When a participle is modified by an adverb, a phrase, or a clause, these modifiers are part of the phrase.

> *Moving closer,* we could see the tiger's teeth.
> (*closer* is an adverb modifying *Moving*.)

> *Walking in pairs*, the elephants lumbered into the ring.
> (*in pairs* is a phrase modifying *Walking*.)

When a participle is completed by objects or predicate words, these words are part of the participial phrase.

> *Having passed the test,* Darla heaved a sigh of relief.
> (*test* is the direct object of *Having passed*.)
> Chet bent over his physics book, *looking perplexed.*
> (*perplexed* is a predicate adjective completing *looking*.)
> *Giving the first mate the charts*, the captain scanned the radar.
> (*first mate* is the indirect object and *charts* is the direct object of *Giving*.)

Like individual participles, participial phrases may modify nouns, pronouns, and words used as nouns.

> *Angered by poor pay and long hours*, the employees decided to strike. (The participial phrase modifies *employees*.)
> We stood in line for three hours, *hoping to get tickets.*
> (The participial phrase modifies the pronoun *We*.)

Generally speaking, a participle or a participial phrase should be placed as close as possible to the word that it modifies. If the word is misplaced so that it modifies the wrong word or group of words, it is called a **dangling participle.**

DANGLING PARTICIPLE: Holsteins are the most popular cows among dairy farmers *producing the most milk.* (The participial phrase *producing the most milk* incorrectly modifies *farmers.*)

CORRECTLY PLACED PARTICIPLE: *Producing the most milk,* Holsteins are the most popular cows among dairy farmers. (The participial phrase now correctly modifies *Holsteins.*)

Diagraming. The participle and the participial phrase are diagramed as follows:

Purring softly, the kitten lay down.

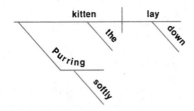

Sailing his boat brilliantly, Jeff won the race.

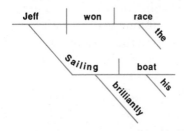

Exercise A: Find the participial phrases. Tell the word each phrase modifies. Remember that phrases can be made from past participles and present participles.

1. Arriving in Philadelphia, Franklin looked for a job.
2. Having finished her required work, Cara began an investigation of her own.

3. Lincoln entered the capital at night, disguised in strange clothing.
4. Alarmed by the condition of the troops, the general ordered a retreat.
5. Appearing before the committee, the accountant admitted her guilt.
6. Both pros, wilting under the hot sun, played a slow game.
7. The girls came into the house, carrying a mysterious package.
8. Woodrow Wilson went to bed, convinced of his defeat.
9. Having studied the chapter, I was ready for the test.
10. Lynn limped out onto the court, determined to finish the game.

Exercise B: Find the participial phrases. Tell what words they modify.

1. Panting heavily, Kris dove across the finish line.
2. The people driving the tractors have a dangerous job.
3. The woman riding the ten-speed bicycle is my teacher.
4. Two nurses, having finished their work, left the ward.
5. The audience grew restless, waiting for the show to begin.
6. Best known for her novels, Willa Cather also wrote stories.
7. Movies intended for a general audience are rated G.
8. The player scoring the most points loses the game.
9. The notice posted on the bulletin board gives the examination schedule.
10. Seared by the drought, the farms looked lifeless.

Exercise C: Writing Identify the incorrectly placed participial phrases in each of the following sentences. Then, rewrite each sentence so that the participial phrase modifies the correct word.

1. Walking across the front lawn, the geraniums looked beautiful to Jack.
2. Broken down and covered with scratches, Paul was able to buy the car very cheaply.

3. Pickled and canned, the family appreciated the kiwi fruit.
4. The posters seemed beautiful to Sally hanging on the wall.
5. Swimming in the aquarium, my cat watched the guppies.
6. The chimpanzees and the other great apes were photographed by the scientist swinging from the branches.
7. Lying on the television, I found the note she had left me.
8. Dried up from too little water, Mark lost two of his plants.
9. He often jogged through the park with his dog singing songs from Italian operas.
10. Flying fantastic formations in the air, I watched the finest single engine plane in the world.

2.16 The Gerund Phrase

A **gerund** is a verb form that is used as a noun and that always ends with -ing: *thinking, hiking, acting.*

A **gerund phrase** consists of the gerund and its modifiers and complements. The modifiers themselves may be phrases.

Proper lighting is necessary for studying.
  (*Proper* is an adjective modifying *lighting.*)
Geraldine likes *walking briskly.*
  (*briskly* is an adverb modifying *walking.*)
Playing without adequate practice demoralizes a team.
  (*without adequate practice* is a phrase modifying *Playing.*)
Swimming after eating a meal is dangerous.
  (*after eating a meal* is a phrase modifying *Swimming.*)

Gerunds may be completed by objects or predicate words. These words are part of the gerund phrase.

Being president of the group is an honor.
  (*president* is a predicate noun completing *Being.*)
Giving Phil those books changed his whole life.
  (*Phil* is the indirect object and *books* is the direct object of *Giving.*)

The gerund phrase is always used as a noun.

> *Finding an apartment* is a difficult task. (The gerund phrase is the subject of the verb *is*.)
>
> One of the most difficult tasks is *finding an apartment*. (The gerund phrase is being used as a predicate word after the linking verb *is*.)
>
> We liked *picnicking on the island*. (The gerund phrase is the direct object of *liked*.)
>
> After *training intensively*, the team was ready for opening day. (The gerund phrase is the object of the preposition *After*.)

Diagraming. The gerund and the gerund phrase are diagramed as follows:

Hiking is her favorite sport.

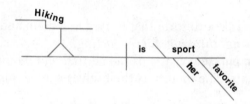

Fine passing won the game.

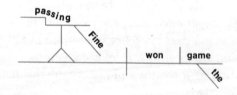

We disliked taking the test.

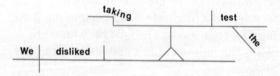

After trudging through the snow, we relaxed.

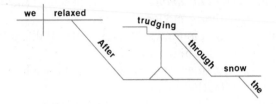

Exercise A: Find the gerund or gerund phrase in each of the following sentences.

1. Cooking is a hobby of many famous men and women.
2. Several football coaches enjoy painting in their spare hours.
3. This young man's hobby was training pigeons.
4. The movies gave dancing its current popularity.
5. After studying, Mike took a long walk.
6. We enjoyed hearing your speech.
7. Getting there is half the fun.
8. Don't blame Sarah for losing the game.
9. Before going to bed, Mr. Harris turned on the radio.
10. Sleeping late on Saturdays is a great luxury.
11. Turn off the water before closing the camp.
12. He made a fortune by collecting and trading comic books.
13. Concentration is most important in playing chess.
14. Climbing the fence is forbidden.
15. Watching the clock is hard work.

Exercise B: Find the gerund phrases in the following sentences and tell whether these phrases are being used as subjects, direct objects, indirect objects, objects of prepositions, or predicate words.

1. Reporting the news can be exciting work.
2. Begin your study of journalism by training your powers of observation.
3. Enormous strength and subtle grace give his dancing a special flair.
4. Arachne was known for weaving beautiful tapestries.

5. Americans love watching European films.
6. After seeing *Flashdance,* everyone at school started wearing tights and leg warmers.
7. Hiking in the mountains helped Justice William O. Douglas overcome his lung ailment.
8. Hank's most spectacular feat was catching a high fly ball over the outfield fence.
9. Willie Shoemaker, the famous jockey, started riding horses at an early age.
10. Penny Dean holds a record for crossing the English Channel in only seven hours and forty minutes.

Exercise C: Identify the verbals and verbal phrases in the following sentences. Label them *Participle, Gerund,* or *Infinitive.*

1. Sitting on our roof, we watched the strange light in the sky.
2. Wounded, the Armada sailed north to its destruction.
3. Anyone can learn to fly a plane by taking lessons.
4. Lost in his thoughts, Perry stepped right over a wallet lying on the sidewalk.
5. Eric stayed behind, hoping to talk to his teacher.
6. Oil companies have started to pump oil through the Alaskan pipeline.
7. We are hoping to see many old friends at the reunion.
8. After landing in Richmond, we had to wait two hours.
9. Finding new sources of water is essential if our cities are to survive.
10. Paul expected to pay his expenses by working after school.

2.17 The Appositive Phrase

An **appositive** is a word placed after another word to explain or identify it. An appositive should be set off by commas.

The police chief, *Carolyn Vance,* spoke to the youth group.
Daniel Keyes, *the novelist,* wrote "Flowers for Algernon."

Appositives are always nouns, pronouns, or other parts of speech acting as nouns. The word that an appositive explains is also always a noun, a pronoun, or another part of speech acting as a noun.

An **appositive phrase** consists of the appositive and its modifiers, which themselves may be phrases.

> Gina's cat, *a streetwise old tiger,* is missing. (The appositive phrase identifies *cat.* The adjectives *streetwise* and *old* modify the appositive, *tiger.*)
>
> The Donnellys bought the house, *a split-level ranch model with a swimming pool.* (The italicized words are the appositive phrase, identifying *house.* The adjectives *split-level* and *ranch* modify the appositive, *model,* as does the adjective phrase *with a swimming pool.*)

Diagraming. The appositive is diagramed as follows:

Mary Alvarez, the new secretary, comes from El Paso.

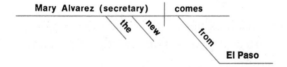

2.18   A Review of Diagraming

Meaning is conveyed in English sentences by word groups arranged in definite ways. Diagraming helps you to show which words go together and how they are arranged. The following is a review of the diagraming presented in this Section.

The simple sentence is composed of subject-verb-complement. These words are placed on the base line of the diagram. The indirect object is placed below the verb.

Subject	Action Verb	Direct Object
		Indirect Object

The introductory word *There* or *Here* is placed on a separate line above the base line. Also note the slant line after the linking verb. This indicates that the predicate word refers back to the subject of the sentence.

The subject of an imperative sentence, *you* (understood), is placed in parentheses.

A single-word modifier is placed on a slant line below the word it modifies. An adverb modifying an adjective or adverb is placed as shown below.

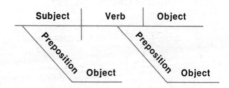

The prepositional phrase is attached to the word it modifies, as follows:

The infinitive phrase is shown in this way:

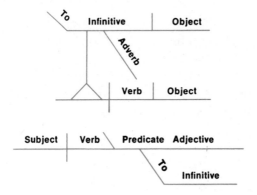

The participial phrase is shown as follows:

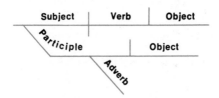

The gerund phrase is placed above the base line unless it is the object of a preposition.

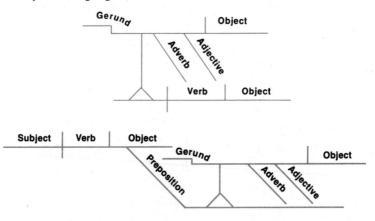

2.19 The Basic Sentence Patterns

As you have seen, there are many different elements that can be used in English sentences. However, there are a limited number of ways in which these elements can be arranged. We call these different arrangements of sentence parts the **basic sentence patterns**. In this Section we will discuss the most important of these patterns.

Pattern One

N	V	(Adverb or Prepositional Phrase)
The fans	cheered.	
Casey	struck	out.
Vinnie	is going	by bus.
They	should hurry.	
That movie	ended	strangely.

Pattern One sentences consist of a noun (*N*) followed by a verb (*V*). Frequently, the pattern is completed by an adverb or a prepositional phrase. Verbs that occur in Pattern One sentences are *intransitive verbs*.

Note: Remember, pronouns, gerunds, and infinitives often can be used in place of nouns. They can therefore be substituted for nouns in any of these patterns.

Pattern Two

N	V	N
The choir	sang	several selections.
The hometown pitcher	hit	a home run.
Someone	has given	the money.
Carelessness	causes	accidents.
We	should win	every game.

The noun that follows the verb in a Pattern Two sentence is a *direct object*. The verbs that occur in this type of sentence are *transitive verbs*.

Most of the thousands of transitive verbs in English occur only in Pattern Two sentences. However, some transitive verbs may occur in sentences that have two nouns following the verb. Such sentences are Pattern Three sentences.

Pattern Three

N	V	N	N
Mother	got	Sybil	that job.
Valerie	gave	us	the keys.
He	wrote	each aunt	a postcard.
Jimmy	should tell	his parents	our plans.

In Pattern Three sentences, the first noun following the verb is the *indirect object*; the second noun is the *direct object*. These two nouns refer to different people or things.

Pattern Four

N	LV	N
My aunt	is	a doctor.
Both books	have become	best sellers.
Luther	remained	my friend.
They	are	exchange students.

Be, become, and *remain* are the verbs that usually appear in Pattern Four sentences. They are *linking verbs (LV)*. The noun following the linking verb in a Pattern Four sentence is a *predicate noun*. The linking verbs that occur in this pattern produce sentences in which two nouns refer to the *same* person or thing.

In Pattern Two (N-V-N), the transitive verbs produce sentences in which the two nouns in each sentence refer to *different* persons or things.

In each pair of sentences below, notice how the relationship between the nouns changes when we replace a linking verb with a transitive verb:

> His sister became a doctor. (N-LV-N)
> His sister needed a doctor. (N-V-N)
>
> Fran was my friend. (N-LV-N)
> Fran snubbed my friend. (N-V-N)

Pattern Five

N	LV	ADJ
Those rocks	are	treacherous.
My overcoat	has become	quite shabby.
His mother	seems	very young.
He	remained	calm.
Her story	sounded	true.

Verbs that occur in Patterns Four and Five are *linking verbs.* There are thousands of intransitive verbs in English, but only a few words are regularly used as linking verbs. The most important are *be* (and its various forms), *become, seem,* and *remain.* The word following the linking verb in a Pattern Five sentence is a *predicate adjective (ADJ).*

English sentences are seldom as simple as the basic sentences listed above. In order to convey meaning adequately, we usually need to expand the basic patterns by adding modifiers and more complicated constructions. No matter how complicated or how long a sentence becomes, however, it will always have one of the basic patterns as a foundation.

Exercise A: Identify the sentence pattern in each sentence below.

1. Our school has a rugby team.
2. Barbara smiled radiantly.
3. Ms. Tortina told the class a funny story.
4. My friends are considerate.

5. Salem is the state capital.
6. The bleachers are full now.
7. Julia mailed her parents a postcard from camp.
8. Someone must have taken my watch!
9. The spark quickly became a blaze.
10. The store detective raced onto the elevator.

Exercise B: Writing Write three different sentences that follow each of the sentence patterns listed below.

1. Noun   Verb
2. Noun   Verb   Noun
3. Noun   Verb   Noun   Noun
4. Noun   Linking Verb   Noun
5. Noun   Linking Verb   Adjective

Exercise C: Writing Identify the pattern of each sentence below. Then, rewrite the sentence so that it follows the sentence pattern in parentheses.

1. The dance hall is large. **(N-LV-N)**
2. Carole writes in a diary. **(N-V-N-N)**
3. Juan reads rapidly. **(N-V-N)**
4. Rembrandt is a famous painter. **(N-LV-ADJ)**
5. Bill grew scared. **(N-V-N)**
6. The teacher gave us a special project assignment. **(N-V-N)**
7. Selina made a bookcase. **(N-V-N-N)**
8. The high school has become a familiar place. **(N-V-ADJ)**
9. The editor-in-chief wrote a controversial editorial. **(N-V-N-N)**
10. The archaeologists found the remains of a past civilization. **(N-V-N-N)**

REINFORCEMENT EXERCISES
The Parts of a Sentence

A. Make complete sentences. All but two of the following groups of words do not express complete thoughts. Identify these groups and change them into sentences. Write *Sentence* for those groups of words that are already complete sentences.

1. The scientist in the laboratory
2. Swayed and trembled in the violent wind
3. The villain with the long, black moustache
4. Stopping abruptly, he turned and stalked away
5. Offered Joyce one scoop of rocky road ice cream and one of butter pecan
6. The scariest movie I have ever seen
7. Rushed toward the goal post while the fans roared
8. Is flying in tonight from Philadelphia on a DC-10
9. Tried unsuccessfully to hold back his tears
10. Working in the emergency ward is exhausting for the staff

B. Use different kinds of sentences. Tell what kind of sentence each sentence below is. Then rewrite each one to be the type indicated in parentheses. Make whatever changes are necessary.

1. A new type of dinosaur skeleton was recently unearthed in England. (Interrogative)
2. You can stop at the post office on your way home. (Imperative)
3. Did William Shakespeare write both *Hamlet* and *Macbeth?* (Declarative)
4. The country music special on television last night was fantastic. (Exclamatory)
5. Many small businesses are now using computers. (Interrogative)
6. What a shock to see John performing in the circus! (Interrogative)

7. Is it illegal to hunt crocodiles in the Florida Everglades? (Declarative)
8. Did you buy a ticket for the matinee performance? (Imperative)
9. Weren't we lucky to find that terrific cassette sale? (Exclamatory)
10. Weren't many of Isaac Bashevis Singer's stories adapted from folk tales? (Declarative)

C. Identify the verb and its simple subject. Find the verb and its simple subject in each of the following sentences.

1. The winner donated her prize money to charity.
2. This circus owns several miniature horses.
3. After they were married, Phillip and Nancy moved to Colorado.
4. Franklin Delano Roosevelt was Theodore Roosevelt's distant cousin.
5. Rudolf Nureyev and Mikhail Barishnikov were both born in Russia.
6. Maurice Sendak writes and illustrates many wonderful children's books.
7. Buckingham Palace and St. Paul's Cathedral are located in London.
8. West Virginia became a state during the Lincoln administration.
9. Some lizards change color when frightened.
10. The panda may eventually become extinct.

D. Find the subject and verb. Find the verb and its simple subject in each of the following sentences.

1. There were thirty-two new players at football practice in August.
2. Along the horizon twinkled the city lights.
3. Between the band and the next float rode six clowns on motorbikes.
4. From inside the vacant house came shrill laughter.

5. Beside him at the ceremony sat Len's little sister.
6. There will be four candidates in the race for vice-president.
7. Into the harbor sailed the double-masted schooner.
8. Here are the videotapes of the game.
9. From the cave entrance flew the bats.
10. On this island grow many carnivorous plants.

E. Identify direct objects, indirect objects, and predicate words.
Find the direct objects, indirect objects, and predicate words in the following sentences. Label each one.

1. Woody Allen has written a new screenplay.
2. The judge granted the defendant a new trial.
3. Leslie was the best forward on our basketball team.
4. One popular kind of puppet is the marionette.
5. Attorney Stephens sent the mayor her resignation.
6. The cougar is a solitary animal.
7. One diver cut his hand on the sharp coral.
8. The curator showed our class a mummy.
9. After the Civil War, Grant became President.
10. Most farmers must rotate their crops every few years.

F. Find the compound parts. Find the compound parts in each sentence. Then identify each part as *Subject, Verb, Direct Object, Indirect Object, or Predicate Word.*

1. Michiko and Alex planned and purchased the refreshments.
2. Miguel sold George and Sherri tickets to the play.
3. Ben Franklin was both witty and practical.
4. Mars and Venus are the planets nearest to Earth.
5. We raced across the beach and dove into the icy water.
6. Uncle Dale gave me a camera and some film for my birthday.
7. The ambassador looked pale and tired after the ten-day trip.
8. The mayor and the council favor a curfew of 10:00 on week nights.

9. The Mississippi flood waters slowed and receded over the weekend.
10. Prince Charles toured Victoria and Vancouver in British Columbia.

G. Use prepositional phrases. To each sentence, add the type of prepositional phrase indicated in parentheses. Then underline the word each phrase modifies.

1. The clowns were satisfied but exhausted. (adjective)
2. One salesperson demonstrated the stereo equipment. (adjective)
3. The volcano spewed out rocks and red-hot lava. (adverb)
4. The farmers harvested thousands of bright yellow pumpkins. (adjective)
5. The band played several Sousa marches. (adverb)
6. Mandy took excellent photographs. (adjective)
7. Columbus had to store several months' rations. (adverb)
8. The private eye found a valuable clue. (adverb)
9. Finally, the skin diver emerged. (adverb)
10. Two giant cedars flanked the solitary cabin. (adjective)

H. Identify the verbal phrases. Find the infinitive, participial, and gerund phrases in the following sentences. Label each phrase. Some sentences contain more than one verbal phrase.

1. Riding his bicycle, Alan can reach Jonesboro in two hours.
2. Once hunted near extinction, the American buffalo is now protected in zoos and animal preserves.
3. Mr. Aldredge wanted to see geysers spouting from the ground in Yellowstone Park.
4. Climbing "El Capitan" will require perseverance and hard work.
5. Raised in China, Pearl Buck loved to write about her experiences there.
6. Geraldo Rivera was the first television reporter to interview Barbra Streisand in seven years.

7. *Sugaring off* is one step in the process of making maple syrup.
8. To live by the ocean is the dream of many Americans.
9. Working at the zoo, Jason was able to learn a great deal about animals.
10. Marcia's hobby is carving chess pieces from blocks of wood.

I. Identify the sentence patterns. Identify the sentence pattern of each of the following sentences.

1. The owl gave me a disdainful look.
2. Doug prepared chicken for Mom's birthday dinner.
3. The car died in the middle of the busiest intersection in Tulsa.
4. My dad told a wildly funny story about his first date.
5. *Divali* is the Hindu festival of lights.
6. Tonya broke her arm on Thursday.
7. The French flag is red, white, and blue.
8. Frank Lloyd Wright lived for years in Spring Green, Wisconsin.
9. The hot air balloon drifted lazily across meadows and woods.
10. My uncle in Alaska sent us a smoked salmon.

The Parts of a Sentence

A. Make six columns. Head them *Subject, Verb, Direct Object, Indirect Object, Predicate Word,* and *Prepositional Phrase.* Place those parts of the following sentences in the proper columns. Some of the sentence parts may be compound.

1. Our class wrote and produced a musical.
2. My aunt in Mexico sent me a piñata and a sombrero.
3. A heavy snowfall stopped trains and buses in the city.
4. During the trial, the defendant admitted his guilt.
5. Four-person bobsledding is one event in the Olympics.
6. The magician showed Willy several card tricks.
7. The Latin class wore togas for a Roman banquet.
8. The babysitter gave the children crackers and cheese.
9. My helicopter ride was much too short.
10. Pigs and cattle were loaded onto railroad cars.
11. This cave seems eerie and hazardous.
12. A gust of wind scattered Jason's homework around the parking lot.
13. Three airplanes performed stunts for the crowd.
14. The gymnastics coach spotted Kendra during her backflip.
15. R. L. Jeffries is the supervisor at the glassworks.
16. Billie Holiday was a famous blues singer.
17. Cindy asked the veterinarian questions about pet care.
18. Dad taught us a new dive.
19. Cassie seems confused about the algebra assignment.
20. Whom did their class elect for president?

B. Complete or expand the following sentences by adding the material indicated in parentheses.

1. The rescue volunteers distributed _____ to the flood victims. (compound direct object)

2. I like my sandwiches with lots of _____. (compound object of a preposition)

3. The President _____ at the photographers. (compound verb)

4. _____ are my favorite writers. (compound subject)

5. Carla discovered that _____ can be a thrilling way to travel. (gerund phrase)

6. The priceless painting, _____, was missing from the museum. (appositive phrase)

7. The committee agreed that the only way _____ was to merge with the Student Council. (infinitive phrase)

8. _____, Marnie decided to make the decision on her own. (participial phrase)

9. The space shuttle landed _____, within inches of the projected target. (prepositional phrase)

10. After the game, Gerri asked her friends _____. (infinitive phrase)

C. Identify the sentence pattern for each of the sentences given below.

1. The temperature remained steady through the afternoon.

2. Our coach taught us a new formation for the next game.

3. The Constitution guarantees equality for all Americans.

4. The movie ended happily after all.

5. These attractive plants are actually poisonous.

6. Mary Stewart is a writer of gothic novels and fantasy stories.

7. Galileo discovered the moons of Jupiter.

8. Something has crawled into our tent!

9. This new stereo sounds wonderful.

10. Mr. Hernandez photographs animals for *National Geographic.*

USING GRAMMAR IN WRITING
The Parts of a Sentence

A. Imagine that you are one of the first civilian passengers aboard a space shuttle. You have been asked to write your impressions of the space flight for NASA's archives. Write the first paragraph of this report, describing your take-off. Use all four kinds of sentences: declarative, imperative, interrogative, and exclamatory.

B. Read the following skeleton of a story. Identify the sentence pattern of each of the sentences. Then, expand and finish the story by adding your own infinitive, participial, appositive, gerund, or prepositional phrases. Underline and label each phrase that you add. Notice how much more interesting the story becomes.

> The moon was full.
> The Arctic air was bitter.
> A dog sled crossed the frozen landscape.
> No village was in sight.
> Suddenly, the driver slumped forward.
> The lead husky howled and stopped in his tracks.
> The dog escaped from its harness.
> It ran for miles.
> Eventually, it found our camp.
> We followed the dog.
> We rescued its owner.

C. Writers must tailor the length and complexity of their sentences to suit different audiences. Write a short magazine article about an interesting subject, such as the Loch Ness monster. Assume that you are writing for a children's magazine. Make all of your sentences short and simple, with no unusual subject-verb order. Now rewrite your article for an adult magazine. This time, vary the subject-verb order. Experiment with starting your sentences using different types of phrases.

3.0 Sentence and Clause

We have seen (Section 2.2) that sentences can be classified according to the purpose of the speaker: *declarative, imperative, interrogative,* and *exclamatory*. This classification can help you to solve problems of proper punctuation.

For help in writing better sentences, there is another classification. This is the classification by form. There are three basic forms of sentences: the *simple sentence*, the *compound sentence*, and the *complex sentence*. A fourth kind, the *compound-complex sentence*, is a combination of basic forms.

3.1 The Simple Sentence

A simple sentence contains only one subject and predicate. Both the subject and the predicate may be compound.

You will recall that *compound* means having two or more similar parts.

COMPOUND SUBJECT: The *producer* and the *playwright* argued about script changes. (The producer argued; the playwright argued.)

COMPOUND PREDICATE: Shakespeare *wrote his own plays* and *acted in some of them.* (Shakespeare wrote his own plays; Shakespeare acted in some of them.)

COMPOUND SUBJECT AND COMPOUND PREDICATE: Both *Mayor Flynn* and the *city council attended the hearings* and *defended the proposals*. (Mayor Flynn and the city council attended; Mayor Flynn and the city council defended.)

All of the preceding sentences are simple sentences. In these sentences both parts of a compound subject go with the same verb, both parts of a compound verb have the same subject, or both parts of a compound subject go with both parts of a compound verb. In each of these sentences there is only one subject-verb connection.

In the following sentence the first subject goes with the first verb, but the second subject goes with the second verb. There are two subject-verb connections. This is *not* a simple sentence:

The *visitors played* tennis; their *host took* a nap.

The Compound Predicate. The compound predicate is useful to combine ideas into clear, smooth sentences.

In a sentence with a compound predicate, both verbs have the same subject.

My *uncle bought* some land and *farmed it*.
The *actors bowed* and *left* the stage.

As a general rule, do not use a comma or semicolon to separate the parts of a compound predicate.

Exercise A: Identify the compound subjects and compound predicates in the following sentences.

1. Both the manager and his assistant were injured in the crash.
2. We left the house early and walked to school.
3. The committee will hire an orchestra and arrange for decorations.
4. The stage crew designed the sets and painted them.
5. Strawberries and asparagus are in season now.

6. The logs were split and stacked in the woodshed.
7. Claire read several books about Marie Curie and wrote a report about the famous chemist.
8. The attendant filled the gas tank and checked the oil.
9. The guitarist and the bass player rehearsed for the concert.
10. Hamilton and Washington wrote the Farewell Address together.

Exercise B: Writing Rewrite the following sentences, making all of the predicates compound.

1. Experts examined the old paintings.
2. A rabbit and a dog raced under the fence.
3. For the parade the children decorated their bikes.
4. Will you and Evan do the dishes?
5. This home computer displays a variety of games.
6. Carolyn brushes her cat's fur once a week.
7. The general gave an order to one of the aides.
8. The guitarist played at a deafening volume.
9. The bus screeched to a stop, inches from the huge hole.
10. Thomas Jefferson wrote books on a variety of subjects.

3.2 The Compound Sentence

The compound sentence consists of two or more simple sentences put together.

The parts of a compound sentence are put together with a semicolon, or with a comma and a coordinating conjunction (*and, yet, so, but, or, for, nor*).

> Chris likes all outdoor sports, *but* she enjoys backpacking the most.
>
> The Revolutionary War had been won, *but* the thirteen states were still far from united.
>
> You can take five hours by bus, *or* you can get there in an hour by plane.

He had known the Governor well, *for* he had been her
campaign manager.
Charlie could not play the guitar, *nor* could he sing.
The fans were ecstatic; their team had won its division.
George watched the line intently; he expected the tuna to
strike.

Conjunctive adverbs such as *then, however, moreover, hence,
consequently,* and *therefore* are also used to join the parts of a
compound sentence. The conjunctive adverb is preceded by a
semicolon.

They went to the stadium; *however,* the game had been
rained out.
She qualified in the Olympic trials; *then* she won a gold
medal.
Jamie's sweater was too small; *therefore,* he gave it away.

Diagraming. The compound sentence is diagramed on two parallel base lines as follows:

The game was close, but we finally won.

Leslie grilled the steaks; Jesse made the salad.

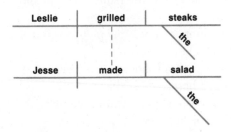

Compound Sentences and Compound Predicates. In the compound predicate, every verb has the same subject or subjects. In the compound sentence, each verb has a different subject. This difference can be seen readily in diagrams.

SIMPLE SENTENCE WITH COMPOUND PREDICATE:

Anne completed three applications and mailed them.

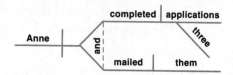

COMPOUND SENTENCE:

Anne completed three applications, and her brother mailed them.

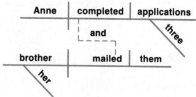

Exercise A: Decide which of these sentences are compound sentences and which are simple sentences. For the simple sentences, identify the compound predicate.

1. The pre-colonial house was small, but the grounds and gardens were spacious.
2. You can begin taking French classes this year or wait until next year.
3. The huge rocket left the launching pad and vanished into the sky.
4. Da Vinci painted only a few pictures, but they are all masterpieces.
5. Our library is small; however, it has a good collection of reference books.
6. We can take the express train tonight or fly to Detroit early in the morning.

7. Peter ate all of the food on his plate but complained about every single bite.
8. The unemployment rate dropped in May, but it rose in June.
9. The class visited the Museum of Modern Art and spent hours studying the new paintings.
10. Stephanie was a successful businessperson; her work was interesting and challenging.

Exercise B: Writing All of the following sentences are compound sentences. Rewrite them as simple sentences. Use compound subjects or compound predicates, following the model of the example.

EXAMPLE: Two deer bolted across the road; they disappeared into a grove of birches. (compound sentence)

EXAMPLE: Two deer bolted across the road and disappeared into a grove of trees. (simple sentence with a compound predicate)

1. The moon turns on its axis every twenty-eight days; therefore, it always presents the same face to the earth.
2. Woody Guthrie wrote about the Oklahoma dust bowl, and John Steinbeck wrote about it, too.
3. Central built a new stadium, and then it started a football team.
4. Sharon teaches modern dance in the evenings; moreover, she choreographs musicals at the high school.
5. Each day, Marion rides his bicycle, or he jogs through the park.
6. Birds are born blind; however, they can recognize their mothers by using their other senses.
7. Anissa enjoys opera, but she also loves folk music.
8. Lou sat by the telephone; he waited for his friend's call for over an hour.
9. Isaac Stern played at the Hollywood Bowl, and Loretta Lynn played there, too.
10. The rain forced us to return to our cabin, and the cold also forced us to go back.

3.3 The Clause

Before you can study complex or compound-complex sentences, you must understand one of their basic elements. This element is the clause.

A clause is a group of words containing a verb and its subject.

According to this definition, a simple sentence is a clause. Indeed, the simple sentence is sometimes defined as consisting of one main clause. However, we shall find it simpler to use the word *clause* to name a *part* of a sentence.

Each part of a compound sentence has its own verb and subject. These parts are therefore called clauses.

Each clause in a compound sentence can be lifted out and written separately as a simple sentence.

A clause that can stand by itself as a sentence is a main clause.

We have defined a compound sentence as consisting of two or more simple sentences put together. We can now also define it as consisting of two main clauses.

A clause that cannot stand by itself as a sentence is a subordinate clause.

When he asked me...(What happened?)

If you don't vote...(Then what?)

While you were away...(What?)

The subject of a subordinate clause is sometimes a relative pronoun.

Were you the person *who ordered the flowers*?
    (*who* is the subject of the clause)
These are the speakers *that came with the stereo*.
    (*that* is the subject of the clause)

Phrase or Clause? A clause has a subject and a verb. A phrase does not.

She saw Jack *playing in the band.* (phrase)

She met Jack *when he was playing in the band.* (clause)

The box *of jewels* was missing. (phrase)

The box *that contained the jewels* was missing. (clause)

Exercise A: Are the italicized words in each sentence a phrase or a clause?

1. *To photograph the ocean bottom,* two women descended in a metal sphere.
2. It was hard to believe *that we would not see him again.*
3. Herb started down the road, *rolling the tire ahead of him.*
4. We had arranged *to meet at the information desk.*
5. Seven women have run *for the Presidency.*
6. *After he had broken several records,* Pete Rose became the baseball hero of the year.
7. Is this the prize *for which you have been working so hard*?
8. Scientists are hopeful now *of finding cures for muscular dystrophy.*
9. *Ferociously barking and pawing at the window,* the dog attracted our attention.
10. We could not see *who was at the door.*
11. *After leaving high school,* Mark will go to a business school.
12. Washoe the ape, *who was trained by her owner,* communicates with sign language.
13. *Simple to learn and to use,* Esperanto was devised as an international language.
14. The men were losing weight, *for they had been too tired to eat properly.*
15. *Moving carefully under the ice,* the submarine inched its way to safety.

Exercise B: Find the main clause and the subordinate clause in each sentence below. Identifying the subject and verb for each part will help you find the clauses.

1. Here is the turn where the accident occurred.
2. Is this the music that you wanted?
3. Do you know what the winning number is?
4. Turn off the lights before you go to bed.
5. Unless the rain stops, the game will be postponed.
6. Who knows where the Millers live?
7. Prices of farm products fell after the Erie Canal opened.
8. Mr. Bruce is the man who bought our house.
9. What will we do if the power fails?
10. When there is a heavy snowfall in the city, everything stops.

3.4   The Adjective Clause

The single-word adjective, the adjective phrase, and the adjective clause are used in the same way. They modify a noun or pronoun.

An adjective clause is a subordinate clause used to modify a noun or pronoun.

Introductory Words. Most adjective clauses begin with an introductory word. There is a growing tendency, however, to use adjective clauses with no introductory word.

This is the town *where Lincoln was born.* (*where* is an introductory word.)

This is the time *when jonquils bloom.* (*when* is an introductory word.)

There is the suit *I need.* (no introductory word)
There is the suit *that I need.* (*that* is an introductory word.)

The boat *you wanted* is out of stock. (no introductory word)
The boat *that you wanted* is out of stock. (*that* is an introductory word.)

In the first two examples, the introductory words *where* and *when* are both used within the subordinate clause as modifiers of the verb; *was born* **where;** *bloom* **when.**

Relative Pronouns. The pronouns *who, whose, whom, which,* and *that* are used to introduce adjective clauses. Used in this way, they refer to a word in the main clause and are used in place of that word. That word is the antecedent of the pronoun. It is also the word modified by the adjective clause.

> Eliza is the one *who got the most votes.*
> (*one* is the antecedent of *who* and is modified by the adjective clause.)
>
> There goes the man *whose daughter is an astronaut.*
> (*man* is the antecedent of *whose* and is modified by the adjective clause.)
>
> Relative humidity is the amount of water vapor *that the air contains.*
> (*vapor* is the antecedent of *that* and is modified by the adjective clause.)

An adjective clause introduced by a relative pronoun is sometimes called a **relative clause**.

The relative pronoun has two functions. It introduces the clause, and it is used as a sentence-part within the clause.

> The letter *to which you refer* has been lost.
> (*which* is the object of the preposition *to.*)
>
> Tina is the girl *whom he asked* to my party.
> (*whom* is the direct object of *asked.*)
>
> Howard Cosell is a public figure *who shrugs off criticism.*
> (*who* is the subject of *shrugs.*)

The case of the pronoun is determined by its function within the clause. Notice, for example, that *who* is used as a subject or a predicate word within the clause. *Whom* is used as a direct object, an indirect object, or an object of a preposition within the clause.

That and *which* also have specific functions. *That* introduces adjective clauses that are essential to the meaning of the sentence. *Which* introduces nonessential clauses.

> Where are the supplies *that I ordered*?
> (*that I ordered* is essential to the sentence.)

> The supplies, *which I ordered last week*, still have not arrived.
> (The clause is not essential to the meaning of the sentence.)

Diagraming. The adjective clause is joined to the word it modifies in the main clause. A dotted line leads from this word to the introductory word. Note that the relative pronoun is placed to show its use in the clause.

The route that they took went through Washington.

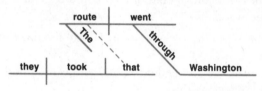

This is the spot where the plane crashed.

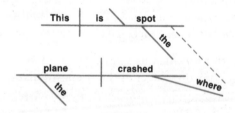

Exercise A: Find each adjective clause and the word it modifies.

1. August is the month when you can see meteors.
2. Is this the record you bought yesterday?
3. Dorothy Hamill is the American figure skater who won the gold medal.
4. This is the spot where the first state capitol stood.

5. Professor Morrison is the person to whom we wrote.
6. The aerial photographs showed outlines of ancient buildings that no one had ever noticed from the ground.
7. He reported seeing objects that came from outer space.
8. The energy you are using came originally from the sun.
9. We need leaders who are honest and fearless.
10. Was it the most embarrassing thing that ever happened?

Exercise B: Writing Add adjective clauses containing the material in parentheses to each of the sentences below.

1. The mynah bird _____ sings in two languages. (My aunt bought the bird.)
2. The store _____ is out of business. (The store sells shoes.)
3. Scientists have invented a light _____ . (The light does not produce heat.)
4. The trip _____ will take us through the West. (We are planning the trip.)
5. The fellow _____ hosts a game show. (We saw the fellow in the restaurant.)
6. This is the chapter _____ . (I told you about this chapter.)
7. William Carlos Williams _____ was also a doctor. (William Carlos Williams was a famous poet.)
8. Here is a book of poems _____ . (You might enjoy it.)
9. The books _____ finally arrived. (We ordered the books.)
10. The lady _____ is the director. (You spoke to the lady.)

3.5 The Adverb Clause

The single-word adverb, the adverb phrase, and the adverb clause are all used to modify verbs, adjectives, and adverbs.

An adverb clause is a subordinate clause used to modify a verb, adjective, or adverb.

Adverb clauses tell *where, when, why, how, how much,* or *to what extent* about the words they modify.

ADVERB CLAUSES MODIFYING VERBS

They **put** the stop sign *where few could see it.* (tells *where*)
When the bell rings, everyone **takes** a break. (tells *when*)
The Senator **talked** *as if she would run for re-election.*
   (tells *how*)
We **left** the beach *because it was too noisy.* (tells *why*)

ADVERB CLAUSES MODIFYING ADJECTIVES

Winter seems twice as **long** *as it used to be.* (tells *how much*)
Kevin is as **funny** *as his uncle is.* (tells *to what extent*)

ADVERB CLAUSE MODIFYING AN ADVERB

Esther worked **harder** *than her sisters did.* (tells *how much*)

Subordinating Conjunctions. Words used to introduce adverb clauses are called **subordinating conjunctions**. These words not only introduce the subordinate clause but link it to the main clause. They make the relationship between the two clauses clear. Subordinating conjunctions show relationships of *time, place, condition, comparison, cause, result, exception,* and *alternative.* The most common subordinating conjunctions are these:

after	because	so that	whatever
although	before	than	when
as	if	though	whenever
as if	in order that	till	where
as long as	provided	unless	wherever
as though	since	until	while

When a subordinating conjunction is placed before a clause, the clause can no longer stand alone.

Your grades are average. (*complete*)
If your grades are average…(*incomplete*)
Since your grades are average…(*incomplete*)

The football season is over. (*complete*)
When the football season is over…(*incomplete*)
Until the football season is over…(*incomplete*)

A subordinating conjunction may be placed before either of two main clauses to tie it to the other. Which clause is subordinate depends upon the meaning the writer wants to express.

> *Although* the chef bakes delicious bread, his cakes are failures.
> *Although* the chef's cakes are failures, he bakes delicious bread.
> *Because* few people had signed up, the trip had been delayed.
> Few people had signed up, *because* the trip had been delayed.

Subordinating conjunctions can be used to show a great variety of relationships between main ideas. Choosing conjunctions carefully will enable you to express your ideas clearly and exactly.

TIME:	as, as soon as, after, before, since, until, when, whenever, while
CAUSE OR REASON:	because, since
COMPARISON:	as, as much as, than
CONDITION:	if, although, though, unless, provided
PURPOSE:	so that, in order that

Note how the meaning changes with the change of conjunctions in these sentences.

> *While* she gave the speech, she seemed confident.
> *Before* she gave the speech, she seemed confident.
> *After* she gave the speech, she seemed confident.

Elliptical Clauses. The word *elliptical* comes from *ellipsis*, which means "omission of a word." An **elliptical clause** is one from which words have been omitted.

> *While she is milking the cows*, she sings folk songs.
> *While milking the cows*, she sings folk songs.
> *When you are applying for a job*, dress appropriately.
> *When applying for a job*, dress appropriately.

Diagraming. The adverb clause is diagramed on a separate line:

When the car stopped, we lurched forward.

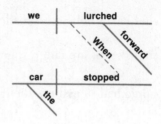

Exercise A: Find each adverb clause and the word or words it modifies.

1. When the girls returned to school, they planned the drama club picnic.
2. As soon as the snow starts falling, the snowplows go out.
3. Whenever there is an accident, a crowd gathers.
4. While she was studying for the test, Jocelyn ate an entire bag of potato chips.
5. John set the table while Martin cooked the hamburgers.
6. The stadium was hushed as Diane Pulcinski went to bat.
7. As soon as the ride started, the people were shrieking.
8. Beans grow best where the soil is sandy.
9. The people on the island are isolated until the spring thaws come.
10. Unless more funds are raised, the school will have no library.

Exercise B: Writing Add adverb clauses containing the information in parentheses to each of the sentences below. You may change the wording or the information somewhat.

1. Bob said very little. (This was his first meeting.)
2. You may return the lamp. (You might not like it.)
3. Everyone in the courtroom rose. (The judge entered.)
4. We walked down the road. (The car was being repaired.)

5. School was cancelled. (The snow fell all night.)
6. Could you help me with my algebra? (You have the time.)
7. The actor would not mention Shakespeare's *Macbeth* in the theater. (He was very superstitious.)
8. Huckleberry Finn leaves home. (His Aunt Sally wants to "sivilize" him.)
9. Morgan had never flown hang-gliders. (At nineteen he began flying them.)
10. There was no light, no sound, no movement. (We approached the house.)

3.6 The Noun Clause

A noun clause is a subordinate clause used as a noun.

The noun clause may be used as subject or object of the verb, as a predicate noun, as object of a preposition, or as an appositive.

> Officer Taylor asked *where the accident occurred.* (direct object of the verb *asked*)
> Angela did not agree with *what José had said.* (object of the preposition *with*)
> Father vetoed my idea *that we go to the fair.* (appositive)
> *Who began the war* is not certain. (subject)
> What I'd like to know is *how this dishwasher works.* (predicate noun)

Introductory Words. As the examples above clearly show, noun clauses may be introduced by some of the same words that introduce adverb clauses: *when, where.* Used in noun clauses, these words are not regarded as subordinating conjunctions. They are introductory words, used as adverbs within the noun clause.

Similarly, noun clauses may be introduced by the same words used to introduce relative clauses: *who, whose, whom, which, that, when,* and *where.* Used in noun clauses, these words are not regarded as relative pronouns, but they may serve as subjects or objects within the noun clause.

Terry knows **where** *Ed is*. (noun clause as the object of *knows*)

We went **where** *we could swim*. (adverb clause modifying *went*)

Are you the one **who** *called*? (adjective clause modifying *one*)

Who *sent this package* is a mystery. (noun clause as the subject of *is*)

Many noun clauses are written without any introductory word. Every direct quotation preceded by words such as *I said, she called, Jo asked* is a noun clause without an introductory word. Every indirect quotation is a noun clause with an introductory word.

He said *that the answer was wrong*. (noun clause as the object of *said*)

He said, *"The answer is wrong."* (noun clause as the object of *said*)

Infinitive Clauses. Unlike other verbals, an infinitive may have a subject as well as complements and modifiers. Such a construction is called an **infinitive clause**. The subject of an infinitive is always in the objective case.

The commander ordered *them to charge.*

The editor urged *her readers to vote.*

Diagraming. The noun clause is diagramed as shown below. Note that the use of the noun clause determines its position.

I know that they are going. (The clause is the object of the verb *know*.)

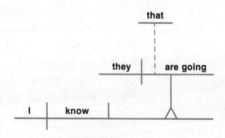

We have a job for whoever is qualified. (The clause is the object of the preposition *for*.)

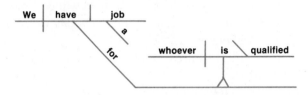

Exercise A: Identify each noun clause. Tell whether it is used as a subject, object, object of a preposition, predicate word, or appositive.

1. Barbara would not tell us where she had been.
2. What the reporter really wanted was a mystery to us.
3. Fred was apologetic about what he had said.
4. The doctor said that Marion could get up tomorrow.
5. Do you know who invented the microscope?
6. We had no idea of what might happen.
7. The police know who wrote the threatening letters.
8. Who will win the game is anyone's guess.
9. Everyone knew that the test would be difficult.
10. We thought the day would never end.
11. What happened to the missing artists was never discovered.
12. The department will be grateful for whatever you can do.
13. You can't get what you want without hard work.
14. We did not know Jim had such powers of concentration.
15. Is your new job what you expected?

Exercise B: In each sentence below, a subordinate clause is italicized. Tell whether each clause is a noun clause, adjective clause, or adverb clause.

1. Literature *that describes future events* is called science fiction.
2. *Whoever returns the stolen wallet* will be rewarded.
3. *When the moon moves between the sun and the earth*, a solar eclipse occurs.

4. Did you ask *what time it is*?
5. One sport *that is very popular in the Midwest* is ice hockey.
6. *If the rain continues*, the baseball field will be swamped.
7. Some of the tools *that the mountain climber uses* are picks, ropes, and crampons.
8. Some students drop out of school *because they are not motivated*.
9. The gymnast felt *that her timing was off*.
10. The laborers returned to work *after the strike was over*.
11. Ms. McKillip emphasized *what she expected of her students*.
12. Mack Sennett, *who developed the Keystone Kops*, was a pioneer in film comedy.
13. Multicolored leaves drifted to the pavement *as a brisk breeze brushed the countryside*.
14. May is the month *when most tulips bloom*.
15. Mark Twain said *that cauliflower is just cabbage with a college education*.

3.7   The Complex Sentence

Now that you understand clauses, you are ready to study the other two classifications of sentences.

The complex sentence consists of one main clause and one or more subordinate clauses.

In a complex sentence, the subordinate clause is used as a noun or a modifier. If it is used as a modifier, the subordinate clause usually modifies a word in the main clause.

When you leave, shut the door. (clause modifies *shut*)

If he quits that job, he will regret it later on. (clause modifies *will regret*)

The book *that you want* is over here. (clause modifies *book*)

In each preceding example, the main clause can stand as a sentence by itself: *Shut the door, He will regret it later on, This is the book.*

The subordinate clauses, however, cannot stand alone because their meaning is incomplete.

> When you leave...(What then?)
> If he quits that job...(What will happen?)
> that you want...(What is it?)

Complex sentences containing noun clauses are somewhat different. The noun clause is used as a noun *within the main clause.* The noun clause, in other words, is part of the main clause.

> *What we saw* is impossible! (Noun clause is subject of *is.*)
> Kira is sorry about *what she said.* (Noun clause is object of preposition *about.*)
> No one knew that *he would be late.* (Noun clause is object of *knew.*)

In these sentences, neither the main clause nor the noun clause can stand by itself. Nonetheless, a sentence containing one main clause and a noun clause is regarded as a complex sentence.

Exercise A: Identify the main clause and the subordinate clause in each of the following complex sentences.

1. This is the house that Frank Lloyd Wright built for himself.
2. If you are finished with your paper by Thursday, we can go to a movie on Friday.
3. The school, which has only 927 students, ordered over 2,000 paperback books last year.
4. Jamie will be able to play center again this year as long as he keeps his grades up.
5. It has been a long time since anyone visited that house.
6. Some scholars believe that writing began as a kind of word magic.
7. In 1494, Spain and Portugal signed the Treaty of Tordesillas, which divided the new world between them.

8. The city that had the first American zoo was Philadelphia.
9. We saw a film on Jack Johnson, who was the first black heavyweight champion of the world.
10. Americans must watch a lot of television because there are more TV sets here than in any other country in the world.

Exercise B: Indicate whether each sentence below is simple, compound, or complex.

1. The world has changed drastically since Edison invented the electric light.
2. The fight against tuberculosis is growing harder because the germs have become resistant to the new drugs.
3. She has wanted to ride on a river boat ever since she read *Life on the Mississippi.*
4. Puerto Rico is called a commonwealth, but just what is a commonwealth?
5. The woman ordered a rose plant for her parents, but the mail-order company sent them a tractor instead.
6. At the South Pole, the sun does not shine for six months.
7. Marysville won the toss and elected to kick.
8. When night came, I lighted a lantern and rolled out our sleeping blankets.
9. The plane taxied out into the takeoff position and started down the runway.
10. Tia stopped talking when the doctor entered the room.

3.8 The Compound-Complex Sentence

A compound-complex sentence consists of two or more main clauses and one or more subordinate clauses.

The main clauses are joined by a coordinating conjunction (preceded by a comma), a conjunctive adverb (preceded by a semicolon), or by a semicolon alone. The subordinate clause modifies a word in one of the main clauses or acts as a noun within one of them.

MAIN CLAUSE	MAIN CLAUSE	SUBORDINATE CLAUSE

It was night,   and we heard the loon   that nested by the lake.

MAIN CLAUSE	MAIN CLAUSE	SUBORDINATE CLAUSE

I will come,   and I will bring José   if he has the day off.

Exercise A: Identify the main clauses and the subordinate clauses in the following compound-complex sentences.

1. The clown looked everywhere for his trumpet, but, since it was in his back pocket, he couldn't find it.
2. Divers sometimes explore the shipwrecks under Lake Superior, but they must be very careful, because these ancient wrecks can be dangerous.
3. After the game is over, a rock band will perform in the school gymnasium, and light refreshments will be served in the cafeteria.
4. Richard Burbage, who was a giant of a man, played the first Hamlet; moreover, he was a shareholder in Shakespeare's theater.
5. While the ship's captain and the first mate were below, a violent storm arose, and a dangerous waterspout was spotted in the distance.
6. There are very few tickets left, but you can still see the Led Zeppelin concert provided you don't mind sitting in the second balcony.
7. Although many of the hits of 1938 have been forgotten, "Jeepers, Creepers" is still popular, and "Flat Foot Floogie with a Floy Floy" has only recently been re-recorded.
8. We enjoyed the jousting at the Renaissance Fair; however, the madrigal singers, who were among the best that I've heard, put on an even more enjoyable show.
9. Van Gogh was one of the greatest painters that Europe has produced; nevertheless, he remained poor all of his life.
10. The white rabbit, who wore a waistcoat and pocket watch, scurried by, and Alice gasped in amazement.

Exercise B: Indicate whether the following sentences are compound, complex, or compound-complex.

1. Wherever you travel on the African sub-continent, you will find people who speak English, French, or Swahili.
2. When the chorus gets into position, the pianist will strike two chords, and the leading man will begin.
3. Rosemary listened to the far-off sound of the calliope, and it seemed that it grew steadily louder.
4. The runner handed the baton to his partner, who took it and ran like lightning.
5. Giorgio is very good with hands, but he lacks patience.
6. Kim loves Martin Leman's paintings of cats, so I bought her one for her birthday.
7. The ski resorts will lose a lot of money unless it snows soon.
8. There are alligators in the swamp, but they will not attack you if you don't bother them.
9. Everyone has some talent, though some people haven't discovered theirs yet.
10. Babe Ruth often hit home runs; accordingly, while he was at the plate, pitchers were usually very nervous.

3.9   The Sentence Redefined

We are now ready to complete the definition of a sentence that we started in Sections 2.1 and 2.3. We may begin by noting once again the differences between phrases and clauses.

A **phrase** is a group of words used within a sentence as a single part of speech. A phrase may be used as a noun, a verb, an adjective, or an adverb. It does *not* contain a subject and a verb.

A **clause** is a group of words that contains a verb and its subject. It may be used as a noun, an adjective, or an adverb.

PHRASE: Walking by the lake...

CLAUSE: When we were walking by the lake...

A main clause can stand by itself as a sentence. A subordinate clause cannot stand by itself.

MAIN CLAUSE   MAIN CLAUSE

The well was dry, and there was no sign of rain.

The well was dry. (*complete*)
There was no sign of rain. (*complete*)

SUBORDINATE CLAUSE   MAIN CLAUSE

Although the well was dry, there was no sign of rain.

There was no sign of rain. (*complete*)
Although the well was dry...(*incomplete*)

Clauses and phrases are sentence parts. Every sentence consists of at least one main clause. A sentence may also include any number of additional clauses or phrases. Our complete definition of a sentence, then, is in three parts:

A sentence is a group of words that

1. expresses a complete thought,
2. contains at least one main clause with a subject and a verb, and
3. may contain subordinate clauses and phrases in addition to the main clause.

REINFORCEMENT EXERCISES
Sentence and Clause

A. Identify the subject and predicate in a simple sentence.
Copy the following sentences. Underline the subject once and the predicate twice. Remember that both subjects and predicates can be compound.

1. The grizzly and the condor are considered endangered species.
2. We will plant the vegetable patch today and paint the fence next weekend.
3. The Kattners often fish for muskies in Wisconsin.
4. The fans and the cheerleaders launched into the school song.
5. Debra took a martial arts class with her cousin.
6. Jenna defeated Sean in ten straight games of ping pong.
7. Luther trains dogs at a local kennel and plays the tuba in the marching band.
8. Bill and his buddy devoured the lasagna.
9. The actors and dancers waited tensely backstage.
10. Squirrels feed in our back yard and make their homes in our trees.

B. Combine simple sentences to form compound sentences.
Combine each pair of simple sentences to form a compound sentence. Use the conjunction in parentheses and add appropriate punctuation.

1. Maria saved us seats on the forty yard line. We saw the action perfectly. (consequently)
2. The library is the oldest building in town. The city council has declared it an historic monument. (therefore)
3. Kara's birthday is next Sunday. We bought her a gift and a card. (so)

4. The antique porcelain platter was cracked. It was still beautiful. (but)
5. José owns a new ten-speed bike. He never rides the bus. (therefore)
6. It was a crisp October day. The squirrels were frantically storing away food for the winter. (and)
7. Smoke curled invitingly from the chimney. The visitors could smell a fantastic dinner being cooked. (moreover)
8. The ground was covered with ice and snow. The deer survived on bark from bushes and saplings. (however)
9. The French club organized a car wash. They didn't make much money because of the rain. (yet)
10. We could go backstage after the show. We could wait for her at the stage door. (or)

C. Identify phrases and clauses. Tell whether the italicized group of words in each of the following sentences is a phrase or a clause.

1. *When I saw the Statue of Liberty,* it was undergoing repair.
2. *After winning the Olympic gold medal,* the U.S. Hockey Team received congratulations from the President.
3. *The most outstanding exhibit at the science fair* was the presentation on the language of bees.
4. *While Gina worked diligently on the crossword puzzle,* Renetta read the national news.
5. *Charging out of the woods,* a six-pronged deer appeared on the path ahead of us.
6. Islam, *the official religion of many Arabic countries,* was founded in the seventh century A.D.
7. *If it rains,* we will have to wear our ponchos on the trip.
8. Professor Gray, *who teaches at Rutgers University,* spoke to the sophomore class about careers in journalism.
9. *Caught in a monstrous traffic jam,* some drivers got out of their cars and began to chat.
10. Some caterpillars live in tent-like webs *that they spin* among tree branches.

D. Identify adjective clauses. Find the adjective clause in each of the following sentences. Then, tell what word each adjective clause modifies.

1. The cat that wandered into our yard three months ago has become a part of the family.
2. Henry Ford, who was a pioneer in the automobile industry, called his first car the "quadricycle."
3. Antarctica, which is the fifth largest continent, contains ninety percent of the earth's ice.
4. Many visitors come each year to Stratford, England, the town where Shakespeare was born.
5. The director chose the actress who seemed most comfortable with the script.
6. Queen Victoria ruled in an age when England was a world power.
7. Dr. Robert Goddard, whose inventions launched the space age, built the first liquid-fueled rocket in 1926.
8. Oberlin, which is located in Ohio, was the first American college for both men and women.
9. The English colony that was established on Roanoke Island in 1587 disappeared without a trace.
10. Benjamin Franklin, who was the author of *Poor Richard's Almanac*, also established the first lending library.

E. Identify adverb clauses. Find the adverb clauses in each of the following sentences. Then, tell what word each clause modifies.

1. Jason finished the oil portrait of his grandmother while she was visiting.
2. Inspector Holmes looked thoughtful as he investigated the scene of the crime.
3. Before we left the reservation, we stopped at a museum of Indian art.
4. After *A Raisin in the Sun* became a hit on Broadway, it was made into a motion picture.

5. Chaing did better on the American history examination than she had expected.
6. If the coach agrees to it, we will wear our new jerseys for the homecoming game.
7. The town will be flooded unless we build a barrier along the river bank.
8. Although his native tongue was Polish, Joseph Conrad became a famous English novelist.
9. The Presidential debates began an hour later than they were expected to.
10. Paul Zindel's popular novel *Pigman* is as serious as it is funny.

F. Identify noun clauses. Find the noun clauses in each of the following sentences. Tell whether each is used as a subject, object, appositive, or predicate word.

1. Who would win the World Series was the question on everyone's mind.
2. Warm Springs, Georgia, is where President Franklin Delano Roosevelt spent the last days of his life.
3. After what the visitor told us about Italy, I became extremely interested in ancient Rome.
4. The shop teacher showed the class how fine, wooden cabinets are made.
5. The article said that the official language of Nigeria is English.
6. Mary scorns the belief that we are being visited by flying saucers.
7. Mountain climbers must remember that snakes sometimes sun themselves on ledges.
8. The crowd wondered which runner would finish the marathon first.
9. That Muddy Waters was a great musician is unquestionable.
10. The anxious competitors wondered whom the judges would select as the winner.

G. Identify complex and compound-complex sentences.
Tell whether each of the following sentences is complex or compound-complex.

1. Because owls sleep during the day, people rarely see them.
2. After they were accepted by the Peace Corps, Coretta went to Peru, and Steven went to Ghana, West Africa.
3. When the tracks were first discovered, the local residents thought that they had been made by an enormous bear.
4. Before he reached the age of twenty-five, John Updike had published many articles and cartoons; moreover, he had also written his first novel.
5. The saraband, which is a slow, graceful dance, originated in Spain.
6. If the weather forces us to cancel our trip, we can still send greeting cards to the rest home, or perhaps some of us could visit the home on our own time.
7. When the trapeze broke, the crowd screamed in panic, but the performers remained calm and leapt to safety.
8. Since the ape house was built, attendance has increased and peanut sales have skyrocketed.
9. I will work for the park district again this summer, provided that the city council approves funds for temporary summer help.
10. The treaty granted Native Americans the land "as long as the rivers flow."

MIXED REVIEW
Sentence and Clause

A. Indicate whether the words in italics are main clauses or subordinate clauses. Then tell whether each subordinate clause is an adjective, adverb, or noun clause.

1. *When you are shopping for winter clothes*, you should consider warmth as well as price and fit.
2. William Pitt was a statesman of great intellect, but *his physical health was poor.*
3. A history play on the career of Henry VIII was the last known work *that Shakespeare wrote.*
4. We will support the candidate *who is the most qualified.*
5. *What career you pursue* will depend upon your interests.
6. *When the referee blows the whistle*, leap for the ball.
7. Although Francis Drake's treatment of Spanish ships sometimes amounted to piracy, *the Queen permitted and encouraged his activities.*
8. The family that you are born into and the people *that you meet* help shape your social behavior and attitudes.
9. Do you know *who wrote the biography of Carrie Chapman?*
10. While the band was playing, *several guards stood in front of the stage.*

B. Identify each sentence as simple, compound, complex, or compound-complex. In addition, find each subordinate clause and tell what kind it is.

1. Blaine demonstrated how she weaves cloth on a loom.
2. The car screeched as it pulled away.
3. Black and white photographs can be very dramatic.
4. Are you on the swimming team, or are you playing basketball this season?

5. A pilot must consider temperature, wind, and visibility.
6. Darryl dropped the bag that contained the two dozen eggs and then he slipped and dropped the bottle of milk.
7. Since she was very young, Bernice has collected hats.
8. Some shoppers hurried through the aisles, but others browsed slowly.
9. While the band members marched, they formed designs on the field.
10. Bert fed the horse oats, and then he placed a blanket on its back while Laura untangled the bridle.
11. The audience cheered wildly when *Stray Cats* appeared on the stage.
12. What annoys Mr. Berman most is tardiness.
13. The Chicago Fire of 1871 destroyed much of the city.
14. If the ice caps melted, much of the earth would be flooded and the temperature would change throughout the world.
15. Joshua wants to drive a car, but he is too young.
16. While everyone slept, snow fell.
17. The man confessed to the crime, but he was innocent.
18. Cobras are poisonous, but pythons are not.
19. The director gave up and sent the camera crew home.
20. The Gutenberg Bible was the first book that was ever printed.

USING GRAMMAR IN WRITING
Sentence and Clause

A. You have just thought of an invention that the whole world is waiting for. You want to sell your marvelous idea to a respected manufacturer so that production can begin on a large scale. Write a few paragraphs to the president of the company explaining why he or she should buy your invention. First try to write an interesting and persuasive letter using only simple sentences. Then expand your letter using complex, compound, and compound-complex sentences. Notice how variation in sentence structure creates a more interesting and exciting writing style.

B. Select a newspaper article that is very interesting or involving. Pretend that you were on the scene or involved in the incident and write your own first person account of it. Use adverb, adjective, and noun clauses to make your writing more interesting to the reader. Label each clause according to its type.

C. If you could move to any part of the world, where would it be? Write an essay explaining why you would like to live there and why everyone else should want to live there, too. Add variety to your writing by using each of the four kinds of sentences: simple, compound, complex, and compound-complex.

D. The types of sentences you use in writing often depend on the audience for whom the piece is intended. An article for children, for example, would contain only short, simple sentences. An article for older students might contain some compound or complex sentences. Finally, an article for adults would probably contain all four types of sentences.

Write a short paragraph on something interesting that you have just learned in science or social studies. First write the paragraph so that an eight-year-old would understand it. Then write it for a junior high student. Finally, write the article as a formal report.

CUMULATIVE REVIEW
Usage (I)

Understanding How Words Are Used. A word or group of words can be used in different ways within a sentence. Study each italicized word, phrase, or subordinate clause. Decide whether it is being used as a *Subject, Verb, Adjective, Adverb, Predicate Word, Direct Object, Indirect Object,* or *Object of a Preposition.* Write each word and your answer next to the number.

1. Turn the *stove off* before the milk boils over.
2. *Walking through the woods* is my favorite *exercise.*
3. Evelyn does not want *to sing at her sister's wedding.*
4. The woman *who is standing on the reviewing stand* is *one* of the judges.
5. *Some* of the Lapps still herd reindeer *across Norway.*
6. Oscar *seems* tired and confused after *staying up all night.*
7. Jack *was walking* up the *stairs* when he slipped on the toy car and fell.
8. The *painting* showed soldiers *leaning wearily against the wall.*
9. Summer never seems to last as long *as it used to.*
10. Scientists *have experimented* with *growing sunflowers in space.*
11. My *Spanish* teacher asked *us* to translate three pages.
12. *Above* we could see several *constellations.*
13. *Few* of us wanted to continue the picnic *in the rain.*
14. The injured player, *who seemed to be in pain,* insisted on *returning to the game.*
15. The veterinarian gave the young *chimp* a bottle *as we watched.*
16. My choir *is singing* at *that* memorial service on Sunday.
17. *Having finished her report,* Mandy went *to bed* and slept.
18. *Here* are *the books* that I borrowed last month.
19. *Who* answered the door *when she rang the bell*?
20. Jack made *himself* a sandwich with the warm garlic *bread.*

4.0 Complete Sentences

Through study and practice, you can learn to write effective and forceful sentences. However, you must learn to avoid two kinds of sentence error: (1) the sentence fragment, and (2) the run-on sentence. Both of these errors cause confusion.

Uncompleted sentences are more often a problem in writing than in speaking. If you use an uncompleted sentence in speaking people can interrupt and ask you what you mean. In writing, however, your reader will simply have to wonder what you meant. This is why you must correct all uncompleted sentences during the revision stage of the writing process.

4.1 Fragments Resulting from Incomplete Thought

An uncompleted sentence is called a **sentence fragment**. It is only a part, or fragment, of a sentence.

You can think much faster than you can write. Many of your sentence errors, if you make them, happen because your mind has raced ahead of your hand. You have started to write a second thought before you have finished writing the first. Or, perhaps in haste, you have left out a key word necessary for a complete sentence. Suppose you intended to say something like this:

In 1939, Ike was a colonel. After war broke out, he soon became commander of American forces in Europe. He later led all Allied forces.

In the hurry to get on with your writing, however, what you put down was something like this:

> In 1939, Ike was a colonel. After he soon became commander of American forces in Europe. He later led all Allied forces.

The second group of words is not a sentence. It causes confusion. The reader may suppose that you meant to say Ike was a colonel after he became commander of American forces in Europe.

Exercise A: Writing Find the sentence fragments. Add the words needed to make each fragment a sentence.

1. The same size as a human child and just as curious
2. A program just like several others
3. After reaching the top of the hill
4. Most of the world's great books available in inexpensive paperback editions
5. Mr. Walters, one of the oldest residents in the city
6. The huge trucks rolling along the nation's highways all night long
7. Finally, in a corner of the garage, the missing boxes
8. Nothing in the newspapers about the robbery
9. There is a reward. Anyone who finds the valuable bracelet
10. After working hard all day, a little relaxation

Exercise B: Writing Three of the groups of words in the following paragraph are sentences. The rest are fragments. Rewrite the paragraph. Add words to make the fragments into sentences.

> Ghost towns all across the country. Pithole, Pennsylvania, one of the most famous. It flourished for a brief ten years. For a time, 20,400 people in the town. Everyone left quickly when the oil wells dried up. Elsewhere, ghost towns in timber country. Modern ghost towns in the iron-mining regions of Minnesota. The most famous of all in the mining sections of the West. Houses full of furniture and offices with papers in the desks. Wherever the resources gave out, there are ghost towns.

4.2 Fragments Resulting from Incorrect Punctuation

The first word of a sentence begins with a capital letter. The sentence is closed by a punctuation mark: *period, question mark*, or *exclamation mark*. A great many sentence fragments occur simply because the writer inserts a period and a capital letter too soon. This error is called a **period fault**.

FRAGMENT:	*Before accepting the invitation.* He called his wife.
SENTENCE:	Before accepting the invitation, he called his wife.
FRAGMENT:	The team was still in the huddle. *When time ran out.*
SENTENCE:	The team was still in the huddle when time ran out.
FRAGMENT:	*At the beginning of this century.* Motoring was an adventure.
SENTENCE:	At the beginning of this century, motoring was an adventure.

Exercise A: Writing Find the fragments. Correct them by changing the punctuation and capitalization or by adding the words needed to make a sentence.

1. Everyone liked the banana cream pie. Except me.
2. Again the sirens wailed. Another accident on the highway.
3. Glenn has been interested in music. For many years.
4. We finally arrived. Just before midnight.
5. Before signing the treaty. The President said a few words.
6. Please send your order. As soon as possible.
7. Linda joined the debate team. Hoping to improve her public speaking skills.
8. The average American teen-ager watches TV. Almost 22 hours each week.
9. The instructor taught yoga three days a week. From 9:00 to 10:30 A.M.
10. Quarterback Ken Stabler, a leader in pass completions. Plays for the Oakland Raiders.

Exercise B: Writing Combine each fragment in Column A with a sentence from Column B to make ten complete sentences. You may have to add additional words.

COLUMN A

1. Singing the theme song from *Fame*
2. Scattering eggs all over
3. A natural talent
4. To work during the Men at Work concert
5. Including the Tidal Wave at Great America
6. And then the barn
7. A thrilling experience
8. Before the deadline
9. Ready for take-off
10. And his tape recorder

COLUMN B

A. Did you finish your project?
B. Larry sold his bike.
C. The haystack caught fire.
D. An article rated the top ten roller coasters.
E. Sixteen ushers were hired.
F. Alice played the piano effortlessly.
G. We did some grammar exercises.
H. The plane taxied down the runway.
I. The truck slid.
J. Susan roller-skated through the park.

4.3 Phrases as Fragments

You know that a phrase is a group of words that does not contain a verb and its subject. A phrase, therefore, cannot be a sentence by itself. It is a *part* of a sentence.

You are not likely to mistake a prepositional phrase for a complete sentence. If you write a long prepositional phrase or a series of phrases as a sentence, it is probably because you have punctuated incorrectly.

FRAGMENT: *In the first place.* He has had no experience in public office.

SENTENCE: In the first place, he has had no experience in public office.

You are more likely to mistake a verbal phrase for a complete sentence. This error occurs because verbals look like verbs and function somewhat like verbs. Like verbs, they may be modified by adverbs and followed by objects or predicate words. They are not complete verbs, however, and cannot be used as such.

The most troublesome verbals are those that end in *-ing*. All gerunds and present participles end in *-ing*. You will avoid many sentence errors if you will remember this fact:

No word ending in *-ing* can be a complete verb unless it is a one-syllable word like *sing, ring,* or *bring*.

If an *-ing* word is preceded by *is, are, was,* or some other form of *be,* the two words together are a verb.

PARTICIPLE	COMPLETE VERB
reading	is reading
running	had been running
studying	were studying

A long infinitive phrase may sometimes be mistaken for a complete sentence. Such a phrase sounds like a sentence since it often has everything that a sentence requires except a subject.

INCORRECT:	Ray has a plan. To go to Greece.
CORRECT:	Ray has a plan. His scheme is to go to Greece.
INCORRECT:	Vera was overjoyed. To be one of the top contenders for a National Merit Scholarship.
CORRECT:	Vera was overjoyed to be one of the top contenders for a National Merit Scholarship.

A noun and an appositive phrase are sometimes written incorrectly as a complete sentence. Although the combination may seem like a sentence, it lacks a verb.

FRAGMENT:	The rocket, *the heaviest ever launched.*
SENTENCE:	The rocket, the heaviest ever launched, roared toward the moon.
SENTENCE:	The rocket was the heaviest ever launched.

Exercise A: Writing Rewrite the following groups of words to make complete sentences. You may need to add words.

1. Margo arranged with the band. To play an extra hour.
2. The leader of the expedition. A scientist of wide experience.
3. Studying the ocean as a source of food and minerals.
4. We had seen the program before. A fascinating explanation of sound waves.
5. Bases loaded with Steve Garvey at bat.
6. Jane delighted with the chance to visit Hawaii.
7. The reporter asked Sen. Glenn. About running for President.
8. Pete and his friends busy making plans for the hike.
9. Sally has a great ambition. To become a surgeon.
10. Was *The Thorn Birds* made into a movie? Starring Richard Chamberlain.

Exercise B: Follow the same directions as for Exercise A.

1. The newspaper story, an unfair statement of what had actually happened.
2. We waited in line for hours. To buy tickets for the Elvis Costello concert.
3. The two books, one a true story and the other a fictional account of Frémont's expedition.
4. The *Mary Deare* found drifting with no crew aboard.
5. The need for more food for the world's population.
6. The boy told his story. Expecting no one to believe him.
7. The class adviser arranged for a bus. To take the group to the contest.
8. The Rose Bowl, the Gator Bowl, the Orange Bowl, and the Cotton Bowl. Only a few of football's "bowls."
9. The unhappy motorist searching her pockets for her license.
10. The book an account of how the mighty Spanish Armada was defeated.

4.4 Clauses as Fragments

A subordinate clause cannot stand alone as a sentence. (See Section 3.3.) A sentence may be changed into a subordinate clause by having a subordinating conjunction placed before it.

> SENTENCE: We were paddling the canoes upstream.
>
> SUBORDINATE CLAUSE: As we were paddling the canoes upstream . . .

Writers sometimes mistakenly place a period before or after a subordinate clause as though it were a sentence.

> INCORRECT: When we saw the smoke. We leaped on our horses.
> CORRECT: When we saw the smoke, we leaped on our horses.

> INCORRECT: Richard was excited. Because he was going to Colorado.
> CORRECT: Richard was excited because he was going to Colorado.

Exercise A: Writing Rewrite the word groups below to eliminate the fragments.

1. Beth is the only one. Who knew the answers.
2. We stayed in the mountains. Until the first snow fell.
3. She took the old painting. Since nobody else wanted it.
4. Although the book is unusually long. It is worth reading.
5. There will be a big celebration in Pittsburgh. When the Pirates win the pennant.
6. Linda is studying forestry. Because she likes outdoor life.
7. Preparing a report on the rock collection that we had started the year before.
8. Ruth decided to buy the red coat. Even though her mother disliked it.
9. We will be glad to see you. Whenever you can come.
10. In the camp, the explorers checked their pitons. Which are spikes used for climbing steep rock faces.

Exercise B: Writing In this exercise you will find examples of many kinds of fragments. Change them into sentences.

1. Thomas Jefferson wrote the final draft of the Declaration of Independence. At the age of thirty-three.
2. A mother rhinoceros always keeps her baby ahead of her. As she walks along.
3. India has over two hundred languages. And many religions.
4. My library at home contains many paperbacks. Also books with beautiful, gold-tooled leather covers.
5. John Updike wrote "A & P." One of the most famous short stories of our time.
6. In a full orchestra, there are four families of instruments. Stringed instruments, woodwinds, brasses, and percussion instruments.
7. She is one of those overly cautious people. Always raising objections.
8. Northern Canada is a vast Arctic wasteland. Has a few people, large herds of caribou, and numerous species of fur-bearing animals.
9. The needle of a compass always points north. Because it is attracted by a center of magnetic force near the North Pole.
10. Edison's first electric light burned for approximately forty hours. The average life of a 100-watt bulb today over 750 hours of service.

4.5   Run-on Sentences

A **run-on sentence** is two or more sentences written as though they were one sentence. That is, the writer fails to use a period or other end mark at the end of each sentence.

RUN-ON:	Carlotta went fishing last month she caught a shoe.
CORRECT:	Carlotta went fishing last month. She caught a shoe.
RUN-ON:	Pedro went to the clinic he had cut his arm.
CORRECT:	Pedro went to the clinic. He had cut his arm.

The most common run-on sentence error is the joining of two sentences by a comma. This error is called the **comma fault**.

COMMA FAULT: The club held a car wash, it was a great success.

CORRECT: The club held a car wash. It was a great success.

COMMA FAULT: The critic read the book, she then wrote a review.

CORRECT: The critic read the book. She then wrote a review.

In all of the foregoing examples, notice that the two sentences are closely related and that the second sentence begins with a personal pronoun: *it, he, she.* Watch for situations like these in your own writing and avoid the comma fault.

4.6   Avoiding the Run-on Sentence

There is no objection to joining two or more closely related statements into one sentence. In fact, it is often better to join them than to write them separately. There are three ways to join sentences to make a compound sentence: (1) with a comma and a coordinating conjunction; (2) with a semicolon; (3) with a semicolon and a conjunctive adverb. A conjunctive adverb is usually followed by a comma.

RUN-ON: Neal has two choices. He can play college football, he can sign with the Yankees.

CORRECT: Neal has two choices. He can play college football, or he can sign with the Yankees.

RUN-ON: Churchill led England through the agonizing war years, then he was defeated in the first postwar election.

CORRECT: Churchill led England through the agonizing war years; then he was defeated in the first postwar election.

RUN-ON: The demonstration was orderly, consequently,
the mayor heard our plea.

CORRECT: The demonstration was orderly; consequently,
the mayor heard our plea.

Exercise A: Correct each of the following run-on sentences in one of these ways: (1) by using a period and a capital letter; (2) by using a semicolon; or (3) by using a comma and *and, but,* or *or.*

1. We flew to Idaho Falls, then we took a bus to the lake.
2. Andy tries to practice the flute every day, however, he doesn't always have time.
3. Ms. Albrecht has a new car, it is a Dodge Challenger.
4. Cooking a turkey takes hours, it has to be started early.
5. Howard University is small, nevertheless, it has an excellent faculty.
6. The station was crowded, we nearly missed our train.
7. It isn't a new dress, I wore it to the Christmas party.
8. Pat hasn't called, he must be lost.
9. We planned a dance, however, the band never arrived.
10. Mom painted the chairs, they look very nice.
11. Mark is color-blind, therefore, he needs help selecting his clothes.
12. Sand the redwood, then you can apply the lacquer.
13. The fog was very heavy, no planes left the airport.
14. Larry started to cross the street, then the light changed.
15. Jim hesitated too long, consequently, he missed his chance.

Exercise B: Writing The first part of a sentence is given on each line. Add a second main clause, starting it with the word in parentheses. If the word is a conjunctive adverb, place a semicolon before it and a comma after it. If the word is a personal pronoun, use a semicolon or a comma with a coordinating conjunction.

1. The deer started to cross the road (then)
2. The author of the article is Mel Brooks (he)
3. We were not expecting you today (however)

4. The road was strewn with heavy branches (it)
5. The class had had plenty of time to study (nonetheless)
6. Jan and Sylvia were late to class (they)
7. The driver had simply been going too fast (moreover)
8. The town's population has been declining (consequently)
9. Eve will be working next summer (she)
10. Willy could scarcely lift the package (it)
11. First you send for an application blank (then)
12. We are rapidly exhausting some of our natural resources (for example)
13. Most words have more than one meaning (therefore)
14. You have seen this book before (it)
15. In the clear desert air, the mountains look very close (they)

Exercise C: Writing Copy this paragraph, correcting the run-on sentences.

None of us could believe that Harry was guilty, he had never been known to do anything dishonest. He had always been careful to give customers the exact change, yet he was now charged with pilfering the cash register at his checkout counter. The manager himself usually picked up the extra cash twice a day, however, on Thursday he waited until the store closed. He put Harry's cash in a separate bag, then he locked it up in the safe. When he counted it the next morning it was ten dollars short. He accused Harry of pocketing the money, however, Harry denied the charge. He thought for a while, then he asked to count the money. The manager agreed, he stood beside Harry while he counted. Harry went through each stack of bills slowly, he found the ten dollars. Two ten-dollar bills had stuck together. The manager and his assistant apologized, they even let Harry pick up the cash from the checkout counters the next week to show that they trusted him.

REINFORCEMENT EXERCISES
Complete Sentences

A. Correct fragments resulting from incomplete thoughts.
Rewrite each of the following fragments. Make each one into a complete sentence.

1. One of the most popular series ever shown on television
2. Brakes screeching and horns honking
3. Scaling the sheer face of the mountain
4. After working in the factory for almost forty years
5. On Halloween, at midnight
6. Lincoln High's star quarterback, Jim Taylor
7. The Pacific salmon swimming upstream
8. After living for years on an isolated mountain top
9. Its windows boarded up
10. Hurtling through outer space at more than six thousand miles per hour

B. Correct fragments resulting from incorrect punctuation.
Decide if the following are complete sentences or fragments. Correct the fragments. Write *S* for complete sentences.

1. The Union Pacific Railroad was completed in 1869. Linking the country from coast to coast.
2. David was pulled over by the police officer. Who gave him his second ticket this year.
3. Michelle went to state in track. For the second year in a row.
4. Scientists have discovered evidence of a new planet. Outside the orbit of Pluto.
5. The four friends were the stars of the basketball team. They had known each other since kindergarten.
6. We bought sponges in Tarpon Springs, Florida. Which is famous for glass-bottomed boats.

7. George Lucas and Steven Spielberg have been responsible for the top-grossing films. In the history of movies.
8. A flag flew from the roof of Shakespeare's theater. It signaled that a play would be performed that day.
9. This plant fossil is sixty-five million years old. It was found in Colorado.
10. The Lipizzan stallions from Vienna. Perform all over the world.

C. Correct fragments that are phrases. Correct the fragments in the following paragraph by connecting them to make complete sentences.

Every year, people from all over America gather in the little community of Bean Blossom, Indiana. To take part in the annual Bill Monroe Bluegrass Festival. The festival is a combination of old and new. A celebration of traditional and contemporary bluegrass music. It offers the finest in good old-fashioned, foot-stomping entertainment. Including music by the best bluegrass bands in the country. Visitors to the festival stroll up and down several acres of lovely Indiana countryside. Listening to melodies with names like "Salty Dog" and "Tea for Texas." They can applaud the skilled musicians. Playing on instruments that range from banjos and mandolins to fiddles, autoharps, and guitars.

D. Correct fragments that are clauses. Rewrite the following word groups to make them complete sentences.

1. While we were at the beach. I collected some sand dollars and conch shells.
2. Coach Monterstelli was extremely pleased. Because Brad and Doug won a trophy.
3. Since it is wrapped in a dense layer of cloud. Jupiter has always been something of a mystery.
4. I saw the *Courier-Journal* photographer. As I was leaving the camera store.

5. Until my bicycle is repaired. I will be taking the bus to school.
6. We put everything inside the tent. Because it was raining.
7. If more tickets are not sold. The promoters will cancel the concert.
8. I will bring paper plates and silverware. Provided that you bring all of the food and refreshments.
9. The West was not settled. Until gold was discovered in California.
10. Marty remembered his keys. After he had locked the car door.

E. Correct run-on sentences.   Correct each of the following run-on sentences.

1. We arrived at Ticketron at 6:00 A.M., we were determined to get good seats for the Police concert.
2. Eaves are the part of a roof that hangs over the outside wall, they help protect the walls from rain and snow.
3. John took a special class in computers he thought it would help him find a summer job.
4. Evelyn and Vicky presented opposing views on the issue, Evelyn favored thin crust pizza, Vicky favored the thick variety.
5. Leonard was chosen captain of the bowling team, his average score was over 220.
6. All race horses have their official birthday on January first, in the Southern Hemisphere the date is August first.
7. Our bus broke down on the way to school, we missed our first class, we were disappointed.
8. Johnny Carson is the highest paid performer in television he makes nearly five million dollars a year.
9. My parents get two weeks' vacation, we usually go to Wyoming.
10. Friendly Plains Indians allowed wagon trains to pass through their hunting grounds, some even helped the pioneers cross rivers.

F. Find and correct run-on sentences. Rewrite the following paragraph, correcting all the run-on sentences. For some run-ons, simply separate the sentences. For others, use commas with coordinating conjunctions, semicolons, or semicolons with conjunctive adverbs.

Many people agree that Wilt Chamberlain is the greatest player in the history of the National Basketball Association, he holds an incredible number of records. In one season, he played the most complete games he played the most on-court minutes of any player. He led the league in scoring for seven straight years, and he has scored the most lifetime points his record is 31,419 points scored. In a game against New York in 1962, Chamberlain scored fifty-nine points in one half, he ended up scoring one hundred points in the game. His lifetime scoring average is over thirty points per game most players don't score that many points in any game. Chamberlain also holds records for the most field goals in one game, thirty-six, and for the most free throws in one game, twenty-eight. He was also a champion rebounder, he led the league in rebounds for eleven seasons, and he made a career total of 23,924. Chamberlain played for Philadelphia, San Francisco, and Los Angeles during his career all three teams wish they had him back now.

MIXED REVIEW

Complete Sentences

A. Rewrite the following paragraph, correcting all sentence fragments and incorrectly placed punctuation.

Africa. A continent of contrast, compelling wonder, and awe-inspiring splendor. Deserts and rain forests. Vast stretches of level land are followed by rolling grasslands. Called *savannas*. There are also lands that dry, crack, and crumble each year when rains cease. Then turn to mud when the rains come. Cool, pleasant highlands.

Africa contains the longest river in the world. This is the Nile. Which courses 4,130 miles from the highlands of East Africa northward to the Mediterranean Sea. The most magnificent falls, mist-shrouded Victoria, a 355-foot plunge of the Zambesi river between Zambia and Rhodesia. And snow-capped mountains, like twin-peaked Kilimanjaro in Tanzania. Rising 19,340 feet above the level of the sea.

B. The following paragraph is one long run-on sentence. Correct the run-ons with proper punctuation and capitalization.

Scott Joplin came from a musical family in Texarkana, Texas, he was interested in music from an early age the future King of Ragtime began to play the piano while he was still a boy eventually, Joplin left his home and began playing his music on steamboats that traveled on the Mississippi after several years of developing his own special style Joplin decided to receive formal training in music Joplin published his "Maple Leaf Rag" in 1899 then he moved to St. Louis to devote himself to the composition of serious full-length works Joplin wrote a ballet and two operas by 1916 his work was never fully appreciated he was a broken man when he died his work faded from public notice but it has been revived in recent years.

C. In this exercise, you will find fragments and run-ons. Rewrite them to make complete sentences.

1. The campers pitched their tent, they had found a perfect spot.
2. They hung their provisions from a tree. To prevent animals from getting the food.
3. Jeanne's favorite foods are spaghetti, steak, and ice cream. Dripping with chocolate sauce.
4. Feeling extremely happy about his high grades in math and computer science this semester.
5. Jon practices karate at home, his sister is an instructor at the community center.
6. Lee has tickets to the Superbowl, it will be held in Miami.
7. The article that I read in *Rolling Stone* about Lacy J. Dalton.
8. Would you like to appear on a TV talk show? Or on a game show?
9. Rosemary felt strange and lonely in her new school. Which was very large.
10. The Lindsays have built an underground home. Because it will conserve heating energy.

D. Rewrite the following paragraph, correcting all sentence fragments and run-ons.

The idea of moving from one level of a building to another without the use of stairs has long been a challenge to inventors. Even before the development of skyscrapers and high-rise buildings. The first machine to answer this challenge was the "Flying Chair" it was built in 18th-century France. For King Louis XV. It took the king from his balcony to the chamber above. Using an intricate system of concealed weights. Early in the 19th century, an elevator was built in London. Known as the "Ascending Room." Towards the middle of the century elevators were being installed in New York hotels and department stores, today they continue to be invaluable to people whose legs will not carry them up long flights of stairs.

USING GRAMMAR IN WRITING
Complete Sentences

A. Imagine that you are the captain of a rescue team searching for a lost group of explorers in the Amazon jungle. You receive a radio communication from the explorers. However, the signal is faint, and you can only hear fragments of what is being said. These fragments are listed below. Try to figure out what is being said by turning these fragments into complete sentences.

> . . . is Captain . . . you read me . . . Julio, of the Amazon exploration team . . . not lost . . . located approximately three miles northeast of the village Quizotl . . . cannot move from our position . . . explosion in our camp . . . most of our party . . . quickly . . . medical supplies and blankets.

B. Imagine that you are an archeologist working among ancient Egyptian ruins. You have discovered a broken tablet covered with hieroglyphics. You translate these, and arrange the pieces of the tablet in the order shown below. The last steps in your translation are to complete any fragments as best you can and to punctuate your final version. Avoid sentence fragments and run-ons.

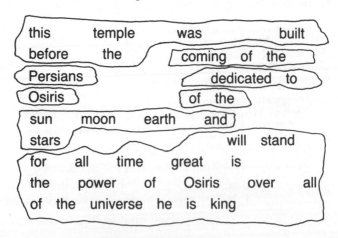

this temple was built
before the coming of the
Persians dedicated to
Osiris of the
sun moon earth and
stars will stand
for all time great is
the power of Osiris over all
of the universe he is king

CUMULATIVE REVIEW
The Sentence (I)

Kinds of Sentences. The paragraphs below contain simple sentences, compound sentences, complex sentences, and compound-complex sentences. Number your paper from 1 to 10. Next to each number, write either *S, CD, CX,* or *CD-CX* to identify the type of sentence it is. Also write *INT* next to the number of the interrogative sentence, and *E* next to the number of the exclamatory sentence.

(1) One person who is always mentioned in discussions of the Renaissance is Leonardo da Vinci. (2) He lived approximately five hundred years ago in Italy, but he is still honored today as a gifted artist and an engineer of great genius. (3) His versatility has long amazed those who study his life, for Da Vinci did research in the areas of mathematics, architecture, music, optics, astronomy, geology, botany, zoology, hydraulics, aeronautics, and anatomy. (4) What an incredible range of interests! (5) How did this man develop such a fascination for the world around him?

(6) Although he was the son of a peasant girl and was only meagerly educated in his father's home, Da Vinci became apprenticed to a painter in Florence as a teenager. (7) As he mastered various mediums of art, the young man continued his studies of nature, but he became more secretive about his studies as he grew older. (8) For example, while working in Milan as a painter and a designer of military devices, Da Vinci began keeping secret notebooks containing drawings and notes written in mirror writing.

(9) In his mature years, Da Vinci worked in Florence, Rome, Milan, and France painting pictures and beginning many more works of art and architecture that were never completed. (10) As death approached, Da Vinci despaired that he had finished so little of what he might have accomplished; he was unaware that the magnificent works that he had completed were enough to ensure his immortality.

CUMULATIVE REVIEW
The Sentence (II)

Correcting Fragments and Run-Ons. On your own paper, re-write the following passage. Correct all sentence fragments and run-on sentences. You may have to change or add a few words, but many of the errors can be corrected with changes in punctuation and capitalization only.

The Old City of Jerusalem is a holy place to Muslims, Christians, and Jews. Containing within its walls the place from which Muslims believe that Mohammed ascended to heaven, the spot where Christians believe Jesus was killed and rose again, and the site where Jews believe Solomon's Temple once stood and will someday be rebuilt. The Old City makes up less than one percent of the modern city of Jerusalem, the larger city is now the home of about 407,000 people. Israel's largest city.

In medieval times, Christian crusaders fought Jews and Muslims for control of the city, these crusaders established a kingdom there in A.D. 1099 that lasted for about one hundred years. For the next six hundred years, the city was inhabited mainly by Muslims from Egypt, Syria, and Turkey. Until 1917, when a British army captured the city. After this, both Jews and Muslims flocked there. Jerusalem was a divided city until 1967, when Israel won control of the entire city. In the Six Day War.

Muslims, Christians, and Jews continue to live in the city, however, relations among these peoples of different faiths are sometimes stormy. Even violent. Despite the violence, Jerusalem continues to be holy land for three of the world's great religions.

5.0 Verb Usage

There are several thousand verbs in our language. Most of these verbs have several forms, each of which is useful for particular purposes. In order to use verbs correctly, you must learn how to recognize and make these forms. You must also learn when each form is appropriate. Mastery of the use of verbs will help you to become an effective speaker and writer.

5.1 The Principal Parts of Verbs

Every verb has many different forms. All of these forms are made from the three **principal parts** of the verb. These principal parts include (1) **the present infinitive** (usually called simply **the present**), (2) **the past,** and (3) **the past participle.**

A **regular verb** is one that forms its past and past participle by adding -ed or -d to the present form of the verb. Most verbs fall into this category.

PRESENT	PAST	PAST PARTICIPLE
talk	talked	talked
dazzle	dazzled	dazzled
arrive	arrived	arrived

An **irregular verb** is one that does not form its past and past participle by adding -ed or -d to the present. Approximately sixty commonly used verbs fall into this category.

PRESENT	PAST	PAST PARTICIPLE
burst	burst	burst
sing	sang	sung
freeze	froze	frozen

Both regular and irregular verbs have one other form, sometimes considered a fourth principal part, called the **present participle.** This form is made by adding -ing to the present form: *see–seeing, play—playing, leave—leaving.*

5.2 Irregular Verbs

Because the principal parts of irregular verbs are formed in unusual ways, people sometimes have trouble choosing the correct form.

The past form is used alone. The past participle form is used with forms of *be* or *have*.

Barbara Walters *began* the interview. (past)
Barbara Walters *had* already *begun* the interview.
    (past participle)

Once you understand this rule, you need only familiarize yourself with the past and past participle forms of the most commonly used irregular verbs.

There are five groups of irregular verbs that you should become familiar with. These groups are determined by how the verbs form their principal parts.

Group 1. The easiest of the irregular verbs are those that have the same form in all principal parts.

PRESENT	PAST	PAST PARTICIPLE
burst	burst	(have) burst
cost	cost	(have) cost
hit	hit	(have) hit
hurt	hurt	(have) hurt
put	put	(have) put
set	set	(have) set
shut	shut	(have) shut

Group 2. A second group of irregular verbs that causes little difficulty is composed of verbs that have the same form for both the past and the past participle.

PRESENT	PAST	PAST PARTICIPLE
bring	brought	(have) brought
catch	caught	(have) caught
dive	dived *or* dove°	(have) dived
fight	fought	(have) fought
flee	fled	(have) fled
fling	flung	(have) flung
get	got	(have) got *or* gotten
lead	led	(have) led
lend	lent	(have) lent
lose	lost	(have) lost
say	said	(have) said
shine	shone	(have) shone
sit	sat	(have) sat
sting	stung	(have) stung
swing	swung	(have) swung

°Where two forms are given, both are standard usage, but the first is more common.

Exercise A: Choose the standard form from those in parentheses.

1. As usual, the plumber's assistant has (brung, brought) the wrong tools.
2. Running at top speed, Cal reached up and (catched, caught) the ball on his fingertips.
3. Last week the baby (hurt, hurted) herself on the sidewalk.
4. If the vampire mask had (cost, costed) less, I would have bought it.
5. Carlotta had never (dove, dived) from a diving platform.
6. When his parents suggested a bath, the child (fleed, fled).
7. Robert Graves's poem (sayed, said) that love is a universal headache.
8. With a little help from a pin, the balloon (burst, bursted).
9. Frank claimed that he had been (stang, stung) by an unidentified flying object.
10. The waiting sharks turned and (fleed, fled) as the ship approached.
11. Someone had (flang, flinged, flung) a burning cigarette from a car.
12. Gail generously (lent, lended) Greg money to buy a taco.
13. Lewis (lead, led) us up the face of the cliff.
14. George returned the book that you (lented, lent) him.
15. The travelers had (losed, lost) their way in the storm.
16. The moon (shone, shined) brightly as we crossed the desert.
17. The hot liquid (stang, stung) my throat.
18. When we had finished, the car (shone, shined) like new.
19. The crane slowly (swang, swung) the girders into place.
20. Lars had (caught, catched) a skunk in his trap.

Exercise B: In the sentences below, the present form of the verb is given in parentheses. Substitute either the past or past participle, whichever the sentence requires.

1. One of the teachers had (bring) a portable television set.
2. A canary (sit) on the classroom window ledge.
3. Rick (get) an invitation in the mail.

4. Ms. Allen (bring) out the fact that we need more books.
5. Two of the escaping convicts were (catch) in the swamp.
6. The twins, the babysitter said, had (fight) all night.
7. Without awaiting an answer, John (flee) from the house.
8. Papers had been (fling) all over the lawn.
9. Suddenly, the lifeguard (dive) into the pool.
10. That purchase (lead) us ever deeper into debt.
11. We had (lend) the wheelbarrow to our neighbors.
12. How many games have we (lose) this year?
13. The light (shine) into my eyes so that I could hardly see.
14. The divers had been badly (sting) by jellyfish.
15. The batter (swing) at the first pitch and popped it into the stands.
16. As we passed, the men in the boat (fling) up their arms in salute.
17. Rosemary has (lead) the band for three years.
18. The sun had (shine) on only one day of our vacation.
19. The crane (swing) crazily out over the street.
20. Ned (lend) me a dollar to buy some notebook paper.

Group 3. Another group of irregular verbs adds *-n* or *-en* to the past form to make the past participle.

PRESENT	PAST	PAST PARTICIPLE
bear	bore	(have) borne°
beat	beat	(have) beaten
bite	bit	(have) bitten
break	broke	(have) broken
choose	chose	(have) chosen
freeze	froze	(have) frozen
speak	spoke	(have) spoken
steal	stole	(have) stolen
swear	swore	(have) sworn
tear	tore	(have) torn
wear	wore	(have) worn

°Note that *borne* retains the final *e*.

Exercise A: Choose the standard form from those in parentheses.

1. Fran (bore, beared, borne) the family burdens all alone.
2. The batter should be (beat, beaten) until it is smooth.
3. I thought I had (bit, bitten) into a piece of metal.
4. All heat records were (broke, broken) last summer.
5. Deirdre had already (chose, chosen) a camera for her birthday present.
6. The car door (froze, frozen) shut.
7. Mr. Davis had (spoke, spoken) against driver education.
8. The stowaways had (stole, stolen) onto the ship at night.
9. The men had (swore, sworn) to hold the fort or die.
10. Two pages had been (tore, torn) out of the index.
11. Dad (wore, worn) the same old hat for five years.
12. The natives (beared, bore) the casket to the top of the hill.
13. The town had (born, borne) the full fury of the tornado.
14. The Cardinals were badly (beat, beaten) in the championship game.
15. A little boy's finger was (bit, bitten) by a big dog.
16. All of our dishes (broke, broken) when the van turned over.
17. Ramona has been (chose, chosen) to give an address at the commencement exercises.
18. Because of the unusually early cold, many ponds were (froze, frozen).
19. The heavy traffic has (tore, torn) up the road.
20. The rocks had been (worn, wore) down by the waterfall.

Exercise B: In the sentences below, the present form of the verb is given in parentheses. Substitute either the past or the past participle, whichever the sentence requires.

1. Betty hasn't (wear) her new suit yet.
2. The new president was (swear) into office by her father.
3. Squirrels (steal) the food you put out for the birds.
4. I have already (speak) to the boss about a raise.
5. On the hike, Steve's ears were badly (freeze).
6. The new coach has already been (choose).

7. Hundreds of windows were (break) by the explosion.
8. When Cindy delivered papers, she was (bite) by that dog.
9. Jim's ankle was (break) in the first play of the game.
10. The flowers had been (beat) down by the rain.
11. The twins (bear) little resemblance to each other.
12. The wreckers (tear) down the old building in two weeks.
13. Someone has (break) the power mower.
14. Derek (swear) he had been at home all day.
15. The pond had (freeze) solid early in November.
16. The reindeer had been (steal) from the hotel's lawn.
17. The wind had (tear) the door off its hinges.
18. Mr. Alvarez has never been (beat) in an election.
19. During the night we were attacked and (bite) by gnats.
20. I think Hilda has (speak) for all of us.

Group 4. Another group of irregular verbs is alike in changing the middle vowel from *i* in the present, to *a* in the past, and to *u* in the past participle. Memorize these seven verbs as a unit. They are the only verbs that follow this pattern.

PRESENT	PAST	PAST PARTICIPLE
begin	began	(have) begun
drink	drank	(have) drunk
ring	rang	(have) rung
sing	sang	(have) sung
sink	sank *or* sunk	(have) sunk
spring	sprang *or* sprung	(have) sprung
swim	swam	(have) swum

Exercise A: Choose the standard form from those in parentheses.

1. As children, we had always (sung, sang) "Auld Lang Syne" on New Year's Eve.
2. Coach Robinson was happy that we had (begun, began) our debate season with such a strong team.
3. Yesterday, Dorothy (sinked, sank) a hole in one.
4. The audience applauded when the rabbit (springed, sprang) from the magician's top hat.

5. When Todd reached the river, he found that his dog had already (swum, swam) to the opposite bank.
6. Whenever the temperature rose above eighty degrees, Wayne (drunk, drank) lots of root beer and iced tea.
7. The trained mice (rung, rang) a bell for food.
8. My dachshund always (sung, sang) along with my Pat Benatar records.
9. The skipper couldn't see the submarine because it had (sunk, sank) beneath the surface.
10. The paramedics had (sprung, sprang) into action even before the alarm sounded.
11. Finally we (begun, began) to see her point.
12. The *Andrea Doria* (sinked, sank) off the coast of Nantucket.
13. The cashier had already (rung, rang) up the charge.
14. Linda had (drunk, drank) too much grape juice at the party.
15. The car's door was (sprung, sprang) in the smashup.
16. Ricardo had (swum, swam) halfway across the lake before anyone noticed him.
17. Susan (begun, began) classes this week at Bethel College.
18. The ship exploded and (sinked, sank) immediately.
19. Have they ever (sung, sang) the "Hallelujah Chorus"?
20. Barry (springed, sprang) out like a jack-in-the-box.

Exercise B: The present form is given in parentheses. Substitute the past or past participle, whichever the sentence requires.

1. Has the voting (begin) yet?
2. The three boys had (drink) a gallon of milk.
3. Sarah walked up the steps and (ring) the bell.
4. Has Alex ever (sing) before an audience?
5. The orchestra had (begin) the overture.
6. All the other swimmers floated; I (sink).
7. The shopkeeper asked if her phone had (ring).
8. The weighted line (sink) quickly to the bottom.
9. The dogs (spring) at each other in great fury.
10. A seventeen-year-old girl has (swim) across Lake Ontario.

11. The snow (begin) to fall shortly after midnight.
12. That alto (sing) off-key in my ear.
13. The toy (sink) slowly to the bottom of the pond.
14. The rescued pilot (drink) the water slowly in tiny sips.
15. In 1979, U.S. Olympic competitor, Cynthia Woodhead, (swim) the 200-meter freestyle in less than two minutes.
16. As the band played, the crowd (sing) the national anthem.
17. Church bells (ring) across the nation when the first transcontinental railroad was completed.
18. Our relay team had (swim) the race in record time.
19. The pipe was (sink) and anchored in concrete.
20. The volunteers had (spring) into action during the fire.

Group 5. Another group of irregular verbs is alike in making the past participle from the present form rather than from the past.

PRESENT	PAST	PAST PARTICIPLE
blow	blew	(have) blown
come	came	(have) come
do	did	(have) done
draw	drew	(have) drawn
drive	drove	(have) driven
eat	ate	(have) eaten
fall	fell	(have) fallen
give	gave	(have) given
go	went	(have) gone
grow	grew	(have) grown
know	knew	(have) known
ride	rode	(have) ridden
rise	rose	(have) risen
run	ran	(have) run
see	saw	(have) seen
shake	shook	(have) shaken
slay	slew	(have) slain
take	took	(have) taken
throw	threw	(have) thrown
write	wrote	(have) written

Exercise A: Choose the standard form from those in parentheses.

1. Carmen sat in the car and (blowed, blew) the horn.
2. Darla (come, came) running down the driveway.
3. By noon we had already (did, done) a day's work.
4. A police car (drawed, drew) up beside the truck.
5. Mr. Cobb had (drove, driven) off to the side of the road for a nap.
6. The birds have (ate, eaten) all the seeds we put out.
7. The old house has (fell, fallen) into disrepair.
8. Ms. Hanley (give, gave) her nephew a ten-year loan to cover college expenses.
9. Our neighbors have (gone, went) to Miami for the winter.
10. One of my friends (grew, growed) four inches in a year.
11. We should have (know, knowed, known) that the stores would be closed today.
12. The girls had (rode, ridden) a bus all morning to get to the capital.
13. This successful business is (ran, run) entirely by students.
14. Nick just (shaked, shook) his head and said nothing.
15. Fewer people were (slew, slain) in medieval battles than in modern ones.
16. Jeff felt that he had been (took, taken) for granted.
17. The road crews (threw, throwed) sand and salt on the icy roads.
18. It's lucky we have (wrote, written) ahead for reservations.
19. Our class has (wrote, written) a news article every week this semester.
20. Phillip had (saw, seen) tigers before at the Cincinnati Zoo.

Exercise B: The present form is given in parentheses. Substitute the past or past participle, whichever the sentence requires.

1. The ships had been (blow) far off their course in the storm.
2. People had (come) from miles around to see the play.
3. Dad (do) his best to discourage us from buying the old car.
4. The Rose Bowl game (draw) a capacity crowd.

5. When the subways were on strike, we all (drive) into town to get work.
6. Moths had (eat) holes in my winter coat.
7. Trees and telephone poles had (fall) across the road.
8. The coach's inspiring talk (give) us all a lift.
9. Two firefighters had (go) quickly into the blazing building.
10. As midnight approached, we (grow) panicky.
11. It was the worst blizzard that Rochester had ever (know).
12. The scouts had (ride) hard all night to reach the fort.
13. As we came down the hill, two deer (run) across the road right in front of our car.
14. By six in the evening, the Governor had (shake) hands with several hundred people.
15. The actor fell down on the stage, pretending that the gunshot had (slay) him.
16. Someone has (take) down the road sign.
17. One of the passengers was (throw) from her seat when the bus stopped suddenly.
18. Has anything been (do) to improve the water supply for the farms in the middle of the state?
19. Your Christmas package finally (come) in February.
20. No signs of the downed pilots were (see).

5.3 The Progressive and Emphatic Forms of Verbs

The Progressive Forms

To show ongoing action, you use the **progressive forms** of the verb. They are made by using the forms of *be* with the present participle.

She *is running.*	Rob *has been sleeping.*
We *are going.*	The water *had been running.*
The cars *were stalling.*	We *must be going.*
Someone *will be arriving.*	They *might have been shouting.*

The Emphatic Forms

You can give special emphasis to a statement by using *do, does,* or *did* with the present form of the verb. These are examples of **emphatic forms.**

PRESENT: I *like* the new cottage.
PRESENT EMPHATIC: I *do like* the new cottage.
PAST: I *enjoyed* your speech.
PAST EMPHATIC: I *did enjoy* your speech.

Exercise A: Find each verb. Decide whether it is a progressive or emphatic form.

1. What has Karen been doing this summer?
2. The punishment does seem a bit severe.
3. We are now exploring new energy sources.
4. We have been hoping for a new school for years.
5. Artificial respiration does save lives.
6. The lawyer will be filing her brief in court.
7. Geologists do not know the exact age of Earth.
8. Many scientists have been working on cures for cancer.
9. Has anyone been doing anything about decorations?
10. The principal did approve the student council's plan.

Exercise B: Writing Rewrite each sentence, changing the italicized verb to the form indicated in parentheses.

1. Though not a famous figure, Mary E. Outerbridge *introduced* the game of tennis to the United States. (emphatic)
2. Investigators found that the Atlantic blue marlin caught by E. J. Fishman in 1968 really *weighed* 845 pounds. (emphatic)
3. French soldiers *used* the crossbow as early as A.D. 851. (progressive)
4. The audience *applauded* wildly for the leading lady. (progressive)

5. Stanley *had bowled* in our league for years. (progressive)
6. Professor Pauling *studied* the aging process. (progressive)
7. Mocha was a little-known city in Arabia, but it *became* famous for exporting coffee. (emphatic)
8. Marco Polo *had worked* for Kublai Khan for seventeen years when he returned to Europe. (progressive)
9. Attendance has been falling, but the promoters *intend* to continue the concert series anyway. (emphatic)
10. I *go* to register for summer classes today. (progressive)

5.4 Verb Tense

Tense means "time." Most verbs change their forms to show present, past, and future time. Each verb has three simple tenses and three perfect tenses. They are formed as follows:

1. Present tense. The present tense is formed from the present or simple form of the verb.

A verb in the present tense usually tells of something that exists at the present moment.

> The mail carrier *is* at the door. (right now)
> The jacket *feels* too tight. (at this moment)

The simple present tense is not the only verb form used to tell of actions that are going on at the moment, however. We do not always say, "I read." In fact, we are more likely to use the **progressive form** "I am reading" or the **emphatic form** "I do read." An exception is the use of the present to describe ongoing sports events:

> Madlock *slides* and Bench *tags* him out.

The present tense is also used to tell of repeated or regular and habitual action.

> We *go* to band practice on Thursday evenings.
> The factory *closes* at five o'clock.

The present tense is also used to tell of something that is generally true at all times.

> All politicians *need* a base of power.
> The sun *rises* in the east.
> Dr. Jane Goodall *writes* about animal behavior.

The **historical present tense** is used to tell of some action or condition in the past as though it were occurring in the present:

> The captain *orders,* "Abandon ship!" as the great vessel *lists* dangerously to starboard, its decks ablaze.

2. Past tense. Past time is usually told by the past tense, which is the second principal part of the verb: *We left, they cheered, nobody asked.* Continuing past action is shown by the **past progressive:** We *were having* a good time. The past progressive is formed by using a simple past tense form of *be* with the present participle.

3. Future tense. Future time is shown by using *shall* or *will* with the present form of the verb: *We shall arrive, you will notice, I will listen.*

Future time may be shown by the present tense together with an adverb or a phrase that tells time. Future time may also be shown by the use of a present tense form of *be* with *going to.*

> We *get* the grades *tomorrow.* (*tomorrow* is an adverb telling time.)
> The planes *are grounded until further notice.* (*until further notice* is an adverb phrase telling time.)
> I *am going to* resign in January.

4. Present perfect tense. The present perfect tense is formed by using *has* or *have* with the past participle (third principal part) of the verb. This tense is used to refer to some indefinite time in the past.

> The mayor *has promised* his support.
> I *have* often *written* letters to the editor.

The present perfect is also used to show action that began in the past and continues into the present.

> We *have worked* here for ten years. (We still work here.)
> We *have been debating* long enough. (present perfect progressive)

5. Past perfect tense. The past perfect tense is formed by using *had* with the past participle (third principal part) of the verb. The past perfect tense tells of an action completed in the past before some other action.

EARLIER	LATER
We *had finished* the harvesting	before the storm *broke.*
Brenda *had been* pessimistic	until the acceptance notice *came.*
We *had been waiting* an hour.	before the bus *arrived.*

6. Future perfect tense. The future perfect tense is formed by using *will have* or *shall have* with the past participle of the verb (third principal part). This tense is used to tell of one action completed in the future *before* some other action in the future.

> Before the season *ends,* the Mets *will have won* eighty games.
> When the campaign *is* over, he *will have made* 150 speeches.

Note: The first verb, in the present tense, indicates far future action. The second verb, in the future perfect tense, indicates future action *before* the action of the first verb.

Conjugation is a list of the forms of a verb. Usually, verbs are conjugated in the order shown here:

Conjugation of *Save*

Principal Parts:	**Present Infinitive:**
save, saved, saved	to save
Present Participle:	**Perfect Infinitive:**
saving	to have saved

Present Tense

FIRST PERSON:	I save	we save
SECOND PERSON:	you save	you save
THIRD PERSON:	he, she, it saves	they save

Present Progressive: I am saving, you are saving, etc.

Present Emphatic: I do save, you do save, he does save, etc.

Past Tense

FIRST PERSON:	I saved	we saved
SECOND PERSON:	you saved	you saved
THIRD PERSON:	he, she, it saved	they saved

Past Progressive: I was saving, you were saving, etc.

Past Emphatic: I did save, you did save, etc.

Future Tense

FIRST PERSON:	I shall (will) save	we shall (will) save
SECOND PERSON:	you will save	you will save
THIRD PERSON:	he, she, it will save	they will save

Future Progressive: I shall be saving, you will be saving, etc.

Present Perfect Tense

FIRST PERSON:	I have saved	we have saved
SECOND PERSON:	you have saved	you have saved
THIRD PERSON:	he, she, it has saved	they have saved

Present Perfect Progressive: I have been saving, you have been saving, he has been saving, etc.

Past Perfect Tense

FIRST PERSON:	I had saved	we had saved
SECOND PERSON:	you had saved	you had saved
THIRD PERSON:	he, she, it had saved	they had saved

Past Perfect Progressive: I had been saving, you had been saving, etc.

Future Perfect Tense

FIRST PERSON:	I shall have saved	we shall have saved
SECOND PERSON:	you will have saved	you will have saved
THIRD PERSON:	he, she, it will have saved	they will have saved

Future Perfect Progressive: I shall have been saving, etc.

Exercise A: Find each verb and tell its tense.

1. We do not know the answer.
2. The workers handled the explosives carefully.
3. Mary always seems restless.
4. At the side of the road stood two state police cars.
5. The crew of the *Mary Jane* had vanished.
6. Will the new offices have air-conditioning?
7. Amateur rock collectors are finding many valuable gems.
8. By the end of the century, scientists will have learned the language of whales.
9. The car had been behaving oddly on hills.
10. There have been lighthouses on our coasts since 1716.
11. At noon, the party will end.
12. I have been taking this same bus for years.
13. Zeb was counting on a check for his birthday.
14. I did shovel the walk; then it snowed again.
15. Evelyn likes to try unusual foods.

Exercise B: **Writing** Find each verb and tell its tense. Then re-write each sentence and change the verb to the form given in parentheses.

1. Sue lived in Duluth as a child. (past perfect)
2. The guests were eating chocolate mousse. (future perfect)
3. A new roller rink will open at the mall by September. (future perfect)
4. The girls' basketball team has won the state title. (future)
5. Curt makes pizza with pepperoni and olives. (present progressive)
6. Martina Navratilova won the Wimbledon tennis tournament. (present perfect)
7. Debra played Beatrice in *The Effect of Gamma Rays on Man-in-the-Moon Marigolds.* (past perfect progressive)
8. Tomorrow morning, we shall practice our mime routine. (future progressive)
9. The band was playing the grand finale. (present perfect progressive)
10. The Detroit Symphony returned from Europe. (present perfect)

5.5 Voice and Mood

You have already seen that verbs can take on many forms—the emphatic forms, the progressive forms, and the forms of the various tenses. The verbs change depending upon the purposes for which they are used. In addition to these common changes in verb form, there are other, more subtle forms that verbs can take to achieve special purposes.

The Active and Passive Voice

When the subject performs the action expressed by the verb, the verb is considered to be in the **active voice**. When the subject receives the action of the verb, the verb is in the **passive voice**.

The passive voice is formed by using some form of *be* with the past participle of the verb.

ACTIVE: Jeanne *threw* the *ball* out-of-bounds.
PASSIVE: The ball *was thrown* out of bounds.

ACTIVE: Fritz *is carving* the *turkey.*
PASSIVE: The turkey *is being carved* by Fritz.

A transitive verb can be put into the passive voice because it has an object. The object in the active form becomes the subject in the passive form.

An intransitive verb cannot be put into the passive voice because it has no object. There is no word to become the subject.

Gertrude Stein *wrote* the introduction. (active)
The introduction *was written* by Gertrude Stein. (passive)

Jim Childs *read* the minutes. (active)
The minutes *were read* by Jim Childs. (passive)

The active voice is usually livelier, more colorful, and more precise than the passive voice. For this reason, good writers try to avoid writing long passages in the passive voice. They also avoid mixing the passive and active voices in the same sentence or passage.

Mood

The mood of a verb shows the speaker or writer's attitude toward his or her statement. The **indicative mood**, which we use most of the time, shows that we are talking or writing about something that has happened, is happening, or definitely will happen.

The **imperative mood** is used to express a command or a request. This mood of the verb has only one tense—the present—and only one person—the second.

Take your books with you.   Please *call* me.
Gather all of your papers.   *Be* quick.

The **subjunctive mood** is used to express some wishes, commands, and conditions that are doubtful or contrary to fact. The forms of the subjunctive mood are identical to those of the indicative mood, with the following exceptions:

1. The *s* is omitted from the verb in the third-person singular.

    INDICATIVE: We *use* safety belts.
    SUBJUNCTIVE: He asked that we *use* safety belts.

    INDICATIVE: He *uses* safety belts.
    SUBJUNCTIVE: We asked that he *use* safety belts.

2. The present tense of the verb *to be* is always *be.*

    Andrew asked that the order *be* canceled.
    Have courage though you *be* alone.

3. The past tense of the verb *to be* is always *were.*

    If she *were* President, she would limit spending.
    I wish I *were* going to Europe this summer.

The following is a list of the major uses of the subjunctive:

1. *Were* and *be* are often used instead of other forms of *to be*
    a. To express wishes

        I wish I *were* king. (uses *I were* instead of *I was*)

    b. To express conditions that are doubtful or contrary to fact after *if, as if, though,* and *although*

        If I *were* you, I would go. (uses *I were* instead of *I was*)

2. *Were, be,* and the third person subjunctive forms of other verbs are often used
    a. To express commands or requests after *that*

        He asked that the bird *be* freed. (uses *be* instead of *is*)
        He requested that Mary *move* her car. (uses *move* instead of *moves*)

b. In certain isolated, ancient phrases that retain the subjunctive

> . . . *come* what may . . .
> . . . far *be* it from me . . .
> . . . Heaven *forbid* . . .
> . . . *come* rain or shine . . .

Exercise A: Writing Find each verb. Tell whether it is active or passive. Then, change the active verbs to passive and passive verbs to active. You may have to add words where no subject exists.

1. The lights had been turned down.
2. We have been invited to the symphony concert.
3. My sister has already picked a career.
4. The next batter was hit by a pitched ball.
5. Many New York school children do not understand English.
6. Several of the games were played at night.
7. A new school will be constructed here.
8. The speaker told of her adventures in Africa.
9. More than one hundred elements have been discovered.
10. Cynthia has bought a new book about sports cars.
11. The speaker will be introduced by the class president.
12. Woodbridge has equaled our tournament record.
13. Our class decorated the gym.
14. The influenza shots were given by the school doctor.
15. The game was ruined by the rain.
16. The team bus was delayed by a flat tire.
17. The citrus fruit was destroyed by frost.
18. The new bridge will be dedicated by the mayor.
19. A flaming explosion interrupted the rock concert.
20. My sister's class elected her president.

Exercise B: Tell the mood of each italicized verb below.

1. If I *were* a rich man, I'd own a dozen cars.
2. The instructor asked that she *hold* the racket in both hands.
3. I wish I *were* in the land of cotton.

4. P. T. Barnum's "Greatest Show on Earth" *opened* in 1871.
5. Chief Joseph requested that the Nez Perce *be allowed* to settle in Canada.
6. Please *help* me carry in the amplifiers and drums.
7. *Don't trip* over the cable!
8. If we *were* never sad, we wouldn't know when we *are* happy.
9. Gondolas *have been used* in Venice since A.D. 1094.
10. Though they *be* friendly, we still *shall be* wary.

5.6 Commonly Confused Verbs

Three pairs of verbs are often confused because the meanings of each pair are closely related. To use these verbs correctly, keep their meanings distinct.

Lie and lay. The verb *lay* means "to put or place something." The verb *lie* has eight or nine meanings, all having the idea of "being in a horizontal position, or to remain, or to be situated."[*]

Lie is always an intransitive verb. It never has an object. *Lay* is a transitive verb. It almost always has an object. The principal parts of these verbs are as follows:

PRESENT	PAST	PAST PARTICIPLE
lie	lay	(have) lain
lay	laid	(have) laid

Sit and set. The verb *sit* usually means "to rest with the legs bent and the back upright," but there are many other related meanings. The verb *set* means "to put or place something."

Sit is an intransitive verb; it never has an object. *Set* is transitive; it almost always has an object. Here are the principal parts:

PRESENT	PAST	PAST PARTICIPLE
sit	sat	(have) sat
set	set	(have) set

---

[*]There is a homonym meaning "to tell an untruth." The principal parts of this verb are *lie, lied, lied.*

Rise and raise. The verb *rise* means "to go to a higher position." The verb *raise* means "to lift to a higher position."

Rise is intransitive; it never has an object. *Raise* is transitive; it almost always has an object. Things *rise* by themselves; they are *raised* by something else. The principal parts of these verbs are as follows:

PRESENT	PAST	PAST PARTICIPLE
rise	rose	(have) risen
raise	raised	(have) raised

Note: It is very difficult to make general statements about English usage that will hold without exception. These are exceptions to the statements given above about the three pairs of verbs:

The sun *sets*. (intransitive)
Gelatin *sets* in three hours. (intransitive)
Sit the doll up. (transitive)

Exercise A: Choose the standard form from those in parentheses.

1. The necessary tools (lay, laid) in a neat row on the table.
2. The fruit had (lain, laid) too long in the sun.
3. The mayor (lay, laid) the cornerstone for the new city hall.
4. Please don't (lie, lay) your wet coats on the chairs.
5. All day, the refugees (lay, laid) hiding in the rice field.
6. The books were (lying, laying) on the floor of the closet.
7. It is impossible for Boots to (lie, lay) still.
8. The beautiful old chest had (lain, laid) in the attic for years.
9. The company is already (lying, laying) plans for further expansion.
10. The city has (lain, laid) new storm drains along the road.
11. The old dog was (lying, laying) in the middle of the road.
12. New duties have been (lain, laid) on the branch managers this year.
13. Here in the cave the wounded trapper had (lain, laid) down to die.
14. Near the beach a new tennis court has been (lain, laid) out.

15. After the earthquake, over half the city (lay, laid) in ruins.
16. We were (lying, laying) in the shade waiting for the bus to come.
17. The union has (lain, laid) plans for a huge demonstration.
18. After dinner, you must (lie, lay) down for a rest.
19. We (lay, laid) out our equipment on the rocks to dry.
20. The revolver was found (lying, laying) in twelve feet of water.

Exercise B: Choose the standard form from those in parentheses.

1. Several of the guests were (sitting, setting) on the floor.
2. Please don't (sit, set) your glass on the table.
3. The superstitious think it is bad luck to (sit, set) a hat on a bed.
4. We will be (sitting, setting) on these chairs for a long time.
5. You will find it easier to (sit, set) still as you grow older.
6. The artist (sat, set) a fresh canvas on the easel.
7. You can (sit, set) the flowers on the hall table.
8. Ms. Donovan (sat, set) two hours today for her portrait.
9. Some of the children were (sitting, setting) on the curb.
10. Leroy (sat, set) his hat carefully on the back of his head.
11. I (sat, set) the brief case on the seat and promptly forgot about it.
12. How long has the coffee pot been (sitting, setting) on this burner?
13. Extra chairs were (sat, set) on the platform.
14. (Sitting, Setting) on one's heels is called hunkering.
15. You can (sit, set) the bag of ice outside.
16. The family (sat, set) at the airport all night, waiting for any plane.
17. The skeleton was (sitting, setting) on a chair in the front row of the auditorium.
18. The empty cartons were (sat, set) in the hall.
19. A warning light had been (sat, set) in the road.
20. The students were (sitting, setting) on the steps, waiting for the library to open.

Exercise C: Choose the standard form from those in parentheses.

1. Early in the day the wind had (risen, raised).
2. The cost of living did not (rise, raise) this last year.
3. Farm prices have not (risen, raised) for several years.
4. The proposal for a new airport (rose, raised) a storm of protest.
5. When the doctor asked for volunteers, five people (rose, raised) their hands.
6. The company's business has (risen, raised) every year.
7. Tonight, the moon is (rising, raising) in the northeast.
8. The fog was (rising, raising) as we left for the airport.
9. The archaeologists (rose, raised) the heavy stone statues by ropes.
10. Will the bus fare be (risen, raised) again this year?
11. Please (rise, raise) the window a few inches more.
12. The club plans to (rise, raise) a fund to send the band to the tournament.
13. Someone was (rising, raising) a disturbance outside the hall.
14. A sigh of relief (rose, raised) from the waiting crowd.
15. It will be Bonita's duty to (rise, raise) the flag every morning.
16. The dough has not (risen, raised) yet.
17. The landlord (rose, raised) our rent again this year.
18. A month ago, no one thought to (rise, raise) those arguments.
19. During the past hour, the water has (risen, raised) three inches.
20. The flock of ducks (rose, raised) gracefully from the lake.

REINFORCEMENT EXERCISES
Verb Usage

A. Use past participles correctly. The present form of the verb is given in parentheses. Substitute the past participle and rewrite the sentence.

1. The painting would have (cost) too much.
2. Have you (see) the riverboats on the Mississippi?
3. She has (bear) the responsibilities of office well.
4. Coach Zelenke has (swim) two miles a day for over twenty years.
5. My dog couldn't find the stick because I had (throw) it over the fence.
6. Loretta Lynn has (sing) at the White House several times.
7. I would have (run) another mile if I hadn't (see) the ice cream truck.
8. The American philosopher and novelist, George Santayana, had (speak) Spanish as a child.
9. The eternal flame on the top of the courthouse has (shine) since World War II.
10. Sheila has (lend) that book to several of her friends.

B. Identify progressive and emphatic forms. Tell whether the verb in each sentence is in the progressive form or the emphatic form.

1. The city council did not approve the mayor's tax proposal.
2. Our history class is studying the colonization of America.
3. I do hope the float will be finished in time for the homecoming parade.
4. William Thomson, the great mathematician, was studying at Glasgow University at the age of ten.
5. By June I shall have been working at the company for six years.
6. My sister Melanie will be completing her medical studies this year.

7. The beekeeper was sowing clover near his hives.
8. Randy does like musicals more than any other type of play.
9. Did Shakespeare really write all of the plays attributed to him?
10. The quarterback and the wide receiver were practicing lateral passes.

C. Identify verb tenses. Find the verb in each of the following sentences and tell its tense.

1. Margarite read several books about India.
2. In recent years, winters have become colder.
3. Our speech team will be going to the state meet next Saturday.
4. The rattlesnake had been sunning itself on a rock.
5. Paul had learned Arabic in college.
6. The seals perform in the main arena every evening.
7. The mountain climbers will leave a flag at the summit.
8. By October, my family will have been in business for twenty-five years.
9. The folksinger was telling us about life in the coal mining country of Kentucky.
10. The new class delegates will report to the president of the student body.

D. Identify passive and active verbs. Find the verb in each of the following sentences and tell whether it is active or passive. Then rewrite sentences containing passive verbs, changing these to the active voice.

1. The dispute was settled by the referee.
2. The drama club banquet has always been catered by Marino's.
3. The Amazon River flows over four thousand miles across the continent of South America.
4. Balboa, the chimpanzee, was often fed peanuts by visitors to the zoo.

5. A new basketball court was installed at the Community Center by the Department of Neighborhood Development.
6. Many television commercials are produced by advertising agencies in Chicago.
7. The name Sophia means "wise."
8. Many strange paintings of melting clocks were produced by Salvador Dali.
9. William Goldman will write the film adaptation.
10. The lost city of Troy was found by Heinrich Schliemann.

E. Use commonly confused verbs correctly. Seven of the sentences below use verbs incorrectly. Rewrite these sentences so that they follow standard form. If the sentence contains no error in usage, write *Correct*.

1. The veterinarian had lain the medicated cloth on the horse's sprained shoulder.
2. Why don't you set on this bench while I get refreshments?
3. The chef laid strips of dough across the top of the pie crust.
4. Sherri carefully sat the fragile china vase on the shelf.
5. The campers had raised with the sun and prepared breakfast.
6. If you have a headache, lay down for a while.
7. The color guard rose the flag up the pole and saluted.
8. Don't set that wax figure by the heater!
9. The doctor had only laid down for a minute before she received an emergency call.
10. One of the breeders had raised collies for over thirty years.

MIXED REVIEW
Verb Usage

A. Choose the standard form of the verb from those in parentheses.

1. Jolita has (gone, went) to the library.
2. Years ago, automobiles (cost, costed) much less to produce.
3. A large trout (swinged, swang, swung) from the end of Jake's fishing line.
4. That blister has (hurt, hurted) for days.
5. The Bee Gees have (sang, sung) in several movies.
6. Each year Aunt Laura has (brought, brung) the pumpkin pies for Thanksgiving dinner.
7. Our dog Zap has never (bit, bitten) anyone.
8. Osaka has (broke, broken) the school record for diving.
9. A dinner bell was (rang, ringed, rung) to call the campers.
10. The candidate (shook, shaked) hands with everyone.
11. Tim (flung, flang, flinged) a dart at the target.
12. The Wildcats were (beat, beaten) in overtime.
13. Lost in the desert, Connors had (drank, drunk) no water for ten days.
14. We should have (knowed, known) that sunrise was earlier.
15. A ten dollar bill (lay, laid) on the sidewalk.
16. A southwest wind (rose, raised) the temperature.
17. Please (lie, lay) your jacket on the couch.
18. The bricklayer (sat, set) the bricks in neat rows.
19. Ryan (sat, set) patiently in the dentist's chair.
20. Emily (rose, raised) her binoculars to view the asteroids.

B. Rewrite the following sentences, changing the verb to the form shown in parentheses.

1. Kareem Abdul-Jabbar constantly moved up and down the court. (present progressive)
2. Poachers have drastically reduced the black rhinoceros population in Kenya. (passive)

3. During the speech, no one applauded. (past progressive)
4. The astronauts spend many hours in a weightless environment. (future perfect)
5. The abusive player was removed from the game by the umpire. (active)
6. I find chess more challenging than video games. (emphatic)
7. Karen and her brother are debating the issue. (past)
8. José's life was saved by Elise's knowledge of CPR. (active)
9. The linesman called the serve out of bounds. (past perfect)
10. The trains pick up new cars at the freight yards. (future)

C. The following paragraph contains thirteen errors in verb usage. Rewrite the paragraph, eliminating these errors.

Jim laid awake most of the night, thinking about the lake and what he had seed there the previous evening. Restless, he got up and springed into his clothes as quickly as he could. He needed to go down to the lake and take another look. Jim had heared about monsters being sighted in other parts of the world, but he had never expected to find one in Cedar Lake, New Jersey. The sun had just rose over the horizon when Jim come down to the dock on his bike. He run to the edge and lied down to look across the water. He throwed a stone into the lake, and it sinked quickly to the bottom, stirring up a family of frogs resting on the rocks. There was no other motion. As the frightened frogs swum by, Jim begun to wonder if the monster he had saw the day before had been nothing more than a floating log or trick of the light.

USING GRAMMAR IN WRITING
Verb Usage

A. Children often make errors in verb usage by trying to apply the rules for regular verbs to verbs that are irregular. Imagine that you are studying this stage of language development. For your records, rewrite the following passage, which is a transcript of the speech of a child. Then explain how the child has learned the rules for making regular verbs, but not the exceptions to these rules.

> Yesterday, when Grandpa comed over to our house, he bringed Mom and Dad a fish that he had catched to cook for dinner. But Mom sayed that she already maked dinner; so, she eated the fish for lunch. Then he gived me some bubble stuff and we blowed bubbles for a while. He wanted to go home then, but his car breaked; so, he goed home on the bus instead.

B. To make your writing livelier, learn to use lively verbs. Rewrite this account of a volcanic eruption. Make it more colorful by replacing dull verbs. Also change passive verbs to the active voice and make any other revisions that might improve the story.

> The force of the explosion could be felt by people miles away. Windows were broken and brick walls cracked. Nearer to the mountain, there was a cloud of dust and ash. It covered trees, houses, and people. Huge rocks and hot gases came from the crater. A red-hot river of lava went down the mountainside.

C. In both speaking and writing we often confuse the verbs *lie,* meaning "to be in a horizontal position"; *lie,* meaning "to tell an untruth"; and *lay,* meaning "to put or place something." Test your knowledge of these words by writing a humorous story about a lazy bricklayer who is given to telling untruths. Be sure that you use each of the italicized verbs at least once. Write the story in the present tense; then rewrite it in the past tense.

CUMULATIVE REVIEW
The Sentence (III)

Writing Different Types of Sentences. Rewrite each sentence on your own paper. Follow the directions given in parentheses.

1. The Y.M.C.A. offers several aerobics classes. (Change the active verb to a passive verb.)
2. Some students discovered the bones of a saber-toothed tiger. (Add a prepositional phrase to modify *students*.)
3. Would you like to meet the celebrated author? (Change this simple sentence to a complex sentence by adding a clause beginning with a relative pronoun.)
4. Maria wished a safe voyage to everyone. (Change this N V N sentence to one with a N V N N pattern.)
5. One of the actors forgot his lines. (Change the form of the verb from past to past participle.)
6. Martin's hobby was speleology. Speleology is the scientific study of caves. (Change these two sentences to one sentence by using an appositive phrase.)
7. Barbara likes painting brightly-colored abstract designs. (Change the gerund phrase to an infinitive phrase.)
8. Carl jogged for two miles along the path, and Sandi ran with him. (Change this compound sentence to a simple sentence with a compound subject.)
9. The circus had to refund the money for the tickets. (Add an adverb clause.)
10. The early American pioneers did not have sophisticated tools. They could build a log house in a matter of days. (Change these two sentences into one compound sentence by using the conjunctive adverb *nevertheless*.)

6.0 Agreement of Subject and Verb

In grammar the word *agreement* means "likeness." To make two words agree is to make them alike in some respect.

A common error in speech is the failure to make subject and verb agree (*they was* instead of *they were*). Errors of agreement in speaking are sometimes difficult to avoid. In writing, however, these errors should be easier to avoid because the writer always has the time and opportunity to revise his or her work before presenting it to a reader.

6.1 Subject-Verb Agreement in Number

There are two numbers in grammar: **singular** and **plural**. A word is singular in number if it refers to one person or thing. A word is plural if it refers to more than one person or thing.

Except for *be*, English verbs show a difference between singular and plural only in the third person and only in the present tense. The third person singular present form ends in *s*.

$$\left.\begin{array}{l} \text{I} \\ \text{you} \\ \text{we} \\ \text{they} \end{array}\right\} \text{see} \qquad \left.\begin{array}{l} \text{he} \\ \text{she} \\ \text{it} \end{array}\right\} \text{sees}$$

A singular verb is used with a singular subject.

A plural verb is used with a plural subject.

The subject determines whether the verb is singular or plural. The verb does not agree with any other part of the sentence.

> The cat (singular) *likes* liver.
> The cats (plural) *like* liver.
>
> The teacher (singular) *works* hard.
> The teachers (plural) *work* hard.

The verb *be* presents several special problems in agreement because it does not follow the regular pattern for English verbs.

PRESENT TENSE		PAST TENSE	
SINGULAR	PLURAL	SINGULAR	PLURAL
I am	we are	I was	we were
you are	you are	you were	you were
he, she, it is	they are	he, she, it was	they were

The most common errors with *be* are *you was, we was, they was.*

6.2 Words Between Subject and Verb

The verb agrees only with its subject. Occasionally, a word with a different number than the subject occurs between the subject and the verb. This word usually has no effect on the number of the verb even though it is closer to the verb than the subject.

> The young *condor,* cared for by a team of scientists, *has* made wonderful progress.
> (*condor* is the subject.)
> *One* of his classmates *is* a guide at the United Nations.
> (*One* is the subject.)

The *Congress* of the United States *is* in session.
   (*Congress* is the subject.)
The *pears* on that old tree *are* not edible.
   (*pears* is the subject.)

The words *with, together with, along with, as well as, in addition to,* are prepositions. The objects of these prepositions have no effect upon the number of the verb.

The *President,* together with his aides, *was* studying the crisis.
   (*President* is the subject.)
Your *dress,* as well as your manners, *is* important.
   (*dress* is the subject.)
The *singer,* along with her band, *is* on tour for six months.
   (*singer* is the subject.)

Exercise: Choose the standard form of the verb for each sentence.

1. When (was, were) you at the doctor's office?
2. Is it true that one of the passengers (is, are) missing?
3. (Is, Are) the book reports due this week or next?
4. The teacher, as well as the class, (was, were) surprised by Ronny's report.
5. The pilot, in addition to the crew, (has, have) your comfort and safety in mind.
6. The age of the huge sequoias (is, are) hard to believe.
7. The high cost of repairs for electronic equipment always (comes, come) as a surprise.
8. The lights in the store window (is, are) turned off at midnight.
9. The decision of the umpires (was, were) hotly disputed.
10. The danger of floods on the Ohio and Allegheny Rivers (has, have) been exaggerated.
11. The president of the company, along with her secretary, (plans, plan) to fly to Boston.
12. The contestants in the skateboarding contest (warms, warm) up before the start of the event.

13. Only one of these old transistor radios (works, work).
14. The scientist's report, together with the photographs, (is, are) very convincing.
15. The older members of the local school board (wants, want) to build a new school.
16. The lights in the valley down below (looks, look) like tiny jewels.
17. The co-captains of our team (has, have) a special responsibility.
18. (Was, Were) you at home all day?
19. The aim of the debates (is, are) to provide important information for the voters.
20. The sale of the school yearbooks (has, have) been disappointing.

6.3 Indefinite Pronouns

Some indefinite pronouns are always singular. Others are always plural. Some may be either singular or plural.

SINGULAR				PLURAL
another	each	everyone	anyone	several
anybody	either	everybody	someone	few
anything	neither	no one	somebody	both
everything	one	nobody		many

Each of the candidates *has* criticized spending.
Neither of the buses *was* full.
Everybody in the fields *was* working.

Several in this class *are* excellent writers.
Few in the student council *have* been re-elected.
Both of the quarterbacks *were* injured.

SINGULAR OR PLURAL

some	all	most
none	any	

Some, all, most, none, and *any* are singular when they refer to a portion or a quantity. They are plural when they refer to a number of individual items.

Some of the cream *was* sour. (a quantity of cream)
Some of the buildings *were* brick. (a number of buildings)

Most of the forest *was* saved from fire. (a portion of the forest)
Most of our friends *are* going to the movie. (a number of friends)

All of the turkey *was* eaten in two days. (a quantity of turkey)
All of the classes *are* taking the test. (a number of classes)

Exercise: Choose the standard form of the verb for each sentence.

1. Either of these hats (suits, suit) you.
2. Most of the television programs (is, are) boring.
3. Not one of the papers (has, have) covered the story.
4. Neither of the drivers (was, were) hurt in the accident.
5. One of the violins (is, are) playing off key.
6. Each of the new cars (comes, come) equipped with safety belts.
7. (Has, Have) either of the buses left yet?
8. Obviously, one of the witnesses (was, were) not truthful.
9. Some of the teams (has, have) new uniforms.
10. The old houses in this block (is, are) being torn down.
11. Everyone in the stands (was, were) sure a touchdown had been scored.
12. Few in this school (knows, know) about his trouble.
13. One of the boats (seems, seem) to have a leak.
14. It was reported that neither of the bridges (was, were) safe.
15. The pilot discovered that one of the engines (was, were) not working right.
16. Each of the balloons (carries, carry) scientific instruments.
17. Everyone in the pictures (is, are) grinning foolishly.
18. Neither of these patterns (is, are) what I want.
19. Several of the listeners (has, have) telephoned the studio.
20. (Has, Have) either of the candidates promised lower taxes?

6.4 Compound Subjects

Compound subjects joined by *and* are plural.°

Overloaded circuits and faulty wiring *cause* fires.

Singular words joined by *or, nor, either-or, neither-nor* to form a compound subject are singular.

Neither your grammar nor your punctuation *is* perfect.
Either Shirley or Pat *has* your baseball.
Is Joe or Olga *baby-sitting* after school?

When a singular word and a plural word are joined by *or* or *nor* to form a compound subject, the verb agrees with the subject that is nearer to it.

Neither the police nor the suspect *wants* to make a
    statement. (*suspect* is closer to the verb than *police*.)
A novel or two plays *meet* the reading requirements.
Neither the songs nor the singer *pleases* him.

Exercise A: Writing Find the errors in subject-verb agreement in these sentences. Write the sentences correctly. Two of the sentences are correct.

1. Neither the train nor the airlines are on schedule.
2. The chairs and the table was loaded with packages.
3. Neither the gloves nor the sweater were the right size.
4. Either Cybil or Jeff have been here.
5. The gloves and the hat is the same color.
6. Either pen or pencil is acceptable.
7. Two books and a notebook is on the desk.
8. The lifeguard or the swimming coach are always on duty.
9. Neither the papers nor the radio have told the story.
10. Either the meat or the potatoes is burning.

°If the words making up the compound subject are habitually used together to refer to a single thing, the subject may be used with a singular verb: *bread and butter, macaroni and cheese*, etc.

Exercise B: Writing Follow the directions for Exercise A.

1. Have either Mr. Barnes or Ms. Brown arrived yet?
2. Neither the doctor nor her nurse were at the office.
3. Two squirrels and a jackrabbit is all we saw.
4. Both skill and constant practice go into the making of a champion.
5. Neither the French fries nor the hamburger were hot.
6. Sandwiches or soup are your only choice.
7. Was the governor or her aide interviewed?
8. Neither the guard nor the police officer were really on the job.
9. Either Jack or his sister have your books.
10. Neither the audience nor the actors was aware of the trouble backstage.

6.5 Subject Following Verb

The most difficult agreement problem in speech arises when the subject follows the verb. The speaker must think ahead to the subject in order to decide whether the verb is to be singular or plural.

This problem arises in sentences beginning with contractions made from *There* and *Here*. It also arises in questions beginning with *Who, Why, Where, What, How*.

NONSTANDARD:	Here's the skis for Kay.
STANDARD:	Here *are* the skis for Kay.
NONSTANDARD:	There's four letters for you.
STANDARD:	There *are* four letters for you.
NONSTANDARD:	Who's the three people at the door?
STANDARD:	Who *are* the three people at the door?
NONSTANDARD:	What's the amendments to the constitution?
STANDARD:	What *are* the amendments to the constitution?
NONSTANDARD:	From out of the blue *comes* three jets.
STANDARD:	From out of the blue *come* three jets.

6.6 Predicate Words

The linking verb agrees with its subject, *not* with the predicate word.

NONSTANDARD: Hamburgers *is* his favorite food.
STANDARD: Hamburgers *are* his favorite food.
NONSTANDARD: Martha's main interest *are* horses.
STANDARD: Martha's main interest *is* horses.
NONSTANDARD: Money and power *is* his goal.
STANDARD: Money and power *are* his goal.

6.7 *Don't* and *Doesn't*

The word *does* and the contraction *doesn't* are used with singular nouns and with the pronouns *he, she,* and *it.* The word *do* and the contraction *don't* are used with plural nouns and with the pronouns *I, we, you,* and *they.*

DOES, DOESN'T	DO, DON'T
the law does	the laws do
he doesn't	we don't
she doesn't	you don't
it doesn't	they don't

Exercise: Choose the standard form from the two in parentheses.

1. (Where's, Where are) the stack of papers I put on the desk?
2. (Doesn't, Don't) the wind sound wild tonight?
3. (Here's, Here are) the books you lent to Robin.
4. (What's, What are) the names of the mountain ranges in California?
5. It seems that there (was, were) two men named Clyde Smith.
6. Hard work and ambition (is, are) the answer.
7. Success and fame (was, were) Wilson's goal.

8. The leader of the expedition (doesn't, don't) dare to take chances.
9. Sunny days and a beautiful beach (is, are) the town's claim to fame.
10. Up the steps (moves, move) the procession.
11. (Doesn't, Don't) the bus stop at this corner?
12. Protein and fats (is, are) the great dietary need in India.
13. (There's, There are) two good restaurants right outside of town.
14. Down into the cave (goes, go) Cousteau and Didi.
15. The wax on the floors (makes, make) them dangerously slippery.
16. The biggest difficulty (is, are) the inexperience and indifference of the workers.
17. Through this door (passes, pass) the lawmakers of our nation.
18. The expedition's task (was, were) to establish a base camp and to begin scientific observations.
19. (Where's, Where are) the people who are coming to help us?
20. (What's, What are) the weather predictions for this week?

6.8 Collective Nouns

A collective noun names a group of people or things: *family, choir, crew, herd, faculty.*

When the writer refers to a group acting together as one unit, the collective noun is used with a singular verb. When the writer refers to the individuals in the group acting separately, one by one, the collective noun is used with a plural verb.

The team *was* the best in the history of the school.
(united action)
The team *were* putting on their uniforms. (separate actions)
The council *is* in emergency session. (united action)
The council *were* debating the proposals. (separate actions)

Once the writer decides whether the collective noun is a unit or a group of individuals, he or she must abide by that choice. Later in the same sentence the writer may not use a verb or pronoun of different number.

NONSTANDARD: The Senate *has* (singular) changed *their* (plural) rules.

STANDARD: The Senate *has* changed *its* rules.

6.9   Nouns Plural in Form

Some nouns are plural in form but are regarded as singular in meaning. That is, they end in *s* as most plural nouns do, but they do not stand for more than one thing: *news, mumps, molasses.* Therefore, they are used with a singular verb.

Bad news *travels* fast.
Mumps *is* more serious for adults than children.

There are many words ending in *-ics* that may be either singular or plural: *economics, athletics, civics, politics.* These words are singular when they are used to refer to a school subject, a science, or a general practice. When singular, they are not usually preceded by *the, his, her, some, all,* or singular modifiers.

Ethics is important in the study of religion. (singular)
The council's ethics in this matter *are* questionable. (plural)

Politics *is* a fascinating game. (singular)
His politics *involve* only a struggle for power. (plural)

6.10   Titles and Groups of Words

The title of a book, play, story, film, musical composition, or other work of art is used with a singular verb. The name of a country is used with a singular verb. Such words, even though they may be plural in form, refer to a single thing.

The Philippines *is* made up of 7,083 islands and islets.
All the President's Men was produced by Robert Redford.
"War of the Worlds" *was* written by H. G. Wells.
The United Nations *is* discussing the problem.
The Four Seasons, by Vivaldi, *was* played at the concert.

Any group of words referring to a single thing or thought is used with a singular verb.

What we need *is* votes.
"Because I said so" *is* a popular phrase with many people.

6.11   Words of Amount and Time

Words or phrases that express periods of time, fractions, weights, measurements, and amounts of money are usually regarded as singular.

Ten dollars *is* too much to pay.
Two-thirds of the money *has* been raised.
Five hours *seems* a long time for that trip.
One hundred pounds of bird seed *is* ridiculous.
Ten yards of curtain material *was* not enough.

Sometimes a prepositional phrase with a plural object falls between the subject and the verb. When this happens, the verb remains singular if the subject is meant as a single thing. The verb is plural if the subject is meant as a plural thing.

Five kilograms of apples *is* plenty.
Five of the bikes *are* missing.

Exercise: Choose the standard form from the two forms given in parentheses.

1. On their hours off duty, the crew (was, were) not allowed to leave the ship.
2. Making their way slowly up the cliff, the relief party (was, were) nearly at the ledge.

3. Next year, economics (is, are) to be taught in ninth grade.
4. Politics (is, are) my aunt's hobby.
5. Two thousand (seem, seems) a low estimate for the number of fans in the crowd.
6. The East Indies (was, were) a source of European wealth.
7. All that we need (is, are) time and money.
8. Two-thirds of the crop (was, were) not even harvested.
9. Two-thirds of the students (wants, want) a weekly paper.
10. Six quarts of milk (is, are) what we ordered.
11. Athletics (is, are) taking too much of Harry's time.
12. With its new plays, the team (was, were) winning.
13. Genetics (make, makes) it possible for scientists to develop new breeds of animals.
14. At its meetings, the group (sees, see) movies.
15. The United States (has, have) started explorations beneath the earth's crust.
16. Pneumatics (deals, deal) with the properties of air and other gases.
17. Two thousand dollars (is, are) a lot to pay for a used car.
18. Sixteen hours on the bus (was, were) too much for us.
19. "By the Waters of Babylon" (is, are) a thought-provoking story.
20. One of the lifeboats (has, have) sunk.

6.12 Relative Pronouns

A relative pronoun stands in place of its antecedent (the word to which it refers). If that antecedent is plural, the relative pronoun is plural. If the antecedent is singular, the relative pronoun is singular.

A relative pronoun agrees with its antecedent in number.

When a relative pronoun is used as subject of the verb in the relative clause, the number of the verb depends upon the number of the pronoun's antecedent.

They are the *candidates* (plural) who (plural) *have* been elected.

Fay is the *girl* (singular) who (singular) *manages* the store.

King is one of those *dogs* who *are* always chasing cars. (*dogs* are always chasing cars.)

Ms. Foss is the only *one* of the teachers who *has* a master's degree. (Only *one* has a master's degree.)

The problem of agreement arises in the last two sentences because there are two words, either of which *might* be the antecedent of the relative pronoun. Remember that the verb in the relative clause will agree with the true antecedent of the relative pronoun.

Exercise A: Choose the standard form from the two forms given in parentheses.

1. Good running shoes are ones that (has, have) firm support.
2. Those are the trees that (produces, produce) juicy apples.
3. This is the only one of the books that (is, are) really worth reading.
4. James is the only one in the class who (has, have) climbed all the way up Mt. Washington.
5. Anne is one of those individuals who (is, are) always finding fault with others.
6. Gibson is one of the members who always (listens, listen) attentively before replying.
7. Juan is the only person in the crowd who (is, are) smiling at the antics of the mime.
8. Mr. Marin is the only one of my teachers who (calls, call) roll at the end of class.
9. Veterans Day is one of the holidays that (falls, fall) on Saturday this year.
10. Sarah is one of the musicians who (marches, march) in the band.

Exercise B: Follow the directions for Exercise A.

1. That is the only one of her wisdom teeth that (aches, ache).
2. Here are two fabrics of the kind that (resists, resist) moisture.
3. He is the only one of the refugees who (speaks, speak) English fluently.
4. Joan is the one person in the group who (has, have) a good record collection.
5. There are three members of our class who (has, have) won prizes.
6. The ivy is the only plant in these rooms that (is, are) poisonous.
7. Laura is one of the students who (has, have) straight A's.
8. He is one of the neighbors who never (fails, fail) to greet us.
9. This is the kind of jeans that (lasts, last).
10. Tim is the only one in the group who (seems, seem) confident.

REINFORCEMENT EXERCISES
Agreement of Subject and Verb

A. Choose the correct verb. Identify the subject in each of the following sentences. Then choose the standard form of the verb from the two given in parentheses.

1. The runners in the marathon (leaves, leave) the starting gate at six o'clock.
2. Which one of the paintings (is, are) missing from the museum?
3. Jerry, along with his brothers Jack and Jim, (is, are) repairing a snowmobile.
4. The thermos, along with the condiments and dessert, (is, are) already packed.
5. The lights at the end of the pier (is, are) easy for the boats to spot at night.
6. Performers in the circus (works, work) odd hours.
7. The demand for more computer classes (has, have) not yet been met by schools and universities.
8. Employees of the city (live, lives) inside the city limits.
9. One of the paramedics, as well as several firefighters, (was, were) hospitalized with injuries.
10. The members of the team (runs, run) ten laps after every practice.
11. One of these candlesticks (is, are) more tarnished than the other.
12. The officials of the Department of the Interior (supports, support) the proposed legislation.
13. Tacos, my favorite food, (is, are) served in the cafeteria every Wednesday.
14. The quality of the photographs (was, were) exceptionally good.
15. The boxer, as well as his trainers, (lives, live) up in the Catskills.

B. Choose verbs that agree with indefinite pronouns. Identify the subject in each of the following sentences. Then choose the correct verb from the two given in parentheses.

1. All of the birds in the neighborhood (gathers, gather) around this feeder.
2. Everyone (is, are) upset about the plans to expand the local airport.
3. Either of these tennis rackets (is, are) acceptable in regulation play.
4. One of the robbers (was, were) caught just outside the store by an alert officer.
5. None of the active volcanoes (has, have) erupted this year.
6. Everybody in the cast (was, were) superb.
7. All of the snow (was, were) cleared from the main highways.
8. Most of the season tickets (has, have) already been sold.
9. Some of the senators (is, are) in favor of providing more support for foreign language education.
10. Each of the contestants (receives, receive) a prize.

C. Choose verbs that agree with compound subjects. Identify the subject in each of the following sentences. Then choose the correct verb.

1. Neither wolves nor coyotes (lives, live) in this area.
2. Either his agent or his business managers (advise, advises) the actor on every contract.
3. Both Adams Street and Monroe Street (is, are) one way.
4. A doe and two fawns (was, were) grazing in the meadow.
5. Neither pasta nor bread (is, are) allowed on my diet.
6. Three farmhands and the cook (shares, share) the bunkhouse.
7. Either the trainer or the coach (has, have) already called the college scouts.
8. Both Nina and Sally (is, are) wearing long dresses to the dance.

9. Neither the President nor his aides (was, were) responsible for the press leak.
10. Either the roller coaster or the Shooting Star (is, are) her favorite ride.

D. Choose verbs that agree with the subjects. Choose the correct word or words from those given in parentheses.

1. (There's, There are) the new computers I was telling you about.
2. In the front row (sits, sit) the playwright, Jim Leonard.
3. The most important thing in the world to him (was, were) sports.
4. (Who's, Who are) the winners of the three-legged race?
5. Into the harbor (sails, sail) the tall ships.
6. (Here's, Here are) the final scores in the gymnastic competition.
7. Manuel (doesn't, don't) live on Van Buren Street anymore.
8. Hard work and energy (is, are) the key to success in that company.
9. Why (was, were) the people on the high wire performing without a net?
10. Where (does, do) squirrels live in the winter?

E. Make subjects and verbs agree. The subjects of some of the following sentences are collective nouns. Identify the subject of each sentence. Then choose the proper verb form.

1. The St. Louis Cardinals (is, are) playing in Los Angeles tonight.
2. Social studies (was, were) my best class last year.
3. Five dollars (is, are) a lot of money to spend for a movie ticket.
4. *The King and I* (opens, open) this Saturday night at the dinner playhouse.
5. Local politics (demands, demand) tact and diplomacy.
6. Mumps (is, are) an illness that can be dangerous for adults.

7. "Bread and Circuses" (sounds, sound) like an interesting title for an article.
8. Twenty yards (is, are) a great gain for a running play.
9. The band (buys, buy) their own uniforms and music.
10. Sixty percent of the ballots (has, have) been counted.

F. Choose correct verbs after relative pronouns. Determine the antecedent of each relative pronoun. Then choose the verb that agrees with this antecedent.

1. Jackson Browne is one of those performers who (uses, use) acoustic instruments.
2. Black holes are objects in space that (doesn't, don't) emit light.
3. John and Harvey are the football players who (deserves, deserve) special recognition.
4. Compassion is one of the qualities that (is, are) necessary in a good leader.
5. She is the only one of the cheerleaders who (hates, hate) football.
6. Dr. Melbourne is one of the doctors who (works, work) in the clinic.
7. This is the only one of the race cars that (run, runs) so quietly.
8. The best pets are ones that (returns, return) your affection.
9. This is the kind of movie that always (ends, end) happily.
10. The newspaper editor is the person who (decides, decide) what articles to print.

MIXED REVIEW
Agreement of Subject and Verb

A. Choose the standard form of the verb for each sentence.

1. A pile of rocks (is, are) blocking Central Street.
2. My backpack, together with its contents, (weighs, weigh) over twenty pounds.
3. Each of these towns (has, have) a yearly festival.
4. One of the new cars (gets, get) over sixty miles per gallon.
5. Everybody (expects, expect) to be treated fairly.
6. Fruit or fruit juice (makes, make) a nutritious snack.
7. The editors or the art director (designs, design) the cover.
8. Around the grounds of the park (struts, strut) a peacock.
9. There (is, are) many ski areas in Colorado.
10. How (does, do) artists make stained glass?
11. Hawaii (is, are) actually several islands.
12. Creativity and enjoyment (is, are) the aim of the program.
13. Les (doesn't, don't) read any magazines except *TV Guide*.
14. The choir (sings, sing) at a special spring concert.
15. Gymnastics (requires, require) precise timing.
16. "Hill Street Blues" (has, have) high viewer ratings.
17. Sixteen dollars (is, are) the price of that shirt.
18. Three-quarters of an hour (is, are) the length of each class.
19. These boots are made of material that (melts, melt) snow.
20. Laverne is one of several class officers who (is, are) meeting with the principal.

B. Choose the correct verb for each of the following sentences.

1. Marc Chagall's *Four Seasons* (was, were) installed in Chicago in 1974.
2. Everyone who (thinks, think) that a reporter's life is romantic should spend time working on a newspaper.
3. There (is, are) some problems that can't be solved without the help of others.

4. Two hundred years of democracy (has, have) made certain changes in the Constitution necessary.
5. She (doesn't, don't) care whether anyone approves of the way she dresses.
6. Neither the station master nor the conductor (speaks, speak) English.
7. Two cups of whole wheat flour (was, were) all the recipe called for.
8. Most of the class members (wants, want) to visit the planetarium again.
9. Athletics (is, are) an important part of the school's curriculum.
10. Either the owner or her manager (is, are) always available to work on Saturday.

C. The following passage contains several errors in the agreement of subjects and verbs. Copy the paragraph, correcting these errors.

Charlie Brown is one of the characters created by Charles Schultz for his much-loved comic strip. "Peanuts" have been around for over a generation now, and there is hardly anyone who don't feel compassion for the struggles of Charlie Brown. Each of his readers, both child and adult, seem to identify with Charlie's tendency to fail. One of the problems that Charlie often has are getting his kites to fly. There's always trees in the way, and the kite invariably gets caught in one of them—on purpose, Charlie believes. Then there is Charlie's inability to kick a football or win even a single baseball game. Either the kite or sports give Charlie trouble in almost every strip. He don't have to worry about being unloved, however. Charlie Brown has millions of friends all over the world.

USING GRAMMAR IN WRITING
Agreement of Subject and Verb

A. Imagine that you are a member of the student council and that the council wishes to hold a variety show. You have been asked to find out what other organizations in your school have helped with the variety show in the past. You gather the following information:

Duties Performed by School Organizations for Past Variety Shows

Ticket sales—the French Club or the Latin Club

Lighting, set, direction—the Drama Club

Music—the Senior Jazz Ensemble and one of the music teachers

Program—the staff of the school newspaper or the staff of the yearbook

Ushers—the Varsity Cheerleaders or the Chess Club

Master of Ceremonies—one of the members of the Speech Team

Write a report to the council on your findings. Use the present tense, and make sure your subjects and verbs agree.

B. Sometimes schools, communities, cities, social groups, or even sections of the country have distinct "personalities." Identify a group to which you belong and which you feel has a very recognizable character. Write about the people in this group. Discuss their beliefs, habits, and attitudes. Write in the present tense, and use indefinite pronouns (someone, everyone, none, all, most, each, every, many, several) wherever possible. Be careful to make your subjects and verbs agree.

7.0   Pronoun Usage

Words often change their forms, depending on how they are used in particular sentences. Sometimes they change their spellings only slightly:

NOUN:	girl — girl's — girls — girls'
VERB:	need — needs — needed — needing
ADJECTIVE:	new — newer — newest
ADVERB:	near — nearer — nearest

At other times, the spellings change completely:

VERB:	do — did — done
ADJECTIVE:	good — better — best

Pronouns also change form, depending on their use in sentences. These changes in pronoun form are called changes in the **case** of the pronouns. There are three major forms that pronouns can take: the **nominative case**, the **objective case**, and the **possessive case**. These case forms, for the personal pronouns and *who*, are as follows:

NOMINATIVE	OBJECTIVE	POSSESSIVE
I	me	my, mine
we	us	our, ours
you	you	your, yours
he	him	his
she	her	her, hers
it	it	its
they	them	their, theirs
who	whom	whose
whoever	whomever	whoever

The pronouns *this, that, these, those, which,* and *what* do not change their forms to indicate case.

Indefinite pronouns change form only in the possessive case. The nominative and objective case forms are identical.

NOMINATIVE	OBJECTIVE	POSSESSIVE
someone	someone	someone's
everybody	everybody	everybody's
no one	no one	no one's

The material in this Section will explain when to use the various case forms of pronouns.

7.1 The Pronoun as Subject of a Verb

The nominative form of the pronoun is used as subject of a verb.

The problem of which pronoun form to use as subject arises chiefly when the subject is compound. The compound subject may be made up of pronouns or of both nouns and pronouns.

To decide which pronoun form to use in a compound subject, *try each part of the subject by itself with the verb.*

Hal and (I, me) went to the movies.
(Hal went; I went, *not* me went.)

The McCarthys and (they, them) are in the club.
(The McCarthys are; they are, *not* them are.)

Kerry and (she, her) read *Huckleberry Finn.*
(Kerry read; she read, *not* her read.)

The plural forms *we* and *they* sound awkward in many compounds. They can be avoided by recasting the sentence.

AWKWARD: The girls and we are going.
BETTER: We and the girls are going.

AWKWARD: We and they planned to swim at dawn.
BETTER: We all planned to swim at dawn.

7.2 The Predicate Pronoun

The verb *be* is a linking verb. It links the noun, pronoun, or adjective following it to the subject. A pronoun so linked is called a **predicate pronoun.**

The nominative pronoun form is used as a predicate pronoun.*

The problem of which form to use in a predicate pronoun occurs primarily after the verb *be*. The rule applies to all verb phrases built around forms of the verb *be* such as: *could have been, can be, should be,* etc.

> It *was* **I** whom they called.
> *Could* it *have been* **she** who won?
> It *must have been* **they** in the sports car.

Sometimes the nominative form sounds awkward. The awkwardness can be avoided by recasting the sentence.

AWKWARD: The winner was she.
BETTER: She was the winner.

AWKWARD: It was we who found the entrance to the cave.
BETTER: We are the ones who found the entrance to the cave.

AWKWARD: It should be they who are chosen.
BETTER: They should be the ones who are chosen.

7.3 The Pronoun as Object of a Verb

The objective pronoun form is used as direct or indirect object.

The problem of which pronoun form to use as object of the verb arises chiefly when the object is compound. The compound object may consist of pronouns or of both nouns and pronouns.

To decide which pronoun form to use in a compound object, *try each part of the object by itself with the verb.*

*Standard usage permits the exception in both speech and writing of *It is me.*

DIRECT OBJECT:

The principal wanted to see George and (I, me).
(see George; see me, *not* see I)
Jenny invited both (they, them) and (we, us) to the party.
(invited them, *not* invited they; invited us, *not* invited we)
Did you ask (he, him) and (I, me) to dinner?
(ask him, *not* ask he; ask me, *not* ask I)

INDIRECT OBJECT:

The counselor gave Janet and (I, me) good advice.
(gave Janet; gave me, *not* gave I)

Exercise A: Choose the standard form from those given.

1. Jeff and (I, me) are applying for scholarships at Syracuse.
2. We invited Mr. Dawson and (she, her) to speak.
3. At the bottom of the waterfall were Roger and (I, me).
4. How much money did Lynn and (she, her) make?
5. Give Marion and (she, her) the extra tickets.
6. Marty and (I, me) are having a party after the game.
7. The Warners and (they, them) are good friends.
8. The last on the program are Herb and (I, me).
9. The coach gave Harold and (I, me) passes to the game.
10. Was it (he, him) who answered the telephone?
11. (She, Her) and the officer were having a loud argument.
12. Can you tell Beth and (I, me) where the party will be?
13. Scott and (I, me) were watching television when you called.
14. Lincoln School and (we, us) are sponsoring the play.
15. We were sure that it was (he, him) at the door.

Exercise B: Follow the directions for Exercise A.

1. The bus met (he, him) and (I, me) at the station.
2. The police telephoned Gary and (they, them) right after
   the accident.
3. The store manager greeted (she, her) and (he, him)
   cordially.

4. The airlines office told (they, them) and (we, us) different stories.
5. Was it (they, them) who wrote you?
6. It might have been (she, her) in that crash.
7. The seniors scarcely noticed Betty and (I, me) as we slipped into the back row of the auditorium.
8. Why don't you let (they, them) and (we, us) take care of decorations?
9. Dad drove Casey and (I, me) into town.
10. Will you and (he, him) study together for the test?
11. It must have been (she, her) in the window.
12. If it were (he, him) who won first place, I would certainly be surprised.
13. What would you do if you were (she, her)?
14. The boss gave Herb and (I, me) a difficult job.
15. We met (they, them) and their parents at the theater after the show.

7.4   The Pronoun as Object of a Preposition

The objective pronoun form is used as object of a preposition.

The problem of which pronoun form to use as object of a preposition arises only when the object is compound. The compound object may consist of pronouns or of both nouns and pronouns.

To decide which pronoun to use in a compound object of a preposition, *try each part of the object by itself with the preposition.*

Will your aunt be going with you and (I, me)?
(with you; with me, *not* with I)
We received Christmas cards from (they, them) and the Clarks.
(from them, *not* from they)
The doctor gave virus shots to both the coaches and (we, us).
(to us; *not* to we)

The preposition *between* causes especially noticeable errors in pronoun usage. Use only the objective pronoun forms after *between*.

between you and him, *not* between you and he
between him and me, *not* between he and I

7.5   The Pronoun Used with a Noun

In a construction such as *we girls* or *us boys*, the use of the noun determines the case form of the pronoun.

We girls can bring the lunch.
   (girls is the subject of *can bring;* the nominative pronoun is therefore required.)
The Kiwanis Club gave the sports equipment to us girls.
   (girls is the object of the preposition *to;* the objective pronoun is therefore required.)

To decide which pronoun form to use in a construction such as *we boys* or *we girls,* try the pronoun by itself with the verb or preposition.

The work was not too difficult for (we, us) girls.
   (for us, *not* for we)
The officer told (we, us) boys not to play ball in the alley.
   (told us, *not* told we)
(We, Us) friends must promise never to part.
   (We must not part, *not* us must not part)

Exercise A: Choose the standard form of the pronoun from those given in parentheses.

1. Make out the check either to Mom or (I, me).
2. On my birthday I received a card and a gift from both Beth and (he, him).
3. Understanding the complex directions was hard for Mark and (I, me).

4. There is a package for you and (she, her) at the post office.
5. Between you and (I, me), that party will never be held.
6. Stacey is going home with Grace and (he, him).
7. The law guarantees the rights of (we, us) students.
8. (We, Us) Americans can learn from other cultures.
9. The doctor recommended complete rest for Mrs. Barry and (he, him).
10. There is no quarrel between (she, her) and (I, me).
11. Will you save tickets for (they, them) and (we, us)?
12. The books have been ordered for (we, us) students.
13. (We, Us) two will have to do most of the work.
14. There were many compliments for you and (she, her).
15. There is a special practice for (we, us) flute players today.

Exercise B: Follow the directions for Exercise A.

1. We had a long visit with Sue and (she, her).
2. The camp counselor asked for help from Jay and (I, me).
3. To (we, us) newcomers, the coach gave special exercises.
4. Sarah, Lynn, and (she, her) are on the committee.
5. The bad news reached Ted and (I, me) just before Christmas.
6. The usher seated Terri and (he, him) way up front.
7. For Lee and (we, us), the party was just a lot of work.
8. There are no secrets between Sally and (I, me).
9. (We, Us) baseball fans were not surprised by the Yankees' record this year.
10. After Wayne and (she, her) had spoken, there was a general discussion.
11. Only (we, us) three have been called to the office.
12. Jack, Nancy, and (I, me) are going to study marine biology in Florida.
13. There is no such thing as a junk car to (we, us) antique automobile enthusiasts.
14. The paintings by you and (I, me) will be exhibited at the Arts Center.
15. The scholarship committee met with Sue and (I, me).

Exercise C: Choose the standard form of the pronoun from those given in parentheses.

1. The counselor told Dick and (I, me) that the government often hires interpreters.
2. Later (she, her) and (I, me) found a rare book at the public library.
3. The guide showed (he, him) and (I, me) some synthetic diamonds.
4. The Clarks and (we, us) are having Thanksgiving dinner together.
5. For (we, us) girls, the lecture on job opportunities was an eye opener.
6. Will the concert management allow (we, us) three backstage?
7. When will Mario and (they, them) finish building the stereo cabinet?
8. The school has given (we, us) tournament winners an extra day of vacation.
9. Just between you and (I, me), I think the actor who played Gus in the musical *Cats* should have won a Tony award.
10. We left the selection of a class ring to (she, her) and Roger.
11. There are starting positions on the debate team for Jeff and (I, me).
12. Tom left ahead of Alice and (I, me).
13. (She, Her) and (he, him) used to tell long, complicated stories in Pig Latin.
14. The girls joined Mary and (we, us) at the bowling alley.
15. The driver called to (he, him) and (I, me) for help.
16. Unfortunately, neither (he, him) nor Brad knew the answer to the trivia quiz question.
17. We have had no letters from Holly or (she, her).
18. The changing of the guard at Buckingham Palace entertained Sue and (we, us) royally.
19. Dad and (I, me) shook hands with the Governor as we left.
20. The elephant herd migrated every year, even though it was a long trip for (they, them).

7.6 *Who* and *Whom* in Questions

Who and *whom* are pronouns that are used either to ask questions or to introduce clauses. When they ask questions, they are called **interrogative pronouns.**

To use *who* and *whom* correctly in a sentence, you must understand how the word functions in the question.

Who is the nominative form of the pronoun. It is used as the subject of the verb or as a predicate pronoun.

Whom is the objective form of the pronoun. It is used as the direct object or as the object of a preposition.

> *Who* wrote this novel? (*who* is the subject.)
> *Whom* will you choose? (*whom* is the direct object.)
> With *whom* did you dance? (*whom* is the object
>   of the preposition *with*.)
> *Whom* did you vote *for*? (*whom* is the object of the
>   preposition *for*.)

Exercise: Choose the standard form from those given in parentheses.

1. (Who, Whom) plays the leading role?
2. (Who, Whom) will the director choose?
3. (Who, Whom) knows how to figure skate?
4. For (who, whom) does Jeff babysit?
5. Perry, (who, whom) gave you those books?
6. (Who, Whom) did you speak to?
7. With (who, whom) will you travel?
8. The attorney general is (who, whom)?
9. (Who, Whom) was your report about?
10. (Who, Whom) plays quarterback for the Rams?
11. (Who, Whom) did Paul Revere warn?
12. For (who, whom) will you vote?
13. (Who, Whom) have we forgotten?
14. (Who, Whom) called Martha Graham the founder of
     modern dance?
15. (Who, Whom) did we leave behind?

7.7 *Who* and *Whom* in Clauses

As explained in Sections 3.4 and 3.6 the pronouns *who, whose,* and *whom* are often used to introduce adjective or noun clauses. When they are used to relate an adjective clause to the noun it modifies, they are called **relative pronouns.**

The pronouns *whoever* and *whomever,* meaning "any person that," are used in the same way as *who* and *whom.*

As a part of a clause, any of these pronouns has two jobs:

1. It introduces the clause.
2. It has a role within the clause.

A pronoun in the nominative form (*who, whoever*) can act as the subject or the predicate pronoun of the clause.

Galileo is the scientist *who invented the thermometer. (who* is the subject of the verb *invented* in this adjective clause.)

No one could guess *who it was. (who is* the predicate pronoun within this noun clause.)

The coach decided *who would play goalie. (who* is the subject of this noun clause.)

A pronoun in the objective form (*whom, whomever*) can act as a direct object or object of a preposition within the clause.

Pearl Buck is an author *whom I admire. (whom* is the direct object of the verb *admire* within this adjective clause.)

I will support *whomever the President appoints. (whomever* is the direct object in this noun clause.)

Venus was a Roman goddess *for whom a planet was named. (whom* is the object of the preposition *for* within this adjective clause.)

Whose functions as the possessive form within the clause.

This is the artist *whose painting I bought. (whose* is a possessive adjective modifying *painting* in the clause.)

Exercise: Choose the standard form from those given.

1. One sportscaster (whose, whom) vocabulary is famous is Howard Cosell.
2. The student (who, whom) found my watch turned it in at the office.
3. Chris is the gymnast (who, whose) specialty is the rings.
4. (Whoever, Whomever) knows how to study has an advantage.
5. The President (who, whom) initiated the New Deal was Roosevelt.
6. The people (who, whom) I resent most are cheaters.
7. Only the judges know (who, whom) the winner is.
8. Ask (whoever, whomever) you want.
9. Geologists (who, whom) study rock formations discover facts about the earth's history.
10. The police asked everyone in the neighborhood (who, whom) the troublemakers were.
11. (Whoever, Whomever) needs advice should talk to a friend or counselor.
12. One prisoner (who, whom) was paroled repeated his crimes.
13. Mr. Lee is the one (who, whom) has a black belt in karate.
14. Persephone was the woman (who, whom) Hades carried away to the underworld.
15. The letter is addressed to (whoever, whomever) lives at 123 Yellow Brick Road.
16. No one (whom, who) was in the audience will ever forget the singer's farewell performance.
17. Stephanie, (who, whom) I told you about, has been awarded a dance scholarship.
18. (Whoever, Whomever) goes on the ski weekend will have a good time even if there's no snow.
19. Faith, Rex, and (whoever, whomever) else is on the committee can be excused from study hall.
20. Doug, (whom, whose) father repairs stereos, has volunteered to fix the speakers in the auditorium.

7.8 Pronouns in Comparisons

Sometimes a comparison is made by using a clause that begins with *than* or *as*.

Fred is better at chess *than George is.*
You have as many A's *as he has.*
Marie likes me more *than she likes you.*

Sometimes the final clause in the comparison is left incomplete making the pronoun choice more difficult.

Fred is better at chess than George (is).
You have as many A's as he (has).

To decide which pronoun form to use in an incomplete comparison, complete the comparison.

Herb plays the trumpet better than (I, me).
(Herb plays the trumpet better than *I play.*)
Betty wrote a better composition than (I, me).
(Betty wrote a better composition than *I wrote.*)
We can sing as well as (they, them).
(We can sing as well as *they can.*)

7.9 The Pronoun with Infinitives

The objective form of the pronoun is used as the subject, object, or predicate pronoun of an infinitive.

The officer told *me to stop.*
(*me* is the subject of *to stop.*)
The official asked *them to observe* the rules.
(*them* is the subject of *to observe.*)
They took *him to be me.*
(*him* is the subject of *to be,* and *me* is the predicate
pronoun following *to be.*)
Reporters were at the airport *to question her.*
(*her* is the object of *to question.*)

7.10 Possessive Case with Gerunds

The possessive form of the pronoun is used when the pronoun immediately precedes a gerund.

All gerunds end in -*ing,* and they are all formed from verbs. The present participle also ends in -*ing,* and it, too, is formed from a verb. If the -*ing* word is used as a modifier, it is a participle. If it is used as a noun, it is a gerund.

The possessive form of the pronoun is used before a gerund. The nominative and objective forms are used before a participle.

His running had improved since the last track meet.
(*running* is a gerund, the subject of the verb *had improved.*)

We saw *him running* toward the finish line.
(*running* is a participle modifying *him.*)

We dislike *their playing* the stereo at midnight.
(*playing* is a gerund, the object of the verb *disliked.*)

We heard *them playing* the stereo at midnight.
(*playing* is a participle modifying *them.*)

7.11 The Pronoun as an Appositive

The form of a pronoun used as an appositive is determined by the use of the noun to which it is in apposition.

The delegates, *Tony* and *I,* want your support.
(*Tony* and *I* are in apposition to *delegates,* which is the subject of *want.* Therefore, the nominative form of the pronoun is required.)

For the two producers, *Margo* and *him,* the show was a hit.
(*Margo* and *him* are in apposition to *producers,* which is the object of the preposition *for.* Therefore, the objective form of the pronoun is required.)

We gave the children, *Toby* and *her*, new tricycles.
(*Toby* and *her* are in apposition to *children*, which is the indirect object of *gave*. Therefore, the objective form of the pronoun is required.)

To determine which form of the pronoun to use in apposition, try the appositive by itself with the verb or preposition.

Her friends, Jackie and (he, him), were always calling.
(Jackie and he were, *not* Jackie and him were.)

The flowers are from two of your friends, Sally and (I, me).
(The flowers are from me, *not* from I.)

7.12   Compound Personal Pronouns

Compound personal pronouns are used only when their antecedents appear in the same sentence.

STANDARD: I carried it up the stairs myself.
STANDARD: We made lunch for ourselves.
NONSTANDARD: The hat belongs to yourself.
STANDARD: The hat belongs to you.
NONSTANDARD: The request was approved by Lara and myself.
STANDARD: The request was approved by Lara and me.

Exercise: Choose the standard form from those given in parentheses.

1. Bill can type much faster than (I, me).
2. Mr. Crofts was disturbed by (our, us) blowing the horn.
3. The class would rather have you for president than (he, him).
4. (Their, Them) shouting kept us awake.
5. We knew the "ghost" would turn out to be (he, him).
6. No one was more frightened than (she, her).
7. Did you hear (our, us) calling you?

8. Binnie and (I, myself) will clean up the yard.
9. We gave the soloists, Jenny and (she, her), bouquets of roses.
10. We had twice as big a squad as (they, them).
11. We kept some of the strawberry shortcake for (us, ourselves).
12. The committee gave two students, Barry and (I, me) first prizes.
13. We were expecting Ms. Kirk rather than (she, her).
14. After the party, please return the unused soft drink cartons to Ted or (me, myself).
15. No one but (you, yourself) saw the accident.
16. I didn't like (his, him) sneaking in through the back door.
17. California played a better defensive game than (we, us).
18. We didn't expect the winner to be (he, him).
19. Write a thank you letter to your hosts, Katie and (he, him).
20. The audience was no more surprised than (they, them).

7.13   Pronouns and Antecedents

A pronoun agrees with its antecedent in number, gender, and person.

Agreement in Number. If the antecedent of a pronoun is singular, a singular pronoun is required. If the antecedent is plural, a plural pronoun is required.

The indefinite pronouns that are singular in meaning cause the greatest difficulty. The following are referred to by singular pronouns:

another	each	everything	one
anybody	either	neither	somebody
anyone	everybody	nobody	someone
anything	everyone	no one	

> *Each* of the boys brought *his* sleeping bag.
> *Everyone* should make up *his or her* own mind.
> *Someone* had left *his or her* briefcase on the bus.

The indefinite pronouns *all, some, any*, and *none* may be referred to by either a singular or plural pronoun, depending upon the meaning intended.

All the furniture *was* in *its* original condition.

All the students *were* taking *their* last examination.

Some of the cider *has* lost *its* tang.

None of the refugee children *have* heard from *their* parents.

Note: In all of the foregoing examples, the collective nouns and indefinite pronouns are used as subjects. The number of the verb and the number of the pronoun referring to them must be the same.

NONSTANDARD: Some of the orchestra *are* playing *its* new instruments.

STANDARD: Some of the orchestra *are* playing *their* new instruments.

NONSTANDARD: None of the singers *was* making *their* debuts.

STANDARD: None of the singers *were* making *their* debuts.

STANDARD: None of the singers *was* making *his or her* debut.

See Sections 1.2 and 6.3 for further information on agreement with indefinite pronouns.

Two or more singular antecedents joined by *or* or *nor* are referred to by a singular pronoun.

Either Bob or Hank will let us use *his* car.
Neither the cat nor the dog had eaten *its* meal.

Collective nouns may be referred to by either a singular or plural pronoun, depending upon the meaning intended.

The track team *has its* new coach.
The track team *have* worked out in *their* spare time.

Agreement in Gender. Masculine gender is indicated by *he, his, him*. Feminine gender is indicated by *she, her, hers*. Neuter gender is indicated by *it* and *its*. A pronoun must be of the same gender as the word to which it refers.

> The lion had fought for *its* life. (neuter)
> The actor rehearsed *his* lines. (masculine)
> The queen was riding in *her* coach. (feminine)

When a singular pronoun must refer to both feminine and masculine antecedents, the phrase "his or her" is acceptable. It is, in fact, preferred by some people who wish to avoid what they consider to be sexist language.

> STANDARD: Every student should have *his* ticket ready.
> STANDARD: Every student should have *his or her* ticket ready.

Agreement in Person. A personal pronoun must be in the same person as its antecedent. The words *one, everyone,* and *everybody* are in the third person. They are referred to by *he, his, him, she, her, hers*.

> NONSTANDARD: *One* should always wear *your* seat belt.
> STANDARD: *One* should always wear *his or her* seat belt.
> NONSTANDARD: *I* find that the baby's crying grates on *your* nerves.
> STANDARD: *I* find that the baby's crying grates on *my* nerves.

Exercise A: Find and correct the errors in agreement in these sentences. Make sure that both the verbs and the pronouns are correct. Three of the sentences are correct as they stand.

1. Someone had left their car in our driveway.
2. Each of the boys promised that they would come early.
3. Either Jane or Peggy left their scarf here.
4. Neither of the persons who complained would give their name.
5. Not one of the crew expected to see his or her home again.

6. Some of the team is wearing their new uniforms.
7. Nobody had done their homework during vacation.
8. Did either your father or grandfather change their name?
9. Neither of the witnesses admitted that they had seen the man.
10. Neither the principal nor the class adviser would give their approval to our plan.
11. None of the students were minding their own business.
12. Everyone on our street had decorated his or her house.
13. The student council has made up their mind to drop the party.
14. The majority of the class plans to buy their rings this year.
15. Everyone was doing their best to make the party a success.

Exercise B: Find and correct the errors in agreement between pronouns and antecedents in these sentences.

1. One should start early to plan your career.
2. I find that moderate exercise makes you feel better.
3. Everyone can now have your own computer terminal.
4. We found that you could hear well even in the back seats.
5. You will find cooking easy if one follows the directions.
6. Everyone brought their own food to the picnic.
7. What happens if one's foot slips when you are driving?
8. Nobody in the club has their own equipment.
9. Everyone in class is busy working on their own project.
10. It is a mistake for anyone to try being your own lawyer.

7.14   Indefinite Reference

To avoid any confusion for the reader, every personal pronoun should refer clearly to a definite antecedent.

INDEFINITE: The yearbook is good, but *they* didn't include enough pictures of the glee club.

BETTER: The yearbook is good, but *the editors* didn't include enough pictures of the glee club.

INDEFINITE:	*It* says in the newspaper that it will rain today.
BETTER:	The newspaper says that it will rain today.
INDEFINITE:	Harry wants to run for office because *it* is exciting.
BETTER:	Harry wants to run for office because *politics* is exciting.
INDEFINITE:	Read what *they* say about headsets.
BETTER:	Read what *this article* says about headsets.

The pronoun *you* is sometimes used when it is not meant to refer to the person spoken to. The effect is usually confusing.

INDEFINITE:	In that course *you* have fewer exams.
BETTER:	In that course there are fewer exams.
INDEFINITE:	From a single corn kernel *you* may grow a corn plant from twelve to fourteen feet high.
BETTER:	From a single corn kernel one may grow a corn plant from twelve to fourteen feet high.

Exercise A: Writing Revise the sentences below to remove all indefinite references of pronouns.

1. It says in the paper that the President vetoed the bill.
2. In English class you write essays.
3. He swung his racket but missed it.
4. During Prohibition, they made the sale of liquor illegal.
5. The tailor asked me to try it on.
6. They said on the radio that the mayor has resigned.
7. Andy wants to become a chef because it interests him.
8. The best show that they broadcast is "Nova."
9. In this school, they make you study a foreign language.
10. When you work in a lab, they expect you to be accurate.

Exercise B: Writing Follow the directions for Exercise A.

1. I missed Carl's birthday, and I'm sorry about it.
2. Kim wants to be a ski instructor because he thinks it's fun.
3. The hotel's exterior is modern, but they ruined its interior.

4. In Hawaii, they greet you with flowers.
5. I have never told a lie, and it makes people trust me.
6. They never tell you the price.
7. The plumber worked hard, but it didn't stop the leak.
8. The temperature is dropping; it may ruin the orange crop.
9. In Colonial days, they preached very long sermons.
10. They expect you to work long, hard hours at that job.

7.15 Ambiguous Reference

The word *ambiguous* means "having two or more possible meanings." The reference of a pronoun is ambiguous if the pronoun may refer to more than one word. This situation arises whenever a noun or pronoun falls between the pronoun and its true antecedent.

AMBIGUOUS: Take the books off the shelves and dust *them*.
BETTER: Dust the books after you take them off the shelves.

AMBIGUOUS: The hounds continued to chase the foxes until *they* were exhausted.
BETTER: Until the hounds were exhausted, they continued to chase the foxes.

AMBIGUOUS: Before they could get the rocket off the pad, *it* had to be repaired.
BETTER: They had to repair the rocket before they could get it off the pad.

AMBIGUOUS: Vince told Joe *he* had won the prize.
BETTER: Vince told Joe, "I've won the prize."

Exercise A: Writing Revise the sentences below to remove all ambiguous pronoun references.

1. When I put the candle in the holder, it broke.
2. Jeff asked Mark about his assignment.
3. Sara told Tanya that she really should try out for track.

4. There's an orange in this lunch bag, but it isn't mine.
5. Alison put the plant in the wagon after she bought it.
6. Before you wash them, separate the clothes from the towels.
7. Tom explained to Fred that his car needed to be overhauled.
8. Julie told Katie that her drawing won an award.
9. I took the money out of my wallet and put it on the counter.
10. Take the tennis rackets out of the presses and dust them.

Exercise B: Writing Follow the directions for Exercise A.

1. I saw the picture in a magazine, but I can't find it.
2. Joan took the belt off her dress and washed it.
3. Although I keep my books with my notebooks, I always lose them.
4. Ellen told Kay that she had made a serious mistake.
5. As the designer talked to the model, she smiled.
6. When the traffic officer spoke to Mom, she frowned.
7. We can choose a different classroom or a different schedule if we want it.
8. Take the groceries out of the bags and put them on the shelf.
9. Uncle Kevin studied acting and journalism but never pursued it.
10. We tried hanging the picture over the bookcase, but it was too big.

REINFORCEMENT EXERCISES
Pronoun Usage

A. Use pronouns as subjects, objects, and predicate words.
Choose the correct pronoun form from those in parentheses.

1. Sandra and (I, me) love to go hiking in the mountains.
2. Was it really (they, them) in that television commercial?
3. My dance instructor took (she, her) and (I, me) to a rehearsal of the American Ballet Theater.
4. (Us, We) and the Blue Demons belong to the same conference.
5. The main attractions were (her, she) and the ventriloquist.
6. (He, Him) and Abraham Lincoln had a law practice in Springfield, Illinois.
7. The pilot allowed (we, us) into the cockpit.
8. Joel met (she, her) at the theater and (they, them) went out for ice cream afterwards.
9. Rick and (her, she) are hoping to go to law school.
10. For the past two years, the leaders of the pep team have been (he, him) and Maria.

B. Use pronouns correctly. Choose the standard form from those given in parentheses.

1. Direct any suggestions to (we, us) committee members.
2. The correct number of jellybeans in the jar was known only by Mr. Hounsel and (me, I).
3. (We, Us) members of the marching band rehearse in all types of weather.
4. Except for my sister and (she, her), no one saw the mysterious light.
5. The President signed a treaty between (they, them) and (us, we).
6. Just between you and (me, I), we could never have met that deadline.

7. Who will serve as French Club officers after David and (she, her)?
8. All of (we, us) runners reached the first checkpoint without any problems.
9. The play, co-authored by (he, him) and Moss Hart, was an enormous success.
10. Will you go to the air show with Marcus and (I, me)?

C. Use *who* and *whom* correctly. Choose the standard form from those given in parentheses.

1. Is Sir John Gielgud the actor (who, whom) you most admire?
2. The winner of the election was (who, whom)?
3. By (who, whom) was the prize-winning essay written?
4. (Who, Whom) is that quiet man in the corner?
5. The new starting quarterback is (who, whom)?
6. (Who, Whom) is going to collect kindling and wood for the bonfire?
7. (Who, Whom) was the documentary about?
8. For (who, whom) was this house built?
9. (Who, Whom) is the highest paid entertainer on television?
10. (Who, Whom) was the part originally created for?

D. Use *who* or *whom* in clauses. Choose the correct pronoun from those given in parentheses.

The inventor (who, whom) got movies off to a roaring start was Thomas Edison. It was Edison, (who, whom) we now consider a genius, who introduced the kinetoscope in 1894. With this instrument, (whoever, whomever) had a nickel could watch a film by peering through a viewer and turning a crank. Two years later, the Lumière brothers, (who, whom) worked in Paris, invented a projector. This enabled large numbers of people to watch the same film at the same time. Consequently, theater owners, (whom, whose) main objective was making a profit, could collect ticket money from (whoever, whomever) they could crowd into their theaters. It was Warner Brothers (who, whom) presented the first all-sound film in 1923. After that, silent films were dead forever. Actors (whom, whose) voices didn't match the audience's expectations were out of jobs. Lillian Gish was one actress (whom, who) audiences loved in both silents and "talkies."

E. Use pronouns correctly. Some of the following sentences contain errors in the use of pronouns. If a sentence is correct as it stands, write *Correct* on your paper. If a sentence is incorrect, change the pronoun as necessary.

1. We resented them talking so loudly in the movie theater.
2. Everyone but yourself knows the answer to that question.
3. Do you advise against his going by himself?
4. The photographers gathered around to take pictures of Harrison Ford and herself.
5. The responsibility for leading the expedition rests with the two counselors, Nell and he.
6. Tai taught himself to play the guitar.
7. Carole is a better goalie than her.
8. The two researchers, Dr. Collins and her, are working on a cure for cancer.
9. The best candidate for the job has to be him.
10. No one understands the situation better than I.

F. Use pronouns that agree with antecedents. Supply a correct pronoun form for each of the following sentences.

1. Neither Hall nor David would budge from _____ point of view.
2. Everyone on the swim team must bring _____ permission form by Thursday.
3. None of the sprinters equaled _____ previous records in the 100-yard dash.
4. Either Louise or Lois will loan me _____ camera.
5. Nobody showed up after the raffle to collect _____ prize.

6. The Martins and the Waldrups took us along on _____ trip out West.

7. One must always be careful when proofreading _____ compositions.

8. All of the construction workers were satisfied with _____ new work schedule.

9. Neither my uncle nor my dad can fit into _____ old Army uniform.

10. Everyone must be responsible for making _____ own arrangements for transportation.

G. Correct indefinite or ambiguous pronoun reference. Rewrite the following paragraphs. Correct all indefinite or ambiguous pronoun references.

It was reported in the *Boston Herald* that smoking is discouraged in the Japanese city of Waki, and they are determined to eliminate it. City officials passed laws prohibiting smoking on three days in each month, and most citizens support them. On other days, sales of tobacco are not totally outlawed, but it is discouraged.

Although anti-smoking posters are all over town, they still smoke a lot. It says in the article that 70.1 percent of Waki's citizens smoke. Women smoke less than men, but their numbers are increasing. These statistics are startling, and legislators hope that the new laws will begin to lower them.

MIXED REVIEW
Pronoun Usage

A. Choose the standard form from those given in parentheses.

1. (They, Them) and we met at the movie theater.
2. The chef trained Britt and (he, him) as assistants.
3. That mysterious caller must be (she, her).
4. The soloists, Marcia and (he, him), vocalized before the concert.
5. (We, Us) girls defeated the other soccer team.
6. (Who, Whom) does Inspector Holmes suspect?
7. Connie runs the mile faster than (I, me).
8. The readers are pleased about (him, his) writing for the paper.
9. (Whoever, Whomever) touches the wet paint will leave fingerprints.
10. The editor encouraged (I, me) to join the newspaper staff.
11. In gym class, (they, them) demonstrated traditional dances.
12. The captain awarded (I, me, myself) a special trophy for sportsmanship.
13. Everyone must provide (his or her, their) own transportation.
14. Sondra asked the ushers, Miguel and (she, her), for directions to the stage door.
15. Neither Cecilia nor Randi had learned (her, their) lines for the play.
16. The passenger in the chauffeured limousine was (I, me).
17. Our teacher encouraged (him, his) setting the poem to music.
18. Alicia knitted a cowl-neck sweater for (me, myself).
19. The jury made its decision after (they, it) had deliberated for two days.
20. Anyone (who, whom) that director casts will see an improvement in (his or her, their) career.

B. Some of the following sentences contain errors in the use of pronouns. Rewrite these sentences, eliminating the errors. If there are no errors in a particular sentence, write *Correct*.

1. The proud owner of the Honda mini-bike was myself.
2. Everyone left the debate feeling pleased with their performance.
3. If you could spend a day with a famous person from history, whom would it be?
4. His playing in the band was a source of satisfaction to Brian's grandfather.
5. Max and me are trying to produce a program for cable television.
6. You made as many errors on the test as me.
7. The contest was between Frank and I.
8. No one wants to give their free time to the project.
9. The principal knew that she would give the award to whoever deserved it most.
10. Some of Hermie's teammates could not believe that the winner was him.
11. The coach gave an inspiring speech to us players.
12. If you don't want your comic book collection any more, give it to my sister and I.
13. Every doctor should attempt to keep their medical knowledge up to date.
14. To whom did you want this message delivered?
15. Although you were shorter than Danny last year, now you are two inches taller than he.

USING GRAMMAR IN WRITING
Pronoun Usage

A. Writers often tie ideas together by using words and phrases called **transitional devices.** Pronouns can be used for this purpose. Note the following example:

> The pterodactyl is an extinct, flying reptile. *It* had a wing span of twenty feet.

Write a paragraph on the peregrine falcon using the notes given below. Tie your sentences together by using pronouns.

> The peregrine falcon—a beautiful bird of prey.
> Can fly at a speed of up to 200 miles per hour.
> Less than twenty years ago, peregrines were nearly extinct.
> Numbers thinned by contamination of eggs with DDT.
> Captive breeding program set up at Cornell in 1970.
> Scientists in program incubated fragile falcon eggs.
> Scientists raised chicks and returned the birds to the wild.

B. Try your hand at science fiction writing. Imagine that in three days, a meteor will strike the Earth, completely destroying life on your planet. The Zarathustrians have decided to move everyone in your school to an uninhabited planet much like earth. There, you will establish a colony. You are to be the governor of this colony and must choose administrators to run the branches of your government:

1. One person to serve as Chief Justice
2. Two people to oversee farming and agriculture
3. Two people to oversee construction of shelters
4. One person to oversee the production of clothing
5. Two people to oversee education and the arts

Write a report explaining which people in your school you will choose for these jobs and why. Demonstrate your understanding of pronoun usage. Use pronouns as both subjects and objects.

8.0 Adjective and Adverb Usage

The similarities between adjectives and adverbs often lead people to mistake them for one another. Many adjectives look like adverbs, and many adverbs look like adjectives. Furthermore, both adjectives and adverbs are used as modifiers. To avoid confusing these two types of words, learn the guidelines in this Section for distinguishing between them.

8.1 Understanding Adjectives and Adverbs

Adjectives modify nouns and pronouns. They are also used as predicate words after linking verbs. Adverbs modify most other parts of speech, including verbs, adjectives, and other adverbs.

Julian met a *dreadful* beast in the woods. (The adjective *dreadful* modifies the noun *beast.*)

This beast was really *dreadful.* (The predicate adjective *dreadful* modifies the noun *beast.*)

The beast howled *dreadfully.* (The adverb *dreadfully* modifies the verb *howled.*)

It was a *dreadfully* noisy beast. (The adverb *dreadfully* modifies the adjective *noisy.*)

To determine whether a modifier is an adjective or an adverb, determine the part of speech of the word that it modifies.

8.2 Using Adjectives and Adverbs Correctly

Most adverbs are made by adding *-ly* to adjectives.

ADJECTIVE	ADVERB
poor	poorly
careful	carefully
sudden	suddenly
happy	happily

However, some adjectives and adverbs have precisely the same spelling:

ADJECTIVE	ADVERB
a *straight* course	thinks *straight*
a *hard* problem	works *hard*
a *high* note	flies *high*

Remember that most adjectives and adverbs that are spelled alike are of one syllable. Adjectives of more than one syllable almost always take an *-ly* ending when used as adverbs.

Sarah disliked eating in the *noisy* restaurant.
The dishes fell *noisily* to the floor.

The coach had a *cheerful* smile.
The children ran *cheerfully* onto the playground.

Some adverbs have two forms, both of which are considered proper. One form is spelled with *-ly*. The other is not.

come *quick*	move *quickly*
drive *slow*	work *slowly*
stay *close*	follow *closely*

Confusion arises because the first adverb in each of the above pairs can also be used as an adjective: a *quick* movement, a *slow* dance, a *close* friendship. Remember that these words are exceptions and that most adjectives, unlike *quick, slow,* and *close,* cannot be used as adverbs unless their spellings are changed.

8.3 The Placement of Adverbs

When a word modifies an action verb, an adjective, or another adverb, it is always an adverb.

Garfield *always* eats Jon's food. (modifies the verb *eats*)

That cat is *rarely* happy. (modifies the adjective *happy*)

He is *rather* unusually independent. (modifies the adverb *unusually*)

When the adverb follows the word that it modifies, there is sometimes a temptation to use an adjective instead, but this is a mistake. Remember that, wherever the modifier is placed, it is an adverb if it modifies a verb.

NONSTANDARD: Workers searched careful through the debris.
STANDARD: Workers searched *carefully* through the debris.

A word that comes after an action verb and that modifies the verb is an adverb.

8.4 Adjectives with Linking Verbs

Linking verbs are usually followed by adjectives rather than by adverbs. The adjective is a predicate adjective and modifies the subject.

There is no problem with modifiers following the form of *be*, the most common linking verb. Most of the other linking verbs, however, may also be used as action verbs. As action verbs, they may be followed by adverbs.

The groundhog *appeared suddenly*.
(*appeared* is an action verb modified by an adverb.)

The actress *appeared nervous*.
(*appeared* is a linking verb followed by a predicate adjective.)

The baby *grew quickly.*
(*grew* is an action verb modified by an adverb.)

The lake *grew dark* and *ominous.*
(*grew* is a linking verb followed by predicate adjectives.)

The following verbs are linking verbs. Most of them may also be used as action verbs.

look	feel	stay	become
sound	smell	remain	seem
appear	taste	grow	

To decide whether a verb is used to link or to show action, try substituting a form of *be*. If the sentence still makes sense, the verb is a linking verb.

The bride *seemed* (happy, happily).
(*The bride was happily* does not make sense. *The bride was happy* makes sense; *seemed* is a linking verb here.)
The bride *looked* (happy, happily) at the groom.
(*was* does not make sense with either modifier; *looked* is an action verb here.)

Exercise A: Choose the standard form from those given.

1. You can find the way (easy, easily) from here.
2. The man seemed (unsteady, unsteadily) on his feet.
3. Larry looked very (happy, happily) in his new job.
4. It rained (steady, steadily) all day long.
5. Jan worked at the fatiguing job as (rapid, rapidly) as possible.
6. Tony felt (uneasy, uneasily) about his mother's illness.
7. Harold found the solution to the first problem (quick, quickly) and turned to the second.
8. We thought the game was (certain, certainly) lost.
9. Your voice sounds (different, differently) over the telephone.
10. Twelve passengers in the first car were hurt (bad, badly).

Exercise B: Decide whether the italicized modifier is standard or nonstandard. If it is nonstandard, substitute the standard form.

1. You can get an office job *easier* if you have learned to take dictation.
2. Harriet seemed *angrily* about the interruption.
3. You must drive more *careful*.
4. Dr. Sanders signs his name *differently* on every prescription.
5. Barbara felt *unhappily* about her choice.
6. The repair shop fixed the radio *perfect*.
7. Skate *cautiously* on thin ice.
8. The old cottage on the dunes smelled *damply*.
9. We were concerned that the Doberman was not behaving *normal*.
10. Herb studied the letter very *careful*.

8.5 *This—These; That—Those*

This and *that* modify singular words. *These* and *those* modify plural words. The words *kind, sort,* and *type* require a singular modifier.

> NONSTANDARD: *These* kind are the best.
> STANDARD: *This* kind is the best.

> NONSTANDARD: *These* sort of gloves wear well.
> STANDARD: *This* sort of glove wears well.

8.6 *Them—Those*

Those may be either a pronoun or an adjective. *Them* is always a pronoun and never an adjective.

> NONSTANDARD: How did you get *them* blisters?
> STANDARD: How did you get *those* blisters? (adjective)
> STANDARD: How did you get *them*? (pronoun)

8.7 Bad—Badly

In standard usage, *bad* is always used after linking verbs. *Badly* follows action verbs.

> I felt bad. (*not* I felt badly)
> The fish tastes bad.
> The team played *badly*.

8.8 Good—Well

Good is used only as an adjective to modify nouns and pronouns.

Well is an adjective when it means "in good health." *Well* is used as an adverb to modify an action verb when it means that the action was performed properly or expertly.

> The Vice-President looks *well*. (adjective)
> The baby walks *well* now. (adverb)

8.9 Fewer—Less

Fewer is used to describe things that can be counted. *Less* refers to quantity or degree.

> Patrick has *fewer* headaches than he used to have.
> There has been *less* rain this year than last year.
> This dishwasher will give you *less* trouble than that one.

Exercise: Decide whether the italicized words are standard or nonstandard usage. Change nonstandard forms to standard ones.

1. There are *less* pupils studying French this year.
2. We enjoy your letters; don't stop writing *them*.
3. The milk tastes *badly* to me.
4. Be careful not to trip over *them* wires.
5. The bush grew *good* after being transplanted.
6. *Those* kind of animal belongs in a zoo.

7. Secretaries should be able to spell *good.*
8. The team felt *badly* about Lindsay's injury.
9. There are *fewer* new students in school this year.
10. *Less* voters turned out than we had expected.
11. You can't buy *those* kind of candy any more.
12. Bob has all *them* power tools in his shop.
13. Mr. Jackson has looked *badly* ever since his operation.
14. Renee gets along very *well* with her co-workers.
15. We had some of *these* kind of apple last year.

8.10   Comparative and Superlative Forms

Every adjective and adverb has one form that is commonly used to describe individual things. Most adjectives and adverbs have two additional forms that are used not only for description, but for comparison. These additional forms are the **comparative**, which is used to compare two things, and the **superlative**, which is used to compare more than two things.

COMPARATIVE: You can have either dress pattern, but I think you will find this one *easier* to follow.

SUPERLATIVE: Of the three speakers, the Jensen brings out the bass notes *best.*

Adjectives in Comparisons

The **comparative** form of the adjective is formed in two ways:

1. Most adjectives of one syllable and a few adjectives with two syllables add *-er.*

   warm—warmer   loose—looser   funny—funnier

2. Most adjectives with two syllables and all adjectives with more than two syllables use *more* to form the comparative.

   careful—more careful   optimistic—more optimistic

The **superlative** form of the adjective is formed by adding -*est* or by using *most*. Adjectives that form the comparative with -*er* form the superlative with -*est*. Those that form the comparative with *more* form the superlative with *most*.

COMPARATIVE	SUPERLATIVE
warmer	warmest
looser	loosest
funnier	funniest
more careful	most careful

Note: Comparatives may also be formed with *less* and superlatives may be formed with *least*.

Irregular Comparisons Using Adjectives

We form the comparative and superlative of some adjectives by changing the words themselves.

	COMPARATIVE	SUPERLATIVE
bad	worse	worst
far	father *or* further	farthest *or* furthest
good	better	best
little	less *or* lesser	least
many	more	most
much	more	most
well	better	best

Adverbs in Comparisons

Like adjectives, adverbs are used in comparisons. The comparative and the superlative are formed as follows:

1. Most adverbs of one syllable add -*er*.

> The wind blew *harder* yesterday.
> The assignment took *longer* than usual.

2. Most adverbs ending in -*ly* form the comparative with *more*.

The second round of talks ended *more fruitfully*.
I walked into the baby's room *more quietly*.

3. The superlative form of the adverb is formed with -*est* or *most*. Adverbs that form the comparative with -*er* form the superlative with -*est*. Those that use *more* for the comparative use *most* for the superlative.

COMPARATIVE	SUPERLATIVE
harder	hardest
longer	longest
more fruitfully	most fruitfully
more quietly	most quietly

Note: As with adjectives, comparative and superlative adverbs may be made using *less* and *least*, respectively.

Irregular Comparisons Using Adverbs

A few adverbs have irregular comparative and superlative forms.

	COMPARATIVE	SUPERLATIVE
far	farther, further	farthest, furthest
late	later	latest, last
little	less	least
much	more	most
well	better	best

Exercise A: Find each adjective. Tell whether it is in comparative form or superlative form. Ignore the articles.

1. We gave the best performance on Friday.
2. Tokyo is now bigger than New York.
3. The pen is mightier than the sword.
4. The world's fastest bird is appropriately called the swift.
5. Jack was the most unhappy boy on the team.

6. Fruit is more plentiful than ever before.
7. Which is harder, calculus or algebra?
8. Where can I find a larger dictionary?
9. That was the worst mistake I ever made.
10. The largest crowds in history witnessed the World Series.

Exercise B: Find each adverb. Tell whether it is in comparative or superlative form.

1. My parakeet roamed more widely than my cat.
2. I always get up earliest on Saturday mornings.
3. Geoffrey has the most distinctly British accent in the class.
4. The veterinarian asked us to feed Nip more frequently.
5. Mr. Spangler explained the problem more patiently than I had expected him to.
6. Several students in our speech class can say the tongue-twister, but Mark can do it most easily.
7. Jill's parents lived more happily than any fairy tale couple.
8. The students began to concentrate more intently.
9. Try to think more positively about your future.
10. Who, among the crowd of people at the audition, sang the most beautifully?

8.11 The Double Comparison

The comparative form of a modifier is made either by adding -*er* or by using *more*. It is nonstandard to use both.

The superlative form of a modifier is made either by adding -*est* or by using *most*. It is nonstandard to use both.

NONSTANDARD: My boat will go much more faster than yours.
STANDARD: My boat will go much faster than yours.

NONSTANDARD: You should find it more easier to do.
STANDARD: You should find it easier to do.

NONSTANDARD: It was the most fanciest house I'd ever seen.
STANDARD: It was the fanciest house I'd ever seen.

8.12 Illogical Comparisons

The word *other*, or the word *else*, is required in comparisons of an individual member with the rest of the group.

ILLOGICAL: Bill has won more honors than any student.
(Bill is also a student.)

CLEAR: Bill has won more honors than any *other* student.

ILLOGICAL: George is as tall as anyone on the team.

CLEAR: George is as tall as anyone *else* on the team.

The words *than* or *as* are required after the first modifier in a compound comparison.

ILLOGICAL: Tim is as tall if not taller than Brad.

CLEAR BUT
AWKWARD: Tim is as tall *as,* if not taller than, Brad.

BETTER: Tim is as tall *as* Brad, if not taller.

ILLOGICAL: Sue had as many examinations to take if not more than Helen.

CLEAR: Sue had as many examinations to take *as* Helen, if not more.

ILLOGICAL: The Dodgers' chances of winning the pennant are as good if not better than the Giants'.

CLEAR: The Dodgers' chances of winning the pennant are as good *as* the Giants', if not better.

Both parts of a comparison must be stated completely if there is any chance of its being misunderstood.

CONFUSING: I miss her more than Sandra.

CLEAR: I miss her more than Sandra *does.*

CLEAR: I miss her more than *I miss* Sandra.

CONFUSING: Harvard beats Yale more often than Brown.

CLEAR: Harvard beats Yale more often than Brown *does.*

CLEAR: Harvard beats Yale more often than *it beats* Brown.

ILLOGICAL: The population of Rio is larger than London.
CLEAR: The population of Rio is larger than *that* of London.
BETTER: Rio has a larger population than London *has*.

Exercise A: Writing Revise the following sentences to correct the errors in comparison.

1. Turn the radio up a little more louder.
2. Our team is more weaker this year because of several minor injuries.
3. Some students can study more easier with the radio turned on.
4. Harry is the tallest of the twins.
5. This down coat was the less expensive of the dozen I looked at yesterday.
6. We watched both programs, but we thought Alistair Cooke's was the best.
7. Please open the window just a bit more wider.
8. The water is more softer now with the new filtration plant.
9. Chuck washes the dishes more often than Lisa.
10. The problem is more clearer to me now than before.

Exercise B: Writing Follow the same directions as for Exercise A.

1. The work of a miner is more dangerous than a carpenter.
2. Joe is the smartest of that pair.
3. Joyce is as knowledgeable as any member of the citizen's committee.
4. In the 1978 World Series, the Yankees had the best team.
5. Beth chose the longest of the two books for her report.
6. Please try to come over a little more earlier than usual.
7. The coach was the better of the three speakers at the banquet.
8. I respect Betty Jean more than Chuck.
9. Our enrollment is more bigger than ever this year.
10. Melissa and Dolores are both good students, but Melissa is the best.

8.13   The Double Negative

A double negative occurs when a negative word is added to a statement that is already negative. The double negative is nonstandard usage.

NONSTANDARD: He did*n't* have *no* soda left.
STANDARD: He did*n't* have *any* soda left.

NONSTANDARD: She did*n't* know *nothing* about the causes of the Civil War.
STANDARD: She did*n't* know *anything* about the causes of the Civil War.

Hardly or *barely*, used with a negative word, is nonstandard.

NONSTANDARD: There was*n't hardly* a ticket left for the show.
STANDARD: There was *hardly* a ticket left for the show.

NONSTANDARD: Terry could*n't barely* hit the ball.
STANDARD: Terry could *barely* hit the ball.

Exercise A: Find examples of nonstandard usage in the following sentences and change them to standard usage. Two sentences are already standard usage.

1. The bus hadn't never been so late before.
2. There hadn't been nothing said about staying out of the water.
3. We have never had any trouble with the ignition.
4. Nobody in the audience couldn't tell what had happened.
5. The doctor hasn't said nothing that should frighten you.
6. By midnight the Thanksgiving turkey hadn't barely begun to thaw out.
7. Bob hasn't none of his brother's charm.
8. We had barely finished cleaning up, when a new crowd came through the door.
9. I'm sure that nobody else couldn't have done as well.
10. We haven't had no response to our letter, but we expect to get one soon.

Exercise B: **Writing** These sentences cover many problems of adjective and adverb usage. Find the nonstandard usages and revise them to show standard usages. Two sentences are correct.

1. You can finish the job easy in five minutes.
2. The roads are slippery. Drive careful.
3. The papers had been stacked neat on the desks.
4. Nomads don't have no homes.
5. Kris looked sad at the empty cage.
6. You will have to speak a little more clear.
7. In every pair of shoes, the right one is the biggest.
8. The score was much more closer than in last year's game.
9. The class requested less assignments.
10. After the party there wasn't hardly any food left.
11. We had peach pie and cherry pie, but the peach was best.
12. The victim's family took the news bad.
13. In a show of great football competition yesterday, the best team finally won.
14. Please don't order any more of them pencils.
15. Don felt bad about forgetting so many lines of dialogue on opening night.
16. There were less cars on the road than we had expected on a holiday weekend.
17. The patient felt far more grateful to the blood donor than the doctors.
18. We stopped using those kind of helmets two years ago.
19. Be sure to clean the metal good before applying the two coats of enamel.
20. The elm has proven to be more susceptible to disease than most other trees.

REINFORCEMENT EXERCISES
Adjective and Adverb Usage

A. Use adjectives and adverbs correctly. Correct any errors in the use of modifiers. Three sentences are already correct.

1. A lone swan flew graceful over the marshes.
2. That incoming wave is moving fast.
3. After all of those syrupy pancakes, the grapefruit juice tasted sourly.
4. Many of the passengers appeared sleepy.
5. Your chimney must be cleaned regular to avoid fires.
6. The baking fish smells wonderful!
7. The President's news conference was broadcast simultaneous over the three main networks.
8. Charlece felt uncomfortably as she walked to the podium.
9. The team of horses trudged slow up the hill.
10. Hold tight and try not to lean to either side.

B. Use troublesome modifiers correctly. Rewrite this paragraph, correcting all adverbs and adjectives used incorrectly.

My brother and I needed money bad, so we convinced our neighbor to let us paint her garage. We told her that we work good together and that we could get more done in less hours than some professional painters could. She finally gave in, and we headed to the hardware store. A hardware store employee told us that we should use long-handled roller brushes so that we wouldn't have to climb ladders. However, my brother told him, "We want to use these kind," and pointed out some short-handled brushes. So, we bought the brushes and used one of them eight-foot construction ladders. Our painting was going good when our neighbor came around to offer us some tea. I turned to her and fell off the ladder. Them cans of paint and the brushes landed on top of me. It didn't hurt bad, but I did get two black eyes and a coat of paint.

C. Correct improper comparisons. Revise the following sentences, correcting nonstandard comparisons.

1. The test was much more harder than I expected.
2. That movie was as bad if not worse than the one we saw last week.
3. I write with a pen better than a pencil.
4. Laura thinks that double chocolate cookies are more tastier than chocolate chip cookies.
5. Saturn has as many satellites if not more than any other planet.
6. This season the Knicks seem more better than any team in the division.
7. The number of assignments in English is more than history.
8. My grandad is as active if not more active than anyone in the family.
9. The pioneer spacecraft has traveled more farther than any other vehicle in history.
10. Jim knows Mark better than Carl.

D. Correct double negatives. Rewrite the following sentences, correcting the double negatives.

1. We couldn't hardly wait to hear Mr. Dunn's lecture.
2. The shortstop said that he didn't know nothing about basketball.
3. Haven't none of the musicians arrived?
4. This restaurant has never had no complaints about its food.
5. We haven't scarcely begun to distribute our posters.
6. There isn't nobody else who writes stories so suspenseful.
7. In complete armor, some medieval knights couldn't barely walk.
8. I would offer you some tea, but there isn't none left.
9. After Wednesday, I won't have no time to work on the history project.
10. No one else couldn't have groomed that horse as well as you did.

MIXED REVIEW
Adjective and Adverb Usage

A. Choose the standard form from those given in parentheses.

1. That cartoonist draws both the characters and the backgrounds extremely (good, well).
2. The food certainly smelled (bad, badly).
3. Would you bring me (them, those) books?
4. I've never seen (this, these) kind of shoe.
5. Diamonds are the (hardest, most hardest) natural substance.
6. Jerry hadn't (never, ever) seen a television studio.
7. Regina waited (nervous, nervously) for the results of her audition.
8. The radio announcer sounded (serious, seriously).
9. Of all mammals on land or in the sea, the whale is the (larger, largest).
10. Because of his cold, Eric (could, couldn't) hardly talk.
11. Most people watch (fewer, less) TV programs in summer than in winter.
12. We planted bean and tomato plants, but the bean plants grew (faster, fastest).
13. Our school library has more books than (any, any other) school library in the state.
14. My schedule of school activities doesn't allow (any, no) time for socializing.
15. Our bike club traveled (fewer, less) miles on Monday than on Tuesday.
16. Anna's scheme for the surprise party sounds (foolish, foolishly).
17. Mark types faster than (anyone, anyone else) in his class.
18. The batter (had, hadn't) barely tipped the ball.
19. Macramé seems (more easily, easier, easiest) than batik.
20. The champion looked (intent, intently) at the chess board before making his move.

B. The sentences below contain errors in the use of adjectives and adverbs. Rewrite these sentences, correcting all errors.

1. My little brother and my youngest cousin always play good together.
2. If you want to try a delicious candy, try these kind of jellybeans.
3. I got less compliments on my report than my sister did, but I also got less criticisms.
4. Dressed in her ballet costume, Felicia looked beautifully.
5. The sailors looked joyful in the direction of the land.
6. We felt badly when we realized that our friends had been waiting at the theatre for an hour.
7. The job will go more quicklier if you get a partner to help.
8. The rate of population growth in some countries is greater than the food.
9. We couldn't scarcely hear the weather report because of the thunder outside.
10. Van Gogh didn't have no idea that he would one day be famous.

USING GRAMMAR IN WRITING
Adjective and Adverb Usage

A. Imagine that you were trapped in a mine shaft for a few days and deprived of sensations from the outside world. When you were finally rescued, the sights, sounds, and smells that greeted you seemed very intense. Write a descriptive paragraph in which you recount the first impressions of the world as you imagine it would appear after such an experience. Use adjectives and adverbs to make your descriptions vivid.

B. *The Guinness Book of World Records* tells about a millionairess named Henrietta Green who had $95,000,000 when she died in 1916. She was a miser who saved little scraps of soap and went to free clinics to avoid paying doctor bills. Write an "interior monologue" in which you put yourself into the mind of Henrietta Green and think her thoughts as she walks down the streets of New York. Use adjectives and adverbs to make the impressions vivid and to communicate in concrete detail how the world's greatest miser saw life.

C. Imagine what the modern world would look like to an ancient historical figure. What would Julius Caesar think of video games and television commercials? What would the Egyptian pharoah Cheops think of skyscrapers and digital watches? Write a paragraph from the point of view of some ancient figure seeing the modern world. Use comparative adjectives and adverbs to contrast the two periods in history.

9.0 The Right Word

In preceding Sections, you may have noticed the labels **standard** and **nonstandard. Standard usages** are appropriate at all times and in all places. **Nonstandard usages** are not acceptable everywhere. In many cases, they mark the user as untrained in the English language. As a general rule, you should attempt to eliminate nonstandard usages from your speaking and writing. (See Chapter 3 at the front of this book for more information about the levels of standard and nonstandard usage.)

This Section will explain many common misuses of individual words and many common errors in word choice. Study the word lists presented in this Section so that you can learn to use the words in these lists correctly. Refer to these word lists whenever you have questions about the proper use of particular words or phrases. If a usage question arises, and it is not covered in this Section, consult a good dictionary.

9.1 Words Commonly Confused

accept, except   To *accept* is "to agree or to receive something willingly." To *except* is to "exclude or omit." As a preposition, *except* means "but" or "excluding."

> Will you *accept* my invitation?
> The new rule *excepts* honor students from final exams. (verb)
> Everybody *except* Jean brought a lunch. (preposition)

adapt, adopt To remember these words, look at the second syllables. *Adapt* means "to make *apt* or suitable; to adjust." *Adopt* means "to *opt* or choose as one's own; to accept."

> The writer *adapted* the play for the screen.
> She *adopted* the latest style of dress.

advice, advise You *advise* someone (verb). What you give that person is *advice* (noun).

affect, effect *Affect* is a verb meaning either "to influence" or "to pretend." *Effect* as a verb means "to accomplish or to produce as a result." As a noun, *effect* means "result."

> The news from South Africa *affected* him deeply.
> The actor *affected* a British accent.
> What is the *effect* of rock music on plants?
> The students tried *to effect* a change in the school policy.

agree to, with, on You agree *to* something, such as a plan. You agree *with* someone else; or something such as spinach does not agree *with* you. You agree with others *on* a course of action.

already, all ready *Already* is an adverb meaning "even now" or "previously." *All ready* is an adjective phrase meaning "completely prepared."

> We are *already* late. We are *all ready* for the tournament.

altogether, all together *Altogether* means "entirely" or "on the whole." *All together* means that all parts of a group are considered together.

> This news story is *altogether* false. (entirely)
> A tug of war is won by a team pulling *all together*.

among, between *Between* expresses the joining or separation of two people or things. *Among* refers to a group of three or more.

> NONSTANDARD: We shared the pie *between* the three of us.
> STANDARD: We shared the pie *among* the three of us.

amount, number   *Amount* is used to indicate a total sum of things. It is usually used to refer to items that cannot be counted. *Number* is used to refer to items that can be counted.

> The chef cooked the *amount* of food we ordered.
> (Food cannot be counted.)
> The chef cooked the *number* of omelets we ordered.
> (Omelets can be counted.)

angry at, with   You are angry *with* a person and angry *at* a thing.

bad, badly   See Section 8.7.

beside, besides   *Beside* means "at the side of." *Besides* means "in addition to."

> Secret Service agents stand *beside* the President.
> There are other motives *besides* greed.

borrow, lend   You *borrow from* someone. You *lend to* someone.

> NONSTANDARD: Will you *borrow* me your book?
> STANDARD: Will you *lend* me your book?
> STANDARD: May I *borrow* your book?

bring, take   *Bring* means motion or movement towards someone or some place; *take* means motion or movement away from someone or some place.

> I will *take* you back to school. (away from here)
> I hope Mom *brings* a newspaper home. (toward here)
> A plane will *take* me to St. Louis. (away from here)

can, may   *Can* means "able or having the power to do something." *May* is used to ask or to grant permission. It also expresses the probability of something happening.

> *Can* you ride a horse? (ability)
> *May* I be excused? (permission)
> Eagles *may* become extinct. (probability)

Could is the past tense of *can; might* is the past tense of *may.*

differ from, with   One thing or person differs *from* another in characteristics. You differ *with* someone when you disagree with him or her.

different from, different than   If you always use *different from,* you will never be wrong. Use *different than* only when *than* introduces a clause. Even then, use *different than* only if it is necessary to avoid awkwardness.

NONSTANDARD: My dog was *different than* hers.
STANDARD: My dog was *different from* hers.
AWKWARD: It thrilled me in a *different* way *from which* it ever had before.
LESS AWKWARD: It thrilled me in a *different* way *than* it ever had before.

Exercise A: Writing Rewrite these sentences to make them follow standard usage.

1. I advice you to be already when our visitors arrive.
2. Everyone accept Monica has agreed with the new plan.
3. Did you take back the rake I borrowed you?
4. May you tell the difference among a peach and a nectarine?
5. Alligators differ with crocodiles in the shape of the snout.
6. I get angry with machines that don't return change.
7. The union members met altogether and agreed between themselves on a strike.
8. An amendment to the Constitution must be adapted by three-fourths of the states.
9. I asked, "Can we go to the library?" but she didn't hear my request.
10. A large amount of students noticed the effect of soothing music in the cafeteria.

Exercise B: Writing Follow the same directions as for Exercise A.

1. The candidate has all ready agreed with a debate with her opponent.
2. This book I borrowed to Tom was different than the rest.

3. Heather adopted the story to suit the young listeners sitting besides her.
4. Now that I've accepted your advise, you're already to change your mind.
5. The weather can effect the amount of planes that land here.
6. If we agree on what we should do, we will except your proposal.
7. My counselor adviced me to take this math course if I plan on going to college.
8. The two leaders disagreed among themselves on the issue of excepting the treaty.
9. Will you four girls please lift the mat altogether and take it toward me?
10. Environment effects a person's personality, but heredity also has an effect.

fewer, less   See Section 8.9.

formally, formerly   *Formally* means "in a formal manner." *Formerly* means "previously."

> The committee *formally* ratified the proposal.
> Our principal was *formerly* a state senator.

further, farther; furthest, farthest   Generally, in good usage, *farther* is used for comparisons of distance, and *further* is used for anything else.

> Robin's punt went *farther* than Jenny's. (distance)
> Pablo has advanced *further* in his study of English than anyone else in the class. (extent)

good, well   See Section 8.8.

hanged, hung   Criminals are *hanged*. Things are *hung* on walls, hooks, or elsewhere.

> The sheriff's men *hanged* the thief.
> The children *hung* decorations on the tree.

imply, infer   A speaker or writer suggests or *implies* something. The reader, listener, or observer comes to a conclusion or *infers* something on the basis of what he or she sees and hears.

> The dealer *implied* that the jewelry was valuable.
> The class *inferred* that the teacher was pleased.

in, into   *In* means "inside something." *Into* tells of motion from the outside to the inside of something.

NONSTANDARD:	Carl dove *in* the water.
STANDARD:	Carl dove *into* the water.
NONSTANDARD:	I drove the car *in* the garage.
STANDARD:	I drove the car *into* the garage.

it's, its   *It's* means "it is." *Its* is a possessive pronoun.

kind, sort, type   See Section 8.5.

lay, lie   See Section 5.6.

learn, teach   To *learn* means "to gain knowledge or instruction." To *teach* is "to provide knowledge" or "to instruct."

> The student *learns* the lessons that the tutor *teaches*.

leave, let   Leave means "to go away from." *Let* means "to permit." The principal parts are *leave, left, left,* and *let, let, let.*

NONSTANDARD:	Please *leave* the usher show you to your seat.
STANDARD:	Please *let* the usher show you to your seat.

like, as, as if   While the use of *like* as a conjunction is common in speaking, its use as a conjunction is not fully established in writing. *Like* is better used as a preposition.

NONSTANDARD:	The soup doesn't taste *like* it should.
STANDARD:	The soup doesn't taste *as* it should.
NONSTANDARD:	*As* most primates, chimpanzees are social animals.
STANDARD:	*Like* most primates, chimpanzees are social animals.

NOT ACCEPTED: I feel *like* Susan Anderson does about consumers' rights.

BETTER: I feel *as* Susan Anderson does about consumers' rights.

NOT ACCEPTED: Ralph looked *like* he had seen a ghost.

BETTER: Ralph looked *as if* he had seen a ghost.

most, almost *Almost* is an adverb meaning "nearly." *Most* is an adjective meaning "the greater part."

NONSTANDARD: *Most* everyone attended the game.

STANDARD: *Almost* everyone attended the game.

of, have When *could have, might have, must have*, and similar phrases are spoken, they usually come out as contractions: *could've, might've, must've*, and so on. Because the contracted form *'ve* sounds like *of*, some people mistakenly write *could of, might of, must of*.

NONSTANDARD: That plant *must of* been overwatered.

STANDARD: That plant *must have* been overwatered.

raise, rise See Section 5.6.

their, they're, there *Their* is a possessive pronoun. *They're* means "they are." *There*, like *here*, refers to a place.

to, too *To* is a preposition. It introduces prepositional phrases such as *to the store*. *Too* is an adverb meaning "overly" or "also."

He was *too* tired. (He was *overly* tired.)
I was tired *too*. (I was tired *also*.)

your, you're *Your* is a possessive pronoun. *You're* means "you are."

Exercise A: Writing Rewrite these sentences to make them follow standard usage.

1. Most everyone must of had less money than formally.
2. An ice rink was formally located besides the field house.

3. My parents left me choose there new car.
4. Blackbeard, the pirate, was hung their, to.
5. Most all of Poe's stories keep the reader in suspense.
6. Our coach learned us how to hit an overhead smash in the corner.
7. Your going to have to rise these up higher.
8. Most everyone felt like Liz did about the game, for there were a lot of unfair decisions.
9. Listening to the radio learned me how to sing good.
10. I imply from the judge's sentence that the murderer will be hung.

Exercise B: Writing Follow the directions for Exercise A.

1. Its to bad you couldn't of come, to.
2. As outfielders, their the best around.
3. Most anyone would have said to leave it go at that.
4. You could of gone farther in school.
5. A farther goal of mine is to learn myself to play the guitar like James Taylor does.
6. He listened good to his director like a serious actor ought to.
7. The horse looked sleek as it moved in the lead.
8. "Leave me get up!" the boy shrieked, like he had been attacked.
9. For the dance we hanged colorful decorations from the ceiling.
10. The ambassador inferred that he wanted to be formerly invited to the reception.

9.2 Words Commonly Misused

a lot This little expression causes *a lot* of trouble. It is two words, not one. The misspelling *alot* is nonstandard. In addition, the phrase itself tends to be overused. Substitute other phrases such as "a great deal" for variety.

all of   The *of* is unnecessary except before pronouns.

> NONSTANDARD: Mickey ate *all of* the bananas.
> STANDARD: Mickey ate *all* the bananas.

all right   The misspelling *alright* is nonstandard usage. The two words are separate.

anywhere, nowhere, somewhere, anyway   *Anywheres, nowheres, somewheres,* and *anyways* are nonstandard.

had of, off of   The *of* is unnecessary and nonstandard.

> NONSTANDARD: If you *had of* played, we would have won.
> STANDARD: If you *had* played, we would have won.
> NONSTANDARD: The child fell *off of* the swing.
> STANDARD: The child fell *off* the swing.

kind of a, sort of a   The *a* is unnecessary and nonstandard.

> NONSTANDARD: What *kind of a* dog is Scout?
> STANDARD: What *kind of* dog is Scout?

majority   This word can be used only with items that can be counted. It is nonstandard if used in speaking of time or distance.

> NONSTANDARD: The *majority* of the film was interesting.
> STANDARD: *Most* of the film was interesting.
> NONSTANDARD: The *majority* of the time was wasted.
> STANDARD: *Most* of the time was wasted.
> STANDARD: The *majority* of the students wasted no time.

seldom ever   The *ever* is unnecessary and nonstandard. Use *seldom, very seldom,* or *hardly ever* instead.

Exercise: Writing   Rewrite the following sentences, correcting any errors in usage.

1. It rained, but I wish we could of gone to the drive-in anyways.
2. The majority of the time, we practice in the choral room.

3. My favorite kind of a movie is the detective mystery.
4. The majority of the townspeople felt that the mayor's plan was alright.
5. Ms. Martin looked for the person who had left the gift, but he was nowheres to be seen.
6. All of my relatives, or nearly all of them, felt that MacArthur Park was a nice place for the reunion.
7. Mott's Amusements, a sort of a miniature circus, is around here somewheres.
8. They seldom ever begin a game without playing the school song.
9. The painter fell off of a high scaffolding, but he was all right.
10. If you had of visited the World's Fair, you would have seen alot of interesting exhibits.

REINFORCEMENT EXERCISES
The Right Word

A. Use commonly confused words correctly. Choose the correct form from those given in parentheses.

1. In order to finish the experiment, we're going to have to work (altogether, all together).
2. The school district (adapted, adopted) a new book for its biology classes.
3. The actress said she wouldn't (accept, except) the Academy Award even if she won it.
4. My older brother is always giving me unasked for (advise, advice).
5. What was the (affect, effect) of the volcanic eruption on the earth's atmosphere?
6. The mayor has (already, all ready) announced the new budget.
7. John looks (like, as if) he has lost a lot of weight.
8. (Between, Among) the six of us, we finally arrived at a compromise.
9. Would another community temporarily (borrow, lend) us some snow removers?
10. The director was (angry with, angry at) the cast for not knowing their lines.
11. Let Mrs. Wilson know the (amount, number) of hamburgers we will need.
12. Can you (bring, take) some fruit to the class picnic?
13. Would you please (let, leave) me alone until I finish this?
14. Will you (learn, teach) me to dance?
15. In the 1880s, almost all horse thieves were (hung, hanged).
16. (Most, Almost) all of the soccer team had injuries.
17. Omaha is (farther, further) from here than Lincoln.
18. Tony pitched (less, fewer) games than Anne.

19. The detective was (implying, inferring) that Mr. Snodley himself was guilty.
20. When it started raining, we all ran (in, into) the restaurant.

B. Use commonly misused words correctly. Rewrite the following sentences, correcting any errors in usage.

1. Mom said that it is alright to phone her at the office.
2. The Roy Acuff Museum has alot of fascinating musical instruments.
3. Anyways, the trappers were snowed in for two days.
4. If we had left earlier, we could of avoided a majority of this traffic.
5. I put out food for the birds, but the squirrels ate all of the nuts.
6. What kind of an electronic game did Penny buy?
7. The score was tied for the majority of the game.
8. Juanita seldom ever makes a mistake with that kind of a math problem.
9. Clark Kent couldn't find a phone booth anywheres.
10. Did James Thurber write all of his stories for the *New Yorker?*

MIXED REVIEW

The Right Word

A. Choose the standard form from the two choices that are given in parentheses.

1. It was (already, all ready) midnight before the runway was clear enough for landings.
2. My parents said that I (can, may) take guitar lessons if I share the expense with them.
3. The three pirates split the treasure (between, among) themselves.
4. John Steinbeck delivered an inspiring speech when he (accepted, excepted) the Nobel Prize.
5. (Most, Almost) everything I liked to do last year seems childish to me now.
6. One decision that is certain to (affect, effect) your later life is your choice of a career.
7. The light of a single torch flickered (besides, beside) the memorial.
8. The President depends a great deal on the (advise, advice) of his Cabinet.
9. Special (affects, effects) are becoming an important part of the movie industry.
10. After practicing for years, I (can, may) finally juggle several eggs without breaking them.
11. Is the lawyer (implying, inferring) that the witness is hiding something?
12. Jill can throw the shotput (farther, further) than anyone else on the team.
13. This is not the (kind of a, kind of) song Hall and Oates usually sing.
14. The mayor (differed with, differed from) her advisors on how to raise money for the schools.
15. The (amount, number) of people currently residing in the city will be determined by the census.

B. Rewrite these sentences to make them follow standard usage.

1. We'll help you bring those books back to the library.
2. The author must of lived somewheres in the South.
3. Will you borrow me some kind of a measuring stick?
4. Most all of the contestants looked like they might of been nervous, to.
5. Mr. Chang learned our class how reptiles differ from amphibians.
6. Mars is alot further from Earth than the moon is.
7. After she went in the building, Gilda hanged her coat, which is different than mine, in her locker.
8. The lifeguard wouldn't leave us jump off of the high dive.
9. Our hockey coach, who formally played for the Blackhawks, seldom ever gives bad advice.
10. The principal has all ready agreed with there plan for changing the school's attendance policy.
11. The officers will except any advise that sounds alright.
12. The counselor left Alicia and her parents decide between themselves.
13. Our team has adapted another mascot in addition to the bulldog.
14. Your going to have to stop playing football all together unless that knee heals.
15. In her speech, the commentator inferred that the majority of the legal system was corrupt.
16. Each year, NASA excepts a few new astronauts from a large amount of candidates.
17. Anyways, no one plays the guitar quite like she does.
18. The majority of the time the Royal Family does not dress formerly.
19. The salesperson inferred that there were only a certain amount of tickets left.
20. The Senator differs from the President about the affect of inflation.

USING GRAMMAR IN WRITING
The Right Word

A. Write a story about a search for the Loch Ness Monster, Big Foot, the Abominable Snowman, or some other legendary creature. In your story use as many of the words from pages 627-635 as you can. Underline each of these words to see how many you were able to include in the story.

B. Folklore experts usually record the stories exactly as they hear them. Later, they may rewrite the stories in standard English. Rewrite the following story, correcting the errors in usage.

A poor woman once asked a rich man to borrow her a big silver spoon so she could entertain a special guest. The rich man told the woman it would be alright to bring the spoon to her little shack if she would be sure to bring it back the next day. The woman left with the spoon and came back the next day with the big spoon and a little silver spoon. When the rich man saw the amount of spoons, he asked the woman what had happened. The poor woman said that the big spoon had had a baby during the night. The greedy rich man excepted both spoons.

A few days later, the poor woman came back and said, "May I borrow your silver candlesticks tonight? I'll use them in my house and nowheres else." The rich man agreed on this plan and secretly hoped the woman would bring back a lot of little candlesticks the next day. However, the poor woman returned the next day empty-handed. She said the candlesticks had both fallen off of the table during dinner and died.

The rich man was very angry and hauled the woman before the three wisest people in town. These three discussed the problem between themselves and decided to formerly adapt this judgment. "If you are willing to except the profits when a spoon has a baby, then you must take the loss when a candlestick dies."

CUMULATIVE REVIEW
Usage (II)

A. Using the Correct Form of Words. Write the correct word from the two given in parentheses.

1. The old comic strips were framed and (hanged, hung).
2. It looks as though (we, us) bowlers will have to begin without a full team.
3. This discussion is between (he and I, him and me).
4. Although the scientist said that she was pleased with the results, she sounded (disappointed, disappointedly).
5. Everyone had finished (their, his or her) news article.
6. It was (she, her) who was chosen to be part of the crew.
7. Ned is one of a dozen dancers who (is, are) performing.
8. A discussion was held (between, among) the cast members.
9. Please (sit, set) the casserole on the trivet.
10. Geoff (raised, rose) the shade and peered into the yard.

B. Finding Errors in Usage. Identify the errors of agreement or form in the following sentences and rewrite each incorrect sentence. Write *C* if a sentence is already correct.

1. Leave me lie this package on the table.
2. Both the cast members and the director seems tired.
3. Neither the students nor the teacher wants to prepare for that there test.
4. That is the officer who the police chief commended.
5. The council members agreed with the plan immediately.
6. Most of the class finished the assignment, and everybody turned in their papers.
7. The audience are members of the Academy.
8. It must have been they whom we saw from the window.
9. We criticized him arriving late for rehearsal.
10. Luis and myself couldn't barely see anything in the fog.

10.0 Capitalization

10.1 Proper Nouns and Adjectives

A **common noun** is the name of a whole group of persons, places, or things. A **proper noun** is the name of an individual person, place, or thing. A **proper adjective** is an adjective formed from a proper noun.

COMMON NOUN	PROPER NOUN	PROPER ADJECTIVE
continent	Europe	European
playwright	Shakespeare	Shakespearean
car	Corvette	

Proper nouns and adjectives occur in many compound words. Capitalize only the parts of these words that are capitalized when they stand alone. Do not capitalize prefixes such as *pro-, un-, pre-* attached to proper nouns and adjectives.

un-American   pro-Leftist   pre-Civil War

Proper nouns occur in great variety. The following rules with their illustrations will help you solve the capitalization problems that proper nouns present.

10.2 Geographical Names

In a geographical name, capitalize the first letter of each word except articles and prepositions.

The article *the* appearing before a geographical name is not part of the geographical name and is therefore not capitalized.

CONTINENTS:	North America, South America, Asia, Europe, Africa
BODIES OF WATER:	the Indian Ocean, Lake Ontario, the Jordan River, Strait of Belle Isle, Cape Cod Bay, the Adriatic Sea, St. George's Channel, the Gulf of Finland
LAND FORMS:	the Pyrenees, the Sinai Peninsula, the Grand Canyon, the Syrian Desert, Mount Constance, the Plains of Abraham, Raton Pass
POLITICAL UNITS:	the District of Columbia, the British Isles, the Commonwealth of Pennsylvania, the State of Maine, the West Indies, San Francisco, the Republic of Texas, the First Congressional District, the Union of Soviet Socialist Republics
PUBLIC AREAS:	Gettysburg National Park, Fort Niagara, the Blue Grotto, Mount Rushmore
ROADS AND HIGHWAYS:	Main Street, Route 447, West Side Highway, Van Buren Avenue, the Ohio Turnpike, Strawberry Lane, Savile Row, Rue de Rivoli

10.3   Common Nouns in Names

A common noun that is part of a name is capitalized. A common noun used to define or refer to a proper noun is not capitalized.

PART OF THE NAME	REFERENCE OR DEFINITION
New York State	the state of New York°
Salt Lake City	the city of Jacksonville
the Western Plains	plains in the West
the Ohio Valley	the valley of the Ohio

10.4   Words Modified by Proper Adjectives

The word modified by a proper adjective is not capitalized unless adjective and noun together are a geographical name.

GEOGRAPHICAL NAME	MODIFIED NOUN
English Channel	English accent
the Indian Ocean	Indian customs
West Germany	German language

10.5   First Words

Capitalize the first word of a sentence, a direct quotation, and a line of poetry.

They handed him a bouquet of daisies.

"No one," he said, "has ever given me flowers before."

I will arise and go now, and go to Innisfree,
And a small cabin build there, of clay and wattles made;
Nine bean rows will I have there, a hive for the honey bee,
    And live alone in the bee-loud glade.

°In official documents, words like *city, state,* and *county* are capitalized when they are part of the name of a political unit: *the County of Westchester, the State of Mississippi, the City of Los Angeles.*

645

10.6 *A.D., B.C., I, O*

Capitalize the abbreviations *A.D.* and *B.C.*, the pronoun *I*, and the interjection *O*.

The abbreviations B.C. and A.D. occur only with the number of a year: 1001 B.C., A.D. 1492. The interjection *O* occurs in poetry, in the Bible, or in prayers or petitions: O Lord, O King, O Master.

O is quite different from the explosive interjection *oh*, which is capitalized only at the beginning of a sentence.

Exercise: Copy the following sentences, supplying necessary capitals.

1. the only german composer i could name was bach.
2. the explorers skirted the gulf of mexico until they came to the mississippi river.
3. there are not many english-speaking people in the indonesian republic.
4. many of the dutch speak german and english as well as their native tongue.
5. the republic of ghana lies on the coast of africa.
6. the amazon river almost bisects the continent of south america.
7. in an old chest found in death valley, there was a copy of a new york newspaper.
8. the old roman walls, many of them built around a.d. 100, may still be seen in the northern parts of great britain.
9. the state of minnesota is supposed to have 10,000 lakes.
10. for years, one part of the western plains was surrounded by texas and oklahoma, but it belonged to neither state.
11. you can now drive from new england to the midwest on throughways.
12. glacier national park lies in the state of montana.
13. some people believe there is a difference between the american language and english.
14. several languages are spoken in the republic of the philippines.
15. the south pole lies under a mass of ice in antarctica.

16. travelers can now go directly from the jersey turnpike to the pennsylvania turnpike.
17. the ohio river forms part of the boundary of the state of ohio.
18. the bus goes down fifth avenue to washington square.
19. several american textbooks have been translated into spanish for use in the schools of the commonwealth of puerto rico.
20. the name *robert* comes from a germanic word meaning "bright fame" and is spelled *roberto* in italian.

10.7 Directions and Sections

Capitalize names of sections of the country but not of directions of the compass.

Cotton was king in the South.
Cities in the Southwest are flourishing.
It is just north of Paris.
They flew east through the storm.
She lives on the north side of the street.
The lake is west of our cottage.
The hurricane moved northward.

Capitalize proper adjectives derived from names of sections of the country. Do not capitalize adjectives derived from words indicating direction.

an Eastern school   a southerly course
a Western concept   an eastern route

Exercise: Copy the following sentences, supplying the necessary capitals. If a sentence is correct, write *C* next to the number.

1. Many factories from the north have moved into the southern states.
2. The people of the southwest think of themselves as neither southern nor western.

3. Many eastern students are going to midwestern colleges.
4. The westbound flight leaves in ten minutes.
5. The southeast and the far west are the most rapidly growing sections of the country.
6. The storm is moving rapidly eastward.
7. In the Pacific there is one great current that flows eastward and another, south of it, that flows in a westerly direction.
8. The civilization of the west has much to learn from that of the east.
9. There are many points at issue in east-west relations.
10. The sunlight moves from east to west, but the prevailing winds move eastward.
11. Water shortage is becoming a serious problem in the southeast.
12. The northern papers were printing outrageous stories about the south, and southern papers retaliated in kind.
13. From Manila, Dr. Sims will fly west to the middle east.
14. The east branch of the Delaware flows into Pennsylvania.
15. We will take the northern route on our trip to the west.
16. One small midwestern town is named peculiar.
17. The candidate for Vice-President will probably be a westerner.
18. Some birds fly south in September but return to the north in April.
19. Is it true that Atlanta lies west of New York?
20. Northern summer resorts attract people from the south.

10.8 Languages, Races, Nationalities, and Religions

Capitalize the names of languages, races, nationalities, and religions and the adjectives formed from them.

English class	Judaism	Protestant
the Italian heritage	Episcopalian	Irish linen
Hungarian	Catholic	Peruvian

Do not capitalize the names of school subjects, except for specific course names. However, languages are always capitalized.

algebra	Algebra 2	history	Women in History
biology	Biology 1	French	Earth Science II

10.9 Organizations and Institutions

Capitalize important words in the names of organizations, buildings, firms, schools, churches, and other institutions. Do not capitalize *and* or prepositions. Capitalize an article (*a, an,* or *the*) only if it appears as the first word in a name.

Pittsburgh Symphony	Carlino Tile Company
Cedars of Lebanon Hospital	Taylor Allderdice High School
Church of the Martyr	Metropolitan Museum of Art
University of Illinois	United Airlines

Note: In brand names, the common noun is not capitalized: *a Volkswagen bus; Indian River grapefruit; Crest toothpaste.*

Exercise: Copy the following sentences. Substitute capital letters where necessary.

1. The boston choral society will appear at the university of maine.
2. The st. louis art museum has a fine collection of dutch paintings.
3. The lerner string quartet will play at the library of congress.
4. The new york public library has a fine collection of books on buddhism.
5. Ship the english books to the richmond field high school.
6. The hungarian people have an asiatic background.
7. The knights of columbus have a new office near st. mary's hospital.
8. The pennsylvania railroad runs under the hudson river into the pennsylvania station.

9. A friend of mine is teaching spanish at stanford university.
10. The anglo-african oil company is not interested in aluminum.
11. My sister bought a secondhand chevy van and furnished it with curtains from bloomingdale's.
12. Suzanne took courses in english, chemistry, and american history at columbus east high school.
13. Louis served us french toast with vermont maple syrup.
14. The junior chamber of commerce will campaign for a new hospital.
15. My mathematics teacher teaches trigonometry as well as geometry II and algebra I.
16. Where are the offices of the american red cross?
17. The oldest english company, faversham oyster fishery, has been in operation for over seven hundred years.
18. Mr. Margolis has worked at the morgan guaranty trust company for twenty years.
19. Our new offices are in the first national bank building.
20. The new business teacher is also a leader in the boy scouts of america.

10.10 Titles of Persons

Capitalize words that show rank, office, or profession when they are used with a person's name.

Doctor Weber	Representative Walsh	Father Forbes
Sergeant Reilly	Rabbi Kahn	Captain Brooks
Private Harrison	Mayor Derrado	Judge Bentley

The titles of high officials are capitalized even when they are used without the official's name.

the President of the United States the Prime Minister
the Secretary of State the Governor

The prefix *ex-* and the suffix *-elect* are not capitalized when attached to titles: *ex-President Nixon,* the *Senator-elect.*

10.11 Family Relationships

Capitalize the name of a family relationship when it is used with a person's name.

Aunt Ruth   Uncle Bill   Cousin Joe

When words like *mother, father, dad,* and *mom* are used alone in place of a particular person's name, they are capitalized. When modified by a possessive pronoun, as in *your mother,* they are not capitalized. When these and other words of family relationship do not stand for a particular person, they are not capitalized.

This sweater is from Aunt Daisy.
We begged Mom to play the piano for us.
His father will meet him at the station.

10.12 Titles of Books and Works of Art

Capitalize the first word and every important word in the titles of books, stories, plays, articles, poems, films, works of art, and musical compositions.

The only words considered not important are conjunctions, articles (*a, an,* and *the*), and prepositions containing fewer than five letters. But even these are capitalized when used as the first word in a title.

Raiders of the Lost Ark	*Death of a Salesman*
Notes of a Native Son	"To Build a Fire"
"White Christmas"	*Mona Lisa*

Exercise: Copy each word that requires a capital in these sentences.

1. Is aunt rachel giving dad a birthday party?
2. There was a radio report of the death of ex-governor jones.
3. My aunt jenny introduced colonel hawkins as our next governor.

4. The president-elect met with the senators from his state.
5. Gershwin's most famous musical work is *rhapsody in blue*.
6. Did your father hear from cousin bert?
7. The judge asked officer swenson to testify.
8. We saw the play *a raisin in the sun* by lorraine hansberry.
9. Our doctor consulted with doctor pamela payne.
10. Was henry kissinger secretary of state when ex-president ford was in office?
11. The author of the article is justice laura larson.
12. We learned that the governors of these states are to meet the secretary of the interior.
13. Have mother and father met judge krantz?
14. My sister gave cousin sandra *webster's new world dictionary*.
15. You will find *art through the ages* a useful reference.
16. Heather wants a copy of *flowers for algernon*.
17. Claire's favorite poem is frost's "stopping by woods on a snowy evening."
18. The meeting will be addressed by chief of police johnson.
19. The party consisted of colonel byrd, lieutenant wojack, and my cousin.
20. Your mother drove us out to see grandfather brown.

10.13 The Deity

Capitalize all words referring to the Deity, the Holy Family, and to religious scriptures.

God	the Holy Spirit	Allah	the Torah
the Father	the Virgin Mary	the Bible	the Talmud
the Son	the Lord	the Gospel	the Koran

Capitalize personal pronouns but not relative pronouns that refer to the Deity.

May God make His blessings plentiful.
Praise God from whom all blessings flow.

10.14 Days, Months, and Holidays

Capitalize the names of days of the week, of months, and of holidays. Do not capitalize the names of the seasons.

Wednesday	Thanksgiving	spring
August	Easter	fall

10.15 Historical Names

Capitalize the names of historical events, documents, and periods.

World War II	the Renaissance	the Homestead Act
the Constitution	the New Deal	Bill of Rights

Exercise: Copy the words in these sentences that require capitals.

1. Edward is reading the chapters on the late middle ages.
2. My favorite period in american history is the age of jackson.
3. Both the declaration of independence and the emancipation proclamation are greatly admired by other nations.
4. Some authorities believe that the battle of the bulge was a decisive battle in world war II.
5. In new york, columbus day is always a holiday.
6. The prohibition era was a time of lawlessness and confusion.
7. We expect to celebrate new year's eve by staying home and watching TV.
8. The convent of st. paul the apostle is the local address of the sisters of the holy ghost.
9. The romantic period began later in american literature.
10. The second continental congress lasted for five years.

REINFORCEMENT EXERCISES
Capitalization

A. Use correct capitalization. Correctly capitalize the following phrases.

1. a champion french poodle
2. a new chrysler
3. rhodes, an island in the aegean sea
4. modern japanese literature
5. the state of georgia
6. hannibal's invasion of italy in 218 b.c.
7. the gulf of mexico
8. the irish sea
9. irish folklore
10. pro-american

B. Use correct capitalization. Correctly capitalize the following phrases. Then use each phrase in a sentence.

1. a buddhist monk
2. the university of virginia
3. the topeka post office
4. the northern part of the midwest
5. woden, a norse god
6. polish sausage and pretzels
7. *my darling, my hamburger,* by paul zindel
8. union carbide corp.
9. halloween, on october 31
10. uncle philip's interest in the history of world war I

C. Use correct capitalization. Rewrite the following sentences, supplying necessary capitals.

1. in 1263 john balliol and his wife, devorgilla, founded a college at oxford university.
2. the story of esther is told in the old testament and commemorated by jews on purim.
3. at purdue this fall, the drama students will put on a play entitled *the time of our lives.*

4. the birds in our backyard are especially fond of eating kellogg's cornflakes and post raisin bran.
5. the famous erie canal, which was built in 1817, connected the great lakes with the hudson river.
6. the death of marc antony, which shakespeare dramatized in the 17th century, actually took place in 30 b.c.
7. the seminary students were doing research in pre-biblical languages.
8. i asked my sister to bring back some irish lace and english tea from her trip.
9. columbus was not the first european to believe he could get to the east indies by sailing west.
10. one of the most mysterious cases of a missing person is the unsolved disappearance of judge joseph f. crater in 1930.

D. Use capital letters correctly. Copy the words that require capitals in these sentences.

1. The vice-president met the french premier at national airport.
2. The social security act is administered by the department of health, education, and welfare.
3. The little group under captain siple observed christmas leave at the south pole.
4. My uncle was on an airplane carrier in the battle of midway.
5. The governor and the senator-elect exchanged cordial greetings.
6. In an address to congress, president monroe announced the monroe doctrine.
7. The settlers rode down the ohio river on their way to the west.
8. Several french communities were founded in the midwest.
9. On the eastbound flight, we were over the rocky mountains very quickly.
10. You can buy irish linen at dayton's department store on fourth street.

MIXED REVIEW
Capitalization

A. Rewrite the following sentences, supplying the necessary capitals.

1. yes, doctor caldwell advised mother to rest.
2. the falklands are a group of british islands east of the southern tip of south america.
3. last christmas uncle daniel gave me richard wright's autobiographical book, *black boy.*
4. majorca is a spanish island resort in the mediterranean sea.
5. in the spring, the chinese emperor traveled down the yangtze by boat.
6. several midwestern high schools are offering local history classes.
7. do brazilians speak spanish or portuguese?
8. the noxell corporation manufactures cover girl liquid makeup.
9. the gulf stream keeps winters mild along cape cod.
10. during world war II grandma worked at a munitions factory.
11. at bakers square i had the dutch apple pie with swiss cheese.
12. the greyhound bus traveled north along the edens expressway.
13. perhaps britain's prince charles and princess diana will visit new england.
14. one reporter asked representative chissom and senator hayakawa for reports of their earnings.
15. mahatma gandhi repeated a famous hindu prayer on the banks of the ganges river.
16. at stevenson high school, advanced algebra II begins with a review of algebra I.
17. headquarters for the united nations are in new york city.

18. ms. ellman asked, "who ruled the world in 100 b.c.?"
19. reciting verses from the bible, the pilgrims celebrated the first thanksgiving day.
20. at appomattox, a village in virginia, general robert e. lee signed the treaty that ended the civil war.

B. Rewrite the following paragraph, supplying the necessary capitals.

of all the horror films that have been made in the twentieth century, probably none has been so popular as r. l. stevenson's story of *dr. jekyll and mr. hyde.* in fact, the first horror film ever released in america was a version of that tale. the movie was made by selig polyscope company of chicago, and it was first seen by american audiences in the spring of 1908. on the other side of the atlantic the same story was made into the first british horror film with two different actors, james cruze and harry benham, taking the title roles. unfortunately for stevenson, he had no reason to think of securing movie rights when he originally wrote *dr. jekyll and mr. hyde.*

C. Rewrite the following paragraph, supplying the necessary capitals.

my grandmother davis had always dreamed of a vacation in the wilderness of california. she said, "i love san francisco, san diego, and disneyland, but i've never been in the mountains." so, for her birthday this july, we drove south from seattle, along the pacific coast highway. she liked the scenery in oregon, but she really lit up when we turned east and headed into the mountains. eventually, we reached our destination, yosemite park. my grandma loved hiking in tuolomne meadows, and she must have taken three rolls of pictures of half dome mountain, el capitan, and all the waterfalls. she was also a good sport about rubber rafting on the merced river. she says the best part of the vacation, though, was her birthday dinner at the beautiful old ahwanee hotel.

USING MECHANICS IN WRITING
Capitalization

A. You can quickly gain insights about a person by asking him or her the right types of questions. Interview four people whom you consider to be interesting personalities. Ask these questions:

1. What is your age?
2. What is your occupation or area of interest?
3. What part of the country are you from?
4. Would you describe yourself as ordinary, different, unique?
5. Which modern figures do you most admire?
6. What magazines or newspapers do you read?
7. What two books and two musical recordings would you take with you to a desert island?
8. What is your favorite movie or television show?

Choose the person whose answers most interest you. Write a short composition analyzing his or her interests and background. Do they fit the type of person that you perceived this individual to be? Be sure to capitalize according to the rules presented in this Section.

B. Imagine that you are the winner of a sweepstakes contest. You will be given the foreign vacation of your dreams. The contest rules state that you must submit a letter containing the following information:

1. What two countries would you most like to visit?
2. What languages are spoken there?
3. What geographical features (mountains, rivers, oceans, waterfalls, and the like) attract you to these countries?
4. What cities or towns would you like to visit there?
5. What sights would you like to see in these countries?

Research the countries of your choice in the library. Write your letter based on this research. One country may be the United States.

11.0 End Marks and Commas

11.1 Periods at the Close of Sentences

Place a period at the close of every declarative sentence and of most imperative sentences.

A period is also used at the close of groups of words that are used as sentences even though they are not complete sentences.

> Don't get too near the fire.
> I'll never go back to that barber. Never.

11.2 Periods in Abbreviations

Place a period after every part of an abbreviation.

U. S. Grant	Ulysses Simpson Grant
Atty. Gen.	Attorney General
N. Dak.	North Dakota
P.M.	*post meridiem*

It has become the custom not to use periods in abbreviations of certain government agencies and international organizations.

NATO	North Atlantic Treaty Organization
FBI	Federal Bureau of Investigation
UN	United Nations
FDA	Food and Drug Administration
IRS	Internal Revenue Service

11.3　Exclamation Points

Place an exclamation point after an exclamatory sentence and after an exclamation set off from a sentence.

Wow! What a hit!　That's enough!
Help! Help!　Look out!
Bravo!　We want Armstrong!

11.4　Question Marks

Place a question mark after an interrogative sentence or after a question that is not a complete sentence.

The word order in questions is sometimes the same as in declarative sentences. In speech, the speaker raises his or her voice at the end of the sentence to show that it is a question. In writing, the question mark performs the same function.

Does Roger ice skate?　You call this hot?
Is this the book you want?　Who made these donuts?
The date? It's the twenty-fifth.　These are yours?

Exercise A: Copy these sentences, using end marks and punctuation as required for sentences and abbreviations. Use question marks only for sentences in normal interrogative form.

1. At what time does the game begin
2. Mr. L V Costello left his office at 4:30 P M Thursday and has not been heard from since
3. I've been robbed
4. Does the plane from San Francisco arrive at 4:10 A M or 4:10 P M
5. Have you ever seen Bogart in "Casablanca"
6. U S Sen J W Fulbright attended Oxford University on a Rhodes Scholarship
7. Emily Ray, D D S, used to work for General Foods, Inc doing research on how sugar affects teeth

8. Dr J A Larson, Jr will attend a nutrition conference in Washington, D C
9. The contract was arranged between Brightons, Ltd of England and Sweetways, Inc of New York
10. Who ruled the area surrounding the Mediterranean from 100 B C to A D 200

Exercise B: Follow the directions for Exercise A.

1. Don't touch that wire
2. When the box arrives, may we open it
3. The book about the life of Jesus was written by the Reverend Thomas Powers, S J
4. Susan B Anthony was a leader in the women's suffrage movement, wasn't she
5. Help The rug is on fire
6. Brig Gen M E Clark is director of the Women's Army Corps
7. Did Dr Martin Luther King, Jr win the Nobel peace prize in 1963 or in 1964
8. Does the IRS check up on the FBI
9. The seminar on international relations was addressed by Asst Dep José Rivera
10. Marilyn Barnard, D Sc was appointed to the ICC

Uses of the Comma

11.5 Introductory Words

Introductory words such as *yes, no, well, why,* and *oh* are followed by a comma.

Yes, I think I would like some soup.
Well, I haven't actually finished the assignment.
Oh, this coat belongs to you.

Adverbs such as *besides, however, anyhow, nonetheless* at the beginning of a sentence are set off by commas.

11.6   Introductory Phrases and Clauses

A participial phrase at the beginning of a sentence is followed by a comma.
An adverbial clause at the beginning of a sentence is followed by a comma.
A succession of prepositional phrases at the beginning of a sentence is set off by a comma.
A single prepositional phrase at the beginning of a sentence may be set off by a comma if it is followed by a natural pause when read.

> *Hoping to be rescued,* they treaded water all night.
>   (participial phrase)
> *When the sun rose the next morning,* our sleeping bags were
>   covered with dew. (adverbial clause)
> *Under the rug at the top of the stairs,* we found Dad's keys.
>   (succession of prepositional phrases)
> *After the brief summer rain,* the desert bloomed.
>   (optional comma after a single introductory prepositional
>   phrase)

11.7   Transposed Words and Phrases

Words and phrases moved to the beginning of a sentence from their normal position are usually set off by a comma.

> There is obviously no exit to this cave. (normal order)
> *Obviously,* there is no exit to this cave. (transposed order)
>
> Call Serena for directions if necessary. (normal order)
> *If necessary,* call Serena for directions. (transposed order)

Exercise A: Copy the following sentences, inserting commas where necessary. Two of the sentences are correct.

1. Honestly we are not justified in complaining.
2. At the start of the campaign Ms. Anson was favored to win.
3. Well no one was more surprised at the outcome than Rob.
4. If possible make the appointment for Wednesday.

5. Wearing sunglasses gives me a headache.
6. After scoring six runs in the first inning the Mets let up.
7. To avoid nervous tension practice physical relaxation.
8. Counting on surprise Greenville passed on the first down.
9. Exploring the wilderness requires preparation and skill.
10. Although the road was icy we made fairly good time.

Exercise B: Follow the directions for Exercise A. Two of the sentences are correct.

1. No there is no other way out of the valley.
2. When Mozart was six he was performing his music in the courts of Europe.
3. Concentrating intensely Lynn went over her report again.
4. Yes Amelia Earhart was the first woman to fly solo across the ocean.
5. Dropping their tools the workers scrambled for safety.
6. To save some of the money is simply good sense.
7. When the tide went out we walked along the sandy beach.
8. Keeping up the morale of the staff was Paul's hardest job.
9. Hard as she worked the younger child could not catch up.
10. Why no one warned us to shut off the water.

11.8 Appositives

An appositive is set off from the rest of the sentence by commas.

Farrell, *our quarterback,* injured his shoulder.
Mother's guest, *Ms. Worthall,* was not amused.

11.9 Words of Direct Address

Words of direct address are set off by commas.

Giles, please stop humming that song.
So, *Dr. Jeffries,* what is your opinion?
Would you come here a minute, *Ms. Chilton?*

11.10   Parenthetical Expressions

Words and phrases used to explain or qualify a statement are called **parenthetical expressions.** These same words and phrases may also be used as basic parts of sentences. It is only when they are parenthetical that they are set off by commas.

> I believe our car is over there.
> Our car, *I believe,* is over there. (parenthetical)
>
> We hope that we'll get back in time for the meeting.
> We'll get back, *we hope,* in time for the meeting.
> (parenthetical)

Parenthetical expressions are set off by commas.

Some expressions often used parenthetically are:

of course	as a matter of fact	for example
in fact	I believe (hope, think)	on the other hand

> Jenny, *on the other hand,* was well prepared.
> You know, *of course,* that Mark Twain was a pseudonym.

Conjunctive adverbs (see Section 1.7) used parenthetically within a sentence are set off by commas: *therefore, moreover, nevertheless, however, consequently,* and so on.

> The principal, *moreover,* was in favor of their plan.
> The students, *however,* did not know this.
> The rally, *consequently,* was attended by very few.

Occasionally, words like *however, therefore,* and *consequently* are used to modify a word in the sentence. As modifiers they are an essential part of the meaning of a sentence. Since they are essential, they are not set off by commas.

> Pat cannot arrive on time *however* hard he tries.
> The cast had performed the play the previous semester.
> They *therefore* needed little rehearsal.
> The club's bylaws were *consequently* altered.

11.11 Dates, Addresses, Geographical Names

In dates and addresses of more than one part, set off every part after the first from the rest of the sentence.

> She comes from a small town in Ohio. (one part)
> I believe that East Liverpool, Ohio, is her home town. (two parts, the second set off by commas)
> V-J Day was in 1945. (one part)
> It was on August 14, 1945, that the fighting with Japan ended. (two parts, the second set off by commas)
> All of his mail is being forwarded to 3144 Camelback Road, Phoenix, Arizona 85016, where his aunt and uncle live. (three parts, the second and third set off by commas)

Note: The day of the month and the month are one item. The name of the street and the house number are one item. The name of the state and the ZIP code are one item.

> May 29   313 West Houston Street   Georgia 30312

Exercise A: Copy these sentences, inserting necessary commas.

1. We visited the Adams Library one of the oldest in America.
2. There is no doubt my friends that hard times are ahead.
3. One field of science computer technology is almost completely devoted to storing and transmitting information.
4. The damage however was less than we had expected.
5. A completely honest person I can assure you is hard to find.
6. In San Francisco California late summer is often chilly.
7. The door was opened by the butler a tall man with brooding eyes.
8. The game was played as a matter of fact just as we planned.
9. Therefore the library will be closed on Saturday March 16.
10. The company has moved to Morristown New Jersey.

Exercise B: Follow the directions for Exercise A.

1. A map will show that Reno Nevada lies farther west than Los Angeles California.
2. Our new address is 41 East Twelfth Street New York New York 10003.
3. The treaty was signed in Geneva Switzerland on December 15 1906 but it was not ratified until March 6 1908.
4. On July 5 1835 there were snowstorms in New England.
5. Lee and his twin brother were born in Omaha Nebraska on December 19 1970.
6. You know my colleagues we may be on the verge of a revolution in printing.
7. This house as you can see was built on a rocky ledge.
8. We will meet you at Canton Ohio on Wednesday January 10.
9. The trapped miners decided therefore to make one more attempt to dig their way out.
10. It is up to you my friends to decide what kind of society you want to live in.

11.12 Nonrestrictive Modifiers

A clause that identifies or points out the person or thing it modifies is a **restrictive clause.** It is essential to the meaning of the sentence. It cannot be dropped without confusing the meaning or making the meaning incomplete.

The car *that I told you about* is parked over there.
(The clause tells *which* car.)
We need a car *that can seat ten.* (The clause tells
an essential characteristic of the car.)
The woman *who called you* is the personnel director
(Without the clause the sentence has no specific
meaning.)

Restrictive clauses are not set off from the rest of the sentence by commas.

A **nonrestrictive clause** does *not* contain information essential to the meaning of the sentence. It merely presents added information. It can be dropped without confusing the meaning of the sentence.

> Lynn, *who had been accepted for admission to several colleges,* was awarded a scholarship to Berkeley.
> The cat, *which recently had kittens,* drinks at least a pint of milk a day.

Nonrestrictive clauses are set off by commas from the rest of the sentence.

Notice that *that* is used to introduce restrictive clauses, and that *which* is used to introduce nonrestrictive clauses.

> The river *that empties into the Gulf of Mexico* is called the Mississippi.
> The Mississippi River, *which empties into the Gulf of Mexico,* has inspired much great American writing.

Participial phrases that identify or point out the thing or person they modify are restrictive.

> The mechanic *lying under that Ford* worked on our car. (Without the phrase, the sentence loses its specific meaning.)
> The tag *sewn into the lining* tells whose coat it is. (The phrase identifies the tag.)

Nonrestrictive participial phrases merely add meaning. They are not essential and can be dropped without making the meaning of the sentence incomplete.

> *Shading my eyes,* I peered across the field.
> Tony, *holding aloft a huge cake,* entered the room.
> The protesters, *circling in front of the store,* sang freedom songs.

Nonrestrictive participial phrases are set off from the rest of the sentence by commas. Restrictive phrases are not set off by commas.

Exercise : Number your paper 1-20. Decide whether the adjective clause or the participial phrase is restrictive or nonrestrictive. After each number write *restrictive* or *nonrestrictive.* Copy and insert commas in the sentences in which commas are needed.

1. Lewis Carroll is the British author who wrote *Alice in Wonderland.*
2. Standing in the doorway Drew asked if he could come in for a moment and get warm.
3. This is the house that we expect to buy.
4. Mr. Salvatore who is a famous singer will train our class.
5. The Carlsbad Caverns which attract sightseers to New Mexico are the largest known underground caverns.
6. My sister Lily who is crazy about airplanes wants to be a pilot someday.
7. The picture now appearing at the Tivoli stars Meryl Streep.
8. We were delighted by the unbiased report that appeared in the morning papers.
9. The new toll road which runs from Zenith to Mt. Zion will save us a great deal of time.
10. Mom's office which has always been dark and gloomy has just been redecorated.
11. The new show which was a musical about cats was a disappointment to us.
12. These are the boxes that you are to return to the store.
13. We waited until the last moment hoping you would appear.
14. The person driving the car had neither insurance nor a valid driver's license.
15. The hills that you see in the distance lie in New Jersey.
16. Our next-door neighbor who is a fine mechanic helped us repair the dishwasher.
17. The horse that is pawing the ground has not been fed.
18. The coach fearing overconfidence put the team through a rigorous practice session.
19. The car that you just passed is a police car.
20. The room which was too small in the first place was now overcrowded.

11.13   Compound Sentences

Place a comma before the conjunction that joins two main clauses in a compound sentence.

It snowed all night, *and* the schools were closed the next day.

Ms. Thomas must leave now, *or* she will miss her plane.

The bill may not pass this time, *but* you can be certain it will be passed soon.

Lucy did not remember where they had planned to meet, *nor* did she know Henry's phone number.

When the clauses are quite short, the comma may be omitted.

The sun rose and we awakened.

Reynolds hit a double and Lane scored a run.

11.14   Series

A **series** is a group of three or more items of the same kind.

SERIES OF NOUNS:	*Clothing, books,* and *papers* were piled on top of Kent's dresser.
SERIES OF VERBS:	The bus driver *honked, slammed* on the brakes, and *swerved* sharply.
SERIES OF ADJECTIVES:	The day that we had so long awaited was *warm, sunny,* and *cloudless.*
SERIES OF PHRASES:	Groups of children were playing *behind the house, on the porch,* and *in the yard.*

Commas are used to separate the parts of a series.

No comma is required after the last item in a series. When the last two items of a series are joined by *and* or *or,* the comma is sometimes omitted. To avoid all possibility of misunderstanding, it is wise to use a comma before the conjunction.

Do not use a comma if all parts of the series are joined by *and, or,* or *nor: All summer the children swam and read and played.*

11.15 Coordinate Adjectives

Commas are placed between coordinate adjectives that modify the same noun.

The long, dull debate seemed endless.
Raging, howling winds whipped the trees.

To determine whether adjectives are coordinate, try placing an *and* between them. If it sounds natural, they are coordinate, and a comma is needed.

PROBLEM:	His loud whining voice made the audience shudder.
NATURAL:	His loud *and* whining voice made the audience shudder.
SOLUTION:	His loud, whining voice made the audience shudder.
PROBLEM:	It was a dark dreary depressing day.
NATURAL:	It was a dark, dreary, *and* depressing day.
SOLUTION:	It was a dark, dreary, depressing day.
PROBLEM:	Our house is the big white one.
NOT NATURAL:	Our house is the big *and* white one.
SOLUTION:	Our house is the big white one.

In general, it is safe to omit the comma after numbers and adjectives of size, shape, and age.

a big round moon   five tiny wafers

Exercise : Copy these sentences, placing commas where they are needed.

1. We asked Marion to come with us but she had another engagement.
2. The lights the movements and the presents make a pretty picture.

3. We had not intended to stay overnight but the snowfall turned into a blizzard.
4. The officer asked for Bob's license looked it over and got out her notebook.
5. The ambulance must come soon or we will have to take Evan to the hospital ourselves.
6. Beethoven wrote symphonies quartets concertos and sonatas.
7. Three trucks four cars and a trailer were tangled on the icy bridge that spanned the Potomac River.
8. The president of the manufacturing company seemed friendly warm and generous.
9. The boss frowned got up from his desk tried to look severe and finally grinned.
10. Every picture on the roll of film was either blurred dark or out of focus.
11. Harry has his pass but he cannot leave the base until tomorrow afternoon.
12. Helen entered the room walked straight to the table and called the meeting to order.
13. Strange noises were coming from the stereo from the water pipes and from the attic.
14. I could not reach the top shelf of the closet nor could I find the stepladder.
15. You had better start for the station now or you will miss the last bus to Davenport.
16. Couples were standing in the streets sitting on telephone poles and leaning out of windows.
17. A flight attendant must be cheerful alert and always pleasant to the passengers.
18. We had expected to arrive in Bismarck by midnight but the plane could not land.
19. All roads bridges and highways into the city have been closed by the heavy snowstorm.
20. Suddenly, the commanding officer picked up a pen reached for my papers signed them and handed them across the desk to me.

11.16 Clarity

Use a comma to separate words or phrases that might be mistakenly joined in reading.

There are three common situations in which words may be mistakenly read together. In these instances, commas are necessary to avoid confusion. The first situation occurs when the conjunctions *but* and *for* are mistaken for prepositions.

CONFUSING: I liked all the speeches but one was superb.
CLEAR: I liked all the speeches, but one was superb.

CONFUSING: Rita listened for she thought she'd heard a cry.
CLEAR: Rita listened, for she thought she'd heard a cry.

A second source of confusion is a noun following a verbal phrase.

CONFUSING: Before waxing Jill washed the car.
CLEAR: Before waxing, Jill washed the car.

CONFUSING: To walk a cat must withdraw its nails.
CLEAR: To walk, a cat must withdraw its nails.

CONFUSING: After painting Vincent wrote his brother.
CLEAR: After painting, Vincent wrote his brother.

A third source of confusion is the word that may be either adverb, preposition, or conjunction at the beginning of the sentence.

CONFUSING: Below the earth looked like a quilt.
CLEAR: Below, the earth looked like a quilt.

CONFUSING: Outside the courtyard was in chaos.
CLEAR: Outside, the courtyard was in chaos.

11.17 Words Omitted

Use a comma when words are omitted from parallel word groups.

Anna baked a pie; Tom, some bread.

Detroit manufactures cars; Hollywood, dreams.
The day became warm, and our spirits, merry.

Exercise A: Copy these sentences, placing commas where necessary to avoid confusion.

1. Ms. Ellis sent four letters; Ms. Harris two dozen postcards.
2. I recognized none of the group but Todd had known one of the boys in summer camp.
3. Once before the stage curtain had stuck halfway up.
4. After cooking Roger cleaned up the kitchen.
5. Amy wore red socks; Melinda blue ones.
6. Luis tasted all the pies but one was too hot.
7. To play a stereo must have speakers.
8. Inside the house smelled of freshly baked brownies.
9. From calling Ben lost his voice.
10. Beyond the residential section extends for ten miles.

Exercise B: Follow the same directions as for Exercise A.

1. Inside the church was beautifully lighted.
2. Above the men were dangling ropes over the cliff.
3. Before leaving the janitor locked the windows.
4. As he wrote the short story became very long.
5. Underneath the boat was covered with slime.
6. John Steinbeck wrote *Of Mice and Men;* Leonard Wibberley *The Mouse That Roared.*
7. When a doctor is called to cure a patient is his or her aim.
8. All the girls went to the game but Sue had to babysit.
9. Skip set out the chairs on the porch for the guests were arriving.
10. Outside the house looked as though no one lived there.

REINFORCEMENT EXERCISES
End Marks and Commas

A. Use end marks correctly. Punctuate the following sentences as necessary.

1. Wow Dave Winfield just hit a grand slam
2. What time is it It's exactly 5:00 P M
3. The spy masqueraded as an FBI agent
4. I can't believe it She just won two hundred dollars in the short story contest that she entered
5. Watch out for that truck
6. José R Sanchez is an interpreter at the UN
7. Help Fire Call the fire department
8. At 8:00 A M, Sen Percy held a news conference
9. Marion Heid, Ph D, was named the President's advisor to NATO
10. Is S Caro the right abbreviation for South Carolina

B. Use commas after introductory words and phrases. Insert commas where needed in the following sentences.

1. Yes Kaskaskia was once the capital of Illinois.
2. Although she looked familiar I couldn't recall her name.
3. However busy he is Dad always makes time to hear our problems.
4. While he was speaking Mr. Sanchez gestured with his hands.
5. Obviously this pair of skates is beyond repair.
6. Yes I would like a ride home after the game.
7. However his mother was born in Chile.
8. Of course few people really believe that there are ghosts in the Tower of London.
9. Until we find our compass we will not be able to make our way back to camp.
10. After the discovery of gold in Victoria many settlers came to South Australia.

C. Use commas correctly. Insert commas where necessary in the following sentences.

1. Luke Skywalker hero of the *Star Wars* trilogy is now a famous figure.
2. Jill Tom has been trying to call you.
3. Jason Robards as a matter of fact has starred in nearly all of Eugene O'Neill's major plays.
4. For information on stamp collecting write to the National Philatelic Society 111 Huron Street Chicago Illinois 60604.
5. On May 3 1765 the first American medical school opened.
6. Ben Franklin I believe was the inventor of bifocal lenses.
7. O. Henry the author of "Gift of the Magi" was born on September 11 1862.
8. Of course Michael you might attend college on a football scholarship.
9. Believe it or not Elvis Presley recorded eighty albums and almost two hundred singles.
10. We will arrive in Tucson Arizona we hope by Labor Day.

D. Use commas to set off nonrestrictive modifiers. Insert commas where needed in the following paragraph. Remember that commas are not used to set off restrictive modifiers.

Commedia dell'arte which is a form of comic theatre was performed all across Europe between the years 1400 and 1600. Performers of the *commedia* did not memorize written dialogue as actors do now. They improvised instead which means that they made up their lines as they went along. The actor who was most important in *commedia* was the clown. He had to be very athletic since much of the humor in *commedia* performances came from his gymnastics. The clown who was very clever usually played tricks on the other characters. *Commedia dell'arte* was very popular; an entire town would often turn out to watch a performance. Audiences could be counted on to fill the hat that was passed around after every show.

E. Use commas correctly. Insert commas in the following sentences as necessary. One sentence is already correct.

1. Crocodiles snakes turtles and lizards all belong to the reptile family.
2. Sherry loves masquerades music and dancing so she really enjoys Mardi Gras.
3. We ate in Chinatown and took a cable car to the Art Institute.
4. Four small children marched up Third Street past the florist shop and into the candy store.
5. Our scout troop took a trip to Eagle River and we swam hiked and canoed every day for two weeks.
6. His blue eyes red hair and freckles made me suspect that his ancestors were Irish Scottish or English.
7. Our history class had questions about a local Revolutionary War hero so we wrote to the Historical Society.
8. The loud insistent knocking sound terrified her as she sat alone in the old house.
9. Three of the contestants at the 4-H fair were college students but most of them were still in high school.
10. Gregory broke his arm sprained his ankle and cut his leg when he fell down the dark dilapidated stairs.

F. Use commas for clarity. Punctuate the following sentences.

1. All of the puppies were cute but one was beautiful.
2. Never worrying Shonta met each day with enthusiasm.
3. Inside the store was crowded with bargain hunters.
4. Kurt was the first performer on the stage; Bart the second.
5. Inside the calf was sleeping on a bed of straw.
6. To make real Italian spaghetti sauce oregano is essential.
7. Dad is a Democrat; Mom a Republican.
8. After fishing my brother cleaned the trout and fried them for dinner.
9. All of the ambassadors spoke French; some Russian or Chinese as well.
10. The first speaker was entertaining; the second dull.

End Marks and Commas

A. Copy these sentences, inserting the necessary end marks and commas.

1. Fortunately Yoshi is much healthier now
2. Hooray Our team made the finals
3. Both of my sisters are successful businesswomen but Angela is I think the more successful of the two
4. When the movie is over will you pick us up
5. Scanning the area the forest ranger noticed a distant cloud of smoke
6. Well leap year of course has an extra day
7. Early settlers landed at Salem Massachusetts on September 6 1628
8. After calling Tina let her brother use the phone
9. J Edgar Hoover I believe was head of the FBI in 1968
10. April Fool's Day a day for harmless pranks and jokes is observed on April 1
11. My uncle trying to lose weight eats a lot of salads fruit and cottage cheese
12. Hank did you go to Paris or did you stay in London
13. The time in San Diego is 9 A M; in Baltimore 12 noon
14. The northern kit fox which is native to Canada is an endangered species
15. The East Building of the National Gallery of Art in Washington D C was designed by I M Pei
16. Traveling through space the astronaut radioed to Earth
17. Undoubtedly Dr. Sayner who is the team doctor will tape your ankle
18. Yes please send my T-shirt to 383 Picardy Rome New York
19. *Nautilus* the first atomic submarine was launched on January 21 1954
20. Wow If the experts are correct Karen we will soon have computerized homes

B. Copy the following sentences, inserting necessary commas and end marks.

1. The reflecting telescope was developed in the machine shop of James Short a Scottish optician in 1730
2. Hindus worship Brahma Vishnu and Shiva
3. The book was published in July 1977 by Bantam Books 666 Fifth Avenue New York New York 10019
4. German shepherds are if I am not mistaken intelligent gentle animals
5. Ordinarily the class would meet in Room 610 on Tuesday
6. Amy's favorite food is pizza; Jenny's ice cream
7. Are you the person looking for an apartment
8. The Almquists who hardly needed any more appliances in their kitchen won a food processor and a microwave oven at the raffle
9. When you read the rules for the game of whist you will see how similar it is to modern bridge
10. How would you like a cool refreshing dip in the pool
11. Wow Did you see that lightning Mr. Shanahan
12. The stage manager the director's assistant is always the busiest person in the theater
13. Before drying Ferne conditioned and set her hair
14. After the local band left the stage Anne Murray appeared and the audience exploded in applause
15. The mammoth which was a kind of prehistoric elephant once roamed the region now known as Texas

USING MECHANICS IN WRITING
End Marks and Commas

A. Advertisers often try to create a sense of excitement regarding very common products that they are trying to sell. To do this, they use sentences and phrases that require exclamation marks and question marks. Write an ad for your house or apartment, describing it as though it were a holiday resort. Use both questions and exclamations to let the buying public know how exciting it would be to spend a whole week where you live.

B. Imagine that you are from a strange country in which absolutely no forms of entertainment exist. You have been sent to the United States to do research on how people enjoy themselves. Write a letter describing your exact location and telling how Americans amuse themselves in their spare time. Remember that most of what you describe will be unknown in your country, so you will have to use appositives and restrictive or nonrestrictive phrases and clauses to explain these things. Also refer to the proper form for letters shown on pages 339 and 340.

C. Write a paragraph about the person whom you think is the most universally-loved figure in all of history. Say why you think so many people love this person. Include in your paragraph at least one parenthetical expression, one appositive, one nonrestrictive modifier, one series of words separated by commas, and one compound sentence. Be sure to punctuate these elements of your composition correctly.

12.0 The Semicolon, the Colon, the Dash, and Parentheses

12.1 Semicolons Between Main Clauses

A semicolon is placed between the main clauses of a compound sentence when they are not joined by a conjunction.

The clauses of a compound sentence are closely related in thought. That is the reason for joining them into one sentence rather than writing them as separate sentences.

In some sentences the semicolon is more effective in joining main clauses than one of the conjunctions. This is especially true when *and* or *but* add little meaning to the joined clauses.

Bonita is good at set shots, *but* I am not.
Bonita is good at set shots; I am not.

The cyclone struck with savage fury, *and* it demolished the little coastal town.
The cyclone struck with savage fury; it demolished the little coastal town.

12.2 Semicolons and Conjunctive Adverbs

A semicolon is used between main clauses joined by conjunctive adverbs or by phrases like *for example, in fact, for instance.*

Our treasury was nearly empty; *accordingly,* we began
 considering various fund-raising projects.
Marge had studied Italian for three years; *yet,* when she
 arrived in Florence, she found herself tongue-tied.
Many of their talents complemented each other; *for
 example,* he played the piano and she sang.
Nick is well liked; *in fact,* he is the most popular person in
 the class.

Note that the conjunctive adverb or phrase is followed by a
comma in the examples above.

12.3   Semicolons Between Word Groups Containing Commas

A sentence containing a great many commas is difficult to read.
If commas precede the conjunction between main clauses, another comma at this point would lose its value as a guide to the
reader.

**A semicolon is used between main clauses joined by a conjunction
if the clause before the conjunction contains commas.**

Jim had done research, taken notes, and made an outline;
 but he didn't feel ready to begin writing.
We put out sandwiches, cider, potato chips, and donuts; and
 still we wondered if there would be enough.

**A semicolon is used between a series of phrases if they contain
commas.**

Members of our class come from as far away as Leeds,
 England; New Delhi, India; and San Juan, Puerto Rico.
Mabel was in charge of the scenery; Roy, the costumes; and
 Charles, the directing of the play.
Eric called the children together; checked their hands, ears,
 and faces; and told them to be back by five sharp.

Exercise: Indicate where a semicolon should replace a comma in the following sentences. Two sentences are correct.

1. We are disappointed in the advertisement, it is too small.
2. The team went to the hospital to see Bud, he had been hurt in Saturday's game.
3. Sylvia is doing very well, in fact, she has a B + average.
4. Dictionaries do not always agree, for instance, they differ on the pronunciation of *duty.*
5. As the game entered the last quarter, Pitt scored twice and won the game handily.
6. We have a factory in Salem, Ohio, an office in Buffalo, New York, and a mill at Andover, Massachusetts.
7. Dave Rotnam won first prize, his sister Joan, second prize, and Davina Belknap, third prize.
8. Eve was surrounded by notebooks, encyclopedias, and dictionaries, but she was reading a letter from Bill.
9. The men at the South Pole rarely got mail, but they could talk to their families by radio.
10. For Christmas, I got a radio, Mark, a typewriter, and Inez, a new suit.
11. We ought to beat Lexington, Bowling Green, and Libertyville, but we may lose to Russell Springs.
12. The building was designed by Frank Lloyd Wright, the famous American architect, but the New York critics, in their newspaper columns, attacked it savagely.
13. The electricity was off for six hours, consequently, everything in our food locker was spoiled.
14. Ms. Novicki has been on the force for twenty-three years, she is almost ready to retire.
15. Ellen has a new camera, it was made in Germany.

12.4 Colons To Introduce Lists

The colon is used to throw the reader's attention forward to what follows. It is in some respects like an equal sign, saying that what follows is the equivalent of what has gone before.

A colon is used to introduce a list of items.

Usually, a colon is required when a list is preceded by the words *the following* or *as follows*. A colon is not used before a series of modifiers or complements immediately following the verb.

> Jim had been a member of the following groups: the Drama Club, the Debate Union, and the Archery Club. (list)
> The following nations were among those represented at the congress: Colombia, Bolivia, Panama, and Ecuador. (list)
> Sue uses cream in cereal, in coffee, and in tea. (series of modifiers)
> The candidate's characteristics were forthrightness, intelligence, and courage. (series of complements)

Do not use a colon with a sentence fragment.

> NONSTANDARD: The reasons are:
> STANDARD: The reasons are as follows:

12.5 Colons with Formal Quotations

A colon is used to introduce a formal quotation or statement.

> Edwin Newman's book *Strictly Speaking* begins with these words: "Will America be the death of English? I'm glad I asked me that. My well-thought-out mature judgment is that it will."

12.6 Colons Before Explanatory Statements

A colon is used between two sentences when the second explains the first. The second sentence begins with a capital letter.

> Then I knew we were in trouble: None of our boys could match the swan dive we had just seen.
> From then on we understood Ms. Gilroy: She was demanding, but she was kind.

12.7   Other Uses of the Colon

A colon is used (1) after the formal salutation of a letter, (2) between hour and minute figures of clock time, (3) in Biblical references, (4) between the title and subtitle of a book, (5) between numbers referring to volume and pages of books and magazines.

> Dear Sir or Madam: Matthew 1:5
> Dear Mr. Berg: *The Raven: The Life of Sam Houston*
> 8:20 P.M.   Volume IV: pages 126-142

12.8   The Dash To Show Break in Thought

A dash is used to show an abrupt break in thought.

In dialogue, the break in thought is often caused by uncertainty or hesitancy as in the first example below.

> "Photosynthesis is an action—I mean, it's what happens—
>   well, it's sunlight doing something to chlorophyll."
> "The movie opens with a shot of the desert—oh, you've
>   seen it."
> "When I talked to her yesterday she said that—oh, I really
>   shouldn't repeat it."

12.9   The Dash with Interrupters

A dash is used to set off a long explanatory statement that interrupts the thought.

> They had searched everywhere—under the seats, in the
>   aisles, in the lobby—before Dan found the keys in his
>   pocket.
> The meeting—between two men who had clashed violently
>   and repeatedly over a period of years—was calm and
>   friendly.

12.10   The Dash Before a Summary

The dash is used after a series to indicate a summarizing statement.

Insufficient heating, leaky roofs, cluttered stairways, and unsanitary corridors—for all these violations of the housing code, the landlord was hauled into court.

Yellowed song sheets, framed photographs of opera stars, programs of long-past performances—these were scattered about her room.

Exercise: Copy the following sentences, inserting semicolons, colons, or dashes where necessary.

1. Beginning next January we shall handle the following foreign cars Datsun, Volvo, Volkswagen, and Honda.
2. The candidate's main qualifications were these twelve years' experience in the Senate, a knowledge of foreign affairs, and the ability to get votes.
3. I am looking for the source of this quotation "Always do right. This will gratify some people and astonish the rest."
4. Our new text is called *Supershopper A Guide to Spending and Saving.*
5. The quotation is found in *The Oxford English Dictionary,* Vol. II page 427.
6. High school students today are more serious they expect to work hard.
7. Alice knew at least she thought she knew what was coming next.
8. It is our obligation there is no choice in the matter to pay all of Frank's expenses to the conventions in Scottsdale and San Diego.
9. It's about well, it's something like I would say it's a good ten miles from here.
10. Having a lot of clothes, owning a fancy car, going to parties are these really suitable goals in life?

11. The prizes are as follows first prize, a movie camera second prize, a portable TV set third prize, a calculator.
12. You have three jobs for today wash the car, clean up the yard, and shop for your mother.
13. The President closed with these words "With God's help, we can face the future hopefully, in full confidence that our problems can be solved."
14. Marion saw the point she was the only one who did.
15. We shall cover the following topics in this conference planning for new products, improving customer relations, and marketing.
16. You will find the statement in *Thomas Jefferson The Man and His Times*, Volume III page 106.
17. You can take this road down but I guess the road is closed, isn't it?
18. There is a strange light a reddish light that moves very fast in the sky to the south of here.
19. Suddenly we had already closed the door the phone rang.
20. It is rather a long walk however, it is a pleasant one.

12.11 Parentheses To Enclose Supplementary or Explanatory Words

Commas, dashes, or parentheses are used to set off words that are supplementary or explanatory. Commas are used when the material set off is fairly close to the main thought of the sentence. Dashes are used to set off material more loosely connected, and parentheses are used to set off material so loosely related to the main thought that it might be made a separate sentence.

There are few occasions in high school writing when parentheses are needed. The safest course for the student is to use commas, or even dashes, to set off parenthetical matter. If the material is so distantly related as to require parentheses, the passage might better be rewritten to place the parenthetical material in a separate sentence.

COMMAS ADEQUATE: Kate's best point, which she saved for the end, was that every group needs leadership.

DASHES REQUIRED: Modern physics no longer deals directly with the visible world—that is, it deals directly only with atoms, electrons, protons, and other particles that are too small to be seen.

PARENTHESES APPROPRIATE: But on the whole, Arthur was a well-behaved little boy; a good pupil and obedient (except when he played with the scruffy boys in the street, whom his parents disliked).—Colin Wilson, *Religion and the Rebel.*

PARENTHESES AVOIDED: But on the whole, Arthur was a well-behaved little boy and a good pupil. He was obedient except when he played with the scruffy boys in the street, whom his parents disliked.

12.12 Punctuation Within Parentheses

Commas, semicolons, and periods are placed outside the closing parenthesis. The question mark and exclamation point are placed inside if the parenthetical material is itself a question or exclamation; otherwise, outside.

Jean (not Martha) was the dancer in the orange leotard.
Leo's speech was on disarmament; Barb's, on acting as a career (her favorite subject); Jim's, on slum clearance.
I never guessed (would you have?) that the maid did it.
Sheldon spoke of his victory over Central's debaters (*his* victory!) as if he had been a one-man team.

The Semicolon, the Colon, the Dash, and Parentheses

A. Use semicolons correctly. The following sentences contain errors in punctuation. Add semicolons as necessary.

1. Tracey threw the Frisbee to Todd José jumped and caught it.
2. The trainer fed the lions, watered the tigers, and exercised the ocelots but he avoided the nervous panthers.
3. The telephone rang it was Ron saying he'd be late.
4. Dolores must have painted this room lavender is her favorite color.
5. One hundred people attended the reception, however, there was only enough wedding cake for ninety-five.
6. The tour included Paris, France, London, England, Glasgow, Scotland, and Dublin, Ireland.
7. The bank president led us to the safety deposit boxes below, the bank's security was strictest there.
8. Dr. Martin Luther King, Jr. was a great leader accordingly, his birthday has been made a national holiday.
9. We have the lantern, a cookstove, and a portable heater however, we forgot to bring matches.
10. The Puritans discouraged merrymaking and festivities for example, they had laws against celebrating Christmas.
11. Miguel brought potato chips, pretzels, and cashews, Rolanda brought napkins, utensils, and paper plates, and the club officers brought hot dogs and hamburgers.
12. This summer I plan to read *My Antonia*, by Willa Cather, *The Golden Apples*, by Eudora Welty, and *Pentimento*, by Lillian Hellman.
13. Cats love peeking into corners, crawling under beds, and getting into bureau drawers, but they don't like being put into confined spaces.

14. Melinkian grabbed the ball then he glanced at the coach, the clock, and the scoreboard and sank a basket.
15. There are many mysteries surrounding the American author Ambrose Bierce for example, no one knows what became of him after he left for Mexico in 1913.

B. Use colons and dashes. The following sentences contain errors in punctuation. Correct these errors by adding colons, dashes, and parentheses as necessary.

1. It was Virginia Woolf who wrote these words "Anonymous was a woman."
2. The following plays are classified as tragedies *Oedipus the King, Macbeth*, and *Death of a Salesman*.
3. Squids, octopuses, snails, and shellfish all these species are classified as mollusks.
4. The popular phrase is a misquotation of this quotation "For the love of money is the root of all evil."
5. William came to a decision He would attend college after all.
6. The solution to the puzzle is wait, you should figure it out on your own.
7. For my report, I need to read Volume 3 pages 166-221 of *English and Scottish Popular Ballads.*
8. The plane leaves Atlanta at 8 30 A.M. and arrives in Washington at 12 48 P.M.
9. Cable TV, laser discs, video recorders all these were unknown to consumers only a few years ago.
10. Ms. Boynton's whimsical work cartoons of animals for greeting cards and calendars rapidly made her a commercial success.

MIXED REVIEW

The Semicolon, the Colon, the Dash, and Parentheses

A. Rewrite the following sentences, inserting necessary semi-colons, colons, and dashes.

1. Evan uses a calculator Lettie uses a slide rule.
2. The movies of Errol Flynn *Robin Hood, Sea Hawk, Captain Blood* are wonderful old swashbucklers.
3. The horse ran, pranced, and galloped and then he rested.
4. The following magazines have the highest circulation *Reader's Digest, National Geographic*, and *TV Guide*.
5. The librarian advised me to check Volume 4 pages 101-105.
6. Panting, the marathon runner crossed the finish line she had come in first.
7. Our school has exchange students from these countries Brazil, Kenya, Sweden, and Chile.
8. Costumes, scrapbooks, toys, and dishes we found them all in the attic.
9. I guessed the trial's outcome The accused murderer would be found guilty.
10. The water ballet routine was precisely choreographed furthermore, it was performed flawlessly.

B. Follow the directions for Exercise A.

1. My class that meets at 9 30 oh, I hope I won't be late will discuss student rights.
2. Alana is the editor-in-chief of the school newspaper Janie, the business manager and Reggie, the staff photographer.
3. The Declaration of Independence ends with these words "We mutually pledge to each other our lives, our fortunes, and our sacred honor."

4. The coach tried everything pep talks, privileges, rallies, toughness to try to improve the team's morale.
5. *Newsweek* magazine we have a subscription features a guest essay called "My Turn."
6. Spiders, ants, fleas they're all part of my insect collection.
7. The following cities have warm winters Miami, Florida Los Angeles, California and Honolulu, Hawaii.
8. Ms. Conti, do you have *JFK The Early Years*, or is it out?
9. Selina prepared for the audition She memorized her lines and practiced her dance.
10. There are many calendars for example, ancient Romans used the Julian calendar.

C. Rewrite the sentences, adding semicolons, colons, and dashes.

1. In his book *On Writing Well*, William Zinsser says the following "Clutter is the disease of American writing."
2. Norway, Finland, Czechoslovakia, Poland, Hungary, Romania, Turkey, Iran, China, North Korea, Afghanistan, and Mongolia all these countries border on the Soviet Union.
3. Three of the club officers were asked to speak Pat, the president Myra, the treasurer and Loren, the secretary.
4. Harry said at least I think this is what he said that everyone would be welcome at the dance.
5. The times of departure for trains to Grand Central Station are 8 30 A.M., 12 00 noon, and 4 30 P.M. every weekday.
6. The veterinarian told us what we all wanted to hear Our cat would not have to have an operation.
7. *The Lord's Prayer* is found in Matthew 6 9-13.
8. What happens in the end no, I won't give it away would surprise even the most devoted reader of spy thrillers.
9. The schedule for aerobics classes has just been issued Monday, Wednesday, and Friday from 9 30-10 30 and Tuesday, Thursday, and Saturday from 12 00-1 00.
10. She did not want to go it was dark and windy to the graveyard at midnight on Halloween.

USING MECHANICS IN WRITING
The Semicolon, the Colon, the Dash, and Parentheses

A. Dashes and parentheses are often used in informal writing, such as personal letters, because they allow the writer to express ideas more as he or she would in casual conversation. The writer can interrupt himself or herself, insert personal reactions, and add a tone of informality. Imagine that a good friend has gone out of the country to study for the year. You are writing a letter to bring him or her up to date on news concerning your family, friends, and school. Use parentheses and dashes (as well as exclamation marks and questions marks) to give your letter a friendly, informal, and conversational tone.

B. Dialogue can be both the easiest and the hardest thing to write. It is easy because you can write exactly the way people speak. You don't have to be concerned with formal language, grammar rules, or usage problems. You do, however, have to make dialogue sound real. This means that you must have an "ear" for the way people speak and be able to re-create the distinctive characteristics that separate one person from the next.

Write a dialogue between two characters. Let one character be a nonstop talker who rambles on and on about trivial ideas, frequently interrupting himself or herself to insert unrelated details. Let the second person be a very polite, relatively quiet person who speaks precisely and correctly, but who keeps being interrupted by the first speaker. Use commas, semicolons, dashes, and parentheses to make the dialogue clear. Make sure that you have a specific situation in mind, and decide whether your "scene" will be serious or humorous.

13.0 The Apostrophe

The **apostrophe** is used with nouns to show possession or ownership: *Arthur's sword, Carl's cat, the lawyer's briefcase.* The apostrophe can also be used to show the following relationships:

MEMBERSHIP:	Aunt Dorothy's golf league, the children's school
LOCATION:	China's Great Wall, Washington's Grand Coulee Dam
SOURCE OR ORIGIN:	Frost's poetry, Charlemagne's laws
IDENTIFYING CHARACTERISTICS:	Lincoln's sorrow, the cheetah's fur

The rules for using apostrophes are quite simple. However, many people still leave out essential apostrophes when they are writing. If you memorize the rules in this Section and proofread your writing, you can avoid most apostrophe errors.

13.1 The Possessive of Singular Nouns

The possessive form of a singular noun is usually made by adding an apostrophe and s ('s) to the noun.

$$dog + 's = dog's \qquad girl + 's = girl's$$
$$Tess + 's = Tess's \qquad town + 's = town's$$

Note: A few proper nouns ending in *s* may take the apostrophe only: *Jesus'* or *Moses'.* In general, however, the correct way to make a singular noun possessive is to add an apostrophe and *s*.

13.2 The Possessive of Plural Nouns

If a plural noun does not end in s, add both apostrophe and s ('s) to form the possessive.

women + 's = women's   men + 's = men's
children + 's = children's   deer + 's = deer's

If a plural noun ends in s, add only the apostrophe to form the possessive.

animals + ' = animals'   members + ' = members'
writers + ' = writers'   soldiers + ' = soldiers'

Exercise: Number from 1-20 on your paper. Write *Correct* for each sentence in which the possessive form is correct. If the form is incorrect, write it correctly.

1. The girls bikes had been locked up in the basement.
2. This year the team's spirit is much better.
3. Toms' minibike was stolen.
4. The girls' friends came to her defense.
5. We found Charles's ski boots in the back of his old station wagon.
6. The regular passengers have formed a passengers committee.
7. The company has put new heaters and visors in the salespersons' cars.
8. The ship's doctor performed the operation at sea.
9. The governors' assistants have their own annual meeting at the same time.
10. The home economics class serves at lunchtime in the teacher's lunchroom.
11. The three reporter's statements differed on most important points.
12. The client's cars are ready for them.
13. Children's toys were scattered over the driveway.
14. The sailor's leaves were suddenly canceled.
15. The actor's voices were loud and harsh.

16. The watchmen's reports make no mention of a disturbance.
17. Les's garage is always open on Sunday.
18. Diplomats and soldiers alike were warmed by the Presidents' smile.
19. The alumni's contributions built the chapel.
20. Cathy's coach has entered her in the womens' tennis tournament.

13.3 The Possessive of Compound Nouns

A **compound noun** is a noun composed of more than one word. Some compound nouns are written with hyphens between the parts.

Only the last part of a hyphenated noun shows possession.

> jack-o'-lantern + 's = jack-o'-lantern's
> sister-in-law + 's = sister-in-law's

Nouns such as *the Queen of England, the President of the United States, the Prime Minister* form the possessive by adding an apostrophe and *s* to the last word only: *the Queen of England's throne.* Often, however, an *of* phrase is less awkward.

> the throne of the Queen of England
> the home of the President of the United States
> the husband of the Prime Minister

13.4 Joint Ownership

When the names of two or more persons are used to show joint ownership, only the name of the last person mentioned is given the possessive form. Add an apostrophe or an apostrophe and s in accordance with the spelling of that name.

> Boris and Ivan's uncle
> Ed and Joanne's home
> Bob and Gregory's project

The rule also applies to firm names and to names of organizations.

> Strawbridge and Clothier's location
> Cross and Hamilton Company's sales force
> Sears and Roebuck's catalog

13.5 Separate Ownership or Possession

If the names of two or more persons are used to show separate ownership, each name is given the possessive form.

> Madison's and Monroe's administrations
> Don's and Jim's grades

This construction may become awkward. It can be avoided by using an *of* phrase.

> the administrations of Madison and Monroe
> the grades of Don and Jim

13.6 Possessive of Indefinite Pronouns

Use an apostrophe and s to form the possessive of indefinite pronouns.

> everyone + 's = everyone's   one + 's = one's
> either + 's = either's   somebody + 's = somebody's

The apostrophe and *s* are added to the last word in forms like *someone else, anybody else, no one else:*

> somebody else's   no one else's

The apostrophe is not used to form the possessive of personal pronouns. (See Section 1.2.)

> NONSTANDARD: your's, her's, it's, our's, their's
> STANDARD: yours, hers, its, ours, theirs

13.7 Expressions of Time and Amount

When used as adjectives, words expressing time and amount are given the possessive form.

a month's time	four days' wait
a week's notice	six months' delay
a day's holiday	thirty seconds' silence
a minute's peace	ten minutes' break
a penny's worth	two centuries' tradition

Exercise: Copy the italicized words, changing them to show ownership or possession.

1. We will meet at my *sister-in-law* house.
2. *Dana* and *Paul* uniforms did not fit.
3. Who will win is *anybody* guess.
4. Ms. Blackmar has three *week* wages coming to her.
5. You can probably find the right kind of truck at *Smith and Weston* store.
6. Because of illness I have missed three *day* work.
7. *Roger and Sons* sale starts next week.
8. *Roosevelt* and *Rockefeller* backgrounds were similar.
9. Buffalo is ten *hours* ride from my town.
10. Where is the *League of Women Voters* office?
11. An *hour* wait now may save a *day* time later.
12. There is an advertisement of *Chase and Maxwell* sale in tonight's paper.
13. Dominic picked up *somebody else* books.
14. What is the *Secretary of the Treasury* salary?
15. The school is sponsoring a *mothers* and *sons* picnic.
16. Have you paid *Lord and Taylor* bill this month?
17. *Andy* and *Marge* mother is a doctor.
18. In two *month* time your leg will be as good as new.
19. *Benét* and *Twain* stories were the best-liked.
20. There is only a *moment* delay before the phone rings at the other side of the continent.

13.8   Apostrophes To Show Omissions

An apostrophe is used to show the omission of letters or figures.

the class of '84   *1984*
they're   *they are*
shouldn't   *should not*

13.9   Plurals of Letters, Words, Numbers, and Signs

An apostrophe is used to show the plurals of letters, numbers, signs, and words referred to as words.

How many *r*'s are there in *embarrass*?
Her speech relies too much on *nice*'s.
Frederick Lewis Allen describes the Roaring '20's in
   Only Yesterday.

Note: The plurals of letters, numbers, signs, and words used as words are always italicized in print. In manuscript and typescript they are underlined (See Section 14.7 for additional information on the uses of italics and underlining).

Exercise : Copy the following sentences, inserting an apostrophe (and *s*) where needed.

1. There are too many *that*s in your sentence.
2. Perrys address has four 3s in it.
3. There should be great prosperity in the 1980s.
4. It was three oclock before we got started.
5. Its not likely that Mars or Venus is inhabited.
6. We dont know the answer, and we cant find it.
7. It is clear now that Dads letter wont come today.
8. Jess short story is being published in *Scholastic Magazine*.
9. Our local papers feature section gives career tips.
10. We dont yet know whos coming.

REINFORCEMENT EXERCISES
The Apostrophe

A. Form possessives of singular and plural nouns. Make a four-column chart. Label the columns *Singular, Plural, Singular Possessive,* and *Plural Possessive.* Fill in those forms of the following nouns.

1. boy
2. antelope
3. university
4. mayor
5. lady
6. buffalo
7. coach
8. city
9. beach
10. senator
11. class
12. saleswoman
13. month
14. goose
15. speech

B. Use apostrophes to show ownership. Some of the sentences below contain errors in the use of apostrophes. Rewrite these sentences, correcting the errors. If the sentence is already correct, write *Correct.*

1. One reporter ignored the editor-in-chiefs warning and revealed one of his sources.
2. Alex's and Andrea's Dance Studio offers classes in ballet, jazz, and tap.
3. I'll buy two dollar's worth of those mixed jelly beans.
4. Pete Rose and George Brett's batting averages are listed in this book of statistics.
5. Somebodys jacket is hanging from the flagpole.
6. There will be a two month's delay before the new equipment is delivered.
7. Were Poe's and Hawthorne's short stories written during the same time period?
8. These guitar strings are her's.
9. My sister-in-law's hobby is collecting old magazines and theater programs.
10. No one elses music captures the feeling of a movie as well as that of John Williams.

The Apostrophe

A. Rewrite the following sentences, correcting all errors in the use of the apostrophe.

1. Bross and Bradys' Gourmet Shop sells pickled eel and chocolate covered grasshoppers.
2. Several golfer's scores were below par.
3. Doesnt the womens locker room have a sauna?
4. It would take two weeks work to get Kellys room clean.
5. The child gleefully turned the jack's-in-the-box handle.
6. Alisons phone number is easy to remember because it has four 8s in a row.
7. This years football squad isn't strong on defense, but the offense has potential.
8. Druid and Companys' policy is never to hire teen-agers.
9. No ones jeans look as new as Terrys.
10. The treasurer of the class of 86 must collect each members' fees.
11. Youll have to borrow someone elses class notes, José.
12. A bird sheds it's feathers during molting season.
13. Katie's and Les' project demonstrates how heredity determines the color of our eyes.
14. Foxes and mink's furs are used for coats, arent they?
15. This seminar is supposed to teach the *ABC*s of ecology in the 1980s.
16. Their clubs skit is a parody of *The Wizard of Oz*.
17. The baseball is Adams, but the bat is her's.
18. During a speech, too many *um*s are distracting to your listener's.
19. Mr. Moran and Ms. Sax's classes are visiting the space museum.
20. Cant you recognize the lilies-of-the-valley fragrance in this perfume?

USING MECHANICS IN WRITING
The Apostrophe

A. You are the leader of a four-person musical group called *The State of the Onion*. Your group is coming out with an album, and you have been asked to write the history of the group for the back cover. In your story, give some background about each person, including what his or her interests and favorite things are. Also describe the group's accomplishments and future plans. Use as many different types of possessive pronouns as possible. Since album notes are a variety of informal writing, you may also use contractions to give your notes a conversational tone.

B. **Personification** is the technique of writing or speaking about a non-human object as though it had human qualities. A poet, for example, might use personification to describe leaves *running along sidewalks*. In a paragraph, describe a commonly-used object as though it were a person. Provide such information as where it lives and what habits it has. Give your readers hints that will enable them to guess the object, but do not make these hints too obvious.

C. Write a short gossip column for your school paper. Include information about the following groups and people. Use the possessive forms of some of the nouns and pronouns.

A new discovery by members of the science club

The plans of Jeffrey Ross, your star football player

Inside information from an anonymous "someone"

A project by the class of 1987

An interesting item about Webster and Lara, a singing team

The mistake of your editor-in-chief

14.0 Quotations

14.1 Direct and Indirect Quotations

Quotation marks are used to enclose a direct quotation.

In a direct quotation, the words of the speaker are directly quoted exactly as spoken.

> Greg said, "The streets should be cleared for our parade."
> "The town," the mayor said, "will be yours that day."

An indirect quotation reports the meaning expressed by the speaker but does not give the exact words.

> INDIRECT: Molly replied that she was always punctual.
> DIRECT: "I am always punctual," Molly replied.

Quotation marks are not used with an indirect quotation.

14.2 Punctuation of Direct Quotations

Punctuation and capitals are used as follows in direct quotations:

1. In dialogue, the first word of the quotation is capitalized. The material quoted from another writer may begin in the middle of a sentence. If so, the first word is not capitalized.

> On January 1, 1863, Lincoln declared the slaves "forever free."

2. The speaker's words are set off from the rest of the sentence.

Note the placement of commas in these examples:

"Let's meet at my house next time," Michael said.
Michael said, "Let's meet at my house next time."

When the end of the quotation is also the end of the sentence, the period falls inside the quotation marks.

3. If the quoted words are a question or an exclamation, the question mark or the exclamation point falls inside the quotation marks.

In this situation no comma in needed.

"May I make the poster?" Lola asked.
"I deny everything!" the suspect cried.

4. If the entire sentence is a question or an exclamation, the exclamation point or question mark falls outside the quotation marks.

Did I hear you say, "Have some cookies"?
It's totally absurd for anyone to consider these thieves
   "responsible citizens"!

5. The colon and the semicolon at the close of a quotation fall outside the quotation marks.

The committee said that the following states contained
   "pockets of poverty": Kentucky, West Virginia, and
   Pennsylvania.
Read the ballad "Sir Patrick Spens"; then study its relation to
   Coleridge's poem "Dejection: An Ode."

6. Both parts of a divided quotation are enclosed in quotation marks. The first word of the second part is not capitalized unless it begins a new sentence.

"Part of my plan," the Governor said, "is to reduce property
   taxes this year."
"You must remember this," the guidance counselor said.
   "Ten hours of casual work will probably be less effective
   than five of real concentration."

7. In dialogue, a new paragraph and a new set of quotation marks show a change in speaker.

"My working habits have no pattern," the author said. "Some writers set themselves strict schedules. I don't."

"But you've written five books in five years," the interviewer replied. "You must work very hard every day."

"On the contrary, some days I spend the entire morning putting in a comma and the afternoon taking it out."

Exercise: For each sentence, write *Direct* or *Indirect* to describe the kind of quotation. Copy and correct the sentences requiring quotation marks, capital letters, or other punctuation.

1. The test was hard said Sam but it was fair.
2. Don replied that he had no one to blame but himself.
3. May I have a new shirt for the party asked Ken.
4. Laura said that she wanted to study advanced science.
5. The teacher asked whether Sam was ready to give his report.
6. No one would think to look in here said Ms. Brown.
7. Ben called out we will be home early.
8. The city is not equipped to deal with a heavy snowfall the guide explained.
9. Does anyone know asked Loretta who is to be the speaker?
10. Well I think I left it on the bus said Jean sadly.

14.3 Quotations Within Quotations

Single quotation marks are used to enclose a quotation within a quotation.

Herb said, "Then she actually said to me, 'I hope I didn't keep you waiting.'"

"The announcer just said, 'More snow tonight,'" Len reported.

Ruth said, "Then Ray looked up from the ground and said, 'I don't think I'll do any more skiing.'"

14.4 Long Quotations

A quotation may be several paragraphs in length.

In long quotations, begin each paragraph with quotation marks. Place quotation marks at the end of the last paragraph only.

Exercise A: Copy the following sentences, adding the necessary punctuation marks and capital letters.

1. Molly asked does anyone know when the reports are due
2. Who shouted look out asked the irate guard
3. Zachary asked may I rewrite this paper
4. There is no excuse for this delay said the customer we gave you our order two months ago
5. Your Honor the defendant pleaded I beg you for another chance
6. In the Sand Creek Massacre the speaker added several hundred Indians were killed
7. Did Captain Perry's message say we have met the enemy and they are ours
8. Look out for a pass Bill shouted
9. Did you finish your homework Sarah asked
10. Do you know asked Jack where we can get a tire

Exercise B: Copy the following passage, correcting any errors in punctuation, capitalization, or paragraphing.

He was very thin and dressed in rags. What I remember are his eyes. He had huge, dark eyes. He did not speak. He just stood there, looking up at me. Who are you I asked in Chinese? I am no one. He said. But what is your name I asked? I have no name he said. Where are your parents? I have no parents. But where did you come from I asked, staring at him? I came from nowhere he said. And you are going nowhere? Nowhere he said. Then why come to me? He shook his head, not able to answer. Come in I said finally, you must be hungry.

—PEARL S. BUCK

14.5 Setting Off Titles

The title of a book, magazine, newspaper, long pamphlet, or bulletin is usually italicized in print. In your own writing, you indicate the italics by underlining.

To distinguish the title of a *part* of a book, magazine, or newspaper, quotation marks are used.

Use quotation marks to enclose the titles of chapters and other parts of books and to enclose the titles of stories, poems, essays, articles, and short musical compositions.

Faulkner's story "The Bear" is as famous as his novels.
The subject of "Auspex" is an incident that occurred
seventy-five years before Frost wrote the poem.

14.6 Words Used in Special Ways

Words used in special ways or special senses are enclosed in quotation marks.

Writers may want to show that they are using a word as someone else has used it. Writers can make clear that they do not accept this use of the word by enclosing it in quotation marks.

Slang words and phrases are also enclosed in quotation marks.

There are always a few people who consider it a shameful
waste to give aid to "inferior nations."
The reporter asked the negotiators to describe what they
meant by "a satisfactory solution."
The senator considered every voter his "pal"; few of his pals,
however, had ever met him.

Note: When a comma or period immediately follows the quoted word, it falls *inside* the quotation marks. A colon or semicolon falls *outside* the quotation marks. See the last example above. If the quoted word appears at the end of a question or exclamation, the question mark or exclamation point falls *outside* the quotation marks: *Is this what you mean by "cool"?*

14.7 Words Used as Words

A word referred to as a word is italicized in print. In writing, the word is underlined.

Until then, I'd never heard the word *boondoggle*.

When a word and its definition appear in a sentence, the word is italicized, and the definition is put in quotation marks.

In music, the word *pianissimo* means "very soft."

Exercise A: Copy the following sentences. Insert quotation marks where necessary. Indicate italics by underlining.

1. What does the word serendipity mean?
2. There are too many and's in your sentences.
3. Read Phyllis McGinley's poem Reflections Dental.
4. The hardest words on the test were quay and spurn.
5. The article Robotics Update was in Time.
6. Doris always has a hard time spelling recommend.
7. The British word for elevator is lift.
8. Rachel will lead a discussion of the story The Open Boat.
9. Epilogue means a concluding part added to a literary work.
10. One of Billy Joel's early songs was Piano Man.

Exercise B: Follow the directions for Exercise A.

1. In Canada the word is spelled colour.
2. Birches is my favorite poem in the book Literature Lives.
3. Todd calls money bread, and Meg calls it the green stuff.
4. Read the chapter called Bacteria Are Your Friends.
5. Why are those islands called The Lesser Antilles?
6. John Denver describes nearly everything as far out.
7. Katie cringes when anyone calls her honey or sweetie.
8. What is meant by the phrase manifest destiny?
9. Would the chef call this meal a gourmet great?
10. How are you using the word break in that sentence?

REINFORCEMENT EXERCISE
Quotations

Use quotation marks correctly. Rewrite the following sentences, correcting any errors in punctuation and capitalization.

1. After seeing Yul Brynner in *The King and I*, Cheri said it was the best play she had ever attended.
2. I'll take Carlysle in four rounds boasted the heavyweight champion.
3. You should buy this beauty said the used car salesman it's a terrific bargain.
4. Almost everyone said the astronomer can find Ursa Major in the sky.
5. Mr. Ortega insisted that he would never again vote for a candidate because of his or her good looks.
6. My little sister said the romantic movie was icky, then she grabbed the remote control and turned off the TV.
7. The supervisor smiled and said the strike is over.
8. Ray Bradbury wrote many marvelous short stories, including The Veldt and The Sound of Thunder.
9. Did the umpire shout The runner is out at first base?
10. I am sure said Jan, that the song What I Did for Love was from a Broadway musical, not a movie.
11. I need a volunteer said the magician which one of you is willing to come up on stage?
12. Have you read Poe's poem The Raven the psychiatrist asked?
13. We have to know how many people are coming Greg explained so we can buy enough food.
14. Oh, no moaned Jennifer I just spilled mustard on my new blazer.
15. Lenny replied Bob Greene's column said life in the 80's isn't nearly as exciting as it was in the 60's but I don't believe that he's right.

MIXED REVIEW
Quotations

Rewrite the following sentences, inserting the necessary quotation marks, capitals, and other punctuation. Indicate italics by underlining. One sentence is correct

1. I'll be a few minutes late Johanna remarked
2. After the feast Bob asked did you get enough to eat
3. I give up said Phil what is the answer
4. Someone in the class asked how we know what people sounded like in Shakespeare's day
5. The consumer expert began her report commercials can make us dissatisfied
6. I did it the contest winner shouted
7. One chapter of The Martian Chronicles is called The Green Morning
8. We read O. Henry's story The Ransom of Red Chief
9. Sabrina asked did you read the poem Fifteen
10. The TV term for an added sound track of people laughing is called canned laughter
11. The word madam is a palindrome, a word that is spelled the same forwards and backwards
12. Thanks to television Fred Allen said the next generation will have four eyes and no tongue
13. Our English teacher said that genre means a kind or type of artistic endeavor
14. Carla asked did Mr. Oldfield say class is dismissed
15. Why do TV emcees say we'll be back after this word from our sponsor
16. Who wrote the book The Long Winter Vivienne asked
17. Whoopee! the announcer shouted the Rangers have won
18. Ms. Armanda, does the word subsequent mean next Sonia asked

USING MECHANICS IN WRITING
Quotations

A. You are a critic for a local paper. Write a review for your readers. Depending on the type of critic you choose to be, your subject may be this season's television shows, the top songs on the radio this week, or some best-selling books. Be sure to mention the names of works you are reviewing. Use at least two quotations in your review as you discuss the content of the work.

B. One of the most popular types of television show is the soap opera. Even prime time hours are filled with these programs. In them, families, and sometimes entire communities, share secrets, problems, and schemes.

Write out the dialogue for one scene from the soap opera "All My Problems." In this scene, Maggie is sitting alone in a booth in the town's only restaurant. She overhears a conversation in an adjoining booth between her brother, the handsome doctor Cliff Noble, and the scheming Erica Lyer. Erica is trying to undermine Cliff's confidence about an upcoming heart transplant operation that he is performing on his sweetheart, Jenny.

Use as many different types of quotations in your dialogue as possible. Make sure that you punctuate correctly.

CUMULATIVE REVIEW
Capitalization and Punctuation

Using Capitalization and Punctuation Correctly. Rewrite the following paragraphs, correcting any errors in capitalization or punctuation.

The first explorer, known to History, was an egyptian named hennu. In 2007 bc Hennu sailed across the red sea to somaliland which is located on the indian ocean. Since this first, courageous voyage over four thousand years ago countless explorers have followed hennus example. Among the most famous of these explorers were the following—marco polo the european, who visited china in ad 1275 christopher columbus the italian navigator who sailed West across the atlantic to discover the americas, and vasco da gama the portuguese sailor who circumnavigated the Globe in ad 1498. Today thanks to such people as these few regions of the earth remain unexplored even the three fifths of the world that is water has been fairly well mapped.

Nonetheless exploration is still very much alive. In october of 1,957 the soviet union launched sputnik I the first artificial satellite and this event launched in turn a new period in the History of Exploration the space age. In may of 1961 president john f. kennedy the man most responsible for getting the american space program 'off the ground' announced, that the united states would land a manned spacecraft on the Moon within a decade.

The culmination of america's early space explorations came on july, 20 1969. On this date neil armstrong a native of wapakoneta ohio became the first Human Being ever to set foot on another World. As his feet touched the surface of the moon, armstrong said one small step for man; one giant leap for mankind. In other words this Modern Day explorer was telling us "that reaching the barren desolate moon was, but a stepping stone to exploration of the universe."

15.0 Spelling

Spelling has been a problem for generations of students. There is no simple way to teach you to spell. There is no easy way to learn. If you are concerned about the problem, however, there are several helpful suggestions:

1. Proofread all your writing. Even the ablest scholar may write "their" for "there" or "here" for "hear" in a first draft. Many apparent errors are not spelling errors at all. They are mistakes caused by carelessness and haste.

2. Learn to look at the letters in a word. Most of us have learned to read by recognizing whole words or parts of words. Spelling errors are errors in the letters that compose a word. You will find it helpful to break a word into its parts to see and to memorize the spelling of each part.

3. Keep a list of your spelling errors. The point is that you can spell correctly most of the words you use. Your errors fall within a narrow range. If you will concentrate on this range—provided by your list—you may show quick improvement.

4. Practice on your own spelling problem. There is no reason why you cannot totally eliminate spelling errors *if you want to*. One recommended procedure is to use a card pack. Print your problem words on cards in large letters. Take a card from the pack. Look at every letter and let the order of the letters sink into your mind. Pronounce each part of the word separately. Turn the card over. Write the word on a piece of paper. Turn the card over again and compare what you have written with the correct spelling.

5. Memorize and apply the few rules of spelling given below. Be sure you understand the rules, or your memory work will be wasted. Practice using the rules so that their use becomes automatic.

Exercise: Divide these words into parts. Do not be concerned as to whether they conform to the dictionary division. Just make sure that every word part has a vowel sound. Study the word parts, looking for unusual patterns.

1. occurrence	7. humorous	13. italicize
2. accidentally	8. specifically	14. miniature
3. accommodate	9. necessary	15. extraordinary
4. incredible	10. disappearance	16. secretarial
5. miscellaneous	11. mimeograph	17. athletic
6. maintenance	12. immediately	18. privilege

15.1 The Final Silent e

When a suffix beginning with a vowel is added to a word ending in a silent e, the e is usually dropped.

deceive + ing = deceiving   traverse + able = traversable
structure + al = structural   dose + age = dosage
trade + ing = trading   narrate + ion = narration
relate + ion = relation   delete + ion = deletion

When the final silent e is preceded by c or g, the e is usually retained before a suffix beginning with a or o.

trace + able = traceable   courage + ous = courageous
charge + able = chargeable   outrage + ous = outrageous

When a suffix beginning with a consonant is added to a word ending in a silent e, the e is usually retained.

grace + ful = graceful   face + less = faceless
love + ly = lovely   hope + ful = hopeful

These words are exceptions: *truly, argument, wholly, awful.*

15.2   Words Ending in *y*

When a suffix is added to a word ending in *y* preceded by a consonant, the *y* is usually changed to *i*.

There are two exceptions: (1) when -*ing* is added, the *y* does not change. (2) Some one-syllable words do not change the *y*: *dryness, shyness*.

happy + ness = happiness	marry + age = marriage
company + es = companies	marry + ing = marrying
carry + ed = carried	dally + ing = dallying

When a suffix is added to a word ending in *y* preceded by a vowel, the *y* usually does not change.

pray + ing = praying	destroy + er = destroyer
enjoy + ing = enjoying	coy + ness = coyness

Exceptions: day + ly = daily, gay + ly = gaily

Exercise A: Find the misspelled words and spell them correctly.

1. We enjoyed sailing lazyly down the bay.
2. Mr. Ray sent us an invitateion to meet a fameous artist.
3. That architectureal work is truly admireable.
4. The negotiators made a couragous effort to achieve a peaceable settlement.
5. There has been a noticable improvement in the safety record of our high school.
6. The caravan was moveing slowly along the icey road.
7. Creative talent can always profit from guideance.
8. Despite our arguements, the judge was immoveable.
9. The statement by the next witness was wholely false.
10. The cave was incrediblely dark and terribly silent.
11. A recluse is lonly, but a hermit is lonelyer.
12. Zonkers is the crazyest dog imagineable.
13. The doctor is continueing an intenseive X-ray treatment.
14. The captain's arrival is useually prompt.

15. On the queen's sixtyeth birthday there was merryment.
16. There was a certain hazyness about Jack's ideas.
17. The heavyer carriages were almost immoveable.
18. The earlyest Mayan writing is not easly deciphered.
19. The guide was very likeable, and her stories were exciteing.
20. We climbed clumsyly up the walls of the old fortifycations.

Exercise B: Add the suffixes as shown and write the new words.

1. mystery + ous	11. worry + ing	21. move + ment
2. relay + ing	12. carry + ed	22. change + able
3. body + ly	13. enjoy + able	23. charge + ing
4. frenzy + ed	14. create + ive	24. hurry + ing
5. appraise + ed	15. copy + ing	25. debate + able
6. waste + ful	16. educate + ion	26. hasty + ly
7. amaze + ing	17. assemble + age	27. merry + ly
8. insure + ance	18. wide + ly	28. easy + ly
9. grease + y	19. constitute + ion	29. day + ly
10. situate + ion	20. like + able	30. argue + ment

15.3   The Suffixes -*ness* and -*ly*

When the suffix -*ly* is added to a word ending in *l*, both *l*'s are retained. When -*ness* is added to a word ending in *n*, both *n*'s are retained.

real + ly = really   plain + ness = plainness
eternal + ly = eternally   mean + ness = meanness

15.4   The Addition of Prefixes

When a prefix is added to a word, the spelling of the word remains the same.

dis + approve = disapprove   dis + place = displace
mis + take = mistake   re + creation = recreation
il + legible = illegible   co + operate = cooperate

15.5 Words with the "Seed" Sound

Only one English word ends in *sede: supersede.*
Three words end in *ceed: exceed, proceed, succeed.*
All other words ending in the sound of *seed* are spelled *cede: secede, accede, recede, concede, precede.*

Exercise A: Find the spelling errors in these sentences. Spell the words correctly. One sentence is correct.

1. Because of the thiness of the paper, the print shows through.
2. Despite hours of work on the project, Bob was disatisfied with the results.
3. Jeff peacefully admired the greeness of the countryside.
4. We usualy get a heavy snow in February.
5. Leaving the door unlocked was an iresponsible act.
6. The uneveness of the lettering ruins the whole sign.
7. The flower girl reentered and preceeded the bride down the aisle.
8. The statement is surly illogical.
9. We reccommend this restaurant; the food is extremly good.
10. Finaly, the stain dissappeared.
11. The lawyer said that the question was imaterial.
12. Naturaly, we were dissappointed with our poor grades.
13. Several words on the ransom note were carefully misspelled.
14. The magician waved gracefuly and succeded in making a rabbit appear.
15. Samantha remained imobile while her sister cooly removed the splinter.
16. Cheating on taxes is not only ilegal but also imoral.
17. Alice proceded to pack the rest of the dishes more carefuly.
18. Actualy, the tests are always preceeded by a review.
19. It is unecessary to excede the speed limit.
20. The doctor conceeded that eventualy an operation would be needed.

Exercise B: Add suffixes and prefixes. Write the new word.

1. thin + ness	6. co + operate	11. happy + ly
2. mis + state	7. incidental + ly	12. re + examine
3. ir + relevant	8. im + mobilize	13. dis + appear
4. im + moderate	9. uneven + ness	14. cordial + ly
5. dis + satisfied	10. im + moral	15. dis + agree

15.6 Words with *ie* and *ei*

When the sound is long e (ē), the word is spelled *ie* except after c.

I BEFORE E

retrieve	pier	chief
belief	shield	field
piece	brief	niece

EXCEPT AFTER C

receive	ceiling	deceive
perceive	conceit	receipt

Exceptions: *either, neither, financier, weird, species, seize, leisure.* Remember these words by combining them into such a sentence as: *Neither financier seized either weird species of leisure.*

Exercise A: Correct the spelling errors in these sentences.

1. The peice in the newspaper about our play was very breif.
2. The preist sheilded the child from the attacking dog.
3. My niece is sitting in the first teir of seats.
4. The sentenced prisoner received a repreive.
5. The cheif carried a handsome sheild.
6. We do not beleive that the crop yeild will be good this year.
7. The banker gave her neice a reciept for the money.
8. You can just barely percieve the spot on the cieling.
9. The naturalist spotted a rare species of bird in the feild.
10. Niether of my parents has much liesure.
11. Conceit causes nearly as much trouble as deciet.

12. The caretaker weilded the mop like a baseball bat.
13. It is hard to beleive that the merchant's grief is real.
14. We were releived when the thief yielded to the police.
15. You could not concieve of a setting more wierd.
16. A chilling shreik peirced the silence.
17. The old lady waved a breif farewell with her handkercheif.
18. The cheif engineer has a peice of iron ore on her desk.
19. On a leisurely stroll to the peir, we retreived our paddle.
20. We percieved that some mischief was afoot.

Exercise B: Copy the words below, filling the spaces with *ie* or *ei*.

1. perc__ve	4. rec__pt	7. n__ce	10. p__ce
2. n__ther	5. ch__f	8. sh__ld	11. hyg__ne
3. c__ling	6. f__rce	9. s__ze	12. p__r

15.7 Doubling the Final Consonant

Words of one syllable, ending in one consonant preceded by one vowel, double the final consonant before adding a suffix beginning with a vowel.

1. Words of one syllable ending in one consonant preceded by one vowel:

    grab   dig   drug   slim

These words double the final consonant if the suffix begins with a vowel.

    grab + ing = grabbing   drug + ist = druggist
    dig + er = digger   slim + est = slimmest

2. Words of one syllable ending in one consonant preceded by *two* vowels:

    treat   feel   loot   clean

The rule does not apply to these one-syllable words because two vowels precede the final consonant.

3. The final consonant is doubled in words of *more* than one syllable:
When they end in one consonant preceded by one vowel.
When they are accented on the last syllable.

> re·gret'   per·mit'   de·ter'

The same syllable is accented in the new word formed by adding the suffix:

> re·gret' + ed = re·gret'ted
> per·mit' + ing = per·mit'ting
> de·ter' + ence = de·ter'rence

If the newly formed word is accented on a different syllable, the final consonant is not doubled.

> re·fer'+ence' = ref'er·ence

Exercise A: Copy these words, indicating with an accent mark (') where each word is accented.

1. control	6. regret	11. forget	16. differ
2. excel	7. allot	12. murmur	17. infer
3. limit	8. impel	13. defer	18. propel
4. resist	9. travel	14. benefit	19. submit
5. omit	10. distill	15. admit	20. begin

Exercise B: Add the ending indicated, and write the new word.

1. control + ing	11. put + ing	21. admit + ance
2. bat + ed	12. get + ing	22. let + ing
3. compel + ed	13. plan + ing	23. pad + ed
4. bed + ing	14. prefer + ed	24. murmur + ing
5. differ + ence	15. sit + ing	25. repel + ed
6. limit + ed	16. remit + ance	26. omit + ed
7. commit + ed	17. transfer + ing	27. add + ed
8. book + ed	18. nod + ing	28. ton + age
9. fur + y	19. begin + ing	29. allot + ed
10. disappear + ed	20. expel + ed	30. defer + ed

15.8   Words Often Confused

capital means "most important." It can also mean the city that is the seat of government.

capitol is a building in which a state legislature meets.

the Capitol is the building in Washington, D.C., in which the United States Congress meets.

des'ert means "a wilderness or dry, sandy region with sparse, scrubby vegetation."

de·sert means "to abandon."

dessert (note the change in spelling) is a sweet such as cake or pie served at the end of a meal.

hear means "to listen to," or "to take notice of."

here means "in this place."

its is a word that indicates ownership.

it's is a contraction for *it is* or *it has*.

loose means free or not fastened.

lose means to mislay or suffer the loss of something.

principal describes something of chief or central importance. It also refers to the head of an elementary or high school.

principle is a basic truth, standard, or rule of behavior.

stationary means "fixed or unmoving."

stationery refers to paper and envelopes used for writing letters.

their means "belonging to them."

there means "in that place."

they're is a contraction for *they are*.

to means "toward," or "in the direction of."

too means "also" or "very."

two is the number 2.

weather refers to atmospheric conditions.

whether helps express choice or alternative.

who's is a contraction for *who is* or *who has*.

whose is the possessive form of *who*.

your is the possessive form of *you*.
you're is a contraction for *you are*.

Exercise A: Choose the right word from those in parentheses.

1. For (desert, dessert) we had strawberry shortcake.
2. The Cubs' loyal fans refuse to (desert, dessert) them.
3. The cat arched (it's, its) back.
4. (It's, Its) too hot to play tennis today.
5. I was (there, their) on time.
6. They said (they're, their) names were Sam and Tamara.
7. (Their, They're) always first in line.
8. I am going (weather, whether) you go or not.
9. The (weather, whether) in August is hot and humid.
10. (Whose, Who's) got the tickets?
11. (Whose, Who's) dollar is this?
12. It's (your, you're) fault as much as mine.
13. Call me by ten if (your, you're) not going.
14. I hope the Hawks don't (lose, loose) tonight's game.
15. Somehow the puppies got (loose, lose).
16. Telling a lie is against my (principals, principles).
17. Ms. Happ is (principal, principle) at Brent High School.
18. We rode our bikes (too, to) the park.
19. The soup was (too, two, to) salty.
20. The North Star is almost (stationery, stationary).
21. Pens are on sale at the (stationary, stationery) store.
22. We got (here, hear) on time; why couldn't you?
23. "Now (here, hear) this," came the voice over the loud speaker.
24. Do you know what the (capitol, capital) of Delaware is?
25. The Senate and the House of Representatives both meet in the (capital, Capitol, capitol) building.

Exercise B: Writing Choose ten words at random from the list that begins on the next page. Use your imagination and incorporate them into a humorous paragraph or two. Refer to a dictionary if you are unsure of the meaning of any of the words.

A List of Commonly Misspelled Words

abbreviate	bargain	contemptible	emphasize
absence	becoming	convenience	enthusiastic
accidentally	beginning	corps	environment
accommodate	believe	correspondence	equipped
accompanying	benefited	courageous	especially
achievement	bicycle	courteous	etiquette
acknowledge	biscuit	criticism	exaggerate
acquaintance	bookkeeper	criticize	excellent
across	bulletin	curiosity	exceptional
address	bureau	cylinder	exhaust
all right	business	dealt	exhilarate
altogether	cafeteria	decision	existence
always	calendar	definitely	expense
amateur	campaign	dependent	experience
analyze	candidate	descent	familiar
annihilate	cellophane	description	fascinating
anonymous	cemetery	desirable	fatigue
answer	certain	despair	February
apologize	changeable	desperate	feminine
appearance	characteristic	dictionary	financial
appreciate	colonel	different	foreign
appropriate	colossal	dining	forfeit
arctic	column	diphtheria	fourth
argument	commission	disagree	fragile
arising	committed	disappear	generally
arrangement	committee	disappoint	genius
ascend	comparative	discipline	government
assassinate	compel	dissatisfied	grammar
associate	competitive	economical	guarantee
attendance	complexion	efficient	guard
audience	compulsory	eighth	gymnasium
auxiliary	conscience	eligible	handkerchief
awkward	conscientious	eliminate	height
bachelor	conscious	embarrass	hindrance
balance	consensus	eminent	horizon

humorous	mischievous	practice	specifically
imaginary	missile	preference	specimen
immediately	misspell	prejudice	strategy
incidentally	mortgage	preparation	strictly
inconvenience	municipal	privilege	subtle
incredible	necessary	probably	success
indefinitely	nickel	professor	sufficient
indispensable	ninety	pronunciation	surprise
inevitable	noticeable	propeller	syllable
infinite	nuclear	prophecy	sympathy
influence	nuisance	psychology	symptom
inoculation	obstacle	pursue	tariff
intelligence	occasionally	quantity	temperament
interesting	occur	questionnaire	temperature
irrelevant	occurrence	realize	thorough
irresistible	opinion	recognize	throughout
knowledge	opportunity	recommend	together
laboratory	optimistic	reference	tomorrow
legitimate	original	referred	traffic
leisure	outrageous	rehearse	tragedy
lieutenant	pamphlet	reign	transferred
lightning	parallel	repetition	truly
literacy	parliament	representative	Tuesday
literature	particularly	restaurant	tyranny
loneliness	pastime	rhythm	twelfth
luxurious	permanent	ridiculous	unanimous
maintenance	permissible	sandwich	undoubtedly
maneuver	perseverance	schedule	unnecessary
marriage	perspiration	scissors	vacuum
mathematics	persuade	secretary	vengeance
matinee	picnicking	separate	vicinity
medicine	pleasant	sergeant	village
medieval	pneumonia	similar	villain
microphone	politics	sincerely	weird
miniature	possess	sophomore	wholly
minimum	possibility	souvenir	writing

REINFORCEMENT EXERCISES
Spelling

A. Add suffixes to words ending in silent e or y. Add the following base words and suffixes, being careful to spell the resulting words correctly.

1. relate + ing
2. cry + ing
3. happy + ly
4. employ + er
5. carry + er
6. grave + ly
7. guide + ing
8. change + able
9. early + er
10. complete + ion

11. true + ly
12. lazy + er
13. hope + less
14. grade + ing
15. peace + ful
16. angry + ly
17. silly + er
18. believe + able
19. lone + ly
20. study + ed

B. Identify misspelled words. Find the misspelled words in the following list and spell them correctly. Two words are correct.

1. procede
2. conceed
3. dissagree
4. necessaryly
5. greeness
6. sucseed
7. awfuly

8. transslate
9. thinness
10. receed
11. supercede
12. missunderstand
13. relocate
14. wholy

15. ireverent
16. uneveness
17. seseed
18. eventualy
19. browness
20. exseed

C. Spell words correctly. Find the misspelled words in the following sentences. Spell them correctly.

1. Mr. Horton spent his liesure time weedding his garden.
2. Ty Cobb, the greatest bater in the history of baseball, recieved many awards for his achievements.
3. The cheif believes that the theif will soon be apprehended.

724

4. The accident occurred while Mr. Garber was plowing in his feilds.
5. The village preist performs several wedings each year.
6. After the drop in the stock market, the financier greived over his losses.
7. Mr. Poe wrote many wierd tales about madmen and fiends.
8. Bobsleding and boatting are my neice's favorite activities.
9. The ballad made referrence to a fierce knight weilding an enchanted sheild.
10. Before diner I was seized by an urge for chocolate puding.

D. Distinguish between words that are commonly confused.
Choose the right word from those given in parentheses.

1. Richmond, Virginia was the (capital, capitol, Capitol) of the Confederacy.
2. The largest (desert, dessert) in the world, the Sahara in northern Africa, covers three and a half million square miles.
3. Savannah is justly proud of (its, it's) historic district.
4. Barley, a type of grain, is one of the (principal, principle) products of Denmark.
5. (Their, They're, There) collection includes unusual weapons such as Samurai swords.
6. Strictly speaking, nothing on Earth is (stationary, stationery) because the planet itself is in constant motion.
7. Paul Laurence Dunbar, (who's, whose) poems now appear in most high school literature anthologies, was the son of an escaped slave.
8. Mr. Davenport told me that (your, you're) the new Assistant Coach.
9. Some scientists fear that dumping pollutants into the air may have drastic effects on (weather, whether) conditions.
10. I, (to, too), wonder what schools will be like in a hundred years.

MIXED REVIEW
Spelling

A. Combine the following word parts using the spelling rules presented in this chapter.

1. remit + ed
2. moral + ize
3. fat + er
4. final + ly
5. re + do
6. swim + ing
7. relate + ion
8. peace + able
9. lovely + er
10. trans + oceanic
11. haste + y
12. plain + ness
13. delay + ing
14. carry + age
15. hurry + ed
16. appraise + al
17. un + necessary
18. psychology + cal
19. prefer + ence
20. original + ly

B. Correct the spelling errors. One sentence is correct.

1. Peter checked the feild carfully for broken glass.
2. Rakeing leaves, I beleive, is Evie's chore.
3. The firefighter's actions were truly couragous.
4. Writteing precisly, Jeff copied the outline from the book.
5. Mother usualy dissapproves of sugared snacks.
6. The caravan proceded on it's journey through the dessert.
7. The crowd claped and cheered as the two winners appearred.
8. Roger exceled at drawing inferrences in a logical way.
9. If these aren't you're books, then who's are they?
10. The pilot landed at one of the busyest airports.
11. Tyrone is enjoying a suspensful novel about ilegal spying.
12. One principle of friendship is openness of communication.
13. "The same wierd dream recured," Kim answerred.
14. The lookout percieved a stationery ship in the distance.
15. Lobbyists are generaly employed by companys and organizations.

USING MECHANICS IN WRITING
Spelling

A. If you had to design an exhibit illustrating life in your town, to be preserved and shown to Earthlings of the 25th century, what would you include? Write an essay of three paragraphs or more in which you use at least fifteen words from the list of commonly misspelled words on pages 722-723. When you have finished, go back and underline each of the words from the list.

B. Children's authors often take ideas or situations from folk tales and reword them in their own ways. Try your hand at this interesting and rewarding kind of writing. Write a children's story about a king who is looking for someone worthy to take over his throne. You may want to have your central character undergo some sort of test. Use as many of the "seed" words listed on page 716 as you can. Once you are finished, find a child to read your story to.

C. Proofreading for spelling errors is one of the last steps in the process of writing. You must train your eyes to catch these errors. Proofread the following short paragraph. Then rewrite it, correcting all errors in spelling.

> Cormorants are large, pelican-like birds with webed feet and hookked bills. They are usualy found along seacoasts, for they exist on a deit composed primaryly of fish which they capture by diveing into shallow water. In the Oreint, cormorants are used on water much as huntting dogs are used on land. By placeing a metalic band around a cormorant's neck and connectting a long cord to this band, a fisherman can keep the bird from fliing away and can control its movments. Siting on the edge of a fisherman's boat, trained cormorants watch the water. Then, when fish are spoted, they procede to do what comes natuaraly: They dissappear below the surface, seize the fish in thier powerful bills, and return to thier master with their catch.

16.0 The Plurals of Nouns

16.1 Regular Formation of Plurals

The plural of most nouns is formed by adding -s.

building + s = buildings   ground + s = grounds
yard + s = yards   carrot + s = carrots

16.2 Plurals Formed with -es

The plural of nouns ending in s, sh, ch, x, and z is formed with -es.

rash + es = rashes   crutch + es = crutches
bus + es = buses   box + es = boxes
waltz + es = waltzes

16.3 Plurals of Nouns Ending in y

When a noun ends in y preceded by a consonant, the plural is formed by changing the y to i and adding -es.

duty   duti + es = duties
party   parti + es = parties
pantry   pantri + es = pantries

When a noun ends in *y* preceded by a vowel, the plural is formed by adding *-s*.

tray + s = trays   envoy + s = envoys
day + s = days   boy + s = boys
pulley + s = pulleys   foray + s = forays

16.4 Plurals of Nouns Ending in *o*

The plural of nouns ending in *o*, preceded by a vowel, is formed by adding *-s*.

studio + s = studios   radio + s = radios
rodeo + s = rodeos   ratio + s = ratios
cameo + s = cameos   duo + s = duos

The plural of most nouns ending in *o*, preceded by a consonant, is formed by adding *-s*, but for some nouns of this class the plural is formed by adding *-es*.

piano + s = pianos   auto + s = autos
solo + s = solos   silo + s = silos
tomato + es = tomatoes echo + es = echoes
potato + es = potatoes hero + es = heroes

There are some words ending in *o* with a preceding consonant that may form the plural with either *-s* or *-es: motto, zero, mosquito*. The safest thing to do is to memorize the few words that add *-es* and to consult the dictionary when in doubt.

16.5 Plurals of Nouns Ending in *f, ff,* or *fe*

The plural of most nouns ending in *f* or *ff* is formed regularly by adding *s*.

roof + s = roofs   dwarf + s = dwarfs
belief + s = beliefs   handkerchief + s = handkerchiefs
gulf + s = gulfs   staff + s = staffs

The plural of some nouns ending in *f* or *fe* is formed by changing the *f* or *fe* to *ve* and adding *-s*.

calf — calves	loaf — loaves
life — lives	self — selves
half — halves	wharf — wharves
shelf — shelves	leaf — leaves
knife — knives	elf — elves

Since most of these words with irregular plurals are in common use, careful listening may help you to spell them correctly. If you are doubtful about spelling, however, look up the singular form of the word in a dictionary. If the plural of a word is irregularly formed, the plural will be given immediately after the singular.

16.6 Nouns with Irregular Plurals

The plural of some nouns is formed by a change of spelling.

tooth—teeth	goose—geese
man—men	mouse—mice
woman—women	ox—oxen
child—children	basis—bases
datum—data	phenomenon—phenomena
crisis—crises	hypothesis—hypotheses

The plural and singular forms are the same for a few nouns.

sheep	corps	Japanese
deer	moose	Swiss

16.7 The Plurals of Names

The plural of a name is formed by adding *-s* or *-es*.

Albert Steele—the Steeles	Jack Amos—the Amoses
Judy Lyons—the Lyonses	Bob Sable—the Sables

16.8   The Plurals of Compound Nouns

When a compound noun is written without a hyphen, the plural is formed at the end of the word.

armful + s = armfuls   teaspoonful + s = teaspoonfuls
cupful + s = cupfuls   skateboard + s = skateboards

When a compound noun is made up of a noun plus a modifier, the plural is added to the noun.

mothers-in-law (the phrase *in law* is a modifier.)
editors-in-chief (the phrase *in chief* is a modifier.)
attorneys-general (*general* modifies *attorneys.*)
notaries public (*public* modifies *notaries.*)
passers-by (*by* modifies *passers.*)
bills of sale (the phrase *of sale* modifies *bills.*)
secretaries of state (*of state* modifies *secretaries.*)

Exercise A: Form the plural of each of the following words.

1. holiday	11. studio	21. tablespoonful
2. herd	12. county	22. father-in-law
3. glass	13. valley	23. drive-in
4. radio	14. belief	24. attorney-general
5. dash	15. potato	25. right of way
6. hero	16. handkerchief	26. chief of police
7. watch	17. grief	27. clerk of court
8. laboratory	18. hypothesis	28. Supreme Court Justice
9. lady	19. datum	29. bill of sale
10. cupful	20. basis	30. notary public

Exercise B: Find the errors in plural forms in the following sentences. Write the plurals correctly.

1. The economists do not have enough datums to explain what has happened.
2. There are several hypothesis to explain the existence of the twin moons of Mars.

3. We have two brother-in-laws living in Elmira.
4. Don't use more than three cupsful of flour.
5. How many leafs are missing from your book?
6. What vegetables shall we grow in the garden besides potatos and tomatos?
7. There are several solos for the sopranoes.
8. It would be hard to find many home studioes big enough for two pianos.
9. Last Sunday after church, we stopped to chat with the March's and the Lyons's.
10. In yesterday's game, Rudi made two sensational catchs.
11. American prisoners have suffered cruelties in some foreign countrys.
12. The two mother-in-laws are great friends.
13. Not many countrys have only two major political partys.
14. There are too many autoes on the streets of our citys.
15. Even during routine dutys, the researchers discovered interesting phenomenons.
16. The Chineses have a very ancient civilization.
17. We need more than two notary publics in this big company.
18. Elena brought several armsful of wood into the house.
19. In the spring the mooses move north through the valleys.
20. The sheeps on the range are carefully protected against attacking wolfs.
21. These heros lost their lifes in scientific research for mankind's benefit.
22. Several hanger-ons were waiting for the partys to break up.
23. There are two boxs of matchs in the kitchen cupboard.
24. The thiefs turned out to be brother-in-laws.
25. With their knifes the workers cut big gashs in the trunks of the rubber trees.

REINFORCEMENT EXERCISES
The Plurals of Nouns

A. Form the plurals of nouns. Give the plural form of each of the
following nouns.

1. garage	7. zero	14. brush
2. switch	8. battery	15. hex
3. Commissioner of Police	9. calf	16. belief
	10. Alice	17. Wednesday
4. donkey	11. nightmare	18. wish
5. wolf	12. president-elect	19. sister-in-law
6. lass	13. fez	20. harmonica

B. Correct improper plurals. Rewrite the following sentences,
correcting all errors in the formation of plurals.

1. In autumn, Martin's brother-in-laws pick persimmones and
   blackberrys for canning.
2. Mr. Eckert says that there are three Smith's in his class's.
3. Both recipes call for two tablespoonsful of oregano and
   three cupsful of tomatos.
4. The Western democracys managed to solve both crisises
   peacefully.
5. Mitzner's Music sells radioes, stereoes, and musical
   instrumentes of all kinds, from pianoes to banjoes.
6. Despite numerous injurys, the German and American
   teames still won several trophys.
7. Former Secretarys of State often become professores.
8. On Wednesdaies, the two attornies meet for lunch outside
   the Superior Court Building.
9. Some dentistes distribute toothbrushs to their patientes.
10. J. R. R. Tolkien wrote fascinating storys about elfs,
    dwarves, and other creature's from medieval folk tale's.

MIXED REVIEW
The Plurals of Nouns

A. Form the plural of each of the following words.

1. desk		11. half	
2. crutch		12. chef	
3. paradox		13. freshman	
4. convoy		14. moose	
5. opportunity		15. crisis	
6. tomato		16. Barnes	
7. echo		17. handful	
8. alto		18. bookcase	
9. radio		19. great grandmother	
10. self		20. brother-in-law	

B. Rewrite each of the following sentences, changing all singular nouns to plurals.

1. The dairyman saved the life of the calf.
2. Without the datum from the security program, the crisis cannot be avoided.
3. The man, woman, and ox labored in the field.
4. The child gave the flower to the returning hero.
5. Only my sister-in-law could play the old piano.
6. The soprano felt satisfied when the solo on the recording came out so well.
7. The freshman built the magnificent castle for the float.
8. The moose can be found in the valley.
9. By what criterion can the political party be judged?
10. The box containing the knife fell off when the convoy drove over the bumpy road.

USING MECHANICS IN WRITING
The Plurals of Nouns

A. Imagine that you are the curator of a museum. While examining one of the storerooms, you notice the edge of a door frame behind some old shelves. You remove the shelves, open the door, and step inside a large, musty room. The room is filled with incredible collections of objects, some of which you cannot even identify. Describe the contents of the room in a report that includes a list of the different collections. Make up names for things you can't identify, but be sure to describe them. Use as many different types of plural forms as you can.

B. Very old recipes often give quantities in nonstandard measurements. For example, a recipe may say to add as much butter as would fill two walnut shells, or to blend in three handfuls of flour. Write instructions for something that you know how to make without referring to a recipe. When you need to describe a quantity, give the measurement in terms of familiar objects.

C. Imagine that you are one of eleven children in a family. Every week you must accompany your parents to the supermarket to help with the weekly grocery shopping. Think about providing meals for eleven children and two adults; then describe the shopping trip and the quantities of food your family has to buy. You will undoubtedly use plural forms in writing about this event. Try to use as many irregular plurals as you can to demonstrate your mastery of them.

CUMULATIVE REVIEW
Spelling

Adding Suffixes and Forming Plurals. Number your paper from 1 to 15. Write the word formed by adding the suffix.

1. enjoy + able
2. deter + ence
3. teaspoonful + s
4. structure + al
5. constitute + ion
6. imply + ed
7. change + less
8. courage + ous
9. shelf + s
10. argue + ment
11. incidental + ly
12. latch + s
13. belief + s
14. company + s
15. father-in-law + s

Using the Correct Word. Number your paper from 1 to 15. Next to each number, write the correct word from the two in parentheses.

1. Did the paper (accept, except) your article on dolphins?
2. Fashions in clothing are strongly (effected, affected) by changes in life styles.
3. My (principal, principle) reason for wanting a new car is that my old one is now shaped like an accordian.
4. In an eclipse, the earth casts (its, it's) shadow on the moon.
5. The (capital, capitol) of the Confederacy was Richmond.
6. The elderly news photographer gave some excellent (advice, advise) on getting started in the business.
7. The guide was (altogether, all together) lost.
8. How much (farther, further) is it to the campsite?
9. I hope you never (lose, loose) your passion for writing.
10. Our new French teacher was (formally, formerly) a quarterback at the University of Texas.
11. Screenwriters have (adapted, adopted) several of S.E. Hinton's novels.
12. Are you sure that (your, you're) ready to join the team?
13. The supermarket manager decided that it was (alright, all right) for some of the employees to wear jackets.
14. Sondra has (already, all ready) completed her research.
15. Mark had a box of jellybeans for (desert, dessert).

17.0 Good Manuscript Form

Readers will surely be more impressed with a paper that is neat and legible than with one that is hard to read. Good manuscript form increases the impact of what a writer says. Many schools have regular forms that students are expected to follow. Others require that students follow the manuscript form described below.

17.1 Legible Writing

Few schools require that student papers be typewritten. A typed paper, however, is easier to read than one written by hand.

If a paper is written by hand, it should be written with pen, in a dark blue or black ink. An ink of any other color is not acceptable. Letters should be formed so that there is no doubt as to what they are: *a*'s and *o*'s should be distinctly different; *u*'s and *i*'s should be distinct; *i*'s should be dotted.

17.2 Margins and Spacing

Leave a margin of an inch at the top, the bottom, and the right side of each page. The left margin should be slightly wider. If a paper is typed, the left-hand margin must be carefully maintained. The right-hand margin should be approximately the same, and it should be as even as possible without an excess of hyphens to show the break in a word. It is a good rule not to permit more than two successive lines to end with a hyphen.

All typed copy should be prepared with a double space between lines. Usually five letter spaces are provided for each paragraph indention. One space separates each word; two spaces follow the end punctuation of a sentence. If material must be deleted, it can be struck out by x's or capital M's.

17.3 Proper Labeling

Your teacher will give you instructions on the heading for your papers. Follow these instructions exactly. Usually, you will be expected to place your name at the upper right-hand corner of the first page. On a line below your name, you will place the name or number of the course, and on a third line, you will place the date.

Number each page beginning with page two. (Do not number the first page.) The number may be placed in the upper right-hand corner. To guard against loss or misplacement, you may place your name under the page number.

17.4 Placement of the Title

The title of a paper appears only on the first page. Place the title two lines below the last line of your heading, and center it. Allow two lines between the title and the first line of your copy.

Capitalize the first word and all important words in the title. See Section 10.12. If you are typing, capitalize only the initial letters. Do not underline the title; do not place it in quotation marks unless it is a quotation from some other source.

If a paper is longer than three or four pages, your teacher may ask you to supply a title page. This is a separate page containing the heading in the upper right-hand corner and the title centered on the page.

17.5 Preparation of Final Copy

It is almost impossible to write a paper exactly as you want it the first time. After you have written your first draft, read it over carefully. Revise and correct it. After you have completed your revision, make a final copy. Then read over this copy, giving it a final proofreading before turning it in.

You may find that you have left out words, or you may find errors. You can insert words neatly by writing above the line where they should appear and by using a caret (∧) to show their position. You can make corrections neatly by drawing a line through a word and writing the correction above it. If more than two or three corrections per page are necessary, recopy the page. See Chapter 6, "The Process of Writing," for more information on revision and proofreading.

17.6 Numbers in Writing

Numbers that can be expressed in fewer than four words are usually spelled out; longer numbers are written in figures.

They gathered *thirty-one* bushels of apples in one day.
The piggy bank yielded *thirteen* dollars.
The tickets are selling for *eight* dollars each.
The loss amounted to $4,280.

A number beginning a sentence is spelled out.

Eight hundred were suddenly made homeless by the flood.
Twenty-five minutes passed without a word from Hugh.
Forty percent of Idaho is covered with forest.

17.7 Figures in Writing

Figures are used to express dates, street and room numbers, telephone numbers, page numbers, temperatures, decimals, and percentages.

Shakespeare's birth date was April 23, 1564.
Carol lives at 5457 Guarino Road.
The English class is in room 312.
Is your telephone number 257-4353?
We were asked to learn the poem on page 80.
Last week the temperature reached 101 degrees.
The earthquake measured 4.5 on the Richter scale.
Fred had 98 percent right in the physics test.

Note: Commas are used to separate the figures in sums of money or expressions of large quantities. They are not used in dates, serial numbers, page numbers, addresses, or telephone numbers.

RIGHT: Terry had saved $1,270 for the trip to Europe.
RIGHT: Bernie now owns more than 100,000 stamps.
RIGHT: Washington died in 1799.
WRONG: Washington died in 1,799.

Exercise: Copy these sentences, correcting any errors in the writing of figures. Some sentences are correct.

1. There are now two hundred thousand volumes in the library.
2. 7 of the students in my class worked on the float for the parade.
3. When we arrived in Duluth, it was twenty degrees below zero.
4. The cost of the land alone is $7,500.
5. Nearly sixty percent of high school graduates now go on to college.
6. The offices are now located at 1,741 Broadway.
7. The satellite whirled about the earth every four and three-tenths minutes.
8. It says on page 646 that New Orleans then had a population of 125,000.
9. Our room number is four twenty-six.
10. We have had 2,275 replies to our letter.
11. The telephone number is 275-4,000.

12. The date on the flyleaf was eighteen hundred ninety seven.
13. Helen's new address is two hundred twenty East End Avenue.
14. We have room for only 700 students in the college.
15. Sixty-three percent of the residents turned out to vote.

17.8 Abbreviations in Writing

Abbreviations may be used for most titles before and after proper names, for names of government agencies, and in dates.

BEFORE PROPER NAMES:	Dr., Mr., Mrs., Ms., Messrs., Rev., Hon., Gov., Sgt.
AFTER PROPER NAMES:	Jr., Sr., M.D., Ph.D.
GOVERNMENT AGENCIES:	CIA, FCC, FDA
DATES AND TIME:	A.D., B.C., A.M., P.M.

Notice that there are no periods after abbreviations of government agencies.

The abbreviations of titles are acceptable only when used as part of a name. It is not acceptable to write *The pres. of the club is a dr.* The titles *Honorable* and *Reverend* are not abbreviated when preceded by *the: the Honorable Lois Tate.* They appear with the person's full name, not just the last name. Also abbreviations are not appropriate for the President and Vice-President of the United States.

In ordinary writing, abbreviations are not acceptable for names of countries and states, months and days of the week, nor for words that are part of addresses or firm names.

UNACCEPTABLE:	We are going to Mich. and Can.
BETTER:	We are going to Michigan and Canada.
UNACCEPTABLE:	Miller's play opened on Thurs., Jan. 23.
BETTER:	Miller's play opened on Thursday, January 23.
UNACCEPTABLE:	Pay your bill to the Bell Tel. Co.
BETTER:	Pay your bill to the Bell Telephone Company.

In ordinary writing, abbreviations are not acceptable for the following: names of school courses, *page, chapter, Christmas,* and words standing for measurements such as *km., mi., ml., hr., lb.*

17.9 The Hyphen

A hyphen is used at the end of a line to divide a word between syllables.

> Tracy Austin has charmed and aston-
> ished fans with a lively brand of ten-
> nis.

Note: Each line should have at least two letters of the hyphenated word.

Many compound words require hyphens. Check a dictionary for correct hyphenation.

trade-in	T-shirt	sister-in-law	show-off
play-off	vice-president	ten-year-old	close-up

Words used together as an adjective before a noun are usually hyphenated.

good-looking bike	two-career family
long-distance call	real-life story

However, when the same words are used after the noun, they often are not hyphenated.

CORRECT: We found a well-informed source.
CORRECT: The source was well informed.

Compound numbers between twenty-one and ninety-nine are hyphenated, as are fractions, such as *two-thirds* and *one one-hundredth.*

Some proper nouns with prefixes and suffixes require a hyphen.

> ex-Governor   all-American   Texas-style

Exercise: Correct the errors in the following sentences.

1. The Rev. Richard Anderson, D. D., is one of the speakers.
2. Your reservation is on Am. Airlines for next Saturday.
3. Twelve-year-old Jennifer is the youngest student at Mather H. S.
4. The Hershey Co. is located in Pa.
5. For twenty one days Anita will be traveling in Ire.
6. Mr. Walsh and Jas. Perrin are at a teachers' convention.
7. Bob has an appointment at 4:00 P M on Fri.
8. Ms. Marks has just been made vice pres. of the bank.
9. Xmas vacation will start on Dec. 21.
10. Our assignment is to read pp. 46 to 62.
11. The well meaning club secy. has very little to do.
12. We used to live in Ill., but then we moved.
13. The dr. delivered a baby that weighed 7lb.
14. Augustus ruled the Roman Emp. from 27 B.C. to A.D. 14.
15. In northern Minnesota, I once caught a pike 16 in. long.

17.10   Italics for Titles

The word *italics* is a printer's term. It refers to a kind of type. When a writer wants to indicate that a word is in italics, he or she underlines it in the manuscript.

Titles of books, plays, newspapers, magazines, motion pictures, works of art, and long musical compositions are printed in italics. The names of ships, trains, and airplanes are also printed in italics.

MANUSCRIPT FORM: I never miss the ads in <u>Seventeen</u>.

PRINTED FORM: I never miss the ads in *Seventeen*.

MANUSCRIPT FORM: Gian Carlo Menotti's best-known opera is <u>Amahl and the Night Visitors</u>.

PRINTED FORM: Gian Carlo Menotti's best-known opera is *Amahl and the Night Visitors*.

MANUSCRIPT FORM:	The front page of <u>The New York Times</u> showed the President boarding <u>Air Force One</u>.
PRINTED FORM:	The front page of *The New York Times* showed the President boarding *Air Force One*.

17.11 Italics for Foreign Words and Phrases

Many foreign words have become so widely used that they are now part of the English language: *wigwam, spaghetti, gourmet.* These naturalized words are printed in regular type. Foreign words and phrases that have not become naturalized in our language are printed in italics: *mañana, Gesundheit.*

The only way to be sure whether a word or phrase of foreign origin should be printed in italics (underlined in manuscript) is to consult the dictionary. Most dictionaries indicate whether or not a word is foreign by using special symbols.

17.12 Italics for Words, Letters, or Figures

Italics are used for words, letters, or figures referred to as such.

In printed works, words, letters, or figures referred to as such are in italics. In writing, they are underlined.

MANUSCRIPT FORM:	In England, <u>either</u> is pronounced <u>eyether.</u>
PRINTED FORM:	In England, *either* is pronounced *eyether.*
MANUSCRIPT FORM:	Road signs have given <u>slow</u> the status of an adverb.
PRINTED FORM:	Road signs have given *slow* the status of an adverb.
MANUSCRIPT FORM:	Dot your <u>i</u>'s and cross your <u>t</u>'s.
PRINTED FORM:	Dot your *i*'s and cross your *t*'s.

17.13 Italics for Emphasis

Italics (underlining) are used to give special emphasis to words or phrases.

The tendency in modern writing is to avoid the use of italics for emphasis. One reason is that italic type is considered harder to read then regular (roman) type, particularly if there is a great deal of it. Another reason is that modern writers are developing a direct, straightforward style which gives emphasis to important words without use of printing devices.

In high school writing, use italics for emphasis only to make meaning clear.

Woman's place *was* in the home; it certainly isn't today.
"Have you *ever* seen such a storm!" Father exclaimed.

Exercise: Copy the following sentences. Underline words that should be italicized.

1. Gina shouted "Arrivederci!" from her window on the Greyhound bus.
2. My Fair Lady is based on George Bernard Shaw's Pygmalion.
3. The Stourbridge Lion was the first locomotive to run on tracks in the United States.
4. Some people spell Elizabeth with an s instead of a z.
5. The pastry chefs at La Parisienne make special Christmas desserts including Buche de Noel and croque-en-bouche.
6. Eine Kleine Nachtmusik for light orchestra is one of Mozart's best known suites.
7. Ken sat down at the counter with a carton of yogurt, a croissant, and a copy of People magazine.
8. Degas' A Woman with Chrysanthemums can be seen at the Metropolitan Museum of Art.
9. That $7.29 has been entered in the wrong column.
10. The USS Ohio is the largest and most powerful of America's nuclear submarines.

17.14   Correction Symbols and Revision

Both in high school and in college your teachers will make marginal notes on your themes and reports before returning them to you. These notes will indicate errors or awkward passages that require rewriting. The correction of errors will make you alert to their recurrence in your later writing.

Many schools and colleges have their own system of briefly indicating writing faults. If your school has such a system of abbreviations, it will be made available to you. Your teachers may prefer to use the symbols listed below. These are symbols used by professional copyreaders. The manuscript bearing the marks is returned to the author, no matter how experienced, for correction and revision before the manuscript is set in type.

ab *Abbreviation.* Either the abbreviation is not appropriate, or the abbreviation is wrong. Consult a dictionary.

agr *Agreement.* You have made an error in agreement of subject and verb, or of pronoun and antecedent. Consult Section 6.1 and 7.13 in your Handbook.

awk *Awkward.* The sentence is clumsy. Rewrite it.

cap *Capital letters.* You have omitted necessary capitals. Consult Section 10 in your Handbook.

cf *Comma fault.* You have joined two sentences with a comma. Change the punctuation.

dang *Dangling construction.* You have written a verbal phrase in such a way that it does not tie up to another word in the sentence. Rewrite the sentence.

frag *Sentence fragment.* You have placed a period after a group of words that is not a sentence. Join the fragment to an existing sentence or add words to complete the thought.

ital *Italics.* You have omitted italics that are needed.

k *Awkward.* See *awk* above.

lc	*Lower case.* You have mistakenly used a capital letter where a small letter is required.
ms	*Manuscript form.* You have not followed the proper manuscript form.
no ¶	*No paragraph.* You have started a new paragraph too soon. Join these sentences to the preceding paragraph.
¶	*Paragraph.* Begin a new paragraph at this point.
nc	*Not clear.* Your meaning is not clear. Rewrite the passage to say what you mean.
om	*Omission.* You have left out words that are needed for clarity or smoothness of style.
p	*Punctuation.* You have made an error in punctuation. Consult Sections 11–14 in your Handbook for sentences like the one you have improperly punctuated.
ref	*Reference.* There is an error or a weakness in the reference of pronoun to antecedent. Consult Section 7 in your Handbook.
rep	*Repetition.* You have repeated a word too often, or you have repeated something you wrote in preceding sentences.
ro	*Run-on sentence.* You have written two or more sentences as one. Change the punctuation.
shift	*Shift.* You have shifted point of view or tense needlessly.
sp	*Spelling.* You have misspelled a word.
t	*Tense.* You have used the wrong tense form. Consult Section 5 in your Handbook.
tr	*Transpose.* Your meaning would be more clear if a sentence or passage were placed at another point.
wd	*Wrong word.* You have confused homonyms, or you have used a word that does not fit the meaning. Consult a dictionary.

REINFORCEMENT EXERCISE
Good Manuscript Form

Correct errors in proper manuscript form. The following are sentences from final drafts. Rewrite these sentences, correcting any errors in manuscript form.

1. European families celebrate the Feast of St. Nicholas on January Six.
2. The planet Pluto has an estimated surface temperature of minus three hundred and sixty degrees Fahrenheit.
3. The heaviest pig ever recorded weighed two thousand five hundred and fifty-two pounds.
4. There are only 2 people alive today who still speak the Eskimo language known as Eyak.
5. The soph. float took 8 and one-half hrs. to construct.
6. Feb. twenty-nine occurs every 4 years, making a leap year of three hundred sixty-six days.
7. Ms. Lamas worked for the Amer. Conservation Assoc., which is located at thirty Rockefeller Plaza, New York, N.Y.
8. Approximately twenty percent of the students (73 students in all) signed up for phys. ed.
9. Chapt. 1, p. one of the novel *Flowers for Algernon* contains many intentional errors in spelling.
10. Some people pronounce the word theatre as thē-ay′-ter; others say thē′-uh-ter.
11. The students toured the Federal Bureau of Investigation office in Indianapolis, Ind.
12. Jocelyn bettered her own long standing record in the play offs.
13. Several of his constituents sent Senator Dole presents for Xmas.
14. Ciao and arrivederci both mean "goodbye".
15. The Rev Arthur Dimmesdale is a central character in Nathaniel Hawthorne's novel, "The Scarlet Letter."

MIXED REVIEW
Good Manuscript Form

Rewrite the following sentences, correcting the errors in italics, abbreviation, hyphenation, and the writing of figures.

1. How many sixteen year olds attend Clemente H.S.?
2. That 15 min. phone call cost $5.12, Doctor Kowinski.
3. Dial 936-1,212 for the Natl. Weather Serv. forecast.
4. A kilogram equals 2.2 lbs., and a gram equals .035 oz.
5. According to The New York Times, the word life style is being overused.
6. 24 well qualified students were elected to the Student Assoc.
7. St. Patrick's Day is celebrated on Mar. seventeenth.
8. The P.T.A. has its headquarters at seven hundred N. Rush St., Chicago, Ill.
9. The chart on page sixty of Modern Biology explains the classification of vertebrates.
10. Canada is divided into 10 provinces, just as the U.S. is divided into 50 states.
11. The largest lake in the world is the Caspian Sea with an area of 143550 sq. mil.
12. The Pres.'s appointments secy. declined three fourths of the invitations.
13. About seventy five percent of all active volcanoes are located in an area called the "Ring of Fire."
14. The ocean liner Queen Elizabeth weighed 83673 tons.
15. Brigitta has that all knowing attitude that some people call savoir-faire.
16. 60,000 people attended the all star benefit performance at Madison Sq. Garden.
17. The Raymonds are a close knit family.
18. Britishers use the word petrol when they refer to gasoline.
19. Is the St. Louis Post-Dispatch a pro Republican paper?
20. All but 4 of the players were under the age of 17.

USING MECHANICS IN WRITING
Good Manuscript Form

A. Imagine that you have been named director of a charitable foundation. You control a fund of ten million dollars that you must spend for the benefit of people whom you do not know. How will you spend the money? Defend your decisions in a composition that follows proper manuscript form.

B. The following is the first draft of an essay. The correction symbols in the margins indicate corrections that need to be made. Copy the essay, making the corrections that are indicated by these symbols.

In 1886, in Prague, Okla., a great grandson was born to Black **ab**
Hawk. The famous Indian chief. Among the Sac and Fox In- **frag**
dians, he was known as *Wa-tho-buck*, or "Bright Path." To the **ref**
rest of the world, he becomes known as Jim Thorpe, the great- **shift**
est athlete in history. Jim Thorpe begun his athletic career as **¶ /+**
an all American football player for the Carlisle Indian Indus- **p**
trial school, located in Carlisle, Pennsylvania. Competing in the
1912 Olympic Games, the world was astounded by Thorpe's **dang**
becoming the first athelete in history to win both the pentath- **sp**
lon and the decathlon. After his Olympic sucesses, Thorpe **sp**
played six seasons of professional Baseball, he then switched **lc/cf**
to football, which he played for fifteen years. In 1920, he became the first president of the American Professional Football
Association, now known as the National League Football. Jim **tr**
Thorpe's unparalleled reputation is the fact of being a well- **awk**
rounded athlete who could perform brilliant in many different **wd**
athletic endeavors and sports. In 1951, Jim Thorpe became one **rep**
of the first people to be elected to the National Football Foun-
dations Hall of Fame.

P

18.0 Outlining

Outlining is a valuable tool. It is used for two purposes: (1) for taking notes and (2) for planning a composition. A good outline helps the note-taker to record information in a concise and logical manner. It helps the writer organize ideas, and provides a speaker with a diagram of the basic course of a talk.

18.1 Outlines as Organizational Tools

An outline is useful for organizing a piece of writing or a talk. Before making an outline, however, you must gather information related to the purpose of your paper. All information in the outline must directly develop a single controlling purpose. Once you have gathered enough relevant information, the outline will give you a scheme for organizing it.

First, study your controlling purpose and your ideas for the paper or talk. Determine which ideas are most important for developing the controlling purpose. These will be the main topics of the outline.

Then group the remaining ideas under the main topics that they relate to. These will be the subpoints and their supporting details.

A final question is how to organize the main points and the subpoints under them. Some ideas are most logically organized in time sequence, in ascending importance, or by increasing complexity. The best order is the one that is clearest and most understandable for the topic.

Your finished outline will be the pattern for a well-organized final product.

18.2 Kinds of Outlines

An outline may be one of two kinds: (1) a **topic outline** or (2) a **sentence outline**.

The topic outline uses words or phrases instead of complete sentences. It is useful for quick note-taking or for informal organizing. The following is an example of a topic outline.

How To Make Pottery

Purpose: to explain how to make clay pottery.

   I. Preparing the clay

      A. Purify clay

      B. Mix clay with water

      C. Knead clay

  II. Shaping the clay

      A. Hand-building

      B. Throwing it on potter's wheel

         1. Design of wheel

         2. Technique of throwing

      C. Molding

 III. Decorating the pottery

      A. Scratching designs

      B. Underglazing

 IV. Firing in the kiln

  V. Glazing the pottery

      A. Brushing

      B. Spraying

      C. Dipping

 VI. Refiring the pottery

The sentence outline, using complete sentences, is most effective for notes that will be studied later or for formal writing.

Painting a Landscape in Oils

Purpose: to show how anyone can paint a simple landscape by following a few step-by-step procedures.

I. Choose materials and a subject.
   A. You must purchase a few basic art supplies.
      1. You will need paints in the primary colors and in white and black.
      2. You will need an eraser and pencils or charcoal.
      3. You will need canvas, a palette, a palette knife, and brushes of various sizes.
   B. You must choose a simple subject.
      1. Beginners should avoid including buildings, people, or animals in their landscapes.
      2. Beginners do best when they paint large areas of water, sky, and forest seen at a distance.

II. Make preliminary sketches of your subject.
   A. Draw several sketches of your subject on paper the size of your canvas.
   B. Transfer the best sketch to your canvas using a light pencil or charcoal.
   C. Make your sketch accurate and complete.

III. Paint your subject.
   A. Using a color chart, mix the colors on your palette.
   B. Using large brushes, paint lighter-colored background areas of sky and land.
   C. Using a palette knife and smaller brushes, add darker-colored details to the background areas.
   D. Using yet smaller brushes, add highlights to provide depth and to indicate light sources.

18.3 Outline Form

In general, the same form applies to both topic and sentence outlining.

 1. Begin by placing the title at the top of the page. Under it, write the purpose. These are not items in the outline. The introduction and the conclusion are usually not part of the outline either.

 2. Use the following arrangement of numerals and letters: Roman numerals for main topics and capital letters for sub-topics, then numbers for points that develop the subtopics. Small letters are for subpoints under these points, numbers in parentheses for details developing the subpoints, and finally, small letters in parentheses for subdetails. Always divide your subtopics in descending order of importance.

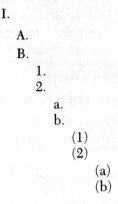

 3. Indent each division of the outline. Put the letter or nu-meral directly under the first letter in the first word of the larger heading above.

4. Do not use a single subheading. There must be at least two. For example, if there is a *1* under *A*, there must also be at least a *2*. An idea cannot be broken down into fewer than two parts.

5. In a topic outline, keep items of the same rank in parallel form. For instance, if *A* is a noun, then *B* and *C* should also be nouns. If *1* is a prepositional phrase, then *2* and *3* should also be prepositional phrases.

6. Begin each item with a capital letter. Do not use end punctuation in a topic outline.

Exercise A: Below is a partial topic outline. Complete the outline by inserting the following headings in the appropriate blanks:

Poisoning	Severe bleeding
Avoiding movement of victim	Burns
Reassuring victim	To prevent worsening
Fractures	For cuts or wounds
Frostbite	Treatment of shock
To ease pain	Symptoms of shock
Situations requiring first aid	

First Steps to First Aid

First aid techniques can provide emergency treatment until medical help arrives.

I. Goals of first aid

    A.

    B.

    C. To soothe fears

II. General techniques of first aid

    A. Staying calm

    B.

    C. Examining the victim
       1. For burns
       2.
       3. For fractures
    D.
    E. Preventing shock
       1.
       2.
          a. Covers
          b. Hot drinks

III.

    A. Animal bites
    B.
    C. Asphyxiation
    D.
    E.
    F. Fainting
    G. Heatstroke
    H.
    I.
    J. Severe cuts

Exercise B: Writing Choose a short nonfiction magazine article and outline it. You may use either a topic or sentence outline, but be sure that you follow correct outline form.

REINFORCEMENT EXERCISES
Outlining

A. **Understand outline form.** Complete the statements below.

1. Every outline must develop a single _____ .
2. There are two kinds of outline: the topic outline and the _____ .
3. Roman numerals are used in outlines before _____ .
4. Capital letters are used in outlines before _____ .
5. The letter or numeral at the beginning of each outline entry should be placed _____ .
6. Immediately following the title should be the _____ .
7. There must always be at least _____ subheadings.
8. In a topic outline, items of the same rank should be in _____ form.
9. _____ outlines do not use end punctuation.
10. The first letter of the first word of every entry is a _____ .

B. **Use proper outline form.** Correct the outline below.

Our Noisy Earth

Controlling purpose: Noise pollution is a threat to our well-being.

I. Causes of Noise Pollution

    A. Vehicles (motorcycles, buses, etc.)

        1. cars

    B. Industrial Machinery

II. effects of noise pollution

    a. Mental Tension and Physical Tension.

III. Solutions for noise pollution

    1. better planning.

    2. stricter laws.

    3. more citizen concern.

Outlining

Below is an article from an encyclopedia. Outline the information as you would if you were taking notes for a speech or composition.

Scientists have described and named approximately a million kinds of animals. Of these, more than eight hundred thousand are insects. Scientists discover from seven thousand to ten thousand new kinds of insects every year. They believe there may be from one million to ten million kinds of insects still undiscovered.

Insects live almost everywhere on earth—from steamy tropical jungles to cold polar regions. They live high on snow-capped mountains and in deserts below sea level. They can be found in caves deep in the earth or flying high in the sky. Only in the oceans are few insects found.

We are constantly at war with insects. They annoy us, bite us, and infect us with deadly diseases. They attack our crops, our pets, and our domestic animals. They invade our homes, eat our food, and damage our property. But insects also have great value to us. For example, they pollinate many of our crops, provide us with honey and other products, and serve as food for fish, birds, and many other kinds of animals. In fact, life as we know it could not exist if all the insects on earth were to disappear.

USING MECHANICS IN WRITING
Outlining

Using the following outline, write a composition in proper manuscript form describing the life and work of Walt Disney.

Controlling Purpose: Walter Elias Disney was an important pioneer in the field of animated film.

I. Walt Disney was interested in cartooning as a youth.
   A. He was born in Chicago in 1901.
   B. At the age of 16, he studied art in Chicago.
   C. At age 19, he worked for the Kansas City Film Ad Company, creating crude cartoon advertisements.

II. Disney started his own film business.
   A. In 1923, he moved to Los Angeles to become an *animator* (someone who draws cartoons for movies).
   B. He started a film studio in his garage.
   C. His first successful character was Mickey Mouse.
   D. Disney achieved several movie-making firsts.
      1. His cartoon *Flowers and Trees* was the first film made in full Technicolor.
      2. His cartoon *Steamboat Willie* was the first to use sound.
      3. His *Snow White and the Seven Dwarfs* was the first full-length cartoon film.

III. Disney became extremely popular and successful.
   A. He created many popular cartoon characters, including Donald Duck, Goofy, and Pluto.
   B. He created such films as *Pinocchio, Fantasia, Bambi, Cinderella,* and *Lady and the Tramp.*
   C. He founded Disneyland Amusement Park.
   D. He produced nature films and films with actors, including *Treasure Island* and *Mary Poppins.*
   E. His studio won more than forty-five Academy Awards.

Sources of Quoted Materials

Cover

Homage to the Square: Intersecting Orange. Josef Albers. Courtesy of The Josef F. Albers Foundation, Inc. Whereabouts of the painting unknown.

Editorial Credits

Editor-in-Chief: Joseph F. Littell
Editorial Director, English Programs: Joy Littell
Managing Editor: Kathleen Laya
Assistant Managing Editor: Geraldine Macsai
Senior Editor: Bonnie Dobkin
Assistant Editor: Robert D. Shepherd

Associate Designer: Mary E. MacDonald
Handwritten Art: Kenneth Izzi
Cover Design: Joy Littell, Debbie Costello
Production Assistant: Julie Schumacher

Index